The King's Two Bodies

THE KING'S
TWO BODIES

A Study in
Mediaeval Political Theology

BY

ERNST H. KANTOROWICZ

WITH A NEW PREFACE
BY WILLIAM CHESTER JORDAN

PRINCETON UNIVERSITY PRESS
PRINCETON, NEW JERSEY

Published by Princeton University Press, 41 William Street,
Princeton, New Jersey
In the United Kingdom: Princeton University Press,
Chichester, West Sussex
Copyright © 1957, by Princeton University Press;
Copyright renewed 1985 by Princeton University Press
Preface by William Chester Jordan copyright © 1997
by Princeton University Press
ALL RIGHTS RESERVED
L.C. Card No. 57-5448
ISBN 0-691-01704-2 pbk.

Princeton University Press books are printed on acid-free paper and
meet the guidelines for permanence and durability of the Committee on
Production Guidelines for Book Longevity of the Council on Library Resources

First Princeton Paperback printing, 1981

Seventh paperback printing, with a new preface by William Chester Jordan, 1997

http://pup.princeton.edu

Printed in the United States of America

10

ISBN-13: 978-0-691-01704-4

ISBN-10: 0-691-01704-2

D. M.

MAXIMI RADIN

(MDCCCLXXX–MCML)

SACRUM

CONTENTS

vii

PREFACE (1997)

THE REACTION to *The King's Two Bodies*, published forty years ago and now reissued in this anniversary edition, was immediate and enthusiastic. Two reviews—one by Peter Riesenberg, the other by William Dunham, Jr.—began with the same simple declaration that Professor Kantorowicz "has written a great book."[1] Dunham went on to compare Kantorowicz's method (arguing back from the known, in this case the Tudor doctrine of the king's two bodies, to its unknown medieval precedents) with that used in Frederic William Maitland's *Domesday Book and Beyond: Three Essays in the Early History of England*.[2] One of the half dozen or so most splendid pieces of historical writing and conceptualization ever published, Maitland's book was an apt comparison; and Dunham intended his readers to appreciate Kantorowicz's similarly bold undertaking.[3] Riesenberg thought *The King's Two Bodies* "perhaps the most important work in the history of medieval political thought, surely the most spectacular, of the past several generations."[4]

Such praise proved to be nearly universal: "ce livre magistral"; the "most important contribution to the history of medieval kingship since Fritz Kern's *Gottesgnadentum und Widerstandsrecht*, published almost a century ago"; "this great study."[5] Among German reviewers the favorite word was *Bewunderung*; Kantorowicz had written a "marvel."[6] In England reactions were similar. "And what a book he has written!" gushed E. F. Jacob on page two of the *Manchester Guardian* of 19 August 1958. In the *Spectator* a

[1] Dunham's review appeared in *Speculum* 33 (1958): 550–53; Riesenberg's in the *American Political Science Review* 52 (1958): 1139–40.

[2] Dunham, p. 550.

[3] Maitland's book, originally published a century ago this year, was reissued by Cambridge University Press in 1987 with a laudatory preface by J. C. Holt.

[4] Riesenberg, p. 1139.

[5] In order of quotation the reviewers cited are the following: Robert Folz in *Revue d'histoire et de philosophie religieuses* 38 (1958): 374–78; Norman Cantor in *American Historical Review* 64 (1958): 81–83; R. E. McNally in *Journal of Religion* 38 (1958): 205.

[6] Thus, Wiebke Fesefeldt in *Göttingische Gelehrte Anzeigen* 212 (1958): 67; Rudolf Kloos in *Historische Zeitschrift* 188 (1959): 364; and Friedrich Kempf, "Untersuchungen über das Einwirken der Theologie auf die Staatslehre des Mittelalters (Bericht über ein neues Buch)," *Römische Quartalschrift* 54 (1959): 233. Although Fesefeldt hoped for a quick German translation, none appeared in that language, so far as I have been able to determine, before 1990.

more subdued, but no less approving Geoffrey Barraclough ruminated on the wonderful appropriateness of the subtitle of the book, *A Study in Mediaeval Political Theology*, which, for him, captured the sincerely reverential and ultimately metaphysical aspects (the theology) of what other scholars, even other reviewers, misleadingly and over-rationalistically called "medieval political thought."[7]

To be sure, there were a few caveats. Not every reviewer delighted in Kantorowicz's phrase "political theology,"[8] which some associated with the German and Nazi-leaning jurist Carl Schmitt's description and endorsement of authoritarian government.[9] Certain historians of England, focusing on quotidian matters, wanted to know more about the ways in which the doctrine of the king's two bodies directly affected court cases that came before Tudor judges. What did it matter in everyday life that jurists conceived of the prince with both a body natural and corruptible, on the one hand, and a body politic and immortal, on the other? There was, for these critics, even when they otherwise lavishly praised the book, a touch too much indulgence in recovering high intellectual discourses in the pages of Kantorowicz's book.[10]

A chorus of commentators also thought that there was more than a touch of what might be called too-much-ness ("nimiety," to use one reviewer's word) in the book as a whole.[11] Read closely *The King's Two Bodies* was a dozen or more studies, all scintillating and at least loosely connected, but which overall

[7] *Spectator*, 1 August 1958, p. 171. The reviewer for the *Review of Metaphysics*, probably Robert Tredwell (but it might have been an associate editor), thought the work was "fascinating" in its treatment of what was also, in his view, a metaphysical theme.

[8] See, for example, Ernst Reibstein in *Zeitschrift der Savigny-Stiftung für Rechtsgeschichte* (Germanistische Abteilung) 76 (1959): 379. Reibstein's lukewarm review was not regarded as very weighty by Friedrich Baethgen, "Ernst Kantorowicz 3.5.1895–9.9.1963," *Deutsches Archiv* 21 (1965): 12 n. 19, "wird, auch wenn die darin erhobenen kritischen Einwände sich mehr oder minder als stichhaltig erweisen sollten, der Bedeutung des Buches im Ganzen keineswegs gerecht."

[9] See the discussion in Alain Boureau, *Histoires d'un historien: Kantorowicz* (Paris, 1990), pp. 162–67.

[10] To Dunham and Cantor (nn. 1 and 5 above), who—in the first case gently, in the second, more harshly—make this criticism, may be added Ewart Lewis in *Political Science Quarterly* 73 (1958), 453–55, and J. F. Costanzo in *Annals of the American Academy* 321 (1959): 203–4.

[11] For the phrase, "touch of nimiety," see H. S. Offler's review in *English Historical Review* 75 (1960): 295–98.

lacked cogency. Reading the book was like trying to decipher a "kaleidoscope," moaned one otherwise laudatory reviewer.[12] A "rich and muddled book" by whose end, complained Beryl Smalley, "I felt as queasy as one would after a diet of jam without bread."[13] Or, in Richard Southern's quite evocative words, to "travel through the Middle Ages with Professor Kantorowicz in search of the king's two bodies is like walking in a strange country by night along unknown ways: the illumination is fitful, though sometimes spectacular, the shape of the country is only dimly discernible." But, he went on to add, "the experience is one which remains more vividly impressed on the memory than many a daylight journey on the beaten track."[14]

Not enough of practical politics (although not everyone subscribed to this criticism[15]); too much crammed in between the covers, but a bit thin on the papacy said one expert on the medieval church;[16] otherwise there were almost unmitigated praise of and awe at the enormous erudition as the author ranged across the whole of the Middle Ages and late Antiquity on his trek back from the Tudor jurists.[17] How had Kantorowicz come to write a book of such authority and sweep?

The story of Ernst Hartwig Kantorowicz's life has of late been written and rewritten by intelligent admirers and at least one crank.[18] At times it is a troubling story. A strong conservative in the old European sense of the term, Kantorowicz was also a non-

[12] Cecil Grayson, *Romance Philology* 15 (1961–62): 179–84. Grayson lavished his praise on the Dante chapter of *The King's Two Bodies*; Kloos (n. 6 above) also called that section "ein meisterlicher Danteexkurs" (p. 363).

[13] *Past and Present*, no. 20 (1961), pp. 30–35.

[14] *Journal of Ecclesiastical History* 10 (1959): 105–8.

[15] Riesenberg (n. 1 above) and Folz (n. 5 above) saw no problem on this point.

[16] Michael Wilks in *Journal of Theological Studies* 10 (1959): 185–88. Cf. Kempf, "Untersuchungen," pp. 213–14, on Kantorowicz's treatment of ecclesiology.

[17] In addition to the reviews already cited, see those by R. J. Schoek in the *Review of Politics* 22 (1960): 281–84, and Hubert Dauphin in the *Revue d'histoire ecclésiastique* 55 (1960): 176–79.

[18] The sketch that follows, both as to details and overall interpretation, has been abstracted from the following (listed in order of publication): Yakov Malkiel, "Ernst H. Kantorowicz," in *On Four Modern Humanists: Hofmannsthal, Gundolf, Curtius, Kantorowicz,* ed. Arthur Evans, Jr. (Princeton, 1970), pp. 146–219; David Abulafia, "Kantorowicz and Frederick II," *History* 62 (1977): 193–210 (reprinted in the author's *Italy, Sicily and the Mediterranean 1100–1400* [London, 1987], no. II, with an important bibliographical supplement in the "Addenda et Corrigenda," p. 1); Boureau, *Histoires d'un historien*; and Norman Cantor, *Inventing the Middle Ages: The Lives, Works, and Ideas of the Great Medievalists of the Twentieth Century* (New York, 1991), pp. 79–117.

practicing Jew, probably an atheist, who developed a fascination for the reputed organic unities of medieval religion and society.[19] A member of the Stefan George circle and a pallbearer at the master's funeral in 1933, he was in many ways an aesthete with some common, but, in hindsight, unhappy ethnic prejudices.[20] Born in 1895 to a prosperous bourgeois family in Posen (Poznań), he served in the German army and was wounded in the First World War. After the war he eagerly took part in the suppression of communists in Germany and was wounded again.

Although he toyed with the idea of doing work in the economic history of the eastern Mediterranean, he later decided to concentrate on medieval history. His first important work was a biography of Emperor Frederick II. Published in 1927 without notes and with a heavy dose of almost Romantic mythmaking, it was a best seller and later a Nazi favorite, but it provoked a torrent of sometimes frenzied criticism from the scholarly old guard. Kantorowicz responded in several ways, not least by publishing a supplementary volume that securely established his claim to know the sources intimately even if it did not answer all the criticisms raised by his opponents.[21]

Kantorowicz seemed about to embark on a more traditional university career after accepting an appointment at Frankfurt in 1930, but the political situation in Germany grew more and more ominous. This arch-conservative with the aristocratic temperament detested National Socialism and its adherents' shrill anti-Semitism and seemingly pointless and philistine roughness, all of which helped to erode his estimation of German political culture. In 1934 he refused to take the oath to Adolf Hitler, gave up his academic post in Frankfurt, and went into a kind of retirement. A brooding melancholy followed during which time he collected and translated a number of English poems on the themes of "death, affliction, and transfiguration" (his personal

---

[19] On the probable atheism, I follow Boureau, *Histoires d'un historien*, p. 137.

[20] Malkiel, a friend, did not try to hide these: "Among Kantorowicz's many, and sometimes conflicting, loyalties and lines of curiosity, even the closest inspection does not uncover the slightest affectionate concern for Slavs, in general, or for Poles, in particular" ("Ernst H. Kantorowicz," p. 154).

[21] The best general sketch of these incidents and their ramifications on future scholarship may be found in the Abulafia article (n. 18 above), along with the important bibliographic supplement in the reprint.

designation for the collection), but it was not until 1938 that he brought himself to leave Germany for good.[22]

He was fortunate to find a safe haven in the United States, was offered a position at Berkeley, and settled down to write his second book, *Laudes Regiae: A Study in Liturgical Acclamations and Mediaeval Ruler Worship* (Berkeley, 1946). But Kantorowicz left the west coast a few years later when he, along with a few other faculty members of the University of California, refused to take a loyalty oath. McCarthyite anti-communism was weighing heavy on state institutions. It was not the substance of the declaration that the regents of the university asked Kantorowicz to make that necessarily offended him. His anti-communism dated at least from his street-fighting days in the immediate aftermath of the First World War. But he regarded the demand to take the oath as an assault on academic freedom, and he fought it hard, mobilizing support as best he could, although with only modest success.

To his great good fortune Kantorowicz again landed on his feet, for he soon received the offer of a permanent position at the Institute for Advanced Study in Princeton along with the privilege, whenever he chose to exercise it, of teaching graduate seminars at the University. It was in Princeton, from 1951 until his death on 9 September 1963, that he did his research. *The King's Two Bodies,* like *Laudes Regiae,* reconstructs some of the visions of organic wholeness articulated by medieval thinkers. Kantorowicz increasingly directed his praise, however, at figures who embodied the religious ideals of the organic model of society. Although Frederick II still fascinated him, Kantorowicz's most sympathetic portrait in *Laudes Regiae,* for example, is not of that mythically heroic emperor but of his saintly contemporary and "rival," Louis IX of France.[23]

In the fall of 1962 Kantorowicz devoted his last seminar to a study of Dante's *De Monarchia.* In a short description written

---

[22] Boureau, *Histoires d'un historien,* p. 124.

[23] *Laudes Regiae,* pp. 3–4, "It was St. Louis, who in every respect enriched that treasure of grace on which all his successors would thrive. It was he whose kingship was elevated to transcendancy by the Spiritualists and Symbolists of his age and who, in turn, bestowed the thin and light air of the angelic kingdoms upon his country. . . . [H]e had, as it were, commended his government to Christ the victorious, the royal, the imperial, whom he himself represented on earth more perfectly, perhaps, than any other king ever did."

by a member of the seminar, the author recalls Kantorowicz's method, particularly his responses to formal queries from his students. He would prepare a small note card directing each questioner to relevant texts and scholarly discussions of whatever he had been asked about. "Invariably, several of the references would point to *The King's Two Bodies*, though seldom, if ever, to the text itself. . . . Rather, Kantorowicz worked from the footnotes, which were the repository of his learning. There he sent us again and again, and we quickly came to respect that source as the treasure trove it was, and remains."[24]

If emphasis were added to the quotation, one might legitimately place it on the word *remains*. The initial enthusiasms for *The King's Two Bodies* have been sustained over the course of four decades.[25] And Friedrich Baethgen's measured evaluation of the book in his memorial for Kantorowicz still commands wide endorsement: *The King's Two Bodies* has been and continues to be indispensable for all investigations of *Staatstheorie* and political theology.[26] This is not to say that the book has achieved a status beyond censure.[27] It is always hard for novices and frequently for senior scholars to follow some of the arguments, let alone to weave them into a coherent whole despite having the advantage of being able to turn to the efforts of earlier scholars to do so.

Nevertheless, for most readers the wonder and fascination of the myriad subjects brilliantly treated in *The King's Two Bodies* and the delight in the notes remain. When social history came to prominence in the 1960s and 1970s, it might have appeared inevitable that a work largely of high intellectual history or at least dependent on sources associated with the traditional history of ideas would be displaced somewhat from center stage.

[24] Professor Michael Mahoney (Department of History, Princeton University), in a memorandum to the author of this preface, 14 January 1997.

[25] Morimichi Watanabe reviewed the paperback reissue in 1983 and in a paragraph summed up initial and some later reactions; *Church History* 52 (1983), 258–59.

[26] Baethgen, "Ernst Kantorowicz," p. 12.

[27] There are a few harsh remarks in Malkiel, "Ernst H. Kantorowicz," pp. 214–15. Malkiel regards *The King's Two Bodies*, because of its lack of overall integration—and, so he believes, lack of vision—as a "stubborn retreat from monumentality"; I do not know what he means. Antony Black in an irreverent and iconoclastic article entitled, "Society and the Individual from the Middle Ages to Rousseau: Philosophy, Jurisprudence and Constitutional Theory," *History of Political Thought* 1 (1980): 147 n. 13, repeats the reservations of an earlier generation when he calls Kantorowicz's book "a masterpiece of erudite confusion."

But because of the artistic, discursive, and symbolic slant Kantorowicz gave to his subject, readers never regarded *The King's Two
Bodies* as "mere" history of ideas. Consequently, the book retained a grip on the historical imaginations of many scholars.[28]
When social history came to be enriched by other disciplines,
especially cultural anthropology, in the course of the 1970s and
1980s there was an even greater surge of interest in *The King's
Two Bodies*, as evidenced, it would seem reasonable to suggest,
from the proliferation of translations:[29] Spanish in 1985; Italian
and French in 1989; German in 1990; Portuguese and Polish in
1997.

In 1957 Ernst Kantorowicz published a book that would be
the guide for generations of scholars through the arcane mysteries of medieval political theology. *The King's Two Bodies* remains
as the fundamental legacy of a great scholar's career. It remains,
indeed, a wonderfully exciting and constantly rewarding book.

William Chester Jordan

Princeton, New Jersey
March 1997

[28] It may not be the best evidence, but a search of citation indexes, like the *Arts and
Humanities Citation Index* (Philadelphia, 1976–), reveals a continuous and relatively high
level of recourse to the book. As I read the citation records, it seems to be "out performing" Lawrence Stone's magisterial *Crisis of the Aristocracy, 1558–1641* (Oxford), whose
original publication date was 1965, and it is not so far behind Fernand Braudel's synthesis, *La Méditerranée et le monde méditerranéen à l'époque de Philippe II* (Paris), whose first
edition appeared in 1949.

[29] Cf. Robert Lerner, "Ernst H. Kantorowicz (1895–1963)," in *Medieval Scholarship:
Biographical Studies on the Formation of a Discipline*, I: *History*, ed. Helen Damico and Joseph
Zavadil (New York and London, 1995), pp. 274–75. Lerner's entire article can be rec-
ommended as a useful assessment on the enduring quality of Kantorowicz's scholarship.

PREFACE

AT the beginning of this book stands a conversation held twelve years ago with my friend MAX RADIN (then John H. Boalt Professor of Law, at Berkeley) in his tiny office in Boalt Hall, brimful floor to ceiling and door to window of books, papers, folders, notes—and life. To bait him with a question and get him off to an always stimulating and amusing talk was not a labor of Hercules. One day I found in my mail an offprint from a liturgical periodical published by a Benedictine Abbey in the United States, which bore the publisher's imprint: *The Order of St. Benedict, Inc.* To a scholar coming from the European Continent and not trained in the refinements of Anglo-American legal thinking, nothing could have been more baffling than to find the abbreviation *Inc.*, customary with business and other corporations, attached to the venerable community founded by St. Benedict on the rock of Montecassino in the very year in which Justinian abolished the Platonic Academy in Athens. Upon my inquiry, Max Radin informed me that indeed the monastic congregations were incorporated in this country, that the same was true with the dioceses of the Roman Church, and that, for example, the Archbishop of San Francisco could figure, in the language of the Law, as a "Corporation sole"—a topic which turned our conversation at once to Maitland's famous studies on that subject, to the abstract "Crown" as a corporation, to the curious legal fiction of the "King's Two Bodies" as developed in Elizabethan England, to Shakespeare's *Richard II*, and to certain mediaeval antecedents of the "abstract King." In other words, we had a good conversation, the kind of talk you would always yearn for and to which Max Radin was an ideal partner.

When shortly thereafter I was asked to contribute to a volume of essays in honor of Max Radin on his retirement, I could do no better than submit an essay on the "King's Two Bodies" (parts of Chapters I-III, and a section of Chapter IV), a paper of which he himself was, so to speak, a co-author or at least the illegitimate father. The *Festschrift* unfortunately never materialized. The contributions were returned to their authors, and though displeased by the fact that a well-deserved recognition was withheld from my friend, I was nevertheless not unhappy to see my manuscript back because in the meantime I had enlarged both my views and my material on the subject. I decided to publish my paper separately and dedicate it to Max Radin (then a temporary member of the Institute for Advanced Study, in Princeton) on his 70th birthday, in the Spring of 1950. Personal affairs such as the exasperating struggle against the Regents of the University of California as well as other duties prevented me from laying my gift into the hands of my friend. Max Radin died on June 22, 1950, and the study, destined to elicit his criticisms, his comments, and his broad laughter, serves now to honor his memory.

In its present, final form, this study has considerably outgrown the original plan, which was merely to point out a number of mediaeval antecedents or parallels to the legal tenet of the King's Two Bodies. It has gradually turned, as the subtitle suggests, into a "Study in Mediaeval Political Theology," which had not at all been the original intention. Such as it now stands, this study may be taken among other things as an attempt to understand and, if possible, demonstrate how, by what means and methods, certain axioms of a political theology which *mutatis mutandis* was to remain valid until the twentieth century, began to be developed during the later Middle Ages. It would go much too far, however, to assume that the author felt tempted to investigate the emergence of some of the idols of modern political religions merely on account of the horrifying experience of our own time in which whole nations, the largest and the smallest, fell prey to the weirdest dogmas and in which political theologisms became genuine obsessions defying in many cases the rudiments of human and political reason. Admittedly, the author was not unaware of the later aberrations; in fact, he became the more conscious of certain ideological gossamers the more he expanded and deepened his knowledge of the early development. It seems necessary, however, to stress the fact that considerations of that kind belonged to afterthoughts, resulting from the present investigation and not causing it or determining its course. The fascination emanating as usual from the historical material itself prevailed over any desire of practical or moral application and, needless to say, preceded any afterthought. This study deals with certain cyphers of the sovereign state and its perpetuity (Crown, Dignity, Patria, and others) exclusively from the point of view of presenting political creeds such as they were understood in their initial stage and at a time when they served as a vehicle for putting the early modern commonwealths on their own feet.

Since in this study a single strand of a very complicated texture has been isolated, the author cannot claim to have demonstrated in any completeness the problem of what has been called "The Myth of the State" (Ernst Cassirer). The study may be none the less a contribution to this greater problem although it is restricted to one leading idea, the fiction of the King's Two Bodies, its trans-formations, implications, and radiations. By thus restricting his subject, the author hopes to have avoided, at least to some extent, certain dangers customary with some all-too-sweeping and ambi-tious studies in the history of ideas: loss of control over topics, material, and facts; vagueness of language and argument; unsub-stantiated generalizations; and lack of tension resulting from tedious repetitions. The tenet of the King's Two Bodies and its history served in this case as a unifying principle easing the assem-blage and selection of facts as well as their synthesis.

The origin of this study will explain how it happened that the author swerved again (as in his study on the *Laudes*) from the normal tracks of the mediaeval historian and broke through the fences, this time, of mediaeval Law, for which he was not prepared by his training. For this trespass he owes apologies to the profes-sional jurist who, undoubtedly, will find many a flaw in this presentation, although the author himself is aware of some of the more likely shortcomings: overlaboring of texts on the one hand, missing of salient points on the other. But those are the hazards to which the outsider will usually expose himself; he will have to pay the fine for intruding into the enclosure of a sister-discipline. The incompleteness of sources is still another point in need of apology. Every student laboring in the vineyard of mediaeval Law will be painfully aware of the difficulty of laying hands on even the most important authors whose works, so far as they are pub-lished at all (there is, for example, no edition of the most influ-ential canonist of the late twelfth century, Huguccio of Pisa), are available only in the both rare and antiquated sixteenth-century prints. Consultations of the Law Libraries at Berkeley, Columbia, and Harvard; the understanding kindness of the head of the Law

Collection of the Library of Congress, Dr. V. Gsovski; the supplies of Princeton's Firestone Library, now enriched by the collection of C. H. McIlwain; finally purchases made for the author by the Library of the Institute for Advanced Study and by the author himself gradually filled some of the most irritating gaps. The value of assistance through Interlibrary Loan, normally inestimable, was, however, considerably reduced in the case of a study which demanded a constant checking and re-checking and comparing of a large source-material, as the problems continually recurred. How much has been missed, how many texts became accessible too late to be used for the present task, will be known to none better than to the author himself. The reader will notice very quickly which authors were permanently available and which ones only occasionally or not at all; whereas the fact that the same works are quoted not uniformly according to the same editions tells yet another story. Fortunately, however, a study intending, as this one does, to make problems visible rather than to solve them, would not have aimed at completeness in any event. The same is true, though for different reasons, with regard to secondary literature which, on the whole, will be quoted only when and where the author felt an immediate indebtedness, a procedure which does not rule out the possibility that relevant, and perhaps very valuable, studies may have been overlooked or come to the author's attention too late to be evaluated here. That the author has quoted his own studies and articles perhaps too frequently does not imply indebtedness to himself, but laziness: he felt disinclined, except in a few cases, to repeat what he had done before.

The documentation has been kept rather full and may at times seem excessive. Since, however, much of the legal material will not be accessible in more than perhaps half a dozen libraries in this country, it seemed advisable in view of the needs of students in the history of political ideas to reproduce text passages lavishly rather than sparingly. Moreover, the material on tangential problems which could not be discussed in the text without encroaching upon its intelligibility and stifling the main argument, was thrown into a footnote where eventually it may become useful to others— although admittedly the temptation of expanding on side-issues was not always easy (and sometimes indeed too great) to resist. It may therefore happen that the reader will find more material appealing to his taste and his interests buried in the footnotes than resuscitated in the text. It remained, however, the author's prime ambition to produce a fairly readable text, to chart a more or less clearly marked way through rarely explored thickets, and to keep the reader's attention, if possible, awake instead of abandoning him to some jungle teeming with scholarly tsetse flies. Whether he succeeded or not, will be up to the reader to decide.

Only hesitatingly and rarely did the author find it necessary to draw conclusions or indicate how the various topics discussed in these pages should be geared with each other; but the reader will find it easy enough to draw his own conclusions and himself combine the cogwheels, an operation facilitated by very numerous cross-references and a full index.* At any rate, the present study will have served its purpose of calling attention to certain problems if the reader detects many more examples or places relevant to the King's Two Bodies and many more interrelations with other problems than the author intimated. It may be regretted also that the dualities present in ecclesiastical offices have not been discussed coherently in a special chapter. While this would have been a subject in its own right, the author never lost sight of the ecclesiastical aspects and believes that in an indirect fashion the ecclesiastical side of the problem has not been neglected.

A book that has been in the making over a long period of time naturally owes much to others. The author gladly confesses his indebtedness for various informations and courtesies to friends, colleagues, and other helpers whose contributions are gratefully acknowledged in the notes and in the List of Plates. His thanks, however, should go in the first place to his younger friends who, formerly his students at Berkeley, succeeded each other as the author's Assistants at the Institute for Advanced Study. Each, in his way, not only helped to put the manuscript into shape and get it ready for the press, but also contributed by counsel, criticism, and advice, and by lively interest which in turn kindled the flagging interest of the author. For these and other services the author is obliged to Professor Michael Cherniavsky, Mr. Robert L. Benson, Dr. Ralph E. Giesey, and Mrs. Margaret Bentley Ševčenko, whereas to Dr. William M. Bowsky goes a separate share of the

---

* The cross-references referring to a footnote refer usually not only to the footnote itself but also to the text, or even to the page, to which the note belongs.

author's gratitude because to him there fell the most uninspiring and unrewarding task of all, that of reading and re-reading the proofs, assembling the Bibliography, and helping to collect the Index. To other former students of his, Professor William A. Chaney and Dr. Schafer Williams, the author is grateful for calling his attention to important points, whereas Professor George H. Williams kindly read the first draft and contributed through his own publication.

Others as well were kind enough to read the greater part of the final manuscript: Professors Dietrich Gerhard, Gaines Post, and Joseph R. Strayer, who obliged the author by a considerable number of suggestions and additions, and, last not least, by their moral support. In this respect, the author's gratitude is due, above all, to Professor Theodor E. Mommsen, who loyally read the whole manuscript as—chapter by chapter—it emerged from the typewriter, who never withheld his opinion and made numerous corrections, and who gave the author a chance to discuss with him on many evenings the broader problems as well as countless details. The author, further, was in the fortunate position of being able to draw from the knowledge of his colleagues at the Institute for Advanced Study and plague them with his questions: Professor Harold Cherniss, who became the chief victim, carrying as he did the brunt of the author's queries in matters of ancient philosophy, and who patiently iterated his explanations of more complicated problems regardless of the tortures he himself suffered from the distortions which not only Plato had suffered at the hands of Aristotle, but also Aristotle at the hands of mediaeval scholastics; Professor Erwin Panofsky, upon whom the author could always rely when questions of art history arose and who would be untiring once the hunt was on; Professor Kurt Weitzmann, who called the author's attention to several items and was always ready to be helpful in matters of photos and plates; and Professor Andreas Alföldi, of whose treasure of knowledge the author could avail himself in matters concerning Late Antiquity. To these names there has to be added that of the author's former colleague at Berkeley, Professor Leonardo Olschki, with whom the author discussed over a long period of time innumerable Dante problems and by whose fruitful criticisms the chapter on Dante profited in many respects. To all these friends the author extends not only his thanks but also his apologies wherever he may have misinterpreted them: the mistakes are the author's own and perhaps most original contribution.

A collaboration of a singular kind developed with Dr. Ralph E. Giesey whose own forthcoming study on "The Royal Funeral Ceremony in Renaissance France" overlapped with some central problems dealt with in Chapter VII. As in all cases of a daily exchange of ideas and material, it would often be not at all easy to separate neatly the partners' contributions. The footnotes, however, will make it manifest how generously Dr. Giesey placed his own material—published as well as unpublished texts and photos—at the disposal of the author who had no qualms about using it, but remains for these sections a grateful debtor.

Finally the author wishes to express his thanks to Dr. J. Robert Oppenheimer who, on the part of the Institute for Advanced Study, generously subsidized the publication of this book, and to Princeton University Press for its willingness to comply in every respect with the author's suggestions and personal wishes.

E.H.K.

Princeton, New Jersey
March 2, 1957

PUBLISHER'S NOTE TO THE SECOND PRINTING:

The author provided a short list of Addenda and Corrigenda at the end of the original printing of this book. The Addenda remain at the end of this reprinting just as he gave them. The Corrigenda, however, have been incorporated into the text of this reprint, as have a score or more of other manifest errors in spelling, usage, and typography which have come to our attention.

Some errors of a substantive nature (sometimes simply typographical but not readily noticeable as such) have been found by examining the author's copy of the book and by consulting with his friends and colleagues. We provide the following list of these substantive corrections, which we have made in this printing, for the benefit of those who possess the original imprint of the book: p. 40, in a quotation, read true king's fall (for great king's); p. 154, n. 194, read C.6,23,19 (for 23,11); p. 169, n. 240, read *C*.7,37,3 (for 37,1); p. 205, n. 35, read Tierney, *Cath. Hist. Rev.*, XXXVI, 428,n.57 (for "Conciliar Theory," etc.); p. 208, n. 43, add to end: [Gierke erred: read *Spec. Doctr.* VII, c. 15.]; p. 223, n. 89, read Prince against trying to (for Prince to try); p. 224, read Bishop of St. Davids (for Bishop of Hereford); p. 241, line 2, read Death itself is Victory and is (for Victory itself is); p. 264, n. 218, read *QFIAB*, XXXIV (for XXIV); p. 269, n. 230, read Seneca, *Ep.* 85,35 (for 85,30); p. 271, n. 235, read Peter of Auvergne (for William); p. 400, n. 295, read tamen (for tantum); p. 414, n. 332, end of line 13, read 1600 (for 1620); p. 420, read Burgh-upon-the-Sands on the Solway (for Burgh in Norfolk); p. 440, n. 405, read John 10:30 (for 10:20); p. 478, in first quotation, read civil affairs (for view of the citizens); p. 541, under Dubois, read 256, n. 194 (for n. 195); p. 552, 2nd column, 2nd line from bottom on right, read 212, n. 55 (for 312).

Ernst H. Kantorowicz died in September, 1963. A collection of twenty-five of his previously published essays have been reprinted under the title *Selected Studies* (Locust Valley, N.Y.: J. J. Augustin, 1965). A complete bibliography of his works is given in that volume.

The King's Two Bodies

INTRODUCTION

MYSTICISM, when transposed from the warm twilight of myth and fiction to the cold searchlight of fact and reason, has usually little left to recommend itself. Its language, unless resounding within its own magic or mystic circle, will often appear poor and even slightly foolish, and its most baffling metaphors and highflown images, when deprived of their iridescent wings, may easily resemble the pathetic and pitiful sight of Baudelaire's Albatross. Political mysticism in particular is exposed to the danger of losing its spell or becoming quite meaningless when taken out of its native surroundings, its time and its space.

The mystic fiction of the "King's Two Bodies," as divulged by English jurists of the Tudor period and the times thereafter, does not form an exception to this rule. It has been mercilessly plucked by Maitland in a highly stimulating and amusing study on "The Crown as Corporation."[1] With a strong touch of sarcasm and irony, the great English historian of law has disclosed the follies which the fiction of the king as a "Corporation sole" could, and did, lead to, and has shown at the same time what havoc the theory of a two-bodied king and a twinned kingship was bound to work in bureaucratic logic. Wittily Maitland puns about the king being "*parsonified*" and styles the theory of the King's Two Bodies "a marvelous display of metaphysical—or we might say metaphysiological—nonsense."

From his admirably stocked garner of juridical *exempla* Maitland was able to produce case after case illustrating the absurdity of that doctrine. He tells us the story about King George III who had to go to Parliament for permission to hold some land as a man and not as a king, "since rights not denied to any of His Majesty's subjects were denied to him." He adds that other delightful case concerning the tenants of one of the traitors of the rebellion of 1715 whose barony had been confiscated and handed over to the king: the tenants were jubilant at this change of lordship, for owing to the fact that the barony now was "vested in His Majesty, his heirs and successors in his politick capacity, which in consideration of law never dies," they believed that henceforth

---

[1] F. W. Maitland, *Selected Essays* (Cambridge, 1936), 104-127, reprint from *Law Quarterly Review*, XVII (1901), 131-146.

they were freed from paying the customary relief on the death of their (hitherto simply mortal) lord. Parliament, however, disappointed them by making the surprising decision that in this case the king was considered a private person who could die, and therefore the tenants continued to pay their taxes as before. And Maitland was even able to bring evidence to show that Louis XIV's famous if apocryphal *l'état c'est moi*—or, for that matter, the scholastic *papa qui potest dici ecclesia*—was officially recognized also in England: a Statute of 1887 decreed that "the expressions 'permanent civil service of the State,' 'permanent civil service of Her Majesty,' and 'permanent civil service of the Crown' are hereby declared to have the same meaning"—which, so Maitland remarks, "is a mess."[2]

The challenge to ridicule the theory of the King's Two Bodies is indeed great when you read, without being prepared for it, the at once fantastic and subtle description of the king's superbody or body politic rendered by Blackstone in a chapter of his *Commentaries* which conveniently summarizes the achievements of several centuries of political thought and legal speculation. From his pages there rises the spectre of an absolutism exercised, not by an abstract "State," as in modern times, or by an abstract "Law," as in the High Middle Ages, but by an abstract physiological fiction which in secular thought remains probably without parallel.[3] That the king is immortal because legally he can never die, or that he is legally never under age, are familiar stage properties. But it goes further than expected when we are told that the king "is not only incapable of *doing* wrong, but even of *thinking* wrong: he can never mean to do an improper thing: in him is no folly or weakness."[4] Moreover, that king is invisible[5] and, though

---

[2] *Ibid.*, 117. That such "mess" was not restricted to England was of course not unknown to Maitland, since Otto von Gierke, *Deutsches Genossenschaftsrecht* (Berlin, 1891), III,294,n.148, quotes a striking parallel. Antonius de Butrio, a 14th-century canon lawyer, claims that it made no difference concerning the ownership of ecclesiastical property "sive dicas Christum, sive praelatum, sive ecclesiam universalem, sive particularem possidere, sive episcopum, sive alium praelatum, sive Papam vicarium Christi."

[3] Sir William Blackstone, *Commentaries on the Laws of England*, I,c.7 (first published in 1765), 237ff.

[4] *Ibid.*, I,246.

[5] The king's invisibility is not mentioned directly by Blackstone, but it belongs to the standard definitions of the body politic; see below, Ch. I, n. 2, for Plowden: ". . . the Body politic is a Body that cannot be seen or handled"; or *Calvin's Case*

he may never judge despite being the "Fountain of Justice," he
yet has legal ubiquity: "His Majesty in the eye of the law is always
present in all his courts, though he cannot personally distribute
justice."[6] The state of superhuman "absolute perfection" of this
royal *persona ficta* is, so to speak, the result of a fiction within a
fiction: it is inseparable from a peculiar aspect of corporational
concepts, the corporation sole. Blackstone gives credit entirely to
the Romans for having invented the idea of corporations—"but
our laws have considerably refined and improved upon the invention, according to the usual genius of the English nation: particularly with regard to sole corporations, consisting of one person
only, of which the Roman lawyers had no notion."[7]

That kind of man-made irreality—indeed, that strange construction of a human mind which finally becomes slave to its own
fictions—we are normally more ready to find in the religious
sphere than in the allegedly sober and realistic realms of law,
politics, and constitution; and therefore Maitland's often caustic
criticisms are understandable and appear fully justified. However,
the seemingly ludicrous, and in many respects awkward, concept
of the King's Two Bodies has not only those physiologically amusing traits. Maitland himself was fully aware that this theorem, to
say the least, provided an important heuristic fiction which served
the lawyers at a certain time "to harmonize modern with ancient
law," or to bring into agreement the personal with the more
impersonal concepts of government.[8] Great mediaevalist that
Maitland was, he knew perfectly well that the curious fiction of
"twin-born majesty" had a very long tradition and complex history which "would take us deep into the legal and political
thoughts of the Middle Ages."[9]

This history, alas, has not been written by Maitland, even

(1608), in Sir Edward Coke, *The Reports*, ed. George Wilson (London, 1777), VII,
10-10a: ". . . for the politic capacity is invisible and immortal" (cf. 12a).

[6] Blackstone, *Comm.*, I,270.

[7] *Ibid.*, I,c.18, 469; Maitland, *Sel.Ess.*, 75.

[8] See Maitland's remarks in: Pollock and Maitland, *The History of English Law*
(2nd ed., Cambridge, 1898 and 1923), I,512, also 495, and *Sel. Ess.*, 105ff; further
his study "The Corporation Sole," *Sel. Ess.*, 73-103, with (p. 264) a valuable list of
Year Book cases (reprint from *LQR*, XVI [1900], 335-354), in which Maitland with
his unique mastership, discloses the effects of the early mediaeval *Eigenkirchenrecht*
on later conditions, including the concept of the corporation sole.

[9] Maitland, *Sel. Ess.*, 105.

though he may have dropped more than one valuable hint in that respect. Nor will the writing of that history, especially with regard to the crucial fifteenth century, cease to remain an interesting and promising task for one of the many learned investigators of legal and constitutional development in England, for the present studies do not pretend to fill the gap. They merely propose to outline the historical problem as such, to sketch in an all too perfunctory, casual, and incomplete fashion the general historical background of the "King's Two Bodies," and to place this concept, if possible, in its proper setting of mediaeval thought and political theory.

CHAPTER I

THE PROBLEM: PLOWDEN'S REPORTS

IN EDMUND PLOWDEN'S *Reports,* collected and written under Queen Elizabeth, Maitland found the first clear elaboration of that mystical talk with which the English crown jurists enveloped and trimmed their definitions of kingship and royal capacities.[1] In order to describe conveniently both the problem and the theory of the King's Two Bodies it may be appropriate to choose as a starting point Plowden, himself a law apprentice of the Middle Temple, and quote some of the most telling passages from the arguments and judgments made in the king's courts and epitomized in his *Reports.*

The *cause célèbre* concerning the Duchy of Lancaster, which the Lancastrian Kings had owned as private property and not as property of the Crown, was tried—not for the first time, to be sure—in the fourth year of Queen Elizabeth. Edward VI, the Queen's predecessor, had made, while not yet of age, a lease of certain lands of the Duchy. Thereupon the crown lawyers, assembled at Serjeant's Inn, all agreed:

> that by the Common Law no Act which the King does as King, shall be defeated by his Nonage. For the King has in him two Bodies, *viz.,* a Body natural, and a Body politic. His Body natural (if it be considered in itself) is a Body mortal, subject to all Infirmities that come by Nature or Accident, to the Imbecility of Infancy or old Age, and to the like Defects that happen to the natural Bodies of other People. But his Body politic is a Body that cannot be seen or handled, consisting of Policy and Government, and constituted for the Direction of the People, and the Management of the public weal, and this Body is utterly void of Infancy, and old Age, and other natural Defects and Imbecilities, which the Body natural is subject to, and for this Cause, what the King does in his Body politic, cannot be invalidated or frustrated by any Disability in his natural Body.[2]

It may be mentioned immediately that the pattern after which

1 Maitland, *Sel. Ess.,* 109: "Whether this sort of talk was really new about the year 1550, or whether it had gone unreported until Plowden arose, it were not easy to say; but the Year Books have not prepared us for it."
2 Edmund Plowden, *Commentaries or Reports* (London, 1816), 212a. The case is referred to by Coke, *Rep.,* VII,10 (*Calvin's Case*).

the King's body politic—"void of Infancy and old Age, and other natural Defects and Imbecilities"—has been modelled, can be gathered readily from Sir John Fortescue's tractate on *The Governance of England*, where he writes:

> ... it is no poiar to mowe synne, and to do ylle, or to mowe to be seke, wex olde, or that a man may hurte hym self. Ffor all thes poiars comen of impotencie ... wherefore the holy sprites and angels that mey not synne, wex old, be seke, or hurte ham selff, have more poiar than we, that mey harme owre selff with all thes defautes. So is the kynges power more. . . .[3]

The passage has not been adduced here in order to prove that the Elizabethan jurists "borrowed" from Fortescue, or that his treatise was their "source," although in other respects this possibility should not be excluded. What matters is that John Fortescue's passage shows how closely the legal speculations were related to theological thought, or, to be more specific, to the mediaeval concept of the king's *character angelicus*.[4] The body politic of kingship appears as a likeness of the "holy sprites and angels," because it represents, like the angels, the Immutable within Time. It has

---

[3] Sir John Fortescue, *The Governance of England*, c.vi, ed. Charles Plummer (Oxford, 1885), 121; cf. 218f, and the quotation from the *Song of Lewes* (p.217). See also Fortescue's *De Natura Legis Naturae*, c.xxvi, which S. B. Chrimes quotes *in extenso* in his admirable edition of Fortescue's *De Laudibus Legum Angliae* (Cambridge, 1942), 154. See also *De Laudibus*, c.xiv, ed. Chrimes, 34,27f, for related ideas.

[4] The king's *character angelicus* has been mentioned in modern literature quite frequently—see, e.g., Eduard Eichmann, "Königs- und Bischofsweihe," *Sitz. Ber. bayer. Akad.* (Munich, 1928), No.6, p.8; Max Hackelsperger, *Bibel und mittelalterlicher Reichsgedanke* (Munich diss., 1934), 28,n.35; E. Kantorowicz, *Laudes Regiae* (Berkeley, 1946), 49,n.126—but the whole problem has as yet not been investigated. The places decisive for that idea are found not only in the Bible, e.g., II. Sam. 14: 17 and 20; of equal or greater importance is probably the Hellenistic strand. See, for the concept according to which the king and the sage represent a distinct third class, intermediary between gods and men, Erwin R. Goodenough, *The Politics of Philo Judaeus* (New Haven, 1938), 98ff, and the same author's "The Political Philosophy of Hellenistic Kingship," *Yale Classical Studies*, I (1928), 55-102, esp. 76ff,100f; the treatises discussed by Goodenough have more recently been edited and commented by Louis Delatte, *Les traités de la royauté d'Ecphante, Diotogène et Sthénidas*, Bibliothèque de la Faculté de Philosophie et Lettres de l'Université de Liège, xcvii (Liège, 1942); see also Artur Steinwenter, "ΝΟΜΟΣ ΕΜΨΥΧΟΣ: Zur Geschichte einer politischen Theorie," *Anzeiger der Akademie der Wissenschaften in Wien*, phil.-hist.Kl., LXXXIII (1946), 250-268, esp. 259ff. For the early Christian concept, see, e.g., Günther Dehn, "Engel und Obrigkeit," *Theologische Aufsätze Karl Barth zum 50. Geburtstag* (Munich, 1936), 90ff; see also the criticism by Harald Fuchs, *Der geistige Widerstand gegen Rom in der antiken Welt* (Berlin, 1938), 58f.

been raised to angelic heights, a fact which is worth being kept in mind.

The judges, after thus having gained a foothold on, so to speak, firm celestial ground, continued their arguments in the case of the Duchy of Lancaster. They pointed out that, if lands which the King has purchased before he was King, namely "in the capacity of his Body natural," later were given away by him, such gift, even when made during his nonage, had to be recognized as the King's act. For—so the Elizabethan judges declared, and herewith their "mysticism" begins—

> although he [the king] has, or takes, the land in his natural Body, yet to this natural Body is conjoined his Body politic, which contains his royal Estate and Dignity; and the Body politic includes the Body natural, but the Body natural is the lesser, and with this the Body politic is consolidated. So that he has a Body natural, adorned and invested with the Estate and Dignity royal; and he has not a Body natural distinct and divided by itself from the Office and Dignity royal, but a Body natural and a Body politic together indivisible; and these two Bodies are incorporated in one Person, and make one Body and not divers, that is the Body corporate in the Body natural, *et e contra* the Body natural in the Body corporate. So that the Body natural, by this conjunction of the Body politic to it, '(which Body politic contains the Office, Government, and Majesty royal) is magnified, and by the said Consolidation hath in it the Body politic.[5]

The King's Two Bodies thus form one unit indivisible, each being fully contained in the other. However, doubt cannot arise concerning the superiority of the body politic over the body natural. "Three Kings [Henry IV, V, VI] held the Duchy of Lancaster in their Body natural, which is not so ample and large as the other, and the fourth [Edward IV] held it in his Body politic, which is more ample and large than the Body natural."[6]

Not only is the body politic "more ample and large" than the body natural, but there dwell in the former certain truly mysterious forces which reduce, or even remove, the imperfections of the fragile human nature.

His Body politic, which is annexed to his Body natural, takes away

---

[5] Plowden, *Reports*, 213; see below, Ch.vii,nos.302ff, for the Case of the Duchy of Lancaster.

[6] Plowden, *Reports*, 220a, likewise a case referred to by Coke (above, n.2). For the Duchy of Lancaster, see below, Ch.vii,nos.302ff.

the Imbecility of his Body natural, and draws the Body natural, which is the lesser, and all the Effects thereof to itself, which is the greater, *quia magis dignum trahit ad se minus dignum.*[7]

The Latin legal maxim saying that "the worthier draws to itself the less worthy" was common among mediaeval jurists. It was regularly invoked when a *persona mixta* (or, for that matter, *a res mixta*) was the issue. Baldus, the great Italian lawyer and legal authority of the fourteenth century, for example, linked that maxim most fittingly to the two sexes of an hermaphrodite: according to the Digest, the more prominent qualities were to determine the sex, for (summarizes Baldus) "if a union of two extremes is produced, while the qualities of each extreme abide, then the one more prominent and striking draws to itself the other one."[8] What

[7] Plowden, *Reports*, 213a. The Latin maxim (see next note) was later repeated, e.g., by Sir Edward Coke, *The Second Part of the Institutes of the Laws of England* (London, 1681), 307: "Omne maius dignum trahit ad se minus dignum." The maxim itself must have been known in England since the 13th century at the latest; see Matthew Paris. ad a. 1216, ed. Luard (Rolls Series), II,657, who reproduces the opinion of Pope Innocent III against French barons venturing to condemn King John: ". . . per barones, tanquam inferiores, non potuit ad mortem condemnari, quia maior dignitas quodam modo absorbet minorem." For legal maxims in English legal language at large, see David Ogg, *Joannis Seldeni "Ad Fletam Dissertatio"* (Cambridge, 1925), Introd., pp.xlii-xlvi.

[8] For the hermaphrodite, see *D.*1,5,10. Baldus refers to this decision of Ulpian when discussing the Gregorian decretal on the right of advowson which, having both a laical and a clerical character, appeared as *quid mixtum* comparable to the hermaphrodite—or to the King's Two Bodies. See Baldus' gloss on c.3 X 2,1,n.7, *In Decretalium volumen* (Venice, 1580), fol.152ᵛ, with many other allegations and the conclusion: "Item quando ex duobus extremis fit unio, remanentibus qualitatibus extremorum, magis principale et magis notabile aliud ad se trahit." See further the (also medically interesting) legal opinion concerning the hermaphrodite in the house of Malaspina; Baldus, *Consilia* (Venice, 1575), III,237,n.1, fol.67ᵛ. The *Glossa ordinaria* (Bernard of Parma) on c.3 X 2,1, alludes also to that maxim: "Nota quod *causa mixta* inter spiritualem et civilem magis sequitur natura[m] spiritualis quam civilis . . . et sic quod est minus dignum in sui substantia, maioris est efficaciae quo ad iurisdictionem." Baldus himself referred to that maxim repeatedly; see, e.g., on *C.*9,1,5,n.4, *Commentaria in Codicem* (Venice, 1586), fol.194ᵛ, or on *C.*6,43, 2,n.1, fol.157ᵛ, which fits the later English theory not badly: "Nota quod in unitis ad invicem, dignius trahit ad se minus dignum. Item quod plurimum potest, trahit ad se quod nimium potest et communicat illi suam propriam dignitatem et privilegia." See also the *Glossa ordinaria* on the Decretals (Johannes Teutonicus), on c.3 X 3,40, where the maxim is applied to the holy oils: "Item oleum non consecratum potest commisceri oleo consecrato et dicetur totum consecratum," to which the glossator remarks, v. *consecratum*: "Et ita sacrum tanquam dignius trahit ad se non sacrum." (I owe the knowledge of this passage as well as that from Lucas de Penna [below] to the kind interest of Professor Gaines Post.) Further, and once more in connection with advowson, Johannes Andreae, *Novella in Decretales*, on c.un. VI 3,19,n.12 (Venice, 1612), fol.126; and, referring to delegate judges, Hostiensis (Henry of Segusia), *Summa aurea*, on X 1,29,n.9 (Venice, 1586), col.297; see also Oldradus

fitted the two sexes of an hermaphrodite, fitted juristically also the two bodies of a king. Hence, the Tudor jurist proceeded logically and in conformity with the rules of his trade when on that occasion he referred to the proper legal maxim.

The underlying idea was emphasized no less vigorously in the case *Willion* v. *Berkley*, which was argued in the preceding year (3 Elizabeth) in Common Bench. The subject was a trespass of Lord Berkley on certain lands for which he claimed to have paid a tax to the court of King Henry VII and which he considered as parcel in his demesne as of fee tail. The judges pointed out that

> although the law should adjudge that King Henry 7. took it in his Body natural, and not in his Body politic, yet they [the judges] said that he [the King] is not void of Prerogative in regard to Things which he has in his Body natural. . . . For when the Body politic of King of this Realm is conjoined to the Body natural, and one Body is made of them both, the Degree of the Body natural, and of the things possessed in that Capacity, is thereby altered, and the Effects thereof are changed by its Union with the other Body, and don't remain in their former Degree, but partake of the Effects of the Body politic. . . . And the Reason thereof is, because the Body natural and the Body politic are consolidated into one, and the Body politic wipes away every Imperfection of the other Body, with which it is consolidated, and makes it to be another Degree than it should be if it were alone by itself. . . . And the Cause [in a parallel case] was not because the Capacity of his Body natural was drowned by the Dignity royal . . . , but the Reason was, because to the Body natural, in which he held the land, the Body politic was associated and conjoined, during which Association or Conjunction the Body natural partakes of the Nature and Effects of the Body politic.[9]

---

de Ponte, *Consilia*, xvii,n.1 (Lyon, 1550), fol.7ᵛ. For the civilians, see, e.g., the Neapolitan jurist Lucas de Penna, *Commentaria in Tres Libros*, on C.10,5,1,n.17 (Lyon, 1597), p. 33: "Quotiens enim maius minori coniungitur, maius trahit ad se minus . . ." See also, for the related idea of the superior judge engulfing the power of the inferior, Frederick II's *Liber augustalis*, 1,41 (Edition: Cervone, Naples, 1773, which contains the gloss), 93: ". . . minori lumine per luminare maius superveniens obscurato," a passage to which the 13th-century glossator Marinus de Caramanico (*ibid.*, 93) remarks: "maior causa trahit ad se minorem," with a reference to D.5,1,54; see also, for the same idea in the form of an hexameter, Nicolaus de Braia, *Gesta Ludovici Octavi*, line 643, in Bouquet, *Recueil des historiens*, xvii,323: "Ut maiore minus cecetur lumine lumen." See also, on the gloss of Marinus de Caramanico, Matthaeus de Afflictis, *In utriusque Siciliae . . . Constitutiones novissima praelectio* (Venice, 1562), I, fol.167. The maxim seems to stem from Paulus, *Sententiae*, 1,12,8: "maior enim quaestio minorem causam ad se trahit"; see *Fontes iuris romani anteiustiniani*, ed. S. Riccobono et alii (Florence, 1940), ii,330, and D.5,1,54.

9 Plowden, *Reports*, 238, a case later referred to by Coke, *Reports*, vii,32. That the body politic "wipes away imperfection" was common opinion; see, e.g., Bacon, *Post-*

The difficulties of defining the effects as exercised by the body politic—active in the individual king like a *deus absconditus*—on the royal body natural are obvious. In fact, Elizabethan jurists sometimes had to proceed with the caution and circumspection of theologians defining a dogma. It was anything but a simple task to remain consistent when one had to defend at once the perfect union of the King's Two Bodies and the very distinct capacities of each body alone. It is a veritable sword-dance that the jurists perform, when they explain:

> Therefore, when the two Bodies in the King are become as one Body, to which no Body is equal, this double Body, whereof the Body politic is greater, cannot hold in Jointure with any single one.[10]

> Yet [despite the unity of the two bodies] his Capacity to take in the Body natural is not confounded by the Body politic, but remains still.[11]

> Notwithstanding that these two Bodies are at one Time conjoined together, yet the Capacity of the one does not confound that of the other, but they remain distinct Capacities.

> *Ergo* the Body natural and the Body politic are not distinct, but united, and as one Body.[12]

Regardless of the dogmatic unity of the two bodies, a separation of one from the other was nevertheless possible, to wit, that separa-

---

Nati, in: *Works of Sir Francis Bacon,* ed. J. Spedding and D. D. Heath (London, 1892), VII,668: "The body politic of the Crown indueth the natural person of the King with these perfections: . . . that if he were attainted before, the very assumption of the Crown purgeth it." See also Blackstone, *Comm.,* I,c.7,248: "If the heir to the crown were attainted of treason or felony, and afterwards the crown should descend to him, this would purge the attainder *ipso facto.*" The theory was fully developed in England by 1485 when, in the Exchequer Chamber, the justices concurred with regard to Henry VII "que le Roy fuist personable et discharge dascun attainder *eo facto* que il prist sur le Raigne et estre roy. . . ." See Chrimes, *Const. Ideas,* Appendix 74, p. 378, cf. p. 51. This doctrine is in fact the secularization of the purging power of the sacraments. See, for Byzantium, the opinion of Theodore Balsamon (*PGr,* CXXXVII,1156), who held that the emperor's consecration had the same effects as baptism, so that in the case of the Emperor John Tzimisces (969-978) that act did away with all the crimes and sins of his former life. The same idea was advocated in France, under King Charles V, by Jean Golein: the king by his anointment is *telement nettoié des ses pechiez* that he likens a newly baptized; see Marc Bloch, *Les rois thaumaturges* (Strasbourg, 1924), 483; also George H. Williams, *Norman Anonymous* (below, Ch.III,n.1), 159f. See, for a few related cases (Matrimony, Holy Orders), Kantorowicz, "The Carolingian King in the Bible of San Paolo fuori le Mura," *Late Classical and Mediaeval Studies in Honor of Albert Mathias Friend, Jr.* (Princeton, 1954), 293.

[10] Plowden, *Reports,* 238a.   [11] *Ibid.,* 242.   [12] *Ibid.,* 233a, 242a.

tion which, with regard to common man, is usually called Death. In the case *Willion* v. *Berkley*, Justice Southcote, seconded by Justice Harper, proffered some remarkable arguments to that effect, as the Law Report shows:

> The King has two Capacities, for he has two Bodies, the one whereof is a Body natural, consisting of natural Members as every other Man has, and in this he is subject to Passions and Death as other Men are; the other is a Body politic, and the Members thereof are his Subjects, and he and his Subjects together compose the Corporation, as Southcote said, and he is incorporated with them, and they with him, and he is the Head, and they are the Members, and he has the sole Government of them; and this Body is not subject to Passions as the other is, nor to Death, for as to this Body the King never dies, and his natural Death is not called in our Law (as Harper said), the Death of the King, but the Demise of the King, not signifying by the Word (*Demise*) that the Body politic of the King is dead, but that there is a Separation of the two Bodies, and that the Body politic is transferred and conveyed over from the Body natural now dead, or now removed from the Dignity royal, to another Body natural. So that it signifies a Removal of the Body politic of the King of this Realm from one Body natural to another.[13]

This migration of the "Soul," that is, of the immortal part of kingship, from one incarnation to another as expressed by the concept of the king's demise is certainly one of the essentials of the whole theory of the King's Two Bodies. It has preserved its validity for practically all time to come. Interesting, however, is the fact that this "incarnation" of the body politic in a king of flesh not only does away with the human imperfections of the body natural, but conveys "immortality" to the individual king as King, that is, with regard to his superbody. In the case *Hill* v. *Grange* (2 and 3 Philip and Mary) the judges argued as follows:

> And then when the Act gives Remedy to the Patentees . . . , and Henry 8. is mentioned before to be King, and so the Relation is to him as King, he as King never dies, but the King, in which Name it has Relation to him, does ever continue.[14]

[13] *Ibid.*, 233a, quoted by Blackstone, *Comm.*, I,249. In common speech, the idiom of the king's *demise*, signifying in a technical sense "a Removal of the Body politic . . . from one Body natural to another," hardly antedates the era of the Wars of the Roses in the 15th century when each transfer of power from Lancaster to York and back was legally interpreted as the *demise* of the defeated king. The word, however, was used before, e.g., in 1388, when a plea was said to have gone "without day" (that is, in court) *par demys le Roy* (Edward III). See below, Ch.vii,n.195.

[14] Plowden, *Reports*, 177a. The mentioning of the title was essential and often

In this case, *King* Henry VIII was still "alive" though Henry Tudor had been dead for ten years.[15] In other words, whereas the manhood of the individual incarnation appeared as negligible and as a matter of indifferent importance, the eternal essence or "godhead" of the monarch was all that counted before the tribunal of those "monophysite" judges.

Contrariwise, the "manhood" or the king's body natural might become of great importance too, as in *Sir Thomas Wroth's Case* (15 Elizabeth).[16] Sir Thomas had been appointed by Henry VIII as Usher of the Privy Chamber to the entourage of Edward VI, when Edward was not yet king. At Edward's accession to the throne, Sir Thomas ceased to receive his annuities because his service, though suitable with a prince, was not considered befitting the estate of the King. Justice Saunders argued that the continuance of service after the king's accession would have been justified, for example, with regard

> to a Physician or Surgeon for his Counsel and Service to the Prince; and if the King dies, and the Prince becomes King, there the Service is not discharged . . . , for the Service is to be done in respect of the natural Body, which has need of Physic and Surgery, and is subject to Infirmities and Accidents as well after the Accession of the Estate-royal to it as before, so that the royal Majesty causes no Alteration as to the Service in this case. And so is it in other like Cases, as to teach the Prince Grammar, Music, *et cetera*, where the Service to be done has Respect merely to the Body natural, and not to the Majesty of the Body politic.[17]

The least that can be said is that there was logic in the arguments of the lawyers. No less logical, though far less simple, were the arguments in *Calvin's Case* (1608) reported by Sir Edward Coke.[18] Here the judges reasoned that every subject sworn to the king is

---

decisive because legally it made a great difference whether persons *celebrati sunt nomine dignitatis* or by their proper names; see Baldus, *Consilia*, III,159,n.5 (Venice, 1575), 45ᵛ, or, for England, Maitland, *Sel. Ess.*, 77, where a chaplain uses only his corporate name, that is, that of his chantry. See below, Ch.VII, nos.298f. See also *Year Books, 8 Edward II (1315)*, Y. B. Series, XVIII (Selden Society, XXXVII; 1920), 202f.

[15] One is reminded of Leo the Great's *Ad Flavianum* (*ep.* XXVIII,c.3), PL, LIV,765: ". . . et mori posset ex uno, et mori non posset ex altero."

[16] Plowden, *Reports*, 455a.

[17] See, for a parallel case, Bacon, *Post-Nati*, 657f: Sir William Paulet, on account of his offices, would have been entitled to have 13 chaplains: "he had but one soul, though he had three offices."

[18] Coke, *Reports*, VII,10-10a.

sworn to his natural person, just as the king is sworn to his subjects in his natural person: "for the politic capacity is invisible and immortal, nay, the politic body hath no soul, for it is framed by the policy of man."[19] Moreover, treason, that is, "to intend or compass *mortem et destructionem domini Regis*, must needs be understood of his natural body, for his politic body is immortal, and not subject to death."

Those arguments certainly reflect sound reasoning, although an attack against the king's natural person was, at the same time, an attack against the body corporate of the realm. Justice Southcote, in the passage quoted (above, p. 13) from the case *Willion v. Berkley*, referred to the simile of the state as a human body, a "Corporation" whereof the king is the head and the subjects are the members. Of course, that metaphor was very old; it pervaded political thought during the later Middle Ages.[20] Nevertheless, the form in which Justice Southcote couched that old idea—"he is incorporated with them, and they with him"—points directly towards the politico-ecclesiological theory of the *corpus mysticum* which actually was quoted with great emphasis by Justice Brown in the case *Hales v. Petit*. The court, on that instance, was concerned with the legal consequences of a suicide, which the judges tried to define as an act of "Felony." Lord Dyer, Chief Justice, pointed out that suicide was a threefold crime. It was an offense against Nature, since it was contrary to the law of self-preservation; it was an offense against God as a violation of the sixth commandment; finally it was a crime committed "against the King in that hereby he has lost a Subject, and (as Brown termed it) he being the Head has lost one of his mystic Members."[21]

"Body politic" and "mystical body" seem to be used without great discrimination. In fact, Coke, when discussing the politic body of the king, added in parenthesis: "and in 21 E.4 [1482] it is called a mystical body."[22] It is evident that the doctrine of theology

---

[19] That the body politic had no soul was a current argument of the lawyers; see, e.g., Coke, *Rep.*, VII,10a ("of itself it hath neither soul nor body"). The argument is very old and goes back to the beginning of corporational doctrines; see Gierke, *Gen.R.*, III,282,n.112.

[20] Gierke, *Gen.R.*, III,517,546ff; Maitland, in the introduction to his translation of Gierke (*Political Theories of the Middle Age* [Cambridge, 1927], p. xi,n.1) styles Plowden's quotations "a late instance of this old concept."

[21] Plowden, *Reports*, 261; cf. Maitland, *Sel. Ess.*, 110.

[22] Coke, *Rep.*, VII,10 (*Calvin's Case*). See below, Ch. VII,n.312.

and canon law, teaching that the Church, and Christian society in general, was a *"corpus mysticum* the head of which is Christ," has been transferred by the jurists from the theological sphere to that of the state the head of which is the king.[23]

It would be easy to extract from Plowden's *Reports*, and from the writings of later lawyers as well, a not too modest number of similar passages.[24] New places, however, would not add new aspects to the general problem; and the passages referred to, rendering, as they do, the pith of the doctrine, will suffice to illustrate the leading idea, the trend of thought, and the peculiar idiom of the Tudor lawyers to whom, understandably, "a king's crown was a hieroglyphic of the laws."[25] Any reader of those passages in the Law Reports will be struck by the solemnity to which the legal language occasionally rises, notwithstanding the seeming drolleries of logic in their argumentations. Nor will the reader have the slightest doubt as to the ultimate source of that parlance which has a most familiar ring to the ear of the mediaevalist. In fact, we need only replace the strange image of the Two Bodies by the more customary theological term of the Two Natures in order to make it poignantly felt that the speech of the Elizabethan lawyers derived its tenor in the last analysis from theological diction, and that their speech itself, to say the least, was crypto-theological. Royalty, by this semi-religious terminology, was actually expounded in terms of christological definitions. The jurists, styled by Roman Law so suggestively "Priests of Justice,"[26] developed in England not only a "Theology of Kingship"—this had become customary everywhere on the Continent in the course of the twelfth and thirteenth centuries—but worked out a genuine "Royal Christology."

This observation is not entirely new, though hitherto hardly evaluated. Maitland made the very appropriate remark that these English jurists were building up "a creed of royalty which shall

[23] For the state as a *corpus mysticum*, see below, Chapter v.

[24] In Coke's *Reports* much information can be found, especially in *Calvin's Case*; see also *Rep.*, VII,32. It is, however, noteworthy that Coke refers in most of those cases to Plowden's *Reports* as evidence.

[25] Coke, *Rep.*, VII,11a.

[26] D.1,1,1 (". . . quis nos sacerdotes appellet. Justitiam namque colimus") was, of course, a frequently quoted passage; see, for England, e.g., Bracton, *De legibus et consuetudinibus Angliae*, fol.3, ed. G. E. Woodbine (New Haven, 1922), II,24; Fortescue, *De Laudibus*, c.III, ed. Chrimes, 8. See below, Ch.IV, nos.94ff.

take no shame if set beside the Athanasian symbol."[27] The comparison which Maitland probably made in a half joking, half serious mood, is perfectly sound and actually hits the main point. Indeed, in the arguments of the Tudor lawyers—"one person, two bodies"—there seem to echo and reverberate the well known definitions of the Symbol: ". . . non duo tamen, sed unus. . . . Unus autem non conversione divinitatis in carnem, sed assumptione humanitatis in Deum. . . . Unus omnino, non confusione substantiae, sed unitate personae." And it may be recalled in this connection that the Athanasian Symbol remained extraordinarily popular among the English laity, since at Cranmer's suggestion it was incorporated into the Book of Common Prayer. Contrariwise, this Creed was not adopted by the continental Protestant Churches and fell somewhat into oblivion even among the members of the Roman Church when it ceased to be recited regularly on Sundays and when the mediaeval *Livres d'Heures*, which usually contained it, went out of fashion.[28]

Reference, admittedly, might be made to other Creeds as well. The legal arguments are reminiscent, above all, of the "Unconfounded, unchanged, undivided, unseparated" of the Chalcedonian Creed.[29] And generally speaking, it is of great interest to notice how in sixteenth-century England, by the efforts of the jurists to define effectively and accurately the King's Two Bodies, all the christological problems of the early Church concerning the Two Natures once more were actualized and resuscitated in the early absolute monarchy. It is revealing, too, to examine seriously that new Creed of Royalty on its "orthodoxy." Any move in the direction of "Arianism" may be excluded almost *a priori*, since the coequality of the king's body natural with the body politic during their "Association and Conjunction" is beyond any question; on the other hand, the inferiority of the body natural *per se* to the body politic is not "Arian," but is in perfect agreement with the *minor Patre secundum humanitatem* of the orthodox Creed and recognized dogma. The danger of a royal "Nestorianism" was certainly great at all times. However, it may be said that the judges

---

[27] Pollock and Maitland, *History*, I,511.

[28] G. Morin, "L'Origine du Symbole d'Athanase," *Journal of Theological Studies*, XII (1911), 169,n.2.

[29] August Hahn, *Bibliothek der Symbole und Glaubensregeln der alten Kirche* (3rd ed., Breslau, 1897), 174ff, for the Athanasian, and 166ff, for the Chalcedonian Creed.

took pains to avoid a split of the two bodies by stressing continuously their unity, whereas the other hidden rock of "Nestorianism"—the concept of a herolike meritorious advancement from *humanitas* to *divinitas*—was not a problem at all in a hereditary monarchy in which the predestination to rulership of the blood royal was not doubted. The frequent assertion that only the king's body natural could suffer from the "Infirmities that come by Nature or Accident," and that his body politic "is not subject to Passions or Death as the other is," does away with any possibility of a royal "Patripassianism" or "Sabellianism," as was proven in 1649. Quite orthodox is also the attitude towards "Donatism," since the king's acts are valid regardless of the personal worthiness of the body natural, its "nonage or old age," which imperfections "are wiped out by the Body politic"; on the other hand, the sacramental problem of the king's *character indelibilis* would always remain a matter open to controversy.[30] A touch of "Monophysitism" has been indicated above and should probably not be denied: it resulted from the relative indifference to the mortal "incarnation" or individuation of the body politic. The cry of the Puritans "We fight the *k*ing to defend the *K*ing" clearly points in the monophysitic direction, and the concept of the jurists concerning the continuity of repetitive incarnation of the body politic in exchangeable bodies natural suggests anyhow a "noetic" interpretation of kingship. Considerable also was the danger of a royal "Monotheletism," since it is difficult to establish a clear distinction "between the will of the Crown and what the king wants"; it must be admitted nevertheless that the crown lawyers sometimes found an opportunity to distinguish also between the two wills, which became the rule of the revolutionary Parliament in the seventeenth century.[31]

The implication of all this is not that the lawyers consciously borrowed from the acts of the early Councils, but that the fiction of the King's Two Bodies produced interpretations and definitions

---

[30] See below, Ch.II, n.22.

[31] See Kenneth Pickthorn, *Early Tudor Government: Henry VII* (Cambridge, 1934), 159, with reference to the *Abbot of Waltham's Case*; for the case itself, see T. F. T. Plucknett, "The Lancastrian Constitution," *Tudor Studies*, ed. by R. W. Seton-Watson (London, 1924), 172ff; see also, concerning the "will" of corporations, Gierke, *Gen.R.*, III,308ff,390ff, and Maitland's Introduction to Gierke, *Political Theories*, p.xi. For Puritan slogans, see below, n.42.

which perforce would resemble those produced in view of the Two Natures of the God-man. Anyone familiar with the christological discussions of the early centuries of the Christian era will be struck by the similarity of speech and thought in the Inns of Court on the one hand, and in the early Church Councils on the other; also, by the faithfulness with which the English jurists applied, unconsciously rather than consciously, the current theological definitions to the defining of the nature of kingship. Taken all by itself, this transference of definitions from one sphere to another, from theology to law, is anything but surprising or even remarkable. The *quid pro quo* method—the taking over of theological notions for defining the state—had been going on for many centuries, just as, vice versa, in the early centuries of the Christian era the imperial political terminology and the imperial ceremonial had been adapted to the needs of the Church.[32]

The religious strand within political theory was certainly strong during the age of the Reformation when the divine right of secular powers was most emphatically proclaimed and when the words of St. Paul "There is no power but of God" achieved a previously quite unknown importance with regard to the subjection of the ecclesiastical sphere to the temporal.[33] Despite all that, there is no need either to make the religiously excited sixteenth century responsible for the definitions of the Tudor lawyers, or to recall the Act of Supremacy through which the king became "pope in his realm." This does not preclude the possibility that corporational and other concepts defining the papal power were directly transferred and purposely introduced into Tudor England to bolster the royal power. However, the jurists' custom of borrowing from ecclesiology and using ecclesiastical language for secular purposes had its own tradition of long standing, for it was a practice as legitimate as it was old to draw conclusions *de similibus ad similia*.

It may be added that the crypto-theological idiom was not the personal spleen of any single one among the Tudor lawyers, nor was it restricted to a small coterie of judges. Individual judges,

---

[32] The numerous studies of A. Alföldi (esp. in *Mitteilungen des deutschen archäologischen Instituts: Römische Abteilung*, vols. XLIX and L, 1934-35) and, more recently, a study by Th. Klauser, *Der Ursprung der bischöflichen Insignien und Ehrenrechte* (Bonner Akademische Reden, I; Krefeld, 1948), have shed much light on that development.

[33] Gierke, *Johannes Althusius* (Breslau, 1913), 64.

such as Justice Brown, perhaps were inclined to push very far into the mystic regions. However, Plowden's *Reports* disclose the names of a respectable number of lawyers indulging in the quasi-theological definitions of the King's Two Bodies. Plowden tells us, for instance, how at "Spooner's," that is, Spooner's Hall in Fleet Street, the justices, serjeants, and apprentices were eagerly discussing the case of the Duchy of Lancaster and arguing about whether the Duchy had been vested in Henry VII in his capacity as king body natural or as King body politic.[34]

This, therefore, must have been the ordinary and conventional terminology of the English jurists of that period and of the generations to follow. It is true that continental jurisprudence, too, arrived at political doctrines concerning a dual majesty, a *maiestas realis* of the people and a *maiestas personalis* of the emperor, along with a great number of similar distinctions.[35] Continental jurists, however, were unfamiliar with parliamentary institutions such as those developed in England, where "Sovereignty" was identified not with the King alone or the people alone, but with the "King in Parliament." And whereas continental jurisprudence might easily attain to a concept of the "State" in the abstract, or identify the Prince with that State, it never arrived at conceiving of the Prince as a "corporation sole"—admittedly a hybrid of complicated ancestry—from which the body politic as represented by Parliament could never be ruled out. At any rate, to the English "physiologic" concept of the King's Two Bodies the Continent did not offer an exact parallel—neither terminologically nor conceptually.

From English political thought, however, the idiom of the King's Two Bodies cannot easily be dismissed. Without those clarifying, if sometimes confusing, distinctions between the *K*ing's sempiternity and the *k*ing's temporariness, between his immaterial and im-

---

[34] Plowden, *Reports*, 212a; cf. 220a, for Spooner's Hall.

[35] See, e.g., Gierke, *Gen.R.*, IV,219,315ff, and passim; also 247ff. Neither the doctrine of the "Dual Sovereignty" (people and king) nor the distinction between the king as King and as private person, which of course was well established also on the Continent, matches exactly the English "physiological" fiction of the King's Two Bodies. Moreover, English custom apparently tried to reduce the king's "privacy" so far as possible by recording all royal actions once the body natural "has the Estate royal united to it, which can do nothing without record"; cf. Plowden, *Reports*, 213a. Some of these differences have been touched upon by Maitland, in his Introduction to Gierke, *Political Theories*, p.xi and passim.

mortal body politic and his material and mortal body natural, it would have been next to impossible for Parliament to resort to a similar fiction and summon, in the name and by the authority of Charles I, King body politic, the armies which were to fight the same Charles I, king body natural.[36] By the Declaration of the Lords and Commons of May 27, 1642, the King body politic was retained in and by Parliament whereas the king body natural was, so to say, frozen out.

> It is acknowledged [ran the parliamentary doctrine] that the King is the Fountain of Justice and Protection, but the Acts of Justice and Protection are not exercised in his own Person, nor depend upon his pleasure, but by his Courts and his Ministers who must do their duty therein, *though the King in his own Person should forbid them*: and therefore if Judgment should be given by them against the King's Will and Personal command, *yet are they the King's Judgments*. The High Court of Parliament is not only a Court of Judicature . . . , but it is likewise a Council . . . to preserve the publick Peace and Safety of the Kingdom, and to declare the King's pleasure in those things that are requisite thereunto, *and what they do herein hath the stamp of Royal Authority, although His Majesty . . . do in his own Person oppose or interrupt the same. . . .*[37]

Shortly after the May resolutions of 1642, medallions were struck showing the King in Parliament. We recognize, in the lower section of the reverse, the Commons with their Speaker; in the upper, the Lords; and uppermost, on a dais of three steps, the royal throne on which the king, visible in profile, is seated under a canopy (fig. 1).[38] He is clearly the King body politic and head of the political body of the realm: the King in Parliament whose task it was to stand together with Lords and Commons, and, if need be,

---

[36] For the Declaration, see C. Stephenson and F. G. Marcham, *Sources of English Constitutional History* (New York, 1937), 488; C. H. McIlwain, *The High Court of Parliament* (New Haven, 1934), 352f and 389f. See also S. R. Gardiner, *The Fall of the Monarchy of Charles I* (London, 1882), II,420 and passim. David Hume, *History of England* (New York, 1880), v,102 (Year 1642), interestingly overrated the originality of Parliament when he assumed that it was "inventing a distinction *hitherto unheard of*, between the office and the person of the king." The distinction, all by itself, was many centuries old and known in England as well (Declaration of the Barons in 1308); but Parliament pushed it to extremes in view of its application.

[37] See McIlwain, *High Court*, 389f, including his quotation from John Allan: ". . . it is obvious that the two houses not only separated the politic from the natural capacity of the King, but transferred to themselves the sovereign authority attributed to him by lawyers in his ideal character."

[38] E. Hawkins, *Medallic Illustrations of the History of Great Britain and Ireland* (London, 1911), pl.xxv,5-6; also E. Hawkins, A. W. Franks, and H. A. Grueber,

even against the king body natural. In this fashion, the parliamentary King did not cease being included in the body of Parliament, nor was the king "in his own Person" as yet excluded. PRO RELIGIONE·LEGE·REGE·ET·PARLIAMENTO said, on the obverse of one of those medallions, the legend surrounding the portrait head of Charles I, king body natural. At the same time, however, this body was admonished (on the portrait side of a similar medallion [fig. 1f]) by the telling inscription: SHOULD HEAR BOTH HOUSES OF PARLIAMENT FOR TRUE RELIGION AND SUBJECTS FREDOM STANDS. This inscription was a verbatim quotation from the Houses' Declaration of May 19, 1642, when Lords and Commons called upon the king "to be advised by the wisdom of both Houses of Parliament."[39] But the king body natural no longer could take advice from parliamentary wisdom; he had left Whitehall and London to take his residence finally at Oxford. Another medallion, issued later in that year, epitomized a fuller story (fig. 2).[40] From the obverse of the new medallion the king's personal image disappeared; we see instead the picture of a ship—not the customary "Ship of the State," but a battleship: the Navy, since 1642, adhered to the parliamentary cause. The reverse remained seemingly unchanged. Again we find the two Houses of Parliament and the King. The King, however, no longer is seated on a dais. Visible to the knees only, he likens a picture framed by the canopy curtains, very much like an apparition of the image of the Great Seal, or of its central part (fig. 3).[41] It was, after all, by the authority of the Seal that Parliament acted against the individual Charles I. The legend PRO:RELIGIONE:GREGE:ET:REGE, "For Religion, Flock, and King," says plainly enough for whom Parliament was fighting; and that remained true also after Charles I's portrait, as well as the ship, had been eliminated to be replaced by the portrait of the commander-in-chief of the Parliamentary forces, Robert Devereux,

---

Medallic Illustrations (London, 1885), I,292f, Nos.108f. Fig.1,c, is a medallion (no reverse image) in the Collection of the American Numismatic Society, in New York. I am greatly obliged to Dr. Henry Grunthal for calling my attention to this piece and providing me with a photo.

[39] *Ibid.*, 292, No.108, and, for the other legend, No.109.

[40] *Ibid.*, pl.xxv,7, and p.292.

[41] *Trésor de numismatique et de glyptique: Sceaux des rois et reines d'Angleterre* (Paris, 1858), pl.xx; W. de Gray Birch, *Catalogue of Seals in the Department of Manuscripts in the British Museum* (London, 1887), I,63,No.597, describing the Fifth Seal, which is identical with the Fourth used 1640-1644.

Earl of Essex (fig. 1d), whereas once more the reverse side, the King body politic in Parliament, survived without change. In other words, the king body natural in Oxford had become a nuisance to Parliament; but the King body politic still was useful: he still was present in Parliament, though only in his seal image—an appropriate illustration of the concept justifying the Puritan cry of "fighting the king to defend the King."[42]

Nor can the fiction of the King's Two Bodies be thought of apart from the later events when Parliament succeeded in trying "Charles Stuart, being admitted King of England and therein trusted with a limited power," for high treason, and finally in executing solely the king's body natural without affecting seriously or doing irreparable harm to the King's body politic—in contradistinction with the events in France, in 1793. There were very great and serious advantages in the English doctrine of the King's Two Bodies. For, as Justice Brown on one occasion explained:[43]

> King is a Name of Continuance, which shall always endure as the Head and Governor of the People (as the Law presumes) as long as the People continue . . . ; and in this Name the King never dies.

[42] See, for the Puritan slogans (some in poetical form), Ethyn Kirby, *William Prynne, a Study in Puritanism* (Harvard, 1931), 60, and, for the badges of Essex, Hawkins, pl.xxv,10-11, and I,p.295, No.113.
[43] Plowden, *Reports*, 177a.

CHAPTER II

SHAKESPEARE: KING RICHARD II

> TWIN-BORN with greatness, subject to the breath
> Of every fool, whose sense no more can feel
> But his own wringing. What infinite heart's ease
> Must kings neglect that private men enjoy! . . . .
> What kind of god art thou, that suffer'st more
> Of mortal griefs than do thy worshippers?

Such are, in Shakespeare's play, the meditations of King Henry V on the godhead and manhood of a king.[1] The king is "twin-born" not only with greatness but also with human nature, hence "subject to the breath of every fool."

It was the humanly tragic aspect of royal "gemination" which Shakespeare outlined and not the legal capacities which English lawyers assembled in the fiction of the King's Two Bodies. However, the legal jargon of the "two Bodies" scarcely belonged to the arcana of the legal guild alone. That the king "is a Corporation in himself that liveth ever," was a commonplace found in a simple dictionary of legal terms such as Dr. John Cowell's *Interpreter* (1607);[2] and even at an earlier date the gist of the concept of kingship which Plowden's *Reports* reflected, had passed into the writings of Joseph Kitchin (1580)[3] and Richard Crompton (1594).[4] Moreover, related notions were carried into public when, in 1603, Francis Bacon suggested for the crowns of England and Scotland, united in James I, the name of "Great Britain" as an expression of the "perfect union of bodies, politic as well as natural."[5] That Plowden's *Reports* were widely known is certainly demonstrated

---

[1] *King Henry V*, IV.i.254ff.

[2] Dr. John Cowell, *The Interpreter or Booke Containing the Signification of Words* (Cambridge, 1607), s.v. "King (Rex)," also s.v. "Prerogative," where Plowden is actually quoted. See, in general, Chrimes, "Dr. John Cowell," *EHR*, LXIV (1949), 483.

[3] Joseph Kitchin, *Le Court Leete et Court Baron* (London, 1580), fol.1r-v, referring to the case of the Duchy of Lancaster.

[4] Richard Crompton, *L'Authoritie et Jurisdiction des Courts de la Maiestie de la Roygne* (London, 1594), fol. 134r-v, reproducing on the basis of Plowden the theory about the Two Bodies in connection with the Lancaster case.

[5] See Bacon's *Brief Discourse Touching the Happy Union of the Kingdoms of England and Scotland*, in J. Spedding, *Letters and Life of Francis Bacon* (London, 1861-74), III,90ff; see, for the print of 1603, S. T. Bindoff, "The Stuarts and their Style," *EHR*,LX (1945), 206,n.2, who (p.207) quotes the passage.

by the phrase "The case is altered, quoth Plowden," which was used proverbially in England before and after 1600.[6] The suggestion that Shakespeare may have known a case (*Hales v. Petit*) reported by Plowden, does not seem far-fetched,[7] and it gains strength on the ground that the anonymous play *Thomas of Woodstock*, of which Shakespeare "had his head full of echoes" and in which he may even have acted,[8] ends in the pun: "for I have plodded in Plowden, and can find no law."[9] Besides, it would have been very strange if Shakespeare, who mastered the lingo of almost every human trade, had been ignorant of the constitutional and judicial talk which went on around him and which the jurists of his days applied so lavishly in court. Shakespeare's familiarity with legal cases of general interest cannot be doubted, and we have other evidence of his association with the students at the Inns and his knowledge of court procedure.[10]

Admittedly, it would make little difference whether or not Shakespeare was familiar with the subtleties of legal speech. The poet's vision of the twin nature of a king is not dependent on constitutional support, since such vision would arise very naturally from a purely human stratum. It therefore may appear futile even to pose the question whether Shakespeare applied any professional idiom of the jurists of his time, or try to determine the die of Shakespeare's coinage. It seems all very trivial and irrelevant, since the image of the twinned nature of a king, or even of man in general, was most genuinely Shakespeare's own and proper vision. Nevertheless, should the poet have chanced upon the legal definitions of kingship, as probably he could not have failed to do when conversing with his friends at the Inns, it will be easily imagined how apropos the simile of the King's Two Bodies would have seemed to him. It was anyhow the live essence of his art to reveal the numerous planes active in any human being, to play them off

---

[6] A. P. Rossiter, *Woodstock* (London, 1946), 238.

[7] About Shakespeare and Plowden, see C. H. Norman, "Shakespeare and the Law," *Times Literary Supplement*, June 30, 1950, p. 412, with the additional remarks by Sir Donald Somervell, *ibid.*, July 21, 1950, p. 453. For the case, see above, Ch.I, n.21.

[8] John Dover Wilson, in his edition of *Richard II* (below, n.12), "Introduction," p. lxxiv; see pp. xlviii ff, for Shakespeare and *Woodstock* in general.

[9] *Woodstock*, V.vi.34f, ed. Rossiter, 169.

[10] See, in general, George W. Keeton, *Shakespeare and His Legal Problems* (London, 1930); also Max Radin, "The Myth of Magna Carta," *Harvard Law Review*, LX (1947), 1086, who stresses very strongly Shakespeare's association "with the turbulent students at the Inns."

against each other, to confuse them, or to preserve their equilibrium, depending all upon the pattern of life he bore in mind and wished to create anew. How convenient then to find those ever contending planes, as it were, legalised by the jurists' royal "christology" and readily served to him!

The legal concept of the King's Two Bodies cannot, for other reasons, be separated from Shakespeare. For if that curious image, which from modern constitutional thought has vanished all but completely, still has a very real and human meaning today, this is largely due to Shakespeare. It is he who has eternalized that metaphor. He has made it not only the symbol, but indeed the very substance and essence of one of his greatest plays: *The Tragedy of King Richard II* is the tragedy of the King's Two Bodies.

Perhaps it is not superfluous to indicate that the Shakespearian Henry V, as he bemoans a king's twofold estate, immediately associates that image with King Richard II. King Henry's soliloquies precede directly that brief intermezzo in which he conjures the spirit of his father's predecessor and to the historic essence of which posterity probably owes that magnificent ex-voto known as the Wilton Diptych.[11]

> Not to-day, O Lord!
> O! not to-day, think not upon the fault
> My father made in encompassing the crown.
> I Richard's body have interr'd anew,
> And on it have bestow'd more contrite tears,
> Than from it issu'd forced drops of blood.
>
> (IV.i.312ff)

Musing over his own royal fate, over the king's two-natured being, Shakespeare's Henry V is disposed to recall Shakespeare's Richard II, who—at least in the poet's concept—appears as the prototype of that "kind of god that suffers more of mortal griefs than do his worshippers."

It appears relevant to the general subject of this study, and also otherwise worth our while, to inspect more closely the varieties of royal "duplications" which Shakespeare has unfolded in the three

---

[11] V. H. Galbraith, "A New Life of Richard II," *History*, XXVI (1942), 237ff; for the artistic problems and for a full bibliography, see Erwin Panofsky, *Early Netherlandish Painting* (Cambridge, Mass., 1953), 118 and 404f,n.5, and Francis Wormald, "The Wilton Diptych," *Warburg Journal*, XVII (1954), 191-203.

bewildering central scenes of *Richard II*.[12] The duplications, all one, and all simultaneously active, in Richard—"Thus play I in one person many people" (V.v.31)—are those potentially present in the King, the Fool, and the God. They dissolve, perforce, in the Mirror. Those three prototypes of "twin-birth" intersect and overlap and interfere with each other continuously. Yet, it may be felt that the "King" dominates in the scene on the Coast of Wales (III.ii), the "Fool" at Flint Castle (III.iii), and the "God" in the Westminster scene (IV.i), with Man's wretchedness as a perpetual companion and antithesis at every stage. Moreover, in each one of those three scenes we encounter the same cascading: from divine kingship to kingship's "Name," and from the name to the naked misery of man.

Gradually, and only step by step, does the tragedy proper of the King's Two Bodies develop in the scene on the Welsh coast. There is as yet no split in Richard when, on his return from Ireland, he kisses the soil of his kingdom and renders that famous, almost too often quoted, account of the loftiness of his royal estate. What he expounds is, in fact, the indelible character of the king's body politic, god-like or angel-like. The balm of consecration resists the power of the elements, the "rough rude sea," since

> The breath of worldly man cannot depose
> The deputy elected by the Lord.
>
> (III.ii.54ff)

Man's breath appears to Richard as something inconsistent with kingship. Carlisle, in the Westminster scene, will emphasize once more that God's Anointed cannot be judged "by inferior breath" (IV.i.128). It will be Richard himself who "with his own breath"

---

12 The authoritative edition of *Richard II* is by John Dover Wilson, in the Cambridge *Works of Shakespeare* (Cambridge, 1939). Mr. Wilson's "Introduction," pp. vii-lxxvi, is a model of literary criticism and information. I confess my indebtedness to those pages on which I have drawn more frequently than the footnotes may suggest. In the same volume is a likewise most efficient discussion by Harold Child, "The Stage-History of *Richard II*," pp. lxxvii-xcii. The political aspects of the play are treated in a stimulating fashion by John Leslie Palmer, *Political Characters of Shakespeare* (London, 1945), 118ff, from whose study, too, I have profited more than my acknowledgments may show. See also Keeton, *op.cit.*, 163ff. With regard to the historical Richard II, the historian finds himself in a less fortunate position. The history of this king is in the midst of a thorough revaluation of both sources and general concepts, of which the numerous studies of Professor Galbraith and others bear witness. A first effort to sum up the analytic studies of the last decades has been made by Anthony Steel, *Richard II* (Cambridge, 1941).

releases at once kingship and subjects (IV.i.210), so that finally King Henry V, after the destruction of Richard's divine kingship, could rightly complain that the king is "subject to the breath of every fool."[13]

When the scene (III.ii) begins, Richard is, in the most exalted fashion, the "deputy elected by the Lord" and "God's substitute . . . anointed in his sight" (I.ii.37). Still is he the one that in former days gave "good ear" to the words of his crony, John Busshy, Speaker of the Commons in 1397, who, when addressing the king, "did not attribute to him titles of honour, due and accustomed, but invented unused termes and such strange names, as were rather agreeable to the divine maiestie of God, than to any earthly potentate."[14] He still appears the one said to have asserted that the "Laws are in the King's mouth, or sometimes in his breast,"[15] and

[13] See also *King John*, III.iii.147f:

> What earthly name to interrogatories
> Can task the free breath of a sacred king?

[14] This is reported only by Holinshed; see W. G. Boswell-Stone, *Shakespeare's Holinshed* (London, 1896), 130; Wilson, "Introduction," p. lii. The *Rotuli Parliamentorum* do not refer to the speech of John Busshy, in 1397. To judge, however, from the customary parliamentary sermons, the speaker in 1397 may easily have gone far in applying Biblical metaphors to the king; see, e.g., Chrimes, *Const.Ideas*, 165ff.

[15] "Dixit expresse, vultu austero et protervo, quod leges suae erant in ore suo, et aliquotiens in pectore suo: Et quod ipse solus posset mutare et condere leges regni sui." This was one of the most famous of Richard's so-called "tyrannies" with which he was charged in 1399; see E. C. Lodge and G. A. Thornton, *English Constitutional Documents 1307-1485* (Cambridge, 1935), 28f. Richard II, like the French king (below, Ch.IV,n.193), merely referred to a well known maxim of Roman and Canon Laws. Cf. *C.6,23,19,1*, for the maxim *Omnia iura in scrinio (pectoris) principis*, often quoted by the glossators, e.g., *Glos.ord.*, on *D.33,10,3*, v. *usum imperatorem*, or on *c.16,C.25,q.2*, v. *In iuris*, and quoted also by Thomas Aquinas (Tolomeo of Lucca), *De regimine principum*, II,c.8, IV,c.1. The maxim became famous through Pope Boniface VIII; see c.1 VI 1,2, ed. Emil Friedberg, *Corpus iuris canonici* (Leipzig, 1879-81), II,937: "Licet Romanus Pontifex, qui iura omnia in scrinio pectoris sui censetur habere, constitutionem condendo posteriorem, priorem . . . revocare noscatur. . . ." (probably the place referred to by Richard if the correctness of the charges be granted). For the meaning of the maxim (i.e., the legislator should have the relevant laws present to his mind), see F. Gillman, "Romanus pontifex iura omnia in scrinio pectoris sui censetur habere," *AKKR*, XCII (1912), 3ff, CVI (1926), 156ff (also CVIII [1928], 534; CIX [1929], 249f); also Gaines Post, "Two Notes," *Traditio*, IX (1953), 311, and "Two Laws," *Speculum*, XIX (1954), 425,n.35. See also Steinwenter, "Nomos," 256ff; *Erg.Bd.*, 85; Oldradus de Ponte, *Consilia*, LII,n.1 (Venice, 1571), fol. 19ʳ. The maxim occasionally was transferred also to the judge (Walter Ullmann, *The Mediaeval Idea of Law as Represented by Lucas de Penna* [London, 1946], 107) and to the fisc (Gierke, *Gen.R.*, III,359,n.17) as well as to the council (see below, Ch.IV,nos.191f,194f). For Richard's other claim (*mutare et condere leges*), the papal and imperial doctrines likewise were responsible; see Gregory VII's

to have demanded that "if he looked at anyone, that person had to bend the knee."[16] He still is sure of himself, of his dignity, and even of the help of the celestial hosts, which are at his disposal.

> For every man that Bolingbroke hath press'd . . . ,
> God for his Richard hath in heavenly pay
> A glorious angel.
>
> (III.ii.60)

This glorious image of kingship "By the Grace of God" does not last. It slowly fades, as the bad tidings trickle in. A curious change in Richard's attitude—as it were, a metamorphosis from "Realism" to "Nominalism"—now takes place. The Universal called "Kingship" begins to disintegrate; its transcendental "Reality," its objective truth and god-like existence, so brilliant shortly before, pales into a nothing, a *nomen*.[17] And the remaining half-reality resembles a state of amnesia or of sleep.

> I had forgot myself, am I not king?
> Awake thou coward majesty! thou sleepest,
> Is not the king's name twenty thousand names?
> *Arm, arm, my name!* A puny subject strikes
> At thy great glory.
>
> (III.ii.83ff)

This state of half-reality, of royal oblivion and slumber, adumbrates the royal "Fool" of Flint Castle. And similarly the divine prototype of gemination, the God-man, begins to announce its presence, as Richard alludes to Judas' treason:

> Snakes, in my heart-blood warm'd, that sting my heart!
> Three Judases, each one thrice worse than Judas!
>
> (III.ii.131)

Dictatus papae, §VII, ed. Caspar (*MGH*, Epp.sel., II), 203; also Frederick II's *Liber aug.*, 1,38, ed. Cervone, 85, with the gloss referring to *C*.1,17,2,18.

[16] For the genuflection, see *Eulogium Historiarum*, ed. Hayden (Rolls Series, 1863), III,378; see Steel, *Richard II*, 278. The annalist mentions it in connection with "Festival Crownings" (which thus were continued during the reign of Richard) and gives an account of the king's uncanny deportment:

In diebus solemnibus, in quibus utebatur de more regalibus, iussit sibi in camera parari thronum, in quo post prandium se ostentans sedere solebat usque ad vesperas, nulli loquens, sed singulos aspiciens. Et cum aliquem respiceret, cuius-cumque gradus fuerit, oportuit genuflectere.

[17] For the body politic as a mere name, see, e.g., Pollock and Maitland, *History*, 1,490,n.8: "le corporacion . . . n'est que un nosme, que ne poit my estre vieu [see above, Ch.I,nos.2-3], et n'est my substance." See also Gierke, *Gen.R.*, III,281, for corporate bodies as *nomina iuris*, a *nomen intellectuale*, and the connections with the philosophic Nominalism.

It is as though it has dawned upon Richard that his vicariate of the God Christ might imply also a vicariate of the man Jesus, and that he, the royal "deputy elected by the Lord," might have to follow his divine Master also in his human humiliation and take the cross.

However, neither the twin-born Fool nor the twin-born God are dominant in that scene. Only their nearness is forecast, while to the fore there steps the body natural and mortal of the king:

> Let's talk of graves, of worms and epitaphs . . .
> (III.ii.145ff)

Not only does the king's manhood prevail over the godhead of the Crown, and mortality over immortality; but, worse than that, kingship itself seems to have changed its essence. Instead of being unaffected "by Nonage or Old Age and other natural Defects and Imbecilities," kingship itself comes to mean Death, and nothing but Death. And the long procession of tortured kings passing in review before Richard's eyes is proof of that change:

> For God's sake let us sit upon the ground,
> And tell sad stories of the death of kings—
> How some have been deposed, some slain in war,
> Some haunted by the ghosts they have deposed,
> Some poisoned by their wives, some sleeping killed;
> *All murdered*—for within the hollow crown
> That rounds the mortal temples of a king,
> Keeps Death his court, and there the antic sits
> Scoffing his state and grinning at his pomp,
> Allowing him a breath, a little scene,
> To monarchize, be feared, and kill with looks,
> Infusing him with self and vain conceit,
> As if the flesh which walls about our life,
> Were brass impregnable: and humoured thus,
> Comes at the last, and with a little pin
> Bores through his castle wall, and farewell king!
> (III.ii.155ff)

The king that "never dies" here has been replaced by the king that always dies and suffers death more cruelly than other mortals. Gone is the oneness of the body natural with the immortal body politic, "this double Body, to which no Body is equal" (above, p. 12). Gone also is the fiction of royal prerogatives of any kind, and all that remains is the feeble human nature of a king:

> mock not flesh and blood
> With solemn reverence, throw away respect,
> Tradition, form, and ceremonious duty,
> For you have but mistook me all this while:
> I live with bread like you, feel want,
> Taste grief, need friends—subjected thus,
> How can you say to me, I am a king?
>
> (III.ii.171ff)

The fiction of the oneness of the double body breaks apart. God-head and manhood of the King's Two Bodies, both clearly out-lined with a few strokes, stand in contrast to each other. A first low is reached. The scene now shifts to Flint Castle.

The structure of the second great scene (III.iii) resembles the first. Richard's kingship, his body politic, has been hopelessly shaken, it is true; but still there remains, though hollowed out, the semblance of kingship. At least this might be saved. "Yet looks he like a king," states York at Flint Castle (III.iii.68); and in Richard's temper there dominates, at first, the consciousness of his royal dignity. He had made up his mind beforehand to appear a king at the Castle:

> A king, woe's slave, shall kingly woe obey.
>
> (III.iii.210)

He acts accordingly; he snorts at Northumberland who has omitted the vassal's and subject's customary genuflection before his liege lord and the deputy of God:

> We are amazed, and thus long have we stood
> To watch the fearful bending of thy knee,
> Because we thought ourself thy lawful king:
> And if we be, how dare thy joints forget
> To pay their awful duty to our presence?
>
> (III.iii.73ff)

The "cascades" then begin to fall as they did in the first scene. The celestial hosts are called upon once more, this time avenging angels and "armies of pestilence," which God is said to muster in his clouds—"on our behalf" (III.iii.85f). Again the "Name" of kingship plays its part:

> O, that I were as great
> As is my grief, or lesser than my *name*!
>
> (III.iii.136)

> Must (the king) lose
> The *name* of king? a God's *name*, let it go.
> (III.iii.145f)

From the shadowy name of kingship there leads, once more, the path to new disintegration. No longer does Richard impersonate the mystic body of his subjects and the nation. It is a lonely man's miserable and mortal nature that replaces the king as King:

> I'll give my jewels for a set of beads:
> My gorgeous palace for a hermitage:
> My gay apparel for an almsman's gown:
> My figured goblets for a dish of wood:
> My sceptre for a palmer's walking-staff:
> My subjects for a pair of carved saints,
> And my large kingdom for a little grave,
> A little little grave, an obscure grave.
> (III.iii.147ff)

The shiver of those anaphoric clauses is followed by a profusion of gruesome images of High-Gothic *macabresse.* However, the second scene—different from the first—does not end in those outbursts of self-pity which recall, not a Dance of Death, but a dance around one's own grave. There follows a state of even greater abjectness.

The new note, indicating a change for the worse, is struck when Northumberland demands that the king come down into the base court of the castle to meet Bolingbroke, and when Richard, whose personal badge was the "Sun emerging from a cloud," retorts in a language of confusing brightness and terrifying puns:

> Down, down I come like glist'ring Phaethon:
> Wanting the manage of unruly jades. . . .
> In the base court? Base court, where kings grow base,
> To come at traitors' calls, and do them grace.
> In the base court? Come down? Down court! down king!
> For night-owls shriek where mounting larks should sing.
> (III.iii.178ff)

It has been noticed at different times how prominent a place is held in *Richard II* by the symbolism of the Sun (fig. 4), and occasionally a passage reads like the description of a Roman *Oriens Augusti* coin (III.ii.36-53; cf. fig. 32c).[18] The Sun imagery, as inter-

---

[18] For Richard's symbol of the "Rising Sun," see Paul Reyher, "Le symbole du soleil dans la tragédie de Richard II," *Revue de l'enseignement des langues vivantes,* XL (1923), 254-260; for further literature on the subject, see Wilson, "Introduction,"

woven in Richard's answer, reflects the "splendour of the catastrophe" in a manner remindful of Brueghel's *Icarus* and Lucifer's fall from the empyrean, reflecting also those "shreds of glow. . . . That round the limbs of fallen angels hover." On the other hand, the "traitors' calls" may be reminiscent of the "three Judases" in the foregoing scene. In general, however, biblical imagery is unimportant at Flint Castle: it is saved for the Westminster scene. At Flint, there is another vision which, along with foolish Phaethons and Icari, the poet now produces.

> I talk but idly, and you laugh at me,

remarks Richard (III.iii.171), growing self-conscious and embarrassed. The sudden awkwardness is noticed by Northumberland, too:

> Sorrow and grief of heart
> Makes him speak fondly like a frantic man.
> (III.iii.185)

Shakespeare, in that scene, conjures up the image of another human being, the Fool, who is two-in-one and whom the poet otherwise introduces so often as counter-type of lords and kings. Richard II plays now the rôles of both: fool of his royal self and fool of kingship. Therewith, he becomes somewhat less than merely "man" or (as on the Beach) "king body natural." However, only in that new rôle of Fool—a fool playing king, and a king playing fool—is Richard capable of greeting his victorious cousin and of playing to the end, with Bolingbroke in genuflection before him, the comedy of his brittle and dubious kingship. Again he escapes into "speaking fondly," that is, into puns:

> Fair cousin, you debase your princely knee,
> To make the base earth proud with kissing it. . . .

---

p. xii, n.3, and, for possible predecessors using that badge, John Gough Nichols, "Observations on the Heraldic Devices on the Effigies of Richard the Second and his Queen," *Archaeologia*, XXIX (1842), 47f. See, for the "Sun of York" (*K. Richard III*, I.i.2), also Henry Green, *Shakespeare and the Emblem Writers* (London, 1870), 223; and, for the *Oriens Augusti* problem, see my forthcoming study.—The "sunne arysing out of the clouds" was actually the banner borne by the Black Prince; Richard II had a sun shining carried by a white hart, whereas his standard was sprinkled with ten suns "in splendor" with a white hart lodged; see Lord Howard de Walden, *Banners, Standards, and Badges from a Tudor Manuscript in the College of Arms* (De Walden Library, 1904), figs. 4, 5, 71. I am greatly obliged to Mr. Martin Davies, of the National Gallery in London, for having called this MS to my attention.

Up, cousin, up—your heart is up, I know,
Thus high (*touching his own head*) at least, although your
 knee be low.

(III.iii.190ff)

The jurists had claimed that the king's body politic is utterly
void of "natural Defects and Imbecilities." Here, however, "Imbecility" seems to hold sway. And yet, the very bottom has not been
reached. Each scene, progressively, designates a new low. "King
body natural" in the first scene, and "Kingly Fool" in the second:
with those two twin-born beings there is associated, in the half-
sacramental abdication scene, the twin-born deity as an even lower
estate. For the "Fool" marks the transition from "King" to "God,"
and nothing could be more miserable, it seems, than the God in
the wretchedness of man.

As the third scene (IV.i) opens, there prevails again—now for
the third time—the image of sacramental kingship. On the Beach
of Wales, Richard himself had been the herald of the loftiness of
kingship by right divine; at Flint Castle, he had made it his "program" to save at least the face of a king and to justify the "Name,"
although the title no longer fitted his condition; at Westminster,
he is incapable of expounding his kingship himself. Another person will speak for him and interpret the image of God-established
royalty; and very fittingly, a bishop. The Bishop of Carlisle now
plays the *logothetes*; he constrains, once more, the *rex imago Dei*
to appear:

> What subject can give sentence on his king?
> And who sits here that is not Richard's subject? . . .
> And shall the figure of God's majesty,
> His captain, steward, deputy-elect,
> Anointed, crowned, planted many years,
> Be judged by subject and inferior breath,
> And he himself not present? O, forfend it, God,
> That in a Christian climate souls refined
> Should show so heinous, black, obscene a deed!
>
> (IV.i.121ff)

Those are, in good mediaeval fashion, the features of the *vicarius
Dei*. And it likewise agrees with mediaeval tradition that the
Bishop of Carlisle views the present against the background of the
Biblical past. True, he leaves it to Richard to draw the final con-
clusions and to make manifest the resemblance of the humbled

king with the humbled Christ. Yet, it is the bishop who, as it were, prepares the Biblical climate by prophesying future horrors and foretelling England's Golgotha:

> Disorder, horror, fear, and mutiny
> Shall here inhabit, and this land be called
> The field of Golgotha and dead men's skulls.
>
> (IV.i.142ff)

The bishop, for his bold speech, was promptly arrested; but into the atmosphere prepared by him there enters King Richard.

When led into Westminster Hall, he strikes the same chords as the bishop, those of Biblicism. He points to the hostile assembly, to the lords surrounding Bolingbroke:

> Did they not sometimes cry 'all hail' to me?
> So Judas did to Christ: But He, in twelve,
> Found truth in all, but one: I in twelve thousand, none.
>
> (IV.i.169)

For the third time the name of Judas is cited to stigmatize the foes of Richard. Soon the name of Pilate will follow and make the implied parallel unequivocal. But before being delivered up to his judges and his cross, King Richard has to "un-king" himself.

The scene in which Richard "undoes his kingship" and releases his body politic into thin air, leaves the spectator breathless. It is a scene of sacramental solemnity, since the ecclesiastical ritual of undoing the effects of consecration is no less solemn or of less weight than the ritual which has built up the sacramental dignity. Not to mention the rigid punctilio which was observed at the ousting of a Knight of the Garter or the Golden Fleece,[19] there had been set a famous precedent by Pope Celestine V who, in the Castel Nuovo at Naples, had "undone" himself by stripping off from his body, with his own hands, the insignia of the dignity

---

[19] The ecclesiastical *Forma degradationis* was, on the whole, faithfully observed; see the Pontifical of William Durandus (ca. 1293-95), III,c.7, §§21-24, ed. M. Andrieu, *Le pontifical romain au moyen-âge* (Studi e testi, LXXXVIII, Rome, 1940), III,607f and Appendix IV, pp. 680f. The person to be degraded has to appear in full pontificals; then the places of his chrismation are rubbed with some acid; finally "seriatim et sigillatim detrahit [episcopus] illi omnia insignia, sive sacra ornamenta, que in ordinum susceptione recepit, et demum exuit illum habitu clericali. . . ." See also S. W. Findlay, *Canonical Norms Governing the Deposition and Degradation of Clerics* (Washington, 1941). For knights, see Otto Cartellieri, *Am Hofe der Herzöge von Burgund* (Basel, 1926), 62 (with notes on p. 272); also Du Cange, *Glossarium,* s.v. "Arma reversata."

which he resigned—ring, tiara, and purple. But whereas Pope Celestine resigned his dignity to his electors, the College of Cardinals, Richard, the hereditary king, resigned his office to God—*Deo ius suum resignavit.*[20] The Shakespearian scene in which Richard "undoes himself with hierophantic solemnity," has attracted the attention of many a critic, and Walter Pater has called it very correctly an inverted rite, a rite of degradation and a long agonizing ceremony in which the order of coronation is reversed.[21] Since none is entitled to lay finger on the Anointed of God and royal bearer of a *character indelibilis*,[22] King Richard, when defrocking himself, appears as his own celebrant:

> Am I both priest and clerk? well then, amen.
> (IV.i.173)

Bit by bit he deprives his body politic of the symbols of its dignity and exposes his poor body natural to the eyes of the spectators:

> Now mark me how I will undo myself:
> I give this heavy weight from off my head,
> And this unwieldy sceptre from my hand,
> The pride of kingly sway from out my heart;
> With mine own tears I wash away my balm,

[20] For Pope Celestine V, see F. Baethgen, *Der Engelpapst* (Leipzig, 1943), 175; for Richard, *Chronicle of Dieulacres Abbey*, ed. M. V. Clarke and V. H. Galbraith, "The Deposition of Richard II," *Bulletin of the John Rylands Library*, XIV (1930), 173, also 146.

[21] Walter Pater, *Appreciations* (London, 1944), 205f; Wilson, xv f; Palmer, *Political Characters*, 166.

[22] Cf. Chrimes, *Const. Ideas*, 7, n. 2, quoting *Annales Henrici Quarti*, ed. Riley (Rolls Series), 286: "Noluit renunciare spirituali honori *characteris sibi impressi* et inunctioni, quibus renunciare non potuit nec ab hiis cessare." The question as to whether or not the king, through his anointment, ever owned in a technical sense a *character indelibilis* is too complicated to be discussed here. In fact, the notion of the "sacramental character" was developed only at the time when the royal (imperial) consecrations were excluded from the number of the seven sacraments; cf. Ferdinand Brommer, *Die Lehre vom sakramentalen Charakter in der Scholastik bis Thomas von Aquino inklusive* (Forschungen zur christlichen Literatur- und Dogmengeschichte, VIII, 2), Paderborn, 1908. For the attitude of the Pope, Innocent III, see below, Ch. VII, nos. 14f, also 18. A different matter is the common opinion about the sacramental character of royal anointings and the inaccurate use of the term *sacramentum*; see, for the latter, e.g., P. E. Schramm, "Der König von Navarra (1035-1512)," *ZfRG*, germ. Abt., LXVIII (1951), 147, n. 72 (Pope Alexander IV referring to a royal consecration as *sacramentum*). See, in general, Eduard Eichmann, *Die Kaiserkrönung im Abendland* (Würzburg, 1942), I, 86ff, 90, 208, 279, II, 304; Philipp Oppenheim, "Die sakralen Momente in der deutschen Herrscherweihe bis zum Investiturstreit," *Ephemerides Liturgicae*, LVIII (1944), 42ff; and, for England, the well known utterances of Peter of Blois (*PL*, CCVII, 440D) and Grosseteste (*Ep.*, CXXIV, ed. Luard, 350). Actually, the lack of precision was great at all times.

> With mine own hands I give away my crown,
> With mine own tongue deny my sacred state,
> With mine own breath release all duteous oaths:
> All pomp and majesty do I foreswear. . . .
>
> (IV.i.203ff)

Self-deprived of all his former glories, Richard seems to fly back to his old trick of Flint Castle, to the rôle of Fool, as he renders to his "successor" some double-edged acclamations.[23] This time, however, the fool's cap is of no avail. Richard declines to "ravel out his weaved-up follies," which his cold-efficient foe Northumberland demands him to read aloud. Nor can he shield himself behind his "Name." This, too, is gone irrevocably:

> I have no name. . . .
> And know not now what name to call myself.
>
> (IV.i.254ff)

In a new flash of inventiveness, he tries to hide behind another screen. He creates a new split, a chink for his former glory through which to escape and thus to survive. Over against his lost outward kingship he sets an inner kingship, makes his true kingship to retire to inner man, to soul and mind and "regal thoughts":

> You may my glories and my state depose,
> But not my griefs, still am I king of those.
>
> (IV.i.192ff)

Invisible his kingship, and relegated to within: visible his flesh, and exposed to contempt and derision or to pity and mockery— there remains but one parallel to his miserable self: the derided Son of man. Not only Northumberland, so Richard exclaims, will be found "damned in the book of heaven," but others as well:

> Nay, all of you, that stand and look upon me,
> Whilst that my wretchedness doth bait myself,
> Though some of you, with Pilate, wash your hands,
> Showing an outward pity; yet you Pilates
> Have here delivered me to my sour cross,
> And water cannot wash away your sin.
>
> (IV.i.237)

It is not at random that Shakespeare introduces here, as antitype of Richard, the image of Christ before Pilate, mocked as King of

[23] IV.i.214ff.

37

the Jews and delivered to the cross. Shakespeare's sources, contemporary with the events, had transmitted that scene in a similar light.

> At this hour did he (Bolingbroke) remind me of Pilate, who caused our Lord Jesus Christ to be scourged at the stake, and afterwards had him brought before the multitude of the Jews, saying, "Fair Sirs, behold your king!" who replied, "Let him be crucified!" Then Pilate washed his hands of it, saying, "I am innocent of the just blood." And so he delivered our Lord unto them. Much in the like manner did Duke Henry, when he gave up his rightful lord to the rabble of London, in order that, if they should put him to death, he might say, "I am innocent of this deed."[24]

The parallel of Bolingbroke-Richard and Pilate-Christ reflects a widespread feeling among the anti-Lancastrian groups. Such feeling was revived, to some extent, in Tudor times. But this is not important here; for Shakespeare, when using the biblical comparison, integrates it into the entire development of Richard's misery, of which the nadir has as yet not been reached. The Son of man, despite his humiliation and the mocking, remained the *deus absconditus*, remained the "concealed God" with regard to inner man, just as Shakespeare's Richard would trust for a moment's length in his concealed inner kingship. This inner kingship, however, dissolved too. For of a sudden Richard realizes that he, when facing his Lancastrian Pilate, is not at all like Christ, but that he himself, Richard, has his place among the Pilates and Judases, because he is no less a traitor than the others, or is even worse than they are: he is a traitor to his own immortal body politic and to kingship such as it had been to his day:

> Mine eyes are full of tears, I cannot see. . . .
> But they can see a sort of traitors here.
> Nay, if I turn mine eyes upon myself,

[24] The passage is found in the *Chronique de la Traïson et Mort de Richard II*, ed. B. Williams, in: *English Historical Society*, 1846, and in Creton's French metrical *History of the Deposition of Richard II*, ed. J. Webb, in: *Royal Society of the Antiquaries* (London, 1819). A fifteenth-century English version, which has been rendered here, was edited by J. Webb, in *Archaeologia*, xx (1824), 179. See, on those sources, Wilson, "Introduction," lviii, cf. xvi f and 211. The crime of treason would naturally evoke the comparison with Judas. The comparison with Pilate was likewise quite common (see, e.g., Dante, *Purg.*, xx, 91), though his role was not always purely negative; see, e.g., O. Treitinger, *Die oströmische Kaiser- und Reichsidee nach ihrer Gestaltung im höfischen Zeremoniell* (Jena, 1938), 231, n. 104, for Pilate's inkpot in the ceremonial of the Byzantine emperor, who on Ash Wednesday symbolically "washed his hands."

> I find myself a traitor with the rest:
> For I have given here my soul's consent
> T'undeck the pompous body of a king. . . .
>
> (IV.i.244)

That is, the king body natural becomes a traitor to the king body politic, to the "pompous body of a king." It is as though Richard's self-indictment of treason anticipated the charge of 1649, the charge of high treason committed by the *k*ing against the *K*ing.

This cleavage is not yet the climax of Richard's duplications, since the splitting of his personality will be continued without mercy. Once more does there emerge that metaphor of "Sun-kingship." It appears, however, in the reverse order, when Richard breaks into that comparison of singular imagination:

> O, that I were a mockery king of snow,
> Standing before the sun of Bolingbroke,
> To melt myself away in water-drops!
>
> (IV.i.260ff)

But it is not before that new Sun—symbol of divine majesty throughout the play—that Richard "melts himself away," and together with his self also the image of kingship in the early liturgical sense;[25] it is before his own ordinary face that there dissolves both his bankrupt majesty and his nameless manhood.

The mirror scene is the climax of that tragedy of dual personality. The looking-glass has the effects of a magic mirror, and Richard himself is the wizard who, comparable to the trapped and cornered wizard in the fairy tales, is forced to set his magic art to work against himself. The physical face which the mirror reflects, no longer is one with Richard's inner experience, his outer appearance, no longer identical with inner man. "Was this the face?" The treble question and the answers to it reflect once more the three main facets of the double nature—King, God (Sun), and Fool:

> Was this the face
> That every day under his household roof
> Did keep ten thousand men?
> Was this the face
> That, like the sun, did make beholders wink?
> Was this the face, that faced so many follies,
> And was at last outfaced by Bolingbroke?
>
> (IV.i.281)

[25] See below, pp. 87f.

When finally, at the "brittle glory" of his face, Richard dashes the mirror to the ground, there shatters not only Richard's past and present, but every aspect of a super-world. His catoptromancy has ended. The features as reflected by the looking-glass betray that he is stripped of every possibility of a second or super-body—of the pompous body politic of king, of the God-likeness of the Lord's deputy elect, of the follies of the fool, and even of the most human griefs residing in inner man. The splintering mirror means, or is, the breaking apart of any possible duality. All those facets are reduced to one: to the banal face and insignificant *physis* of a miserable man, a *physis* now void of any metaphysis whatsoever. It is both less and more than Death. It is the *demise* of Richard, and the rise of a new body natural.

> *Bolingbroke*:
>> Go, some of you, convey him to the Tower.
>
> *Richard*:
>> O, good! convey? conveyors are you all,
>> That rise thus nimbly by a true king's fall.
>>> (IV.i.316f)

> *Plowden*:
>> Demise is a word, signifying that there is a Separation of the two Bodies; and that the Body politic is conveyed over from the Body natural, now dead or removed from the Dignity royal, to another Body natural.[26]

The Tragedy of King Richard II has always been felt to be a political play.[27] The deposition scene, though performed scores of times after the first performance in 1595, was not printed, or not allowed to be printed, until after the death of Queen Elizabeth.[28] Historical plays in general attracted the English people, especially in the years following the destruction of the Armada; but *Richard II* attracted more than the usual attention. Not to speak of other causes, the conflict between Elizabeth and Essex appeared to Shakespeare's contemporaries in the light of the conflict between Richard and Bolingbroke. It is well known that in 1601, on the eve of his unsuccessful rebellion against the Queen, the Earl of Essex ordered a special performance of *Richard II* to be played in the Globe

---

[26] Plowden, *Reports*, 233a; above, Ch. I, n.13.

[27] Palmer, *Political Characters*, 118f.

[28] Wilson, "Introduction," xvi ff, xlix; also Child (*ibid.*), lxxvii ff; cf. Keeton, *Legal Problems*, 163.

Theatre before his supporters and the people of London. In the course of the state trial against Essex that performance was discussed at some length by the royal judges—among them the two greatest lawyers of that age, Coke and Bacon—who could not fail to recognize the allusions to the present which the performance of that play intended.[29] It is likewise well known that Elizabeth looked upon that tragedy with most unfavorable feelings. At the time of Essex' execution she complained that "this tragedy had been played 40 times in open streets and houses," and she carried her self-identification with the title character so far as to exclaim: "I am Richard II, know ye not that?"[30]

Richard II remained a political play. It was suppressed under Charles II in the 1680's. The play illustrated perhaps too overtly the latest events of England's revolutionary history, the "Day of the Martyrdom of the Blessed King Charles I" as commemorated in those years in the Book of Common Prayer.[31] The Restoration avoided these and other recollections and had no liking for that tragedy which centered, not only on the concept of a Christ-like martyr king, but also on that most unpleasant idea of a violent separation of the King's Two Bodies.

It would not be surprising at all had Charles I himself thought of his tragic fate in terms of Shakespeare's *Richard II* and of the king's twin-born being. In some copies of the *Eikon Basilike* there is printed a lament, a long poem otherwise called *Majesty in Misery*, which is ascribed to Charles I and in which the unfortunate king, if really he was the poet, quite obviously alluded to the King's Two Bodies:

> With my own power my majesty they wound,
> In the King's name the king himself uncrowned.
> So does the dust destroy the diamond.[32]

[29] Wilson, xxx ff; Keeton, 166, 168.   [30] Wilson, xxxii.

[31] Wilson, xvii; Child, lxxix.

[32] According to Rosemary Freeman, *English Emblem Books* (London, 1948), 162, n.1, the poem was first printed in the *Eikon Basilike*, edition of 1648. Margaret Barnard Pickel, *Charles I as Patron of Poetry and Drama* (London, 1938), who prints the whole poem in Appendix C, seems to assume (p. 178) that it was first published in Bishop Burnet's *Memoirs of the Duke of Hamilton* (London, 1677), a work dedicated to Charles II. A few stanzas have been published also by F. M. G. Higham, *Charles I* (London, 1932), 276.

CHAPTER III

CHRIST-CENTERED KINGSHIP

1. The Norman Anonymous

WHILE undoubtedly it is true that the legal fiction of the King's Two Bodies was a distinctive feature of English political thought in the age of Elizabeth and the early Stuarts, it would be unfortunate to imply that those speculations were restricted to the sixteenth and seventeenth centuries or were lacking antecedents.

It may not have been generally known, but it was probably known to at least one prominent Elizabethan, Archbishop Matthew Parker, that almost five centuries before his own times an anonymous mediaeval author had developed some curious ideas about the "twinned" person of a king. For Archbishop Parker, who shortly before his death in 1575 bequeathed his precious library to his old College, Corpus Christi at Cambridge, had among his treasures the only extant manuscript of some highly interesting theological and political tractates which, around A.D. 1100, had been written by an unknown cleric. The tractates reveal in daring language the author's passionately anti-Gregorian and vigorously royalist sentiments; they still breathe the fire kindled by the Investiture Struggle. Since their first publication some fifty years ago, those pamphlets have attracted increasing attention from historians; but despite all scholarly efforts it has not been possible to ascertain the name of their author, although the most recent study leaves no doubt that the "Anonymous" was a Norman from Normandy and perhaps even a member of the Duchy's high clergy.[1]

There are few problems in the field of ecclesiology and policy which the Norman Anonymous, who had a good knowledge of

---

[1] The bulk of the anonymous Tractates was published in 1899, by Heinrich Böhmer, in *MGH,LdL*, III,642-678, and in his *Kirche und Staat in England und in der Normandie im 11. und 12. Jahrhundert* (Leipzig, 1899), 436-497, with a full discussion of the Tractates and suggestions as to the authorship (177-269). For the whole problem, including a *bibliographie raisonnée*, see now, in addition to Harald Scherrinsky, *Untersuchungen zum sogenannten Anonymus von York* (Würzburg-Aumühle, 1940), George H. Williams, *The Norman Anonymous of ca. 1100 A.D.: Toward the Identification and the Evaluation of the So-called Anonymous of York* (Harvard Theological Studies, XVIII; Cambridge, 1951), on whose work I have drawn perpetually in the following pages. See Williams, 125ff, for the authorship of the tractates.

theological literature, liturgy, and canon law, failed to treat in his always original, always surprising, and always lively fashion. Among the many topics which he saw fit to discuss, there was also what later would be defined as *persona mixta*, the "mixed person" in which various capacities or strata concurred. "Mixtures" of all kinds of capacities, of course, may be found today as in every other age and under almost any conditions. However, the yoking of two seemingly heterogeneous spheres had a peculiar attraction for an age eager to reconcile the duality of this world and the other, of things temporal and eternal, secular and spiritual. We need only think of the "mixture" of monk and knight postulated in the orders of spiritual chivalry to grasp the pattern of ideals by which that time might have been moved; and when an abbot of Cluny was said to be *angelicus videlicet et humanus*, it was more than just a metaphor chosen by chance, because we have to remember that the monk claimed to exemplify, while still in this world and in the flesh, the *vita angelica* of the celestial beings.[2]

What matters here is only the *persona mixta* in the religio-political sphere where it was represented chiefly by bishop and king, and where the "mixture" referred to the blending of spiritual and secular powers and capacities united in one person. Dual capacity in this sense was a feature customary and rather common with the clergy during the feudal age when bishops were not only princes of the Church but also feudatories of kings. We do not need to look for such extreme cases as that French bishop who claimed to observe strictest celibacy as a bishop while being duly married as a baron, or the case of Odo of Bayeux who, at Lanfranc's suggestion, was tried by the Conqueror as an earl, and not as a bishop;[3] for

---

[2] See John of Salerno, *Vita S. Odonis*, c.5, *PL*, cxxxiii, 63C: "Erat enim velut lapis angularis quadrus, angelicus videlicet et humanus," whereby it has to be known that according to Christian exegesis the Biblical "Corner Stone" was identified with Christ joining together "two walls," that is, Jews and Gentiles. In this sense, then, Odo of Cluny not only receives an epithet due to Christ, but also is said to join together "two walls," those of angels and men. See, for the concept, Gerhart B. Ladner, "The Symbolism of the Biblical Corner Stone in the Mediaeval West," *Mediaeval Studies*, ii (1940), 43-60. For monachism as *vita angelica*, see, e.g., Kassius Hallinger, "Zur geistigen Welt der Anfänge Klunys," *DA*, x (1954), 417-445, esp. 429f; and, for *Angelus tuus* as an address, Henri Grégoire, " 'Ton Ange' et les Anges de Théra," *BZ*, xxx (1929-30), 641-644.

[3] T. F. Tout, *The Place of Edward II in English History* (Manchester, 1914), 130, n. 1; James Conway Davies, *The Baronial Opposition to Edward II* (Cambridge, 1918), 22. For Odo of Bayeux, see Ordericus Vitalis, *Historia ecclesiastica*, iii, c.vii,

shortly after 1100 the dual capacity of bishops had been spelled out in legal terms in a number of concordats which the Holy See concluded with the secular powers. It is significant, however, that a seemingly so obvious distinction as that between the spiritualities and temporalities of a bishop, with which the problem of investiture had been almost hopelessly entangled, could be established only with great difficulty, and that it was due chiefly to the clear thinking of a legal authority, Ivo of Chartres, that the logical conclusion finally was drawn: the recognition of a bishop's dual status. Under Ivo's sponsorship the problem of the bishops' investiture with the temporalities, sided by the ecclesiastical consecration, was regulated in England by the concordat of 1107, and from that time onwards the dual status of the English bishop-barons was clearly defined. *Habet duos status* declared the royal judges under Edward I concerning the Bishop of Durham, who was at the same time count palatine; and the judges formulated thereby, though with greater precision, only what had been described already in the Constitutions of Clarendon (1164) as well as on other occasions.[4]

Not only the bishop, but also the king appeared as a *persona mixta*, because a certain spiritual capacity was attributed to him as an effluence of his consecration and unction. It is true that the papal doctrine finally denied to the king a clerical character, or relegated it to some insignificant honorary titles and functions.[5] Nevertheless, the late mediaeval authors continued to emphasize that the king was "not purely laical" or, in the language of the law, was "not an ordinary person."[6] Around 1100, however, when the

---

8, *PL*, CLXXXVIII,529f, ed. A. Le Prevost (Paris, 1845), III,191: "Ego non clericum nec antistitem damno, sed comitem meum, quem meo vice mea preposui regno."

[4] *Constitutions of Clarendon*, §11, ed. Stubbs, *Select Charters* (Oxford, 1921), 166; *Close Rolls, 1296-1302*, 330ff; *Rot.Parl.*, I,102ff; cf. Davies, *op.cit.*, 23; Pollock and Maitland, I,524. The dual character of the bishops is stressed also by Francis Accursius; see G. L. Haskins and E. H. Kantorowicz, "A Diplomatic Mission of Francis Accursius," *English Historical Review*, LVIII (1943), 436, 446, §27. The capacities of the pope, of course, are almost innumerable. Bernard of Clairvaux addressed the pope: "Quis es? Sacerdos magnus, summus Pontifex: Tu princeps episcoporum, tu haeres Apostolorum, tu primatu Abel, gubernatu Noe, patriarchatu Abraham, ordine Melchisedech, dignitate Aaron, auctoritate Moyses, iudicatu Samuel, potestate Petrus, unctione Christus"; and St. Bernard did not even mention the judicial and administrative capacities. Cf. Bernard, *De consideratione*, II,8,15, *PL*, CLXXXII,751.

[5] Eichmann, *Die Kaiserkrönung*, I,203,282f,319, for the king's functions of subdeacon and lector; see also next note. For the Norman Anonymous on the *persona mixta*, see also below, n.30.

[6] See above, Chapter II, n.22. For the formula *imperator (rex) non omnino laicus*,

Norman Anonymous wrote his tractates, the concept of the king as a person endowed with spiritual qualities was still in bloom and had hardly passed its heyday; and therefore much of what that writer discusses has to be viewed against the background of mediaeval priest-kingship ideals.

With the King's Two Bodies the doctrine of the *persona mixta* seems to have no direct relation. The duplication expressed by the concept of the *persona mixta* refers to temporal and spiritual capacities, but does not refer to bodies natural and politic. Or could it be that the king's impersonal and immortal super-body appeared, during the earlier Middle Ages, in some way or the other, embedded in that very idea of his spiritual character resulting from the clericalization of the royal office?[7] In fact, it is in that direction that the Norman Anonymous, one of the staunchest defenders of the spiritual essence of a Christ-like kingship, sends us, and we can do nothing better than to take his hint and follow his guidance.

The best known, and perhaps the most remarkable, of the

---

see Eichmann, "Königs- und Bischofsweihe," 58, also 52ff; cf. *Die Kaiserkrönung,* I, 105ff, 203, and passim. See also the Order of Cencius (*Cencius II*), ed. P. E. Schramm, "Die Ordines der mittelalterlichen Kaiserkrönung," *Archiv für Urkundenforschung,* XI (1929), 379: " (Papa) faiit eum clericum," referring to the emperor's reception among the Canons of St. Peter's; see A. Schulte, "Deutsche Könige, Kaiser, Päpste als Kanoniker an deutschen und römischen Kirchen," *Historisches Jahrbuch,* LIV (1934), 137ff; also Schramm, "Sacerdotium und Regnum im Austausch ihrer Vorrechte," *Studi Gregoriani,* II (1947), 425ff. In connection with the right of investiture, see the Norman Anonymous, *MGH,LdL,* III,679, 16ff: "Quare (rex) non est appellandus laicus, quia christus Domini est" (cf. 685,42ff). Some later jurists held the same view; see below, Ch.VII, n.16; for Sicily, e.g., Marinus de Caramanico, *Prooemium,* in *Lib. aug.,* ed. Cervone, xxxv, and ed. F. Calasso, *I glossatori e la teoria della sovranità* (Milan, 1951), 189,26: "Reges enim non sunt mere laici in quos . . . spiritualia iura non cadunt." That the king is not an "ordinary person" was repeated over and over again; see, for England, e.g., G. O. Sayles, *Select Cases in the Court of King's Bench* (London, 1939), Introd., xliii,n.3. For the king as *persona mixta,* see Schramm, *A History of the English Coronation* (Oxford, 1937), 115,n.1; also Chrimes, *Const. Ideas,* 8, and *ibid.,* 387, the interesting statement of Chief Justice Brian (10 Henry VII): "*quod Rex est persona mixta car est persona unita cum sacerdotibus* saint Eglise." From this general concept there derives, ultimately, the doctrine within the Protestant countries concerning the prince as a *duplex persona, saecularis et ecclesiastica;* see Gierke, *Gen.R.,* IV,66f,n.20; and, in general, Hans Liermann, "Untersuchungen zum Sakralrecht des protestantischen Herrschers," *ZfRG, kan.Abt.,* XXX (1941), 311-383.

[7] For the "clericalization" of the royal office, beginning, by and large, with Hincmar of Reims and Charles the Bald, see Schramm, *Der König von Frankreich* (Weimar, 1939), 17f, 26ff; cf. Kantorowicz, *Laudes regiae,* 78ff, and passim.

anonymous tractates is the one *De consecratione pontificum et regum*. As the title suggests, the author's discussion is centered on the effects of the ordination anointings of both kings and bishops. The Norman Anonymous proceeds very logically from the Old Testament to the New, and therefore starts with the anointings of the Kings of Israel. For the moment, we may disregard the fact that the author is referring not only to the anointment of Israel's kings but also to that of Aaron and the Israelitic high-priests, when he writes:

> We thus have to recognize [in the king] a *twin person*, one descending from nature, the other from grace. . . . One through which, by the condition of nature, he conformed with other men: another through which, by the eminence of [his] deification and by the power of the sacrament [of consecration], he excelled all others. Concerning one personality, he was, by nature, an individual man: concerning his other personality, he was, by grace, a *Christus*, that is, a God-man.[8]

This passage parallels strikingly, if in theological rather than constitutional language, the arguments of the Tudor lawyers. Those jurists, of course, did not talk about grace but about the polity of the English people, and they would have said probably "one [body] descending from nature, the other from the polity"; but both the Norman author and the Tudor jurists arrived at a similar fiction of a royal super-body conjoined in some mysterious way to the king's natural and individual body. The similarities between the two concepts, however, should not tempt us to overlook the fact that some perplexing "physiological" difference prevails between the mediaeval "geminate" king and his two-bodied Tudor descendant.

The kings whom the Anonymous refers to are the *christi*, the anointed kings of the Old Testament, who have been foreshadowing the advent of the true royal *Christus*, the Anointed of Eternity. After the advent of Christ in the flesh, and after his ascension and exaltation as King of Glory, the terrestrial kingship underwent, very consistently, a change and received its proper function within

---

[8] *MGH,LdL*, III,664,26ff: "Itaque in unoquoque gemina intelligitur fuisse persona, una ex natura, altera ex gratia, una in hominis proprietate, altera in spiritu et virtute. Una, qua per conditionem nature ceteris hominibus congrueret, altera qua per eminentiam deificationis et vim sacramenti cunctis aliis precelleret. In una quippe erat naturaliter individuus homo, in altera per gratiam Christus, id est Deus-homo."

the economy of salvation. The kings of the New Covenant no longer would appear as the "foreshadowers" of Christ, but rather as the "shadows," the imitators of Christ. The Christian ruler became the *christomimētēs*—literally the "actor" or "impersonator" of Christ—who on the terrestrial stage presented the living image of the two-natured God, even with regard to the two unconfused natures. The divine prototype and his visible vicar were taken to display great similarity, as they were supposed to reflect each other; and there was, according to the Anonymous, perhaps only a single—though essential—difference between the Anointed in Eternity and his terrestrial antitype, the anointed in Time: Christ was King and *Christus* by his very nature, whereas his deputy on earth was king and *christus* by grace only. For whereas the Spirit "leaped" into the terrestrial king at the moment of his consecration to make him "another man" (*alius vir*) and transfigure him within Time, the self-same Spirit was from Eternity one with the King of Glory to remain one with him in all Eternity.[9] In other words, the king *becomes* "deified" for a brief span by virtue of grace, whereas the celestial King *is* God by nature eternally.

This antithesis is applied by the Anonymous over and over again. It is not his own invention, but merely reproduces theologically familiar concepts. The antithesis of *natura* and *gratia* was commonly used to indicate not only that the weakness of man's nature was remedied by grace, but also that grace disposed man to participate in the divine nature itself. In the latter sense the antithesis of *natura* and *gratia* actually formed the vehicle for the early Christian "deification" of man in general, and not just for consecrated and anointed kings. The Anonymous, however, applied that "deification by grace" pre-eminently to the king as an effluence of his anointment and the ritual act of consecration, and used the antithesis to point out that the "eminence of deification" provided his king with a body of grace by which he became "another man" excelling all others—a deification which he describes as coterminous with the Greek *apotheosis* and the ancient Roman

---

[9] *Ibid.*, 665,2f: "Post unctionem vero insilivit in eum spiritus Domini, et propheta factus est, et mutatus est in virum alium." From this "leap" of the Holy Spirit the king's two personalities actually derived; cf. 664,20ff: "[Ad unctionem] insiliebat in eos spiritus Domini et virtus deificans, per quam Christi figura fierent et imago et que mutaret eos in viros alios, ita ut . . . *in persona* sua esset *alius* vir, et *alius in spiritu.* . . .”

consecratio.[10] The antithesis served the Anonymous, it is true, to observe very strictly the inherent difference between the God and the king; but it served him also to blur that line of distinction and to show where the difference between "God by nature" and "god by grace" ended; that is, in the case of *potestas*, of power. Essence and substance of power are claimed to be equal in both God and king, no matter whether that power be owned by nature or only acquired by grace.

> The power of the king is the power of God. This power, namely, is God's by nature, and the king's by grace. Hence, the king, too, is God and Christ, but by grace; and whatsoever he does, he does not simply as a man, but as one who has become God and Christ by grace.[11]

Thus, the king appears the perfect *christomimētēs* also with regard to power, since his power is the same as that of Christ. The author may add, therefore, that the One who is God and Anointed by nature, acts through his royal vicar who is "God and Christ by grace," and who *in officio figura et imago Christi et Dei est.*[12] That is to say, the king, otherwise an individual man, is *in officio* the type and image of the Anointed in heaven and therewith of God.

---

10 For Christian deification, see, e.g., M. Lot-Borodine, "La doctrine de la déification dans l'église grecque," *Revue de l'histoire des religions*, CV-CVII (1932-33); J. Gross, *La divinisation du chrétien d'après les pères grecs* (Paris, 1938); also G. W. Butterworth, "The Deification of Man in Clement of Alexandria," *Journal of Theological Studies*, XVII (1916), 157ff, and Cuthbert Lattey, *ibid.*, 257ff; A. D. Nock, in: *Journal of Religion*, XXXI (1951), 214ff, and Kantorowicz, "Deus per naturam, deus per gratiam," *Harvard Theological Review*, XLV (1952), 253-277. For *apotheosis* and *consecratio*, see below, n.13.

11 *MGH,LdL*, III,667,35ff. The priest instituted by the king is not instituted by the power of man, but by the power of God: "Potestas enim regis potestas Dei est; Dei quidem est per naturam, regis per gratiam. Unde et rex Deus et Christus est, sed per gratiam, et quicquid facit non homo simpliciter, sed Deus factus et Christus per gratiam facit." See also 676,14ff: "Summi et celestis imperatoris et secundi terrenique una eademque potestas est, sed celestis principaliter, terreni secundarie." The ruler as *a Deo secundus* (so already Tertullian, *Apologeticus*, XXX,1) and Christ as δεύτερος θεός (see, e.g., Origen, *Contra Celsum*, V,39, and VII,57) belong to another cycle of problems for which some relevant material has been collected by H. Volkmann, "Der Zweite nach dem König," *Philologus*, XCVII (1937), 285-316. It is interesting, however, that the Byzantine emperor was sometimes addressed as "second God *by grace*" (ὄντος σοῦ τοῦ κατὰ χάριν καὶ δευτέρου θεοῦ); see Spyridon P. Lampros, Μιχαὴλ Ἀκομινάτου τοῦ Χωνιάτου τὰ σωζόμενα (Athens, 1879), I,221,11f; M. Bachmann, *Die Rede des Johannes Syropulos an den Kaiser Isaak II. Angelos (1185-1195)* (Munich diss., 1935), 11 and 26.

12 *MGH,LdL*, III,667,8f: ". . . in spiritu et Christus et deus est, et in officio figura et imago Christi et Dei est." *Ibid.*, 667,39: "Immo ipse, qui natura Deus est et Christus, per vicarium suum hoc facit, per quem vices suas exsequitur."

These reflections on both the bipolarity and the potential one-ness of nature and grace led the author to the concept of his Christ-impersonating king as a "twinned" being. He, the anointed by grace, parallels as a *gemina persona* the two-natured Christ. It is the mediaeval idea of Christ-centered kingship carried to an extreme rarely encountered in the West.[13] The king is a twinned being, human and divine, just like the God-man, although the king is two-natured and geminate by grace only and within Time, and not by nature and (after the Ascension) within Eternity: the terrestrial king *is* not, he *becomes* a twin personality through his anointment and consecration.

The expression itself, *gemina persona*, does not represent a poetical metaphor, but is a technical term derived from and re-lated to christological definitions. That actually this term was rarely applied to Christ is a different matter. According to the orthodox dogma, Christ is *una persona, duae naturae*. "Twin per-son," therefore, was an expression to be avoided as dogmatically unsafe; it was just as bad as "two Persons," since it did not safely preclude a Nestorian or Adoptionist interpretation. It is note-worthy, however, that the image of "twinship," generally rare in that connection, occurs with relative frequency in the acts of the early Hispanic councils. A certain wavering may be found in the numerous Creeds which the Hispanic synods have produced, but their wording is dogmatically correct. The second Hispanic Coun-

---

[13] *Ibid.*, 665,19f: "Erat enim . . . christus Domini et unus cum Domino spiritus. Christus etenim Deus et homo est." And more explicitly, *ibid.*, 665,28ff, a passage showing that king and Christ have the "Two Natures" in common:

Rex autem . . . *huius* Christi, id est Dei et hominis, imago et figura erat, quia . . . totus homo erat, totus deificatus erat et sanctificatus per gratiam unctionis et per benedictionis consecrationem. Nam et si Graeci sermonis utaris ethimologia, conse-cratio, id est *apotheosis*, sonabit tibi deificatio. Si ergo . . . rex . . . per gratiam deus est et christus Domini, quicquid agit et operatur secundum hanc gratiam, iam non homo agit et operatur, sed deus et christus Domini.

I have constantly omitted the references to the bishop; see below, n.30. For the Anglo-Saxon king as *christus Domini*, see the legatine report of 787, in Haddan and Stubbs, *Councils and Ecclesiastical Documents* (Oxford, 1871), III,454.§12; and, for Henry II, Peter of Blois, *PL*, ccvII,440D; in general, see Leonid Arbusow, *Liturgie und Geschichtsschreibung im Mittelalter* (Bonn, 1951), 95,n.60. It should be added that according to the Anonymous (670,5ff) only the king is a true and genuine *christomimētēs*; for the bishops act *interposita vice et imitatione apostolorum*; they are quasi-*apostolomimētai* and only indirectly, through the Apostles, also *christo-mimētai*. The "etymology" of the Anonymous is perfectly correct: in Rome the *consecratio* of the emperor was his *apotheosis*, whereas the word *deificatio*, like the Greek θεοποιία, belongs almost exclusively to Christian terminology.

cil (619) emphasized the *gemina natura* of Christ and added correctly that "this *gemina natura* still forms one person."[14] The Sixth Toledan Council (638) decided also correctly that "man and God are One Christ in two natures . . . lest there acceded a Quaternity to the Trinity, if Christ were a *geminata persona*."[15] In 675, the Eleventh Council of Toledo returned to the term of "twinship" but shifted it from *gemina natura* and *geminata persona* carefully to *gemina substantia,* and explained: "Therefore he has in himself a *gemina substantia,* that of his divinity and of our humanity." And in this connection the Council coined the remarkable sentence: *Item et major et minor se ipso esse credendus est.*[16] Finally the Fourteenth Toletanum (684) introduced a new variety of gemination. The truth is, so the bishops declared, that Christ has a "twin will"—*gemina in eo voluntas, et operatio*—though he is not divided by the twinship of natures—*non naturarum geminatione divisus*—but is wholly God and wholly man.[17] Thereafter the terms of twin-nature, twin-person, twin-substance, or twin-will seem to go out of fashion in the Creeds. Rhabanus Maurus mentions them once more, if in a negative sense;[18] and only the *gigas geminae substantiae* turns up occasionally in the christological writings of the twelfth century as a means of refuting the thesis that Christ was *geminatus* before the Incarnation.[19]

---

14 *PL,* LXXXIV,599C; Hinschius, *Decret. Ps.Isid.,* 440b, cf.441a.

15 *PL,* LXXXIV,395A; Hahn, *Symbole,* 237; Hinschius, 376b.

16 *PL,* LXXXIV,456BC; Hahn, 246f; Hinschius, 407a.

17 *PL,* LXXXIV,506Df, cf.508B.

18 Hahn, *Symbole,* 357: "quia nec geminavit utriusque substantiae integritas personam, nec confudit geminam unitas personae substantiam." See also Leo the Great, *ep.*33, *PL,* LIV,797 ("gemina natura"), and Gregory the Great, *Moralia,* XVIII,85, *PL,* LXXVI,90B ("nec naturarum distinctione geminatus"), against Nestorius. Very specific about the danger of the *geminatio* is Bede, *Expositio Actuum Apostolorum,* ed. M. L. W. Laistner (Cambridge, Mass., 1939), 51: ". . . ne Christi naturam geminare et in Nestorii dogma cadere videamur."

19 Christ as *gigas* derives from Psalm 18:6 ("tanquam sponsus procedens de thalamo suo, exsultavit ut gigas ad currendam viam"), the applications of which cover unexpected grounds, from the Armenian Liturgy to the 17th-century French cult of kings; see, for a few early applications, F. J. Dölger, *Sol salutis* (2nd ed., Münster, 1925), 217, and *Die Sonne der Gerechtigkeit* (Münster, 1918), 102ff; see also A. Alföldi, "Der iranische Weltriese auf archäologischen Denkmälern," *Jahrbuch der Schweizerischen Gesellschaft für Urgeschichte,* XL (1949-50), 24. The expression *gigas geminae substantiae* may have become known through (Pseudo[?]-) Ambrose, *Hymns,* IV,15, *PL,* XVI,1474: "Procedens de thalamo suo,/Pudoris aula regia,/Geminae Gigas substantiae,/Alacris ut currat viam." See below, nos.63ff. The metaphor is found sporadically to designate the *natura duplex* of Christ; see, e.g., Rangerius of Lucca (d. ca. 1112), *Liber de anulo et baculo,* lines 26f, *MGH,LdL,* II,509. Later in the 12th

The Norman Anonymous was well acquainted with the Acts of the Spanish Councils, which formed a section of certain redactions of the Pseudo-Isidorian Decretals. The Norman used and quoted this collection repeatedly; he even evaluated the Spanish councils with some circumspection in order to prove that the Visigothic kings—as kings, not as emperors—customarily summoned, directed, and presided over the synods of their territorial Church just as the emperors summoned, directed, and presided over the councils of the universal Church. Hence, the Visigothic model was an important precedent which, more easily than the imperial model, was applicable to Anglo-Norman conditions in a time when the claim *rex est imperator in regno suo* was not yet formulated.[20] And from the Toledan Councils the Anonymous

---

century, the "giant of twin substance" seems to become a characteristic of the school of so-called Christological Nihilianism, rejected by the Third Lateran Council, in 1179 (cf. Hefele, *Konziliengeschichte*, v[1886], 616, 719). See, e.g., Peter of Poitiers, *Sententiae*, IV,7, *PL*, CCXI,1161C: "Viam quam geminae gigas substantiae exsultando cucurrit. . . ." Further, *Quaestiones Varsavienses trinitariae et christologicae*, ed. F. Stegmüller, in *Miscellanea Giovanni Mercati* (Studi e Testi, 122; Vatican, 1946), II,306,§15: "Coepit esse gigas geminae substantiae biformisque naturae, divinae scilicet et humanae." Peter the Lombard, *In Ep. ad Romanos*, c.1, *PL*, CXCI,1307C, 1308A, seems to use only the expression *gemina substantia*. See, however, the *Prooemium* of Magister Vacarius' *Opusculum de assumpto homine*, edited by Maitland, "Magistri Vacarii Summa de Matrimonio," *Law Quarterly Review*, XIII (1897),143, which was directed against the nihilianism of the Lombard: "Et quod homo cum sit persona, ipse [Jesus] tamen assumptus dicitur et non ipsa persona. Et quod Christus et dominus glorie et gigas gemine substantie duarum sint substantiarum nomina." See, in general, Joseph de Ghellinck, "Magister Vacarius: Un juriste théologien peu aimable pour les canonistes," *Revue d'histoire ecclésiastique*, XLIV (1949), 173-178, with full bibliography.

20 *MGH,LdL*, III,675,16ff, where the Anonymous works out very neatly the difference between the emperor and the kings (see also below, n.47). He remarks, however, that the Visigothic kings exercised the same power over the Church as the emperors did, and concludes (675,27ff) that therefore kings at large have quasi-imperial power over the Church: "Unde manifestum est reges habere sacrosanctam potestatem ecclesiastici regiminis super ipsos etiam pontifices Domini et imperium super eos." The *rex imperator* concept was developed relatively early in England, even though some of the places adduced by Carl Erdmann, *Forschungen zur politischen Ideenwelt des Frühmittelalters* (Berlin, 1951), 15ff,38ff, have turned out to be forgeries of, presumably, the 12th century; see Richard Drögereit, "Kaiseridee und Kaisertitel bei den Angelsachsen," *ZfRG*, germ.Abt., LXIX (1952), 24-73; see also W. Holtzmann, "Das mittelalterliche Imperium und die werdenden Nationen," *Arbeitsgemeinschaft für Forschung des Landes Nordrhein-Westfalen*, VII (1953), 19, n.20, for a remark made, according to John of Salisbury, by Henry II; also Post, "Two Notes," 303. For the doctrine itself, see Calasso, *Glossatori*, 35ff (for England), and, in general, Sergio Mochi Onory, *Fonti canonistiche dell'idea moderna dello stato* (Milan, 1951), including the most recent discussion by Gaines Post, "Two Notes," *Traditio*, IX (1954),296ff. The right of summoning councils does not seem to

probably borrowed also the metaphor of royal "twinship." It may seem curious that he transferred to his definitely christocentric doctrine of kingship the only expression which had, christologically, a Nestorian and Adoptionist flavor, *gemina persona*. But he could not possibly attribute to the king a divine "nature" after having repeated over and over again that the king was *not* divine by nature, but by grace. The axiom of *deificatio*, of becoming god as opposed to being God, brought about in the royal christology of A.D. 1100 a certain affinity with Nestorian and Adoptionist formulae.[21]

The author thoroughly explored the possibilities implicit in his idea of the dual capacities of the Christlike king. This concept, in fact, became the vehicle for all his other constructions which were no less consistent and skillfully developed than the theories of the Tudor lawyers. The Anonymous likes to juggle with the king's two persons; but after the same fashion he incessantly plays off against one another the figures of Jesus *Christus* and Jesus *christus*, the Anointed from Eternity and the one anointed in Jordan during his ministry on earth.[22] The author carries those dichotomies even further, that is, to pagan Antiquity, and thereby obtains the most curious results. It may be acceptable, though strange, when

---

have been included in the bulk of claims which the *rex imperator* would normally make, though in England this would change with the Reformation; see, e.g., Bishop John Jewel's *Apology of the Church of England* (1560) against Thomas Harding (in *The Works of John Jewel* [Cambridge, 1848], III,98f; cf. Frances A. Yates, "Queen Elizabeth as Astraea," *Warburg Journal*, x[1947],39f), whose arguments are sometimes reminiscent of those of the Norman Anonymous.

21 If the Anonymous mentions (667,6) that king and bishop "sunt et dii et christi per adoptionis spiritum" and (675,12) that the king is "alter Christus per adoptionem post Christum," these and similar utterances have nothing to do with "Adoptionism" but with Romans 8:15, and consequently with the *Spiritus adoptionis* effective at Baptism. See, about the "gods" by adoption, Kantorowicz, "Deus per naturam," 256,262; there should be added, however, Honorius of Augustodunum, *Summa gloria*, c.5, *MGH,LdL*, III,66f, who claims that priests are called *filii Dei, dii, christi, angeli*, whereas kings are only *filii hominum*, which proves "[quantum] divina auctoritate sacerdotes in dignitate reges precellunt."

22 The anointment of Christ in Jordan (Acts 10:38; cf. Isaiah 61:1 and Luke 4:18) was interpreted also as "Coronation of Christ," a topic in need of historical and, above all, archaeological investigation. See, for the Dove descending with a crown, the gold-box lid of the 5th or 6th century in the Dumbarton Oaks Collection, reproduced in *The Walters Art Gallery: Early Christian and Byzantine Art* (Baltimore, 1947), pl. cxix,B; further Adolf Goldschmidt, *Karolingische Elfenbeinskulpturen* (Berlin, 1914), I, No. 154, pl. lxv; and, for England, the Benedictional of Aethelwold (963-984), in J. Strzygowski, *Iconographie der Taufe Christi* (Munich, 1885), 59, pl. xviii,4.

he implies that the *reges christi* of the Old Testament, who prefigured the exalted *Christus regnaturus* in Heaven, should be considered—as kings—in a sense superior to the lowly Christ of Nazareth before the Ascension. But it is truly baffling to find a similar relationship between the Roman emperor and the incarnate God; to be exact: between Tiberius and Jesus.[23]

It is Jesus, the Son of man, who submits to Tiberius when rendering the tribute money.[24] But to which Tiberius was the money rendered? The Anonymous creates another *gemina persona* in the Emperor Tiberius, as he interprets the story:

[23] For the interpretation of the following passage, see Williams, *Norman Anonymous*, 131f. It may be that the Anonymous considered the Roman emperor likewise an "anointed" in the sense in which Cyrus was a *christus Domini* according to Isaiah 45:1. See, e.g., Haymon, Bishop of Halberstadt (841-853), *Commentarium in Isaiam*, c.45, *PL*, CXVI,942D: "Christus interpretatur unctus. Antiquitus enim in populo Judaeorum, quemadmodum apud Romanos diadema, faciebant et regem. . . . Quare ergo appellatur Cyrus christus, cum non sit perunctus de oleo benedictionis? Quia *dignitas imperialis* [Cyrus was the founder or "emperor" of the second—that is, the Persian—World Monarchy] pro chrismate ei fuit. Haec dicit Dominus 'christo meo' pro eo quod est 'christo suo': vel uncto suo, hoc est, regi suo." To Bede, *In Esdram et Nehemian Prophetas*, c.1, *PL*, XCI,811, Cyrus appears as a prefiguration of Christ: "At vero juxta mysticos sensus Cyrus rex Dominum Salvatorem et nomine [κύριος?] designat et factis. . . . Assimilavit namque eum Deus filio suo, quamvis ipse Deum se assimilantem minime cognoverit; primum in eo quod Christum suum eum cognominare dignatus est. . . . Assimilavit ergo Cyrum Dominus unigenito Filio suo, Deo et Domino nostro Jesu Christo. . . ." The Greek authors usually confine themselves to explain that Cyrus was styled "anointed" as a king called to government by God; see, e.g., Cyrill of Alexandria, *In Isaiam*, IV, *Oratio* ii (= *Is.*, 45), *PGr*, LXX,950D-951A; Procopius of Gaza, *In Isaiam*, c.45, *PGr*, LXXXVII, 2418. The Greeks, being in permanent conflict with the Persian power, had apparently less sympathy with Cyrus, although he was recognized as a fulfiller of the divine dispensation. See, e.g., the Scholion of Cyril, ed. F. C. Conybeare, *The Armenian Version of Revelations and Cyril of Alexandria's Scholia on the Incarnation and Epistle on Easter* (London, 1907), 169: "And though the man [Cyrus] was an idolater, he is called Anointed by reason of his being so anointed unto kingship by the decree from above: he was designed by God, mightily to subdue the Babylonians." In this sense, then, Tiberius had certainly a prominent place within the economy of salvation.

[24] Matthew 22:21 played, as is well known, an enormous role in mediaeval political theory; see, e.g., Max Hackelsperger, *Bibel und mittelalterlicher Reichsgedanke* (diss., Munich, 1934), 29f, for the tribute to Caesar in the literature of the Investiture Struggle. The Anonymous is perhaps closest to (Pseudo-) Ambrose, *In epist. ad Roman.*, XIII,6, *PL*, XVII,172AB: ". . . principi enim suo, qui vicem Dei agit, sicut Deo subiiciuntur . . . Unde et Dominus: 'Reddite etc.' Huic ergo subiiciendi sunt sicut Deo. . . ." The author of this commentary was probably the so-called Ambrosiaster; cf. E. Dekkers and A. Gaar, *Clavis patrum Latinorum* (Sacris erudiri, III, Bruges and Hague, 1951), 30, No. 184. That the tribute was paid *ad scandalum vitandum* is a surprisingly paltry interpretation which does not seem to antedate Thomas Aquinas, *Summa theol.*, IIa-IIae,q.10,a.10,ad 1: "Sicut etiam Dominus Matth. XVII ostendit, quod poterat se a tributo excusare, quia liberi sunt filii; sed

He said "Render unto Caesar the things that are Caesar's," and did not say "unto Tiberius the things that are Tiberius'." Render to the power (*potestas*), not to the person. The person is worth nothing, but the power is just. Iniquitous is Tiberius, but good is the Caesar. Render, not unto the person worth nothing, not unto iniquitous Tiberius, but unto the righteous power and unto the good Caesar the things that are his. . . . "Give," said he [unto Peter], "for me and thee to the righteous power and to the good Caesar, to whom according to our manhood we are subjects. . . ." For he knew that this pertained to justice to render unto Caesar the things that are Caesar's. . . . In all that he fulfilled justice. For it was just that the human weakness succumbed to the *divina potestas*. Namely, Christ, according to his humanity, was then weak; but divine was Caesar's *potestas*.[25]

The least that can be said for this passage is that it is an extraordinary overlaboring of a principle, and that, though keeping within the range of customary concepts, it is nonetheless opposed to them. All by itself, the exaltation of *potestas* is as much in agreement with the teaching of the Church as the doctrine of "suffering obedience."[26] There comes to mind the touching story about the bishop of a city at whose gates the fierce King of the Huns was knocking: "I am Attila, the Scourge of God." The bishop replied simply: "May there enter the Servant of God," and opened the gate only to be slain while murmuring to the invader the blessing:

tamen mandavit tributum solvi ad scandalum vitandum." See, for the problem, also E. Gilson, *Dante the Philosopher* (New York, 1949), 208,n.1.

[25] *MGH,LdL*, III,671,35ff: "Reddite potestati, non persone. Persona enim nequam, sed iusta potestas. Iniquus Tyberius, sed bonus cesar. Reddite ergo non persone nequam, non iniquo Tyberio, sed iuste potestati et bono cesari que sua sunt . . . 'Da,' inquit, 'pro me et te, iuste potestati et bono cesari, cui secundum hominem subditi sumus' . . . Sciebat enim hoc pertinere ad iusticiam, ut redderet cesari que sunt cesaris. . . . Sed in iis omnibus implevit iusticiam. Iustum quippe erat, ut humana infirmitas divine subderetur potestati. Christus namque secundum hominem tunc infirmus erat, cesaris vero potestas divina."

[26] Authoritative for this attitude was, e.g., I Peter 2:13-18. Obedience toward tyrants was certainly opposed to Greek political thinking, though it does not seem to have disagreed with Jewish tradition: tyrants, like earthquakes and plagues, are a visitation of God and a form of punishment according to Philo; see Erwin R. Goodenough, *The Politics of Philo Judaeus* (New Haven, 1938), 100. A poem on the tribute money by Amarcius (ca.1080-1100) says explicitly:

Reges ergo boni venerandi et sunt imitandi,
Perversi non sunt imitandi, sed venerandi.

Cf. Erdmann, *Ideenwelt*, 133. See, in general for the age of the Investiture Struggle, G. Tellenbach, *Church, State, and Christian Society at the Time of the Investiture Contest* (Oxford, 1938), in addition to Hackelsperger (above, n.24).

Benedictus qui venit in nomine Domini. The bishop had worshipped, even in an Attila, divine Majesty.[27]

This legend, no doubt, reflects an extreme case of passive obedience and of Christian submission to power in the spirit of the Apostle's advice: "The powers that be are ordained by God." But to a like extreme did the Norman Anonymous carry the divinity of power *per se* when he placed above the manhood of the God-man the divinity of the Caesar manifest in Tiberius the man. Here, as elsewhere, the writer starts from his *idée fixe* of the "gemination" of rulership in general, no matter whether the ruler be a Jewish king, a Christian prince, or a pagan emperor. He integrates that dual personality of gods and of kings into his clever system and skilfully makes the *geminatio* the mainspring of all his arguments. The Emperor Tiberius appears as a "twinned" being just as much as the God-man himself. Tiberius as man is iniquitous; but he is divine as Caesar, is divine as the incarnation of Power, is *deus* and, with regard to Jesus, at once *dominus*. And Tiberius' dual personality becomes all the more, and almost hopelessly, involved as this imperial *gemina persona* is set over against another *gemina persona*, Jesus Christ, the *unigenitus* according to his divinity and the *primogenitus* according to his humanity—distinctions which in turn the Anonymous will apply also to his king.[28]

Thus, the strangest chiasmus imaginable results from that confrontation of two dual personalities. It is as though the *potestas* of Tiberius *qua* Caesar were "haloed," whereas Christ, in his human serfdom, remains without halo. At the same time, however, the iniquitous Tiberius in his individual natural body is without halo, whereas the incarnate and individuated God, though a *Deus absconditus*, is haloed even as man.[29]

The anonymous Norman, however, does not halt at this point. With similar arguments he points out that the bishop, too, is a *gemina persona* so that, in this respect, there is no difference between king and bishop. There is, however, a difference of rank,

[27] John of Salisbury, *Policraticus*, 514b, ed. Webb (Oxford, 1909), I,236.

[28] *MGH,LdL*, III,669,35ff: ". . . sacerdotes quidem unxit [Deus] sicut apostolos suos unctione spirituali, regem vero sicut filium suum primogenitum et ante secula genitum pre omnibus participibus suis" (cf. Psalm 44:8).

[29] Maitland, who had at his disposal a felicity for describing accurately such orderly disorder, has devoted unfortunately only a line to the Anonymous, "who was writing sentences that Marsiglio and Wyclif would not have disowned"; see his Introduction to Gierke, *Political Theories*, xliv.

and the author substantiates that difference of *ordo* between king and bishop by means of a new gemination: while distinguishing the *King* Christ from the *Priest* Christ, he turns this duality into an antithesis and equates it not only with the divine and human natures of the God-man (as was the custom), but also with the royal and sacerdotal offices on earth.

> Both [king and bishop] are in spirit *Christus et Deus*; and in their offices they act as antitypes and images of Christ and God: the priest of the Priest, the king of the King: the priest acts as the antitype of the inferior office and nature, that is, His humanity: the king, as that of the superior office and nature, that is, His divinity.[30]

And even this is not all, for the Anonymous drives the wedge of his personality-splitting method into any and every being, person, or institution. There was that old struggle and competition between Canterbury and York about the supremacy of either one or the other see. What is it, asks the Anonymous, that may claim supremacy? Is it the bricks and stones of the church of Canterbury?

[30] *MGH,LdL*, III,667,8ff: "Unde et uterque in spiritu et Christus et deus est, et in officio figura et imago Christi et Dei est. Sacerdos sacerdotis, rex regis. Sacerdos inferioris officii et naturae, id est humanitatis, rex superioris, id est divinitatis." Most of the arguments quoted hitherto and proving the king's *gemina natura* are valid also with regard to the bishop. For although the bishop is the image of "Christ the Priest" he yet shares also to some extent in the "superior office and nature," the kingship and divinity of Christ, and vice versa; see *ibid.*, 665,36ff: ". . . et rex sacerdos et sacerdos rex . . . iure potest appellari. Nam et sacerdotis est in spiritu Christi regere populum." Similarly Hugh of Fleury, *De regia potestate*, I,10, *MGH, LdL*, II,477,21: "Hic [sacerdos] . . . sal terrae vocatur, et rex propter ducatum, quem praebere populo debet, et *angelus*, quia bona nuntiat, et pastor, quia divini verbi dapibus homines explet"; *ibid.*, 477,38: "Nam et regalem dignitatem habere . . . videtur episcopus." But the bishop has to act as mediator "inter regem et oves sibi creditas." The priest as *rex* has a long history which parallels that of the king as *sacerdos*. See, e.g., *Didascalia Apostolorum*, II,34, ed. R. Hugh Connolly (Oxford, 1929), 96,17ff, or the Pseudo-Clementine *Recognitiones*, I,46, *PGr*, I,1234A: "pontifex Aaron, chrismatis compositione perunctus, princeps populi fuit, et tanquam rex . . . iudicandi plebem sorte suscepta de mundis immundisque iudicabat"; cf. Hinschius, *Decret.Ps.Isid.*, 53. From those premises, however, the opposite conclusions could be drawn. See, e.g., James of Viterbo, *De regimine christiano*, II,c.4, ed. H. X. Arquillière, *Le plus ancien traité de l'Église: Jaques de Viterbe, 'De regimine christiano'* (Paris, 1926), 199, who admits that Christ the King is more dignified than, and superior to, Christ the Priest: "Est enim sacerdos in quantum homo, rex autem est et in quantum Deus et in quantum homo . . . et sic maior dignitas importatur ex eo, quod rex dicitur, quam ex eo, quod sacerdos." But then he concludes: "Quare et in prelatis ecclesie superior est potestas regalis, que dicitur iurisdictionis, quam sacerdotalis, que dicitur ordinis." See R. Scholz, *Die Publizistik zur Zeit Philipps des Schönen und Bonifaz' VIII.* (Stuttgart, 1903), 144f; Martin Grabmann, "Die Lehre des Erzbischofs und Augustinertheologen Jakob von Viterbo," *Episcopus: Festschrift für Kardinal Michael von Faulhaber* (Regensburg, 1949), 190f.

Or is it the cathedral building of Canterbury that claims supremacy over the cathedral building of York? Apparently it is neither the stones nor the material building of the church of Canterbury, but it is the immaterial Church of Canterbury, the Archbishopric, which claims superiority. And wherein should the superiority of one archbishop over another archbishop be found? *In eone quod homo est, an in eo quod archiepiscopus est?*

True, at the end the author comes to reject the claims altogether; but the main point is that in employing his usual tactics he sets the *homo* against the *archiepiscopus*, the man against the office, and the "bricks" of Canterbury against the "See" of Canterbury, just as on another occasion he sets the "corporeal sky" against the "incorporeal heaven."[31] And in a similar fashion he rends asunder the unity of the Roman pontiff, sets the office against the person of the pope, and confronts, as we might say by analogy, the pope's "body politic" with the pope's "body natural"—adding, however, in this case, an "infra-human" stratum for a pope who should happen to be a *peccator*.[32]

What is the main problem underlying the political theories of the Norman Anonymous which so clearly betray the influence of the dialectical method at the bend of the eleventh to the twelfth centuries, and what is the significance of those innumerable "geminations"? It is not really the distinction between Office and Person which is so startling; for that was not quite unknown in the earlier Middle Ages. The author himself quotes St. Augustine's saying about the king's obligation to serve God: "It is one thing when he serves [God] because he is a man, and it is another thing when he serves because he is a king."[33] The distinction between office and person was stressed strongly also in a law of King

---

[31] *Tractate XXIX*, in Böhmer, *Kirche und Staat*, 479. Arguments of that kind are not too rare. See, e.g., Isidore, *Etym.*, xv,2,1 ("civitas autem non saxa, sed habitatores vocantur"); see also below, n.99; further, Maitland, *Sel.Ess.*, 90 ("the church is not the house nor the walls, but is to be understood as the *ecclesia spiritualis*"). See below, n.47, for heaven and sky.

[32] Böhmer, *Kirche und Staat*, 436f.

[33] *MGH,LdL*, III,673,24: "Aliter enim servit quia homo est, aliter quia etiam rex est." Augustine, *Ep.* CLXXXV,c.5,19, ed. A. Goldbacher (*CSEL.*, LVII), 17,21, the very frequently quoted letter *Ad Bonifacium*; see, for the place cited here, the *Decretum Gratiani*, c.42,C.XXIII,q.4, ed. Friedberg, I,923, though it is found also in earlier collections, e.g., in Ivo of Chartres, *Decretum*, x,121, *PL*, CLXI,727, interesting in so far as there are other relations between Ivo and the Anonymous; see Williams, *Norman Anonymous*, 55ff.

Reccesvinth of 653, which, through the medium of the Spanish material in the Pseudo-Isidorian Decretals, was widely known. In that law, the Visigothic king pointed out that honor was due, not to the king's person, but to the royal power: not to the king's personal mediocrity, but to the honor of his sublimity: "The rights, not the person, make a king."[34] With due alterations, such distinction was formulated also in a letter of Humbert of Silva Candida to the Patriarch Kerullarios: [Papa] qualis Petrus officio . . . non qualis Petrus merito—"The pope is like Peter by his office . . . he is not like Peter by his merits."[35] And during the great conflict between Empire and Papacy the Emperor Henry IV drew a clear line separating the papal office from the individual Hildebrand when pronouncing his sentence of deposition against Gregory VII.[36]

All those features are found, overtly or latently, in the writings of the Norman pamphletist, too. Where he seems to differ from others is in the philosophy which supports, and builds up, his theory, and in the fact that the king's duplication of persons is not founded in law or constitution, but in theology: it mirrors the duplication of natures in Christ. The king is the perfect impersonator of Christ on earth. Since the king's divine model is at once God and man, the royal christomimētēs has to correspond to that duplication; and since the divine model is at once King and Priest,

---

[34] PL, LXXXIV,431A; Hinschius, Decret.Ps.Isid., 392: "Regalis proinde ordo ex hoc cuncta sibi deberi convincit, ex quo se regere cuncta cognoscit; et inde conquisita non alteri quam sibi iuste defendit; unde non personae, sed potentiae suae haec deberi non ambigit. Regem enim iura faciunt, non persona; quia nec constat sui mediocritate sed sublimitatis honore. Quae ergo honori debent, honore serviant, et quae reges accumulant, regno relinquant." The notion of honor comes very close to the meaning of dignitas in later political theory (below, Ch.VII). The principle disclosed in the last words—"what kings accumulate, they leave to the realm"—was certainly disregarded in Carolingian times and thereafter. An exception is formed by the words which Wipo, Gesta Chuonradi, c.7, ed. H. Bresslau (MGH,SS.r.Germ.), 29f, probably following antique authorities, attributes to Conrad II: "Si periit rex, regnum remansit, sicut navis remanet cuius gubernator cadit. Aedes [destroyed by the people of Pavia] publicae fuerunt, non privatae"; cf. A. Solmi, "La distruzzione del palazzo regio in Pavia nell' anno 1024," Rendiconti dell' Istituto Lombardo di scienze e lettere, LVII (1924), 97ff.

[35] Anton Michel, Die Sentenzen des Kardinals Humbert, das erste Rechtsbuch der päpstlichen Reform (MGH, Schriften, VII; Leipzig, 1943), 32,n.1.

[36] See the king's letters of 1076 (H. dei gratia rex Hildebrando), ed. C. Erdmann, Die Briefe Heinrichs IV. (MGH, Deutsches Mittelalter, I, Leipzig, 1937), 14f, nos. 11 and 12; see also C. Erdmann and D. von Gladiss, "Gottschalk von Aachen im Dienste Heinrichs IV.," DA, III (1939), 168.

kingship and priesthood of Christ have to be reflected in his vicars as well, that is, in the King and the Bishop, who are at the same time *personae mixtae* (spiritual and secular) and *personae geminatae* (human by nature and divine by grace).[37] At any rate, the theories of the Anonymous are not centered in the notion of "office" as opposed to man, nor in constitutional or social considerations; they are christological and christocentric.

Supported by the new dialectical movement and influenced, perhaps directly, by Ivo of Chartres,[38] the Anonymous applied his unity-splitting method to the two natures of Christ and then transferred the results, by a bold analogy, to the royal *imago Christi* on earth. The overemphasis upon the idea *Rex imago Christi* (rather than *Dei!*) makes it evident that the analogy prevailing between the God-man and his image should not be sought in a functional distinction between "office" and "man." For it would be difficult, nay, impossible, to interpret the divine nature of Christ as an "office," since the divine nature is his "Being." And the Anonymous likewise visualizes in his king two different forms of "being": one natural or individual, and the other consecrated or (as the author calls it) deified and apotheosized.[39] In short, the Norman author's vision of the king as a *persona geminata* is ontological and, as an effluence of a sacramental and liturgical action performed at the altar, it is liturgical as well. His vision is, on the whole, more closely related to the liturgy, to the holy action which itself is image and reality at the same time, than to the distinction of functional capacities and constitutional competencies, or to the concepts of office and dignity as opposed to man. That the author's dialectic threatens to break up the ontological oneness by playing off the two natures against each other there is no doubt. This dangerous facility the Anonymous has in common with the intellectual development of his time. But it would be a grave error to ignore the primarily ontological stratum upon which the Norman Anonymous founded the structure of his unambiguously Christ-centered, and therewith liturgical, philosophy of kingship.[40]

---

[37] The passage quoted above, n.9, refers also to the bishops or high-priests; cf. n.30.

[38] On Ivo of Chartres and the Anonymous, see Williams, *Norman Anonymous*, 55ff.

[39] See above, n.13.

[40] A few brief, but very good remarks on the Tractates of the Anonymous (for-

This philosophy was not that of the times to come. It has often been noticed and held against the Norman Anonymous that his passionately anti-hierocratic pamphlets, carried by a mystical belief in the power of sacramental anointings, had no practical effects on the age in which they were written. This is correct. Indeed, the victory of the revolutionary Reform Papacy in the wake of the Investiture Struggle and the rise of the clerical empire under papal guidance, which monopolized the spiritual strata and turned them into a sacerdotal domain, negated all efforts to continue or renew that king-priestly pattern of liturgical kingship which the Anonymous so fiercely defended. On the other hand, the new territorial states which began to develop in the twelfth century were avowedly secular despite considerable borrowings from the ecclesiastical and hierarchical model; secular law, including secularized canon law, rather than the effects of the holy chrism, were henceforth to justify the holiness of the ruler. The ideas of the Norman Anonymous, therefore, found no resonance in either the ecclesiastical or the secular camps. His image of rulership was inacceptable to the hierarchy and it no longer was of major interest to the secular state. Hence, despite the modernism of his dialectical and antithetical method, the pattern of Christ-centered kingship for which he fought belonged to the past. He is the champion of ideals of the Ottonian and early Salian period as well as of Anglo-Saxon England, and in his tractates he actually sums up the political ideas of the tenth and eleventh centuries. But like every bard who glorifies a bygone age, he overlabors and overstresses past ideals, and thus becomes the chief exponent of the christocentric theory of kingship in its most concentrated, most consistent, and most extreme form. His tractates, therefore, have to be used, not as a

---

merly called the York Tractates) have been made by Wilhelm Berges, *Die Fürstenspiegel des hohen und späten Mittelalters (MGH, Schriften, II, Leipzig, 1938), 28ff: "Nie zuvor und nie nachher hat der Christus König-Gedanke die politische Theorie so beherrscht wie im Yorker Tractat."* Williams, *Norman Anonymous,* 190, is a little more precise when he comes to the following conclusion: "The Anonymous' ecclesio-political theory is Christocentric, but the Christ whom his king imitates and whose power he shares is the Royal Exalted Eternal Christ, for whom the Crucifixion was but an incident to be pondered over by priests. Christology has become almost completely regalized." That this development towards an over-emphasis of the Exalted Christ should be viewed against a generally European background, of which Williams is aware, has been recently discussed by Josef Andreas Jungmann, "Die Abwehr des germanischen Arianismus und der Umbruch der religiösen Kultur im frühen Mittelalter," *Zeitschrift für katholische Theologie,* LXIX (1947), 36-99.

reflection of ideas valid in his time or foreshadowing the future, but as a kind of mirror that magnifies, and thereby slightly distorts, the ideals current in the preceding era.[41] Iconographic evidence will bear out this assertion.

2. *The Frontispiece of the Aachen Gospels*

A Romanesque type of crucifix, known as the *Volto santo* and showing the Crucified with an imperial diadem on his head and the purple around his shoulders, renders perhaps the briefest iconographic formula of at once the regal and the sacrificial characters of the God-man.[42] The compact brevity and terseness of that formula is so striking that the image cannot fail to impress directly: the *Volto santo* is signally *una persona, duae naturae*. The theme of the two natures of Christ, of course has often formed the subject of artistic representations, though normally each nature would be figured individually: the newly-born or the cross-bearing Jesus in the lower part of the panel, and in a superimposed register, the King of Glory. In the *Volto santo*, however, the duality is so stirring, and it is expressed so powerfully, that the effect is much stronger here than in the images displaying the two natures separately.[43]

Only in the full flush of the uncompromisingly christocentric period of Western civilization—roughly, the monastic period from 900 to A.D. 1100—could it happen that also the two natures of the imperial *christomimētēs* ruling on earth were depicted in a similarly brief, if iconographically very different, fashion. The famous miniature in the Gospel Book of Aachen, executed about A.D. 973 in the Abbey of Reichenau, shows the Emperor Otto II enthroned

[41] See the "Summary" of Williams, *Norman Anonymous*, 199ff.

[42] For the *Volto Santo*, see A. Kingsley Porter, *Spanish Romanesque Sculpture* (New York, 1929), II,pls.63ff; G. Schürer and J. M. Ritz, *Sankt Kümmernis und Volto Santo* (Forschungen zur Volkskunde, XIII-XV, Düsseldorf, 1934), with full bibliography; see also Clairece Black, "The Origin of the Lucchese Cross Form," *Marsyas*, I (1941), 27-40.

[43] Later Byzantine art, however, produces similar effects in the startling imagery of the Divine Liturgy and in the illustration of the Cherubic Hymn: "Thou art he that offerest and art offered; and that acceptest and art distributed." See J. D. Stefanescu, "L'Illustration des liturgies dans l'art de Byzance et de l'Orient," *Annuaire de l'institut de philologie et d'histoire orientales*, I (1932), 72ff; for the formula itself, cf. J. M. Hanssens, *Institutiones liturgicae de ritibus orientalibus* (Rome, 1932), III,289, §1117.

(fig. 5).[44] He is seated on a throne-bench decked, as usual, with a roll-shaped cushion, while his feet rest on a footstool. It is certainly a representative imperial image of state, conventional in the West since Carolingian times; but there is much disregard of artistic custom and convention in the Aachen Codex. The throne is not standing on firm ground as normally it would in the state images of the precious Carolingian and Ottonian manuscripts. It is seemingly poised in mid-air, for the throne as well as the emperor's whole figure are surrounded by a mandorla. Yet the throne stands on earth; it is carried by a crouching *Tellus*, Earth herself, whose hands support the feet of the footstool. At the same time, the Hand of God is reaching down from above, from heaven, either to impose or to touch and bless the diadem on the emperor's head. The divine aureola framing the Hand of God intersects with the imperial aureola, thus allowing the emperor's head to be placed in the spandrel which is formed by the intersecting haloes.

The image shows three superimposed planes. The upper part of the emperor's figure is surrounded by the four beasts of the Apocalypse, symbols of the four Evangelists, holding a white banderole or drapery. Deep below the emperor's feet, in the foreground of the image, four dignitaries are seen, two archbishops and two warriors, apparently representing the princes spiritual and secular.[45] In the central part, right and left of the footstool, there stand, flagstaffs with purple pennants on their shoulders, two male figures in a gesture of veneration, if not adoration. That they are of very high rank is suggested by their crowns—feudatory dukes or perhaps rulers of the *regna*, the plurality of which was

[44] Stephan Beissel, *Die Bilder der Handschrift des Kaisers Otto im Münster zu Aachen* (Aachen, 1886), 61ff,pl.3; Adolph Goldschmidt, *German Illumination, II: Ottonian Period* (New York, n.d.), pl.I; P. E. Schramm, "Das Herrscherbild in der Kunst des Mittelalters," *Vorträge der Bibliothek Warburg 1922-3*, I (1924), 198ff, a full discussion with bibliography; see also his *Die deutschen Kaiser und Könige in Bildern ihrer Zeit* (Leipzig, 1928), 81ff,191, and pl.64; K. Vöge, *Eine deutsche Malerschule um die Wende des ersten Jahrtausends* (Westdeutsche Zeitschrift, Ergänzungsheft, VII, Trier, 1891), 7f; A. Boeckler, "Die Reichenau Buchmalerei," in *Die Kultur der Abtei Reichenau, Erinnerungsschrift* (Munich, 1925), II,982ff.

[45] The remark has been made that the clergy has its place on the left side of the emperor, similar to the Justinian mosaic in San Vitale and to its weaker replica in Sant' Apollinare in Classe at Ravenna; see Schramm, "Herrscherbild," 198f; Beissel, *Bilder*, 62, for a few other parallels. The distribution of secular and spiritual officers, however, is not influenced by the Byzantine model, but by the imagery of Carolingian Apocalypses; see below, n.82.

needed to indicate the imperial dignity.[46] At any rate, they are princes or *reguli* dependent on the young kosmokrator who himself is raised towards heaven or into heaven. We may think of the description of the emperor's power—the power as such—offered, a century later, by the Norman Anonymous. He calls the imperial *potestas* grand and holy, the *cooperatrix* of the grace of God and therefore entitled "to treat with the sacraments of the Catholic faith and matters celestial." Then he draws his conclusions:

> Therefore the emperor, by the Lord Jesus Christ, is said to be elevated even unto heaven. Even unto heaven, I say, not unto the corporeal sky which is seen, but unto the incorporeal heaven which is unseen; that is, unto the invisible God. Truly, unto God he has been elevated, since so much so is he conjoined to Him in power that no other power is more nigh unto God or more sublime than that of the emperor; yea, all other power is inferior to his.[47]

These are the very ideas which the miniature displays: the emperor elevated unto heaven (*usque ad celum erectus*), all earthly

[46] Schramm, "Herrscherbild," 199, and *Die Deutschen Kaiser*, 83, calls those crown-wearing princes "dukes" on account of the flagstaffs with pennants which they shoulder. Their models, however, are found in the Carolingian *Codex Aureus* (Schramm, *Kaiser*, pl.29a; below, fig.16b), where the corresponding figures are described as *Francia* and *Gothia*: the same drooping knees (more so with the right figure than with the left), the mural crowns replaced by princely crowns, and the cornucopiae by lances. Hence, the idea seems to be that those princes are *reguli* of dependent kingdoms; for the old-fashioned idea of "empire" in the sense of a hegemonial "super-kingship" over a plurality of kingdoms was still very strong in Ottonian times, despite all the advances which the Roman empire idea had made in the meantime; see C. Erdmann, *Forschungen*, 43ff, and passim; also his study, "Das ottonische Reich als Imperium Romanum," *DA*, VI (1943), 412-441.

[47] "Et utique magna et sancta imperatoris potestas, que cooperatrix est gratie Dei in pascendis ovibus eius veritatis germinibus et cui a Deo omnes regere concessum est, cui totius mundi pontifices ad concilium convocare, cui de sacramentis catholice fidei et celestibus negotiis tractare et ipsis pontificibus, ut inde tractent, imperare per cooperantem sibi eandem gratiam collatum est. Propter quod usque ad celum a domino Iesu Christo erectus esse dicitur. Ad celum, inquam, non utique istud corporeum quod videmus, sed incorporeum quod non videmus, id est invisibilem Deum. Usque ad Deum quippe erectus est, quia ei in potestate ita coniunctus est, ut nulla potestas Deo sit propinquior, imperatore sublimior, sed omnis sit alia inferior." *MGH,LdL*, III,676,5ff. For the holiness of the imperial *potestas*, see above, n.25. The distinction between "sky" and "heaven" was conventional because the exegetics had to distinguish between the ascension of Elijah and that of Christ, the former a being taken up to the sky of air (*caelum aereum*) and the latter to heaven (*caelum aethereum*); see Gregory the Great, *Homiliae in Evangelia*, II,29,5f, *PL*, LXXVI,1216f; also Bede, *Expositio Actuum Apostolorum*, I, 11, ed. M. L. W. Laistner, Cambridge, Mass., 1939, 9: ". . . ut vere in caelum illum (Christum) ire monstrarent, et non quasi in caelum sicut Eliam." See, for the problem, Meyer Schapiro, "The Image of the Disappearing Christ," *Gazette des Beaux Arts*, LXXXV (1943), 140.

powers inferior to his, and he himself nearest to God. Most startling, in view of the miniature, is the concept of the *imperator ad
celum erectus*, since this is exactly what the artist painted. Could
he have known that phrase? Chronologically, there would be no
difficulty. The phrase is taken from the so-called *Collectio Hispana*
or *Isidoriana*, a collection of canons composed probably in the
seventh century, ascribed to Isidore of Seville, and later fused with
the Pseudo-Isidorian collection. That the phrase actually originated in the *Hispana* is obvious for a simple reason: only in that
collection do we find a textual corruption of the acts of the Council of Chalcedon at which one of the bishops modestly said that
God *imperatorem erexit ad zelum* [i.e., *fidei*]. In other words, a
scribe copying the canons of Chalcedon misread the text and
changed *ad zelum* into *ad celum*; and this erroneous reading must
have reached, perhaps through the channels of Pseudo-Isidorus,
the Norman Anonymous for whom even that great forgery in favor
of the hierarchy could turn into grist brought to his royalist mill.[48]
The reading is merely an error, though an error remarkable by
itself, since it shows how easily any extravagant exaltation of the
imperial power could flow from the pen of a scribe in those
centuries.

For the present purpose we may forget about the *Hispana* text,
for it is most unlikely that the Reichenau painter knew that corrupt reading when he pictured the *imperator ad celum erectus*.
Nevertheless, it remains a fact that the glorification of the emperor
as displayed by the miniature of the Aachen Gospels by far sur-
passes anything that was customary in Eastern or Western art. The
image shows the emperor in the *maiestas* of Christ, on the throne
of Christ, holding his open and empty left hand like Christ, with
the mandorla of Christ, and with the animal symbols of the four
Gospels which are almost inseparable from the images of Christ in
Majesty. An ivory book cover from St. Gall (fig. 7), and another
one of the early tenth century, now at Darmstadt (fig. 6), may

---

[48] See Hinschius, *Decret.Ps.Isid.*, 283, also the note of Boehmer, in *MGH,LdL*,
III,676,41. Dr. Schafer Williams, who is studying the MSS of Pseudo-Isidorus, kindly
informed me that the misreading is found only in the pure *Hispana* text edited by
F. A. Gonzalez, *Collectio canonum ecclesiae Hispaniae* (Madrid, 1808) and reprinted
in *PL*, LXXXIV,163C; see also G. Williams, *Norman Anonymous*, 189,n.640. The
Norman Anonymous, in that passage, paraphrases throughout the Acts of Chalcedon.

bear out this assertion.[49] These parallels demonstrate that the emperor appears not simply as the *vicarius Christi* and human antitype of the World Ruler above, but almost like the King of Glory himself—truly the *christomimētēs*, the impersonator and actor of Christ. It is as though the God-man had ceded his celestial throne to the glory of the terrestrial emperor for the purpose of allowing the invisible *Christus* in heaven to become manifest in the *christus* on earth.

Related ideas were carried through iconographically by other means as well. Attention has been called recently to the mosaic in the Martorana at Palermo, representing the coronation of King Roger II at the hands of Christ, where the desired effect of making the God manifest in the king was achieved by a striking facial resemblance between Roger and Christ—a duplication (*Zwillingsbildung*) which has its parallel in certain images of the Ottonian period, and has its precursors in imperial coins of the third and early fourth centuries (see fig. 32).[50] In the Aachen Gospels, however, the emperor's assimilation with Christ is indicated, not by means of facial and physiological resemblance between ruler and divine prototype, but rather by a christological and indeed meta-physiological resemblance: the image, to say it immediately, represents the emperor's two natures, human and divine, or rather, in the language of that age, a ruler "human by nature and divine by grace."

[49] Adolf Goldschmidt, *Die Elfenbeinskulpturen aus der Zeit der karolingischen und sächsischen Herrscher* (Berlin, 1914), pl.LXXV, Book Cover from St. Gall (c. A.D. 900), where the right hand is open and empty "like on representations of the Last Judgment" (cf. p.80, No.162); see *ibid.*, pl.LXXIV, for a Book Cover from Belgium, now in Darmstadt, and p.80, No.163a; Christ holds the scroll in his right hand whereas the left is open "to show the stigmata." See also Vöge, *Malerschule*, 282, who likewise thinks of representations of the Last Judgment and of the Ascension. In fact, the gesture performed by Otto II, though not at all rare in the iconography of Christ, seems to be unique in mediaeval imperial iconography. Beissel, *Bilder*, 62f, mentions that the image of the emperor in the Aachen Gospels has actually been mistaken for an image of Christ; Schramm, *Die deutschen Kaiser*, 82, briefly indicates the impossibility of that hypothesis.

[50] See Ernst Kitzinger, "On the Portrait of Roger II in the Martorana in Palermo," *Proporzioni*, III (1950), 30-35; for Ottonian parallels, see the remarks by Schramm, *Die Deutschen Kaiser*, 94f,112, for Otto III and Henry II (also pl.65); similar observations were made by Georg Leidinger, *Miniaturen aus Handschriften der bayerischen Staatsbibliothek in München*, Munich (n.d.), VI,25 and pl.XIII. For a few coin specimens (Postumus, Probus, Constantine the Great), see Kantorowicz, "The Quinity of Winchester," *Art Bulletin*, XXIX (1947), figs.27-29 (following p.78); also H. Usener, "Zwillingsbildung," *Kleine Schriften*, IV (1913), 334ff. See *Panegyrici*

Any interpretation of the image must proceed from the mysterious white banderole or scarf-like drapery which so obtrusively demands the attention of the spectator. It is carried by the four Evangelists represented by the apocalyptic symbols, and it is carried in such a fashion that the two tips of the banderole barely touch the crowns of the *reguli*. A fold of the band itself seems to divide the emperor's body: head, shoulders, and chest are above the borderline; arms, trunk, and feet remain below. The observation was made long ago that the white drapery separates heaven from earth.[51] In fact, the emperor's head not only touches heaven, but is in heaven, or beyond the heavens, whereas his feet on the footstool are carried by the subservient *Tellus*, a feature of world dominion reminiscent of the Barberini Diptych, of Gandhara and later Buddhist monuments, or, above all, of a contemporary ivory in which *Terra* supports the feet of the crucified Christ (fig. 8).[52]

---

latini, VI,21 (Paneg. Constantino Aug. dictus, ed. Baehrens, 1911), 218,6: "Vidisti [Apollinem] teque in illius specie recognovisti." See below, Epilogue, pp. 503f.

[51] Schramm, "Herrscherbild," 199; for the "band" or drapery, see also Vöge, *Deutsche Malerschule*, 282f. Beissel, *Bilder*, 62, is in some respects more correct than others when he compares that drapery with the curtains of the Carolingian throne images (Vivian Bible, *Codex aureus*) where the hand of God is always *separated* from the head of the king by the curtain. See below, n.83, and figs. 16a-b.

[52] See André Grabar, *L'Empereur dans l'art byzantin* (Paris, 1936), 48ff, and pl.IV, for the Barberini Diptych; cf. Beissel, *Bilder*, 61, and Schramm, "Herrscherbild," 195,n.172. For Gandhara, see Hugo Buchthal, "The Western Aspects of Gandhara Sculpture," *Proceedings of the British Academy*, XXXI (1945), fig.29, a feature repeated over and over again. For the Gotha Crucifix carried by a crouching *Terra*, see Goldschmidt, *op.cit.*, II,pl.IX,fig.23. It is likewise *Tellus* which carries, as a cariatyde, Christ in the "Tree of Life" of the Evangeliary from Bamberg, now in Munich (Clm.4454); cf. Leidinger, *op.cit.*, VI,26,pl.XIII. See further the strange miniature in a Byzantine 10th-century MS (Homilies of John Chrysostom: Athens, Bibl. Nat.MS 211,fol.34ᵛ) where Adam, carrying Christ in a clay lamp, is himself carried by Earth; Grabar, "À propos du nimbe crucifère à Castelseprio," *Cahiers archéologiques*, VII (1954), pl.54,fig.1 (facing p.161). Quite frequently Earth is found together with Ocean (e.g., Goldschmidt, I,pl.LXXV) in order to indicate the lordship of Christ *terra marique*. See, for this formerly imperial title, A. Momigliano, "Terra marique," *Journal of Roman Studies*, XXXII (1942), 53-64. It was applied again to Frederick II ("nobis Roma subiaceat, quibus terra servit, mare favet"; "hunc terra et pontus adorant"; "dominatur in terra, principatur in mari et imperat in utroque"); cf. *Erg.Bd.*, 204f. That this lordship over earth and sea, and indeed over the elements, was considered a strictly imperial prerogative became evident when Guillaume de Plaisian, a crown jurist of Philip IV, asserted the king's jurisdiction over the bishop of Gévaudan in these terms: "Item quod dominus Rex sit imperator in regno suo et imperare possit terre et mari," a claim to which the bishop mockingly answered: "Porro utrum dominus Rex sit imperator in regno suo et utrum possit imperare terre et mari et elementis et, si obtemperarent ipsa elementa, si eisdem imperaret, . . . nichil ad propositum nec contra Episcopum facit." See the highly important

The interpretation of the image actually hinges on the interpretation of the banderole, and the understanding of both the details and the whole will be considerably simplified once we know what the banderole designates.

The white scarf is not a band or a banderole at all, nor is it merely an ornamental drapery: it is a veil. It is actually THE VEIL, that is, the curtain of the tabernacle which, according to the oldest Eastern tradition, symbolizes the sky separating earth from heaven. Speculation about the meaning of the veil was at all times alive in the East, since the curtains of the iconostasis, which have a definite function in the rites of all Eastern Churches, actually demanded some explanation.[53] However, the interpretation of the veil of the tabernacle as "sky" was very common in the West as well. Bede, for example, in his work *On the Tabernacle*, explains in full agreement with the Eastern expositors that "the veil figures the sky." He adds that when once a year on the Day of Expiation the high priest of Israel passed through the sky-curtain of the tabernacle in order to offer (Leviticus 16: 12ff), he—like Christ, the eternal Highpriest—actually "entered into heaven itself" (*in ipsum coelum intravit*).[54] Now the sky-curtain, according to Exodus (26: 31f), was hung before four pillars. Those pillars were often identified with the four corners of the world, but full scope was also given to other interpretations. Bede, for example, identified the

---

Mémoire relatif au Paréage de 1307, ed. A. Maisonobe, in *Bulletin de la société d'agriculture, industrie, sciences et arts du Département de la Lozère* (Mende, 1896), 521 and 532; cf. Strayer, "The Laicization of French and English Society in the Thirteenth Century," *Speculum*, xv (1940), 82,n.5, who was kind enough to call my attention to this interesting passage.

[53] For the interpretation of the curtains, see Carl Schneider, "Studien zum Ursprung liturgischer Einzelheiten östlicher Liturgien: ΚΑΤΑΠΕΤΑΣΜΑ," *Kyrios*, I (1935), 57-73; J. Sauer, *Die Symbolik des Kirchengebäudes* (Freiburg, 1902), 133f; also Robert Eisler, *Weltenmantel und Himmelszelt* (Munich, 1910), 191 and 250f.

[54] Bede, *De Tabernaculo*, II,8, *PL*, XCI,445f; see 446D: "velum quo coelum figuratur"; 445C: "Velum hoc, coelum interpretatur." For the passage quoted, see 445D: "Summum vero sacerdotem, qui semel in anno sancta sanctorum cum sanguine victimarum ingrediebatur, ipsum intellegi esse pontificem magnum, cui dictum est: 'Tu es sacerdos in aeternum. . . .' Qui semel oblatus pro peccatis nostris, ipse sacerdos et hostia per proprium sanguinem in ipsum coelum intravit." Bede's *Tabernacle* follows Eastern sources; see M. L. W. Laistner, in A. H. Thompson, *Bede, his Life, Times and Writings* (Oxford, 1935), 246. It remained authoritative, was copied, paraphrased, and quarried by a great number of continental writers; see, e.g., Peter of Poitiers, *Allegoriae super Tabernaculum Moysi*, ed. P. S. Moore and J. A. Corbett, in *Publications in Mediaeval Studies*, III (Notre Dame, Indiana, 1938), 122f.

four pillars with "the powers of the celestial hosts, adorned with the four virtues," and later interpreters of the tabernacle claimed that the pillars signified Apostles.[55] In the Reichenau miniature it is neither the celestial hosts nor the virtues nor the Apostles that are credited with representing the four pillars holding the veil of the tabernacle, but the four animal *virtutes*, the Evangelists— logically, insofar as the picture precedes a Gospel Book.[56]

It would be pleasant to think that the artist, when introducing the four Gospel animals, intended also to allude to the emperor's missionary task. After all, the emperor was "crowned by God" *ad praedicandum aeterni regis evangelium*, "to preach the Gospel of the Eternal King." This idea was expounded in the official "Mass for the King," it was repeated in many a Coronation Mass, and it was programmatically adhered to by the Ottonians in their missionary policy.[57] The combination of veil and animals, however, derived directly from the Carolingian models which the artist followed. These technicalities, interesting though they are, shall

---

[55] Bede, *op.cit.*, 446A: "Quatuor autem columnae, ante quas appensum est hoc velum, coelestium sunt potestates agminum, quatuor virtutibus eximiis praeclarae." Gregory the Great identified the four animals with the four Virtues, and in Byzantium they were mainly "angelic powers"; see Gregory the Great, *In Ezech.*, I, Homil. III,8, *PL*, LXXVI,809A, and F. van der Meer, *Maiestas Domini* (Vatican City, 1938), 227f. For other interpretations, see Sauer, *Symbolik*, 134.

[56] For a survey of the literary tradition concerning the four animals, see van der Meer, *Maiestas Domini*, 223ff; see also Irenaeus, *Adversus haereses*, III,11,8.

[57] For the prayer "Deus, qui ad praedicandum aeterni regis (regni) evangelium Francorum (Romanum) imperium praeparasti," see Gerd Tellenbach, *Römischer und christlicher Reichsgedanke in der Liturgie des frühen Mittelalters* (S.-B. Heidelberg, 1934-35), Abh.1, to whose texts there may now be added the 8th-century *Sacramentarium Pragense*, ed. Alban Dold and Leo Eizenhöfer (Texte und Arbeiten der Erzabtei Beuron, 1.Abt.,Heft 38-42; Beuron, 1949), II,137*,No.246,4. See also Hans Hirsch, "Der mittelalterliche Kaisergedanke in den liturgischen Gebeten," *MÖIG*, XLIV (1930), 9ff, against whom C. Erdmann, "Der Heidenkrieg in der Liturgie und die Kaiserkrönung Ottos I.," *MÖIG*, XLVI (1932), 129-142 (also *Ideenwelt*, 19f,nos. 6-7), emphasizes that the *praedicatio evangelii* was the task of every Christian king, and not only that of the Roman emperor. See, e.g., the acclamations to King Reccared (Third Council of Toledo, in 589): "Ipse mereatur veraciter apostolicum meritum, qui apostolicum implevit officium"; *PL*, LXXXIV,345CD. For the missionary ideology under the Ottonians, see Joseph Kirchberg, *Kaiseridee und Mission unter den Sachsenkaisern und den ersten Saliern von Otto I. bis Heinrich III.* (Historische Studien, 259 [Berlin, 1934]); also M. Bünding, *Das Imperium Christianum und die deutschen Ostkriege vom zehnten bis zum zwölften Jahrhundert* (Historische Studien, 366 [Berlin, 1940]). For the prayer in the Coronation *Ordines*, see, e.g., Schramm, "Die Ordines der mittelalterlichen Kaiserkrönung," *ArchUF*, XI (1929), 371, and "Die Krönung bei den Westfranken und Angelsachsen von 878 bis um 1000," *ZfRG*, kan.Abt., XXIII (1934), 220; Paul L. Ward, "An Early Version of the Anglo-Saxon Coronation Ceremony," *EHR*, LVII (1942), 360.

not occupy us here.[58] Nevertheless, it should be mentioned that in several Carolingian Bibles a picture is found showing the four animals with the throning figure of a man who holds a veil over his head (figs. 9, 10). This miniature conveniently supports the interpretation of the banderole as "sky," for the veil billowing above the head of that male figure descends directly from the veil which the ancient Roman god *Caelus* holds over his head to indicate the sky (fig. 11).[59]

Symbolically the veil of the tabernacle was said to separate heaven from earth. According to its original function, the curtain separated, within the Temple, the sanctuary from the Holy of Holies (Exodus 26: 33). To Bede, who again argues along customary lines, this division of the Temple appeared as a symbol of the Church which itself was twofold: men peregrinating below on earth, and saints as well as angels ruling above in the heights. At this reflection about the twofold Church, Bede arrived because the veil reminded him of the two natures of Christ the Mediator who was, at the same time, on earth the man Jesus and in celestial eternity the co-ruler of God.[60] Bede, at least, offers a clue to help us understand the separating curtain as an indication of the two natures of Christ.

Bede's seemingly strange association will become less cryptic when we turn to another peculiar item of the Aachen miniature: the apparently gigantic stature of the emperor whose feet rest on earth while his head is in heaven. Incidentally, there exists a miniature of Otto's contemporary in the East, Emperor Basil II, who likewise towers like a giant from earth to heaven (fig. 12) while his defeated enemies crouch below.[61] The giant figure, of course, was a distinguishing mark not only of Hellenistic and Roman or By-

---

[58] I may discuss those problems separately.

[59] The three representations of that type (Vivian Bible, Grandval Bible, and San Paolo Bible) have been studied carefully by J. Croquison, "Une vision eschatologique carolingienne," *Cahiers archéologiques*, IV (1949), 10-129, with full bibliography (see p.116f, for Caelus), whose identification of the bearded man on the throne with John the Evangelist is suggestive, but not fully convincing.

[60] Bede, *De Tabernaculo, PL*, XCI,447AB: "Intra hoc velum templi posita est arca testamenti; quia mediator Dei et hominum, homo Christus Jesus, qui solus paternorum est conscius arcanorum, . . . super coelos coelorum ascendens (see below, nos.72ff), sedet ad dexteram Patris. Hoc velo sanctuarium et sanctuarii sanctuaria dividuntur; quoniam Ecclesia, quae ex angelis sanctis et hominibus constat, partim adhuc peregrinatur in infimis, partim in aeterna patria regnat in supernis."

[61] Grabar, *L'Empéreur*, pl.XXIII,1, and p.60.

zantine emperors honored by colossal monuments, but also of Christ. It was a feature well known in early Christian popular belief, especially in the gnostic and docetic circles which may even have drawn from a Rabbinic tradition concerning Adam: "The first man extended from the earth to the firmament."[62] However, the vision of a giant Christ was orthodox as well. It was kept alive within the Church through the 18th Psalm: "He hath rejoiced as a giant to run his course." And although in the Psalm the giant stature of God—Justin parallels him with the mythical Heracles—has no obvious relation to the two natures, Saint Ambrose nevertheless speaks in that connection of Christ as the *gigas geminae substantiae*. The Psalm has been taken subsequently as an allusion to either the Incarnation or the Resurrection and Ascension of Christ.[63] And perhaps the Ambrosian "Giant of two substances" should be linked to a standard interpretation of the head and feet of Christ which was current in the East. "The head means the godhead of Christ; the feet, his manhood," writes Cyril of Jerusalem;[64] and it was quite common, especially in connection with

[62] Decisive is the *Gospel of Peter*, c.40 (see below nos.79ff), ed. Léon Vaganay (Paris, 1930), 298ff, with the parallels, most of which were enumerated already by H. B. Swete, Εὐαγγέλιον κατὰ Πέτρον: *The Ahmim Fragment of the Apocryphal Gospel of St. Peter* (London, 1893), p.18,n.2. See H. L. Strack and P. Billerbeck, *Kommentar zum Neuen Testament aus Talmud und Midrasch* (Munich, 1928), IV, 888, for Rabbi El'azar according to whom the first man extended from earth to heaven, but "inasmuch as he sinned, the Holy One . . . placed his hand upon him and made him small." Since Christ undid the sin of Adam, it is logical that the new Messiah should have had again the original size of Adam, and the rabbinic tradition has it that "the messianic time shall restore to the Israelites more than giant stature." See also Strack-Billerbeck, IV,947f, for additional material; cf. III,851.

[63] For the *gigas geminae substantiae*, see above, n.19; see also Justin, *Apologia*, I,54, who claims that the whole pagan myth of Heracles was stolen from Psalm 18:5, although in fact the versicle referred to Christ. For the interpretation of the Psalm in the sense of Ascension and Resurrection, see Dölger, *Sonne der Gerechtigkeit*, 102ff, and *Sol Salutis*, 217f; also Pseudo-Bede, *In Psalmorum librum exegesis*, XVIII, *PL*, XCIII,581D. See further, Hubert Schrade, "Zur Ikonographie der Himmelfahrt Christi," *Bibliothek Warburg: Vorträge 1928-29* (Leipzig, 1930), 119f, and *Ikonographie der christlichen Kunst: Die Auferstehung Christi* (Berlin and Leipzig, 1932), 39; also Helena Gutberlet, *Die Himmelfahrt Christi in der bildenden Kunst* (Strassburg, 1934), 70f.

[64] Cyril of Jerusalem, *Catechesis*, XII,1, *PGr*, XXXIII,726: ". . . κεφαλὴν μετὰ τῶν ποδῶν μεταλάβωμεν· κεφαλῆς μὲν τῆς θεότητος νοουμένης, ποδῶν δὲ τῆς ἀνθρωπότητος ἐκλαμβανομένης." The passage may reflect *Odes of Solomon*, XLII,13; see Rendel Harris and Alphonse Mingana, *The Odes and Psalms of Solomon* (Manchester, 1920), II,55f. Pseudo-Chrysostomos, *In Pascha*, II, *PGr*, LIX,728, sees in "head and feet" of Exodus 12:9, an allusion to the two Advents of Christ. Bede, *In Exodum*, c.12, *PL*, XCI,306D, does not seem to know that exegesis, but interprets "head and feet" as *Christus cum duabus legibus*.

"the feet like unto fine brass" of the Revelation (1: 15), to explain
that the feet of Christ indicated the Incarnation.[65]

The intellectual climate of the Ottonian period would probably
allow us to take Greek writings into consideration. However, we
do not need to seek succour from either Gnostic authors or Eastern theologians to explain the Reichenau miniature. *A priori* it
would appear unlikely that the master of the Aachen Gospels
should have been inspired by other than conventional material for
his unconventional image. Decisive, in fact, is a source not at all
obscure: Augustine's *Enarrationes in Psalmos*, which may serve
also to illustrate the Ambrosian *gigas geminae substantiae*. When
interpreting Psalm 91, Augustine exclaims: "Oh Christ, who sit-
test in heaven on the right side of the Father, but art with thy feet
and thy limbs struggling on earth."[66] Augustine, on that occasion,
repeated only an idea treated by him at greater length in his exposition on the preceding 90th Psalm. Here he discusses the word
"tabernacle" (v.10), and points out that the word was used of the
human flesh.[67] "The tabernacle of God is the flesh. In the flesh the
Word has dwelt, and the flesh was made a tabernacle for God."
Augustine then continues: "In this very tabernacle the Emperor
[i.e. Christ] has militated for us—*In ipso tabernaculo Imperator
militavit pro nobis*." Once more he remarks on that occasion: "He
is far above all heavens, but his feet he has on earth: the head is
in heaven, the body on earth." And so as to preclude every possibility of a dichotomy and preserve the dogmatic "One person, two
natures," he adds: "But we should not believe that the head is

[65] Andreas of Caesarea, *In Apocalypsim* (on 1,15), *PGr*, CVI,229A, referring to
Gregory Nazianzen: πόδες γὰρ αὐτοῦ ἡ σάρξ; Arethas of Caesarea, *Comm. in Apoc.*
(on 1,15), *ibid.*,519AB. See, for the 12th century, Michael Akominates, *Comment. in
Apocalypsim*, ed. Dyovouriotis, in Ἐπετερὶς ἑταιρείας βυζαντινῶν σπουδῶν, V (1928),
24,19: νοήσωμεν πόδας τὴν διὰ σαρκὸς ἐπιδημίαν. See, for the West, e.g., Haymon of
Halberstadt, *PL*, CXVII,956B: "[pedes] aliquando significant stabilitatem aeternitatis,
aliquando vero humanitatem per quam ad nos venit cognitio divinitatis, aliquando
praedicatores." For the feet as *praedicatores*, see also Victorin of Pettau, *In Apocal.*,
PL, V,319. See further R. J. H. Jenkins and C. A. Mango, in *Dumbarton Oaks
Papers*, IX-X (1956), 132,n.52.

[66] Augustine, *Enarrationes in Psalmos*, XCI,11, *PL*, XXXVII,1178: "O Christe, qui in
coelis sedes ad dexteram Patris, sed pedibus tuis et membris tuis laboras in terra."

[67] For *tabernaculum* (σκηνή, σκᾶνος) in the figurative sense, see II Cor. 5: 4, and
II Peter 1: 13. The human flesh as the "tabernacle of the soul" has its philosophical
antecedents; see Delatte, *Traités de la royauté*, 181; cf. Kantorowicz, "Deus per
naturam," 270,n.56.

separate from the body: there is a discretion in space, but a conjunction in love."[68]

It should be mentioned that the Augustinian exegesis of that Psalm was repeated many times and was generally known. It passed into the ordinary gloss on the Psalter; it is found in the Psalm Commentary ascribed to Bede; it appears later in the marginal glosses of the Canterbury Psalter and in the Exposition on the Psalter by Peter the Lombard, and can probably be found in many other writings as well.[69]

The Reichenau artist did not come about those passages merely by chance. Commissioned, as apparently he was, to design a triumphal image of the emperor, he naturally turned to Psalm 90 and consulted Augustine's commentary. For Psalm 90 was the great Victory Psalm, the "imperial" Psalm *par excellence* according to oldest tradition, because it contains the famous versicle (v.13): "Thou shalt tread upon the adder and the basilisk, the lion and the dragon shalt thou trample under feet."[70] In fact, this Psalm was for many reasons so irresistibly imperial that the very few and rather exceptional representations of Christ in the full uniform of a Roman emperor—golden armour and imperial shoulder fibula with three pendents (fig. 13)—are all connected with Psalm 90: 13, although otherwise "gods in uniform" were a sub-

---

[68] Augustine, *op.cit.*, xc,5, *PL*, xxxvii,1163: "Tabernaculum Dei caro est. In carne inhabitavit Verbum, et caro facta est tabernaculum Deo: *in ipso tabernaculo Imperator militavit* pro nobis . . . Longe est super omnes coelos, sed pedes habet in terra: caput in coelo est, corpus in terra . . . Sed ne putemus quia separatum est caput a corpore: discretum est enim locis, sed iunctum est affectu." The title *imperator* for Christ is found less frequently than *rex*, though of course it is well known, especially in early Christianity; see, e.g., Erik Peterson, "Christus als Imperator," in his *Theologische Traktate* (Munich, 1951), 151-164, quoting also places from Augustine, though not the one mentioned here. The title is found with the later jurists; see, e.g., the Summa *Inperatorie maiestati*: ". . . inperator noster, Christus Jesus, ventis imperans et mari . . ." See Stephan Kuttner, *Repertorium der Kanonistik* (Studi e Testi, 71; Vatican, 1937), 179f; S. Mochi Onory, *Fonti canonistiche dell'idea moderna dello stato* (Milan, 1951), 112f,n.3.

[69] Pseudo-Bede, *In Psalmos*, xc, *PL*, xciii,975C-976B; Anselm of Laon [falsely Walafrid Strabo], *Glossa ordinaria*, Ps. xc, *PL*, cxiii,999; *Canterbury Psalter*, fols. 163ᵛ-164ʳ, ed. M. R. James (London, 1935); Peter the Lombard, *Comm. in Psalmos*, xc,10 (cf. titulus), *PL*, cxci,852C (cf.847D).

[70] See Grabar, *L'Empereur*, 237ff; and, for the West in Carolingian times, also Josef Deér, "Ein Doppelbildnis Karls des Grossen," *Forschungen zur Kunstgeschichte und christlichen Archäologie*, II (1953), 103-156, esp. 118ff. In the *Utrecht Psalter*, fol.53ᵛ, ed. E. T. DeWald (Princeton, [1932]), the illustration of Ps. 90 shows Christ not only stepping on lion and adder, but also receiving a crown.

ject not too rarely depicted in late Antiquity.[71] There cannot be the slightest doubt, therefore, but that the Augustinian exegesis of Psalm 90 prompted the artist to represent the living emperor Christ-like as *Imperator in tabernaculo militans.* As a result, he turned the ambivalent word *tabernaculum* from its figurative meaning ("flesh") back to its original meaning of tabernacle: thence in his picture the "veil of the tabernacle," which became to him also an essential stage property for dividing the emperor's body and indicating the geminate nature—*pedes in terra, caput in coelo.*

To understand the specific function of the veil, another iconographic pattern has to be considered: the image of the Ascension of Christ showing only the feet of the Incarnate whereas body and head have already disappeared in heaven.[72] Perhaps, though not necessarily, the concept of *Christus Gigas* was influential too.

Maximus ecce gigans scandit super astra triumphans
(Lo, the greatest giant strides over the stars in his triumph)

reads a verse inscription explaining an Ascension picture in the Gospels from Bamberg of the early eleventh century.[73] At any rate, the new type of Ascension imagery, very common in the thirteenth century and the later Middle Ages, made its first appearance around A.D. 1000 in two Anglo-Saxon manuscripts as well as in the

[71] See, for the Neon Baptistry in Ravenna, Grabar, *op.cit.,* pl.xxvii,1, and for the representation in the Archiepiscopal Palace, J. Wilpert, *Die römischen Mosaiken und Malereien* (Freiburg, 1917), I, pl.89, and p.47. For the *fibula,* see below, Chapter vii,n.341. For "gods in uniform," see, for the time being, R. Paribeni, "Divinità straniere in abito militare romano," *Bulletin de la société archéologique d'Alexandrie,* xiii (1910), 177-183, also E. Breccia, *ibid.,* xvii (1919-20), 184ff; there are very many monuments to be added. See, in that connection, also A. D. Nock, "Studies in the Graeco-Roman Beliefs of the Empire," *Journal of Hellenic Studies,* xlv (1925), 93, for the *augustus* title of gods, which was carried over to Christian times; see, e.g., Petrus Chrysologus, *Sermo CXXX, PL,* lii,557B: *augusta Trinitas.*

[72] See E. G. Millar, *English Illuminated Manuscripts* (Paris and Brussels, 1926), pl.13a (and p.73), for the Missal of Robert of Jumièges, and pl.29a, for an 11th-century Troper; for the Bernward Gospels, see Gutberlet, pl.xxix; Schrade, "Ikonographie der Himmelfahrt," pl.xv, fig.30; and, for the Morgan Library Gospels of St. Bertin (MS 333), Schapiro, "Disappearing Christ," 147. For the new type in general, see Gutberlet, 243ff; Schrade, 165ff; Schapiro, 140ff. I am greatly indebted to Professor Erwin Panofsky who suggested the combination of that Ascension type with the Reichenau miniature.

[73] Goldschmidt, *German Illuminations,* II, pl.40B; see also Stephan Beissel, *Geschichte der Evangelienbücher in der ersten Hälfte des Mittelalters* (Stimmen aus Maria-Laach, 92-93, Freiburg, 1906), 218.

Bernward Gospels from Hildesheim (fig. 14).[74] It marks a complete break with the whole Western tradition as well as with Eastern iconography. Hitherto the Ascension had been depicted in the forms of an antique apotheosis or of an epiphany; now, however, Christ does not become manifest, he disappears in Heaven.[75] That is to say, whereas *caput et corpus Christi* are in heaven, the feet alone—the symbol of the Incarnation—remain as a visible token of the historical fact that the Incarnate has migrated on earth. Moreover, it is the sky that divides the body of Christ and suggests the two natures,[76] just as the "sky" divides, in the Reichenau picture of Otto II, the body of the emperor.

The sky—that is, the veil of the tabernacle—in the emperor's image still demands some comment. The veil is held by the Eagle of John and the Angel of Matthew in such a fashion that the fall of the fold leaves head, breast, and shoulders as well as the brachial joints of the emperor "above," that is, in heaven, whereas the body, including the hands, remains "below." We have to remember that head, breast, shoulders, and brachial joints were the places where the emperor was anointed with holy oil. Those parts of his body therefore refer, so to speak, to the *christus domini*, whereas trunk and limbs are those of an ordinary man. One might be surprised to find that the hands are below, not above, the veil, since the hands of kings were anointed too. But this detail happens to be correct: the anointment of the hands was not the custom at the imperial coronation nor was it as yet used at the German coronation of Otto II in Aachen (961), though it was introduced a little later, in an Order of the Coronation dated between A.D. 980 and 1000.[77]

[74] Gutberlet, pl.xxix; Schrade, "Ikonographie der Himmelfahrt," pl.xv, 30 (see above, n.72).

[75] Schrade, *op.cit.*, 166.

[76] Augustine, *Enarrat.*, Ps. CIX,7, *PL*, XXXVII,1450: "in eadem [carne] ascendit in coelum et sedet ad dexteram Patris." That is, Christ, who rules together with the Father from Eternity and as God, sits at the right hand of the Father *as man*, which is often forgotten; see Jungmann, "Die Abwehr des germanischen Arianismus," 75,n.8. Most significant is, in this connection, Helinand of Froidmont (late 12th century) who, quoting Leo the Great, says: "Christus ascendens in altum, miro modo, ut ait Leo papa, factus est divinitate praesentior, et humanitate longinquior." *PL*, CCXII,606D, quoted by Schrade, *op.cit.*, 177.

[77] The Coronation Order of ca. A.D. 961 has no anointment of the hands; see Schramm, "Die Krönung in Deutschland bis zum Beginn des Salischen Hauses," *ZfRG*, kan.Abt., XXIV (1935), 254f, and 315, §12; the hand anointment was introduced later (Schramm, 255, and 328, §12a), and only for the coronations at Aachen; the Roman

More difficult is the explanation of the remaining parts of the veil. The Lion of Mark and the Ox of Luke dangle the ends of the curtain so skilfully that the tips just touch the crowns of the two *reguli* who flank the emperor's footstool, that is, his feet which "militate on earth." This feature has been borrowed from the Carolingian models in which we notice that the tips of the veil just touch the mouths of Lion and Ox who, playfully like little dogs, snap at the loose ends (fig. 10).[78] In the Aachen Gospels, however, the touching of the crowns of the *reguli* apparently has a more definite meaning. No better explanation could be found than the words of the Gospel of St. Peter where the author narrates the events at Christ's Resurrection: The soldiers, on guard at the tomb, see two angels descending from above and entering into the sepulchre; then they see "how there come back from the tomb three men [instead of two]; and the two support the One; and of the two, the heads reach *unto* heaven; but the head of the One, whom they support, towers *beyond* the heavens."[79] This would fit almost perfectly the scene as depicted by the Reichenau master. The heads of the two *reguli* "reach unto heaven," that is, unto the tips of the veil representing the sky; but the head of the central figure, the emperor, "towers beyond the heavens."

Unfortunately the painter of the Aachen Gospels could not possibly have studied the apocryphal Gospel of Peter of which no evidence shows us that it was available in the West.[80] But even if we have to rule out the Gospel of Peter as a possible source of inspiration,[81] it may yet help us understand the intentions of the artist. In accordance with Augustine's interpretation of Psalm 90,

---

imperial coronation had no hand anointment anyhow, nor was it customary in France before the 14th century; see Schramm, *Der König von Frankreich* (Weimar, 1939), 157,nos.5-6.

[78] So in the Bible of San Paolo; the interpretation of W. Köhler, *Die karolingischen Miniaturen* (Berlin, 1930-33), I,141, according to whom the animals are tearing at the veil, is hardly acceptable.

[79] *Gospel of Peter*, 36-40, ed. Vaganay, 294ff; above, n.62.

[80] For the influence of the Gospel of Peter, see Vaganay, 163ff, who, however, does not take works of art into consideration.

[81] Gutberlet, *Himmelfahrt*, 226, does not exclude the possibility of an influence of the Gospel of Peter even as late as the early 12th century. An influence may be possible in very early times (see Dölger, *Sol Salutis*, 212ff; Kantorowicz, "The King's Advent," *Art Bulletin*, XXVI [1944], 226), although probably the Apocalypse of Peter was more influential than the Gospel; but without some new and striking evidence, an influence—at least, a direct influence—cannot be assumed in later times.

the artist had to show that the emperor's head was *longe super coelos*. He could, however, demonstrate most conveniently that the head was "far above all heavens" by allowing the sky to touch the crowns of the princes dependent on the emperor: their heads reach *unto* heaven or unto the sky, but the head of the emperor towers *beyond* the heavens. It is a purely artistic expedient which does not seem to demand further textual interpretation; it was supposed to be self-explanatory.

Therewith another detail of the picture falls in its proper place: the four figures below, the princes spiritual and secular. If the uppermost plane represents a sphere "above all heavens," and the middle plane a sphere below heaven but reaching "unto the sky," then the lowest tierce would plainly indicate sub-celestial "earth." In fact, this particular meaning of the tripartition is countenanced by Carolingian manuscripts. The Trier Apocalypse, for example, or the Bible of San Paolo (figs. 15a-b) show the *Maiestas Domini* in a similar fashion: in the uppermost tierce we see Christ with the four animal symbols; in the middle tierce, there are the twenty-four elders, their bodies on the level of the knees and feet of the Saviour and their haloes touching the sky; and in the lowest tierce moves the unhaloed crowd with John or Isaiah respectively in the right corner where in the Aachen Gospels the clergy has its place.[82]

The Carolingian models are important to us because they are a commentary where the Reichenau artist follows them, and they are most revealing where he chooses to deviate. A comparison of the Aachen miniature with the famous Carolingian throne images—for example, of Charles the Bald in the Vivian Bible (fig. 16a) and in the *Codex Aureus* (fig. 16b)[83]—exhibits that point very clearly. True, there is a veil also in the Carolingian minia-tures; it is attached to the pillars of the canopy-*ciborium* vaulting the throne. But the veil does not overcut and divide the ruler's body; it separates his head *from* the Hand of God. In the Reiche-nau miniature, however, the emperor's head pushes through the curtain or "sky" so that the *dextera Dei* is now in direct contact with the head of Otto; moreover, the sky-line itself now divides

---

[82] The scheme is very obvious, e.g., in the Bible of San Paolo, f.115; van der Meer, *Maiestas Domini*, 336f, fig.78; see also 147ff (fig.34), 287f (fig.67), for the Trier Apocalypse.

[83] Schramm, *Die deutschen Kaiser*, figs.26,29a-b, also fig.28.

the emperor's body in two sections, one supra-celestial and the other sub-celestial. The comparison explains also the function of the four animal symbols as carriers of the veil: the curtain attached to the pillars of the throne canopy does not suggest the word "tabernacle" nor could it convey the meanings of "sky" and "far above all heavens" which the Reichenau painter obviously wished to express. Moreover, the very presence of the animals as well as the mandorla surrounding the emperor indicate that he is in the place of Christ, the Emperor "militating for us in the tabernacle." Finally, the veil dividing the body emphasizes that the emperor on earth has in common with Christ the two substances—human by nature, but divine by grace and by consecration.

All this results from a philosophy of state which is very different from that suggested by the Carolingian throne images. It is true, the Hand of God the Father emanates the divine blessing and grace also on the Carolingian monarch, and there is a relationship between the ruler on his throne and the far remote Father in Heaven; but Christ is absent from those scenes. The Carolingian concept of a David-like kingship was decisively theocentric: "Thou art the vicegerent of God, and the bishop is in the second place only, the vicegerent of Christ," as the English scholar Cathwulf wrote to Charlemagne.[84]

Nothing could have been more contrary to the Reichenau painter. His emperor is in the place of Christ, and the hand stretching down from above is surrounded by a cross-halo: it is probably not the hand of the Father, but rather that of the Son.[85] In short,

---

[84] *MGH, Epp.*, IV.503,3ff: ". . . tu [rex mi] es in vice illius [Dei regis tui] . . . et episcopus est in secundo loco, in vice Christi tantum est." M. Buchner, in *Hist.Jhb.*, LV (1935), 604, claims without evidence that the Cathwulf letter is a fiction of the 9th century. There is no reason whatever for this assumption, but even if correct, it would make little difference here: the otherwise unknown Cathwulf would be replaced by the otherwise unknown contemporary author of a "school exercise" who (and this is all that matters) reflected the so-called "Ambrosiaster"; see Williams, *Norman Anonymous*, 175ff. See below, Ch.IV,n.12, for Ambrosiaster in Canon Law.

[85] It is, of course, impossible to tell whether it is the Hand of God stretching down from heaven (Beissel, *Evangelienbücher*, 211) or that of the Son. The crossed nimbus surrounding the hand, however, is a very suggestive feature, since it is very rare in that period, though very common in the later Middle Ages. There seem to be no more than three earlier examples: an ivory plaque of the 10th century (Goldschmidt, *Elfenbeine*, II,pl.IX,24b: Incredulity of Thomas); an antiphonary from Prüm of the same century (Paris, Bibl.Nat., MS.lat.9448, fol.10ᵛ: St. Stephen in the Synagogue); and the Bamberg Apocalypse of ca.1000-1010 (Bamberg, Staatsbibl., MS 140,fol.24ᵛ, ed. H. Wölfflin, 1921, pl.24: Rev. 9: 13). To these there may be added,

the Ottonian concept of rulership displayed by the Reichenau artist was not theocentric: it was decisively christocentric. A hundred years or more of Christ-centered monastic piety[86] have affected also the image of rulership. In fact, the unique Reichenau miniature is the most powerful pictorial display of what may be called "liturgical kingship"—a kingship centered in the God-man rather than in God the Father.[87] As a result, the Reichenau artist ventured to transfer to the Ottonian emperor also the God-man's "two natures in one person." No less distinctly than the Norman Anonymous in his tractates has the master of the Aachen Gospels expounded the concept of the ruler's *gemina persona*.

3. The Halo of Perpetuity

Things difficult and circumstantial to describe in words are sometimes more easily and succinctly expressed by an iconographical formula. It has been stated above that in the tractate of the Norman Anonymous Tiberius *qua* "Caesar" appeared, so to say, with a halo whereas "iniquitous Tiberius," the individual man, was certainly without a halo. This metaphor, not chosen at random, may actually help us to clarify yet another aspect of the mediaeval concept of the ruler's *gemina persona*.

In late antique art, we often find the halo bestowed on such figures as might impersonate a supra-individual idea or general

---

as the definitely earliest one, a representation of the Hand *on* the Cross in the Bible of Charles the Bald (Bibl.Nat., MS.lat.1,fol.317ro, see W. Köhler, *Die Schule von Tours* [1930], pl.89,fig.n: the upright Hand flanked by two angels). Whether in those cases the hand is meant to be that of God or of Christ is not at all clear in every case. However that may be, of major interest is the fact all by itself that the symbol of Christ begins to be passed on to God the Father, an impossible feature in Byzantine iconography of that period, especially in coronation scenes. Contrariwise, Christ as coronator is very common; see, e.g., the Sacramentary of Emperor Henry II, in Schramm, *Die deutschen Kaiser*, fig.85a; and, for Byzantium, Grabar, *L'Empereur*, pl.XIX,1-2, and also (below, fig.12; see above, n.61) the triumph of Basil II. In the Aachen Gospels, where the full figure of Christ could hardly have been represented, the cross-haloed hand therefore seems to imply the abbreviated formula of the Crowning Christ.

[86] This problem is in need of a thorough investigation, although Georg Schreiber, *Gemeinschaften des Mittelalters* (Münster, 1948), touches upon it time and time again; see also Hallinger, *DA*, X,430f. Jungmann, of course (above, n.76), especially in his fundamental book *Die Stellung Christi im liturgischen Gebet* (Liturgiegeschichtliche Forschungen, 7-8; Münster, 1925) is fully aware of the general problem, but does not seem to have dealt with monastic piety in particular.

[87] See below, Ch.IV, pp. 89f.

notion. This special mark of distinction indicated that the figure was meant to represent in every respect a continuum, something permanent and sempiternal beyond the contingencies of time and corruption. Roman provinces such as Egypt, Gaul, Spain, and others were sometimes represented with a halo—for example, in the late antique *Notitia dignitatum.*[88] In that case, we usually call these haloed females "abstractions" or "personifications," which is correct so far as it goes; but we have to be aware that the most significant feature of all abstractions and personifications is their supra-temporal character, their continuity within time. In fact, it was not so much the personification which was made conspicuous by the halo, as the *Genius* of the individual province, that is, its perennial creative and seminal power, since *genius* derives from *gignere*. Much of what we today are inclined to associate with slogans such as *Roma aeterna* or *La France éternelle,*[89] was very precisely expressed by the *Aegyptus*, the *Gallia*, the *Hispania* when adorned with the nimbus. The same was true with regard to notions or virtues: *Justitia* or *Prudentia*, who were goddesses in pagan Antiquity, were meant to represent forces perpetually effective or forms of Being perpetually valid when depicted in Christian art with the halo.[90] In other words, whenever we capitalize a notion and, in the English language, even change the gender from neuter to feminine, we actually are "haloing" the word or the notion and are indicating its sempiternity as an idea or power.

In this sense, and very much in the sense of the anonymous Norman pamphleteer, the Byzantine emperors, until and beyond the Fall of Constantinople, were represented haloed. The origin

[88] It is not intended here to discuss in any detail the function or origin of the halo; see the standard work on the subject by A. Krücke, *Der Nimbus und verwandte Attribute in der frühchristlichen Kunst* (Strassburg, 1905) and K. Keyssner, "Nimbus," *RE*, XXXIII (1936), 591ff, esp. §§18,24.cols.611,622. See *Notitia Dignitatum*, ed. Seeck (Berlin, 1876), e.g., 108 (*Italia, Illyricum, Africa*), 101 (*Felicitas, Virtus, Scientia militaris*), 102 (the Four Seasons, with *Autumnus* cross-haloed[!]); see, for the haloed Seasons, George M. A. Hanfmann, *The Season Sarcophagus in Dumbarton Oaks* (Dumbarton Oaks Studies, II, Cambridge, Mass., 1951), I,266; II,115, n.29,3; also 45,46,48,52, and passim.

[89] The expression "Eternal France" does not seem to antedate the 16th century, and we may wonder whether it was not transferred from "Eternal Rome," just as the notion *Roma communis patria* was transferred, in the 13th century, to France: "corona regni [Franciae] est communis patria." See Gaines Post, "Two Notes," *Traditio*, IX, 288ff (n.44), also 301.

[90] See, for a few remarks on a related subject, my note "Σύνθρονος Δίκῃ," *American Journal of Archaeology*, LVII (1953), 65-70.

of the imperial halo and its tradition from a pagan symbol of divinity to a Christian symbol of holiness shall not occupy us here.[91] The halo of the Byzantine emperor, which even in Christian times still referred to the τύχη, the *genius imperatoris*, referred in later times mainly to the imperial power as such which was considered perpetual and sempiternal and, therewith, venerable and holy also in the Christian sense, regardless, of course, of the presence or absence of venerable or holy qualities in the individual bearer of the diadem. Admittedly, an emperor might be worshipped also individually and independently as a saint as, for example, Constantine the Great;[92] the nimbus, however, did not depend upon an emperor's enrollment in the catalogue of hagiarchs. It indicated the bearer and executive of perpetual power derived from God and made the emperor the incarnation of some kind of "prototype" which, being immortal, was *sanctus*, regardless of the personal character, or even the sex, of its constituent. For example, the Empress Irene, when governing (790-802) the empire as regent for her son Constantine VI, was spoken of in official documents, not as "empress," but as "Emperor"—Εἰρήνη πιστὸς βασιλεύς.[93]

[91] For the imperial halo, see, above all, Alföldi, "Insignien und Tracht der römischen Kaiser," *RM*, L(1935), 139ff. See also H. U. Instinsky, "Kaiser und Ewigkeit," *Hermes*, LXXVII(1942), 313-355; Treitinger, *Oström.Reichsidee*, 122,n.372. Byzantine art represented the emperor adorned with the halo practically without exception—even when he is shown in prostration before a group of likewise haloed saints; cf. Paul Buberl, *Die Miniaturhandschriften der Nationalbibliothek* (Denkschriften der Wiener Akademie, LX,2, Vienna, 1917), 6, pl.IV,fig.7.

[92] His veneration is usually linked to that of his mother, St. Helen; their images and names appear even on hosts; see Carl Maria Kaufmann, "Konstantin und Helena auf einem griechischen Hostienstempel," *Oriens Christianus*, N.S.IV (1915), 85-87.

[93] See J. B. Bury, *The Constitution of the Later Roman Empire* (Cambridge, 1910), 24; also F. Dölger, in *Byz.Zs.*, XXXVI (1936), 129ff. Similar considerations, no doubt, were effective in Hungary when Maria, daughter of Louis the Great (1342-1382), took the title "King" ("quae quidem Maria appellabatur *Rex Hungariae*") and was crowned as "King" (*coronata fuit in regem*); only after her marriage to Sigismund did she accept the title *regina*; see Du Cange, *Glossarium*, s.v. "rex." As late as the 18th century the enthusiastic Hungarians acclaimed their queen *Moriamur pro rege nostro Maria Theresia*. The peculiarly abstract concept of the "Crown of Hungary" may have produced also the abstractness of the title; see, for the vast modern literature on the Hungarian *Sacra Corona*, Patrick J. Kelleher, *The Holy Crown of Hungary* (Papers and Monographs of the American Academy in Rome, XIII [Rome, 1951]), and, in general, Fritz Hartung, *Die Krone als Symbol der monarchischen Herrschaft im ausgehenden Mittelalter* (Abh. Berl. Akad., 1940, No. 13 [1941]), 35ff. Twisting St. Jerome's statement *In divinitate nullus est sexus*, it might be said that also *In corpore politico nullus est sexus*: Gallienus, who vested his supra-personal body with the insignia of Ceres, had coins struck with the legend

Moreover, the Middle Ages were perhaps more aware than we are of the various categories or measures of time. Amalar of Metz, for example, in his acclamations to Emperor Louis the Pious, very acutely distinguishes the individual emperor from the sempiternal prototype; he wishes "long life" to the "divine Louis," but wishes sempiternity to the "new David" as impersonated by the Carolingian emperor:

> *Divo Hludovico vita!*
> *Novo David perennitas!*

In other words, Louis was "haloed" not as an effluence of the epithet *divus*, but through the *perennitas* of the pious King of Israel in whom the Carolingian empire idea, the *regnum Davidicum*, culminated and became manifest.[94] It was perhaps in competition with the Byzantine emperor that Pope Gregory VII claimed the "halo" for every pope, as it were, *ex dignitate officii*, because the court poet of Theodoric the Great, Ennodius of Pavia, had said: "Who can doubt that he be holy whom the apex of so great a dignity has enhanced!"[95] The exact meaning of that kind of holiness *ex officio* has been expressed very neatly by Peter Damiani: "It is one thing to *be* holy by the merits of life, and it is another thing to be *called* holy owing to the ministry of one's

---

Galliena Augusta; see A. Alföldi, "Zur Kenntnis der Zeit der römischen Soldatenkaiser," *Zeitschrift für Numismatik*, XXXVIII (1928), 174ff.

[94] See *PL*, CV,988; Kantorowicz, *Laudes*, 69,n.15. For Louis the Pious haloed, see Schramm, *Die deutschen Kaiser*, pls.15a-b, where the halo has the inscription: *Christe, corona tu Hludovvicum* (Schramm, 171). Carolingian representations of rulers adorned with a nimbus are not too rare. The mosaics of Charlemagne in the Lateran and in S. Susanna, in Rome, showed the square halo; see G. B. Ladner, *I ritratti dei papi nell'antichità e nel medioevo* (Vatican, 1941), I,114f,127. Most impressive is the haloed king in the Sacramentary fragment of MS lat.1141, of the Bibliothèque Nationale, whom A. M. Friend, "Two manuscripts of the School of St. Denis," *Speculum*, I (1926), 59-70, esp.64f, identified with Charles the Bald, while J. Croquison, "Le 'Sacramentaire Charlemagne,'" *Cahiers archéologiques*, VI (1952), 55-71, interprets the picture as a youthful Charlemagne between Saints Gelasius and Gregory; see my remarks on "The Carolingian King in the Bible of San Paolo fuori le Mura," *Late Classical and Mediaeval Studies in Honor of Albert Mathias Friend, Jr.* (Princeton, 1955), 298ff. Also Schramm, *op.cit.*, fig.67 (and p.86, also 192); Hermann Beenken, *Romanische Skulptur in Deutschland* (Leipzig, 1924), 76f,pl.38a.

[95] Gregory VII, *Regist.*, II,55a,§23, ed. Caspar, 207, cf.560,n.1; also Hinschius, *Decret.Ps.Isid.*, 666. Julia Gauss, "Die *Dictatus*-Thesen Gregors VII. als Unionsforderungen," *ZfRG*, kan.Abt., XXIX (1940), 1-115, overlabors her thesis, but has called attention to several interesting items of byzantine-papal rivalry worth being studied separately.

rank."[96] We may wonder whether the mediaeval square nimbus or *nimbus perfectionis*, which so often adorns nameless bishops, priests, or deacons as representatives of their ecclesiastical *ordo*, does not refer to the perfection and sempiternity of the consecrated office *per se*, or of the *dignitas*, regardless of its constituent.[97]

Further, the Norman pamphleteer, when setting the "bricks of Canterbury" over against the "See of Canterbury," was far less original than it may seem. The Byzantines, long before, had claimed that the so-to-speak "haloed" essence of ancient Rome on the Tiber, or her sempiternal *genius*, had been transferred to New Rome on the Bosphorus, and that whatever remained on the banks of the Italian river, was bricks and stones and the rubble of buildings out of which the *genius loci*, the life perennial, had evaporated.[98] The so-called *Versus Romae*, an anti-Roman poem probably of the late ninth century, reflects those feelings very distinctly.

> Thine emperors have, so long ago, deserted thee, Roma,
>> And to the Greeks there has vanished thy honor and name . . .
> Flowering Constantinople is now styled the newer Roma,
>> Moral and mural collapse is, ancient Roma, thy lot.

And with an old palindrome, the poet concludes the first half of the distichs: *Roma tibi subito motibus ibit amor*, "Roma, Amor will suddenly vanish from thee."[99] Rome's haloed body will leave

---

[96] Petrus Damiani, *Liber gratissimus*, c.10, *MGH,LdL*, 1,31,29: "Aliud namque est ex vitae meritis sanctum esse, aliud ex ministerio conditionis dici"; and, very similar to the Anonymous, who in other respects seems to have borrowed from Damiani, *ibid.*, 31,9ff: "licet persona . . . indigna, officium tamen . . . bonum"; see above, n.25.

[97] G. B. Ladner, "The so-called Square Nimbus," *Mediaeval Studies*, III (1941), 15-45, especially the lists, 38ff, which show that very often the square nimbus referred to the office only, and not to the individual person.

[98] Franz Dölger, "Rom in der Gedankenwelt der Byzantiner," *Zeitschrift für Kirchengeschichte*, LVI (1937), 1-42, esp.24ff; also *Byzanz und die europäische Staatenwelt* (Ettal, 1953), 93ff.

[99] William Hammer, "The Concept of the New or Second Rome in the Middle Ages," *Speculum*, XIX (1944), 50-62; *ibid.*, 53,n.6, for the *Versus Romae*, of which I have cited lines 4f,9f:

> Deseruere tui tanto te tempore reges,
>> Cessit et ad Graecos nomen honosque tuus . . .
> Constantinopolis florens nova Roma vocatur
>> Moribus et muris, Roma vetusta, cadis. . . .

The palindrome (line 12 of the poem's 24 lines) is the axis of the poem. The play *Roma-Amor* is very old. It is actually found on coins of the Constantinian period which show the inscription ΕΡΩΣ; see H. Dressel, "Numismatische Analekten," *Zeitschrift für Numismatik*, XXIII (1900), 36ff.

her material body or, as the jurists of a much later period would have put it, will be "transferred and conveyed over from the Body natural now dead to another Body natural." Thus it happened that "Rome" migrated from incarnation to incarnation, wandering first to Constantinople and later to Moscow, the third Rome, but also to Aachen where Charlemagne built a "Lateran" and apparently planned to establish the *Roma futura*.[100] We should not be mistaken: those were not comparisons or allegories after the fashion of "Geneva, the Protestant Rome."[101] Constantinople and Aachen and others claimed to be each a *nova Roma*, just as a Hellenistic king or Roman emperor might claim to be a νέος Διό-νυσος or a νέος Ἥλιος, and a Carolingian ruler, a *novus David* and *novus Constantinus*—temporal incarnations of the god's or hero's image, his perpetual substance and power of life. They were time-bound owners of the "halo" of their divine or heroized proto-types.[102]

All that seems even more true with regard to Jerusalem, although transcendental Jerusalem means timeless Eternity rather than continuity within Time. The original city of Christ, Jerusalem's material body, had been destroyed by Titus; Aelia Capitolina, Hadrian's new foundation on the ruins of David's city, was void of *metaphysis*. Yet, "Jerusalem haloed" might descend to earth at any moment, if for no longer than the festal hour in which a new shrine was consecrated, and then bestow the lustre of Eternity on any insignificant town or even on the village church.[103]

---

[100] Concerning Aachen, see Hammer, *op.cit.*, 56; R. Krautheimer, "The Carolingian Revival of Early Christian Architecture," *Art Bulletin*, xxiv (1942), 30ff, 34ff; Kantorowicz, *Laudes*, 63, where the Aachen Idea is interpreted as both anti-Roman and anti-Byzantine. Similar observations were advanced, quite independently, by C. Erdmann, "Das ottonische Reich als Imperium Romanum," *DA*, vi (1943), 418f, and, on a broader basis, *Ideenwelt*, 22ff ("Die nicht-römische Kaiseridee").

[101] See Hammer, *op.cit.*, 62, for this and many similar expressions.

[102] For the *novus* titles, see A. D. Nock, "Notes on Rulercult," *Journal of Hellenic Studies*, xlviii (1928), 35ff. There was no reason why there should be only one re-incarnation of the prototype at a time; the Emperors Heraclius Father and Son, e.g., were acclaimed as the "new Constantines" (Κωνσταντίνων τῶν νέων . . . πολλὰ τὰ ἔτη); see Henri Grégoire, *Recueil des inscriptions grecques chrétiennes d'Asie Mineure* (Paris, 1922), Fasc.i,21f,Nos.79,80. See, for Carolingian and other examples, Kantorowicz, *Laudes*, 57,n.148, and 69,n.15.

[103] For the descent of Celestial Jerusalem at the dedication of a church, see the Hymn *Urbs beata Hierusalem dicta pacis visio* in its original form, containing the line *Nova veniens e caelo . . .* ; see C. Blume, *Analecta hymnica medii aevi*, li (1908), 110. For the distorting "improvements" of this hymn by the post-Tridentine

Hence, the "halo" always indicated, in some way or another, a change of the nature of Time. It signified that the haloed individual, person or place, participated also in a category of "Time" which was different from the one determining the natural life on earth as the mediaeval mind understood it. The halo, it is true, did not remove its bearer into the *aeternitas Dei* which is without continuity because in it all times, past and future, are present. Yet, the halo removed its bearer too: removed him, scholastically speaking, from *tempus* to *aevum*, from Time to Sempiternity, at any rate, to some continuum of time without end: the haloed person, or rather the person *qua* halo, his *ordo,* "never died." The halo further signified that its individual bearer stood vicariously for a more general "prototype," for some Immutable within the mutable time of this earth, and that, conjoined and associated with him, there was some image or power whose true abode was that endless continuum which the Middle Ages came to call *aevum*. And since *aevum* was the habitat of the Ideas, *Logoi,* or Prototypes as well as of the "Angels" of alexandrianized Christian philosophy, it becomes comprehensible that finally the king's "Body politic" of the Tudor lawyers betrayed so much resemblance to the "holy sprites and angels," and that the *rex christus* of the Norman Anonymous was endowed also with the superior nature of the Mediator, a king human by nature and divine by grace.[104]

It would be difficult to find a more suitable, and at the same time more delightful, illustration of the general problem of the King's Two Bodies in its early mediaeval setting than the little story inserted in a homily wrongly ascribed to John Chrysostom. It is a Palm Sunday sermon, and the unknown preacher discusses, very fittingly, the important rôle which in the economy of salvation was played by the little ass that carried the Expected One into

---

Church, see A. L. Mayer, "Renaissance, Humanismus und Liturgie," *JLW*, XIV (1938), 166f; also the criticisms of X. Schmid, "De Breviario Romano reformando commentatio," *Ephemerides Liturgicae,* XLIII (1929), 308ff. The hymn, incidentally, had its political bearings as well; the medallion of an Emperor "Otto," soldered on a liturgical dish, has the legend *Jerusalem visio pacis*; see Schramm, "Die Magdeburger Patene mit dem Bilde Ottos des Grossen," *Thüringisch-Sächsische Zeitschrift für Geschichte und Kunst,* XVII (1928); also Gerd Tellenbach, *Die Entstehung des Deutschen Reiches* (Munich, 1946), pl.IX (facing p.128). For the manifestations of timeless Jerusalem on earth, see also Kantorowicz, "The King's Advent," 209f.

104 See, for a broader discussion of this subject, below, Ch.VI.

the city of Jerusalem on that day.[105] The loyal creature is mentioned not too rarely in the writings of the Fathers, who generally
held that the *animal messianum* finally was returned to its former
owner; and the Palm Sunday preacher formed no exception to the
rule when he came to speak about the ass.

> It is true (said he), the animal after having made its entrance into
> Jerusalem Judaea, was returned to its owner; but the prophecy, re-
> lated to the animal, remained in Judaea. For of that animal, Christ
> had needed not the visible, but the intelligible nature; that is, not
> the flesh, but the idea. Hence, the flesh was returned, but the idea
> retained: *caro remissa est, ratio autem retenta est.*[106]

In other words, the little ass "body natural," after having served
its task to fulfill to the letter the prophecies of Isaiah (62: 10) and
Zachariah (9: 9), was sent to its former owner; for its visible and
material body no longer was needed by the Lord. The ass's messianic sempiternal body, however, its *ratio* or idea or prototype, as
well as the prophetic vision it stood for and helped to fulfill: these

[105] The sermon, transmitted in Latin only, is found in the *Opus imperfectum in
Matthaeum* (*PGr*, LVI,836), attributed to John Chrysostom, of which Thomas
Aquinas supposedly said he would prefer its possession to that of the whole city of
Paris; cf. Oldradus de Ponte, *Consilia*, LXXXIV,n.1 (Venice, 1571), fol.31v: "Et narra-
tur quod beatus Thomas dixit, quod magis vellet habere Chrysostomum super
Mattheum, quam civitatem Parisii. Expedit enim cuilibet studioso habere multos
libros." See, for the work itself, G. Morin, "Quelques aperçus nouveaux sur l'Opus
imperfectum in Matthaeum," *Rev.bénéd.*, XXXVII (1925), 239-262 (also *ibid.*, LIV
[1942], 9ff), who suggests as place of origin Ravenna, or at least some place in
Northern Italy; cf. K. Jordan, "Der Kaisergedanke in Ravenna zur Zeit Heinrichs
IV.," *DA*, II (1938), 111ff. The Palm Sunday homily of Aelfric, otherwise a paraphrase of the *Opus imperfectum*, does not contain the passage quoted here; see the
Aelfric edition by Benjamin Thorpe (London, 1844), I,206ff. The ass is mentioned
quite often in the writings of the Fathers. Ephrem, e.g., permits the ass and her
colt to offer acclamations in praise of the King of Heaven; see *In festum Epiphaniae
hymnus*, II,27, ed. T. J. Lamy (Mecheln, 1882), I,23; also *Hymni de miraculis*, XIII,
6, ed. Lamy, II,720, where the ass has a twofold meaning: "Pullus durae cervicis
portavit Dominum in figura, cor gentium portavit eum in veritate." According to
later legends, the holy animal died, very advanced in years and after long migra-
tions, in Verona where a local cult developed; see E. Staedler, "Über das Eselsrelief
am Dome zu Como: Ein Beitrag zur Überlieferung des *caput asininum*," *Theologische Quartalschrift*, CXXIII (1942), 177-188, with full literature; see also Leclercq,
"Âne," *DACL*, I,2063f; and, for the ass with colt on later Roman coins, A. Alföldi,
"Asina: Eine dritte Gruppe heidnischer Neujahrsmünzen im spätantiken Rom,"
Schweizerische Münzblätter, II (1951), 57-66.

[106] *PGr*, LVI,836: "Animal quidem postquam ingressus est in Jerusalem Judaeae,
ad dominum suum remissum est, animalis autem prophetia in Judaea remansit.
Nam de animali illo non hoc, quod videbatur, necessarium erat Christo, sed illud,
quod intelligebatur, id est, non caro, sed ratio: ideoque caro remissa est, ratio
autem retenta est."

were indispensable within the course of salvation and inseparable from the image of the Messiah. Thus, the animal's immortal "body politic" remained in the Holy City with the Messiah: it was "haloed," enveloped by the divine light of its Rider.

Caro remissa, ratio retenta! In this sense, Charles I in the flesh could be dismissed to Oxford, but his "haloed" *ratio* in the shape of his seal image remained in Parliament—which does not imply that the unhaloed ass temporal should always be sought at "Oxford," nor the haloed ass perpetual always in "Parliament."

CHAPTER IV

LAW-CENTERED KINGSHIP

1. From Liturgy to Legal Science

THE KING a *gemina persona*, human by nature and divine by grace: this was the high-mediaeval equivalent of the later vision of the King's Two Bodies, and also its foreshadowing. Political theology in that early period was still hedged in by the general framework of liturgical language and theological thought, since a Church-independent secular "political theology" was as yet undeveloped. The king, by his consecration, was bound to the altar as "King" and not only—we may think of later centuries—as a private person. He was "liturgical" as a king because, and in so far as, he represented and "imitated" the image of the living Christ. "Thou art the vicar of Christ; none but his imitator is the true lord," proclaimed the historian Wipo in the imperial camp.[1] "In his king, truly, Christ is recognized to reign," echoed the saintly Cardinal Peter Damiani,[2] while Cardinal Deusdedit, his younger contemporary, included in his canonical collection the words with which Pope John VIII, in an assembly of bishops, had praised the Carolingian Emperor Charles II as the *salvator mundi*, "the saviour of the world constituted by God," whom "God established as the Prince of His people in imitation of the true King Christ, His Son, . . . so that what he [Christ] owned by nature, the king might attain to by grace."[3]

---

[1] Wipo, *Gesta Chuonradi*, c.3, ed. Bresslau (*MGH,SS.rer.germ.*, 1915), 23: "Ad summam dignitatem pervenisti,/vicarius es Christi./Nemo nisi illius imitator/verus est dominator." Cf. c.5,p.26,18; also his *Tetralogus*, line 19,p.76,21, and lines 121f, p.79,15f, where the emperor is called *alter post Christum* and *secundus post dominum caeli*. See above, Ch.III,n.11, for the Prince as a *Deo secundus*.

[2] Petrus Damiani, *Ep.*, VII,2, *PL*, CXLIV,436: "in rege suo vere Christus regnare cognoscitur."

[3] Deusdedit, *Collectio canonum*, IV,92, ed. Victor Wolf von Glanvell, *Die Kanonessammlung des Kardinals Deusdedit* (Paderborn, 1905), 1,439; the passage is quoted also by his contemporary Anselm of Lucca (ca. 1083), *Coll.can.*, 1,79, ed. M. Thaner (Innsbruck, 1906-1915), 52f (*PL*, CXLIX,489, numbered 1,78). See, for the Pope's address at Ravenna, in 877, Mansi, *Concilia*, XVII,App.172; also Bouquet, *Recueil*, VII,695C: ". . . unxit eum Dominus Deus . . . principem populi sui constituens ad imitationem scilicet . . . veri Regis Christi filii sui . . . , ita ut, quod ipse [Christus] possidet per naturam, iste [imperator] consequeretur per gratiam." See also Schramm, *König von Frankreich*, 1,40 and 45, II,36,n.3; Eichmann, *Kaiserkrönung*,

Very naturally this Christ-imitating king was pictured and expounded also as the "mediator" between heaven and earth, a concept of some importance here because every mediatorship implies, one way or another, the existence of a twin-natured being. Kings and bishops, wrote the Norman Anonymous in his customary fashion, "are consecrated and sanctified for the purpose that . . . they be saints; that is, outside the earth and outside the world be they set apart as mediators between God and the people, having communion in heaven and moderating their subjects on earth."[4] Related ideas of a royal mediatorship, though with a significant shift of the point of reference, were expressed in that period by the Coronation Orders: "In analogy with the Mediator between God and men shall the king act as the mediator between clergy and people"—for the king, who in some respect belonged also to the clergy, "bears as the *christus Domini* the type [of Christ] in his name."[5]

It was the language of christological exemplarism which was used throughout to proclaim the king a *typus Christi*.[6] This typol-

---

1,88. The passage could easily have been known to the Norman Anonymous; see Williams, *Norman Anonymous*, 57f,n.169; Kantorowicz, "Deus per naturam," 258.

[4] *MGH,LdL*, III,669,8ff: "Ideo igitur consecrantur sacerdotes et reges et sanctificantur, ut . . . sancti sint, id est extra terram et extra mundum segregati, inter Deum et populum mediatores effecti, et in celis conversentur [Philippians 3:20] et in terris subditos moderentur." See Williams, *op.cit.*, 158ff, and especially p.225ff, the *Magna digressio de voce 'sanctus,'* which explains that passage (e.g., "in Greca lingua quod dicitur *hagios* quasi extra terram esse significat"). See also Peter of Blois: ". . . sanctus et christus Domini rex est nec in vacuum accepit [II Cor. 6:1] unctionis regiae sacramentum"; *PL*, CCVII,440; cf. Eichmann, *Kaiserkrönung*, I,208,n.74. For related places, see Philipp Oppenheim, "Die sakralen Momente in der deutschen Herrscherweihe bis zum Investiturstreit," *Ephemerides Liturgicae*, LVIII (1944), 46f; also Leonid Arbusow, *Liturgie und Geschichtsschreibung im Mittelalter* (Bonn, 1951), 95,n.60.

[5] Schramm, "Krönung in Deutschland," 320, §19: ". . . quatenus mediator Dei et hominum te mediatorem cleri et plebis in hoc regni solio confirmet." See also 317, §14: ". . . cum mundi Salvatore, cuius typum geris in nomine"; and 319, §17: ". . . cum redemptore ac salvatore Iesu Christo, cuius nomen vicemque gestare crederis." See also Schramm, "Austausch," 425ff,450, for the king as *sacerdotalis ministerii particeps*. The phrase *personam Christi gerere* and its equivalents is the technical term for "impersonate, represent," and in that sense it is used also in Pope Pius XII's encyclic *Mediator Dei* defining the place of the priest in the liturgy; see Joseph Pascher, "Die Hierarchie in sakramentaler Symbolik," *Episcopus*, 278ff. The bishop, of course, was not rarely styled the mediator between king and people; see, e.g., Hugh of Fleury, *Tractatus de regia potestate et sacerdotali dignitate*, I,c.10, *MGH,LdL*, II,477,43ff.

[6] A striking example is offered by Otto of Freising, *Gesta Friderici*, II,c.3, ed. G. Waitz (*MGH,SS.rer.germ.*, 1912), 105,7ff, where he reports on the double consecra-

ogy actually covered two aspects of the royal office, one ontological and the other functional, and both were reflected in the honorary titles which so often exalted the mediaeval ruler: "Image of Christ" and "Vicar of Christ." While the former designation referred perhaps more to his Being, the latter stressed juristically his administrative functions and referred primarily to his Doing. Neither of these titles was, by itself, specific about the two natures or emphatic about any "physiological" resemblance between ruler and God-man; but so long as these titles linking the ruler to Christ prevailed, the king could appear, at least potentially, as a *gemina persona* paralleling the two natures of the human-divine prototype of all earthly kingship. However, even the purely potential relationship of the king with the two natures of Christ was forfeited when the high-mediaeval designations of "rex imago *Christi*" and "rex vicarius *Christi*" became evanescent and gave way to those of "rex imago *Dei*" and "rex vicarius *Dei*."

To be sure, the Prince figuring as a simile or an executive of God was an idea supported by the antique ruler cult as well as by the Bible.[7] Hence, the *Deus* titles and metaphors may be found in any century of the Middle Ages. When finally, in the wake of the clericalization of the royal office in the later ninth century and under the influence of the language of the Coronation *Ordines* and their liturgical ideal of kingship, the royal *Christus* titles began to predominate, the difference between a *vicarius Dei* and a *vicarius Christi* was probably not always felt, or not felt at all.[8]

---

tion at Aachen (March 9, 1152) of a king (Frederick I) and a bishop (Frederick of Munster): on the same day, in the same church, by the same consecrators there were anointed two *christi Domini*, both having the same name, so that the *summus rex et sacerdos* himself (that is, Christ), seemed to be present at that celebration. Cf. Arbusow, *Liturgie und Geschichtsschreibung*, 26ff, who rightly emphasizes that Otto of Freising was clinging to an ideal of by-gone days.

[7] The fusion of *homo imago (vicarius) Dei* and *rex imago (vicarius) Dei*, carried through already by the so-called Ambrosiaster, has its long and complicated history; see Kantorowicz, "Deus per naturam," 264ff, and passim; the importance of Ambrosiaster for the later development has been stressed by Berges, *Fürstenspiegel*, 26f. See also G. B. Ladner, "The Concept of the Image in the Greek Fathers and the Byzantine Iconoclastic Controversy," *Dumbarton Oaks Papers*, VII (1953), 1-34.

[8] For the influence of the Coronation *Ordines* on language and thought, the Norman Anonymous is the foremost example; see *MGH,LdL*, III,677ff. It would be wrong to say that in his brilliant study Michele Maccarrone, *Vicarius Christi: Storia del titolo papale* (Lateranum, N.S.,XVIII, Rome, 1952), was heedless of the difference between the two designations, but he was indifferent to the historical implications and to a problem which, in another connection, Jungmann (above, Ch.III,n.86) has

Nevertheless, it is remarkable for the changing patterns of piety and for the general religious mood that after the Carolingian period, during which the *vicarius Dei* predication seems to have been the rule, a definite preference for *vicarius Christi* becomes noticeable in the christocentric age of the Ottonians and early Salians.[9] The difference between the two designations, however, became articulate and therewith historically meaningful when the vicariate of Christ was claimed as a prerogative of the hierarchy—"Where are there emperors found obtaining the place of Christ"?[10]—until finally the *vicarius Christi* title became a monopoly of the Roman Pontiff.

As usual, many strands of political, religious, and intellectual life concurred to bring about the general shift and to dissolve the image of Christ-centered kingship. The spell of the Coronation *Ordines* waned under the impact of the Investiture Struggle. That struggle itself, on the one hand dismantling the secular power of spiritual authority, ecclesiastical competency and liturgical affiliation, and, on the other, imperializing the spiritual power, had certainly its share. However, the dogmatic-theological development of the twelfth century towards defining the real presence of Christ in the Sacrament also produced a new accentuation of the ancient idea of the presence of Christ in the person of the vicariously mass-celebrating priest.[11] Moreover, the new impetus of Canon Law

---

so acutely discussed. The christological problem was definitely visualized, though purposely not treated in detail, by Berges, *Fürstenspiegel*, 26ff. The texts for *vicarius Dei (Christi)* collected by J. Rivière, *Le problème de l'église et de l'état au temps de Philippe le Bel* (Louvain, 1926), 435ff, are discussed in Maccarrone's comprehensive study which also fills considerable gaps in A. von Harnack's famous study *Christus praesens—Vicarius Christi* (S. B. Berlin, 1927, No. xxxiv),415-446. For the interrelations between christology and rulership in earlier times, see G. H. Williams, "Christology and Church-State Relations in the Fourth Century," *Church History*, xx (1951), No. 3,3-33, and No.4,3-26.

[9] Among the Carolingian examples collected by Maccarrone, *op.cit.*, 79f, there is only one referring to the ruler as vicar of Christ (Smaragdus, *Via regia*, c.18, *PL*, cii,958), though in fact more are to be found (see above, n.3). The shift from *vicarius Dei* to *vicarius Christi* should probably be sought in the later ninth century as a result of the clericalization of the royal office (*imitatio sacerdotii* according to Schramm, "Austausch," 404f), of the language of the *Ordines*, and of the spirit of monastic piety.

[10] *De ordinando pontifice*, MGH,LdL, I,14,4: "Ubi enim inveniuntur imperatores locum Christi obtinere?"

[11] Pascher, "Die Hierarchie in sakramentaler Symbolik," 285f; J. Geiselmann, *Die Eucharistielehre der Vorscholastik*, Forschungen zur christlichen Literatur- und Dogmengeschichte, xv,1-3 (Münster, 1926).

studies made itself felt. The *Decretum Gratiani* quoted in two places—one from Hesych of Jerusalem, and the other from Ambrosiaster—bishops and priests alike as *vicarii Christi*,[12] a fact which prompted the decretists to enlarge upon that designation, even though not necessarily in the papal sense.

> Where are now those who say that only the pope is the vicar of Christ? With regard to the plenitude of power, this is true; but otherwise every priest is vicar of Christ and of Peter. . . .[13]

So wrote, between 1187 and 1191, Huguccio of Pisa in his *Summa super Decreto* when glossing the Ambrosiaster passage, and his words show that by his time the almost exclusive application of the "vicar of Christ" title to the pope must have been common enough. Some ten years later, Pope Innocent III tightened the notion of *plenitudo potestatis* in regard to which even Huguccio did not deny that only the pope had the right to style himself vicar of Christ. Furthermore, with the decretals of Innocent III the papal *vicarius Christi* made its first official appearance, not in common language, but in the collections of Canon Law.[14] Henceforth the decretalists, theologians, and scholastic philosophers concentrated on interpreting this title in that exclusively papal sense in which, by and large, it is used today.[15] Vice versa, the civilians, relying upon the vocabulary of Roman Law and some Roman

---

[12] Cf. c.35,D.3, *De penitencia* (C.33,q.3), ed. Friedberg, I,1222: ". . . quos [sacerdotes] Christus vicarios suos in ecclesia constituit" (Hesych), to which the *Glossa ordinaria* remarks: "sacerdotes etiam simplices." Further, from Ambrosiaster, c.19,C.33, q.5, ed. Friedberg, I,1255f: "Quasi ergo ante iudicem Christum, ita ante episcopum sit, quia vicarius Domini est . . ." Maccarrone, who quotes these passages (*op.cit.*, 106), adds also c.13,C.33,q.5, Friedberg, 1254, a passage from Ambrosiaster, cvI,17 (cf. Kantorowicz, "Deus per naturam," 265,n.40), where it is said that man in general has "imperium Dei quasi vicarius eius," but the *Decretum* omits the following "quia omnis rex Dei habet imaginem." The passages are characteristic of the Ambrosiaster's tenet saying that the king is the vicar of God, and the priest that of Christ. Ambrosiaster in canonical literature would deserve a special investigation. In the *Decretum*, Ambrosiaster is quoted many times (see Friedberg, p.xxxiv, s.v. Augustinus, *Questiones veteris et novi testamenti*; there should be added, though, the quotations [*ibid.*, p.xxxii] s.v. Ambrosius, *In S. Pauli epistolas*, since they are also by Ambrosiaster; see above, Ch.III,n.24), and Friedberg's annotations to those passages show that Ivo of Chartres, Anselm of Lucca, the *Collectio Caesaraugustana*, the *Collectio trium partium*, as well as Peter the Lombard, quoted from Ambrosiaster, directly or indirectly. The Norman Anonymous, therefore, could easily have been acquainted with those writing through legal, and not through literary, sources; cf. Williams, *Norman Anonymous*, 175ff.

[13] Maccarrone, *op.cit.*, 106,n.87; cf. 107,n.89.

[14] Maccarrone, 119ff.

[15] Maccarrone, 118ff,129ff.

authors such as Seneca and Vegetius, began to style the emperor
almost without exception *deus in terris, deus terrenus,* or *deus
praesens.* Apparently they took it for granted on the basis of their
sources that the Prince was above all vicar of God; for as an imperial designation, the expression *vicarius Christi* would not have
been within the range of their language at all.[16] Thus it came to
pass that the christocentric ideal of rulership dissolved also under
the influence of Roman Law. Henceforth a papal *Christus in
terris*[17] was sided by an imperial *deus in terris.* As a *pater sub-
jectorum,* "father of his people," the Prince, it is true, was granted
a faint resemblance with the invisible Father in Heaven;[18] but the

[16] The references are usually *D.*35,2,1,5 (*lex Falcidia:* ". . . quae Deo relinquun-
tur," to which the *Glossa ordinaria* remarks: "celesti, idem in terreno"), *D.*14,2,9
(*lex Rhodia de iactu,* where the emperor says of himself: "Ego quidem mundi
dominus"), or *C.*7,37,3,5 (*de quadriennii praescriptione:* ". . . nutu divino imperi-
ales suscepimus infulas"), though there are other relevant places as well. Baldus,
e.g., who uses those places too, quotes very often for *Deus in terra (terris) Nov.*105,
2,4, saying that the emperor is the *lex animata;* see, e.g., *Consilia,* 1,333,n.1,fol.105,
in addition to the places quoted by Gierke, *Gen.R.,* III,563,n.122. Other favored
places were Seneca, *De clementia,* I,1,2: "[Ego, Nero,] . . . qui in terris deorum vice
fungerer," a passage (though without quoting precisely these words) used by Frederick II, *Lib.aug.,* prooem., ed. Cervone, 4, with the gloss of Marinus de Caramanico,
v. *Velut executores;* cf. A. Marongiu, "Concezione della sovranità ed assolutismo di
Giustiniano e di Federico II," *Atti del Convegno Internazionale di Studi Federiciani*
(Palermo, 1952), 43,n.70, and "Note federiciane," *Studi Medievali,* XVIII (1952), 298.
Quoted was also Vegetius, *De re milit.,* 2,5: ". . . nam imperator cum Augusti nomen
accepit, tamquam praesenti et corporali deo est praestanda devotio"; see, e.g.,
Andreas of Isernia, on *Authentica 'Habita'* (cf. *MGH,Const.,* 1,249,No.178), n.3, in
In usus feudorum commentaria (Naples, 1571), fol.318, and the places quoted by
Gierke, *loc.cit.,* but also John of Salisbury, *Policraticus,* IV,c.1, and VI,c.7, ed. Webb,
I,235f, and II,20. A number of places from legal sources may be found in M. A.
Peregrino, *De privilegiis et iuribus fisci,* 1,2,n.46, and 1,3,n.2 (Venice, 1587), pp.26
and 52 (Venice, 1611), fols.7 and 14ᵛ, mostly applied to kings not recognizing a
superior; see also Andreas of Isernia, on *Feud.* II,56 ('Quae sunt Regalia'), n.63,
fol.301: "et dicitur 'nostri numinis,' quia Imperator vel Rex in Regno dicitur
habere numen divinum, quia est in terris sicut Deus in coelo, inde dicitur rescriptum
suum coeleste oraculum. . . ."

[17] See the passage from Arnald of Villanova, in Carl Mirbt, *Quellen zur Geschichte
des Papsttums und des römischen Katholizismus,* 4th ed. (Tübingen, 1924), 211,
no.373.

[18] The place usually quoted is *Nov.*98,2,2: "hoc post deum communis omnibus
pater (dicimus autem qui imperium habet) per legem . . . servet." See *Glos.ord.,*
v. *Dicimus autem;* also Marinus de Caramanico, on *Lib.aug.,* 1,74, v. *Post Deum,*
ed. Cervone, 134; also Andreas of Isernia, on *Lib. aug.,* prooem., ed. Cervone, 6:
"Rex est pater subiectorum in regno suo." In his gloss on *Lib.aug.,* III,26, Cervone,
355, Andreas says: "Princeps legislator, qui est lex animata in terris . . . et pater
subiectorum," and refers to *C.*3,28,34,1: "Sed nos qui omnes subiectos nostros et
filios et nepotes habere existimamus adfectione paterna et imitatione. . . ." For the
origins of the notion "father of his people," see A. Alföldi, "Die Geburt der kaiser-

vicar of the visible incarnate God, of the God-*man*, was the priest, the supreme hierarch.

These shifts in late mediaeval nomenclature, often hardly perceptible and yet very telling, were only the surface symptoms of evolutions in far deeper strata of Western religious sentiment. Official and popular piety, after the era of Saint Francis, became both more spiritualized and more material; and concomitantly there took place an evasive, and yet quite distinct, transformation of christological concepts. Man's relation with God retired from the "realism" of the object-centered mystery to an inner haze of subject-centered mysticism characteristic of the later Middle Ages. Those changes are most obvious in the domain of iconography where, the later the more so, the God-man—unless represented purely "in the flesh"—becomes almost indistinguishable from God the Father.[19] Within the political sphere there resulted the replacement of the more christocratic-liturgical concept of kingship by a more theocratic-juristical idea of government, while from the divine model which later rulers claimed to follow there gradually slipped away the "manhood" of the deity, and therewith the quasi-priestly and sacramental essence of kingship. To put it in another fashion: as opposed to the earlier "liturgical" kingship, the late-mediaeval kingship by "divine right" was modelled after the Father in Heaven rather than after the Son on the Altar, and focused in a philosophy of the Law rather than in the—still antique—physiology of the two-natured Mediator.

The change was not abrupt; in fact, it was slight and subtle like most evolutionary changes in history. There was, nevertheless, a period of transition from the earlier liturgical kingship to the late-mediaeval kingship by divine right, a period, clear in its contours, during which a royal mediatorship, though strangely secularized, still existed, and during which the idea of royal priesthood was vested in the Law itself. The former ontological aspects of a royal

---

lichen Bildsymbolik: 3. Parens patriae," *Museum Helveticum*, IX (1952), 204-243, and X (1953), 103-124.

[19] Although the fact itself is well known—see, e.g., V. Leroquais, *Les sacramentaires et les missels manuscrits* (Paris, 1924), I, p. xxxvii, and pl.87, where the "King of Glory" appears like God the Father—the development itself and its connection with christological changes does not seem to have been investigated.

christomimēsis inherent in the concept of the king's *gemina persona* may have grown paler, but functionally the ideal of the Prince's twin-like duplication was still active; it became manifest in the king's new relationship to Law and Justice, which replaced his former status in regard to Sacrament and Altar.

Jurisprudence as a science was barely existent, and certainly not yet effective, when the Norman Anonymous composed his challenging tractates. When some fifty years later, around 1159, John of Salisbury wrote his *Policraticus*, legal idioms had already penetrated scholarly language and legal notions were applied frequently, though as yet without overturning the modes of mediaeval thought.[20] John of Salisbury, to be sure, was not a professional jurist, but he handled the volumes of the Justinian Corpus and Gratian's Decree with the same ease as the bulky load of classical authors and patristic writings.

In some often-quoted chapters at the beginning of the Fourth Book of the *Policraticus*, John of Salisbury developed his doctrine of the *rex imago aequitatis*. The metaphor of the king as an "Image of Equity" or "Image of Justice" is very old;[21] nor does it in any respect invalidate, by itself, the notion of the *rex imago Christi* or

[20] For a brief but profound analysis of the *Policraticus* and its ontological essence, see Berges, *Fürstenspiegel*, 131-143, whereas W. Kleineke, *Englische Fürstenspiegel vom Policraticus Johanns von Salisbury bis zum Basilikon Doron König Jacobs I.* (Studien zur Englischen Philologie, Heft xc, Halle,1937), 23-46, remains on the surface. The most recent study by Hans Liebeschütz, *Mediaeval Humanism in the Life and Writings of John of Salisbury* (Studies of the Warburg Institute, xvii, London, 1950), hardly touches upon the problems discussed here. For bibliographical items, see Berges, *op.cit.*, 291-293, to which there should be added Fritz Schulz, "Bracton on Kingship," *EHR*, lx (1945), 164ff, and the study by W. Ullmann, "The Influence of John of Salisbury on Mediaeval Italian Jurists," *EHR*, lix (1944), 384-393; also Ullmann, *Lucas de Penna*, Index, s.v. John of Salisbury; through Lucas de Penna and Matthaeus de Afflictis the *Policraticus*, especially the Pseudo-Plutarch chapters, exercised considerable influence on the later French jurists; cf. on the Plutarch problem, H. Liebeschütz, "John of Salisbury and Pseudo-Plutarch," *Warburg Journal*, vi (1943), 33-39, who, convincingly to me, identifies Ps.-Plutarch with John himself; see, however, A. Momigliano, "Notes on Petrarch, John of Salisbury and the *Institutio Traiani*," *ibid.*, xii (1949), 189f. How the old and the new interpenetrated each other in the *Policraticus* has been shown by John Dickinson, "The Mediaeval Conception of Kingship as Developed in the Policraticus of John of Salisbury," *Speculum*, i (1926), 307-337.

[21] The briefest formula of these metaphors is, of course, that of the *lex animata* and the *iustitia animata*; see below. There are, however, related expressions of which Louis Robert, *Hellenica* (Paris, 1948), esp. vol.iv, gives many examples from late antique governor inscriptions, a most fruitful source for the knowledge of political thought also in the Middle Ages; see my paper, quoted above, Ch.iii,n.90.

encroach upon it—after all: *Christus ipse ipsa iustitia.*[22] John of Salisbury's version indicates merely a slight variation of the old theme, a seemingly insignificant shift from the more liturgical to the more legal aspect of Christ as represented by the ruler. In the case of John of Salisbury that variation becomes so noticeable only because he integrated maxims of Roman Law into the impressive building of his thought in which hierocratic and humanistic features blended.

John of Salisbury tried to solve what may appear to us self-contradictory or an effort to square a circle; for he attributed to his Prince both absolute power and absolute limitation by law. The essence of this alleged antinomy is exposed in a chapter-heading which reads:

> That the Prince, although he be not bound by the ties of Law, is yet Law's servant as well as that of Equity; that he bears a public person, and that he sheds blood without guilt.[23]

John of Salisbury does not deny the essential validity of the Roman Law maxim proclaiming the Prince as *legibus solutus;* for the Prince he thinks of is indeed free from the ties of Law. This, however, does not imply that he is permitted to do wrong. He is free from the ties and restrictions of Law just as he should be free from the fetters of sin. He is free and *legibus solutus* because he is "expected to act on the basis of his innate sense of justice,"[24] and because he is bound *ex officio* to venerate Law and Equity for the love of justice herself, and not for the fear of punishment.[25] He is without guilt when he sheds blood in his capacity as judge; for what he does as the ordinary he does as "the minister of the public utility" and for the benefit of the common weal. He is, and acts as, a *persona publica.* And in that capacity he is expected to consider all issues with regard to the well-being of the *res publica,* and not with regard to his *privata voluntas.* Thus, when Roman Law maintains that the Prince's *voluntas* has the power of Law, the reference

---

[22] Honorius Augustod., *Elucidarium,* III,19, *PL,* CLXXII,1150A.

[23] IV,c.2, ed. Webb, I,237: "Quid lex; et quod princeps, licet sit legis nexibus absolutus, legis tamen servus est et aequitatis, geritque personam publicam, et innocenter sanguinem fundit."

[24] Ullmann, "Influence of John of Salisbury," 389.

[25] *Policraticus,* IV,c.2, ed. Webb, I,238,2ff: ". . . dicitur absolutus, non quia ei iniqua liceant, sed quia is esse debet, qui non timore penae sed amore iustitiae aequitatem colat . . ."

appears to be made not to his arbitrary private volitions, but to the *voluntas* active in him as a *persona publica*.[26] As a public person, however, the Prince serves public utility; and therewith the bearer of the *imago aequitatis* becomes at the same time the "servant of Equity"—*aequitatis servus est princeps*.[27]

John of Salisbury's antithesis of *persona publica* and *privata voluntas* seems to contain, by implication, the distinction between the Prince as a public person and the Prince as a private person. We might expect some theory saying that the Prince as a private person is under the Law, *legibus alligatus*, whereas his public person is above the Law, *legibus solutus*. This, however, is not the conclusion which John of Salisbury draws. He, like the Norman Anonymous, is not particularly interested in the Prince as a *persona privata*, at least not in that connection, since every private person is under the Law anyhow. He is interested in the *persona publica*, that portentous notion introduced from Roman Law upon which political theory in the later Middle Ages and thereafter hinged. In the passages of John of Salisbury's *Policraticus* under discussion here, the inner tension is found within the Prince's *persona publica* itself: as a public person he, the Prince, is at once *legibus solutus* and *legibus alligatus*, is at once *imago aequitatis* and *servus aequitatis*, at once lord and serf of the Law. The duality is in the office itself, a conclusion at which John of Salisbury was almost bound to arrive on the basis of two contradictory laws of the Roman Corpus, the *lex regia* and the *lex digna*, as shall be explained presently.[28]

It may be correct to say that the Prince of John of Salisbury is not a human being in the ordinary sense. He is "perfection" if at all he be Prince and not tyrant. He is—in good mediaeval fashion, and yet in a new juristic sense—the very Idea of Justice which itself is bound to Law and yet above the Law because it is the end of all Law. Not the Prince rules, but Justice rules through

---

[26] The whole passage (p.238) deals with the various aspects of *voluntas* and with the distinction between private and public will.

[27] "Eius namque voluntas in his vim debet habere iudicii; et rectissime quod ei placet in talibus legis habet vigorem, eo quod ab aequitatis mente eius sententia non discordet . . . Judex etenim incorruptus est cuius sententia ex contemplatione assidua imago est aequitatis. Publicae ergo utilitatis minister et aequitatis servus est princeps, et in eo personam publicam gerit."

[28] The *lex digna* is quoted IV,c.1, Webb, 237,1ff. See below for *lex regia* and *lex digna*.

or in a Prince who is the instrument of Justice and, though Salisbury does not quote Justinian to that effect, is at the same time the *lex animata.*

All that may appear hazy and ambiguous today. But in that ambiguity we shall learn to recognize the king's *gemina persona* mirrored by Law as well as the idea of royal mediatorship transferred from the liturgical to the juristic sphere.

2. Frederick the Second

PATER ET FILIUS IUSTITIAE

Two generations after John of Salisbury, legal thought unmistakably prevailed over the spirit of the liturgy: Jurisprudence now felt invited to create its own secular spirituality.

The *locus classicus* of a new pattern of *persona mixta* emerging from the Law itself is found in the *Liber augustalis,* the great collection of Sicilian Constitutions which (at Melfi, in 1231) Frederick II published as a Roman Emperor, though in his capacity of King of Sicily—a king truly competent to act as *imperator in regno suo.*[29] Title I,31 of this lawbook is inscribed "On the Observation of Justice."[30] It is a juristic and philosophic discussion of both the origin of the imperial right to legislate and the emperor's obligation to protect and observe the Law. Those, of course, were topics which the lawyers of that age had dealt with frequently, and doubt could not arise about prerogatives and duties at large of the Prince

[29] Frederick II, publishing his laws as emperor in his kingdom, was in fact the only monarch of the 13th century who literally acted in accordance with the new maxim *Rex est imperator in regno suo,* or its equivalents. For the development of that maxim in the Sicilian kingdom, see the latest study of Francesco Calasso, *I glossatori e la teoria della sovranità* (2nd ed., Milan, 1951), who (26ff) reviews the earlier literature, and (179ff) reprints also the Prologue of Marinus de Caramanico's gloss on the *Liber augustalis;* see also *Liber aug.,* ed. Cervone, pp. xxxiii-xl; the same ideas, of course, were developed also in the Prologue of Andreas of Isernia's *Lectura* on the *Liber aug.,* ed. Cervone, pp. xvii-xxxii. The problem of the origin of that phrase and its equivalents has been greatly clarified by Sergio Mochi Onory, *Fonti canonistiche dell'idea moderna dello stato* (Pubblicazioni dell' Università del Sacro Cuore, xxxviii, Milan, 1951); see further the highly important contributions (on the basis of legal material not used by Mochi Onory) and corrections by Gaines Post, "Two Notes on Nationalism in the Middle Ages: II. Rex Imperator," *Traditio,* ix (1953), 296-320; also his study, "Blessed Lady Spain—Vincentius Hispanus and Spanish National Imperialism in the Thirteenth Century," *Speculum,* xxix (1954), 198-209.

[30] *Lib.aug.,* I,31, ed. Cervone, 81 (this edition is used throughout on account of the glosses); see Huillard-Bréholles, iv,33; also Theseider, *L'Idea imperiale* (cf. below, n.44), 179.

who was recognized as the "fountain of Justice."[31] However, the current ideas and formulae were reformulated, succinctly and clearly, in the *Liber augustalis*, and the majestic language in which Frederick's statement was couched appeared impressive enough to make the glossator Andreas of Isernia exclaim: *Pulchre dictata est haec lex*,[32] whereas a later glossator, Matthaeus de Afflictis, suggested that, for the elegance of the wording, young men should learn the whole constitution by heart.[33] In this law the emperor harked back to the ancient right of legislation owned by the Roman Quirites, and declared:[34]

> Not without great counsel and wise deliberation have the Quirites, by the *lex regia*, conferred on the Roman Prince both the right to legislate and the *imperium*, that from the very same person (ruling . . . over the people by his Power) there might progress the origin of Justice, from whom also the defence of Justice proceeds.[35] Pro-

[31] *Lib.aug.*, 1,38, Cervone, 85f, on the offices of the *magister iustitiarius* and the judges of the *Magna Curia*. The preamble of that law follows *C*.1,17,2,18; the last sentence ("a qua [sc. Curia], velut a fonte rivuli, per regnum undique norma iustitiae derivetur") repeats a metaphor used by the jurists (see *Erg.Bd.*, 84f), e.g., by Placentinus, Thomas of Capua, and also Bracton, who draws from Azo, *Summa Institutionum*, on *Inst*. I,1,rubr. (Lyon, 1530),fol.268ᵛ, ed. Maitland, *Bracton and Azo* (see below, n.175), 18. The jurists, however, say: "Ex iustitia omnia iura emanant," which would imply that the *Magna Curia*, or the emperor himself (below, n.133), as it were, impersonated *Iustitia*. It is remarkable to what extent the metaphor of the *fons iustitiae* was repeated in the later theories of French absolutism; see William Farr Church, *Constitutional Thought in Sixteenth-Century France* (Harvard Historical Studies, XLVII; Cambridge, 1941), 38,n.50, also 53,n.30, and passim.

[32] On *Lib.aug.*, 1,31, Cervone, 81; see also (*ibid.*) the gloss of Marinus de Caramanico: "et pulchra est haec constitutio, et continet ius commune."

[33] Matthaeus de Afflictis, *In Utriusque Siciliae Neapolisque sanctiones et constitutiones novissima praelectio* (Venice, 1562), I,fol.147ʳ, on *Lib.aug.*, 1,31,rubr.: "Ista constitutio est multum elegans, et tota esset memoriae commendanda a iuvenibus, et continet ius commune." Cf. above, n.32.

[34] "Non sine grandi consilio et deliberatione perpensa condendae legis ius et imperium in Romanum Principem lege regia transtulere Quirites, ut ab eodem, qui commisso sibi Caesareae fortunae fastigio per potentiam populis imperabat, prodiret origo iustitiae, a quo eiusdem defensio procedebat. Ideoque convinci potest non tam utiliter quam necessario fuisse provisum, ut in eiusdem persona concurrentibus his duobus, iuris origine scilicet et tutela, ut a iustitia vigor et a vigore iustitia non abesset. Oportet igitur Caesarem fore iustitiae patrem et filium, dominum et ministrum: Patrem et dominum in edendo iustitiam et editam conservando, sic et in venerando iustitiam sit filius, et in ipsius copiam ministrando minister."

[35] Cf. *Quaestiones de iuris subtilitatibus*, 1,16, ed. H. Fitting (Berlin, 1894), 56: "Qui enim nomen gerit inperii, gerere debet auctoritate quoque eiusdem, qua tuenda sunt eadem iura, que sunt ab ea profecta." See, for the authorship (probably Placentinus) of this 12th-century tractate, below, n.57. The passage is printed also by Sergio Mochi Onory and Gianluigi Barni, *La crisi del Sacro Romano Impero: Documenti* (Milan, 1951), 150, where it appears as the work of an anonymous author.

vision, therefore, was made for reasons of utility and necessity, as can be proved, that there concur in the selfsame person the origin as well as the protection of Justice, lest Vigor be failing Justice, and Justice, Vigor.[36] The Caesar, therefore, must be at once the *Father and Son of Justice,* her lord and her minister: Father and lord in creating Justice and protecting what has been created; and in like fashion he shall be, in her veneration, the Son of Justice and, in ministering her plenty, her minister.

While the antiphrasis *pater et filius Iustitiae* seems to be a new formula, metaphors of intellectual parentality of that kind were common property of the jurists' idiom of that age. The emperor a *pater legis,* Justice a *mater iuris,* and *ius* itself the *minister vel filius Iustitiae*: all that may be found in contemporary legal literature.[37] It was perhaps, in addition to the obvious paradox, chiefly the concentration of these metaphors in the person of the living emperor that gave a peculiar ring to the language of the *Liber augustalis.* Moreover, in Frederick's stately and solemn proclamation two orbits seem to overlap, one legal and one theological. The document, after all, originated at a time when the tide of the movement labeled "Jurisprudence emulating Theology" ran highest. A quasi-theological undertone, therefore, would not appear as something quite unexpected in an imperial law; nor, for that matter, did it escape the ear of a later glossator of the Sicilian law-book: the emperor acts *exemplo Dei patris et filii,* wrote Matthaeus de Afflictis, who on that occasion recalled also that the emperor, according to Roman Law, was *pater legis* as well as *lex animata.*[38]

[36] Roman Law was influential, not only with regard to the *lex regia* and the Quirites. See, for *vigor* and *iustitia,* C.10,1,5,2, including the *Glos.ord.* on that paragraph, v. *vigorem:* "id est principem, qui est vigor iustitiae, unde dicitur lex animata (= *Nov.*105)." This remained the standard interpretation; see, e.g., Andreas de Barulo, on C.10,1,5,n.5 (*Commentaria super tribus libris Codicis,* Venice, 1601), p. 6: "Imperator est vigor iustitiae . . . (reference to *Nov.*105), ubi dicitur lex animata. Et iura dicuntur ab eo oriri . . . et in pectore suo esse . . . Et pater est legum. . . ." It is this law the *Liber augustalis* alludes to rather than the famous saying that the Prince's *voluntas legis habet vigorem.*

[37] For *pater legis,* see *Nov.*12,4: ". . . aestimavimus recte se habere nos tamquam legis patres" (the plural is one of majesty), including *Glos.ord.,* v. *Patres:* "Nota imperatorem vocari patrem legis, unde et leges sunt ei subiectae," followed again (see above, n.36) by an allegation of *Nov.*105 (the emperor as *lex animata*). The phrase *pater legis* was repeatedly referred to by the glossators; see, e.g., *Glos.ord.* on *Nov.*99,2, v. *Dicimus autem,* as well as below, n.38. For *Iustitia* as *mater iuris,* see, for example, *Glos.ord.* on D.1,1,1, also below, nos.60, 69; but the image was repeated over and over again; see, e.g., Ullmann, "Baldus," 389, n.9. For *minister et filius,* see *Glos.ord.* on D.1,1,1, v. *Et iure:* "ius iustitiam prosequitur ut minister vel filius."

[38] Matthaeus de Afflictis, on *Lib.aug.,* 1,31,n.8, fol.147ᵛ: ". . . exemplo Dei patris et

All that, however, does not yet explain the antiphrastic formula itself which the *Liber augustalis* produced and by which the emperor was represented definitely *et maior et minor se ipso*, that is as a "mediator," as the father and son of Justice, whereby Justice herself was attributed likewise an intermediate position: she was, by implication, at once the mother and daughter of the emperor. The peculiar wording of that paragraph is not warranted by Roman Law. It reminds us rather of certain laudatives applied to princes, and perhaps prelates as well, who were sometimes styled *filius et pater Ecclesiae*.[39] However, the seemingly paradoxical formula describing the relationship between Prince and Justice may have easily evoked other associations in the minds of Frederick's contemporaries: they were accustomed to hear not only the praise of the Holy Virgin as "mother and daughter of her Son" (*Vergine madre, figlia del tuo figlio*), but also the praise of Christ himself as father and son of his virginal mother: "I am your Father, I am your Son," sang Wace, who merely echoed a motif repeated in many variations by a whole chorus of poets.[40]

It would be beside the point to assume that by means of the

filii, ut patet in psal. LXXI: 'Deus iudicium tuum regi da et iustitiam tuam filio regis.' Et ideo dicitur [imperator] *lex animata in terris*, ut in Auth. de consulibus. §.fin. [= *Nov.*105,2,4], et *pater legum*, ut in Authen. de fide instrum. in princ. [= *Nov.*73,praef., actually a wrong allegation; see *Nov.*12,4, and above, n.37]."

39 A. L. Mayer (see next note), p.65, quotes Froumund of Tegernsee's *susceptaculum* for Emperor Henry II: *filius ęcclesię . . . pater aecclesię*; cf. *Die Tegernseer Briefsammlung*, ed. Karl Strecker (*MGH, Epist.sel.*, III; Berlin, 1925), No.XX, p.57; further a tomb inscription for a Count Theobald, from a Zürich MS (C.58/275, fol.8ᵛ): *Ecclesiae matris filius, immo pater*. It seems most likely that prelates, too, were praised as *filius Ecclesiae* and at the same time *pater ecclesiae*, that is, father of their own prebend or church.

40 The very rich material for that antiphrasis has been carefully collected and studied by Anton L. Mayer, "Mater et filia," *Jahrbuch für Liturgiewissenschaft*, VII (1927), 60-82 (*Toletanum*, XI: *ipse et pater matris et filius*, might be added; A. Hahn, *Bibliothek der Symbole und Glaubensregeln der alten Kirche* [2nd ed., Breslau, 1877], 176), who indicates (81f) that this kind of speech, while extremely rare in earlier times, especially in the East, became very common in the 12th century resulting from the new devotion to St. Mary (therefore St. Bernard addresses the Virgin with the words quoted above from Dante's *Paradiso*, XXXIII,1) and that it reached the climax of popularity in the "gothic age"; see p.78, for Wace's *Je suis ton fil, je suis ton père*. See also Helmut Hatzfeld, "Liturgie und Volksfrömmigkeit in den südromanischen Dichtersprachen," *Jahrbuch für Liturgiewissenschaft*, XII (1935), 72. Jungmann, "Arianismus," 81,n.31, quotes L. E. Wels, *Theologische Streifzüge durch die altfranzösische Literatur* (Vechta, 1937), 1,33-51 (not accessible to me), who considers that antiphrasis almost a kind of Sabellianism. If we recall, however, that the Virgin Mary symbolized at the same time the Church, the antiphrasis would imply that Christ, too, was *Ecclesiae matris filius, immo pater* (see above, n.39).

formula of "father and son of Justice" the imperial legislator intended to put himself in the place of Christ or to ascribe to the virgin Justice—the *Virgo Astraea* of Vergil's messianic Eclogue and other classical sources to which the jurists occasionally referred—the place of the Virgin Mary, although admittedly any kind of *quid pro quo* became possible in allegorical interpretation.[41] The emperor's antiphrastic formula belonged to a different world of thought. It fell in with the intellectual climate of the "Jurists' Century" in general, and in particular with that of Frederick's *Magna Curia* where the judges and lawyers were expected to administer Justice like priests; where the High Court sessions, staged with a punctilio comparable to Church ceremonial, were dubbed "a most holy ministry (mystery) of Justice" (*Iustitiae sacratissimum ministerium [mysterium]*); where the jurists and courtiers interpreted the "Cult of Justice" in terms of a *religio iuris* or of an *ecclesia imperialis* representing both a complement to and an antitype of the ecclesiastical order; where, so to speak, the robe of the law clerk was set over against the robe of the ordained cleric; and where the emperor himself, "whom the Great Artificer's hand created man," was spoken of as *Sol Iustitiae*, the "Sun of Justice," which was the prophetic title of Christ.[42] Within

---

[41] For *Astraea*, see, e.g., Baldus, on c.34 X 1,6 (*Venerabilem*), n.13, *In Decretales* (Venice, 1580), fol.78ᵛ, quoting Huguccio: "dicit Ugutio quod Astraea, id est, iustitia que de coelo descendit, dicta est ab astris, id est, a stellis, quia lumen suum naturaliter communicat universae creaturae." Allegorical misrepresentations were not rare. In the *Gesta Romanorum*, c.54, ed. Oesterley (Berlin, 1872), 349f, the Capuan triumphal arch of Frederick II, whose throne image seems to have been flanked by a male and a female figure (a Virtue?), is interpreted in the following fashion: "Carissimi, imperator iste est dominus noster Jhesus Christus, porta marmorea est sancta ecclesia . . . In qua porta sculpta est imago . . .[scil. imperatoris] cum duobus collateralibus, i.e. cum Maria matre Jhesu et Johanne evangelista, qui designant nobis eius misericordiam et iustitiam." The allegorizing cleric thus interpreted the three figures in terms of a *Deésis*. See Carl A. Willemsen, *Kaiser Friedrichs II. Triumphtor zu Capua* (Wiesbaden, 1953), 68f,103,n.222, who, without solving the problem either, corrects me on an important point; see *Kaiser Friedrich II.*, 486, and *Erg.Bd.*, 210f. See, for much later times, Frances A. Yates, "Queen Elizabeth as Astraea," *Warburg Journal*, x (1947), 27-82, who collects interesting material on the triangle of *Virgo Astraea*, *Virgo Maria*, and *Virgo Regina*; see esp. pp.75 and 62 with pl.20a, where *Iustitia*, depicted in the center of the Virtues, wears a dress similar to that of Elizabeth. For a twelfth-century enamel from Stablo displaying *Iustitia* where Mary or the Church would be expected, see below, n.73.

[42] For the material of this summary, see, in general, *Erg.Bd.*, 88ff. For the jurists as *sacerdotes iustitiae*, see below, nos. 94ff, and for *Christus iurisconsultus*, Hermann Kantorowicz, *Studies in the Glossators of the Roman Law* (Cambridge, 1938), 21. For *mysterium iustitiae* (*Erg.Bd.*, 88) and the interchangeable use of *ministerium* and *mysterium*, see F. Blatt, "Ministerium-Mysterium," *Archivum latinitatis medii aevi*,

this political theology, or politico-religious hybridism, the words of the *Liber augustalis*—written by the Bologna-trained jurist and stylist Petrus de Vinea[43]—have their definite place.

However, Frederick's imperial "theology of rulership," though pervaded by ecclesiastical thought, touched by Canon-Law diction, and infused with quasi-christological language to express the arcana of government, no longer depended on the idea of a Christ-centered kingship. The chief arguments of Frederick and his legal advisers derived from or were determined by Law—more accurately by Roman Law. In fact, the emperor's dual function of "lord and minister of Justice" descended from the *lex regia* or was linked to it, as the passage cited from the *Liber augustalis* shows quite unambiguously; that is, it descended from that famous law by which the Quirites of olden times used to confer the *imperium* together with a limited right of creating law, and of law exemption, on the Roman *princeps*.[44] And therewith a strictly Law-centered ideology begins to supersede the stratum of the mystery-like *christomimēsis* predominant in the earlier centuries.

IV (1928), 80f, and my study "The Absolutist Concept *Mysteries of State*, and its Late Mediaeval Origins," *Harvard Theological Review*, XLVIII (1955), 71,n.22. For *religio iuris*, see below, n.159, and for the *ecclesia imperialis*, *Erg.Bd.*, 208. For Vinea addressing the emperor "pacator iustissimus, quem supremi manus opificis formavit in hominem," see Petrus de Vinea, *Epistolae*, III,44, ed. Simon Schard (Basel, 1566), 469, ed. Huillard-Bréholles, *Vie et correspondance de Pierre de la Vigne* (Paris, 1865), 426, no. 107, and for some remarks on the history of that phrase, my study "Kaiser Friedrich II. und das Königsbild des Hellenismus," *Varia Variorum: Festgabe für Karl Reinhardt* (Münster and Cologne, 1952), 171-174. For Frederick II as *Sol Iustitiae*, see Huillard-Bréholles, VI,811, also my study "Dante's Two Suns," *Semitic and Oriental Studies Presented to William Popper*, ed. W. J. Fischel (Berkeley and Los Angeles, 1950), 221f,227ff; for the application of that title to the King of France, see Berges, *Fürstenspiegel*, 263; Johannes Haller, *Papsttum und Kirchenreform* (Berlin, 1903), I,470,n.1. See further the quite recently discovered eulogy on Frederick II by Nicholas of Bari, ed. Rudolf M. Kloos, "Nikolaus von Bari, eine neue Quelle zur Entwicklung der Kaiseridee unter Friedrich II.," *DA*, XI (1954), 166-190, esp.169ff.

43 Hans Niese, "Zur Geschichte des geistigen Lebens am Hofe Kaiser Friedrichs II.," *Hist. Ztschr.*, CVIII (1912), 535, stresses that Vinea "has formulated all the laws incorporated in the *Liber augustalis*," and I agree with him today even more than in former days. The rhetorical "hybridism" with its tendency towards building up "theologies" of all sorts (political theology as well as a theology of science or rhetoric) was actually taught in Bologna; see, e.g., my study "An 'Autobiography' of Guido Faba," *Mediaeval and Renaissance Studies*, I (1941-43), 253-280.

44 For a useful collection of extracts concerning the *lex regia*, see Eugenio Dupré Theseider, *L'Idea imperiale di Roma nella tradizione del medioevo* (Milan, 1942), 255ff. For the older literature, see *Erg.Bd.*, 85ff; see also Karl Jordan, "Der Kaisergedanke in Ravenna," *DA*, II (1938), 110ff; F. Schulz, "Bracton on Kingship," *EHR*, LX (1945), 153ff; Ullmann, *Lucas de Penna*, 48ff.

The twofold possibility of interpreting the *lex regia* as the basis of either popular sovereignty or royal absolutism is too well-known as to require consideration here. In Justinian's *Institutes* and elsewhere the *lex regia* was quoted in order to substantiate the claim that in addition to the very numerous other ways of legislating "also (*et!*) what pleases the Prince has the power of law."[45] But in Justinian's lawbooks there was inconsistency and ambiguity insofar as it was not clearly said whether the *lex regia* implied a full and permanent *translatio* of power to the emperor *in genere* or only a limited and revocable *concessio* to the individual emperor *in persona*.[46] It was that ambiguity which in the later Middle Ages led, among other solutions, to the construction of a dual sovereignty, a *maiestas realis* of the people and a *maiestas personalis* of the Prince.[47] Frederick II did not arrive at a duality of that kind. Nor did he, as yet, come to the formulation which, by the end of his century, described the ruler's position as one deriving equally from the people and from God, *populo faciente et Deo inspirante*.[48] Nor would he have made the distinction between empire and emperor which his contemporary Accursius suggested and Cynus of Pistoia later accentuated: "The emperor stems from the people; but the empire is from God, and because he presides over the empire, the emperor is called divine."[49] Frederick may

[45] The passages referring to the *lex regia* (D.1,4,1,1, and C.1,17,1,7) have been recently discussed, with regard to the Middle Ages, by Schulz, "Kingship," 154ff; the importance of the word *et* (*Inst.*1,2,5; Gaius' *Institutions* [cf.1,1,3,5] were unknown during the Middle Ages except through the Justinian *Corpus*), so often neglected, has been stressed by Max Radin, "Fortescue's *De Laudibus*: A Review," *Michigan Law Review*, XLIV (1944), 182. For the *lex de imperio Vespasiani*, see S. Riccobono, *Fontes iuris Romani antejustiniani* (Florence, 1941), I,154ff, No.15 (with literature); also Theseider, *op.cit.*, 256; the law restricts the emperor's exemption to those cases which were already customary under Augustus and his first successors. The inscription was unknown in the Middle Ages before being rediscovered by Cola di Rienzo; see Burdach, *Rienzo und die geistige Wandlung seiner Zeit* (Berlin, 1913), 304ff, and passim.

[46] *Inst.*1,2,5: *potestatem concessit; C.*1,17,1,7: *translata sunt*. For the problem, see E. Schoenian, *Die Idee der Volkssouveränität im mittelalterlichen Rom* (Leipzig, 1919), esp.17 and 58ff; also A.-J. Carlyle, "The Theory of the Source of Political Authority in the Mediaeval Civilians to the Time of Accursius," *Mélanges Fitting* (Montpellier, 1907), I,181-194, who connects the dispute of the jurists rightly with the conflict between customary and statutory laws.

[47] Gierke, *Gen.R.*, IV,215ff,315ff, and passim.

[48] John of Paris, *De potestate regia et papali*, c.XIX, ed. Dom Jean Leclercq, *Jean de Paris et l'ecclésiologie du XIIIe siècle* (Paris, 1942), 235,11; see below, Ch.VI, nos.51ff.

[49] *Glos.ord.*, on *Nov.*73, rubr.1, v. *De caelo* (below, Ch.VI, n.53). For Cynus, see

have anticipated the essence and main idea of those formulae; but they were neither coined nor applied by him, nor were they quite his. Moreover, with regard to his power of legislator he depended on the Roman Law experts of his own age who, on the whole, ruled out an independent legislative power of the people because they considered the Prince the sole legitimate legislator and ultimate interpreter of the law. Nevertheless, Frederick II derived from the *lex regia* a twofold obligation which he expressed in one clear sentence maintaining, not unlike John of Salisbury, that the Caesar was at once "Father and Son of Justice."

Frederick's interpretation of the ruler's relations with Law was based, so far as the Justinian Law was concerned, not only on the *lex regia* to which he alluded quite often and gave much prominence in his law-book and letters,[50] but also on the *lex digna*. This law, which the glossators customarily cited in connection with the *lex regia* (John of Salisbury, in that respect, was not an exception), did not abolish the ambiguities, nor did it alleviate them. The emperors Theodosius and Valentinian, from whom the *lex digna* issued, had made a statement implying that morally the Prince was obligated to observe even those laws to which legally he was not subjected; but they did not intend to bind themselves to Law without reservations or to deny the validity of the claim according to which the emperor was *legibus solutus*. The sixth-century compilers of the Justinian Code, however, suggested in their summary a more substantial binding to the Law on the part of the emperor when they reproduced the edict:

> It is a word worthy of the majesty of the ruler that the Prince professes himself bound to the Law: so much does our authority depend upon the authority of the Law. And truly, greater than the imperium is the submission of the principate to the laws.[51]

Theseider, *L'Idea imperiale*, 262; Ullmann, *Lucas de Penna*, 175. Cynus makes a clear distinction between the emperor who is *a populo* and the empire which is *divinum a Deo*, the latter a current definition.

[50] For the places, see *Erg.Bd.*, 86 and 183.

[51] C.1,14,4: "Digna vox maiestate regnantis *legibus alligatum se principem profiteri*: adeo de auctoritate iuris nostra pendet auctoritas. Et re vera maius imperio est submittere legibus principatum." See the brief and concise remarks of Schulz, "Kingship," 160f, according to whom the italicized words are an insertion of the later compilers. My translation of the last sentence differs from the one offered by Professor Schulz (p.161), who translates *maius imperio* with "It is nobler for the emperor" (*imperium = imperator*). I prefer the literal translation (*imperio* an ablative dependent on *maius*) because it preserves the antithesis *imperium-princi-*

The mediaeval lawyers could not possibly fail to notice the antinomy prevailing between the maxims *princeps legibus solutus* and *princeps legibus alligatus.* By this antinomy, in addition to other considerations, John of Salisbury was prompted to interpret the Prince as at once *imago aequitatis* and *servus aequitatis*; and this solution, in its turn, appeared to him as a reflection of the biblical model, namely, of Christ who, though King of Kings, "was born under the Law, fulfilled all justice of the Law, and was subjected to the Law *non necessitate, sed voluntate.* For in the Law was his will."[52]

That was, by and large, the expedient to which substantially many mediaeval lawyers resorted when they tried to reconcile the seemingly irreconcilable maxims of the *lex regia* and the *lex digna.* They pointed out that the emperor, though not legally bound by the laws, yet bound himself to the Law and lived voluntarily in accordance with the Law: his subjection to the Law was considered a *velle*, and not an *esse.*[53] Frederick II followed the customary legal exegesis. He, too, referred on one occasion to the *lex digna*, voluntarily recognized a superior judgment, and made a formal account as to the kind of Law to which he considered himself obligated. To the senators and people of Rome he wrote:

> Both all-powerful Reason, who commands the kings, and Nature impose upon us the obligation to enhance in the times of our imperium the glory of the City. . . . In accordance with Civil Law we

---

patus which appears to me as the axis of the whole sentence. See also W. Ensslin, "Der Kaiser in der Spätantike," *Hist.Ztschr.*, CLXXVII (1954), 465. The *lex digna* was paraphrased also in an arenga of Frederick's son, King Henry (VII) in 1228; see J. F. Böhmer, *Acta imperii selecta* (Innsbruck, 1870), I,283, No.326, where one should read *digna voce* (for *vice*).

[52] It was common practice of jurists and political philosophers to link the *lex digna* together with the maxim *legibus solutus*, and thereby to solve that dilemma; see, e.g., Azo, *Summa Instit.*, prooem. ("Quasimodo geniti," the author of which was Boncompagno), fol.267ᵛ: "Licet romanus princeps sit legibus solutus, tamen digna vox ex maiestate regnantis legibus alligatum se principem profiteri." See also Carlyle, *Political Theory*, v,97, and 475f; A. Esmein, "La maxime *Princeps legibus solutus est* dans l'ancien droit public français," *Essays in Legal History* (Oxford, 1913), 203,n.1; 208,n.4; 209,n.1. See also below, n.54, for Frederick II. The difficulty was sometimes overcome by indicating the model of Christ who, though *Rex regum*, was nevertheless *sub lege*; see, e.g., John of Salisbury, *Policraticus*, 523bc, ed. Webb, I,252,6ff: ". . . sicut Rex regum, factus ex muliere, factus sub lege, omnem implevit iustitiam legis, ei non necessitate sed voluntate subiectus; quia in lege voluntas eius."

[53] Schulz, "Kingship," 168 (including n.6) and 163,n.1; cf. above, n.52, for John of Salisbury. See also Esmein, *op.cit.*, 203,n.1.

profess our obligation with a word most worthy [of majesty]. . . .
For although our imperial majesty is free from all laws, it is nevertheless not altogether exalted above the judgment of Reason, herself
the Mother of all Law.[54]

What that statement amounts to may be called the Prince's *voluntas ratione regulata*, his "Will directed by Reason."[55] The
emperor, in his manifesto, strongly emphasized that he was *legibus
solutus*, but at the same time he acknowledged that he was bound
to Reason which commands all kings. The general proportions
were similar to those which he established when he expounded in
his law-book the *lex regia* and proclaimed himself the father and
son of Justice. The passage again reveals the emperor, theoretically, as the intermediate part: he is free from all laws; he is above
the ties of Positive Law, which Reason, complying with public
Utility and changing Necessity, may alter at any time, and of

---

[54] "Ad extollendum imperii nostri temporibus decus Urbis . . . et ratio prepotens,
que regibus imperat, et natura nos obligat, et civiliter obligatos voce dignissima
profitemur . . . Sed quamquam soluta imperialis a quibuscumque legibus sit maiestas,
sic tamen in totum non est exempta iudicio rationis, que iuris est mater." Huillard-
Bréholles, v,162; Theseider, *L'Idea imperiale*, 187. The submission to Reason on the
part of every authority was emphasized by the early glossators; see, e.g., the 12th-
century *Quaestiones de iuris subtilitatibus*, IV,4, ed. Fitting, 58: "Dicat ipsa Ratio,
qua et ipse nituntur auctoritates . . ." See next note. The word *civiliter*, which
might appear ambiguous, obviously refers to *D*.1,1,8: "viva vox est iuris civilis,"
so that we have to consider a contamination of *digna vox* and *viva vox*; see, for
the related law *viva vox*, Steinwenter, "Nomos," 266f, and, for the combination of
ius civile with the *lex digna*, Boncompagno, *Rhetorica novissima*, IX,5, ed. Gaudenzi,
Bibliotheca juridica medii aevi (Bologna, 1892), II, 289. By chance, we have a gloss
of one of Frederick's judges of the *Magna Curia*, Guillelmus de Vinea, on *Lib.aug.*,
III,5, v. *iure proprio*: ". . . quod princeps sit absolutus legibus, tamen iure pri-
vato(?) vivere debet, ut C.de leg.et cons.l.digna vox." Cf. B. Capasso, "Sulla storia
esterna delle costituzioni di Federico II," *Atti della Accademia Pontaniana*, IX
(1871), 439,n.2. To quote another Sicilian, see Andreas de Barulo, on *C*.10,8,3,n.1,
pp.24f: "Nota quod licet Princeps sit legibus solutus, vivit tamen secundum leges,
ut . . . de legib. digna."

[55] See A. P. D'Entrèves, *The Mediaeval Contribution to Political Thought* (Oxford, 1939), 39, for the *voluntas ratione regulata* in the sense of Thomistic doctrines,
and Ullmann, *Lucas de Penna*, 54f, for the principle of the Civilians: "cum voluntas
principis ab aequitate, iustitia et ratione deviet, non est lex." For the emperor's
subjection to Reason, Baldus was later to some extent the authority; see Baldus,
on *D*.4,4,39,n.45, fol.234ᵛ: "magnus est Caesar, sed maior est ratio"; also, *Cons.*, 1,36,
n.6, fol.100ᵛ: "Praeterea princeps potest se subiicere rationi" (with reference to
D.2,1,14); also *Cons.*, 1,333,n.1, fol.105ᵛ: "Item princeps iura utilia potest con(ce)dere
sine causa . . . nam ipse [princeps] et ratio idem sunt." See also Matthaeus de
Afflictis, on *Lib.aug.*, 1,7,n.37, fol.57ᵛ, who refers continuously to Baldus: ". . . Imperator licet sit solutus legibus, tamen non est solutus a praeceptis divinis et sanctae matris ecclesiae . . . Item non est solutus a dictamine rationis, quia est animal
rationale . . . Ideo princeps etiam ligatur naturali ratione. . . ."

which Reason is the mother as he is the father; but Reason is also above the Prince as she is above any king, and to her the emperor is bound: he is *legibus solutus*, but *ratione alligatus*.

The doctrine was not without danger, since the interpretation of Reason might easily depend on the Prince alone. Indeed, less than a century later this semi-divine *Ratio* will become a *ratio regis et patriae*, synonymous with Reason of State, and what formerly was a goal in itself will turn into a tool, a mere instrument of statecraft. Reason, in many respects, was all that already under Frederick II; yet, in legal philosophy she still showed the features of a goddess—a manifestation of Nature equal to God.[56]

IUSTITIA MEDIATRIX

To worship the absolute power of legal Reason was nothing peculiar to Frederick II and his advisers. The lawyers, and especially the Civilians (who were also the true rediscoverers of a non-ecclesiastical Stoicism and therewith the initiators of the later humanistic Neo-Stoicism of Petrarchan pattern), were generally fond of playing with the notion of Reason, and of hallowing Reason as well as Justice like ancient deities. The leading lawyer of the generation just before Frederick II, the great Placentinus (died 1192), was in all probability the author of a legal dialogue called *Quaestiones de iuris subtilitatibus*, the poetical prologue of which is of some relevance here.[57] In this prologue, the author actually erected a literary monument of the goddesses of Law when describing, solemnly and in glowing colors, the beauty and majesty of the *Templum Iustitiae* which he pretended to have dis-

[56] For the necessity of producing new laws caused *per rerum mutationes et temporum*, see *Lib.aug.*, I,38, ed. Cervone, 85, the preamble of which was framed after C.1,17,2,18; the leading idea, found already in the *Dictatus papae* (§7), was of course repeated over and over again. See also, for the parallelism of divine Law (*ius gentium*) and natural reason, the preamble of *Lib.aug.*, I,16, Cervone, 35: "Iuris gentium induxit auctoritas et naturalis haec ratio non abhorret, ut tutela cuilibet sui corporis permittatur"; further *Lib.aug.*, I,31, where the emperor claims ("Hac igitur consulta ratione commoniti . . .") to be prompted by the advice of Reason.

[57] The *Quaestiones de iuris subtilitatibus* were ascribed by their editor, H. Fitting (see above, n.35), to Irnerius, and more recently, for indeed very good reasons, to Placentinus; see Hermann Kantorowicz, *Glossators*, 181-205, and also his study, "The Poetical Sermon of a Mediaeval Jurist: Placentinus and his 'Sermo de Legibus,'" *Warburg Journal*, II (1938-39), 22ff; the *Sermo* betrays a poetical spirit similar to that of the prologue of the *Quaestiones* and quite alien to Irnerius. Absolute certainty as to the authorship cannot, of course, be established at present.

covered, by chance, in a pleasant grove on the top of a hill.[58] In that imaginary shrine he saw Reason, Justice, and Equity dwelling together with the six civic Virtues—a "celestial banquet," so it seemed to him, rather than anything on earth. *Ratio* ranked highest; she was seated on the head of Justice from where she observed "with her star-like eyes and her flashing keenness of mind" the remotest things, even those far beyond the precincts of the temple. *Iustitia,* "in her ineffable habit of dignity,"[59] was the central figure "observing with many sighs the things of both God and men."[60] She embraced her last-born daughter, *Aequitas,* whose features mirrored nothing but kindness and good-will as she tried to balance the scales held by her mother. The other daughters, the six civic Virtues,[61] surrounded Justice like guardians. Within the shrine some space was reserved for the inaccessible Holy of Holies, the *adytum,* which was separated by a wall of glass on which, with golden letters, the full texts of Justinian's law-books were inscribed. It was only through that glass wall that the spectator viewed the deities "as in a mirror." Inside the *adytum,* "a not too

[58] The prologue of the *Quaestiones,* ed. Fitting, 53f, has been edited also by Hermann Kantorowicz, *Glossators,* 183f. The concern here is not the literary genre in general of poetical visions, which was very common in 12th-century literature, but its application to a juristic technical tractate. A less philosophical variety of *templum Iustitiae* is described by Anselmus de Orto, *Iuris civilis instrumentum,* prol., ed. Scialoja, in: *Bibliotheca iuridica medii aevi,* II,87; cf. Fitting, *op.cit.,* 7f.

[59] ". . . michi visa est ineffabili dignitatis habitu Iustitia." The author alludes to the customary definition of Justice: "Iustitia est *habitus* mentis bonus vel bene constitutae" (e.g. Azo, *Summa Institutionum,* on *Inst.*1,1, fol.269); cf. Fitting, *Schriften,* 160 (also 34); H. Kantorowicz, *Glossators,* 60ff,240, also 272,16. See further *Glos.ord.* on *Inst.*1,1, v. *Iustitia:* ". . . quasi habitus mentis bonus. Sed Tullius sic definit: 'Iustitia est habitus animi . . . suam cuilibet tribuens dignitatem.'" The reference of all glossators is Cicero, *De invent.,* II,159. See below, n.61.

[60] ". . . causas enim et Dei et hominum crebris advertebat suspiriis." The melancholy of Justice is traditional; see below, n.64, for Gellius. *Aequitas,* though partly identical with *Iustitia,* belongs to the sphere of practical *Ius;* cf. *Glos.ord.* on *D.*1, 1,1, v. *Iustitia:* "Ius est ars boni et aequi, ut subiicit; et iustitia nihil aliud est quam ipsa aequitas et bonitas: ergo iustitiam habet matrem."

[61] The six Virtues enumerated by the author are *Religio, Pietas, Gratia, Vindicatio, Observantia, Veritas,* again in agreement with Cicero, *De invent.,* II,159ff (above n.59). That they are daughters of Justice agrees with the common opinion (ultimately deriving from Aristotle) according to which all Virtues may be reduced to Justice; see *Nicom. Ethics,* 1129b, with the Latin version by William of Moerbeke: "In iustitia autem simul omnis virtus est, et perfecta maxime virtus"; cf. Thomas Aquinas, *In decem libros Ethicorum Aristotelis ad Nicomachum expositio,* ed. R. M. Spiazzi (Turin and Rome, 1949), 246f (No.642 for Aristotle's text, and No.907 for Thomas' commentary: "in ipsa iustitia simul comprehenditur omnis virtus"). See also below, n.156.

modest number of honorable men," apparently the Clergy of Justice, was in attendance at the glass wall, ever ready to revise the texts of the golden lettering whenever a passage appeared disarrayed to the examining eyes of law-weighing Equity.[62] Outside the *adytum*, finally, a venerable teacher of Law discussed with his auditors difficult legal problems, and it was the discussion between this interpreter of the Law and his audience which the author of the *Quaestiones* pretended to reproduce in his learned tractate.

What the author described in the story framing his story was actually a vision of Jurisprudence at work within the shrine of Justice. The vision itself was stimulated by Justinian's letter to Tribonian in which the emperor disclosed that he ordered "to build up the matter of Law in a most beautiful work and, as it were, to consecrate a proper and most holy temple to Justice," and by his slightly later letter to the Senate in which he declared he wished to show from how many thousands of books "the temple of the *Iustitia Romana* was built."[63] Some additional colors for depicting this goddess may have been borrowed from Aulus Gellius, the second-century jurist and rhetor, who, in his *Attic Nights*, reproduced from Stoic sources a similar literary portrait of *Iustitia*, "an awe-inspiring virgin with penetrating eyes and with some venerable grief in her dignity," and attended by the perfect judge whom Gellius called *Iustitiae antistes*, "the priest of

---

[62] Hermann Kantorowicz, *Glossators*, 185, was surely correct when he suggested that the *honorabiles viri, non quidem pauci*, were the "priestly ministers of the law." Apparently they were identical with the *galaxia* which the 12th-century author of a *Materia Institutionum*, ed. Fitting, *Schriften*, 148,10, mentioned as the inhabitants of the *templum*: "Sicut quidam philosophus ait: 'Qui iusticiam tenuerint, coluerint, auxerint, illum incolunt locum, quem in templo hoc medium vides,' et ostendit galaxiam." The passage refers undoubtedly to the *templum Iustitiae*, though it is not obvious who the *philosophus quidam* may have been.

[63] C.1,17,1,5, and 1,17,2,20a; also the constitution *Deo auctore* (§5) preceding the *Digest*. The *templum Iustitiae* is often quoted and interpreted by the mediaeval jurists; see, e.g., Marinus de Caramanico, on *Lib.aug.*, 1,prooem., v. *Et iura condendo*, ed. Cervone, 6, whereas Andreas of Isernia, *In usus feudorum commentaria*, praeludia, n.16 (Naples, 1571) fol.2v, consecrates his own work as a *proprium et sacratissimum templum iustitiae*. Interesting are the later jurists who connect the *sacerdotes iustitiae* (that is, the *iurisconsulti*) with the *templum*, as, e.g., Cujas, on *D.*1, 1,1, *Opera* (Prato, 1839), vii,col.11f, or François Hotman, on *Inst.*1,1 (Venice, 1569), p.7; whereas Louis d'Orléans, *Les Ouvertures des Parlements faictes par les Roys de France* (Lyon, 1620), 399-446, devotes his whole long-winded "Second Remonstrance" (1590) to the subject of the Temple of Justice, especially to the *Temple eternal de la justice Françoise* (see below, Ch.vii,n.334). See also my remarks in *American Journal of Archaeology*, lvii (1953), 67, concerning the non-architectural character of these and other temples of Justice.

Justice."[64] Placentinus, or the author of the *Quaestiones*, may have been inspired also by other sources,[65] and in later times reflections on the *Templum Iustitiae* were anything but rare.[66] What matters here, however, is that the author not only used the metaphor of the Temple of Justice, but integrated the personifications into the customary hierarchic system of legal philosophy. Reason, in his tractate, eventually revealed herself as identical with the Law of Nature which was practically one with Divine Law.[67] Equity belonged without question to the sphere of Positive Law, the human or man-made laws issued for the government of the state. That left Justice, the most prominent figure to whom the shrine was dedicated, in an intermediate position.[68] She alone had a share in both the Natural Law above and the Positive Law below her, although she was equal to neither. Justice, to be sure, was the end and the ultimate test of every judgment, of every state and of every human institution. But *Iustitia* herself was, properly speaking, not Law at all, although she was present in every law and existed before any law ever was issued.[69] *Iustitia* was an Idea, or a goddess.[70]

[64] Gellius, *Noctes Att.*, xiv,4, renders mainly Chrysippus' description of Justice: "Forma atque filo virginali, aspectu vehementi et formidabili, luminibus oculorum acribus, neque humilis neque atrocis, sed reverendae cuiusdam tristitiae dignitate." See above, n.60, for the *tristitia*. Gellius' description of the ideal judge, *qui Iustitiae antistes est*, and of whom he demands "oportere esse gravem, sanctum, severum, incorruptum . . . , vi et maiestate aequitatis veritatisque terrificum," has exercised considerable influence on mediaeval jurists; see, e.g., Bonaguida of Arezzo (ca.1255), *Summa introductoria super officio advocationis*, I,c.1, ed. Agathon Wunderlich, *Anecdota quae processum civilem spectant* (Göttingen, 1841), 136f, who like others emphasizes the *gravitas* which the judge should display. The Gellius passage certainly impressed the 16th-century jurists such as Cujas and Hotman (above, n.63) as well as Guillaume Budé, *Annotationes in XXIIII Pandectarum libros* (Lyon, 1551), 70 (on *D.*1,1,1).

[65] The so-called *Mythographus III* (12th century) seems to have demanded that *Iustitia* be represented as *puella erecta in coelum*, having *vultum virgineum, aureum vel vitreum*; cf. Hans Liebeschütz, *Fulgentius Metaforalis* (Studien der Bibliothek Warburg, IV, Berlin and Leipzig, 1926), 53. The "glassy" face lets us recall the glass wall of the *Quaestiones*; however, such *cubicula holovitrea* were popular in visionary literature; see, e.g., *Acta S. Sebastiani*, in *Patr.Lat.*, xvii,1045A-B, quoted by Laistner, in *Harvard Theological Review*, xxxiv (1941), 260.

[66] See above, n.58, and nos. 62-64.

[67] *Quaestiones*, iv,6, ed. Fitting, 59,4; H. Kantorowicz, *Glossators*, 185.

[68] *Quaestiones*, iv,6: ". . . Iustitia quam pro officii dignitate potiori gradu collocavi."

[69] The sentence *Prius fuit iustitia quam ius* (*Glos.ord.* on *D.*1,1,1, v. *Iustitia*) was repeated over and over again; see, e.g., Bartolus, on *Inst.*1,1,n.1 (Venice, 1567), fol.68v: "Iustitia est prius quam ius sicut abstractio vel abstractum ante concretum . . ." Similarly Baldus: "Iustitia creatoris fuit ab aeterno antequam orbis crearetur et formaretur" and "[Iustitia in abstracto] est mater et causa iuris"; cf.

She was, in fact, an "extra-legal premise" of legal thought.[71] And like every Idea she had also the function of a mediator, a *Iustitia mediatrix*, mediating between divine and human laws, or between Reason and Equity.

One is tempted to inquire into contemporary art to discover whether perhaps some sculpture or painting rendered the mediaeval lawyer's vision of Justice and her shrine. It is true, the *Iustitia Caesaris* is said to have been represented in the triumphal arch of Frederick II at Capua, where her more than life-sized bust was placed in a key position below the throne of the emperor and directly above the entrance of the gate, and where, so we are told, she was flanked, right and left, by the busts of judges (fig. 17).[72] However, the whole composition of the figures of the Capuan Gate is too uncertain to draw final conclusions, and the arrangement was at any rate very different from what the author of the *Quaestiones* described.[73]

Ullmann, "Baldus," 389,n.9, and 390,n.16. *Iustitia in abstracto* is mentioned already in *Glos.ord.* on *Inst.*1,1, v. *Iustitia*: "Aliquando consideratur iustitia prout est in abstracto, ut tunc iustitia est constans et perpetua."

[70] *Iustitia* as an abstract idea: above, n.69. Justice as a *Virtus* is among the oldest definitions; e.g., Placentinus, *Summa Institutionum*, 24, ed. Fitting, *Schriften*, 221: "ius est preceptum vel scientia, set iusticia virtus est"; also in the *Glos.ord.* on *Inst.*1,1. The definition of Justice in the *Institutes* as *constans et perpetua voluntas* led, on the one hand, to interpret her as a *habitus* (above, n.59), and, on the other, to interpret her as equal with God or the divine *voluntas*; see, e.g., *Glos.ord.* on *Inst.*1,1: "Haec iustitiae definitio potest intelligi de divina iustitia, quasi dicendum: Divina iustitia est voluntas constans et perpetua." The 16th-century jurists, while still depending on the *Glossa ordinaria*, asked whether Justice was a *virtus* or a *dea*, and decided (on the basis of *D.*1,1,1) for the goddess because the jurisprudents were called *sacerdotes* and there were no *sacerdotes virtutum humanarum*; hence, Justinian must have defined *Iustitiam deam, Iovis filiam* (Hotman, *loc.cit.* [above, n.63]); and Cujas (*ibid.*, col. 12) says straightforwardly: "*Iustitiam namque colimus, quasi Deam sanctissimam.*"

[71] Ullmann, *Lucas de Penna*, 35ff, also his study "Baldus," 388ff.

[72] Willemsen, *Triumphtor*, 65ff, has adopted my interpretation (*Kaiser Friedrich II.*, 485f) which I purposely refrained from repeating in *Erg.Bd.*, 211; cf. Baethgen, in *DA*, XI (1955), 624, on Willemsen's hypothesis. The interpretation of the flanking busts as judges ("hinc et hinc imagines erant duorum iudicum") goes back to Lucas de Penna, on *C.*11,41 (40),4 (Lyon, 1582), 446, glossing on the words *imagines consecrari*: "id est, consecratas apponi, vel in porta collocari, ut in porta civitatis Capuae." It is interesting at any rate that in connection with the "consecration of images" the jurist thinks of the "apposita statua Frederici Imperatoris," a ruler he otherwise dislikes as an enemy of the Church. Lucas concludes his description of the Capuan Gate, saying: "Ex his operibus possent dici regales statuae consecrari; alias cessante in regibus iustitia, dicendi sunt potius execrari quam consecrari." His allegation to Andreas of Isernia, *In usus feudorum*, on *De statutis et consuetudinibus*, n.28, fol.315ᵛ, refers to the parallelism between images of kings and images of saints or of Christ.

[73] For a reconstruction, see Willemsen, *Triumphtor*, pl.106, and, for the magnifi-

Far more suggestive is a representation of the early fourteenth century: Ambrogio Lorenzetti's fresco of the *Buon Governo* in the Palazzo Pubblico at Siena.[74] The allegorical contents of the picture, complicated and even obscure as they are, shall not bother us here. It will be sufficient to point out the two main figures, Justice and Good Government (fig. 18a-b). Justice is more than life-sized, indeed a *puella erecta in coelum* and *aspectu vehementi et formidabili*.[75] She is enthroned on a raised platform. Hovering above her head is *Sapientia* who is synonymous with, or takes the place of, *Ratio* in the *Templum Iustitiae* and to whom Justice raises her eyes; at least we now understand what the author of the *Quaestiones* had in mind when he said that Reason "reclined on the head of Justice."[76] Below the feet of *Iustitia* is another "last-born" daughter, *Concordia*, whom the jurists often

---

cent female head which can be appreciated now only after the plaster "embellishments" have been removed, see pls.44-49. That *Iustitia* actually could take the place normally reserved for the Virgin or *Ecclesia*, is shown in a 12th-century enamel from Stablo (Collection of Mr. and Mrs. Alistair Bradley Martin), published by Yvonne Hackenbroch, "A Triptych in the Style of Godefroi de Clair," *Connoisseur*, CXXXIV (1954), 185-188. The iconographic problem is involved, and I may discuss it in another connection; see, however, Francis Wormald, "The Crucifix and the Balance," *Warburg Journal*, I (1937-38), 276-280, for the idea *Crux statera corporis Christi, quod est Ecclesia*. It is, of course, the balance (*statera*) which suggested the representation of *Iustitia* in that place. See fig.19, a reproduction kindly placed at my disposal by permission of the owners through Dr. R. H. Randall, Jr.

[74] For a description, see Ernst von Meyenburg, *Ambrogio Lorenzetti* (Heidelberg diss., 1903), 51ff; for bibliography, see Giulia Sinibaldi, *I Lorenzetti* (Siena, 1933), 209ff. See also L. Zdekauer, "IUSTITIA: Immagine e Idea," *Bullettino Senese di storia patria*, XX (1913), 384-425, esp.400ff, who connects the *ideale nuovo della Giustizia* with the new spirit of the Italian Communes in and after the thirteenth century and who from this angle discusses also the Lorenzetti paintings, but unfortunately omits to consider seriously the new jurisprudence. I am very much obliged to Professor T. E. Mommsen for reminding me of Lorenzetti's *Iustitia mediatrix*.

[75] See above, n.65. Justice occasionally seems to have been represented like a crown-wearing man, for in *Paris, Bibl.Nat. MS.lat.541* (late 13th or early 14th century) we find the remark: "Iustitia pingitur ut vir habens coronam auream"; see *Catalogue général des MSS latins de la Bibl.Nat.*, ed. Ph. Lauer (Paris, 1939), I,190.

[76] The text says: "cuius in vertice recumbebat." H. Kantorowicz, *Glossators*, 185, interprets: "*Ratio* finally, seated gloriously, if uncomfortably, on the head of *Iustitia*." I wonder, however, whether *in vertice* has not simply the meaning "above." The efforts of H. Kantorowicz, p.186, to connect the figures of the *templum* with representations of the "Virgin in Majesty" (e.g., Duccio's Madonna Rucellai) are not fortunate, and the image of the Virgin with the Dove perched on her head in a New Minster MS belonging, as it does, to the filiations of the Utrecht Psalter, should not have been mentioned in that connection at all; see, for the New Minster drawing, my study "The Quinity of Winchester," *Art Bulletin*, XXIX (1947), 73ff.

mention in that connection.[77] On the same platform we find *Buon Governo* enthroned, a gigantic emperor-like figure surrounded by six Virtues. Hovering above the head of "Government" is *Caritas*, flanked by *Fides* and *Spes*. While it is obvious that the Christian Cardinal Virtues are represented, it should yet be indicated that Charity may refer also to *Amor patriae*, according to the definition common around 1300: *Amor patriae in radice Charitatis fundatur*, "Love of the Fatherland is founded in the root of Charity."[78] This patriotic meaning is perhaps alluded to by the emperor-like figure in black and white, the colors of Siena, below whose feet we find the Roman twins with the she-wolf, Siena's coat-of-arms symbolizing the city's foundation by Rome.

The Lorenzetti painting, admittedly, is late and—charged as it is with artistic obscurities of Renaissance allegorism—less limpid than the vision of the twelfth-century jurist. Nevertheless, the picture conveys some notion of what, by and large, the mediaeval lawyer may have had in mind. The fresco certainly displays Justice in the role of a *Iustitia mediatrix*, and the "emperor" or Good Government as the counterpart of *Iustitia*.

In connection with the visionary Temple of Justice of Placentinus, attention has been called occasionally to a miniature of an earlier date showing the emperor as mediator in legal matters. The miniature is found in the magnificent Gospelbook which Emperor Henry II, in 1022 or 1023, donated to the Abbey of Monte Cassino (fig. 20).[79] The folio preceding the Fourth Gospel,

[77] See, e.g., Bartolus, on *Inst.*1,1,n.1, fol.68: [Iustitia] tribuens . . . Deo religionem, parentibus obedientiam, paribus concordiam . . ." See also Baldus, on *D.*1,1,5,n.4, fol.10ᵛ, and innumerable other places.

[78] Tolomeo of Lucca, in his continuation of Aquinas' *De regimine principum*, III,c.4, ed. J. Mathis (Rome and Turin, 1948), 41; see below, Ch.v, n.151. Lorenzetti's *Caritas* reminded Meyenburg rightly of *Amor*; see R. Freyhan, "The Evolution of the Caritas Figure in the Thirteenth and Fourteenth Centuries," *Warburg Journal*, XI (1948), 68ff, who, however, misses *Caritas* as *Amor patriae*. The connection of the *Buon Governo* with the *Amor patriae* is mentioned by Zdekauer (above, n.74). Millard Meiss, *Painting in Florence and Siena After the Black Death* (Princeton, 1951), 51, interprets the Lorenzetti Caritas as both *amor dei* and *amor proximi*.

[79] See Schramm, *Deutsche Kaiser*, pl.86 and pp. 112ff,198, and the very thorough study by Herbert Bloch, "Monte Cassino, Byzantium, and the West in the Earlier Middle Ages," *Dumbarton Oaks Papers*, III (1946), 177ff (full bibliography, p.181, n.53). A. Gaudenzi, "Il tempio della Giustizia a Ravenna e a Bologna e il luogo in esso tenuto dal diritto longobardo," *Mélanges Fitting* (Montpellier, 1908), II,699ff, who combined the miniature with Placentinus' vision (then still attributed to Irnerius), has been misled to rather extravagant conclusions. It may be mentioned

where a representation of St. John would be expected, shows instead a full-page image of the emperor with a number of personifications. It is a highly political and legal-philosophical picture. In the center, within a big circle, the emperor is enthroned in full regalia. In the upper corners we recognize *Iustitia* and *Pietas*; to. the right and left, placed in smaller circles, are *Sapientia* and *Prudentia*, attendants and throne companions of kingship since earliest times. In the corners below the ruler are *Lex* and *Ius*, the symbols of Positive Law.[80] They depend upon the emperor and execute his will. "At the emperor's behest Law and Right condemn the tyrant," reads the verse inscription around the circle below the emperor's feet: the tyrant shall be executed if the emperor so wills.[81] The emperor's will, however, is directed by inspiration from above. To be sure, it is not *Ratio*, the star-eyed goddess of the lawyers, who gives advice to the Prince; however, *Ratio* is not absent from the image. In the circle above the emperor's head we recognize the Holy Spirit descending from heaven in the shape of the dove, the symbol also of Divine Wisdom and Reason.[82] The dove infuses right judgment into the mind of the emperor who, in turn, imparts his inspiration to the executive forces of Law and Right.

In this scene of judgment Henry II clearly functions as mediator between divine Reason and human Law. But, as behooves an Ottonian Prince, the emperor's mediatorship is expressed "liturgically," that is, by the *epiklesis* of the Spirit. The picture's language

---

obiter that Emperor Henry III had the by-name *Linea Iustitiae*; see Wipo, *Gesta Chuonradi*, prol., ed. Bresslau, p.8,5.

[80] See, for personifications in general, Adolf Katzenellenbogen, *Allegories of the Virtues and Vices in Mediaeval Art* (Studies of the Warburg Institute, x; London, 1939—cf. p.36 for the important Monte Cassino Gospels), and, for the important late-antique centuries, Glanville Downey, "Personifications of Abstract Ideas in Antioch Mosaics," *Transactions of the American Philological Association,* LXIX (1938), 349ff; also my study in *American Journal of Archaeology,* LVII (1953), 65ff, for Virtues as throne companions. The most important authority on the Virtues during the Middle Ages was probably Cicero, *De finibus,* 2,21 (cf. Augustine, *De civitate,* 5,20), and especially *De invent.,* 2,159ff, a place frequently expounded by the mediaeval lawyers; see H. Kantorowicz, *Glossators,* Index s.v. "Cicero." Since Justice appeared as the aggregate of all virtues, the lawyers took some interest in systematizing and discussing the virtues at large, and their discussions may have given new impulses to the artists as well.

[81] "Caesaris ad nutum dampnunt Lex Iusque tyrannum." For the political situation and the tyrant referred to, see Bloch, "Monte Cassino," 185f.

[82] H. Kantorowicz, *Glossators,* 186.

is theological, and not jurisprudential: the emperor is mediator and executor of the divine will through the power of the Holy Spirit, and not through the secular spirit of legal science.

The Ottonian miniature may not be as relevant to the twelfth-century lawyer's vision of the Temple of Justice as has been assumed occasionally; it is instructive nevertheless. For it illustrates extremely well to what extent the concept of rulership has drifted away from the liturgical sphere in the span of time separating that miniature from the Hohenstaufen period. It would be quite amiss, however, to assume that the transcendental values distinguishing rulership in the liturgical age were simply abandoned in the following period when political theories began to crystallize around learned jurisprudence. The contrary is true; and it is true not only with regard to the ruler's mediatorship, but it is true in general. The mediaeval patterns and concepts of kingship were not simply wiped out, neither by Frederick II nor by others: practically all the former values survived—but they were translated into new secular and chiefly juristic modes of thinking and thus survived by transference in a secular setting. Moreover, the patterns and values were rationalized not by means of theology, but preferably by means of scientific jurisprudence.

Emperor Henry II was shown as a judge receiving advice through the dove of the Spirit. It would be difficult indeed to imagine the dove alighting on the head of Frederick II whose images—we may recall his statue from the Capuan Gate or his famous gold *augustales*—betray ideas and ideals far remote from sacrament, altar, and unction. If nevertheless this emperor could claim, as he repeatedly did, that in all official acts of state, in legislation and jurisdiction, he was directly inspired by the Divinity, then the justification for this assertion was taken mainly from the law-books of Justinian whose example he followed.[83] Apart from celestial inspiration, Frederick II like every mediaeval ruler claimed also to be the vicegerent of the Deity. In the most prominent place—in the great Prologue of his *Liber augustalis*—the emperor stated that after the Fall of Man kings and princes were

---

[83] Cf. *Erg.Bd.*, 84; *C.*1,1,1, also *C.*5,4,28,1, and other passages. The Holy Spirit, to be sure, was not absent from eulogies praising Frederick II; see, e.g., Kloos, "Nikolaus von Bari," 171, §8: ". . . super quem almus spiritus quasi apis super florem oderiferum requiescit."

created by natural Necessity as well as by divine Providence, and
that they were given the task,

> being arbiters of life and death for their peoples, to establish what
> each man's fortune, lot, and state shall be, as though they acted in
> a certain way as the executors of the divine Providence.[84]

It is most significant, however, that this traditional royal office of
executor divinae Providentiae was couched, not in the words of
Scripture or patristic texts of which any number would have been
available, but in the words which, according to Seneca, the
Emperor Nero could have said:

> Have I not been chosen to act on earth as vicar of the gods? I am
> the arbiter of life and death for the peoples. What each man's lot
> and state shall be is laid into my hands. And what Fortune would
> bestow on any mortal, she makes known through my mouth.[85]

Frederick's chancery, it is true, mitigated what perhaps might
appear as haughty and arrogant language; but it remains a fact
that the office of vicar of God was interpreted by Frederick's legal
advisers after the model of Seneca's emperor, and was couched in
words which were supposed to have been spoken by Nero, who in
mediaeval lore was not considered a model ruler.

It was no less significant that the glossators liked to gloss on
purely biblical quotations by referring to Digest and Code, Novels
and Institutes. Marinus de Caramanico (to take an example
picked at random), when pointing out in his gloss on the Prologue
of the *Liber augustalis* that "kings and princes are from God,"
does not quote Romans 13, as would have been natural, but quotes
Justinian's *Code*; and in order to gloss on the famous words *Per
me reges regnant* he sends his reader not to Proverbs 8: 15 but to

---

[84] *Lib.aug.*, prooem., Cervone, 4: "Qui [principes gentium] *vitae necisque arbitri
gentibus qualem quisque fortunam, sortem, statumque haberet*, velut executores
quodammodo divinae providentiae stabilirent . . ." The italics indicate the words
borrowed from Seneca. See next note.

[85] Seneca, *De clementia*, 1,1,2: "Egone ex omnibus mortalibus placui electusque
sum, qui in terris deorum vice fungerer? Ego *vitae necisque gentibus arbiter; qualem
quisque sortem statumque habeat*, in mea manu positum est; quid cuique mortalium
fortuna datum velit, meo ore pronuntiat." The borrowing on the part of the imperial jurists was noticed immediately; see Marinus da Caramanico, on the Prooemium, v. *Statumque haberet*. More recently, the conformities have been indicated
by Antonio Marongiu, "Concezione della sovranità," 42f, and "Note federiciane,"
296ff (above, n.16). Seneca's *De clementia* was quoted by the jurists over and over
again; see, e.g., below, Ch.VII,n.405.

Code 1,1,8,1, where these words are cited, and to the rubric of
Novel 73, where a related idea is expressed.[86] And Marinus de
Caramanico merely followed the general custom of the Civilians.
In other words, the secular authority of the Roman law-books
appeared to the jurists, as jurists, more valuable and important
and more convincing an evidence than the sacred literature, so
that even straight quotations from the Bible were reached, preferably, by a detour; that is, by citing the volumes of Roman Law.
To be sure, the glossators and post-glossators also quoted Scripture
often enough whenever it fitted their purpose; but their supreme
authority was the Law.

It now fell to Justinian's law-books to replace and restore the
religious values of kingship which, as an effluence of liturgical and
sacramental concepts, had been generally acknowledged until the
Struggle of Investiture. At the height of that struggle, the Norman
Anonymous, as we recall, defended more vigorously than any other
writer the priestly character of the king whom he interpreted as
the genuine *rex et sacerdos* "by grace"; that is, by the power of
the sacrament of consecration.[87] He even conceded to the royal
christus Domini the ministration of the chief sacrificial acts. The
Israelitic king of the Old Testament, declared the Norman,
"offered himself a living host, a holy host, a host that pleases God";
he alone is said to have immolated spiritually because along with
the sacrifices of praise and of the afflicted spirit he brought the true
sacrificium iustitiae. Contrariwise (said the Anonymous), the Levi-
rate only reproduced the king's spiritual sacrifice by symbolic
actions when they offered on the altar the non-spiritual visible
sacrificium carnale.[88]

---

[86] See v. *Divinae provisionis,* ed. Cervone, 4: "Nota quod reges et principes sint
a Deo, ut ... [C.7,37,3,5] et ... [C.1,17,1,1] et ... [C.1,1,8,1]; ibi, per me reges regnant
etc. et in ... [Nov.73, rubr.]." It is not to the contrary if Andreas of Isernia,
Usus feudorum, prael.,n.46, fol.8, says: "Item attendendum, quod in hoc opusculo
producuntur plerunque authoritates sacrae Scripturae: nam illae allegantur in
causis sicut leges scriptae," a statement which he bolsters again by quoting Roman
Law passages. Cf. McIlwain, *The High Court of Parliament* (New Haven, 1910),
99,n.2, for a relevant statement in 17th-century England, though for very different
reasons: " 'Tis from the Statute Book, not the Bible, that we must judg of the Power
·our Kings are invested withal ..."

[87] Above, Ch.III,n.13, also n.21.

[88] *MGH,LdL,* III,665,38: "... et regis est sacrificare et immolare in spiritu. Ipsius
etenim est exhibere se ipsum hostiam vivam, hostiam sanctam, hostiam Deo pla-
centem (Rom. 12: 1), et immolare Deo sacrificium laudis, sacrificium iusticie (Ps.
4: 6), sacrificium spiritus contribulati, quod totum significatum est per carnale

Very different from that emotional author's proximity to the altar were the new ideas about both the royal *sacrificium iustitiae* and the ancient ideal of the *rex et sacerdos*. The Prince did not cease to be "king and priest," but he regained his former priestly character—shattered, or at least reduced, after the Investiture Struggle—through the high pretensions of Roman legal philosophy which compared the jurisprudents with priests. The ancient solemnity of liturgical language mingled strangely with the new solemnity of the Civilians and their idiom when King Roger II of Sicily, in the Prologue of his Assizes (1140), called his collection of laws an offering of mercy and justice and an oblation to God, and then added:

> *In qua oblatione*—By this oblation the royal office presumes for itself a certain privilege of priesthood; wherefore some wise man and jurisprudent called the law interpreters "Priests of the Law."[89]

A few words in this Prologue are reminiscent of the Canon of the Mass.[90] But the chief source of the Prologue was Justinian who

---

sacrificium, quod sacerdos offerebat iuxta ritum visibilem sacramenti." The author may have drawn from the *Liber responsalis*, attributed to Gregory the Great, and the *Antiphonae de suceptione regum* (*PL*, LXXVIII,828B); cf. Williams, *Norman Anonymous*, 168,n.566. In that responsory the *rex et sacerdos* ideal is stressed quite powerfully: "℞. Elegit te Dominus sacerdotem sibi, ad sacrificandum ei hostiam laudis. ℣. Tunc acceptabis sacrificium iustitiae, oblationes et holocausta. *Ad sacrificandum (ei hostiam laudis). ℣. Immola Deo sacrificium laudis et redde Altissimo vota tua." The plural *regum* in the rubric of this *susceptaculum* suggests a considerable age, since it stands probably for the plurality of the Eastern emperors; see, for this plural in the political prayers, G. B. Ladner, "The Portraits of Emperors in Southern Italian *Exultet* Rolls and the Liturgical Commemoration of the Emperor," *Speculum*, XVII (1942), 189ff.

89 F. Brandileone, *Il diritto Romano nelle leggi Normanne e Sveve del regno di Sicilia* (Turin, 1884), 94: "In qua oblatione regni officium quoddam sibi sacerdotii vendicat privilegium: unde quidam sapiens legisque peritus iuris interpretes iuris sacerdotes appellat." See also Hans Niese, *Die Gesetzgebung der normannischen Dynastie im Regnum Siciliae* (Halle, 1910), 46, who rightly stresses the phrase *regni officium*, that is, the office character of kingship. See also Gierke, *Gen.R.*, III,563,n.123; Maitland, *Political Theories*, 34 and 141f.

90 Compare the first words of King Roger's Prooemium—*Dignum et necessarium est*—with the Preface of the Mass: *Vere dignum et iustum est*, and the relative junction *In qua oblatione* with *Quam oblationem* before the Consecration. Neither the similarities nor the slight variations are incidental; one wanted the assonance with the Mass, but refrained from profanation. These scruples were less prominent under Frederick II; see, e.g., the letter about the victory over the Lombards (Vinea, *Epp.*, II,1): "*Exultet iam* Romani Imperii culmen, *et pro tanti victoria* principis mundus gaudeat universus"; also Vinea, *Epp.*, II,45: "*Exultet iam* universa turba fidelium . . . et pro tanta victoria principis precipue gaudeatis"; and compare the *Praeconium paschale*: "*Exultet iam* Angelica turba caelorum . . . et pro tanti Regis

issued one of his laws as a *piisima sive sacrosancta oblatio quam Deo dedicamus.*[91] Similar ideas were expressed in other sections of his law-books, and they were repeated by Frederick II and others.[92] That is to say, the source and point of reference no longer were the Book of Kings and the Psalter, but the laws of Justinian; and it was after the model of this emperor that the new books of codified law represented the *sacrificium iustitiae*: the books themselves were the rulers' oblation and offering.[93]

Moreover, from the first paragraph of the *Digest* sprung the

---

victoria tuba insonet salutaris. Gaudeat et tellus . . ." Hans-Martin Schaller, *Die Kanzlei Kaiser Friedrichs II.: Ihr Personal und ihr Sprachstil* (Göttingen diss., typescript, 1951), 84ff, has assembled from the letters and manifestoes of Frederick II a great number of similar liturgical phrasings, and has pointed out that, though a tendency to that liturgified language may be detected sporadically also in the *arengae* of Frederick I and Henry VI, it was nevertheless only under Frederick II that the dictators of the imperial chancery applied the liturgical language systematically for the *Sakralisierung des Kaisertums*, and that papal partisans actually had some reason to complain of the imperial notaries who indulged in *matutinas et laudes in preconia Cesaris . . . commutando* (*Vita Gregorii* IX,c.31, in *Liber censuum*, ed. P. Fabre and L. Duchesne [Paris, 1889ff], II,30). See also *Erg.Bd.*, 206f, for the *Salvatorstil* used by the courtiers for which some striking parallels are found in late Antiquity when the Roman imperial style was "liturgified." Schaller (p.96) is perfectly correct when he writes: "Friedrich II hat nicht Geistliches verweltlicht, sondern sein profanes Herrschertum vergeistlicht und verkirchlicht." It should be noted, however, that this tendency prevailed also with the lawyers and that the Bolognese *dictatores* applied liturgified language abundantly; see my study "An 'Autobiography' of Guido Faba," *Mediaeval and Renaissance Studies*, I (1943), 253ff, esp. 260ff, 265; also Hermann Kantorowicz, "The Poetical Sermon of a Mediaeval Jurist," *Warburg Journal*, II (1938-9), 22ff.

[91] *Nov.*9, epil.; see also the prologue of this law: "lex propria ad honorem Dei consecrata"; further, Justinian's *De confirmatione Digestorum*, §12: "omnipotenti Deo et hanc operam ad hominum sustentationem piis optulimus animis."

[92] *Lib.aug.*, prooemium: ". . . colendo iustitiam et iura condendo mactare disponimus vitulum labiorum." Marinus de Caramanico quotes promptly a parallel: *Nov.*8,11 ("valeamus domino deo vovere nosmet ipsos"), and adds, v. *Mactare*: "Et sic ipsi Deo pro quodam odore suavitatis praesentem librum constitutionum offerre . . . ut sic per iustitiam, quae est in lege, Imperator iste domino Deo voverat seipsum. . . ." See also *Erg.Bd.*, 85. See further Chrimes, *Const. Ideas*, 69, where the English king's promise in Parliament to protect the Church and to have the laws observed appeared to the Speaker "like the sacrifice of the Mass." The idea *Rex debet offerre legem Deo* still pervades the writings of the French jurists in the 16th century; see, e.g., Church, *Constitutional Thought*, 60,n.51.

[93] The ultimate source, of course, was biblical; see Ps. 50:21: "Tunc acceptabis sacrificium iustitiae, oblationes et holocausta; tunc imponent super altare tuum vitulos," which has to be connected with II Kings 14: 17: "fiat verbum domini mei regis sicut sacrificium; sicut enim angelus Dei, sic est dominus meus rex." Several other places could be referred to as well. Accordingly, already Ephrem the Syrian, *Hymni de Resurrectione*, XIX, ed. Lamy, II,754, could say: "Offerant Domino nostro . . . pontifex suas homilias, presbyteri sua encomia . . . , principes sua acta."

idea according to which lawyers and judges were "Priests of Justice."

> Deservedly may we be called of this art the priests: for we worship Justice and profess the knowledge of what is good and fair. . . .[94]

The *Digest* quoted Ulpian, and Ulpian quoted Celsus, who wrote under Hadrian. Hence, the language of an earlier age has been preserved. We recall that Aulus Gellius epitomized the moral and ethical qualities of the judge as those of an *antistes iustitiae*.[95] A century before him, Quintilian styled one of the great lawyers of the classical period *iuris antistes*.[96] In the Greek orbit other metaphors were used to express a similar idea—for example, "Throne-sharer of Dike" or "Coachman of the throne of Dike"—although in the fourth century a governor was praised also as "Temple of Justice."[97] The Latin language was more solemn and less visual: by the end of the fourth century, Symmachus—or rather Roma herself—addressed the emperors: *Iustitiae sacerdotes*.[98] Whether the change from *antistes* to *sacerdos* really suggests patristic influence is more than doubtful.[99] At any rate, the compilers of the *Digest* eternalized a well-known metaphor when, through Ulpian, they designated the legal experts *sacerdotes*.

The mediaeval glossators could not fail to comment upon that passage. "Deservedly the Law is called holy, and those dispensing the Law are therefore called priests," wrote Azo.[100] Accursius, in the *Glossa ordinaria*, drew a clear parallel between the priests of the Church and the priests of the Law.

---

[94] *D.1,1,1, De iustitia et iure.* See, for an excellent discussion of that title, Ulrich von Lübtow, "De iustitia et iure," *ZfRG*, rom. Abt., LXVI (1948), 458-565. See below, n.99.

[95] See above, n.64.   [96] Quintilian, *Inst.orat.*, XI,1,69.

[97] Louis Robert, *Hellenica* (Paris, 1948), IV,24 and 103: νηὸς Εὐδικίης for a Cretan governor; see also my paper in *AJA*, LVII (1953), 65ff, for the other titles mentioned.

[98] Symmachus, *Epist.*, x,3,13, the famous letter of 384 to Theodosius the Great concerning the altar of Victory, ed. Otto Seeck (*MGH, Auct. ant.*, VI), 282,28. Actually, *sacerdos iustitiae* is found also in an inscription: *CIL*, VI,2250.

[99] G. Beseler, *Beiträge zur Kritik der römischen Rechtsquellen* (Tübingen, 1920), IV,232f, considers the passage an interpolation: "Gedanklich ist es von schönem Ethos, aber (vor allem durch das Gleichnis [*sacerdotes*]) kirchenväterlich, nicht klassisch-juristisch." For objections against Beseler's theory, see Félix Senn, *De la Justice et du Droit* (Paris, 1927), 38,n.3, and Lübtow, "De iustitia et iure," 461,n.12.

[100] *Glos.ordin.* on *D.1,1,1*, v. *Cuius*: "Meruit enim ius appellari sacrum, et ideo iura reddentes sacerdotes vocantur." The gloss is attributed to Azo, who, however, in the prologue of his *Summa Institutionum* simply quotes the passage from the *Digest*.

Just as the priests minister and confection things holy, so do we, since the laws are most sacred . . . And just as the priest, when imposing penitence, renders to each one what is his right, so do we when we judge.[101]

Guillaume Budé, three centuries later, still praised the acuteness of Accursius for this parallel.[102] But the parallelism of spiritual and secular priesthood was common language long before the *Glossa ordinaria*. We may recall the Prologue of the Assizes of Roger II, or think of the twelfth-century author of a collection of legal word definitions who expounded, under the heading *De sacris et sacratis*, the new, or old, dualism:

There is one thing holy which is human, such as the laws; and there is another thing holy which is divine, such as things pertaining to the Church. And among the priests, some are divine priests, such as presbyters; others are human priests, such as magistrates, who are called priests because they dispense things holy, that is, laws.[103]

[101] *Ibid.*, v. *Sacerdotes*: "quia ut sacerdotes sacra ministrant et conficiunt, ita et nos, cum leges sint sacratissimae, ut C. de legi. et consti.l.leges (*C*.1,14,9); et ut ius suum cuique tribuit sacerdos in danda poenitentia, sic et nos in iudicando." In the Gothofredus editions of the *Digest* a few additional glosses are found: "Qui iustitiam colit, sacris Dei vacare dici potest"; and *ex altera Ulpiani collectione* he quotes: "Omnis iurisconsultus est iustitiae sacerdos, et quidem verus et non simulatus: Iustitiam enim colit . . . Hoc vere est iustitiam colere et sacris temploque eius ministrare."

[102] Budé, *Annotationes in Pandectarum libros*, on *D*.1,1,1 (Lyon, 1551), p.29: "Accursius peracute sane (ut solet plerunque) sacerdotes hoc in loco absolute intelligit . . . , ut ipse inquit, poenitentiam dantes." For the formulae used by the judge when passing his sentence, see Durandus, *Speculum iuris*, II,part.iii,§5,n.13 (Venice, 1602), II,787: ". . . talem condemno vel *absolvo*. Vel aliter proferat, sicut viderit proferendum . . ." See, for such alternatives, *ibid.*, §6,n.8,p.790. Also, of course, the judge hears the "confession" of a culprit; cf. *ibid.*, §6,n.2,p.788: "Ego talis iudex, *audita confessione tua*, praecipio tibi . . ." For the preceding *invocatio nominis Dei*, see §6, nos.6-7,pp.789f; it is the custom also today in ecclesiastical courts (cf. *Codex Iuris Canonici*, ca.1874,§1: "Sententia ferri debet divino Nomine ab initio semper invocato"), but it was the custom also in secular courts in the 13th century and thereafter; see, e.g., F. Schneider, "Toscanische Studien," *QF*, XII (1909), 287, for a sentence passed by the imperial vicar general of Tuscany in 1243. That sentences were pronounced "In the Name of the King," so that the king (or emperor) replaced God as the supreme legal authority, belongs to a later period, though it is found sporadically around 1500. See, e.g., in the *Decisiones Sacri Regii Consilii Neapolitani* (Lyon, 1581), p.3, Matthaeus de Afflictis, *Decisio* I,n.1: "utrum praesidens in consilio possit ferre sententiam sub nomine Regiae maiestatis . . . ," or *ibid.*, p.457, Antonius Capycius, *Decisio* CXI,n.1: ". . . quod facerem iustitiam nomine regio, etiam nomine Caes. maiest. protuli sententiam . . ." In modern republics, of course, the sentence is pronounced "In the Name of the People of . . ."

[103] *Petri Exceptionum appendices*, I,95, ed. Fitting, *Jurist.Schriften*, 164: "Sacrum aliud humanum, ut leges, aliud divinum, ut res ecclesie. Sacerdotes alii sacerdotes divini, ut presbyteri, alii humani, ut magistratus, qui dicuntur sacerdotes, quia

To distinguish between the *sacerdos temporalis, qui est iudex*, and the *sacerdos spiritualis, qui dicitur presbyter*, remained the custom for many centuries.[104] Other authors produced parallels which were more in the line of Accursius, as, for example, the imperial judge John of Viterbo, who (about 1238) wrote a *Mirror of the Podestà*. He extracted from Roman Law not only the customary passage according to which judges were quasi-priests, but also passages inferring that "the judge is hallowed by the presence of God," or that "in all legal matters the judge is said, nay, believed to be God with regard to men," whereby the fact that the judge administered a *sacramentum*, the oath, and had a copy of Holy Scripture on his table, served—or was pressed to serve—the purpose of exalting the jurist-priest religiously.[105]

---

dant sacra, id est leges." Those ideas, deriving from the parallelism prevailing between things holy and things public, between priests and magistrates, according to Roman Law (*D.*1,1,1,2), were repeated over and over again, often with reference to *Nov.*7,2,1 (". . . nec multo differant ab alterutro sacerdotium et imperium, et sacrae res a communibus et publicis"), and were lapidarily summarized in the formula: "nam ius divinum et publicum ambulant pari passu"; see Post, "Two Notes," 313,n.81, quoting Jacques de Révigny (ca.1270-80); also Post, "Statute of York," 421,n.18. See also *Glos. ord.*, on *D.*1,1,1,2, v. *in sacris*. Further, Dante, *Monarchia*, III,10,47ff; below Ch.VIII,n.35.

104 *Lib.aug.*, I,72, ed. Cervone, 131, forbids clerics and judges to act as local bailiffs. Marinus de Caramanico, in his gloss, explains that judges are treated like clerics "forte illa ratione, qua quis [iudices] merito sacerdotes appellat." Hence, the parallelism was carried over—at least, on the part of the glossators—to practical administration. Matthaeus de Afflictis, glossing on that law (numbered 1,69, vol.I,228) goes much further; he refers to Marinus and adds: "[iudices laici] quando iuste iudica[n]t, possunt dici sacerdotes temporales. Et sic duplex est sacerdos: temporalis, qui est iudex, et spiritualis, qui dicitur presbyter; vel ibi iudex est sacerdos, quando componit iussu principis sacras leges . . . Et subdit [Albericus de Rosate; see below] quod iudices, qui iuste iudicant, non solum appellantur sacerdotes, sed etiam angeli Dei, et plus merentur quam religiosi." See Albericus de Rosate, on *D.*1,1,1,n.11 (Venice, 1585), fol.10: "ibi, 'iustitiam namque colimus' etc., quia labia sacerdotis custodiunt iustitiam et leges requiruntur ex ore eius. Malachiae. c.2 [Mal. 2: 7: '. . . quia angelus Domini exercituum (sacerdos) est'], ubi dicit Hieronymus [?] quod sunt angeli Dei." Albericus simply quotes, and transfers to the judges, the classical place for the *character angelicus* of priests; cf. Friedrich Baethgen, *Der Engelpapst* (Schriften der Königsberger Gelehrten Gesellschaft, x:2, Halle, 1933), who has collected rich material on that subject; see also Henri Grégoire, " 'Ton Ange' et les anges de Théra," *Byzantinische Zeitschrift*, xxx (1929-1930), 641-645. Albericus then quotes Hostiensis "quod advocati et iudices exercentes recte eorum officia plus merentur quam religiosi." Cf. Hostiensis, *Summa aurea*, prooem.,n.8 (Venice, 1586), col.6: ". . . iusti iudices vitam activam sine plica ducentes, quae si bene duceretur, magis fructifera esset, quam contemplativa."

105 John of Viterbo, *De regimine civitatum*, c.25, ed. Gaetano Salvemini, in: *Bibl. jurid. med. aevi*, III,226: ". . . nam iudex alias sacerdos dicitur quia sacra dat (cf. above, n.103) . . . ; et alias dicitur: Iudex dei presentia consecratur (*C.*3,1,14,2) . . . ;

Distinctions, antitheses, parallelisms, and adaptations such as these, repeated over and over again, were contributive in creating the new holiness of the secular state and its "mysteries,"[106] and therefore have an importance far beyond the mere effort of hallowing the legal profession, of placing legal science on equal footing with theology, or of comparing legal procedure with the rites of the Church. The professional pride of the jurists certainly played an important role. Already Accursius answered the self-posed question whether it be necessary "that everyone who wants to become a jurisprudent or legal expert is bound to study theology," with a straight "No; because all that is found in the body of Law."[107] Baldus, when raising the question whether the Doctors of Law should be included among the higher dignities, answered: "Why not, since they discharge the office of priesthood";[108] and, being himself a professor of Law at Bologna, very neatly said: "Professors of Law are called priests."[109] Professors of Law, of course, wanted to be called "Counts" as well, for the juristic *quid pro quo* method of so-called "equiparations" led to practical success in the field of social stratification: by the end of the thirteenth century the jurists really acquired the quasi-knighthood which they claimed as their due on the basis of some wrongly interpreted passages of Jus-

---

dicitur etiam, immo creditur, esse deus in omnibus pro hominibus (*C.*2,58[59],2,8)." Cf. *C.*2,58(59),1,1 for the Holy Scripture handled by the judge.

[106] See, for the problem in general, my study "Mysteries of State," *Harvard Theological Review*, XLVIII (1955), esp.72ff.

[107] *Glos.ord.* on *D.*1,1,10, v. *Notitia*: "Sed numquid secundum hoc oportet quod quicumque vult iurisprudens vel iurisconsultus esse, debeat theologiam legere? Respondeo, non; nam omnia in corpore iuris inveniuntur."

[108] Baldus, on c.15 X 1,3,n.9, *In Decretales*, fol.37ᵛ: "Sed numquid includantur legum Doctores [inter maiores et digniores]? Dic quia non, quia funguntur sacerdotio."

[109] Baldus, on *D.*1,1,1,n.5, fol.7: "Item nota quod legum professores dicuntur sacerdotes." Even the priestly rank of doctors may be defended; *ibid.*, n.17, fol.7ᵛ: "Quarto opponitur et videtur quod Doctores non sint sacerdotes quia non habent ordines sacros. Solutio: sacerdotium aliud spirituale, et sic loquitur contra; aliud temporale, et sic loquitur hic." Besides, adds Baldus, the *doctoratus* is *publici iuris* and is a *dignitas auctoritate publica*, and "in signum huius datur infula tanquam Principi seu praeceptori legum," so that the doctor may have a "priestly" rank similar to that of the professor of Law. See also Paulus Castrensis, on *D.*1,1,1,n.3 (Venice, 1582), fol.2: "propter quod iuris professores dici possunt sacerdotes, quia administrant leges sacratissimas . . . ; quia professores iuris colunt iustitiam." These and similar considerations finally prompted Thomas Diplovatatius to write his compendium on the great jurists and their right of precedence at ceremonies; see Diplovatatius, *De claris iuris consultis*, ed. H. Kantorowicz and F. Schulz (Berlin and Leipzig, 1919), 145,cf.28ff. See next note.

tinian's *Code.* Henceforth, the promotion of a doctor and the dubbing of a knight were paralleled because they conferred the same grade of social dignity. A new nobility ranked now together with the *militia coelestis* of the clergy and the *militia armata* of the gentry, the so-called *militia legum* or *militia litterata*, which Baldus occasionally called a *militia doctoralis*, a "doctoral knighthood."[110] Needless to say, nothing comparable was achieved with regard to the fiction of the sacerdotal character of the jurists. The jurists never even attempted to materialize their claim to "legal priesthood" in the way they materialized their claim to "legal knighthood." The whole talk about their priesthood reflected the long drawn battle between theology and jurisprudence, ending in the *de facto* victory of the laical spirit. Only in one respect did that talk about legal priesthood come close to the real problem of clerical status: with regard to the ruler.

What held good for the judges held good for the Prince who, after all, headed the legal hierarchy. In the *Digest*, it is true, only the jurisprudent is called a *sacerdos*; but the transfer of this quasi-sacerdotal character from "judge" to "king" was no problem: already King Roger II had utilized the words of Ulpian when he presumed for the royal office "a certain privilege of priesthood."[111] Strangely enough, this legal priesthood of the king eventually served even to prove the clerical status of the ruler *within* the Church and thus to bolster the common assertion that the king was, ecclesiologically, *non omnino laicus* or, as Pierre d'Ailly once put it, *une personne moyenne entre spirituelle et temporelle*, referring thereby to the anointings of kings.[112] On the other hand,

---

[110] The material has been summed up by Fitting, *Das Castrense peculium in seiner geschichtlichen Entwicklung und heutigen gemeinrechtlichen Geltung* (Halle, 1871), who mentions (p.543,n.1) that already Placentinus styled the jurists *milites inermi militia, id est, literatoria militantes*; see for *militia doctoralis*, Baldus, on C.7,38,1,n.1, fol.28, who holds that in this *militia* Hebrews and non-Christians could not militate. Placentinus' contemporary Ralph Niger, a friend of John of Salisbury, stresses that the lawyers were called *domini* and scorned the titles of doctor or master, a complaint sided by Stephen Langton's remark: "Sacerdotes etiam magis volunt vocari *domini* quam sacerdotes vel capellani." See H. Kantorowicz, "An English Theologian's View of Roman Law: Pepo, Irnerius, Ralph Niger," *Mediaeval and Renaissance Studies*, I(1943), 247 (n.2), and 250,32f.

[111] Andreas of Isernia, on *Feud.* II,56 ("Quae sunt regalia"), n.64, fol.301: "Princeps est iudex iudicum . . ." See above, n.89, for Roger II.

[112] Dom Jean Leclercq, "L'idée de la royauté du Christ pendant le grand schisme," *Archives d'histoire doctrinale et littéraire*, XXIV (1949), 259f.

it was not uncommon—apparently ever since Irenaeus—to say that "every just king has sacerdotal rank."[113] A new version, however, became popular by the end of the thirteenth century. William Durand, great lawyer and liturgical expert that he was, did not express his own opinion, but quoted others, presumably some glossators, who held "that the emperor ranked as a presbyter according to the passage where it is said: 'Deservedly we [the jurisprudents] are called priests.' "[114] It is truly remarkable that here a positive effort was made to prove the Prince's non-laical character within the Church, not as a result of his anointing with the holy balm, but as a result of Ulpian's solemn comparison of judges with priests. It is less baffling that William Durand referred also to the pontifical rank which the emperor was said to hold.[115] For in this case his source was either Gratian's *Decree* quoting Isidore of Seville,[116] or any one of the numerous glossators on the *Institutes* of Justinian, all of whom customarily recalled the former

[113] Irenaeus, at least, was quoted by Antonius Melissa, *Loci communes*, II,1 (= CIII), *PGr*, CXXXVI,1004B, as having said: πᾶς βασιλεὺς δίκαιος ἱερατικὴν ἔχει τάξιν ("rex omnis iustus sacerdotalem obtinet ordinem"). The idea itself is found repeatedly; see, e.g., the Norman Anonymous on the *rex iustitiae* (Melchizedek); *MGH,LdL*, III,663,7ff.

[114] Durand, *Rationale divinorum officiorum*, II,8,6 (Lyon, 1565), fol.55ᵛ: "Quidam etiam dicunt ut not.ff.de rerum divis.l.sancta (D.1,8,9) quod fit presbyter, iuxta illud, 'Cuius merito quis nos sacerdotes appellat' (D.1,1,1)." Cf. Marc Bloch, *Rois thaumaturges*, 188,n.3; also Eichmann, *Kaiserkrönung*, I,283 (where, however, the word added in brackets should read *iurisperitos* and not *imperatorem*). The reference to the *iudices sacerdotes* was not customary with the glossators on that occasion, though it does occur; see, e.g., the Memorandum of John Branchazolus, a Doctor of Law from Pavia and Ghibelline partisan, who (in 1312) wrote: ". . . et talis rex appellabatur pontifex et sacerdos, ut . . . (follow references to D.1,1,1; D.1,8,9; and *Inst*.2,1,8);" see Edmund E. Stengel, *Nova Alemanniae* (Berlin, 1921), I, No.90,1,§2, p.46. Durand's other allegation is normal; see next note.

[115] Durand, *loc.cit.*; "Imperator etiam pontifex dictus est"; also *Rationale*, II,11, with reference to ancient Rome: "Unde et Romani imperatores pontifices dicebantur," a quotation from Gratian's *Decretum* (see next note). The Civilians traditionally discussed the imperial character of *sacerdos* and *pontifex* in connection with the dedication of holy places mentioned in D.1,8,9 (see *Glos.ord.*, v. *Dedicavit*) and *Inst*.2,1,8 (*Glos.ord.*, v. *Pontifices*); see also next note.

[116] *Decretum*, c.1,D.XXI, ed. Friedberg, I,68: "Nam maiorum haec erat consuetudo, ut rex esset etiam sacerdos et pontifex. Unde et Romani Imperatores pontifices dicebantur." What the *Decretum* quoted, through the medium of Isidorus, was actually Servius, on *Aeneis*, III,268, which may have been known to the jurists anyhow. The Civilians rarely failed to refer to the *Decretum* when discussing the former priestly character of the emperors; see Azo, *Summa Inst.*, on *Inst*.2,1, n.6, fol. 273ᵛ: "Imperatores enim antiquitus erant sacerdotes, ut fertur in canonibus, et ideo poterant dedicare." Also *Glos.ord.* on *Inst*.2,1,8, v. *pontifices*: "ut in canonibus dicitur."

imperial office of *pontifex maximus* when discussing the dedication of temples and other *res sacrae* at the hands of *pontifices*.[117]

Guillaume Budé, one of the founders of the humanistic historical school of jurisprudence in the sixteenth century, was perfectly correct when he ridiculed the error of Accursius and the glossators in general who were inclined to confuse the *sacerdotes* and *pontifices* of ancient Rome with the presbyters and bishops of their own time.[118] However, it was by means of these objectively false equivocations of which the works of the mediaeval jurists abound, that completely new insights were gleaned and conclusions were drawn which in many respects were to shape our own age and remain highly influential even today. The mediaeval jurists, as natural, were struck by the grave solemnity of the ancient Roman Law which, of course, was inseparable from religion and things sacred in general. They now were eager to apply also the Roman religious ethos of Justinian's collections to the conditions of their own world of thought. Hence, it was through the agency of the jurists that some of the former attributes and cherished similes of kingship—the divinely inspired king, the offering king, the priestly king—were carried over from the age of liturgical and Christ-centered kingship and were adapted to the new ideal of rulership centered on scientific jurisprudence. It is true, of course, that the former liturgical values of kingship did not cease to exist and that, with varying degrees of intensity, they lingered on also in their original setting—though their substance grew paler as both the legal and the religious importance of royal consecrations decreased. But it may be said nevertheless that the jurists salvaged much of the mediaeval inheritance by transferring certain peculiarly ecclesiastical properties of kingship to the legal stage setting, thereby preparing the new halo of the rising national states and, for good or evil, of the absolute monarchies.

In one case, however, the mediaeval theory of kingship was actually brought into bolder relief by the introduction of a secular

---

117 The places were *Inst.*2,1,8; *D.*1,8,9; occasionally also *D.*1,1,1 (see above, nos. 114-115). They were quoted also by the canonists; see also Baldus, on *Rex pacificus*, n.5, *In Decretales*, p.5 (Prooemium of the Decretals of Gregory IX).

118 Budé, *Annotationes*, p.30: "Similis est ignorantia Accursii vel saeculi potius Accursiani, quae hac aetate ridicula est . . . Ubi pontificum Ulpianus meminit, de collegio pontificum loquens, a quo ius pontificium apud antiquos dictum, quod Accursius ad nostros pontifices retulit."

concept which derived from Roman Law and strengthened the idea of royal mediatorship. The earlier Middle Ages had attributed to the legislating Roman Emperors an instrumentality comparable to that of inspired Prophets and Sibyls: "Through the mouths of pious Roman Emperors, inspired by God, there were promulgated the venerable Roman Laws," wrote Pope John VIII, and his words later penetrated into the collections of Canon Law.[119] The miniature of Henry II in the Monte Cassino Gospels apparently reflected a related idea; and the never-failing Norman Anonymous naturally used the mediaeval idea of royal mediatorship for his purposes. When, however, the influence of Roman Civil Law became effective, the Prince not only appeared as the *oraculum* of the divine power: he himself became the *lex animata*, the living or animate Law, and finally an incarnation of Justice.

The concept of the Prince as the "animate Law" was a denizen with regard to Roman legal thought. The notion itself, νόμος ἔμψυχος, derived from Greek philosophy; it was blended with the idea of the Roman Emperor being the embodiment of all Virtues and all else worth the living; and perhaps it was not free from Christian influence either—at least in the form in which Justinian finally applied the metaphor to his own person. At the end of one of his *Novels*, the emperor proclaimed:

> From everything we have decreed [in the preceding edict] there shall be exempt the *Tychē* of the emperor, to whom God has submitted the laws themselves by sending him down to men as the *living Law*.[120]

It has often been noticed and stressed in recent years that most likely the phrasing of Justinian's *Novel* depended on an oration of the philosopher and orator Themistius addressing, in 384, the Emperor Theodosius I.[121] The influence of Themistius on Byzantine thought can be doubted as little as the influence of Hellen-

---

[119] See *MGH,Epp.*, VII,281,11, for John VIII: "venerande Romane leges divinitus per ora piorum principum promulgate." Through Gratian's *Decretum*, c.17,C.XVI, q.3, ed. Friedberg, I,796, the passage became widely known; cf. Ullmann, *Lucas de Penna*, 78,n.2.

[120] *Nov.*105,2,4. The most thorough monograph on the whole subject is Steinwenter, "Nomos," 250ff, where also the modern literature will be found; one might add Pietro de Francisci, *Arcana Imperii* (Milan, 1948), III:2,114ff, as well as the new study by Delatte, *Traités de la Royauté*, 245ff; also Schulz, "Kingship," 157ff. Cf. my study on "Kaiser Friedrich II. und das Königsbild des Hellenismus," 171ff.

[121] Steinwenter, "Nomos," 260; Themistius, *Orat.*, XIX, ed. Dindorf, 277. De Francisci, *Arcana Imperii*, III:2,208.

istic political philosophy on this late imperial orator.[122] But apparently it has been generally overlooked in this connection that already Lactantius, in his *Divine Institutes*, a work dedicated to Constantine the Great as a Christian complement of the Institutes of Civil Law, produced a very similar version of that idea. God, writes Lactantius,

> sent his ambassador and messenger to instruct mortal mankind with the precepts of his Justice . . . For since there was no justice on earth, he sent a teacher, as it were a living Law, to found a new name and temple. . . .[123]

Lactantius, of course, was not talking about an emperor; he spoke of the incarnate Son of God as the intermediary between divine Justice and justice on earth. Common though the topic of the "animate Law"—or its equivalents—was in Greek philosophy, it was not explicitly connected with the idea of an intermediary "sent down" from heaven. The amalgamation of the two ideas seems to go back to Lactantius: in his interpretation of the Incarnation he combined the evangelical image of Christ as teacher in the Temple "sent" by the Father (John 7: 14ff) with the Greek political philosophy of the "living Law." In fact, the later versions of Themistius and Justinian seem to presuppose the doctrine of the Incarnation with which Lactantius was concerned.[124]

However that may be, the doctrine of the Prince as the *lex*

---

[122] Delatte, *Traités*, 152ff, for the influence on Byzantium; also Vladimir Valdenberg, "Le idee politiche di Procopio di Gaza e di Menandro Protettore," *Studi Bisantini e Neoellenici*, IV (1935), 67ff (esp.73f), and "Discours politiques de Thémistius dans leurs rapport avec l'antiquité," *Byzantion*, I (1924), 557-580, esp. 572f; Johannes Straub, *Vom Herrscherideal in der Spätantike* (Stuttgart, 1939), 160ff. Themistius, *Oratio*, xv, Dindorf, 228f, may have influenced the Prologue of Justinian's *Institutes*; cf. Kantorowicz, "On Transformations of Apolline Ethics," *Festschrift für Ernst Langlotz* (Bonn, 1957).

[123] Lactantius, *Divinae Institutiones*, IV,25,1ff: ". . . quare Deus summus, cum legatum ac nuntium suum mitteret, ad erudiendam praeceptis iustitiae suae mortalitatem, mortali voluerit eum carne indui . . . Nam cum iustitia nulla esset in terra, doctorem misit, *quasi vivam legem*, ut nomen ac templum novum conderet . . ." My attention was called to this important passage through the study of Arnold Ehrhardt, "Das Corpus Christi und die Korporationen im spät-römischen Recht," *ZfRG*, rom.Abt., LXXI (1954), 29,n.9, who was kind enough to allow me to peruse the manuscript of his study before publication.

[124] Lactantius' *Christus doctor* is certainly inspired by *Christus docens* of John 7:14ff, where the one *qui me misit* is referred to five times; where v.24 refers to justice: *iustum iudicium iudicate*; and where the setting of the scene in the Temple suggested the *novum templum* of Lactantius. The problem itself will be discussed separately.

animata, practically unknown in the West during the earlier Middle Ages,[125] was revived through the revival of scientific jurisprudence and the literary style of Bologna. If we may trust Godfrey of Viterbo, the famous Four Doctors of Bologna addressed Barbarossa at the Diet of Roncaglia, in 1158, with the following words:

> You, being the living Law, can give, loosen, and proclaim laws; dukes stand and fall, and kings rule while you are the judge; anything you wish, you carry on as the animate Law.[126]

Whether these words were really spoken or not makes little difference here, because by the end of the twelfth century the doctrine of the Prince as *lex animata*, or *lex viva*, must have been common enough anyhow to be known to Godfrey of Viterbo, who died in 1191. Moreover, the English Canonist Alanus, writing between 1201 and 1210, transferred, even at that early date, the notion to the pope. Talking about the fact that a marriage may be forbidden sometimes by the judge, and sometimes by the law, Alanus asserts that the judge's decision stands, "unless you wish to say something about the prohibition on the part of the supreme pontiff, who is the living law or living canon."[127] To refer also to the pope as the *lex animata in terris* was not uncommon in the later thirteenth century and thereafter;[128] but it was a more natural thing to refer

---

[125] An allusion may perhaps be detected in Benzo of Alba, *Ad Heinricum*, vi,7, *MGH,SS.*, xi,669,1: *De coelo missus, non homo carnis* (cf. *Nov.*105: *eum mittens hominibus*). But the similarity is very vague.

[126] *MGH,SS*, xxii,316, line 388:

> Tu *lex viva* potes dare, solvere, condere, leges,
> Stantque caduntque duces, regnant te iudice reges;
> Rem, quocumque velis, *lex animata* geris.
>
> Cf. Steinwenter, "Nomos," 255.

[127] ". . . nisi quid speciale dicere volueris circa prohibitionem summi pontificis, qui est *lex vel canon vivus*." Cf. Franz Gillmann, "Magister Albertus, Glossator der Compilatio II," *AKKR*, cv (1925), 153, a passage to which Mochi Onory, *Fonti*, 76, called attention.

[128] Cf. Joannes Andreae, on c.11 VI 1,14, v. *Iuris*: "[arbitri electi] ad ipsum ius a quo potestatem habent, oportet appellari: et sic ad Papam qui est *lex animata in terris*." See Steinwenter, "Nomos," 251, for this and later examples to which there might be added Oldradus, *Consilia*, 328,n.6 (Venice, 1571), fol.164, who simply refers to *Nov.*105. See also F. Gillmann, "Dominus Deus noster papa?," *AKKR*, xcv (1915), 270,n.3. It may be mentioned in this connection that the papal political theory in general was constructed in analogy to the imperial theories. The pope, though the lord of the *ius fori*, was bound as a minister to the *ius poli* (cf. Rudolph Sohm, *Das altkatholische Kirchenrecht und das Dekret Gratians* [Munich and Leipzig, 1918], 611f); of him, too, it was expected that he submit voluntarily to the Law; see, for example, Hostiensis, *Summa aurea*, on X 1,30 (*De officio legati*), n.3 (Venice, 1586), 324, who quotes for that purpose the *lex digna* together with the maxim *princeps*

to the emperor in these terms. The *Glossa ordinaria* quoted the emperor repeatedly as the "animate Law on earth," sometimes even in connection with the *lex digna*, which represented a different ideal.[129] Around 1238, John of Viterbo recited in his *Mirror of the Podestà* Justinian's *Novel* almost verbatim:

> The emperors have received from God the permission to issue laws; God subjected the laws to the emperor and sent him as the animate Law to men.[130]

In a similar vein, the South-Italian jurists, including the glossators of the *Liber augustalis*, defined the emperor as the living Law.[131]

---

legibus solutus, as was the custom observed by both Civilians and Canonists; see also Johannes Teutonicus, on c.20,C.XII,q.2, v. *papae*: "sed certe licet sit solutus legibus, tamen secundum leges vivere debet." Aegidius Romanus, *De eccles. pot.*, III, 8, ed. Scholz, 190, sums up the theory: "Nam licet summus sacerdos sit animal sine capistro et freno et sit homo supra positivas leges, ipse tamen debet sibi imponere capistrum et frenum et vivere secundum conditas leges" (cf. III,c.7, Scholz, 181). See, for the related right of resistance against the pope, the competent study of Brian Tierney, "Grosseteste and the Theory of Papal Sovereignty," *Journal of Ecclesiastical History*, VI (1955), 1-17.

[129] *Glos.ord.*, on *D.*1,3,22, v. *cum lex*: "lex, id est imperator qui est *lex animata in terris*"; on *D.*2,1,5, v. *alieno beneficio*; on *C.*10,1,5,2, v. *vigorem* (see above, n.36); on *Nov.*12,4, v. *Patres* (above, n.37); on *Nov.*105,2,4, v. *legem animatam*, where the *lex digna* is quoted. Cynus, on *D.*2,1,5,n.7, fol.26ᵛ, polemizes not quite justly against the *Glos.ord.* (on the same law, v. *alieno beneficio*) when, in connection with sub-delegation (possible, if original jurisdiction was derived directly from the law, and impossible, if deriving from another person), he says: "dicit glossa qui habet [iurisdictionem] beneficio alieno, scilicet hominis, non potest demandare [in the sense of 'delegare'] . . . Sed qui habet [iurisdictionem] beneficio legis, bene potest delegare . . . , et *princeps non est homo, sed est lex animata in terris* . . . Ista responsio est derisibilis, quia licet princeps sit lex animata: tamen non est homo." Quite good on that point is Albericus de Rosate, on *D.*1,3,31,n.10, fol.31: "propter quod princeps non debet dici proprie sub lege, sed in lege positus, et ideo dicitur lex animata in terris."

[130] John of Viterbo, *De reg. civit.*, c.128, ed. Salvemini, 266; cf. *Erg.Bd.*, 86; Steinwenter, "Nomos," 254.

[131] Karolus de Tocco, *Apparatus in Lombardam*, on 1,3,1 (*Leges Longobardorum cum glosis Karoli de Tocco*, Venice, 1537, fol.8ᵛ), v. *non possibile*: "nam et si legibus sit princeps solutus, legibus tamen vivere debet . . . (*C.*6,23,3), cum omnis imperialis maiestas et eius auctoritas a lege pendeat et ab ea sit inducta.l.digna vox etc. (*C.*1,14,4); nam cum ipse sit *lex animata* . . . (*Nov.*105,2,4), non debet in legem committere . . . quia frustra legis invocat auxilium qui contra legem committit." Cf. F. Calasso, "Origini italiane della formola 'Rex in regno suo etc.,'" *Rivista di storia del diritto italiano*, III (1930), 241,n.91; also Heydte, 324,n.23. See further Andreas of Isernia, on *Lib.aug.*, III,26, ed. Cervone, 355b: "Princeps legislator, qui est *lex animata in terris* . . . est pater subiectorum." See also Matthaeus de Afflictis, above, n.38.—If, however, Marinus de Caramanico, *Prooem. in Const.*, ed. Cervone, xxxiii, ed. Calasso, *Glossatori*, 182,10ff, says: "Quid enim aliud est lex quam rex?", he does not have Justinian's *Novel* 105 in mind, but sends his reader to *D.*1,3,2, the Chrysippus fragment concerning the νόμος βασιλεύς, a concept (it derives from Pindar, fr.169) related to, though not identical with, that of the *lex animata*; see Steinwenter, "Nomos," 261ff, and, for the problem in general, Hans Erich Stier,

And, of course, Frederick II himself resorted to that definition of his legislating power. In 1230, the "Lord Emperor" was styled in a South-Italian document the *lex animata*.[132] Two years later, the emperor referred to his own person when declaring a decision void because it was directed against "the majesty which is the animate Law on earth and from which the civil laws originate."[133] With the last phrase, the diction comes close to the legal maxim saying that the emperor has all laws in *scrinio pectoris*, "in the shrine of his breast," a maxim likewise deriving from Roman Law and belonging to the same general compound of ideas.[134] Hence, a Bolognese teacher of the *dictamen*, the famous Magister Boncompagno, deemed it correct to address (ca. 1235) the emperor as "Most serene Emperor of the Romans, who keepest all the natural and civil laws in the innermost of thy breast."[135] The tenet of the *lex animata*, however, penetrated the most unexpected areas. Johannes de Deo, writing his *Liber poenitentiarius* about 1245, declared that the emperor may confess to any confessor he chooses, "for the Prince is not subject to laws: He himself is the animate Law on earth."[136] It was probably due to the fact that Frederick II's son, King Henry (VII), acted in Germany as his father's deputy when, in 1231, he stressed "the plenitude of royal power by which we as

---

"ΝΟΜΟΣ ΒΑΣΙΛΕΥΣ," *Philologus*, LXXXIII (1928), 225-258; see also below, n.148, for a fusion of the two theories in the writings of Aegidius Romanus. That the Chrysippus fragment (ὁ νόμος πάντων ἐστὶ βασιλεὺς θείων τε καὶ ἀνθρωπίνων πραγμάτων ...) exercised relatively little influence on mediaeval political theory may have been caused by the translation; for whereas Marinus de Caramanico translated the decisive phrase correctly (*lex est rex*), the official version says *lex est regina*, an allegorizing metaphor no longer suggesting a realistic identification of the Law with the Prince. Baldus, it is true, refers to it (on *D.*1,3,2,n.2, fol.17ᵛ) in the literal sense: "Nota quod lex est Princeps, Dux et regula," but then he returns immediately to the more familiar formulation of *Nov.*105,2,4, and says: "Rex est lex animata: et . . . subditi possunt tunc dicere: Ego dormio et cor meum, id est, Rex meus, vigilat (Cant.5,2)," which neatly illustrates the ruler's omnipresence (see below, n.167). For the *vigilans iustitia*, see below, n.146; I shall discuss the new ideal of the *rex exsomnis* in another connection.

[132] Wolfram von den Steinen, *Das Kaisertum Friedrichs des Zweiten* (Berlin and Leipzig, 1922), 63, quotes the relevant places; see also Steinwenter, "Nomos," 255, n.28.

[133] Böhmer, *Acta imperii*, I,264,No.299: "(maiestas nostra) que est *lex animata in terris* et a qua iura civilia oriuntur." Cf. *MGH, Const.*, II,184,n.1; *Erg.Bd.*, 86f.

[134] See above, Ch.II,n.15.

[135] *Erg.Bd.*, 85.

[136] See Gaines Post, "Blessed Lady Spain," *Speculum*, XXIX (1954), 200, n.10; perhaps the passage quoted by Post, "Two Notes on Nationalism in the Middle Ages," *Traditio*, IX (1953), 299,n.11, belongs to the same compound of ideas.

the living and animate Law on earth are above the laws."[137] For it seems to belong to a slightly later period that, in the course of the customary development, the national king, too, was styled, and himself claimed to be, *in terra sua lex animata*; and this designation played a considerable role in the later political theory of royal absolutism.[138] Nor will it be surprising to find the *lex animata* theory applied to the *universitas*, the legislating community.[139]

That in all these cases Justinian's *Novel* was the common source of Civilians and Canonists is obvious. In the latter half of the thirteenth century, however, one of the ultimate sources of Justinian himself became no less important: Aristotle. In the *Nicomachean Ethics*, Aristotle called the perfect judge a δίκαιον ἔμψυχον (*iustum animatum*), which in English usually is rendered by "animate justice." The judge, in this capacity of animate justice, is the intermediate between the litigant parties who seek nothing but justice itself. Hence, concludes Aristotle, "justice is something intermediate, and so is the judge," who is the living justice.[140]

What matters here is not so much Aristotle himself as his interpreters in the thirteenth century. In his commentary on the *Nicomachean Ethics*, Aquinas, of course, recognized that the judge was *quoddam iustum animatum*; but to the definition of the judges as "intermediates" (*medios*) he added: *vel mediatores*, "or mediators," which is not quite the same thing.[141] In the *Summa*

---

[137] Cf. *MGH,Const.*, ii,184,n.1; Huillard-Bréholles, iii,469.

[138] See Church, *Const.Thought*, 58,70,193, and passim (see Index, s.v. "King"); also Esmein, "Princeps legibus solutus," 206,n.1. Cf. Matthaeus de Afflictis, on *Lib. aug.*, 1,6,n.32, fol.52ᵛ: "et rex in regno dicitur lex animata." See, for an early example (Charles II of Naples, 1295), Romualdo Trifone, *La legislazione angioina* (Naples, 1921), 119, No.LXII.

[139] Lucas de Penna, on *C.11,69,1,n.4* (Lyon, 1582), 613: "nam si potest hoc [sc. aedificare in publico permittere] lex municipalis, fortius ipsa universitas quae legem municipalem constituit . . . , quia potentior est lex viva quam mortua sicut excessive animatum potentius est [in]animato." Lucas thereby implies that the *universitas* is a living being or animate "person," a concept which presupposes the *persona ficta* theory. For his distinction between *lex viva* and *lex mortua* he refers to his own commentary on *C.11,41,n.20*; see below, n.150.

[140] *Eth.Nicom.*, v,1132a,20ff: τὸ δ᾽ἐπὶ τὸν δικαστὴν ἰέναι, ἰέναι ἐστὶν ἐπὶ τὸ δίκαιον· ὁ γὰρ δικαστὴς βούλεται εἶναι οἷον δίκαιον ἔμψυχον. Cf. Delatte, *Traités*, 246; Goodenough, "Hellenistic Kingship," 63; Steinwenter, "Nomos," 260. Justice herself, of course, is an intermediate like all virtues, though of a different and most august kind, because she does not hold the balance between two extremes each of which is a vice (e.g., Fortitude as the mean between Cowardice and Rashness); see *Eth.Nicom.*, v,1129a, 1ff; 1133b, 30ff.

[141] Aquinas, *In Ethicorum Aristotelis ad Nicomachum Expositio*, §955, ed. R. M.

132

theologica, Aquinas brings the king into this image and says that "the judge is animate Justice, and the king the guardian of what is just."[142] In the later section of the commentary on the *Politics*, written by Aquinas' continuator, Peter of Auvergne, the judge has dropped out completely and there remained the king whose office it was "to be the guardian of *Iustitia* . . . and therefore, to resort to the king is to resort to the *iustum animatum*."[143] The transition from judge to king worked as smoothly here as in the case of Ulpian's *sacerdotes Iustitiae*. It is pardonable that Aristotle's simile of *iustum animatum*, referring to the judge or Prince as an intermediate between subjects, was taken to be a mere variant of Justinian's well-known definition of the Prince as the *lex animata*, referring to the Prince as a mediator between heaven and earth. At any rate, the Prince was soon identified with the "living Justice." John of Paris, around 1300, refers quite bluntly to the Prince as *Iustitia animata* and guardian of what is just.[144] And the confusion of Aristotle with Justinian is finally borne out by Baldus who styled the king the *iustum animatum* and referred, not to Aristotle, but to Justinian's *Novel*.[145] However that may be, the Prince appeared not only as the living Law but also as the living Justice. Already Albertus Magnus demanded that the king be neither torpid nor sleepy, but be the "living and vigilant Justice," adding that the king was above the Law because he was the "living form of the Law."[146] And Dante, thoughtfully, lets Justinian him-

---

Spiazzi (Turin and Rome, 1949), 261f: ". . . nam iudex debet esse quasi quoddam iustum animatum, ut scilicet mens eius totaliter a iustitia possideatur. Illi autem qui refugiunt ad iudicem, videntur quaerere medium inter partes quae litigant; et inde est quod iudices vocant medios vel mediatores." See, however, Arist., *Nic. Eth.*, 1132a,22-23: καὶ ζητοῦσι δικαστὴν μέσον, καὶ καλοῦσιν ἔνιοι μεσιδίους.

[142] Aquinas, *Summa theol.*, II-IIae, q.LVIII, a.l, ad 5: "iudex est iustum animatum et princeps est custos iusti." For the king as "guardian," see next note.

[143] Aquinas, *In Politicorum Aristotelis Expositio*, §849, ed. Spiazzi (Turin and Rome, 1951), 284: "Et dicit [Aristoteles] quod officium regis est esse custodem iustitiae. Et vult custos esse iusti. Et ideo recurrere ad regem est recurrere ad iustum animatum." See Arist., *Pol.*, V,1311a,1, who does not use the term "guardian of justice," but simply says: βούλεται δὲ ὁ βασιλεὺς εἶναι φύλαξ ("Vult enim rex esse custos"; §706, ed. Spiazzi, p.282), although the meaning is that of *custos iusti*.

[144] John of Paris, *De potestate*, c.XVII, ed. Leclercq, 225,6: ". . . ad principem pertinet qui est *iustitia animata* et custos iusti." For the two aspects of the king as intermediate between subjects and as intermediate beween God and men, see Valdenberg, in *Byzantion*, I,572f.

[145] See Baldus, on c.33 X 2,24,n.1, *In Decretales*, fol.261: "Item debet esse iustum animatum, ut in Auth. de consulibus (= *Nov.*105,2,4)."

[146] Albertus Magnus, *In Matthaeum*, VI,10, ed. A. Borgnet (Paris, 1893), XX,266f:

self use the expression *viva Giustizia* to designate the Godhead which inspired him.[147]

It may be claimed that the theory about the ruler as the living Law or living Justice was brought to some conclusion by Aquinas' pupil and follower Aegidius Romanus who dedicated, between 1277 and 1279, his political tractate *De regimine principum* to the son of the King of France, later King Philip IV. Since this "Mirror of Princes" was one of the most-read and most-quoted works on a political topic during the later Middle Ages, the main problems were, so to speak, settled by its author for many centuries to come. Aegidius Romanus, having digested Aristotle very thoroughly, likewise styled the Prince "Guardian of Justice" and defined him as the "organ and instrument of the just Law." Moreover, referring directly to the *Nicomachean Ethics*, he quoted the passage concerning the judge who represented a *iustum animatum*, though not without adding: *et multum magis ipse rex*, "and much more so the king himself." For, so Aegidius explained,

> the king or prince is a kind of Law, and the Law is a kind of king or prince. For the Law is a kind of inanimate prince; the prince, however, a kind of animate Law. And in so far as the animate exceeds the inanimate the king or prince must exceed the Law.[148]

In this description of the interrelations between Law and Prince we find an antithesis of *animate* king and *inanimate* Law which, in the last analysis, goes back to Plato's *Politicus*; and also the

---

"Haec autem potestas animata debet esse iustitia, quia rex non tantum debet esse iustus . . . , non torpens vel dormiens, sed *viva* et vigilans *iustitia* . . . Et licet rex supra legem sit, tamen non est contrarius legi: et est supra legem, eo quod ipse est *viva forma legis*, potius formans et regulans legem quam formatus et regulatus a lege . . ." See, for the *rex exsomnis* or *vigilans*, above, n.131, and below, n.167.

[147] Dante, *Parad.*, vi,88: "Chè la viva Giustizia che mi spira." By letting Justinian quote the decisive words in the right place, Dante, as none but he could, interlaces Empire, Church, Roman Law, Aristotle, the emperor as a divinely inspired antitype of God, and many other related matters and ideas.

[148] "Si lex est regula agendorum: ut haberi potest ex 5 Ethic., ipse iudex, et multum magis ipse rex cuius est leges ferre, debet esse quedam regula in agendis. Est enim rex sive princeps quaedam lex; et lex est quaedam rex sive princeps. Nam lex est quidam inanimatus princeps. Princeps vero est quaedam animata lex. Quantam ergo animatum inanimatum superat, tantum rex sive princeps debet superare legem . . . Rex quia est quaedam animata lex, est quaedam animata regula agendorum . . ." See, on Aegidius, Carlyle, *Political Theory*, v,70ff, esp.75f, where the texts are cited in full; Steinwenter, "Nomos," 253f; Berges, *Fürstenspiegel*, 211ff, esp.218f, who gives a succinct analysis of the tractate; cf.320ff, for the literature and for the incredible number of mediaeval translations into at least ten different languages.

superiority of the living king over the rigidity of the lifeless Law has its predecessors.[149] The definitions of Aegidius were repeated over and over again,[150] and his additional conclusion holding that "it is better to be ruled by a king than by the Law," was finally boiled down by the jurists to the maxim *Melius est bonus rex quam bona lex*—a total reversal of what Aristotle had said and meant to say.[151] Furthermore, these reflections on the King-Law mediator led Aegidius to summarize also the numerous discussions about the ruler's position with regard to Natural and Positive Laws. He could arrive practically at one conclusion only: "The Positive Law is under the ruler just as Natural Law is above him." Or, as he remarks in that connection: "The ruler is the intermediate between Natural Law and Positive Law."[152] The tenets of mediatorship and duality of Laws thus were fused.

A Prince who was the intermediate between the two Laws, who was the *lex animata* sent by God down to men, and who was both *legibus solutus* and *legibus alligatus*, was for obvious reasons a not uncommon concept in that period. For every legal philosophy of the Middle Ages was inevitably founded on the assumption that there existed a, so to speak, meta-legal Law of Nature the existence of which did not depend on the existence of kingdoms and states— in fact, of any kingdom or state at all—because the Law of Nature existed self-sufficiently *per se* and apart from any Positive Law.

---

[149] Plato, *Politicus*, 294-296; Steinwenter, "Nomos," 262ff.

[150] See, for Engelbert of Admont, Steinwenter, "Nomos," 253; also George B. Fowler, *Intellectual Interest of Engelbert of Admont* (New York, 1947), 170f. Cf. Lucas de Penna, on C.11,41,n.20 (Lyon, 1582), 453, "Et sicut animatum excessive potentius est inanimato, sic princeps excessive potentior est ipsa lege, dicit [frater Aegidius] ibidem lib.1, parte 2. Et periculosius est contemnere legem vivam, maiusque crimen, quam legem mortuam."

[151] Carlyle, *Political Theory*, v,75,n.2: ". . . quod melius est regi rege quam lege." Cf. Baldus, on D.1,1,5,n.5, fol.10v; also Matthaeus de Afflictis, on *Lib.aug.*, 1,30,n.8, fol.147v. Aquinas, *Summa theol.*, I-IIae, q.xcv, art.1, ad 2, who follows Aristotle, is more sceptical, at least with regard to the judge: he thinks it better to have everything ordered by the laws "quia *iustitia animata iudicis* non invenitur in multis."

[152] Carlyle, *loc.cit.*: "Sciendum est regem et quemlibet principantem esse medium inter legem naturalem et positivam . . . Quare positiva lex est infra principantem sicut lex naturalis est supra . . ." Cf. Gierke, *Gen.R.*, III,614,n.264. Since Aegidius referred, in the preceding sentence, to *5 Ethicorum*, it is certainly the Aristotelean image of the "judge as an intermediate" which prompted him to interpret the ruler likewise as an "intermediate." Aquinas (see next note) interpreted the ruler's position in a similar fashion, and in his commentary on Aristotle's *Politics* (§15, ed. Spiazzi, p.7) he explains that the political power "quasi secundum partem principetur . . . , et secundum partem sit subiectus."

About this fundamentally dualistic aspect of the Law there was no serious disagreement between jurists and theologians. It was actually Thomas Aquinas who made at least one essential point perfectly clear when he declared that indeed the Prince was *legibus solutus* with regard to the coercive power (*vis coactiva*) of Positive Law, since the Positive Law received its power from the Prince anyhow; on the other hand, however, Aquinas held (in full agreement with the *lex digna* which for this purpose he quoted) that the Prince was bound to the directive power (*vis directiva*) of the Law of Nature, to which he should submit voluntarily.[153] This cleverly phrased definition, which apparently offered an acceptable solution of a difficult problem (acceptable to both adversaries and defenders of the later royal absolutism and still quoted by Bossuet),[154] conformed essentially not only with John of Salisbury, but also with Frederick II when he stated that the emperor, though above the Law, was yet bound to the directive power of Reason.

It will be rather obvious by now to what extent the duality of Laws, natural and human, was interlocked with the idea of an intermediate in matters of Law and with the dualities inherent in Justice herself as well as in the Prince. And it is at this point that, philosophically, also Frederick's self-definition as "father and son of Justice" becomes meaningful, since his claim to mediatorship in

---

[153] Aquinas, *Summa theol.*, I-IIae,q.XCVI,a.5,ad 3; see the discussion of that passage by Carlyle, *Political Theory*, v,475f.; also Jean-Marie Aubert, *Le droit romain dans l'oeuvre de Saint Thomas* (Bibliothèque thomiste, xxx [Paris, 1955]), 83f.

[154] *De iure magistratuum* (quoted by Esmein, "Princeps legibus solutus," 209, n.1): the Prince is "solutus nonnisi de legibus civilibus . . . , non autem de iure publico et ad statum(!), ut dici solet, pertinente, multoque minus de iure naturali et divino." The references to Aquinas' distinctions are innumerable; they do not begin with Andreas of Isernia, on *Feud.* II,51 ('De capit. qui'), n.29, fol.231 ("nam quantum ad vim directivam legis, Princeps est subditus legi, sicut quilibet . . ."), nor do they probably end with Bossuet, *Politique tirée des propres paroles de l'écriture sainte*, IV, proposition 4 (ed. H. Brémond, *Bossuet: Textes choisis et commentés*, Paris, 1913, II,115), who, after having quoted the *lex digna* ("cette belle loi d'un empereur romain"), said: "Les rois sont donc soumis comme les autres à l'équité des lois . . . ; mais ils ne sont pas soumis aux peines des lois: ou, comme parle la théologie [sc. Aquinas], ils sonst soumis aux lois, non quant à la *puissance coactive*, mais quant à la *puissance directive*." See also the distinction made by Albericus de Rosate, on *D*.1,3,31,n.10, fol.31: the Prince being the *lex animata* is placed not really *under* the Law, but *in* the Law (above, n.129); then, quoting Ps.1:2 ("In lege Domini voluntas eius"), he explains: "dicit aliud est esse in lege, aliud sub lege. Qui enim in lege est, secundum legem agit voluntarie obediendo legi; qui autem sub lege est, secundum legem agit necessitatis timore coactus." He finally refers to the *lex digna*. See also above, nos.25 (John of Salisbury), 52ff, and, for the later theory, Church, *Constitutional Thought*, 197, 232, passim.

matters of Law resulted from, and fell in with, the political thought of his century. If Justice was the power "intermediate between God and the world,"[155] then the Prince as the *Iustitia animata* necessarily obtained a similar position. Hence, by the combined efforts of Roman Law and Aristotle, of legal and political philosophies, supported by traditional theological maxims, Justice and Prince as well as their mutual relationship appeared in a new light.

It is true that the conventional features characteristic of the image of Justice during the earlier Middle Ages remained untouched and were hardly affected even by the eulogizing effusions of philosophizing jurists. If the lawyers defined Justice most emphatically as a *Virtus* "triumphant over all other Virtues" and almost equal to God himself, there was nothing new in that statement except a certain emphasis and, perhaps, a greater specificness.[156] Nor was the stress incessantly laid upon the two natures of Justice—*alia divina, alia humana*—new by itself; for the distinction was always made between a celestial and a terrestrial Justice, one absolute and immutable, ruling the universe and preceding in time all created laws, and the other imperfectly materialized in the laws of man and mutable in her appearance according to the fickle conditions on earth—therefore "observing with many sighs the things of both God and man."[157] Furthermore, when the jurists distinguished between Justice *in abstracto* and Justice *in concreto*, we easily recognize in the former the "Idea" or the "Universal," and in the latter the actual application of that Idea to human laws. To be sure, new distinctions were derived from Aristotle and his categories of Virtues; but the definition of Justice, for instance, as a *habitus* was known through the agency of Cicero long before the revival of Aristotle.[158]

All that was not decisive. What actually changed in the age of

---

[155] *Siete Partidas*, II,9,28, ed. Real Academia de la Historia (Madrid, 1807), II,84: "la justicia que es medianera entre Dios e el mundo."

[156] Baldus, on c.36 X 1,6, n.4, *In Decretales*, fol.79: "Nota quod iustitia triumphat super omnem aliam virtutem, vitam, famam et scientiam." See also the paraphrase of his glosses on *D.*1,1, by Ullmann, "Baldus," 388ff; further Ullmann, *Lucas de Penna*, 35ff, for a collection of likewise relevant passages. For Justice as the aggregate of all virtues, see further the pompous arenga of a letter of King Robert of Naples concerning the promotion of a Doctor of Law at the University of Naples, ed. G. M. Monti, "Da Carlo I a Roberto di Angiò," *Archivio storico per le province napoletane*, LIX (1934), 146. See also above, n.70.

[157] Above, n.60, also 64.

[158] Above, nos.59ff,80.

the jurists was not Justice herself, but the mood of her new interpreters, who wrote about Justice not for theological or spiritual benefit, but for professional purposes and in a scientific manner. Decisive, then, was that a scientific and professional Jurisprudence had come to life, and that Justice thereby became the special scientific object of scholarly interpreters who concentrated on investigating the nature of *Iustitia* and *Ius* with the same professional devotion and the same inner urge with which theologians would interpret professionally the nature of the triune God or the working of divine dispensation. The opening titles of Justinian's *Digest*, fraught with philosophy as they were, as well as the likewise philosophical introductions of the books of the *Institutes* challenged, by their profound seriousness and their aura of holiness, generations of jurists to ponder about the very essence of their own doing and to reflect or comment on the dignity of their profession. Justice, after all, vindicated the ultimate *raison d'être* of her adepts who, in return, not only stressed the moral and ethical values of their learned occupation, but also made Justice the chief object of their cult and the live center of their *iuris religio*.[159]

---

[159] The term *iuris religio* is regularly used by the glossators when interpreting Justinian's *prooemium* of the *Institutes*, where the emperor is called *iuris religiosissimus* (also *D*.31,1,67,10); see, e.g., Placentinus, *Summa Inst.*, ed. Fitting, *Schriften*, 222,21; also Azo, *Summa Inst.*, fol.268; ed. Maitland, *Bracton and Azo*, p.6; further *Glos.ord.*, v. *religiosissimus*: "Nota quem fieri religiosum per leges; nam ipsae sunt sacrae." Since the emperor mentions the duality of *arma* and *leges*, the glossators expand on that topic; see, e.g., *Glos.ord.*: "Item nota hic quatuor proportionalia: scilicet arma, usus armorum, victoria, triumphus; item leges, usus legum, calumniae, repulsio, et iuris religio"; military triumph and religion of law are put into parallel. Since *religio* was defined according to Cicero (*De invent.*, II,161) as *virtus curam ceremoniamque afferens* (see H. Kantorowicz, *Glossators*, 19), it was not difficult to apply this notion in a secular sense to the care for justice and to the ceremonial of court sessions (see *Lib.aug.* 1,32, Cervone, 82: *Cultus iustitiae silentium reputatur*; cf. *Erg.Bd.*, 89) or, in later times, to the quasi-religious court ceremonial of absolutist kingship. Moreover, the first of the six civic Virtues, the daughters of Justice, was *Religio* (see above, n.61) according to Cicero. Hence, it was common enough to point out that "Iustitia in subiecto infusa vel acquisita informat ad religionem, pietatem, etc." See Baldus, on *D*.1,1,10,n.2, fol.15v; also Ullmann, "Baldus," 390f. Finally, *Inst*.4,16, rubr., the *iurisiurandi religio* is mentioned. See, e.g., Andreas of Isernia, on *Lib.aug.*, 1,99, Cervone, 168: "Iustitia habet multas partes, inter quas est religio et sacramentum secundum Tullium in Rhetorica sua. Ponitur ergo totum pro parte: nam sacramentum est religio: unde dicitur iurisiurandi religio (with a reference to *C*.2,58,1-2; see above, n.105)." It is worth mentioning that Cuias, on *Inst.*, prooem. (*Scholia*), says: "Religiosissimus fere idem est, quod sanctissimus iuris sacerdos." See Cuias, *Opera* (Prato, 1836), II,607. Fortescue (see below, Ch.v,n.89) also talks about *legis sacramenta* and *mysteria legis Angliae*, and he thereby falls in with the lingo of the

Jurisprudence was, according to Roman Law, "the knowledge of things divine and human."[160] Jurisprudence was defined not only as a "science" (*scientia*) but also as an art. And art was for the jurists—long before Renaissance artists picked up that definition—"Imitation of Nature."[161] Of this art, said Ulpian, we jurists may be called the priest, "for we worship Justice" (*Iustitiam namque colimus*), to which a late gloss added explainingly: *ut Deam*, "as a goddess."[162] Whether a Virtue, or a Universal, or an Idea, or a Goddess, the worship of Justice on the part of the jurists was semi-religious, and a great lawyer such as Baldus would later almost apotheosize Justice, which he called "a habitus which does not die (*non moritur*)," which is perpetual and immortal like the soul, and which leads to religion and to God. But already the *Liber augustalis* was carried, unmistakably, by the same semi-religious ethos; and the tenor of its language was as high-strung as that of any legal language in later times. In fact, it was the same language which a judge would use who, when deciding an important case, might wish to preface his sentence by pointing out that "the command of Reason presides in the mind of the judge," that "Justice herself examining truth sits on the bench," and that "Righteousness of Judgment is seated like a king on his throne," or by paralleling the judge on earth with the eternal Judge from

---

Italian jurists; see, e.g., Baldus, on *Liber Extra*, prooem., rubr.,n.7, fol.3: "Quaedam [nomina] misterio iuris sunt introducta," whereas other *nomina* exist "quibus non est datum certum mysterium a iure."

160 *D.*1,1,10,2: "Iuris prudentia est divinarum atque humanarum rerum notitia, iusti atque iniusti scientia"; repeated verbatim in *Inst.*1,1,1.

161 "Ius est ars boni et aequi"; *D.*1,1,1. The glossators, since Irnerius, interpreted these words time and time again; see, for the early glosses, H. Kantorowicz, *Glossators*, 63f. In the earlier times it seems to have been customary to define *ars* according to a phrase attributed to Porphyrius; see Azo, *Summa Inst.*, on *Inst.*1,2,n.2, fol.269; ed. Maitland, p.24; and *Glos.ord.* on *D.*1,1,1, v. *ius est ars*: "id est scientia finita, quae arctat infinita; nam ars est de infinitis finita doctrina, secundum Porphyrium." Later on the definition of Aristotle, *Physics*, II,2,194a,21 ("art mimics nature"), began to prevail; see below, Ch.vi,n.81; see also Berges, *Fürstenspiegel*, 218,n.1, for Aegidius Romanus.

162 Marginal gloss on *D.*1,1,1. In later times, this became the custom; see, e.g., Cujas on that place, in *Opera*, vii,12: "quasi Deam sanctissimam"; and Budé, *Annotationes*, 28f, who compares Justice with the Greek goddess *Dikē*, and adds: "eiusque Deae diaconi et ministri . . . Iudices dicuntur." This, of course, is already the historical school which understands Justice as a goddess of ancient Greek or Roman religion, whereas the mediaeval lawyers understood her as *Dei motus* or *Dei spiritus*; Ullmann, *Lucas de Penna*, 36.

whose features the right judgments proceed.[163] Hence, this language acquired an unexpected degree of reality by its application in court, and what may have seemed to be no more than a presumptuous metaphor could be brought to life and gain actuality through the pronouncement of the judge.

It is against the background of these and many related ideas that we have to understand Frederick II's antiphrasis "father and son of Justice, her lord and her minister." It would be ridiculous to deny the perpetuation and unbroken effectiveness in the thirteenth century of the ancient ideal of the *rex iustus* which had held sway in the earlier Middle Ages, for Frederick II himself would easily enough activate the ancient ideal of the biblical and messianic King of Justice whenever it seemed useful to him. However, like so many other notions, the eschatological image of the *rex iustus* grew paler in the political world of the later Middle Ages, and it was perpetrated politically not in its former Augustinian attire but rather in the guise of the jurists: it survived at the price of being transferred from the altar to the bench, from the realm of Grace to that of Jurisprudence, while the king *gerens typum Jesu Christi* was gradually superseded by a Prince *gerens typum Iustitiae*. The Prince of the juristic century, however, no longer typified Justice in the sense of Melchizedek (whose name means *rex Iustitiae*), but in the sense of Accursius, or (to quote Maitland) of "a priest for ever after the order of Ulpian."[164] And this new type derived its strength not from the effects of consecration, but from learned jurisprudence. The Prince was "mediator" as an impersonator or antitype of *Iustitia mediatrix* rather than an impersonator and antitype of the God-man. It cannot, however, be emphasized strongly enough that the former values continued to stand unabated, even though in juxtaposition with the new values; that the interrelations between Christ and Justice were so obvious

---

[163] Above, n.160; Ullmann, "Baldus," 388f, for Justice as a *habitus*. See the forms of sentences quoted by Durandus, *Speculum iuris*, II,part.iii, §6,n.19 (Venice, 1602), II,791f, who recommends "si autem arduum sit negotium, incipias cum praefatione sic" and then offers the following form: "Presidente rationis imperio in animo iudicantis, sedet in examine veritatis pro tribunali iustitia et quasi Rex in solio iudicii rectitudo . . . Haec enim recti fuit eterni providentia iudicis, de cuius vultu recta iudicia procedent, ut recti iudices eligentur in orbe. . . ."

[164] Pollock and Maitland, *English Law*, I,208 (= p.187), n.3, referring to Bracton, who added to "iustitiam namque colimus" the words: "et sacra iura ministramus," following thereby Azo; cf. Maitland, *Bracton and Azo*, 23f.

and so numerous that the transition was often imperceptible;[165] and that the formerly valid features contributed to shape the image, messianic or apocalyptic, of the Prince also during the "jurists' century."

What matters here is the obvious secularization of royal mediatorship through the new jurisprudence, a development comparable to the secularization of the *rex et sacerdos* ideal and of many another notion. It is true, Frederick II's formula defining the Caesar as both *pater et filius Iustitiae* still had in its phrasing a quasi "physiological" content which would seem to link the emperor to the interpretations of earlier times, to the ruler as a *gemina persona*. Undeniably there evolved some superficial conformities between the Christ-centered and the Law-centered concepts of rulership. But those similarities, if such they be, should not deceive us. The essence of every liturgical kingship, Grace, had no share in the metaphysical superworld which the jurists constructed and into which they placed the Prince as the "living Justice." To the Norman Anonymous, the anointed king appeared as a "twinned person" because *per gratiam* this king reflected the two natures of the God-man, "Man by nature and, through his consecration, god by grace." That is to say, the king's ambivalent appearance was founded theologically on the tension between "human nature and divine Grace." And it was Grace which bestowed upon the individual man that super-body of which the anointed king appeared as the living image.

In the Law-centered era, however, and in the language of the jurists, the Prince no longer was "god by grace" or the living image of Grace; he was the living image of Justice, and *ex officio* he was the personification of an Idea which likewise was both

[165] See above, n.22. See also c.84,C.XI,q.3, ed. Friedberg, 1,666 ("Christus sapientia est, iustitia . . ."), a passage to which, e.g., Lucas de Penna, on C.12,45,1,n.61 (ed. 1582), p.915, refers when explaining that the selling of justice is simony: "gravius crimen est vendere iustitiam quam praebendam. Legimus enim Christum esse iustitiam . . . Non legitur autem esse praebendam . . . Vendere iustitiam quae Christus est, gravissimum est censendum" (see, for the underlying problem, Gaines Post, "The Legal Theory of Knowledge as a Gift of God," *Traditio*, XI [1955], 197-210); see also on C.10,70,4.n.8, p.345, and *ibid.*, n.4: "Iustitia quidem (sicut verissime Trimegistus diffinit) nihil aliud est quam Dei motus." Further, *ibid.*, n.5, where he refers to Pseudo-Chrysostomus' *Opus imperfectum super Matthaeum*: "qui omne iustitia facit et cogitat mente sua, Deum videt, quoniam iustitia figura Dei est. Deus enim iustitia est . . ." And he alludes to Prov. 11: 4, when he says (n.7): "Qui vero iustitiam sectatur, non moritur."

divine and human. The new duality of the Prince was founded on a legal philosophy which indeed was interspersed with theological thought; it was founded on the goddess of the *religio iuris*. However, the field of tension no longer was determined by the polarity of "human nature and Divine Grace"; it had moved towards a juristically formulated polarity of "Law of Nature and laws of man," or to that of "Nature and man," and, a little later, to that of "Reason and society," where Grace no longer had a discernible place.

Baldus, in one of his ethically most high-toned legal opinions, talked about the Prince who surrendered himself to Justice, "that is, to the Substance of what is good and right; for the person who judges, may err, but Justice never errs." And yet (Baldus pointed out), "wanting a person, Reason and Justice act nothing"; they are incapacitated without the personator of their substance, wherefore, if controversy arises, "wanting an official dignitary Justice is buried."[166] Hence, the Prince in his capacity of a *Iustitia animata* had to make that goddess manifest, and as her constituent he could claim for himself with some inner logic a virtual omnipresence in his courts: through his officers he owned, as Frederick II repeatedly termed it, "potential ubiquity" even though in his individual body he could not be present everywhere.[167]

---

[166] Baldus, *Consilia*, III,218, fol.64 (col.b, in fine): "Et certum est quod submittit se iustitiae, id est, substantiae boni et aequi ['realitati iustitiae' in the preceding sentence]. Ius enim reddens quandoque errat, sed iustitia nunquam errat . . . Item certum est quod ratio et iustitia sine persona nihil agit . . . Unde sine magistratu iustitia in controversiam posita sepulta est." See below, Ch.VII,n.420. The underlying idea is that Justice, being a "potentiality," has to be "actualized" by a person or dignity; cf. Petrus de Vinea, *Epp.*, III,68, ed. Schard, 507: "quod in potentia gerimus [the emperor] per eos [judges and officials] velut ministros iusticiae [above, n.162] deduceretur ad actum." We recognize, of course, the Aristotelian categories ("de potentia ad actum").

[167] *Lib.aug.*, I,17, Cervone, 41: "Et sic nos etiam, qui prohibente individuitate personae ubique praesentialiter esse non possumus, ubique potentialiter adesse credamur." See also Vinea, *Ep.* II,8, ed. Schard, 271; *MGH,Const.*, II,306,37f, No.223; cf. *Erg.Bd.*, 94. Further Nicholas of Bari, ed. Kloos, *DA*, XI,175,§16, the encomium in praise of Frederick II: the author demands that every subject serve the emperor "quia omnia novit et falli non potest [see above, n.166, for Baldus on *Iustitia*] . . . , quia ubique eius potentia invenitur et ideo fuge aditus denegatur." Baldus, *Consilia*, I,333,n.1, fol.105ᵛ, uses very similar words to explain the nature of delegations ("Ipse [Imperator] personaliter ubique esse non possit . . ."). See also above, n.131, for the ubiquity of the emperor because he is the *lex animata*: "I sleep, and my heart, that is, my king, watches." The image was not uncommon; see Philip of Leyden, *De cura reipublicae*, VI,1, p.36: ". . . princeps, qui ad quietem subditorum praeparandam noctes transire consuevit insomnes . . ." All those ideas (the Prince's ubiq-

To summarize, the Prince as the animate Law or living Justice
shared with *Iustitia* the duality which inheres in all Universals or
"Ideas." It was this double aspect of Justice, human and divine,
which was mirrored by her imperial vicar on earth who, in his
turn, was mainly through *Iustitia* also the vicar of God. Justice
herself, at least in the language of learned jurisprudence, no longer
was quite identical with the God of the altar, though still inseparable from God the Father; nor was she as yet subordinated to
an absolute or deified State: she was, for that short period of transition, a. living *Virtus* in her own right, the goddess of the age in
which jurisprudence took the lead and became intellectually the
great vivifier of almost every branch of knowledge. By analogy, the
Prince no longer was the *christomimētēs*, the manifestation of
Christ the eternal King; nor was he, as yet, the exponent of an immortal nation; he had his share in immortality because he was the
hypostasis of an immortal Idea. A new pattern of *persona mixta*
emerged from Law itself, with *Iustitia* as the model deity and the
Prince as both her incarnation and her *Pontifex maximus*.

3. Bracton

REX INFRA ET SUPRA LEGEM

The seemingly self-contradictory concept of a kingship at once
above and below the Law has been criticized as "scholastic and
unworkable."[168] Whatever that criticism may mean, and from

---

uity, his character of *lex animata*, his infallibility ["the king can do no wrong"],
and his perpetual vigilance) are summarized by Matthaeus de Afflictis, on *Lib.aug.*,
1,6,n.32, fol.52^v: "(reference to Baldus, *Consilia*, 1,141,n.4, fol.42^v) ubi dicit quod
rex quoad suos subditos in regno suo est tanquam quidam corporalis Deus . . . ,
quod lex non exequitur aliquod iniustum, vel iniquum: quia oculus legis sicut
oculus Dei omnia videt, omnia intuetur . . . et rex in regno dicitur lex animata . . .
Et ideo antiquitus dicebatur quod corona imperialis invisibilis imponebatur a Deo
ipsi principi . . . quia ius divinum concessit principibus supremam potestatem, ut
patet in evangelio. . . ." See also, for the imperial and royal ubiquity, my paper
"Invocatio nominis imperatoris," *Bollettino del Centro di Studi Filologici e Lin-
guistici Siciliani*, III (1955), 35-50, and, for some additions, "Zu den Rechtsgrundlagen
der Kaisersage," *DA*, XIII (1957), nos.6 1ff.

[168] See Schulz, "Bracton on Kingship," *EHR*, LX (1945), 165, about the theory of
John of Salisbury. Schulz, for one thing, underestimates the influence of Salisbury,
which was not restricted to Helinand of Froidmont and Gilbert of Tournai (see,
e.g., Post, "Two Notes," 293, n.53), but can be traced in legal literature to the 16th
century; see Ullmann, "Influence of John of Salisbury," *EHR*, LIX (1944), 384ff, whose
interesting survey, restricted chiefly to Italy, does not pretend to be complete. Salisbury's fiction was, by and large, that of the *rex iustus*, which, in the treatise of

whatever point of view that verdict may have proceeded, the only thing that is of interest here is whether or not those self-contradictions appeared scholastic and unworkable at the time they were introduced and during the centuries they were recognized valid. Men such as John of Salisbury, Frederick II, or Thomas Aquinas were not lacking experience; and if they considered, as apparently they did, those contradictions less unworkable and scholastic than the modern critic, we may safely assume that certain conditions of thought, or perhaps "limitations of thought," forced them to shape their opinions in the way they did. After all, the idea of a state existing only for its own sake was foreign to that age.[169] The very belief in a divine Law of Nature as opposed to Positive Law, a belief then shared by every thinker, almost necessitated the ruler's position both above and below the Law. Finally, we may wonder whether those self-contradictions were not conditioned, directly or indirectly, also by the divine model of mediaeval kings who, being extra-legally God and man at the same time, was likewise above and below the Law; or whether the Virgin Mary, frequently referred to by Canon Law to illustrate legal conditions, did not as "Virgin and mother, daughter of her Son"—*Nata nati, mater patris*—likewise imply certain self-contradictions which would not easily be accommodated to the definitions of any customary law of inheritance.[170]

Gilbert of Tournai, a representative of the political mysticism of 13th-century France, was turned into that of a king to rule supposedly *angelico more* (see the careful analysis of Gilbert's *Erudito regum et principum* by Berges, *Fürstenspiegel,* 150ff, esp.156f). Whether the *rex iustus* or *rex angelicus* is more workable or less workable than the *rex imago Christi* or the king as *lex animata* is, of course, not at all the question, since for a modern "political platform" those ideals are all equally useless. What matters here is the change of the metaphor of "Perfection" which, in the 13th century, entered into a new phase: the image of perfection was either spiritualized (*rex angelicus, papa angelicus*, messianic emperor) or secularized (*lex animata, Iustitia animata*, Crown, Dignity, etc.), which did not exclude mutual overshadowing. I do not believe that any mediaeval political theory could work without some fiction or some "metaphor of perfection," and there is every reason to wonder whether a modern one can.

169 For the whole problem, see Gierke, *Gen.R.,* III,610: "The thought that State and Law exist by, for and under each other was foreign to the Middle Age. It solved the problem by opposing to Positive Law the idea of Natural Law." The translation is Maitland's (*Political Theories,* 74), who captioned the paragraph in the margin: "Law above State and State above Law."

170 See, for *mater et filia,* above, n.40, and, for the juristic evaluation of these terms on the part of the Canonists, Gierke, *Gen.R.,* III,278f, n.96, also 332,n.272 (Goffredus of Trani). John Fortescue, when discussing the problem of the succession

In any case, to the political thinkers and legal philosophers of the late Middle Ages those contradictions did not appear unworkable at all; they appeared, on the contrary, as the only solution of the divine and human duality within the realms of Natural and Positive Laws. If viewed against that background, Frederick II's definition of the emperor's place in the system of mediaeval Law as "father and son of Justice" appears as a highly finished and mature formula; and if one keeps it in mind, as one should, it may turn out to be extremely useful and helpful for the understanding of some further "contradictions of our own making"[171] in the political doctrines of other lawyers of that period, and above all of Bracton. For it appears that in the present lively discussion about "Bracton on Kingship" a focal point has been sometimes unduly slighted.[172]

Frederick II and Henry of Bracton were contemporaries. The great emperor died about the time when Bracton began to write his *De legibus et consuetudinibus Angliae.*[173] No available evi-

---

to the throne, argued along the following lines: since "the father's royalty cannot be inherited by the daughter, she cannot be a medium for its inheritance by her son," because she cannot pass on to her son something she herself does not possess (Chrimes, *Const.Ideas*, 10ff). Fortescue was guided by Roman Law; had he been guided by theology-inspired jurisprudence, his argument would have been hardly convincing, for theology found it less difficult to maintain that the Theotokos did not impair her Son's divine nature, though she herself did not possess it.

[171] Charles H. McIlwain, *Constitutionalism Ancient and Modern* (Ithaca, N.Y., 2nd ed., 1947), 83, whose brilliant discussion of Bracton (pp. 67ff) is itself a great step in delineating the so-called "contradictions" and in understanding them within the setting of thirteenth-century thought.

[172] The present lively interest in Bracton was perhaps stimulated by the controversial book of Hermann Kantorowicz, *Bractonian Problems* (Glasgow, 1941) and the very fruitful discussion was kept alive by Fritz Schulz' numerous studies: "Critical Studies on Bracton's Treatise," *LQR*, LIX (1943), 172-180; "A New Approach to Bracton," *Seminar*, II (1944), 42-50; "Bracton and Raymond of Penafort," *LQR*, LXI (1945), 286-292; "Bracton as Computist," *Traditio*, III (1945), 264-305; his study "Bracton on Kingship" (above, n.168) refers directly to the problems of the present study; see p.136, n.2, for the earlier literature. In addition to two articles by H. G. Richardson ("Azo, Drogheda, and Bracton," and "Tancred, Raymond, and Bracton," *EHR*, LIX [1944], 22-47, 376-384), Gaillard Lapsley in his study, "Bracton and the Authorship of the 'Addicio de Cartis,'" *EHR*, LXII (1947), 1-19, deals with Bracton's concepts of kingship. See further the highly instructive and illuminating studies by Gaines Post, especially "A Romano-Canonical Maxim, *Quod omnes tangit*, in Bracton," *Traditio*, IV (1946), 197-251. For McIlwain's contribution see above, n.171, to which there may be added his text-critical remarks "The Present Status of the Problem of the Bracton Text," *Harvard Law Review*, LVII (1943), 220-240.

[173] The general assumption was, and probably still is, that Bracton finished his book around 1259; H. Kantorowicz, *Bractonian Problems*, 29ff, suggested an earlier

dence permits us to assume that the English lawyer was familiar with the *Liber augustalis,* although the 'fifties of the thirteenth century marked the high-tide of indeed most intense diplomatic and political interchanges between England and the kingdom of Sicily.[174] Similarities between the utterances of the emperor and of Bracton are anything but rare; they are, however, easily accounted for by the fact that the Sicilian lawyers as well as the English relied often on the same material to support their concepts of rulership—especially with regard to Roman Law. The works of Azo, for example, were used equally in the South and in England.[175] The *lex regia,* the maxim *quod principi placuit,* the *lex digna,* and other famous passages of the Justinian law-books have been adduced and evaluated in both countries, and in one way or another the great intellectual problems of that age imprinted their marks unfailingly on every contemporary legal writer.

For all these obvious congruencies, the differences between the imperial and the English concepts of rulership and Law were considerable. The Hohenstaufen emperor was, in many respects, far less cryptic than Bracton. Frederick II described his place above and under Justice in very definite terms, admitting frankly that in some respects the emperor was bound to Law, but emphasizing very firmly that the Prince exclusively had legislative power by divine inspiration as well as by the *lex regia.* He took it for granted that he himself was "The Law," the *lex animata* and incarnation of the very Idea of Justice—a concept of many hues, distinct enough to be valuable in matters legal and political, indistinct enough to be useful, when given a spiritual or messianic interpretation, for purposes of political and anti-papal propaganda.

Of these high-flown ideologies and metaphysics we find little, if anything, in Bracton. To be sure, the idea of Justice also pervades

---

date; see, however, Post, *op.cit.,* 217, n.104, and Stephan Kuttner and Beryl Smalley, "The 'Glossa ordinaria' to the Gregorian Decretals," *EHR,* LX (1945), 97-105.

[174] See, for those relations, my study "Petrus de Vinea in England," *Mitteilungen des Österreichischen Instituts für Geschichtsforschung,* LI,74ff, 81ff. See below, n.209.

[175] See Maitland, *Select Passages from the Works of Bracton and Azo* (Selden Society, VIII, London, 1894), who offers at the same time a useful edition of large passages of Azo's *Summa Institutionum.* See, for Azo and the imperial *curia,* e.g., Niese, in *HZ,* CVIII (1912), 521,n.2, and Capasso, "Storia esterna," 442 (William of Vinea, a pupil of Azo).

his work; but *Justitia* is far from being the Virgo of the Golden Age, and even farther from being incarnate in King Henry III or, for that matter, in any English king. England in the thirteenth century was less messianically minded than Italy and the rest of the Continent, and the doctrine of the ruler as a *lex animata* descending at the command of God from high heaven down to men seems to have fallen on particularly barren ground in England before the age of Queen Elizabeth, the new Astraea.[176] To accept domination by an abstract idea has never been a weakness of England, though a useful fiction might more readily be accepted. Hence, also in Bracton's work the Idea of Justice is eclipsed by the concreteness of Law. The question was not whether the king was at once "father and son of Justice," but whether he was "above or under the Law."

Bracton, though quite unwilling to diminish the sublimity of the Crown or impair the royal prerogative by binding it without qualification to the Positive Law of which the king was the lord, nevertheless emphasized strongly what Frederick admitted only with some reservation: that the king was "under the Law." In other words, where Frederick deduced from the Roman law-books a confirmation of his personal prerogative rights while conceding to some degree his subjection to Natural Law and to Reason, Bracton deduced from the same passages that the king was under the Law of the land, but acknowledged at the same time the unique position of the king against whom Law could not legally be set in motion. Hence, Bracton's king, too, was in some respects above and beyond the Law. There is, not to mention many other points of divergency between Frederick and Bracton, a very tangible difference of emphasis concerning the Prince and the Law; but it is nevertheless a difference within the same general system of politico-legal thought in which the Law as such, incarnate in the ruler or not, appeared as the true sovereign.

One difficulty with Bracton and with so many another political theorist of that age is the equivocal usage of the word *lex*. It may

---

[176] This does not exclude philosophizing on Justice. Bracton has many passages about *pax et iustitia* in the mediaeval sense, that is, as the genuine *raison d'être* of the state; also political and parliamentary sermonizing on Justice will be found at any time (see, for an interesting example, Chrimes, *Const.Ideas*, 121f,197); for the Elizabethan period, see Yates, "Queen Elizabeth as Astraea," *Warburg Journal*, x (1947), 27-82.

cover both the Divine or Natural Law and the Positive Law, written or unwritten. There certainly was a strong tendency in thirteenth-century England to subject the king, in the language of Aquinas, not only to the *vis directiva* of Natural Law, but also to the *vis coactiva* of Positive Law, and thus to establish that "tyranny of the Law" which, in the very days of Bracton, and so often thereafter, threatened to paralyze the orderly functioning of government. It is certainly going much too far to maintain that Bracton endeavored to bind the king to Positive Law without discrimination or restriction. This has been clearly recognized by Professor McIlwain who ingeniously extracted from Bracton's work the distinctions of *gubernaculum* and *iurisdictio*—the former being the sphere of Government within which the king was "absolute," and the latter the sphere of Right, over which the king had no power. And it is most gratifying to find that others also laid stress on the fact that even when *lex* seemed to encompass also the *leges humanae* the term would often refer to that part of the Positive Law only which "corresponds to the Divine Law and has been approved by the continuing consent of past generations."[177] Or, as Aegidius Romanus later formulated the problem most accurately:

> When it is said that some Positive Law is above the Prince, such language does not refer to the Positive Law as such, but to the fact that in the Positive Law there has been preserved some strength of the Natural Law.[178]

That is to say, the king was bound only to the Divine or Natural Law. However, he was bound to the Natural Law not merely in

[177] McIlwain always emphasizes that the Bractonian king was both above and below the Law; see *Growth of Political Thought*, 361ff.,367 (the king "absolute but limited"), and even stronger *Constitutionalism*, 75ff. His distinction between *gubernaculum* and *iurisdictio* is closely related to the problems outlined here and in the following pages. If I do not avail myself of these notions, the reason is that the notions of "Crown" and "King" do not really coincide with *gubernaculum* and *iurisdictio*. The "Crown," above Law and Time, is not identical with *gubernaculum* in regard to which the ruler is "absolute," nor is *iurisdictio* identical with the king body natural, nor could the identifications easily be reversed. It would render a complicated problem even more complicated if the notions *gubernaculum* and *iurisdictio* were integrated here, since the resulting chiasm would make things almost incomprehensible. For the other quotation, see Lapsley, *op.cit.* (above, n.172), p.8f.

[178] "Si dicitur legem aliquam positivam esse supra principantem, hoc non est ut positiva, sed ut in ea reservatur virtus iuris naturalis." Aegidius Romanus, *De regimine principum*, III,2,c.25 and c.29, quoted by Gierke, *Gen.R.*, III,612,n.259; Maitland, *Pol.Theories*, 175.

its transcendental and meta-legal abstraction, but also in its concrete temporal manifestations which included the rights of clergy, magnates, and people—a very important point in an England which relied predominantly on unwritten laws and customs.

It is probable, or even quite certain, that in practice the body of Law by which Bracton considered his king bound, was materially much larger than that to which Frederick II had professed his allegiance. For all that, however, Bracton's expansion of the king's status "under the Law" did not abolish a status of the king also "above the Law." Nowhere can we deduce from Bracton's political theories an intention to invalidate or even reduce those *res quasi sacrae* which pertained to the Crown and which were to form what soon would be called the "Prerogative," that is, more or less undefined rights, along with clearly defined ones, which were not subjected to the customary Positive Law. It appears that not only modern, but already mediaeval overemphasis of the Bractonian maxim *lex supra regem* has led to obscuring unfairly the opposite aspect of Bracton's doctrine: the king "above the Law."[179]

Needless to say, the king's status "above the Law" itself was perfectly "legal" and guaranteed by Law. His supra-legal rights, serving "those things which pertain to jurisdiction and peace" and their protection, were granted to the king by Law itself.

> They pertain to none except only to the Crown and the royal dignity, nor can they be separated from the Crown, since they make the Crown what it is.[180]

Also Bracton's most renowned maxims—*lex facit regem*, or that typical Bolognese lawyer rime *Facit enim lex, quod ipse sit rex*—have an obverse side and are not to be read exclusively in the sense of restrictions.[181] Similar statements were not too rare during the

[179] The *Addicio de cartis*, e.g., may be an addition of the times of the Baronial War; see Schulz, "Kingship," 173ff; Lapsley, "Addicio de Cartis," *EHR*, LXII (1947), 1-19.

[180] "Ea vero quae iurisdictionis sunt et pacis, et ea quae sunt iustitiae et paci annexa, ad nullum pertinent nisi tantum ad coronam et dignitatem regiam, nec a corona separari poterunt, cum faciant ipsam coronam." Bracton, *De Legibus*, f.55b, ed. G. E. Woodbine (New Haven, 1922), II,167. Notice that the emphasis is on Crown, and not on the *rex regnans*.

[181] Bracton, f.5b (Schulz, C,2), Woodbine, II,33, and f.107 (Schulz, A,31), Woodbine, II,306. Passage and paragraph of the texts discussed by Schulz, "Kingship," 137-145, are henceforth added in parenthesis. For the little rimes of Bolognese

Middle Ages. *Regem iura faciunt, non persona*—"Laws, and not the person, make the king"—ran a statement well known to Canonists;[182] and according to the *lex digna* itself the emperors confess: "On the authority of the Law our authority depends."[183] Nor should we forget that the binding of the king's *Person* would usually allow, in the reverse proportion, an increase and even exaltation of the royal *Power*. The king is bound to the Law that makes him king; but the Law that made him king enhances also his royal power and bestows upon the ruler extraordinary rights which in many respects placed the king, legally, above the laws.

The king-making law *par excellence* was for Azo and the Civilians at large, very logically, the *lex regia* by which the Roman People had conferred all its power and imperium on the Prince. Bracton was far from rejecting the opinion of his master Azo.

> The king has no other power, since he is the vicar of God and his minister on earth, save that alone which he has of right. And this is *not* to the contrary of that passage which says "What pleases the Prince has the power of Law"; for there follows at the end of that law (*D.*1,4,1): "because by the *lex regia*, which has been laid down concerning his imperium, [the people transferred to him and on him all its power and authority]."[184]

---

lawyers, see, e.g., for Placentinus, Hermann Kantorowicz, "Poetical Sermon," 22ff, 36ff; or, for Roffred, Ferretti, "Roffredo Epifanio da Benevento," *Studi medievali,* III (1908), 236f.

[182] See the acts of the 8th Council of Toledo, in *PL*, LXXXIV,431A; Hinschius, *Decretales Pseudo-Isidorianae*, 392; Schulz, "Kingship," 169, n.4. This Visigothic concept did not curtail the royal power, but rather exalted the power by binding the person. Also the famous maxim *Nemo potest facere se ipsum regem* led, though for different reasons, to an enormous increase of the king's power: "Facto enim rege de regno eum repellere non est in potestate populi, et sic voluntas populi postea in necessitatem convertitur." For the history of this theory, which first appears in Pseudo-Chrysostomus' *Opus imperfectum* (above, Ch.III, n.105), see Jordan, "Der Kaisergedanke in Ravenna," 111-126, and, for its spreading to England (Aelfric, in: *Homilies of the Anglo-Saxon Church*, ed. B. Thorpe [1844], I,212) through the *Collectio monumentorum*, see Walter Holtzmann, "Zur Geschichte des Investiturstreites: Englische Analekten, 2," *Neues Archiv*, L (1934), 282ff.

[183] For the *lex digna*, see above, nos.51ff, also 128,131,153; Schulz, "Kingship," 141 (A,31), also 168f, where he emphasizes the reciprocity prevailing between law and power. The idea of the *lex digna* is reflected also by Dante, *Monarchia*, III,10: "Imperator ipsam [iurisdictionem] permutare non potest, in quantum Imperator, quum ab ea recipiat quod est."

[184] Bracton, fol.107 (Schulz, A,16f), ed. Woodbine, II,305: "Nihil enim aliud potest rex, cum sit Dei minister et vicarius in terris, nisi id solum, quod de iure potest. Nec obstat quod dicitur: 'Quod principi placet, legis habet vigorem,' quia sequitur in fine legis: 'cum lege regia, quae de imperio eius lata est [, populus ei

The passage is not quite simple, even if we disregard the difficulties arising from Bracton's omission of the bracketed passage.[185] What Bracton obviously wished to express is this: The king's power extends only to what he derived from Law (which, by the way, was not little); this restriction, however, does not disagree with the famous saying "What pleases the Prince has the power of Law"—for, the very fact that "What the Prince wills is Law" is derived from Law, is therefore legal, because it is based on the *lex regia* by which the people conferred on the Prince, among other rights, exactly this power to make Law "at his pleasure." Hence, from the *lex regia* Bracton deduced, like Frederick II and others before and after him, not only the king's allegiance to the king-making *lex regia* and his dependence on it, but also the king's legal power and legal authority to legislate on behalf of the people and interpret the Law *as he pleases.*

This, to be sure, might have led to a sound absolutism, as indeed Ulpian's *Quod principi placuit* very often did. We know that the jurists as well as the political philosophers customarily warded off that danger by quoting the *lex digna* in which the emperors asserted their allegiance to the Law; and Bracton was not an exception: he, too, referred in the same paragraph to the *lex digna* and interpreted it rather thoroughly.[186] But before citing this law, he inserted a qualification of the maxim *Quod principi placuit* by qualifying the very word *placuit,* "pleases." Unlike Frederick II, Bracton gave Ulpian's words a most significant twist to fit "constitutionalism": he deduced from the word *placuit* not an uncontrolled and God-inspired personal rule of the Prince, but a council-controlled and council-inspired, almost impersonal or supra-personal, rule of the king. What "pleased the Prince" was Law; but what pleased him had, first of all, to please the council of mag-

---

et in eum omne suum imperium et potestatem conferat].'" For Azo, see Maitland, *Bracton and Azo,* p.2; also Schulz, 141 (A,31). For the bracketed section, added from *D.*1,4,1, see next note.

185 See the ingenious and elegant solution of a Bractonian *insolubile* by Schulz, 153-156, who eliminated the awkward interpretation going back to John Selden and according to which the words *cum lege regia* were to mean "together with the *lex regia*" thus replacing the conjunction (*cum*) by the preposition; see Ioannis Seldeni, *Ad Fletam Dissertatio,* III,2, ed. David Ogg (Cambridge, 1925), 24f. McIlwain, *Constitutionalism,* 158f, is reluctant to accept Professor Schulz' solution.

186 Bracton, *loc.cit.,* for the *lex digna;* cf. Schulz, 141 (A,28-31); above, n.183.

nates, and therefore Bracton elaborated this argument, when he continued:

[What has pleased the Prince is Law]—that is, not what has been rashly presumed by the [personal] will of the king, but what has been rightly defined by the *consilium* of his magnates, by the king's authorization, and after deliberation and conference concerning it. . . .[187]

The importance of Bracton's constitutionalist qualification of the dangerous word *placuit* cannot be minimized, especially in view of the contemporary and later constitutional struggles in medi-aeval England whose focus was, over and over again, the problem of the king's council and its composition. In practice, of course, few kings of the thirteenth century could or would have legislated without counsel; nor is legislation without counsel encouraged by Roman Law and the Civilians, and even less so by Canon Law and the Canonists: no prelate, no bishop, not even the pope could proceed without taking counsel, though they were not compelled to follow it.[188] Bracton, therefore, was in agreement with common practice, and actually followed the lead of Glanvil, the great English jurist of the twelfth century, when he quoted and used Ulpian's words, but qualified their tenor by relegating the king's pleasure to the *placet* of his legitimate counsellors.[189]

For all that, Bracton differed nevertheless from the Italian

[187] Bracton, *loc.cit.* (Schulz, A,18): "id est, non quidquid de voluntate regis temere presumptum est, sed quod magnatum suorum consilio, rege auctoritatem praestante et habita super hoc deliberatione et tractatu, recte fuerit definitum." The word *consilium*, meaning both counsel and council, may be left untranslated. Also, the *Addicio de cartis*, containing a different concept of the council's power and functions, shall be ignored here; see above, n.179.

[188] For Roman Law, see *C.1,14,8*, quoted by Schulz, 139 (A.18), and, in general, John Crook, *Consilium Principis* (Cambridge, 1955). See also below, nos.194f. A good remark was made by Gerhoh of Reichersberg, *De edificio Dei*, c.21, *MGH,LdL*, III,152,17, who claimed that Constantine the Great could not have made his famous donation *nisi consultis consulibus ceterisque regni maioribus*, because *publica* can be given away only *communicato principum consilio*. Canon Law, of course, had well-defined rules concerning counsel; see, e.g., the decretals united under the title *De his quae fiunt a praelato sine consensu capituli* (X 3,10), ed. Friedberg, II,501ff, including the glosses. The problem is too unwieldy to be discussed here; but a comparative study of the practices observed in various European countries and of the theories of Roman and Canon Laws would be rewarding; cf. Brian Tierney, "A Conciliar Theory of the Thirteenth Century," *Catholic Historical Review*, XXXVI (1950-51), 424f. The older works (e.g., V. Samanek, *Kronrat und Reichsherrschaft im 13. und 14. Jahrhundert*, Freiburg, 1910) are completely out of date.

[189] For Glanvil and Bracton, see Schulz, 171.

jurists also with regard to the council. A maxim of Roman Law, adopted eventually by Canon Law, said that "the Prince (or Pope) has all the laws in the shrine of his breast," which meant that the Prince when legislating was supposed and expected to have all the relevant laws present to his mind, that is, to act competently within his sphere.[190] This, perhaps, was demanding too much, for (said Matthaeus de Afflictis) *raro princeps iurista invenitur*, "rarely will there be found a Prince who is a professional jurist."[191] Whether Bracton had that maxim in mind when he said that the king "has all the rights in his hand, which pertain to the crown and the laical power, and to the material sword which pertains to the government *(gubernaculum)* of the realm," is not certain: the decisive phrase *(habet omnia iura in manu sua)* was liturgical.[192] It is possible nevertheless; for a French jurist claimed that the French king, like the Roman emperor, "had all the rights, especially the rights pertaining to his kingdom, shut in his breast."[193]

---

[190] See, for this maxim, Steinwenter, "Nomos," 256f, and, for its meaning, F. Gillmann, "Romanus pontifex iura omnia etc.," *AKKR*, XCII (1912), 3-17, and CVI (1926), 156-174 (see above, Ch.II,n.15); Post, "Two Notes," *Traditio*, IX,311, and "Statute of York," *Speculum*, XIX,425,n.35.

[191] See below, n.195. Cf. Andreas of Isernia, on *Feud.*I,3,n.16 ("Qui succes. ten."), fol.21ᵛ: "Potest dici, quod quia princeps multos habet in suo consilio peritos . . . et ideo dicitur Philosophiae plenus . . . : raro enim invenitur princeps Iurista." The whole passage deals with the council.

[192] Talking about the king as the ordinary judge, Bracton (fol.556, ed. Woodbine, II,166) says: "habet enim omnia iura in manu sua, quae ad coronam et laicalem pertinent potestatem et materialem gladium, qui pertinet ad regni gubernaculum." Bracton, as Gaines Post (above, n.190) cautiously suggested, may have "paraphrased or vaguely recalled" the famous maxim. The wording, however, is liturgical; see the prayer following after the intercession for the emperor in the *Orationes solemnes* on Good Friday: ". . . Deus, *in cuius manu* sunt . . . *omnia iura regnorum*." Those words, while absent from the Gelasian Sacramentary, were added in the Gregorian Sacramentary; cf. H. A. Wilson, *The Gelasian Sacramentary* (Oxford, 1894), 78,n.28, and *The Gregorian Sacramentary under Charles the Great* (Henry Bradshaw Society, 49; London, 1915), 52; also *PL*, LXXVIII,80A. They are found furthermore in the Frankish Coronation Order of ca. 900, where they appear in the *Oratio super regem* at the end of the mass: "Deus omnipotens, per quem reges regnant et *in cuius manu omnia iura regnorum* consistunt." Cf. Schramm, "Die Krönung bei den Westfranken und Angelsachsen," *ZfRG*, kan.Abt.XXIII (1934), 206,§18; *Sacramentarium ad usum aecclesiae Nivernensis*, ed. A.-J. Crosnier (Nevers, 1873), 112. The phrase is found also in the arenga of a charter of Frederick II; cf. Huillard-Bréholles, I,261; Schaller, *Kanzlei Friedrichs II.*, 83,n.123.

[193] See the Memorandum of a French jurist (perhaps Thomas of Pouilly?) of 1296-1297, ed. F. Kern, *Acta Imperii Angliae et Franciae* (Tübingen, 1911), 200,13f, No.271,§5: "Cum rex Francie omne imperium habet in regno suo, quod imperator habet in imperio . . . et de eo potest dici, sicut de imperatore dicitur, videlicet quod omnia iura, precipue iura competentia regno suo, in eius pectore sunt inclusa. . . ." It is certainly an imperial prerogative which the jurist transfers to the French king;

However that may be, in connection with this maxim the Italian jurists liked to refer to the councillors. Cynus of Pistoia (1270-1336), for example, warned of a literal interpretation because, said he, "shrine of his breast" was to be understood in the sense of "in his court which should abound of excellent Doctors of Law through whose mouths the most law-abiding Prince himself speaks";[194] and Matthaeus de Afflictis explained that "on account of his councillors, who are part of his body, the Prince is said to have all laws in the shrine of his breast."[195] In other words, the council of experts and crown jurists, who are the "shrine of the king's breast" because they really have all the relevant laws present to their mind, appears here as the "mouth of the Prince," who speaks through his councillors, as had been the custom also of Frederick II.[196] Contrariwise, to Bracton the councillors do not appear as the "mouth of the Prince," but it was rather the Prince, or king, who appeared as the "mouth of the council," who promulgated laws "as he pleased" only after discussion with the magnates and on their advice; that is, the king's "pleasure" is Law only insofar as it is "an authoritative promulgation by the king of what the magnates declare to be the ancient custom."[197]

However, even the fact that legislation itself was to emanate from the council of magnates, at their advice and counsel, should again not be interpreted exclusively in the sense of royal restriction, since it was after all "by the authorization of the king" (*rege*

---

but he qualifies the *iura* in the king's breast: *iura competentia regno suo*, which is a phrasing vaguely related to Bracton's *iura quae ad coronam . . . pertinent* and *ad regni gubernaculum*.

[194] Cynus, on C.6,23,19 (Frankfurt, 1578), fol.367r: "Quod [princeps debet habere omnia iura in scrinio sui pectoris] non intelligas ad litteram . . . , sed intelligi debet in scrinio sui pectoris, id est, in curia sua, quae debet egregiis abundare Doctoribus, per quorum ora loquatur iuris religiosissimus princeps." See, for the *religiosissimus princeps*, above, n.159. The Prince speaks through the mouth of the Doctors as formerly God spoke through the mouth of the Roman emperors; see above, n.119. Cynus' pupil Lucas de Penna, on C.12,16,n.1, p.706 ("De silentiariis"), then interprets the apostles as the council of Christ; see below, Ch.vii,n.341.

[195] Matthaeus de Afflictis, on *Lib.aug.*, I,37,n.12, fol.157: "quia isti [the councillors of the *consilium regis*] tales consiliarii sunt pars corporis ipsius regis: ut in l.quisquis.C.ad.l.iul.maiest. [C.9,8,5 rubr.]: et propter istos consiliarios dicitur rex habere omnia iura in scrinio pectoris sui . . . quia raro princeps iurista invenitur." See also on *Lib.aug.*, II,30,n.1, vol.II,fol.65v, where he repeats verbatim Andreas of Isernia (the passage quoted above, n.191).

[196] See *Erg.Bd.*, 89f, for the role of the logothetes Petrus de Vinea.

[197] See McIlwain, *Constitutionalism*, 71.

auctoritatem praestante) that a law became Law. Besides, it is the king who bears the responsibility, since he is—Bracton stresses it in his next sentence—the *auctor iuris*:

> The king's power refers to making Law and not Injury. And since he is the *auctor iuris*, an opportunity to *iniuria* should not be nascent at the very place where the laws are born.[198]

Emphatically Bracton declared that it pertained to the king to interpret the laws, because it pertained to him to make them.[199] And Bracton, like Frederick, emphasized that origin and protection of the Law concur in one hand, that of the king.[200] In short, the king's power to legislate derived from the Law itself, more precisely, from the *lex regia* which made the king a king. Thus a king-making Law and a law-making King mutually conditioned each other, and therewith the well-known relations between the king and the Law reappear in Bracton: the king, Law's son, becomes Law's father. It is the kind of reciprocity and interdependence of Law and Prince which may be found in practically all politico-legal theories of that period.

This spirit pervades the treatise of Bracton wherever he deals with kingship. We might be inclined to admire the impartiality of the judge who tries to distribute evenly the elements restricting and those exalting the king. In fact, however, restriction and exaltation of the king seem evenly distributed only because they were interdependent; for his restriction alone produces also, and justifies, his exaltation: he is recognized as the "vicar of God" only when and where he acts "God-like" by *submitting* to the Law which is both his and God's.

> The king has no other power, since he is the vicar of God and His minister on earth, except this alone which he derives from the Law.[201]

---

[198] Bracton, f.107, Schulz, 140 (A,20): "Potestas itaque sua iuris est et non iniuriae, et cum ipse sit auctor iuris, non debet inde iniuriarum nasci occasio, unde iura nascuntur."

[199] Bracton, f.34, ed. Woodbine, II,109: ". . . cum eius sit interpretari, cuius est condere." The king is not only *auctor* and *conditor legis*, but also *legis interpres* and (see next note) *protector*.

[200] Bracton, f.107 (Schulz, A,7), Woodbine, II,305: "et supervacuum esset, leges condere et iustitiam facere, nisi esset, qui leges tueretur." Cf. *Lib.aug.*, I,31 (above, n.34): ". . . in eiusdem persona concurrentibus his duobus, iuris origine scilicet et tutela."

[201] Bracton, f.107 (Schulz, A,16): "Nihil enim aliud potest rex, cum sit Dei minister et vicarius in terris, nisi id solum, quod de iure potest." Cf. Schulz, 147ff.

Even more telling and clarifying is yet another passage. Bracton starts by pointing out that the king has no peer in his kingdom, not to mention a superior, and then continues:

The king himself must be, not under Man, but under God and the Law, because the Law makes the king. . . . For there is no king where arbitrary will dominates, and not the Law. And that he should be *under* the Law because he is God's vicar, becomes evident through the similitude with Jesus Christ in whose stead he governs on earth. For He, God's true Mercy, though having at His disposal many means to recuperate ineffably the human race, chose before all other expedients the one which applied for the destruction of the devil's work; that is, not the strength of power, but the maxim of Justice, and therefore he wished to be under the Law in order to redeem those under the Law. For he did not wish to apply force, but reason and judgement.[202]

"Christ under the Law" is of course a frequently quoted and, in art, frequently represented episode. The Norman Anonymous, for example, referred to the submission of Christ under the Law to prove the superiority of Tiberius as Caesar over Jesus as man.[203] John of Salisbury stressed that the *Rex regum* submitted to the Law because "in the Law was his will."[204] From Orosius to Dante mediaeval authors reflected on the supposed fact that Christ had chosen to be enrolled "as a *civis Romanus* in that unique register of the human race" and, accordingly, succumbed like any Roman citizen to a Roman judge.[205] Rarely, however, if at all, has the

---

202 Bracton, f.5b, ed. Woodbine, II,33. Schulz, 173, considers this passage, which he has bracketed (p.144, C,4), "possibly an interpolation," since "the long theological parallel seems to be out of place." I cannot follow this argument. Bracton's Introduction is full of theological outlooks and parallels, so that Maitland remarked: "He soars even higher than Azo" (*Bracton and Azo*, 15). Theological parallels are not so rare in Bracton that on this ground alone the assumption of an interpolation seems justified. See below, n.212, for "theological" additions which Bracton made to Azo's text.

203 Above, Ch.III, n.25; see also Pollock and Maitland, 1,182,n.3.

204 Policraticus, 523bc, Webb, 1,252,6ff; above, n.52.

205 See Orosius, *Adversus paganos*, VI,c.20, ed. Zangemeister (*CSEL*, v),418f, for Christ as a Roman citizen. The argument was used quite frequently during the Middle Ages; see, e.g., *Liber de unitate Ecclesiae*, I,c.3, *MGH,LdL*, II,188,7; Dante, *De Monarchia*, II,c.12; *Purg.*, xxxII,102. For the efforts to "romanize" Christ and "christianize" Augustus, see the brilliant discussion by Erik Peterson, "Kaiser Augustus im Urteil des antiken Christentums: Ein Beitrag zur Geschichte der politischen Theologie," *Hochland*, xxx (1933), 289ff. The registration of Christ was a familiar topic both in art (C. Diehl, *Manuel d'art byzantin* [2nd ed., Paris, 1925], II,797 [fig.394], 832 [fig.415]) and in literature: The scribe of the Roman Legate Quirinus, asking Mary who the father of the child was, received the answer "God is

early christocentric concept of kingship arrived at demonstrating a Christ-likeness of the anointed king for the reason that both king and Christ were submitted to the Law, whereas similar arguments are found with regard to the pope, who was held to pay the tribute money like Christ.[206] Bracton's comparison implied— indeed in best mediaeval tradition—that only the *servus legis* could be, or become, also the *dominus legis*. It implied furthermore that the king was exalted above all others as *vicarius Dei* only if, and so far as, he submitted to the Law like the only-begotten Son Himself, and that all royal prerogatives depended on the king's acknowledgment of being bound to the Law which granted to him those very prerogatives. In that case, indeed,

> the king shall have no peer, not to mention a superior, especially when exercising Justice, that there truly of him may be said 'Great is our Lord, and of great power' [Psalm 147: 5], although in receiving justice [as plaintiff] he shall compare with the least man of his realm.[207]

The king, though peerless as God's vicar, is yet bound by the Law, and he shall be like the least of his subjects before the judge—of course, only when being plaintiff, since it belonged to his prerogative that there lies no action against the king.[208]

Bracton's method is always the same: exaltation through limitation, the limitation itself following from the king's exaltation,

---

his father"; whereupon the scribe registered the child "Son of God." See, e.g., John of Euboea, *Sermo in conceptionem Deiparae*, c.18, *PGr*, xcvi,1489. Bracton mentions a *singulare privilegium* of the Virgin Mary to be *supra legem* although in her humility she submitted voluntarily to *legalibus institutis*. The history of this privilege is unknown to me, but it is mentioned in the acts of the Council of Trent, *Sessio* vi, *canon* 23, where it is said that no human being can avoid during his life venial sins "nisi ex speciali Dei privilegio, quemadmodum de beata Virgine tenet Ecclesia." See H. Denzinger, *Enchiridion symbolorum* (Freiburg, 1937), 298, No.833.

206 Two passages in Gratian's *Decretum* were usually quoted in this connection: c.10,C.xxv,q.1, and c.22,C.xxiii,q.8, ed. Friedberg, I,1009 and 961. See, e.g., Marinus de Caramanico, *Prooem. in Const*, ed. Cervone, p.xxxiv, ed. Calasso, *Glossatori*, 186, 47ff: "Papa etiam regi obsequitur et ei se subesse fatetur . . . Et ipse Christus Dei filius terreno regi subditum se ostendit qui cum pro se solvi tributum faceret. . . ." The Canonists shared this opinion; see, e.g., the Gloss on c.10,C.xxv,q.1, v. *subditos* (a gloss of Johannes de Fantutiis[?]).

207 Bracton, f.107 (Schulz, A,11-13), Woodbine, II,305; see fol.5b, Woodbine, II,33: the king is "minimus, vel quasi, in iudicio suscipiendo."

208 For the king as plaintiff, cf. Schulz, 149; Pollock and Maitland, I,515ff. For the history of the non-suability of the Crown and for the state as plaintiff in England, see Robert D. Watkins, *The State as a Party Litigant* (Johns Hopkins diss., Baltimore, 1927).

from his vicariate of God, which the king would jeopardize were he not limited and bound by the Law. This method may be called dialectical. It relies upon the logic that there cannot be a genuine "Prerogative" on the one hand without submission to the Law on the other, and that a legal status above the Law could legitimately exist only if there existed also a legal status under the Law. The Law-abiding king, therefore, becomes *ipso facto* a "Vicar of God"; he becomes a legislator (*auctor iuris*) above the Law and according to the Law; and he becomes the responsible expounder of the existing laws and of royal actions which may not be disputed by either officials or private persons.[209] For were the king not Law-abiding, he were not a king at all but a tyrant.[210]

[209] For the king as *auctor iuris*, see above, nos.198f. The interpretation of laws (above, n.199) belonged, of course, also to the king; Bracton, f.34, Woodbine, II,109: "De cartis vero regiis *et factis regum* non debent nec possunt iustitiarii nec privatae personae disputare, nec etiam, si in *illis* dubitatio oriatur, possunt *eam* interpretari. Etiam in dubiis et obscuris . . . domini regis erit expectanda interpretatio et voluntas, cum eius sit interpretari cuius est condere." Schulz, 173, puts the words *et factis regum* in brackets because they "must be interpolated." Further, he claims that the following *illa* (above: *illis*) and *eam* "show that originally only *cartae* were mentioned in the beginning." It is difficult to follow this argumentation. The word *eam* clearly refers to *dubitatio*, and the word preceding *dubitatio* is not *illa* but *illis* (at least according to the, so to say, standard text of Woodbine, who indeed failed to mention in his apparatus the reading *illa* found in the edition of Sir Travers Twyss [Roll Series, London, 1878] I,268). For grammatical reasons there is no need to assume an interpolation. Moreover, *et factis regum* is perfectly sound. Cf. *Lib.aug.*, I,4, ed. Cervone, 15: "Est enim pars sacrilegii disputare de eius iudiciis, *factis* et constitutionibus atque consiliis. . . ." Frederick II repeated almost verbatim Assize XVII of the "Vatican Assizes" and Assize XI of the "Cassino Collection" of King Roger II of Sicily; see Brandileone, *Diritto Romano*, 103 and 122; Niese, *Gesetzgebung*, 66. This was the current reading; see, e.g., Rudolf M. Kloos, "Ein Brief des Petrus de Prece zum Tode Friedrichs II.," *DA*, XIII (1957), where an imperial notary writes: ". . . eo quod sacrilegii quodammodo censetur ad instar *de factis principum* disputare." The source of all those laws is *C.*9,29,2, a decree of the Emperors Gratian, Valentinian, and Theodosius, addressed in 385 to the *praefectus Urbi* Symmachus: "Disputari de principali iudicio non oportet; sacrilegii enim instar est dubitare, an is dignus sit, quem imperator elegerit." The word *facta* is not found here, nor in the related decree *C.*12,17,1, nor in *Cod.Theod.*, 1,6,9. It appears, however, in both the Sicilian and English adaptations of the imperial decree, of which the Sicilian one is a century older (it was only *re*-issued in 1231). Finally, Schulz remarks: "*Regum* instead of *regis* is conspicuous," and believes again in an interpolation. I do not think so. The title of *Lib.aug.*, I,4, reads: "Ut nullus se intromittat *de factis* seu consiliis *regum*." The plural may have slipped in because *C.*9,29,2, has the heading: *Idem AAA.* (= *Augusti*) *ad Symmachum pu.* (= *praefectum Urbi*); and the Byzantine plurality of emperors influenced South-Italian scriptoria and chanceries not rarely; see Ladner, "Portraits of Emperors," *Speculum*, XVII,189ff. The plural, however, made sense, because it generalized the statement and made it refer also to former kings; it meant: "actions of kings shall not be disputed," and this is the meaning also in Bracton: "royal charters and actions of

On these seeming contradictions Bracton's political theory hinged. Such as the system of mediaeval Law was, with its dualism of Divine and Positive Laws, a reasoned political theory other than the one put forth by John of Salisbury, Frederick II, or Bracton could probably not have developed at all. In one way or the other, it would always result in the concept of a ruler who was at once "under and above the Law," or was "father and son of Justice," or "image and servant of Equity." Also the English king in Bracton's treatise appears *et maior et minor se ipso.*

Bracton's comparison of the king with the humbled Christ before the Roman judge may lead us to yet another problem of Bracton's concept of kingship, a problem of political "christology." He writes:

> For that end has he been created and elected a king that he may give justice to all, and that in him the Lord be seated [Ps. 9: 5; also 88: 15] and that through him the Lord discerns his judgement [III Kings 3: 11].[211]

It would appear from the biblical passages, which Bracton quotes, that the "Lord" who dwells in the king and decrees justice through the king, is God the Father rather than the Son, although admittedly in the later Middle Ages it becomes increasingly difficult to distinguish clearly between the first and second persons of the Trinity. However, in Bracton's treatise the king seems to be styled rather consistently *vicarius Dei* and not *vicarius Christi*, if we except the comparison with Christ submitting as man to the Roman judge. In fact we find that the vicariate of the Son of God has been reserved by Bracton for others. In his *Introduction* Bracton discussed, in full agreement with the rules of legal rhetoric and *ars dictandi*, the "utility" of his treatise. On the whole

---

kings shall not be disputed." How to explain the similarities between Bracton and the Sicilian Law Codes is a different matter; however, when Bracton wrote his treatise, England was swamped by Sicilians; see my study "Petrus de Vinea in England," 74ff, 81ff, and also my forthcoming paper on "The Prologue to *Fleta* and the School of Petrus de Vinea," *Speculum*, XXXII (1957).

[210] For "king and tyrant," see Schulz, 151ff, who has conveniently summed up the essential material.

[211] Bracton, f.107 (Schulz, A,3-4), Woodbine, II,305: "Ad hoc autem creatus est rex et electus, ut iustitiam faciat universis, et ut in eo Dominus sedeat et per ipsum sua iudicia discernat."

he restricted himself to copying Azo almost verbatim. However, he added a few significant words (italicized here), as he wrote:

> The utility [of the treatise] is that it ennobles the apprentices and doubles their honors and profits, and that it makes them to rule in the kingdom, and to sit in the royal hall, *on the very seat of the king, as it were, on the throne of God*, judging tribes and nations, plaintiffs and defendants in a lordly order, *in the king's stead, quasi in the stead of Jesus Christ, since the king is the vicar of God.*[212]

What Bracton added to Azo are a few phrases, seemingly edifying, about the Throne of God which the king occupied.[213] The second addition, at the end of the passage, is related to the first, and though it may sound confused, in fact it is not confused at all. In that whole section the king appears as one acting *vice Dei*, in the place of God and on the throne of God. Contrariwise, for example, the Ottonian miniature (fig. 5) showed the emperor in the place of Christ and on the throne of Christ. Bracton, however, in the second addition to Azo's text, makes a very clear distinction between the Father and the Son. He says that those acting *vice regis*—that is, the royal judges—act *quasi vice Jesu Christi*, whereas the king as the vicar of God acts *quasi vice Dei*. In other words, the judges are in the place of the Son of God whereas the king is in that of God the Father.[214]

---

[212] "Utilitas autem est, quia nobilitat addiscentes et honores conduplicat et profectus, et facit eos principari in regno et sedere in aula regia et in sede ipsius regis quasi throno Dei, tribus et nationes, actores et reos ordine dominabili iudicantes, vice regis quasi vice Ihesu Christi, cum rex sit vicarius Dei. Iudicia enim non sunt hominis sed Dei . . ." Bracton, f.1b, Woodbine, II,20. For a comparison with Azo, see Maitland, *Bracton and Azo*, 3 and 7, and the notes on p.15.

[213] Bracton, in calling the royal throne metaphorically the throne of God, remains within the tradition; see, e.g., the Norman Anonymous, *MGH,LdL*, III,669,45, and 670,1f. Bracton apparently liked that simile, since he repeated it several times; see f.1b, Woodbine, II,21: "Sedem quidem iudicandi, quae est quasi thronus Dei, non praesumat quis ascendere insipiens et indoctus . . . , ne ex alto corruat quasi a throno dei, qui volare inceperit antequam pennas assumat." Again Bracton added the phrase *quasi a throno Dei* to a metaphor (the fall of him who tries to fly before his feathers have grown) which he borrowed from Azo and which is typical for the lingo of the Bolognese masters of the *ars dictandi*; see for Thomas of Capua, Guido Faba, and the *Formularium* of Arnold of Protzan my study "Guido Faba," 280,n.1. It may be noted that Bracton in his more literary and less technical passages abounds in similes deriving from the Bolognese *dictamen*, though he may have borrowed most of this material from the jurists.

[214] In other passages (above, n.213) Bracton calls the judge's seat the "throne of God" without special reference to the king. In a similar spirit, John Fortescue, *De laudibus*, cc. III and VIII, ed. Chrimes, pp.8,22, quotes II Chron. 19: 6, where Jehosha-

This distinction is indeed of greater interest than may appear at first glance, since it seems to reflect a doctrine of particular significance for mediaeval England. It was probably the so-called "Ambrosiaster," in the fourth century, who coined the maxim: *Dei imaginem habet rex, sicut et episcopus Christi.*[215] This doctrine—the king an antitype of God the Father, and the bishop typifying God the Son—reappears with great consistency in the English orbit whereas it does not seem to occur elsewhere. It was quoted by an English scholar, Cathwulf, in a letter to Charlemagne.[216] It turns up, unfailingly, in the tractate of the Norman Anonymous, though in a more christocentric version: "The priest prefigures one nature in Christ, that of the man; the king, the other, that of the God."[217] Finally the whole doctrine, which later will be repeated by John Wycliffe,[218] is found, around 1100, in Hugh of Fleury's *De regia potestate et sacerdotali dignitate*, a tractate written for and dedicated to Henry I of England. The monk of Fleury wrote:

> Verily, the king, within his realm, seems to take the place of God the Father, and the bishop that of Christ. All the bishops, therefore, appear to be rightly subjected to the king, just as the Son is found to be subjected to the Father—not according to his nature, but to his rank.[219]

The bishops thus are said to govern *vice Jesu Christi* while the king rules *vice Dei.*

---

phat, King of Juda, "praecipiens iudicibus, 'Videte, ait, quid faciatis; non enim hominis exercetis iudicium sed Domini.'" See also above, n.102.

[215] *Quaestiones Veteris et Novi Testamenti*, c.xxxv, ed. A. Souter, *CSEL*, 50 (1908), 63.

[216] See above, Ch.III, n.84.

[217] *MGH,LdL*, III,667,8ff (above, Ch.III, n.30); see also p.663,11f, where full eternity is only with the royal, and not with the sacerdotal Christ: "Ipse Christus rex est iusticie, qui ab eterno regnat, et regnabit in eternum *et ultra.* Qui sacerdos dicitur in eternum, *non ultra.* Neque enim in eterno vel ultra eternum sacerdotium erit necessarium." The equation of the human Christ with the sacerdotal office is among the oldest traditions, and so is the conception of God the Father as king; see, e.g., Augustine, *In Psalmos*, CIX,4, *PL*, XXXVII,1459; or, for the English orbit, Beda, *Retractatio*, II,36, who follows Isidorus, *Etym.*, VII,2,2; cf. M. L. W. Laistner, *Bedae Venerabilis Expositio Actuum Apostolorum et Retractatio* (Cambridge, Mass., 1939), 105.

[218] Wycliffe, *Tractatus de officio regis*, ed. A. W. Pollard and C. Sayle (London, 1887), 13 and 137; also *De fide catholica*, c.1, in Wycliffe's *Opera minora*, ed. J. Loserth (London, 1913), 102. Cf. W. Kleinecke, *Englische Fürstenspiegel* (Halle, 1937), 82,n.5; F. Kern, *Gottesgnadentum und Widerstandsrecht* (Leipzig, 1915), 112, n.198, and 119: "Die Gedanken des Anonymus von York, in ihrer Zeit fast ketzerisch, triumphierten an der Schwelle der Neuzeit."

[219] *MGH,LdL*, II,468, also 472,33 and 490,6.

It is most unlikely that the tractate of the Norman Anonymous was known to Bracton; but the pamphlet of Hugh of Fleury may have come to his eyes.[220] At any rate, in Bracton's work the doctrine *rex imago Dei, sacerdos Christi* was changed to *rex imago Dei, judex Christi*. It was transferred from the theological to the legal sphere, from the clerics to the law clerks, or from the *sacerdotes Ecclesiae* to the *sacerdotes Iustitiae*.[221] It is the "priests of Justice" who now act in the image and likeness of the judging Christ and who become the "throne-sharers" of the Father, represented on earth by the royal *vicarius Dei*.

Hence the king, in Bracton's work, is in the first place the vicar of God. However, we should recall that as a *vicarius Dei* the king is claimed to be also the antitype of the humbled Christ whose manhood has been submitted to the Law and to a Roman judge. In other words, the king, together with his judges, typified God the Father with the divine Christ on the Throne of Heaven; but also the king is the antitype of the human Christ whenever he is not the judge, but one who submits to the Law. He is at once God-like above the Law when judging, legislating and interpreting the Law, and is, like the Son or any ordinary man, under the Law because he, too, submits to the Law. We realize that the christological substratum, so powerfully effective in the Ottonian miniature, and in the tractate of the Norman Anonymous and still perceptible in the *Liber Augustalis* of Frederick II, lingered on also in Bracton's work. It may even be gathered from the angry outburst of the Countess of Arundel who openly rebuked King Henry III: "Oh Lord King, why do you turn your face away from justice? . . . In the midst between God and us are you placed [*medius inter Deum et nos constitueris*], but neither yourself nor us do you rule sanely."[222]

To sum up: the Bractonian king had a dual position above and under the Law. In that respect he may appear comparable to Frederick II. But the resemblance, should it exist, would be quite

220 Schulz, 137 and 148.

221 Bracton, f.3, Woodbine, II,24, quotes the famous passage from *D*.1,1,1,1, following Azo; see Maitland, *Bracton and Azo*, 24. See also Fortescue, *De laudibus*, c.III, ed. Chrimes, 8.

222 Matthew Paris, *Chronica maiora* (ad a.1252), ed. Luard, V,336. There is, toward the end, a certain similarity between the outcry of the countess and the *addicio de cartis*. I owe the knowledge of this passage to Professor B. C. Keeney, of Brown University.

superficial. The emperor, even when theoretically submitting to the directive power of Reason, which anticipated to some extent the later Reason of State, remained in fact undisputedly above the Law; whereas in Bracton's England the king *sub lege* was intended to have a very real and definite meaning, albeit not often clearly defined. Moreover, the serious efforts to define the king's status "under the Law" produced correspondingly the other effort, that is, to define in what respects he was, and perforce had to be, also "above the Law." By the end of the century, the royal judges, in the often quoted case of *Humphrey of Bohun* v. *Gilbert of Clare* (1292), argued that

> for the common utility he [the king] is in many cases by his prerogative above the laws and customs usually recognized in his realm . . . But also the Lord King is, in view of all and sundry of his kingdom, the debtor of justice.[223]

Here the king's court itself seemingly arrived at a self-contradiction by stating that the prerogative sometimes puts the king above the laws whereas at other times he was *debitor iustitiae*, that is, under the Law. Again we are reminded of the Caesar's duty to be at once "father and son of Justice." However, the most genuinely English version of that lapidary formula should be sought in a totally different direction, in the no less lapidary formula of the famous writ *Praecipe Henrico Regi Angliae*—a writ in which allegedly *K*ing Henry III enjoined *k*ing Henry III through his officers to remedy some act or else show cause why he refused to do so.[224] This writ, which a fourteenth-century lawyer claimed to

---

[223] *Rotuli Parlamentorum*, 1,71: "[rex] qui pro communi utilitate per prerogativam suam in multis casibus est supra leges et consuetudines in regno suo usitatas"; and p.74: "dominus rex qui est omnibus et singulis de regno suo iusticie debitor." Cf. E. C. Lodge and G. A. Thornton, *English Constitutional Documents, 1307-1485* (Cambridge, 1935), 9. The term *debitor iustitiae* seems to derive from a decretal of Innocent III (c.11 X 2,2, ed. Friedberg, II,251) and was often repeated; see, e.g., Andreas of Isernia, *Usus feudorum*, fol.235ᵛ (*De prohibita feudi alien.*, § *Quoniam inter dominum*, n.5: "Princeps quidem est debitor iustitiae"), and fol.301 (*Quae sunt regalia*, § *Ad Iustitiam*, n.64: "Quia sunt debitores iustitiae Principes et praelati"). The "king above the Law" found defenders in various strata of society; see, e.g., G. O. Sayles, *Select Cases in the Court of King's Bench under Edward I* (Selden Society, LVIII; London, 1939), III,xli; cf. xlviii. From a totally different point of view, Walter Burley, in his *Commentary on Aristotle's Politics* (written ca. 1338), could say: "Est enim rex supra legem et supra se ipsum"; see Cranz, *Aristotelianism*, 166f.

[224] Pollock and Maitland, I,516ff; the writ, embellished by one *Praecipe Jacobo Regi*, was ridiculed by Francis Bacon, "Argument on the Writ *De non procedendo*

have seen, was—if really it existed—either a joke or a school exercise of the times of the Barons' War, for no action lies against the king nor can he be summoned. Nevertheless, this jocular product displays most strikingly the idea of a king who was both above and under the Law, both greater and lesser than himself. Moreover, writs in which the King gave order to the king must have been at least within the range of human imagination in mid-thirteenth-century England. After all, Master Simon, the Norman, a high government official, was dismissed—if we may trust Matthew Paris—because he refused to seal a charter *contra coronam domini regis*, a charter which the king wished to issue, but which the officer found contrary to the Crown and its interests, and therefore contrary also to the officer's oath.[225] Nothing comparable to that incident could have happened in Frederick's Sicilian monarchy. It will be within the field of administration, of legal practice rather than of legal theory that we have to look for the king's impersonal *alter ego*.

CHRISTUS-FISCUS

In Bracton's work christological reflections were peripheral. His thinking and his true interest circled around legal, administrative, and constitutional matters rather than metaphysical ideas and theological distinctions. For all that, however, it is undeniable that in Bracton's days certain theologisms of the state were developing which we would not expect to encounter in that sober constitutional and legal orbit of which Bracton was the exponent. The seemingly irrational maxims were there nevertheless. They were partly the result of the adaptation of theological language and thought to the new conditions of the secular state, and partly the result of the establishment of an impersonal public sphere which emerged from the proper needs of the community of the realm itself.

The maxim *Nullum tempus currit contra regem*, "Time run-

---

rege inconsulto," *Works*, ed. Spedding (London, 1870), VII,694. See, for the general problem, L. Ehrlich, *Proceedings against the Crown, 1216-1377* (Oxford, 1921); also R. D. Watkins, *The State as a Party Litigant* (Baltimore, 1927), 5ff; for the history of the writ itself, see Fritz Schulz, "The Writ *Precipe quod reddat* and its Continental Models," *Juridical Review*, LIV (1952), 1ff.

[225] Sir Maurice Powicke, *King Henry III and the Lord Edward* (Oxford, 1947), II,780ff.

neth not against the king," is of peculiar interest because the idea of sempiternity, or of a supra-personal perpetuity, is involved. The maxim itself presupposes the conceptual existence of at least two notions, "prescription" and "inalienability." Prescription usually meant loss, as its correlate "usucaption" usually meant acquisition, of a title or right to property by uninterrupted, unchallenged, and peaceful possession in good faith over a variable, long or short, period of time as defined by law. The English royal judges of the twelfth century most certainly were familiar with the legal concept of prescription, which had capital importance in Canon Law and to which Gratian in his *Decretum* devoted a whole section on which naturally the Decretists commented over and over again. But the English judges apparently saw no need themselves to reflect upon the idea of prescription, since they seem not to mention it at all.[226] This indifference towards prescription changed in the following century: Bracton dealt repeatedly, and in a scholarly manner, with the principle *Longa possessio parit ius*, "Long possession creates right." Bracton's dependence on Roman Law is revealed by the technical term *Usucapio* heading the chapter in which he discusses the problem of prescription; but this is of minor interest here.[227] What does matter is that, by his time, reflections upon claims to prescriptive possession had become momentous to the royal judges. In fact, prescription attained actuality within the public sphere once a certain complex of royal lands

[226] The passages on prescription collected by Gratian (C.XVI,q.3, ed. Friedberg, 1,788ff) are found, with few exceptions, already in the works of Ivo of Chartres and others. For English Canonists, see Stephan Kuttner and Eleanor Rathbone, "Anglo-Norman Canonists of the Twelfth Century," *Traditio*, vII (1949-51), 279-358, and, for prescription, pp.345,354,355. It seems to be the common opinion that "prescription was unknown to the Old English Law and also to Glanvil," as Carl Güterbock, *Bracton and his Relations to the Roman Law*, trans. by Brinton Coxe (Philadelphia, 1866), 118ff, pointed out; cf. Pollock and Maitland, II,140ff ("Our mediaeval law knows no acquisitive prescription for land"). I was not able to verify the origin of the maxim *Nullum tempus currit contra regem* (or *occurrit regi*) although similar phrases are found in Gratian's *Decretum* (c.14,C.XVI,q.3); the Civilians and Feudists are usually more specific: "centenaria praescriptio currit contra fiscum" (Andreas of Isernia, *Usus feudorum*, on *Prohibita feudi alienatio per Fredericum*, n.51, fol.271ᵛ), or "nulla praescriptio currit contra fiscum regium nisi centenaria" (Matthaeus de Afflictis, on *Lib.aug.*, III,31,n.4, fol.186); but I did not chance upon an exact parallel of the Bractonian formula.

[227] See, above all, Bracton, fol.52, Woodbine, II,157: "Longa enim possessio sicut mater ius parit possidendi"; also fols.40,43a,45b, Woodbine, II,126,134,140, and passim; Güterbock, *Bracton*, 118; W. S. Holdsworth, *A History of English Law* (3rd ed., London, 1923), II,284; Pollock and Maitland, II,141ff.

and rights had been set aside as "inalienable." In that moment, prescription and the prescriptive effects of time acquired considerable importance because they clashed, or might clash, with the notion of inalienability. That is to say, the royal judges frequently faced situations in which they had to decide not only whether or not a private person could legally claim possession by prescription, but also to what extent such claims would affect royal rights and lands which were labelled "inalienable." Hence, the concept of inalienability of royal rights and lands, together with that of prescription, forms the premise for the formula *Nullum tempus currit contra regem*, by which private prescriptive claims to inalienable Crown property were quashed.

It has often been noticed that the principle of inalienability, implying the existence of certain imprescriptible rights of the Crown, developed slowly and with great restraint on the Continent.[228] In England, too, the first official document stating clearly and succinctly that the royal demesne was inalienable, was relatively late: the Councillors' Oath, containing the clause "Item, I will consent to the alienation of none of those things which belong to the ancient demesne of the Crown," falls in the year 1257, that is, in the times of Bracton.[229] This, however, should not be read to mean that the principle itself of non-alienation did not exist before; it actually developed in England much earlier than on the Continent. It is, of course, perfectly true that in the first half of the twelfth century the concept of inalienability was completely absent from English governmental practice. A change, however,

---

[228] Georges de Lagarde, *La naissance de l'esprit laïque au declin du moyen âge, I: Bilan du XIIIe siècle* (Vienna, 1934), 158,n.23, remarks that the idea of inalienability of rights of the state "a été une des plus lentes à pénétrer." For a few remarks on the continental development, see Schramm, *English Coronation*, 198f, and "Das kastilische Königtum in der Zeit Alfonsos des Weisen," *Festschrift Edmund E. Stengel* (Münster and Cologne, 1952), 406; for Spain, also Gifford Davis, "The Incipient Sentiment of Nationality in Mediaeval Castile: The Patrimonio real," *Speculum*, XII (1937), 351-358. The non-alienation clause was added to the French coronation oath in 1365 only (Schramm, *König von Frankreich*, I,237f, nos.1 and 7), but the principle was much older. See, in general, my paper "Inalienability," *Speculum*, XXIX (1954), 488-502, and the latest study on that subject: Peter N. Riesenberg, *Inalienability of Sovereignty in Medieval Political Thought* (New York, 1956).

[229] J. F. Baldwin, *The King's Council in England during the Middle Ages* (Oxford, 1913), 346, §3; Powicke, *King Henry III*, I,336f; Robert S. Hoyt, *The Royal Demesne in English Constitutional History: 1066-1272* (Ithaca, N.Y., 1950), 162, one of the most important and informative discussions of the problems touched upon here.

came with the accession of Henry II whose consolidation of the royal demesne, together with his other administrative and legal reforms, bred the understanding that certain domanial rights and lands were inalienable.[230] The two Laws, Roman and Canon, were certainly contributive factors in making the idea of inalienability of state property articulate;[231] but the essential factor was that Henry II created a *de facto* inalienable complex of rights and lands which later, in the thirteenth century, came to be known as the "ancient demesne" and which formed, in the language of Roman Law, the *bona publica* or fiscal property of the realm.[232] Moreover, the sheer existence of the "ancient demesne"—a supra-personal compound of rights and lands which was separate from the individual king and definitely not his private property—gave substance to the notion of an impersonal "Crown" which developed simultaneously.[233] The officers of Henry II were compelled to distinguish administratively "between lands falling into the monarchy by feudal right, and lands which were more properly the royal demesne of the king, or of the Crown."[234] The result of this development may be gathered from an unofficial proposition made at the very beginning of the thirteenth century. The anonymous compiler of a legal memorandum, jotting down his ideas about what the king's coronation oath should contain, suggested that the king swear to "preserve all the lands of the Crown of this realm in their wholeness (*in integrum cum omni integritate*), and without diminution," and also to recover all that had been alienated or lost.[235]

---

[230] Hoyt, *Demesne*, 84ff,123f.

[231] For the influence of Canon Law, see my paper "Inalienability," 498ff. Civil Law, of course, clarified the difference between *patrimonium* and *fiscus*; but the first reflections on inalienability seem to have emanated from a less technical problem, that is, from the word *augustus* which was traditionally discussed along with the other titles of Justinian (*perpetuus, sacratissimus* etc.); see, e.g., Fitting, *Jurist. Schriften*, 148. *Augustus* (from *augere*, as was generally assumed) meant an "increaser" of the empire; hence, the emperor could not be a "diminisher," that is, he could not alienate property of the empire; cf. Gerhard Laehr, *Die Konstantinische Schenkung in der abendländischen Literatur des Mittelalters bis zur Mitte des 14. Jahrhunderts* (Berlin, 1926), 64,n.44, cf.99.

[232] See Hoyt, *Demesne*, 134ff, who has considerably clarified the meaning of "ancient demesne" and related subjects; see also his "The Nature and Origins of the Ancient Demesne," *Engl.Hist.Rev.*, LXV (1950), 145-174.

[233] See below, Ch.VII,2.

[234] Hoyt, *Demesne*, 124.

[235] See the memorandum *De iure et de appendiciis corone regni Britannie*, forming a portion of the *Leges Anglorum saeculi XIII ineunte Londiniis collectae,*

Bracton, as might be expected, was an ardent defender of the maxim *nullum tempus*. That in practice some of the most seignorial powers and franchises were derived from prescription against the king, would make little difference to Bracton,[236] since the *de facto* situation could not detract from a principle valid *de iure*; and Bracton's arguments, in that respect, were purely juristic. He explained, and reiterated his explanation, that things pertaining to the king's peace and jurisdiction were "things quasi holy," *res quasi sacrae*, which could no more be alienated than could *res sacrae* pertaining to the Church.[237] Those things quasi-holy were "things public" existing for some common utility of the realm, such as the preservation of justice and peace. Bracton held that those things belonged to the Crown as a royal privilege descending from the *ius gentium* which, in its turn, had a semi-divine, or even divine, character similar to the *ius naturale*.[238]

With regard to the *res quasi sacrae* the royal power was definitely above the Law. The king, for example, was not in need to offer a proof when challenging a franchise, since he owned his royal rights not *ex longo tempore* but, as we may say, *ex essentia coronae*; and therefore his challenge would be made, not for private comfort, but for the common utility of the realm.[239] More-

---

edited by F. Liebermann, *Die Gesetze der Angelsachsen* (Halle, 1903-1916), 1,635f. Cf. Schramm, *English Coronation*, 197; Hoyt, *Demesne*, 146,n.47. See also above, n.225.

[236] Bracton, fols.14,56,103, Woodbine, II,58,167,293, and passim. Cf. Pollock and Maitland, 1,572ff.,584, II,140-44; Maitland considers the principle of *Nullum tempus* "a very wholesome maxim" but has his doubts concerning its validity in practice. Ogg, in his Introduction of Selden's *Ad Fletam*, p.xliv, quotes the maxim *Nullum tempus* as being "his [Bracton's] own or at least indigenous." Bracton, however, only repeated or paraphrased a well known doctrine.

[237] The most important place is Bracton, fol.14, Woodbine, II,57f; a free man, too, is a *res quasi sacra* because he can be sold as little as fiscal or Church property. Bracton (fol.407, Woodbine, III,266) calls *quasi sacra* also everything *spiritualitati annexa* which was not *per pontifices Deo dedicata*. Drawing throughout from the *Institutes* of Justinian (*Inst.*,2,1) and from Azo, Bracton confuses somewhat *res sacrae* and *res religiosae*, as has been indicated by Güterbock, *Bracton*, 85; see also below, n.302.

[238] "De iure gentium pertinent ad coronam propter privilegium regis"; Bracton, fol.103, Woodbine, II,293; cf. fol.55b, p.167, and *Inst.*,2,1,4f. See also Gierke, *Gen.R.*, III,211,n.72, also 611f, for the *ius gentium*; further, for the whole problem of "public utility," the observations of Gaines Post, "Public Law," 42ff, and "Two Laws," 421ff.

[239] Bracton, fol.103, Woodbine, II,293f: "et in quibus casibus nullum tempus currit contra ipsum si petat, cum probare non habeat necesse, et sine probatione obtinebit . . . quia se ex longo tempore non defendet." Cf. Maitland, *Bracton and Azo*, 175.

over, concerning the things public or *quasi sacrae* the king would become practically *iudex in causa propria*, which was true anyhow in the case of lese majesty or high treason, since his own cause would appear as a *causa publica* or *causa regni*.[240] Finally, wrongs committed against the *res quasi sacrae* would not underlie the otherwise valid law of prescription—*Demanium nullo tempore praescribitur*, as the Italian jurists explained[241]—because, writes Bracton, "length of time, in that case, does not diminish the wrong but makes it worse."[242]

[240] Treason was judged by "court and peers," but with the king, too, acting as judge; Bracton, fol.119b, Woodbine, II,337 (*De crimine laesae maiestatis*): "debent pares associari, ne ipse rex per seipsum vel iusticiarios suos sine paribus actor sit et iudex." Cf. Lapsley, "Bracton," *Engl.Hist.Rev.*, LXII (1947), 10. That the king with regard to the fisc, or the *fiscus* itself, can be judge *in causa propria*, is stressed perpetually; see, e.g., Cynus, on *C.7,37,3* (Lyon, 1547), fol.306ᵛ: "Imperator causas suas non ipse cognoscit: sed iudices alios facit. Licet quando velit et ipse possit in re sua iudex esse." This was, by and large, also the opinion of Andreas of Isernia, *Usus feudorum* (on *De prohib. feudi alien.*, nos.84ff), fol.281. Further, Lucas de Penna, on *C.11,58,7*, n.16 (Lyon, 1582), 564, who holds that "princeps est iudex in causa sua" with regard to the fisc and whenever he revokes things alienated "in praeiudicium dignitatis et coronae." For later times, see Gierke, *Gen.R.*, IV,247,n.149. This is basically the idea also when the English king is judge in a cause *de antiquo dominico corone Anglie*; he is not judge in his own, private cause as an individual, but in a *causa rerum quasi sacrarum*, just as the bishop would be judge *in causa ecclesiae (quae nunquam moritur)* which again is not identical with a *causa propria* of the bishop; see Gierke, *Gen.R.*, III,257,n.41.

[241] See, for example, Marinus de Caramanico, *gl.* on *Liber aug.*, III,39, Cervone, 399. More cautious is Andreas of Isernia, on the same law, p.400; also p.312 (on *Liber aug.*, III,8) where he states: "Demania sunt publica quia fiscalia sunt publica. Fiscus, Populus Romanus et Respublica Romana idem sunt." See also Andreas of Isernia, *Usus feudorum, loc.cit.*, n.51, fol.272: "Demania sunt principis sicut publica populi Romani, quia fiscus est respublica idem sunt." Everything fiscal was public; see *Glos.ord.*, on *D.1,1,2*, v. *in sacris*; cf. Post, "Two Laws," 421,n.18. Also, e.g., Cynus, on *D.1,1,rubr.,n.17* (Lyon, 1547), fol.2: ". . . lex dicit quod fiscale dicitur ius publicum." Bracton does not indulge in those identifications and equations of fisc, people, state, crown, king, but implies essentially the same ideas, since to him likewise *res quasi sacrae* are things public to which the ancient demesne belonged; see Hoyt, *Demesne*, 232ff, also 188.

[242] Bracton, fol.14, Woodbine, II,58: "Diuturnitas enim temporis in hoc casu iniuriam non minuit, sed auget." The principle referred to by Bracton is canonical; see c.11 X 1,4 (*De consuetudine*), ed. Friedberg, II,41: "Quum tanto sint graviora peccata, quanto diutius infelicem animam detinent alligatam . . ." The decretal, dealing with the problem of old custom (*longaeva consuetudo*) as opposed to Natural and Positive Laws, and with the prescriptive power of custom, is frequently quoted in connection with prescription; see, e.g., Andreas of Isernia, *Usus feudorum*, praeludia, n.30, fol.4ᵛ: "Ea quidem quae nullo titulo, sed sola usurpatione tenuntur, nullo tempore praescribuntur . . . , maxime iure poli, ubi tanto gravius peccatur, quanto diutius." The glosses on c.11 X 1,4 say (*rubr.*): "Contra ius naturale nulla consuetudo valet. Item contra ius positivum praevalet consuetudo rationabilis et praescripta," and (v. *naturali iuri*): "et naturalia quidem iura immutabilia sunt, civilia vero mutabilia." Bracton, by applying that whole complex of

In short, the maxim *nullum tempus* placed the king and his imprescriptible rights above the Law that bound all other men. Others, in the course of some limited time, ran the risk of loss by prescription; not so the king, who was protected even where minor rights were concerned which he was entitled to give away. Certain regalian rights, for example, wreckage, treasure troves, or big fish (tuna, sturgeon, and others), which indeed pertained to the Crown, were of no concern to "common utility" so that the king, if he pleased, could transfer these rights, or parts of them, to private persons; because, says Bracton, "such translation would not do damage to any person except to the king or Prince himself."[243] Here Bracton arrives at a clear distinction between the essentials "which make the Crown what it is," and the accidentals pertaining to the king; or, between rights vested in the king for his public and common benefit of the community of the realm, and others serving the benefit of the king's person. However, even these minor regalian rights, as they, too, descended allegedly from the *ius gentium*, could be acquired only by a special royal grant; they could not be acquired by prescription.[244]

This general protection against alienation through the effects of time did not prevent the king from being himself subjected to the law of prescription whenever *res non ita sacrae*, "things less holy," were concerned, things such as tolls or manorial jurisdictions,[245] which did not belong to the ancient demesne or fall among the regalian rights, things which the Civilians would call *patrimonialia* as distinguished from *fiscalia*.[246] That is to say, with

---

ideas to the demesne or fisc, thus equates the *res quasi sacrae*, as it were, with Natural Law.

243 "Sunt etiam aliae res quae pertinent ad coronam propter privilegium regis, et ita communem non respiciunt utilitatem, quin dari possunt et ad alium transferri, quia, si transferatur, translatio nulli erit damnosa nisi ipsi regi sive principi." Bracton, fol.14, Woodbine, 11,58; see also fol.56, p.167. This is essentially the opinion of all jurists.

244 Bracton, fol.14,p.58: ". . . quia si warantum non habuerit specialem in hac libertate se defendere non poterit, quamvis pro se praetenderit longi temporis praescriptionem . . . huiusmodi de iure gentium pertineant ad coronam." See above, n.238.

245 The *res non ita sacrae* are mentioned on fol.14, p.58; cf. fol.55b, Woodbine, 11,166f.

246 The distinction between *fiscus, patrimonium*, and *res privatae* of the emperor was lacking clarity even in ancient times (see Vassalli, "Fisco" [below, n.272], 97ff), and the Civilians did not always realize that the terms were used with a different meaning at different times. Peregrinus, *De iure fisci*, I,1,n.8,fol.1ᵛ, sums up cor-

regard to some rights, lands, and liberties, which he was entitled to give away at his pleasure, which did not touch the essence of his office and therefore did not "touch all,"[247] and which were said to serve only to strengthen his position (*per quae corona regis roboratur*), the king himself was bound to the law of prescription: "With regard to those things, time runs against the king as against any private person."[248]

To summarize, in some respects the king was under the law of prescription; he was a "temporal being," strictly "within Time," and subjected, like any ordinary human being, to the effects of Time. In other respects, however, that is, with regard to things *quasi sacrae* or public, he was unaffected by Time and its prescriptive power; like the "holy sprites and angels," he was beyond Time and therewith perpetual or sempiternal. The king, at least with regard to Time, had obviously "two natures"—one which was temporal and by which he conformed with the conditions of other men, and another which was perpetual and by which he outlasted and defeated all other beings.[249]

---

rectly the glossators when he says: "Fisci autem res sunt, quae in Principatus sunt patrimonio [not in the *patrimonium Principis*], quorum administratio, quasi stipendia laboris, in usum et usufructum Principi concessa est, pro tuitione imperii et populorum bono regimine." It is from this point of view that Accursius, on C.7,37,3, v. *omnia principis*, explained: "Vel verius omnia sua sunt, scilicet fiscalia et patrimonialia." This opinion was represented also by Andreas of Isernia, on *Lib.aug.*, III,4, Cervone, 293: "Item, licet postquam bona sunt incorporata, omnino sunt Principis"; however, he insists: "Differentia tamen est inter res Demanii et alia bona Curiae . . . , sic inter fiscalia et patrimonialia." I refrain from pushing this complicated problem, especially since in Bracton feudal concepts interfere everywhere with the terminology of the Civilians.

247 This, of course, is the gist of the problem: "What touches all" belongs to things public and cannot be affected by time; see Gaines Post's famous paper "Quod omnes tangit," *Traditio*, IV (1946), 197ff.

248 Bracton, fol.14: "et in quibus currit tempus contra regem sicut contra quamlibet privatam personam." Cf. fol.56: "In aliis enim, ubi probatio necessaria fuerit, currit tempus contra ipsum sicut contra quoscumque alios." The king's private property, needless to say, was likewise exposed to prescription.

249 We may recall the Norman Anonymous who placed his *rex sanctus* beyond time and space (cf. Williams, *Norman Anonymous*, 160, and 225ff, the *Digressio de voce "sanctus"*), though not for fiscal reasons; see above, n.4. Bracton seems to have been somewhat conscious of the problem of Time. On one occasion (fol.102b-103, Woodbine, II,293), he distinguishes, following Justinian, *Inst.*4,12, between perpetual and temporal actions; that is, actions valid perpetually (laws, decrees of the senate, or imperial constitutions) and actions limited by time. Quite unexpectedly, however, he inserts—apparently challenged by the notions of perpetuality and time limitation—a paragraph on *nullum tempus*, although the *Institutes* offer not the slightest foundation for this excursus; cf. Maitland, *Bracton and Azo*, 175.

In other words, concerning Time the king was a *gemina persona*; he was Time-bound in some respects, and was above or beyond Time in others. At this point, however, a warning is needed. Bracton did not seem to make a distinction between the king as King who is sempiternal and above Time, and the king as a *private* person who is temporal and within Time. The idea of the king as a purely private person was, it seems, within the range of Bracton's political thought as little as it was within that of John of Salisbury or Frederick II.[250] Nor is the cleavage conditioned by the king's "body natural": it is a duality within the concept of rulership itself. This new *geminatio* of the king results from the establishment of a (so to say) extra-territorial or extra-feudal realm within the realm, an "eminent domain" the continuity of which, beyond the life of an individual king, had become a matter of common and public interest because the continuity and integrity of that domain were matters "that touched all."[251] The line of distinction, therefore, has to be drawn between matters affecting the king alone in his relations to individual subjects, and matters affecting all subjects, that is, the whole polity, the community of the realm. Better than distinguishing between the king as a private person and the king as a non-private person, would be to distinguish between a king feudal and a king fiscal, provided that we mean by "feudal" preeminently matters touching individual relations between liege lord and vassals; and by "fiscal," matters "that touch all."

Bracton himself seems to support this discrimination in the passage in which he explained the term *res quasi sacrae* and defined to what matters precisely he attributed sempiternity and

---

[250] See above, p.96. This does not imply that a distinction between public and private capacities was entirely lacking in earlier times. Around 1130, for example, Gerhoh of Reichersberg, *De edificio Dei*, c.21, *MGH,LdL*, III,152,12, when discussing the Donation of Constantine (above, n.231), remarked: "De regni autem facultate, quae est res publica, non debet a rege fieri donatio privata. Est enim aut regibus in posterum successuris integre conservanda aut communicato principum consilio donanda. De re autem privata tam a regibus quam a ceteris principibus potest fieri donatio privata." Irene Ott, "Der Regalienbegriff im 12. Jahrhundert," *ZfRG*, kan. Abt., XXXV (1948), 262f, certainly goes much too far when she deduces from that passage an implication concerning the state as a "juristic person." In later times, the Civilians as well as the Canonists mention, time and time again, things owned privately by the king "non tanquam rex, sed tanquam homo et animal rationale," as Baldus, *Consilia*, I,271,n.6, fol.82, says. However, those *res privatae* are hardly discussed by Bracton.

[251] Post, "Public Law," 46ff,49; also "Two Laws," 421ff.

immutability. He obviously chose his words with consideration; for he distinguished carefully between the *rex regnans* (the "ruling king") and the "Crown" while identifying at the same time the *res quasi sacrae* with the *res fisci*.

> A thing *quasi-sacred is a thing fiscal*, which cannot be given away or be sold or transferred upon another person by the Prince or ruling king; and those things make the Crown what it is, and they regard to common utility such as peace and justice.[252]

Bracton clearly referred to the public sphere, to "common utility," when speaking about the Crown and the fisc. Above all, however, he attributed immutability and sempiternity not only to church property, the *res sacrae* or (as others called them) the *res Christi*, but also to the *res quasi sacrae* or *res fisci*. And therewith there emerges that seemingly weird antithesis or parallelism of *Christus* and *Fiscus* to which hitherto little or no attention has been paid and which nevertheless illustrates most accurately a central problem of political thought in the period of transition from mediaeval to modern times.

In 1441, a monastery of Austin Friars was tried before the Court of the Exchequer because rector and monks claimed, in the case of some public emergency, tax exemption on the basis of a royal franchise granted by Edward III. It was a case of estoppel, since the judges felt that the king's personal grant to the monks was prejudicing the king's normal rights to taxation for the public welfare. In the course of that trial, John Paston, Justice of the Court of Common Pleas, and later well known as the collector of the letters of the Paston family, threw into the discussion an illustrative example. The details are of no interest here, but Paston supposed the case of a man who died a felon after having turned his lands to the dead hand, the Church. In such a case,

---

[252] Bracton, fol.14, Woodbine, II,58: "Est etiam *res quasi sacra res fiscalis*, quae dari non potest neque vendi neque ad alium transferri a principe vel a *rege regnante*, et quae faciunt ipsam *coronam* et communem respiciunt utilitatem, sicut est pax et iustitia quae multas habent species." Unfortunately Bracton does not discuss the various species of "Peace and Justice" coherently, but they are congruent with notions such as *usus publicus* or *communis utilitas* which Post ("Public Law," 50ff) has discussed. The "Crown" in Bracton's treatise is certainly not the "personified state" nor is it as yet even a *persona ficta*, although crypto-corporative concepts begin to make their appearance in Bracton, as Post, in his study "Quod omnes tangit," has demonstrated.

ran Paston's remarkable argument, the felon's chattels would be forfeited to the king "because what is not snatched by *Christus*, is snatched by the *Fiscus*"—*quia quod non capit Christus, capit fiscus.* The learned interpreter of that law-suit took this remark apparently as a *bon mot* of Paston and quoted it in a footnote because he considered it "too good to be lost."[253] But Paston's remark would not have been lost anyway. In his collection of emblems of 1531, the great Italian jurist and humanist Andrea Alciati presented an emblem showing a king (*fiscus*) who squeezes a sponge to the last drop, and the motto: *Quod non capit Christus, rapit fiscus* (fig. 21).[254] Alciati's book was singularly influential; in its wake some 1300 authors published more than 3000 similar emblem books, while Alciati's original work was translated into all European languages.[255] Hence also the *Christus*-and-*fiscus* motto wandered into a good many of those collections of emblems, devices, and proverbs of which the Renaissance was so fond.[256]

Did Justice Paston coin that phrase? Or did he think of, or happen to know, a disposition frequently repeated in the Dooms of Anglo-Saxon kings to the effect that certain fines were to be split between "King and Christ," the latter meaning the episcopal

---

[253] T. F. T. Plucknett, "The Lancastrian Constitution," *Tudor Studies Presented to A. F. Pollard* (London, 1924), 168,n.10. For the principle involved (invalidation by a *casus necessitatis* of the king's private contract with an individual), see Post, "Two Laws," 424, and "Public Law," 53; see also the succinct formula of Philip of Leyden (below, n.259), *Tabula*, rubr.I,n.9, p.370: "In rebus reipublicae consuetudo vel statutum non praeiudicant," which would apply also to charters and privileges. Miss Elizabeth Weigel, in London, was kind enough to copy for me the complete text of Paston's argument from the *Black Letter Vulgate* (London, 1679), II, parts 7-8, p.63. Donations of felons were always legally interesting cases; see, e.g., Selden, *Ad Fletam*, III,1, ed. Ogg, p.22. Paston actually complicated his hypothetical case by assuming that the *felo de se* (self-murderer) died intestate so that legally the fisc was the heir also for lack of a last will, a feature interesting in so far as Philip of Leyden (see below, n.259) likewise mentions the *Christus-fiscus* parallelism in connection with intestate death. See, in general, my brief note "Christus-Fiscus," *Synopsis: Festgabe für Alfred Weber* (Heidelberg, 1948), 225ff, then written without a knowledge of either the origin or the later history of the comparison.

[254] Andrea Alciati, *Emblemata* (Lyon, 1551), No. CXLVII, p.158. The motto, not yet found in the supposedly planned edition of 1522, first appeared in the *editio princeps* of 1531; see Henry Green, *Andrea Alciati and the Books of Emblems* (London, 1872), 324.

[255] Green, *Alciati*, p.viii.

[256] See, e.g., Johannes Georgius Seyboldus, *Selectiora Adagia latino-germanica* (Nürnberg, 1683), 306; K. F. W. Wander, *Deutsches Sprichwörterlexikon* (Leipzig, 1867), I,538, Nos.54,56,57; V,1102, No.95, cf. Nos.103f; see also Gustavo Strafforello, *La sapienza del mondo ovvero dizionario universale dei proverbi di tutti popoli* (Turin, 1883), II,86, s.v. "Fisco."

chest?[257] The answer is simple enough: neither was the motto a felicity of Paston nor did Alciati borrow it from the English judge; but both Alciati and Paston merely quoted a phrase proverbially used by lawyers. Matthaeus de Afflictis, writing around 1510, quoted it repeatedly in connection with tithes.[258] A century before Paston, around 1355, the Flemish civilian Philip of Leyden, author of a legal tractate on government, wrote about the rights of the fisc to intestate inheritance, and on that occasion he, too, dropped somewhat unexpectedly the remark: *Bona patrimonialia Christi et fisci comparantur,* "One compares the patrimonial possessions of Christ and the fisc."[259] The Dutch jurist apparently produced his comparison as a common usage of legal language; and in that he was correct. For the ultimate source of all these lawyers was the *Decretum* of Gratian: *Hoc tollit fiscus, quod non accipit Christus,* "What is not received by *Christus,* is exacted by the *fiscus.*"[260] With these words Gratian concluded a brief discussion about tithes due God and Caesar, borrowing the whole passage from a Pseudo-Augustinian sermon in which the unknown preacher argued that taxes rendered to the fisc became the more burdensome the less tithes were rendered to God.[261]

---

[257] See Edward and Guthrum, *Prol.,* cc.2 and 12; VIII Aethelred, cc.2,15,36,38; I Canute, cc.2 and 4; ed. Felix Liebermann, *Die Gesetze der Angelsachsen* (Halle, 1903), I,128f,134f,263,265,267,280f.

[258] Matthaeus de Afflictis, on *Lib.aug.,* 1,7 (*De decimis*), fol.53ᵛ; also *praeludia,* q.XV,n.3, fol.14ᵛ.

[259] Philippus de Leyden, *De cura rei publicae et sorte principantis,* I,n.9, ed. R. Fruin and P. C. Molhuysen (The Hague, 1915), 13, a text to which my attention was called by Berges, *Fürstenspiegel,* 265; see, for Philip, also F. W. N. Hugenholtz, "Enkele Opmerkingen over Filips van Leydens *De cura rei publicae et sorte principantis* als historische bron," *Bijdragen voor de Geschiedenis der Nederlanden,* Nos. 3-4, 1953. On the basis of C.10,10,1, the author discusses the right of the fisc to intestate inheritance and rejects claims on the part of cities or other local corporations (see, on the altercations between fisc and cities, Cecil N. Sidney Woolf, *Bartolus of Sassoferrato* [Cambridge, 1913], 120ff, and on the *successio ab intestato* on the part of corporations, Gierke, *Gen.R.,* III,291,n.139); a legacy snatched by a city must be revoked by the Prince: "Et quasi bona patrimonialia Christi et fisci comparantur. Ut administratores rerum Christi pauperum cibos ad libitum non disponant . . . , sic bona fisci in protectionem et conservationem reipublicae servanda sunt." Philip of Leyden, I,n.15, p.14, actually quotes the relevant passage from the *Decretum* (see next note). For the very common legal concept according to which the poor are the owners of Church property, see Gierke, *Gen.R.,* III,293,n.143.

[260] See c.8,C.XVI,q.7, ed. Friedberg, I,802. This passage, of course, was widely known, and it was cited, in the 1340's, by Albericus de Rosate in his *Dictionarium Iuris tam Civilis quam Canonici* (Venice, 1601), fol.120, s.v. *Fiscus:* "Quod non accipiet Christus, ubi aufert fiscus."

[261] [Pseudo-]Augustine, *Sermones supposititii,* LXXXVI,3, *PL,* XXXIX, 1912.

However, perfectly authentic words of St. Augustine referring to the *fiscus* of Christ are available; they are found in his commentary on the Psalter: *Si non habet rem suam publicam Christus, non habet fiscum suum*, "Unless Christ has his state [or community] he lacks his fisc."[262] In this case, the political notions of *res publica* and *fiscus* were used in a figurative and spiritualized sense: the community of mutual love and charity depended upon the spiritual treasure, and the one who practiced charity and gave alms thereby contributed to the "fisc" of Christ without needing fear the temporal "fiscal dragon," that is, the "exactor of the fisc" of the empire.[263] This passage, too, was received by the lawyers; Lucas de Penna, for example, quoted it in full when discussing ecclesiastical property.[264] Actually those places were not unimportant to the Church, because in the course of the Poverty Struggle in the times of Pope John XXII they served with other material to prove that Christ, since he had a *fiscus*, must have owned property.[265]

It is not difficult to detect what made *Christus* and *fiscus*—incomparable magnitudes to modern ears—comparable to mediaeval jurists. The comparison hinged upon the inalienability of both ecclesiastical property and fiscal property.[266] Alongside of the spiritual "dead hand" of the Church there had come into being, or into legal awareness, a secular "dead hand" of the state: the fisc. Or perhaps, following a suggestion of Lucas de Penna, it might

[262] Augustine, *Enarrationes in Psalmos*, CXLVI,17, *PL*, XXXVII, col.1911.

[263] "Ne putetis quia aliquis draco est fiscus, quia cum timore auditur exactor fisci; fiscus saccus est publicus. Ipsum habebat Dominus hic in terra, quando loculos habebat; et ipsi loculi Judae erant commissi (John 12: 6). . . ."

[264] Lucas de Penna, on *C.*10,1,1,n.7 (Lyon, 1582), p.5; (Lyon, 1597), fol.11v.

[265] The decisive passages are c.12 and c.17,C.XII,q.1, ed. Friedberg, 1,681,683: "Quare habuit [Christus] loculos cui angeli ministrabant, nisi quia ecclesia ipsius loculos habitura erat"? and "Habebat Dominus loculos, a fidelibus oblata consecrans. . . ." Both passages are taken from Augustine, *In Johannem*, 12,6 (above, n.263). These places were referred to by Pope John XXII in his decretals against the Spirituals; cf. *Extravagantes Ioannis XXII*, tit.XIV,c.5, ed. Friedberg, II,1230ff, esp.1233. The word *loculus*, meaning "purse," could be taken to mean "fisc" as demonstrated by Augustine (above, n.263). The jurists then elaborated on the question whether or not Christ had a fisc in the proper sense of the word; see, e.g., Matthaeus de Afflictis, *Praeludia*, q.xv,nos.7-9, fol.14v.

[266] The designation *Christus* for the possessions of the Church is explained by the fact that Christ was considered the owner (Gierke, *Gen.R.*, III,250,n.18), or God (below, n.298), or the poor (above, n.259). See, for the early mediaeval history of inalienability of Church property, Arnold Pöschl, "Kirchengutsveräusserungen und das kirchliche Veräusserungsverbot im früheren Mittelalter," *AKKR*, CV (1925), 3-96,349-448.

be recommendable to replace the term "dead hand," *manus mortua*, by "perpetual hand," *manus perpetua*, since the perpetuality was the truly significant feature common to both Church and fisc: they "never died."[267] Indeed, "Church and fisc walk together on equal terms,"[268] as the jurists remarked, for "there is no prescription against the Empire and the Roman Church."[269] It was on this basis that the lawyers began to challenge, not the genuineness, but the validity of the Donation of Constantine because, ran their argument, the Prince was not entitled to alienate property of the Empire, not to mention whole provinces; nor could the Church claim that by now the lands donated by Constantine were prescribed, since there was no prescription against the property of the Empire.[270] At any rate, by the thirteenth century the concept had gained general acceptance that the fisc represented within empire or kingdom some sphere of supra-personal continuity and perpetuality which depended on the life of the individual ruler as little as Church property depended on the life of an individual bishop or pope.

That Roman Law and its complex *ius fisci* were responsible for the new way of expounding the existence of an "immortal fisc"

---

[267] "Unde fiscales regni dicunt quod feudum pervenit ad manus mortuas; sed verius et proprius diceretur manus perpetuas; nam ecclesia nunquam moritur . . . sicut nec sedes apostolica . . . sic nec imperium quod semper est." See Lucas de Penna, on *C*.11,69,5,n.2 (Lyon, 1582), p.515, who refers to Andreas de Isernia, on *Feud*., 1,13,n.3, v. Ecclesiae, fol.49ᵛ. Cf. Gierke, *Gen.R.*, III,365,n.43. See, for the phrase *fiscus nunquam moritur*, below, n.292.

[268] Bartolus, on *C*.11,62 (61),4,n.1, fol.45ᵛ: ". . . cum ecclesia et fiscus paribus passibus ambulent," with an allegation of *C*.1,2,23, where we find *divinum publicumque ius* set over against *privata commoda*. Accordingly, it was common among lawyers to emphasize that "ius divinum et publicum ambulant pari passu"; cf. Post, "Two Notes," 313,n.81, quoting Jacques de Révigny (*ca*.1270-80). See n.267, and below, nos.283,285.

[269] See, e.g., Baldus, on *C*.7,38,1, fol.29: ". . . nullo tempore praescribitur res Caesaris . . . Contra Imperium et Romanam Ecclesiam non praescribitur" (below, n.280); also Baldus, on *C*.prooem.,n.38, fol.3: "quod non potest prescribi, non potest alienari."

[270] For the attitude of the jurists and the problem in general, see Laehr, *Konstantinische Schenkung*, 98ff,129ff,184f; also B. Nardi, "La *Donatio Constantini* e Dante," *Studi Danteschi*, XXVI (1942), 81ff; Ullmann, *Mediaeval Papalism*, 107ff, 163ff; Woolf, *Bartolus*, 94ff, also 343ff. Baldus, on c.33 X 2,24, fol.261, supported the validity of the Donation only because it was a "miracle," but admitted that it was not legal; see also *Consilia*, III,159,n.3, fol.45ᵛ, where he is rather outspoken: "nam quicquid dicatur de donatione Constantini, quae fuit miraculosa, si similes donationes fierent a regibus, non ligarent successores, quibus regni tutela, non dilapidatio est commissa." See, for England, Schramm, *English Coronation*, 197ff; Hoyt, *Demesne*, 146.

detached from the person of the ruler is obvious; at the same time, however, Canon Law concepts about the inalienability of Church property served as a model for the establishment of an independent and impersonal fisc.[271] From the twelfth century onward the legists made efforts to interpret the meaning of that strange thing called "the fisc."[272] The word, of course, was very common in Carolingian times when it meant the private property of the king;[273] and the jurists of the twelfth century were inclined to interpret, in a similar fashion, the fisc as the *sacculus regis*, "the king's purse into which the king's money was received," an interpretation which was repeated for centuries.[274] But from this more

[271] See above, n.226. Whereas the perpetuality of Church property was stressed, time and again, during the Investiture Struggle (see, e.g., Placidus of Nonantula, *De honore ecclesia*, c.7, *MGH,LdL*, 11,577,30: "Quod semel aecclesiae datum est, in perpetuum Christi est, nec aliquo modo alienari a possessione aecclesiae potest"), the defenders of the imperial cause, who denied the perpetuality of the temporal properties of the Church, came to deny also the perpetuality of the secular power as such; they insisted on ever-repeated investiture, that is, confirmation of grants to the Church, on the accession of every new king and new bishop; see, e.g., Wido of Ferrara, *De scismate Hildebrandi*, ii, *MGH,LdL*, 1,564,42: "Sicut enim imperium et regnum non est successorium, sic iura quoque regnorum et imperatorum successoria non sunt, nec regibus et imperatoribus perpetim manere possunt. Si vero perpetim non manent illis, qualiter his [sc. episcopis], quibus traduntur, perpetim manere possunt?" Wido, it is true, tries to construct perennial *imperialia iura*, but he does not carry this notion far enough to overcome the break of continuity which he was bound to construct in order to maintain the necessity of new investitures of the bishops at the hands of every new emperor.

[272] For the following, see Gierke, *Gen.R.*, iii,209ff; for the history of the fisc, see Filippo E. Vassalli, "Concetto e natura del fisco," *Studi Senesi*, xxv (1908), 68-121, 177-231. Very useful is the work of a Venetian canonist, Marcus Antonius Peregrinus, *De privilegiis et iuribus fisci libri octo* (Venice, 1611), who, in his references, conveniently sums up the opinions of the mediaeval glossators.

[273] The frequency of the word fisc in the Frankish documents, laws, and chronicles implies no more than a survival of the ancient administrative language; the former impersonal character of the fisc had given way to a purely personal concept already in the writings of Gregory of Tours. See the remarks of Vassalli, "Fisco," 181ff. It is significant that in a work such as James Westfall Thompson's *The Dissolution of the Carolingian Fisc in the Ninth Century* (Berkeley, 1935), not the slightest effort has been made to determine what "fisc" meant.

[274] See, e.g., Fitting, *Juristische Schriften*, 200: "Fiscus dicitur regius sacculus, quo recipiebatur pecunia regis. Per translationem vero dicitur omne dominium regie maiestatis." This definition, of course, was quite unoriginal. For the personal concept of the fisc, see the charter for Speier, of 1111, in which the Emperor Henry V talks about his rights "in locis fiscalibus, id est ad utilitatem *imperatoris* singulariter pertinentibus"; cf. Vassalli, "Fisco," 186,n.2, who records also the change from *imperatoris* to *imperii* in the confirmation of the charter in 1182. For the survival of the definition *sacculus regis*, see, e.g., Bartolus, on *C.*10,1,rubr.,n.11 (Venice, 1567), fol.2ᵛ: "Fiscus est saccus cesaris vel regis vel reipublicae"; but (n.13) he calls it also *camera imperii*, and (n.17) he makes a clear distinction between private and public: ". . . aut accipimus cameram imperatoris prout est impera-

personal and private aspect of the fisc, the lawyers proceeded quickly to a more impersonal and public exposition of fiscal property. They tried to find out what the fisc really was, and to whom it belonged. Was it identical with the *respublica?* Or was the *respublica* only the usufructuary of the fisc, as Placentinus maintained, or the owner of the fisc, with full *dominium* over it, as Azo believed? Moreover, what was the relation between the Prince and the fisc? Had, by the *lex regia*, the fisc been conferred upon the Prince together with the imperium? And if that were so, would the fisc then be the property of the Prince or was he merely the administrator and vicar of the fisc, assuming the privileges which derived from it, but responsible for its undiminished preservation for the benefit of his successors? And how did the fisc compare with the other appurtenances which the Prince was entitled to alienate, of which he could freely dispose, and which actually were subject to the prescriptive effects of time? Finally, if one assumed that the fisc was neither identical with the *respublica* nor with the Prince, was it perhaps a fictitious person *per se*, a "person" having its own patrimony, having experience, its own council, and "all the rights in its breast"—that is, did the fisc have an independent existence all by itself as a body corporate?[275]

---

tor . . . , aut prout est privatus, et tunc differt camera imperii a camera sua." See below, n.276, for considerably earlier distinctions of that kind; also Peregrinus, *De iure fisci*, 1,1,n.6.

[275] For Placentinus and Azo, see Gierke, *Gen.R.*, III,211; also Post, "Public Law," 49, and, in general, Vassalli, "Fisco," 189ff. The *lex regia* was quoted, e.g., by Cynus, on *C.*2,54,4 (Lyon, 1547), fol.81, and (Frankfurt, 1678), fol.114ᵛ: "Praeterea negari non potest, quin Respublica fisci successerit in locum Reipublicae Romanorum per legem regiam, quae omne ius populi transtulit in principem. . . . Ergo eius privilegia et conditionem assumpsit." The identity of fisc and Prince found support, e.g., in *D.*43,8,2,4: "res enim fiscales quasi propriae et privatae principis sunt." Baldus, on *C.*10,1, nos.11-13, fol.232ᵛ, discusses practically every possible interpretation, including the pros and cons; he, too, considers the results of the *lex regia* (n.12) and draws the conclusion that, on this basis, ultimately the Roman people owned the fisc "quia princeps repraesentat illum populum, et ille populus Imperium, etiam mortuo principe." Baldus, of course, recognizes the difficulty of identifying the fisc with the Prince (n.18): "Quaero, mortuo imperatore, ubi est iste fiscus, cum sit mortuus ille qui erat fiscus? Responsum: fingitur non mortuus, donec alius creetur imperator, sed vice personae fungetur." The fiscal interregnum, of course, was non-existent in the hereditary monarchies and in the Italian republics. Baldus, like many another jurist, defined the fisc as the *camera imperii* (see next note). On the other hand, Bartolus, on *D.*49,14,2,n.2, fol.254ᵛ, and elsewhere, in pursuance of his well known ideas about "sovereignty," held that "populus liber est sibi ipsemet fiscus." Cf. Vassalli, "Fisco," 191,n.3. See, for the relation of *populus* and *fiscus*, also P. W. Duff, *Personality in Roman Private Law* (Cambridge, 1938),

There could not be any one answer to satisfy all those questions and solve the problems involved, nor could there be unanimity among the jurists concerning the interpretation of "fisc." It became apparent, however, that the lawyers were trying to distinguish between "private" and "public" more effectively than had been done in an earlier era, and that they were about to create by their definitions the new sphere of things pertaining to Public Law—as it were, a new realm within the realm—which then could be set against, or compared with, the things pertaining to the Church under Ecclesiastical Law and likewise forming a realm within the realm since earliest times. Already the *Glossa ordinaria* had made the fisc public: the fisc was considered to be the *aerarium*, the treasury, not of the people or the Prince, but of the empire. Unanimity there was in one respect: that fiscal property was normally inalienable and that the fisc was perpetual or immortal.[276]

A very different matter, of course, was the practical problem of how to recover fiscal losses and fiscal rights or possessions which had been in the hands of private persons, landlords and others for a very long time—"beyond which the memory of man runneth not to the contrary."[277] The *tempus memoratum* had been fixed

---

52-61. For the personification of the fisc, see Gierke, *Gen.R.*, III,359,n.17; and, in general, Vassalli, "Fisco," 211ff.

[276] See *Glos.ord.* on D.1,1,1,2, v. *in sacris*, and also on C.10,1,rubr.: "Fiscus dicitur ipsa imperialis vel imperii camera, non dico patrimonii Imperatoris." The last words were often repeated with particular stress, e.g., by Odofredus, on C.10,9,1,n.10 (Vassalli, "Fisco," 189), who added to the words *camera imperii* the remark: "non patrimonialis [camera] principis." Bartolus, glossing the words *patrimonii Imperatoris*, made a clear distinction: "Quia tunc Imperator capitur ut privatus, et tunc eius [patrimonii] procurator differt a procuratore fisci." Baldus, on C.10,1,n.13, fol.232, makes a generalizing remark: "Fiscus est camera imperii: ubi ergo est fiscus, ibi est Imperium." See, in general, Peregrinus, I,1,nos.2,4,8, and passim, fol.1v; Post, "Public Law," 48ff, also "Two Laws," 421f, nn.18f; and, for the perpetuality of the fisc, Vassalli, "Fisco," 215, also for the customary etymology of *fiscus* from *fixus* in the sense of perpetual; cf. Peregrinus, I,1,n.37,fol.3v: "fiscus est fixus et stabilis, quia perpetuus et nunquam moritur, . . . et quamvis mutetur domini persona, semper tamen idem est fiscus."

[277] For the *tempus memoratum* see, e.g., C.7,39,4,2. Bracton, fol.230, Woodbine, III,186, gives a very specific reason for the validity of prescription against the fisc: "Item docere oportet longum tempus et longum usum qui excedit memoriam hominum. Tale enim tempus sufficit pro iure, non quia ius deficiat sed quia actio deficit vel probatio." Andreas of Isernia, on *Feud.*, II,55 (*De prohib. alien.*), n.50, fol.271v, discusses whether or not prescription against the fisc is possible: "Item quaeritur an demania regni vel imperii possint praescribi: periti regni Siciliae dicunt, quod non, sicut glossator [Marinus de Caramanico] in constitutione 'Si

by Justinian at a hundred years with regard to the Roman Church:[278] prescription, so far as it could be claimed against the Roman Church and ecclesiastical property in general, was valid only after a period of a hundred years, which was more than any human being could remember.[279] This prescription of a hundred years was in the West a privilege of the Roman Church alone; it served to protect the Church property and make it in practice inalienable. Baldus, however, like other jurists remarked repeatedly that "the same prerogative against prescription, which the Roman Church enjoys, is enjoyed by the Empire," or that "the Roman Empire enjoys the same prerogative [of a hundred-years prescription] as the Church." He declared even more specifically: *"Today* one does not seem to recognize a prescription of less than a hundred years [running against the Empire], which shows that the empire is treated as on a level with the Church"—or, when stressing the hundred-years prescription against the Church, he added: "And the same prerogative seems to be enjoyed *today* by the Empire."[280]

---

dubitatio' [*Lib.aug.*, III,8, Cervone, 307ff]. . . . Videtur ergo dicendum quod praescriptio temporis cuius non extat memoria, procedat et in demaniis. . . ." The same view is expressed also in Andreas' gloss on *Lib.aug.*, III,8. See below, n.283.

[278] See *Nov.*9 (for the Roman Church), and *C.*1,2,23,3-4 (for churches in general in certain cases). Despite changes and a reduction to 40 years (cf. *Nov.*111, also *Nov.*131,6), the *praescriptio centum annorum* remained valid in Rome and in Canon Law; see Gratian's *Decretum*, c.17,C.XVI,q.3, ed. Friedberg, I,796.

[279] The *Glos.ord.* on c.14 X 2,26, v. *centum annorum*, stresses that a prescription of 100 years is equal to no prescription at all: "Sed videtur certe impossibile probari praescriptionem centum annorum. Idem est ac si diceret Papa: Nolo quod currat praescriptio contra Romanam ecclesiam." The glossator adds that a witness had to be at least 114 years old to prove possession of 100 years, because he had to be 14 years old to be admitted as witness. This, then, remained the customary interpretation of this Innocentian decretal; see, e.g., Baldus, on c.14 X 2,26,n.2, fol.273ᵛ; also Matthaeus de Afflictis, on *Lib.aug.*, III,7,n.6, fol.122, who discusses the question with regard to the demesne "an autem sit aliqua differentia inter praescriptionem centum annorum, et praescriptionem tanti temporis, cuius initii memoria non existit." Those arguments were all raised by the early glossators of the Sicilian Constitutions; see Marinus de Caramanico, on *Lib.aug.*, III,39, Cervone, 399, and also Andreas of Isernia (*ibid.*, p.400).

[280] Baldus, on *C.*7,39,3,n.17, fol.31: ". . . ecclesia sancta Romana, contra quam non praescribitur nisi spatio centum annorum; contra vero alias ecclesias praescribitur spatio 40 [annorum]." *Ibid.*, 17b: "Item ecclesiae Romanae et Imperio non praescribitur super his quae reservata sunt in signum universalis dominii." *Ibid.*, 17d: "Qua enim praerogativa gaudet Romana ecclesia contra praescribentem eadem gaudet Imperium." *Ibid.*, 18: "Sed *hodie* non videntur praescribi minore tempore centum annorum ex quo imperium aequiparatur ecclesiae." See also Baldus, on *C.*7,30,2,n.2, fol.19ᵛ: "*Hodie* vero de iure authenticorum non sufficit minus tempus

It is true that the word *hodie,* "today," meant very often the times of Justinian to which the Civilians referred.[281] This, however, is not true in the present case, since Roman Law, where it did recognize prescriptive rights against the fisc, was ignorant of a hundred-years prescription; the fisc was normally protected by a period of forty or (according to Lombard Law) of sixty years. Therefore, the emphasis which Baldus laid repeatedly on the word "today" is noteworthy, because it seems to imply that only since relatively recent times were Church and imperial-royal fisc "equiparated" with regard to the hundred-years prescription. In fact, this "equiparation" of Church and fisc does not seem to antedate Frederick II who transferred the ecclesiastical privilege to the secular state. In his *Liber augustalis* he states in plain words:

> We extend the prescription of forty and sixty years, which hitherto was appropriate in public matters [to run] against the fisc, to a space of time of hundred years.[282]

And the Sicilian glossators made it perfectly clear that the fiscal hundred-years prescription was established by Frederick's law and that this emperor transferred an ecclesiastical privilege to the fisc.[283] The *aequiparatio* of Church and fisc was thus carried

---

centum annorum, quia sicut Romanum imperium gaudet [ecclesia Romana] eadem praerogativa. . . . Attende tamen quod nec centum annorum sufficit praescriptio contra imperium vel Romanam ecclesiam in his quae etiam sibi reservavit imperium in signum praeeminentiae et superioritatis. . . ." Also on *C.*7,40,1,n.7, fol.34: "non enim praescribitur [contra Romanum ecclesiam] nisi spatio centum annorum. . . . Et eadem praerogativa videtur *hodie* gaudere imperium." See also Peregrinus, vi,8,n.6,fol.145ᵛ, who refers to Baldus and others, and who, being a Venetian, includes the Signoria of Venice as enjoying the hundred-years prescription like Empire and Roman Church.

[281] Hermann Kantorowicz, *Glossators,* 135.

[282] *Lib.aug.,* iii,39, Cervone, 398: "Quadragenalem praescriptionem et sexagenariam, quae contra fiscum in publicis hactenus competebat, usque ad centum annorum spatium prorogamus."

[283] Marinus de Caramanico, v. *Quadragenalem:* "Sed haec constitutio prorogat quadragenalem in centum annos, et sic redit ad ius antiquum. C.de sacrosan.eccles. l.fin. (*C.*1,2,23; see above, n.279)." That is to say, Frederick reverted to conditions valid for churches and cities alike according to a law which in its preamble places *divinum publicumque ius* on one level; see the *Glossa ordinaria* on this law. That Frederick's law was a novelty seems to be indicated also by Andreas de Isernia, on *Feud.,* ii,55,n.51, fol.271ᵛ, where he makes the general statement: "Centenaria praescriptio currit contra fiscum per constitutionem 'Quadragenalem.'" On the other hand, Azo, on *C.*7,38,n.7, fol.216ᵛ, seems to be as yet ignorant of a fiscal prescription of a hundred years; he apparently approves of Justinian's reduction of the hundred-years prescription valid against the Roman Church (*Nov.*111; above, n.278) and argues: "Absurdum enim esset civitatem [Romam] maioris esse privilegii quam

through at an early date in Sicily, where it fell in with other related measures of Frederick II and his Norman predecessors. A similar idea, however, must have existed also in England where the "time beyond which the memory of man runneth not to the contrary" likewise was defined as a period of roughly a hundred years: it was set, before 1237, to the year 1135 when Henry I died; thereafter it was moved to the year 1154, the accession of Henry II; finally, in 1275, the year of the coronation of Richard I (1189) became the starting point of man's memory," and there it remained.[284]

Christus and *fiscus* thus became comparable with regard to both inalienability and prescription. The juristic basis of that "equiparation" was found in many places of the Roman Law, for example, in Justinian's *Code* where things belonging to the *templa*, the churches, were treated on equal footing with things belonging to the *sacrum dominium*, the "sacred demesne" of the emperor.[285]

principem." See, however, *Glos.ord.* on *Nov.*7,2,1, v. *nec multum* (see below, nos. 285,296), discussing the differences and similarities between *res sacrae* and *res publicae*, which says: "similitudinem autem habent; nam utriusque res iure isto adhuc centum annis praescribuntur." That the fisc was among the things public (*res publicae*) was said by Frederick himself in his law; see Marinus de Caramanico's gloss on *Lib.aug.*, III,39, Cervone, 398, v. *in publicis*: "Id est, fiscalibus rebus, quae dicuntur publicae (see above, n.241)." He later adds (p.399): "Item intellige principium constitutionis, quod praescriptio centum annorum, sicut dictum est, locum habeat contra fiscum, tam in feudis, quam in aliis bonis. . . . Omnia enim feuda publica sunt." The same words are repeated by Andreas of Isernia, *ibid.*, p.400; see also on *Lib.aug.*, III,8, Cervone, 308: "Feuda quidem de publico sunt." This is, unless I am mistaken, not in agreement with the English concept concerning "things public." The prescription of 100 years against the empire must have been common knowledge by the end of the 13th century, because the French use it to prove France's independence of the empire by right of prescription; see Lagarde, *Bilan du XIIIe siècle*, 248,n.56; Ullmann, "Sovereignty," 14.

[284] Pollock and Maitland, II,81, also 141; W. Holdsworth, *A History of English Law* (3rd ed., London, 1923), III,8, also 166ff.

[285] "Loca ad sacrum dominium pertinentia." See *C.*7,38,3, whose title indicates the parallelism: "Ne *rei dominicae* vel *templorum* vindicatio temporis exceptione submoveatur." Another place frequently quoted to prove the *aequiparatio* of divine and public spheres was *C.*1,2,23 (above, n.283); also *Nov.*7,2,1; "Nec multo differant ab alterutro sacerdotium et imperium, et sacrae res a communibus et publicis," with the *Glos.ord.*, v. *nec multum* (above, n.283); cf. Bartolus, on *Nov.*7,2, v. *sinimus*, n.4, fol.13ᵛ: "dicitur enim hic quod imperium et sacerdotium aequiparantur." See also Baldus, on *C.*10,1,3,n.3, fol.236: "aequiparantur enim ecclesia et fiscus." Of course, Church and fisc equalled also a minor and a madman because all of them were under age; see, e.g., Baldus on *C.*4,5,1,n.6, fol.12: ". . . nisi talis sententia esset lata contra fiscum, ecclesiam, vel pupillum, vel furiosum, quia aequiparantur pupillo." Cf. Gierke, *Gen.R.*, III,483, for this comparison. Bracton (fol.12, Woodbine, II,51f), shows that he was quite familiar with these categories.

Accordingly, the jurists would talk about the *sacratissimus fiscus* or *fiscus sanctissimus*, "the most holy fisc," a phrase having a curious ring only in modern ears, but explaining the ease with which *Christus* and *fiscus* were put into parallel.[286] Perhaps it sounds more convincing to us if Baldus, though holding that the fisc was *quoddam corpus inanimatum*,[287] nevertheless called it the "soul of the state."[288]

The parallelism between things holy and things fiscal, however, was not restricted to Time; it referred also to Space. The lawyers ascribed ubiquity to the fisc. *Fiscus ubique praesens* said Accursius in a gloss on the law of prescription to point out that the argument of "absence of the owner" was worthless in the case of the fisc, because the fisc was "everywhere and ever present."[289] The same words were repeated a little later by Marinus de Caramanico in his gloss on the *Liber augustalis*.[290] And Baldus, who likewise pointed out that the fisc could never be claimed to be "absent" from the realm, drew the final and logical conclusion: "The fisc is omnipresent and in that, therefore, the fisc resembles God."[291]

---

[286] In *C*.7,37,2, the *sacratissimus fiscus* and *sacratissimum aerarium* are mentioned, the adjective meaning nothing but "imperial." To this law reference is made, e.g., by Lucas de Penna, on *C*.10,1,n.8 (Lyon, 1582), p.5: "Fiscus dicitur sanctissimus."

[287] Baldus, *Consilia*, 1,363,n.2, fol.118: ". . . fiscus per se est quoddam corpus inanimatum consensum per se non habens, sed simpliciter repraesentans." See Gierke, *Gen.R.*, III,281 (with n.110), for the origin of this doctrine.

[288] Baldus, *Consilia*, 1,271,n.2, fol.81ᵛ: "et, ut ita loquar, est [fiscus] ipsius Reipublicae anima et sustentamentum." The comparison of the fisc with the stomach, in analogy with the story of Menenius Agrippa, is found at an early date in Corippus' *In laudem Iustini*, II,249ff, *MGH, Auct.ant.*, III,2,p.133; it is repeated by Lucas de Penna, on *C*.11,58,7,n.10 (Lyon, 1582), 564: the fisc is *instar stomachi*.

[289] *Glos.ord.* on *C*.7,37,1, v. *continuum*; also in the margin: "Fiscus ubique praesens est."

[290] Marinus, on *Lib.aug.*, III,39, v. *in publicis*, Cervone, 399: "et specialiter ubi dicit 'praesente in regno adversario suo' etc.; sic non loquitur de fisco, qui semper est praesens," with allegation of the *Glos.ord.* (preceding note). See also Matthaeus de Afflictis, on the same constitution (III,39), n.3, fol.186: ". . . nec requiritur probare de praesentia fisci, quia fiscus semper est praesens." Cf. Peregrinus, 1,2,n.42, fol.7.

[291] Baldus, on *C*.7,37,1,n.2, fol.37: ". . . quod fiscus est ubique, et sic in hoc Deo est similis. Et ideo fiscus non potest allegare absentiam." See also Baldus on *C*.4,27,1,n.27, fol.74ᵛ: "quia fiscus est ubicunque." A similar ubiquity was attributed to the Roman Church and its fisc; see Peregrinus, 1,2,n.22, fol.6: "In spiritualibus et inde dependentibus Papa, qui est caput Romanae Ecclesiae, fiscum generalem ubique habet, ut pro delicto in his commisso . . . bona delinquentis sint confiscanda; in fiscum Romanae Ecclesiae bona illius, ubilibet sint, cogantur, quia sicut Romana Ecclesia ubique est, sic fiscum Ecclesiae Romanae ubique existere oportet." Baldus, on c.9 X 2,14,n.38, fol.190ᵛ, "equiparates" fisc and Church: "Fiscus est persona

We are familiar with that kind of language reflecting merely another version of the *Christus-fiscus* theme. It does not imply, of course, that these metaphors were taken seriously, at their face value: *sanctus Fiscus* was never included in the official catalogue of saints. The metaphors do not (or not yet) betray an effort on the part of the jurist to "deify" the fisc, but to explain the perpetuity and general nature of the fisc; and for this purpose they availed themselves of theological terms, whereby "God" or "Christ" took the place of symbols or ciphers of fictitiousness serving to expound the fictitious nature of the fisc, its ubiquity and eternity: "Concerning its essence the fisc is a thing eternal and perpetual . . . , for the fisc never dies."[292] We should not forget that, vice versa, imperial terminology was applied to the papal fiscal possessions which, probably since the eleventh century, appeared as the *regalia beati Petri,* "the regalian rights of Blessed Peter," which emperors and papal feudatories swore to defend[293]—a technical term used occasionally also to bolster the *rex et sacerdos* doctrine of the hierarchy: the bishop a *rex* because he enjoyed *regalia.*[294] Imperialization of the papacy and sanctification of the secular state and its institutions ran in parallels.[295]

---

incorporalis et ideo ubique . . . Quandoque est [possessio] de non corpore in non corpus, ut fiscus vel ecclesia in abstracto . . . ," which may own something incorporeal, e.g., an easement, and thus *possidetur mistice.*

[292] Baldus, *Consilia,* I,271,n.3, fol.81ᵛ: ". . . cum respublica et fiscus sint quid eternum, et perpetuum quantum ad essentiam, licet dispositiones saepe mutentur: fiscus enim nunquam moritur." Concerning the "changing dispositions" and the "identity despite changes," see Gierke, *Gen.R.,* III,365,n.43; below, Ch.VI,2.

[293] See, for a brief discussion of the problem and for some material, my study "Inalienability," 492,n.26. There is a high degree of probability that the notion was introduced, by the Reform Papacy, at the time of the infeudation of the Normans. Irene Ott, "Der Regalienbegriff im 12. Jahrhundert," *ZfRG,* kan.Abt., XXXV (1948), 234-304, rightly distinguishes between the *regalia* in the sense of the *temporalia* of bishops (the predominantly German version), and the *regalia* in the sense of royal prerogative rights or *fiscalia* (the predominantly legalistic version in the sense of *fiscus*); unfortunately, however, she omitted to discuss the *regalia S. Petri,* which belonged definitely to the second category. Arnold Pöschl, "Die Regalien der mittelalterlichen Kirchen," *Festschrift der Grazer Universität für 1927* (Graz, 1928), was not accessible to me. See, for a few remarks, Niese, *Gesetzgebung,* 54,n.1.

[294] The political pamphleteers picked that notion up and elaborated on it. See, e.g., Gerhoh, *De investigatione,* I,69, *MGH,LdL,* III,388,45: the bishops have not only the *sacerdotalia* of tithes and oblations, but a¹so the *regalia* on the part of the king; they may claim, therefore, to be *quodammodo et reges et sacerdotes Domini,* and are entitled to demand of the people not only obedience, but also an oath of fealty "ad defensionem videlicet regalium simul et pontificalium beati Petri." See also Gerhoh, *ibid.,* 389,10; *Dialogus de pontificatu, ibid.,* 538,30.

[295] Schramm, "Sacerdotium und Regnum," discusses excellently the problem for

A Novel of Justinian has to be mentioned here. It was often cited to prove the parallelism of Church property and state property, since in it the legislator stated in clear words that between *imperium* and *sacerdotium* the difference was not too great, nor between *res sacrae* and *res communes et publicae*.[296] At this point Bracton fell in with the budding fiscal "theology" of his age. Bracton, to be sure, was remote from the subtle distinctions of the Bolognese who argued whether the fisc was identical with the people or with the ruler or with itself; nor did it occur to him to conceive of the fisc as a *persona ficta* although that concept was introduced in his days.[297] And yet he came very close to the concept of a fictitious person when he used the technical term of *nullius*, stating that both the *res sacrae* and the *res quasi sacrae* were "property of none," *bona nullius*. "That is, they are not property of any single person, but only property *of God or the fisc*."[298] We discover—owing to our long digression into later legal thought—that Bracton likewise produced that strange combination of divine and fiscal. The common denominator for *Deus* and *fiscus* was, in his case, the *res nullius*; and this notion covered the legal synonymity of both ecclesiastical and fiscal possessions just as effectively as any "equiparation" of the later jurists who compared *Christus* and *fiscus*. It was in that connection, too, that Bracton distinguished between the *rex regnans* and the Crown[299]— wisely so, because the Crown itself, rather than the mortal king, appeared to have, in many respects, an inner relationship with the *res nullius*, that is, with the impersonal and supra-personal fisc. The development of the abstract notion of "Crown"—to anticipate here some results of a later chapter—was, after all, con-

---

the earlier Middle Ages (secular *imitatio sacerdotii*, spiritual *imitatio imperii*), but for the later Middle Ages little has been done; for a few remarks, see my study "Mysteries of State," *Harvard Theological Review*, XLVIII (1955), 65-91.

296 *Nov.*7,2,1; see above, n.285.

297 See, concerning the concept of *persona ficta*, Gierke, *Gen.R.*, III,279ff, for Innocent IV, and *ibid.*, 204, for some forerunners; also Maitland, *Political Theories*, xviii f; below, Ch.VI.

298 Bracton, fol.14, Woodbine, II,57f: "Huiusmodi vero res sacrae [including *res quasi sacrae*] a nullo dari possunt nec possideri, quia in nullius bonis sunt, id est, in bonis alicuius singularis personae, sed tanquam in bonis *Dei vel* bonis *fisci*." Cf. fol.12, Woodbine, II,52f, where Bracton emphasizes that "primo et principaliter fit donatio Deo et ecclesiae, et secundario canonicis," that is, God or the Church are the true owners, whereas the clerics "nihil habent nisi nomine ecclesiae suae."

299 See above, n.252.

comitant with the development of the fisc or "royal demesne" under Henry II. And just as Bracton paralleled God and the fisc, so would his contemporary fellow-judges tend to refer to the abstract Crown rather than to the king whenever they wanted to juxtapose the public sphere of the state and the public sphere of the Church.[300]

About the sources of Bracton very few words are needed. Even were it quite unknown to what extent Bracton actually depended on Azo's *Summa Institutionum*, the legal notion of *res nullius* in connection with *res sacrae* would make it perfectly clear that the English lawyer was following, or paraphrasing, the Law of Things of Justinian's *Digest* and *Institutes*.[301] Bracton called the non-ecclesiastical things owned "by none" *res quasi sacrae*, whereas Roman Law called them *res publicae*.[302] His technical term for things public or fiscal (*res quasi sacrae*) was not popular among the Bolognese, and there may have been some misunderstanding on the part of Bracton.[303] However, the designation he chose was

300 It seems that the references to "Crown" and "Dignity" were chosen with some regularity when the king's courts were set against the courts Christian as, e.g., in Bracton's chapter *De exceptionibus* (fols.399b-444b). See, e.g., fol.400b, Woodbine, IV,248: "Est etiam iurisdictio quaedam ordinaria, quaedam delegata, quae pertinet ad sacerdotium et forum ecclesiasticum. . . . Est et alia iurisdictio, ordinaria vel delegata, quae pertinet *ad coronam* et *dignitatem* regis et ad *regnum* . . . in foro saeculari." Cf. fol.401,p.249; fol.401b,p.251: "Vice versa non est laicus conveniendus coram iudice ecclesiastico de aliquo quod pertineat *ad coronam, ad dignitatem regiam* et *ad regnum*." The same phrases occur in the writs, e.g., fol.402, p.252 (three times); fol.403b, and 404, p.257f; fol.404b, p.259; fol.406b, p.264, and passim. Bracton, to be sure, uses *dignitas regis et corona* also elsewhere, e.g., fol.103, Woodbine, II,293. The problem needs further investigation. See below, Ch.VII,nos.107f.

301 *D*.1,8,1: "Quod autem divini iuris est, id nullius in bonis est. . . . Quae publicae sunt, nullius in bonis esse creduntur." Cf. *Inst*.2,1,7: "Nullius autem sunt res sacrae et religiosae et sanctae."

302 Bracton (fol.14) confuses (above, n.237) *res sacrae, religiosae,* and *sanctae,* because he uses the term *quasi sacrae* for both the *res publicae* and the *res sanctae*: "Donari autem non poterit res quae possideri non potest, sicut res sacra vel religiosa vel quasi, qualis est res fisci [= res publicae], vel quae sunt quasi sacrae sicut sunt muri et portae civitatis [= res sanctae]." The basis is *Inst*.2,1,10, or *D*.1,8,11, where walls and city-gates are repeatedly called *res sanctae*, not *res quasi sacrae*. The "holiness" of city-walls could not have meant very much to Bracton, nor the fact that it was a sacrilegious act to leap over a wall, although the death of Remus is mentioned in *D*.1,8,11, and the glossators liked to comment on that place.

303 *Inst*.2,1,8, explains that only such things are *res sacrae* which have been consecrated *rite et per pontifices*, and then adds: ". . . si quis vero auctoritate sua *quasi sacrum* sibi constituerit, sacrum non est, sed profanum." The term *quasi sacrum* has here a somewhat derogatory meaning, and it is highly improbable that Bracton knowingly applied it in this sense to the *res publicae*; but the term may

convenient for bringing property of the Church and property of the fisc juristically into parallel, even though Bracton on the whole shows hardly a tendency to exalt the secular state in general, or to raise its immutable Time-defeating essence to the quasi-holy stratum to which Frederick II and his advisers aspired in many respects.

Res sacrae and *res quasi sacrae* could be reduced to the same denominator because as *res nullius* they were the property, not of a natural person, but of a legally fictitious person ("Christ" or "fisc"), which was not exposed to the contingencies of Time. In the last analysis, the seemingly weird parallelism of *Christus* and *fiscus* goes back to the earliest layers of Roman legal thought. To the Romans the property of the gods and the property of the state appeared by legal definition on the same level: *res divinae* and *res publicae* were beyond the reach of any individual because they were *res nullius*.[304] In later times, the pagan notion of "things pertaining to the gods" was logically transferred to the Christian Church, so that St. Ambrose could remind the young Emperor Valentinian II that "things divine are not subjected to the imperial power,"[305] meaning, of course, that the *res divinae* were beyond the reach even of the Prince, since they were *res nullius*. During the feudal age, with its patriarchal concepts of social organisms, those notions, especially that of *res publicae*, lost their former significance and became practically irrelevant despite occasional recollections.[306] It was under the impact of the

---

have been in his mind in some other connection. In the writings of the glossators, I did not find the term *res quasi sacrae* replacing *res publicae*.

[304] See above, n.301, also my study, "Christus-Fiscus," 234f.

[305] Ambrose, *Ep.*, xx,8, *PL*, xvi,1039A: "quae divina sunt, imperatoriae potestati non esse subiecta." The passage is later found in canonical collections; see, e.g., Deusdedit, iii,c.211, ed. Victor Wolf von Glanvell, *Die Kanonessammlung des Kardinals Deusdedit* (Paderborn, 1905), 1,511,19; Gratian, c.21,C.xxiii,q.8, ed. Friedberg, 1,959. For the interpretation, see H. Lietzmann, "Das Problem Staat und Kirche im weströmischen Reich," *Abh.preuss.Akad.* (Berlin, 1940), Abh.11, p.8; also Kenneth M. Setton, *Christian Attitude towards the Emperor in the Fourth Century* (New York, 1941), 110.

[306] One is reminded of the famous remark which, according to Wipo, *Gesta Chuonradi*, c.7, ed. H. Bresslau, 29f, Emperor Conrad II was supposed to have made when, after the death of his predecessor, the people of Pavia destroyed the palace fortress in their city because, they claimed, the owner had died and the palace now belonged to no one. Conrad is said to have made a distinction between *domus regis* and *domus regalis*, admitting that not the king's house was destroyed because at that time there was no king, but stressing the destruction of the "royal

Bolognese movement only, and as a result of the recovery of learned jurisprudence, that, in the twelfth and thirteenth centuries, the ancient complementary notions of *res sacrae* and *res publicae* reclaimed their former significance under new conditions. They became applicable, not only to the property of the Church, therein following the late-antique and mediaeval tradition, but also to things pertaining to the nascent sovereignty of the secular state. And again, as in ancient Roman times, the technical term *res nullius* gave expression to the idea that things public and fiscal were *sacer*, were as "untouchable" and therewith as perpetual and "beyond Time" as the things belonging to the gods, betokened in the later Middle Ages by the legal cipher of "Christ."

Hence, the formula *Christus-fiscus* appears simply as a shorthand expression for a long and complicated development by which something definitely secular and seemingly "unholy" in the Christian and every other sense, namely the fisc, was turned into a thing "quasi holy." The fisc finally became a goal in itself. It was taken as a hall-mark of sovereignty, and, by a total reversal of the original order, it could be said that "the fisc represents State and Prince."[307] Moreover, already Baldus pointed out that not only fisc and commonwealth were on one level, but also *fiscus* and *patria*.[308] We may wonder whether it is logic or irony of history that the solemn Roman cult of gods and public functions should be found at the root of modern deification and idolization of state mechanisms.

---

building," and then continued: "Si rex periit, regnum remansit, sicut navis remaneat, cuius gubernator cadit. Aedes *publicae* fuerant, non *privatae*." This is legal terminology; see, on the issue, A. Solmi, "La distruzione del palazzo regio in Pavia nell'anno 1024," *Rendiconti dell'Istituto Lombardo di Scienze e Lettere*, LVII (1924), 97ff. See also above, n.250, for the distinction between *publica* and *privata* in the writings of Gerhoh, or the remark in the *Annales Disibodenbergensens*, ad a.1125, *MGH,SS*, XVII,23, according to which Lothar III ordered concerning confiscated property "potius regiminis subiacere ditioni, quam regis proprietati." Cf. Vassalli, "Fisco," 187.

[307] Vassalli, "Fisco," 213,n.4, quotes Pierre Grégoire (Tholosanus), *De re publica*, VII,20,31, as saying: "Fiscus repraesentat principem et rempublicam." This is the rubric quoted in the index (s.v. *Fiscus*); the text (Lyon, 1609, p.237) shows the reading: "Fiscus publicam rem et principis refert."

[308] *Glos.ord.*, on *D*.3,1,10, has a marginal note saying that Baldus considered this law unique "quia *fiscus*, *respublica* et etiam *patria* aequiparantur quoad reverentiam eis exhibendam." I was not able to spot the place, though it is most likely that Baldus made this remark because *patria* is mentioned in that law.

In Bracton's political theory the notion of *res nullius* did not serve as the main lever for moving the problems of Public Law. However, together with a great number of other impulses originating from Romano-Canonical practice, the parallelism of God and fisc contributed to articulate the concept of a sempiternal public sphere within the realm. A split, as yet hardly visible, between the "reigning king" and the financial "holy district" within the realm began to show up. But while the English kings reigning in the thirteenth century tried to ignore even the existence of a cleavage between themselves and the things public, the various baronial opposition groups were ready to widen that split and to pit the *res publicae* against the *rex regnans*. It is significant that during the constitutional struggles of the thirteenth and fourteenth centuries, the baronial objections were always centered on the fiscal-domanial sphere, including the prerogative rights attached to it, whereas the strictly feudal sphere—including feudal aids and other rights exercised by the king as personal liege lord—remained, on the whole, unchallenged. Within the orbit of public affairs, however, and especially public finances, the barons could venture to control the king, to bind him to a council of their own choice, and thus to demonstrate that things of public concern no longer touched the king alone, but "touched all," the king as well as the whole community of the realm.[309] In fact, the Bolognese lawyers also considered the ruling Prince in many respects only the administrator and vicar of the fisc;[310] and the English barons looked upon their king certainly not as the personal

---

[309] Post, "Quod omnes tangit," 235f, 250, and passim; also "Two Laws," esp. 425ff (with n.35), for things touching (1) the head principally, (2) the members principally, and (3) head and members equally. Those distinctions do not coincide with *res privatae* and *res publicae*, since the king's private estate was, or could become at any moment, a matter of public concern.

[310] The tenet of the Prince as administrator of the fisc was based on *D*.41,4,7,3: "nam tutor in re pupilli tunc domini loco habetur, cum tutelam administrat, non cum pupillum spoliat." For the fisc as a minor, see above, n.285; in general, Gierke, *Gen.R.*, III,226f,332,482. That the Prince was not the owner, but the *legitimus administrator* of the fisc, was a maxim repeated over and over again; see, e.g., Baldus, *Consilia*, I,271,nos.2-3, fol.81ᵛ; Peregrinus, 1,2,n.47, fol.7ᵛ. The maxim served also to refute the legality of Constantine's Donation (above, n.270); see, e.g., John of Paris, *De potestate*, c.21, ed. Leclercq, 244f: a private donation would have been valid, but "non quando donat de patrimonio fisci quod semper debet manere," because the Prince is "administrator imperii et reipublicae. . . . Sed si imperii administrator est, donatio non valet" (reference to the *lex regia* and to *D*.41,4,7,3).

owner, but as the guardian of the public appurtenances which served the benefits and the security of the whole body politic, and were supposed to serve that polity in perpetuity—far beyond the life of the individual king.

Whatever the angle from which we may wish to inspect the development of English political thought, and whatever the strand we may choose to study and isolate for this purpose, always will the Bractonian age stand out as the most critical period. It was then that the "community of the realm" became conscious of the difference between the king as a personal liege lord and the king as the supra-individual administrator of a public sphere—a public sphere which included the fisc that "never died" and was perpetual because no time ran against it. Religious thought, which had profoundly influenced, or even determined, the concepts of government in an earlier phase, was carried over to the new orbit of public affairs in a seemingly scurrilous fashion—by comparing the sempiternity of the fisc to the eternity of God or of Christ. The Norman Anonymous had expressed the king's supra-temporal qualities by attributing to him a divine and God-like nature by grace. But the ideas of the Norman Anonymous propounding the king as a *gemina persona* because he was the "image of Christ" even with regard to the two natures, belonged to the past. Frederick II, as the *lex animata*, had sought the sempiternal essence of his rulership somewhere in an undying Idea of Justice, and had changed, so to speak, from a *vicarius Christi* to a *vicarius Iustitiae*, an office which still had semi-religious connotations. However, the metaphysical concepts and eschatological ideas of the imperial court may have fitted the conditions of Italy and of the great war against the papacy; they did not fit Bractonian England. Bracton himself was more sober and, in a way, more secular than were the lawyers at the court of Frederick II. To be sure, the king in the Bractonian age changed also; and if we were to make an overstatement and understand by "fisc" the public sphere at large, we might perhaps say that he changed from a *vicarius Christi* to a *vicarius Fisci*. That is, the perpetuality of the supra-personal king began to depend also on the perpetuality of the impersonal public sphere to which the fisc belonged. At any event, what ultimately the rulers of the thirteenth century had in common was that they borrowed their touch of sempi-ternity not so much from the Church as from Justice and Public Law expounded by learned jurisprudents—be it by name of *Iustitia* or *Fiscus.*

The ancient idea of liturgical kingship gradually dissolved, and it gave way to a new pattern of kingship centered on the sphere of Law which was not wanting its own mysticism. The new "halo" began to descend upon the nascent secular and national state, headed by a new *pater patriae,* when the state began to claim for its own administrative apparatus and public institutions a sempiternity or perpetuity which hitherto had been attributed only to the Church and, by Roman Law and the Civilians, to the Roman Empire: *Imperium semper est.*[311] Clearly, the mediaeval dichotomy of *sacerdotium* and *regnum* was superseded by the new dichotomy of the King and the Law. In the Age of Juris-prudence the sovereign state achieved a hallowing of its essence independent of the Church, though parallel to it, and assumed the eternity of the Roman empire as the king became an "emperor within his own realm." But this hallowing of the *status regis et regni,* of state institutions and utilities, necessities and emer-gencies, would have remained incomplete had not that new state itself been equated with the Church also in its corporational aspects as a secular *corpus mysticum.*

[311] See, e.g., *Nov.*6,epil., in addition to many other places (see below, pp. 291ff).

CHAPTER V

POLITY-CENTERED KINGSHIP: CORPUS MYSTICUM

INFINITE cross-relations between Church and State, active in every century of the Middle Ages, produced hybrids in either camp. Mutual borrowings and exchanges of insignia, political symbols, prerogatives, and rights of honor had been carried on perpetually between the spiritual and secular leaders of Christian society.[1] The pope adorned his tiara with a golden crown, donned the imperial purple, and was preceded by the imperial banners when riding in solemn procession through the streets of Rome. The emperor wore under his crown a mitre, donned the pontifical shoes and other clerical raiments, and received, like a bishop, the ring at his coronation.[2] These borrowings affected, in the earlier Middle Ages, chiefly the ruling individuals, both spiritual and secular, until finally the *sacerdotium* had an imperial appearance and the *regnum* a clerical touch.

A certain state of saturation was reached by the beginning of the thirteenth century, when both the spiritual and secular dignitaries were rigged with all the essential attributes of their offices. The borrowings between the two orbits, however, did not then come to an end; only the objectives changed during the later Middle Ages when the center of gravity shifted, as it were, from the ruling personages to the ruled collectives, the new national monarchies, and the other political aggregates of human society. In other words, the exchanges between Church and State continued; but the field of mutual influence, expanding from individual dignitaries to compact communities, henceforth was determined by legal and constitutional problems concerning the structure and interpretation of the bodies politic. Under the *pontificalis maiestas* of the pope, who was styled also "Prince" and "true emperor,"[3] the hierarchical apparatus of the Roman Church

[1] See, in general, Schramm, "Austausch," for the earlier period; also my *Laudes regiae*, 129ff.

[2] For the imperial mitre and other symbols, see Schramm, *Herrschaftszeichen und Staatssymbolik* (Schriften der MGH, XIII [Stuttgart, 1954]), esp.68ff.

[3] For the title *pontificalis maiestas*, see Mochi Onory, *Fonti*, 113; cf. *Laudes regiae*, 140, nos. 94, 95.

tended to become the perfect prototype of an absolute and rational monarchy on a mystical basis, while at the same time the State showed increasingly a tendency to become a quasi-Church or a mystical corporation on a rational basis.

While it has often been felt that the new monarchies were in many respects "churches" by transference, it has far less often been pointed out in detail to what extent late mediaeval and modern commonwealths actually were influenced by the ecclesiastical model, especially by the all-encompassing spiritual prototype of corporational concepts, the *corpus mysticum* of the Church.

1. Corpus Ecclesiae mysticum

The corporational doctrine of the Roman Church has been summarized and dogmatized, in 1302, by Pope Boniface VIII in the lapidary sentences of the bull *Unam sanctam*:

> Urged by faith we are bound to believe in one holy Church, Catholic and also Apostolic . . . , without which there is neither salvation nor remission of sins . . . , which represents one mystical body, the head of which is Christ, and the head of Christ is God.

The general context of the bull leaves no doubt about the meaning of the introductory sentence. It betrays the supreme effort on the part of the spiritual power to answer and, if possible, to overcome the challenge of the nascent self-sufficiency of the secular bodies politic. Pope Boniface was bent upon putting political entities in what he considered their proper place, and therefore stressed, and overstressed, the hierarchical view that the political bodies had a purely functional character *within* the world community of the *corpus mysticum Christi*, which was the Church, whose head was Christ, and whose visible head was the vicar of Christ, the Roman pontiff.[4]

[4] Ladner, "Aspects," esp. 409ff, also his more recent study, "The Concepts: Ecclesia, Christianitas, Plenitudo Potestatis," *Sacerdozio e regno da Gregorio VII a Bonifacio VIII* (Miscellanea Historiae Pontificiae, XVIII; Rome, 1954), 49-77, esp. 53ff. The literature on *corpus mysticum* is very extensive, especially after the publication of the encyclical *Mystici corporis* in 1943; see, for a more recent comprehensive study, Émile Mersch, *Le corps mystique du Christ, études de théologie historique* (2 vols., Louvain, 1933). An excellent evaluation with regard to the history of ideas is owed to Henri de Lubac, *Corpus mysticum* (2nd ed., Paris, 1949), also in *Recherches de science religieuse*, XXIX (1939), 257-302, 429-480, and XXX (1940), 40-80, 191-226; in the following pages I have merely ransacked the wealth of his material (much of which was inaccessible to me) and his ideas. For early

The Church as the mystical body of Christ—and that means: Christian society as composed of all the faithful, past, future, and present, actual and potential[5]—might appear to the historian so typically mediaeval a concept, and one so traditional, that he would easily be inclined to forget how relatively new that notion was when Boniface VIII probed its strength and efficiency by using it as a weapon in his life-and-death struggle against Philip the Fair of France. The concept of the Church as *corpus Christi*, of course, goes back to St. Paul;[6] but the term *corpus mysticum* has no biblical tradition and is less ancient than might be expected. It first came into prominence in Carolingian times and gained some importance in the course of the controversy about the Eucharist carried on over many years by Paschasius Radpertus and Ratramnus, both of the monastery of Corbie. On one occasion, Ratramnus pointed out that the body in which Christ had suffered, was his "proper and true body" (*proprium et verum corpus*) whereas the Eucharist was his *corpus mysticum*. Perhaps Ratramnus relied on the authority of Hrabanus Maurus, who had stated, shortly before, that within the Church the *corpus mysticum*—meaning the Eucharist—was administered by the priestly office.[7]

Here then, in the realm of dogma and liturgy, there originated that notion whose universal bearings and final effects cannot easily be overrated. *Corpus mysticum*, in the language of the

---

scholasticism, see also Ferdinand Holböck, *Der Eucharistische und der Mystische Leib Christi in ihren Beziehungen zueinander nach der Lehre der Frühscholastik* (Rome, 1941). The very important book of Brian Tierney, *Foundations of the Conciliar Theory: The Contribution of the Medieval Canonists from Gratian to the Great Schism* (Cambridge Studies in Medieval Life and Thought, N.S., IV; Cambridge, 1955), appeared too late to be considered here; see esp. Part II, 87ff, 106ff, 132ff.

[5] Aquinas, *Summa theol.*, III, q.VIII, a.3.

[6] For St. Paul's metaphor, see I Cor. 12: 12, and 27, also 6: 15; Eph. 4: 4,16,25, and 5: 30; Col. 2: 19. The study of T. Soiron, *Die Kirche als der Leib Christi nach der Lehre des hl. Paulus* (Düsseldorf, 1951), was not yet accessible to me. For the place of St. Paul's organological concept within antique philosophical tradition, see Wilhelm Nestle, "Die Fabel des Menenius Agrippa," *Klio*, XXI (1926-27), 358f, also in his *Griechische Studien* (1948), 502ff; also the study of A. Ehrhardt, "Das Corpus Christi und die Korporationen im spät-römischen Recht," *ZfRG*, rom.Abt., LXX (1953), 299-347, and LXXI (1954), 25-40, is relevant for the present problem, and so is M. Roberti, "Il corpus mysticum di S. Paolo nella storia della persona giuridica," *Studi in Onore di Enrico Besta* (Milan, 1939), IV, 37-82.

[7] For the Carolingian controversy, see Lubac, *Corpus mysticum*, 39ff; cf. 41f, for Hrabanus Maurus, *De clericorum institutione*, I,c.33, *PL*, CVII,324A.

Carolingian theologians, referred not at all to the body of the Church, nor to the oneness and unity of Christian society, but to the consecrated host. This, with few exceptions, remained, for many centuries, the official meaning of the "mystical body," whereas the Church or Christian society continued to be known as the *corpus Christi* in agreement with the terminology of St. Paul. It was only in the course of a strange and perplexing development—*un curieux chassé-croisé*[8]—that finally, around the middle of the twelfth century, those designations changed their meaning. The change may be vaguely connected with the great dispute of the eleventh century about transubstantiation. In response to the doctrines of Berengar of Tours and to the teaching of heretical sectarians, who tended to spiritualize and mystify the Sacrament of the Altar, the Church was compelled to stress most emphatically, not a spiritual or mystical, but the *real* presence of both the human and the divine Christ in the Eucharist. The consecrated bread now was termed significantly the *corpus verum* or *corpus naturale*, or simply *corpus Christi*, the name under which also the feast of *Corpus Christi* was instituted by the Western Church in 1264.[9] That is to say, the Pauline term originally designating the Christian Church now began to designate the consecrated host; contrariwise, the notion *corpus mysticum*, hitherto used to describe the host, was gradually transferred—after 1150—to the Church as the organized body of Christian society united in the Sacrament of the Altar. In short, the expression "mystical body," which originally had a liturgical or sacramental meaning, took on a connotation of sociological content. It was finally in that relatively new sociological sense that Boniface VIII defined the Church as "one *mystical* body the head of which is Christ."

Concomitant with the new emphasis laid upon the real presence of Christ in the sacrament—a doctrine finally culminating in the dogma of transubstantiation of 1215, by which the Eucharist was officially designated as *corpus verum*—was the development of

[8] Lubac, 88.

[9] For the reaction against Berengar, see Lubac, *Corpus mysticum*, 104ff, 162ff, and, for the "inversion" in general, p.19. For the institution of the feast of *Corpus Christi*, see P. Browe, "Die Ausbreitung des Fronleichnamsfestes," *Jahrbuch für Liturgiewissenschaft*, VIII (1928), 107-143, who has collected also the early sources in his *Textus antiqui de festo Corporis Christi* (Münster, 1934); and for the most recent studies, Anselm Strittmatter, in *Traditio*, V (1947), 396ff.

the term *corpus mysticum* as a designation of the Church in its institutional and ecclesiological aspects. It was adopted at a critical moment in Church history. After the Investiture Struggle there arose, for many reasons, the "danger of too much stress being laid on the institutional, corporational side of the Church" as a body politic.[10] It was the beginning of the so-called secularization of the mediaeval Church, a process which was balanced by an all the more designedly "mystical" interpretation even of the administrative body and technical apparatus of the hierarchy. The new term *corpus mysticum*, hallowing, as it were, simultaneously the *Corpus Christi Juridicum*,[11] that is, the gigantic legal and economic management on which the *Ecclesia militans* rested, linked the building of the visible Church organism with the former liturgical sphere; but, at the same time, it placed the Church as a body politic, or as a political and legal organism, on a level with the secular bodies politic which were then beginning to assert themselves as self-sufficient entities. In that respect the new ecclesiological designation of *corpus mysticum* fell in with the more general aspirations of that age: to hallow the secular polities as well as their administrative institutions. When in the twelfth century the Church, including the clerical bureaucracy, established itself as the "mystical body of Christ," the secular world sector proclaimed itself as the "holy Empire." This does not imply causation, either in the one way or the other. It merely indicates the activity of indeed interrelated impulses and ambitions by which the spiritual *corpus mysticum* and the secular *sacrum imperium* happened to emerge simultaneously—around the middle of the twelfth century.[12]

By that time, it is true, the expression *corpus mysticum* as a designation of the ecclesiological body corporate was found only sporadically. Nevertheless, it was then that both theologians and

---

[10] Ladner, "Aspects," 415, who noticed, and vigorously stressed, the connections between the new *corpus mysticum* interpretation and the ecclesio-political and constitutional development of the thirteenth century; see, for some related observations, G. Le Bras, "Le droit romain au service de la domination pontificale," *Revue historique de droit français et étranger*, XXVII (1949), 349.

[11] This useful notion, quoted by Ladner, "The Concepts of Ecclesia, etc.," 53,n.2., was introduced by Alfons Stickler, "Der Schwerterbegriff bei Huguccio," *Ephemerides Iuris Canonici*, III (1947), 216, who sets it against the *corpus Christi mysticum*.

[12] The term *sacrum imperium* seems to appear programmatically first under Frederick I, in 1157; MGH, *Const.*, I,224, No.161; cf. Kern, *Gottesgnadentum*, 134, n.245.

canonists began to distinguish between the "Lord's two Bodies"—one, the individual *corpus verum* on the altar, the host; and the other, the collective *corpus mysticum*, the Church.[13] Around 1200, Simon of Tournai, who began to teach at Paris in 1165, could write:

> Two are the bodies of Christ: the human material body which he assumed from the Virgin, and the spiritual collegiate body, the ecclesiastical college.[14]

The question shall be left aside here whether, or to what extent, corporational diction may have been contributive when Simon of Tournai described the supra-personal body of Christ as a *spirituale collegium*, a *collegium ecclesiasticum*. What matters here is that the distinction between Christ's *Two Bodies* was not simply identical with the ancient christological distinction between the *Two Natures* of Christ, divine and human. What Simon of Tournai produced was rather a sociological distinction between an individual body and a collective body, a distinction put forth very clearly by his contemporary Gregory of Bergamo, who explained:

> One is the body which is the sacrament, another the body of which it is the sacrament . . . One body of Christ which is he himself, and another body of which he is the head.[15]

In the writings of other authors of that period we find a similar dichotomy. Guibert of Nogent, for example, discussed the "bipartite body of the Lord" (*corpus dominicum bipertitum*) and distinguished between the *corpus principale*, the individual body as the prototype, and the *corpus mysticum* which he called also the *corpus figuratum*; he claimed that Christ had intended to lead mankind from his individual *corpus principale* to his supra-individual *corpus mysticum*.[16] The scholars around 1200—Sicard of

[13] Lubac, *Corpus mysticum*, 116ff.

[14] "Duo sunt corpora Christi. Unum materiale, quod sumpsit de virgine, et spirituale collegium, collegium ecclesiasticum," quoted by Lubac, *Corpus mysticum*, 122.

[15] Gregory of Bergamo, *De veritate corporis Christi*, c.18, ed. H. Hurter, *Sanctorum patrum opuscula selecta* (Innsbruck, 1879), vol. XXXIX, 75f: "Aliud est corpus, quod sacramentum est, aliud corpus, cuius sacramentum est. . . . : Christi corpus, quod videlicet ipse est, aliud autem corpus, cuius ipse caput est." Cf. Lubac, *Corpus mysticum*, 185.

[16] Guibert of Nogent, *De pignoribus sanctorum*, II, *PL*, CLVI,629,634C (*corpus figuratum*), and 650A: ". . . a principali corpore ad mysticum Dominus noster nos

Cremona, for example, or Lothar of Segni (later Innocent III)—in their discussions of the Sacrament of the Altar almost customarily distinguished between the individual body (*corpus personale*) and the collective body (*corpus mysticum*) of Christ. And in the first quarter of the thirteenth century, William of Auxerre reflected upon the *duplex corpus Christi* and contrasted the body natural (*corpus naturale*) with the *corpus mysticum*.[17]

Here, at last, in that new assertion of the "Lord's Two Bodies"—in the bodies natural and mystic, personal and corporate, individual and collective of Christ—we seem to have found the precise precedent of the "King's two Bodies." It will remain to be seen whether interrelations between the ecclesiological and the political spheres were effective.

It should be recalled that the definitions quoted above were still connected, more or less directly, with the Eucharist and with the liturgical sphere at large. However, the terminological change by which the consecrated host became the *corpus naturale* and the social body of the Church became the *corpus mysticum*, coincided with that moment in the history of Western thought when the doctrines of corporational and organic structure of society began to pervade anew the political theories of the West and to mold most significantly and decisively the political thinking in the high and late Middle Ages.[18] It was in that period—to mention only the classical example—that John of Salisbury wrote those famous chapters of his *Policraticus* in which he compared, under the guise of Plutarch, the commonweal with the organism of the human body, a simile popular also among the jurists.[19] Similar comparisons of the Church with a human body, stimulated by St. Paul (I Corinthians 12: 14ff), are found sporadically through-

---

voluit traducere." Cf. Lubac, *Corpus mysticum*, 46, who explains (p.93) the word *principalis* as the equivalent of the Greek πρωτότυπον.

[17] Lubac, *ibid.*, 123f, also 185 (n.155), with additional examples for the *duplex corpus Christi*.

[18] For the following, see Gierke, *Gen.R.*, III,546ff; also Nestle, "Menenius Agrippa" (above, n. 6), for the ancient model.

[19] John of Salisbury, *Policraticus*, v,2ff,540a, Webb, I,282ff, pretends to borrow his metaphors from Plutarch's *Institutio Traiani*; see H. Liebeschütz, "John of Salisbury and Pseudo-Plutarch," *Warburg Journal*, VI (1943), 33-39, who suggests that Pseudo-Plutarch was none but John of Salisbury himself; see, however, A. Momigliano, *ibid.*, XII (1949), 189ff: For contemporary jurists, see, e.g., Fitting, *Jurist. Schriften*, 148,23ff, gloss on "*princeps*" (below, n.42).

out the Middle Ages, and it was only an adaptation to the new terminology that Isaac of Stella, a contemporary of John of Salisbury, applied the metaphor of the human body with great precision to the *corpus mysticum* the head of which was Christ and whose limbs were the archbishops, bishops, and other functionaries of the Church.[20] That is to say, the anthropomorphic imagery was transferred as a matter of course to both the Church as the "mystical body of Christ" in a spiritual sense and the Church as an administrative organism styled likewise *corpus mysticum*.

The organic pattern furnished the standard interpretation of the *corpus mysticum* during the thirteenth century, especially after Thomas Aquinas had started to apply the term "mystical body" rather freely to the Church as a social phenomenon. In many respects he remained within the tradition. Like Isaac of Stella and others he compared the *corpus mysticum* with man's body natural:

> Just as the whole Church is styled one mystical body for its similarity to man's natural body and for the diversity of actions corresponding to the diversity of limbs, so is Christ called the "head" of the Church. . . .[21]

Aquinas, to be sure, was still fully aware of the fact that the mystical body really belonged to the sacramental sphere, and that *corpus mysticum* was to be set over against the *corpus verum* represented by the consecrated host. Even he, however, spoke of both bodies—the true and the mystical—without reference to the Eucharistic bread. In his teaching, the "true body" repeatedly signified not at all the Eucharistic Christ of the altar but Christ as an individual being, physical and in the flesh, whose individual

---

[20] Isaac de Stella, *Serm.* xxxiv, *PL*, cxciv,1801C; Lubac, *Corpus mysticum*, 120. Isaac compared Christ with the root of a tree ("in hoc mystico corpore *sub* uno capite Christo et *una radice* . . . membra multa sunt"), a tree having the roots above while branching down to earth; Lubac, very correctly, calls this mystic body "semblable à un arbre renversé." That strange inverted tree, however, has a long history which may be traced back to Plato's *Timaeus*, 90a, where—in agreement with ancient plant physiology according to which the root of a plant is its "head"—man's head is called also $ \dot{\rho} i \zeta a $, the root, which is suspended and which "directs the whole body" ($ \dot{o} \rho \theta o \hat{\imath} \pi \hat{a} \nu \tau \dot{o} \sigma \hat{\omega} \mu a $). The metaphor has a very complicated history; see the forthcoming study of Otto J. Maenchen-Helfen, *The Inverted Tree*, who has collected, above all, the archaeological material.

[21] Aquinas, *Summa theol.*, iii,q.viii,1; Gierke, *Gen.R.*, iii,518,n.7; Lubac, *Corpus mysticum*, 127ff,nos.60-64, who has collected the relevant places.

"body natural" became sociologically the model of the supra-individual and collective mystical body of the Church: *corpus Christi mysticum . . . ad similitudinem corporis Christi veri.*[22] In other words, the customary anthropomorphic image comparing the Church and its members with a, or any, human body was sided by a more specific comparison: the Church as a *corpus mysticum* compared with the individual body of Christ, his *corpus verum* or *naturale.* Moreover, *corpus verum* gradually ceased to indicate solely the "real presence" of Christ in the Sacrament, nor did it retain a strictly sacramental meaning and function. The individual body natural of Christ was understood as an organism acquiring social and corporational functions: it served with head and limbs, as the prototype and individuation of a super-individual collective, the Church as *corpus mysticum.*

The development did not stop here. Aquinas, quite frequently, used the term *corpus Ecclesiae mysticum,* "the mystical body of the *Church.*" Hitherto it had been the custom to talk about the Church as the "mystical body of Christ" (*corpus Christi mysticum*) which sacramentally alone makes sense. Now, however, the Church, which had been *the* mystical body of Christ, became *a* mystical body in its own right.[23] That is, the Church organism became a "mystical body" in an almost juristic sense: a mystical corporation. The change in terminology was not haphazardly introduced. It signified just another step in the direction of allowing the clerical corporational institution of the *corpus ecclesiae iuridicum* to coincide with the *corpus ecclesiae mysticum* and thereby to "secularize" the notion of "mystical body." In that development Aquinas himself holds a key position. For it is not devoid of some inner logic that the *Doctor angelicus* on several occasions saw fit to replace, straightforwardly, the liturgical idiom by a juristic idiom.

The term *corpus mysticum,* despite all the sociological and organological connotations it had acquired, nevertheless preserved its definitely sacramental ring simply because the word "body" still recalled the consecrated sacrifice. That last link to the sphere of the altar, however, was severed when Aquinas wrote: "It may be said that head and limbs together are as though one mystical

---

[22] Lubac, *Corpus mysticum,* 129, n.71.
[23] Lubac, *Corpus mysticum,* 128,n.63, stresses these changes emphatically.

person."[24] Nothing could be more striking than this *bona fide* replacement of *corpus mysticum* by *persona mystica*. Here the mysterious materiality which the term *corpus mysticum*—whatever its connotations may have been—still harbored, has been abandoned: "The *corpus Christi* has been changed into a corporation of Christ."[25] It has been exchanged for a juristic abstraction, the "mystical *person*," a notion reminiscent of, indeed synonymous with, the "fictitious person," the *persona repraesentata* or *ficta*, which the jurists had introduced into legal thought and which will be found at the bottom of so much of the political theorizing during the later Middle Ages.[26]

Undeniably the former liturgical concept of *corpus mysticum* faded away only to be transformed into a relatively colorless sociological, organological, or juristic notion. It has been observed—correctly, it seems—that this "degeneration" made itself felt very strongly in the circle of theologians around Pope Boniface VIII.[27] This is certainly true with regard to the papally-minded pamphleteers of the early fourteenth century. In their writings, the Church appeared, the later the more so, as a "Christian polity"—*regnum ecclesiasticum* or *principatus ecclesiasticus, apostolicus, papalis*[28]—so that even a Civilian as, for example, Lucas de Penna,

[24] Aquinas, *Summa theol.*, III.q.XLVIII,a.2: "Dicendum quod caput et membra sunt quasi una *persona mystica*." See Lubac, *ibid.*, 127,n.60, for a number of similar places.

[25] Rudolph Sohm, *Das altkatholische Kirchenrecht und das Dekret Gratians* (Munich and Leipzig, 1908), 582: "Aus dem Körper Christi hat sich die Kirche in eine Körperschaft Christi verwandelt."

[26] See Gierke, *Gen.R.*, III,246ff, for the general development; also G. de Lagarde, *Ockham et son temps* (Paris, 1942), 116ff, for the *persona representata*. See also the remark of Le Bras, "Le droit romain" (above, n.10), 349, concerning the political *corpus mysticum* which he styles "un concept . . . que l'on en venait à classer dans l'album des personnes juridiques."

[27] Lubac, *Corpus mysticum*, 130ff, sums up most interesting material concerning the degeneration of the *corpus mysticum* idea. The legalistic interpretation of this idea is anything but surprising in an age when the question was frequently discussed whether the souls of Christians were better taken care of by a jurist, or by a theologian, as supreme pontiff; see M. Grabmann, "Die Erörterung der Frage, ob die Kirche besser durch einen guten Juristen oder durch einen Theologen regiert werde," *Eichmann Festschrift* (Paderborn, 1941), who discusses Godfrey of Fontaines and Augustinus Triumphus; some additions (Francesco Caracciolo) have been made by Michele Maccarone, "Teologia e diritto canonico nella *Monarchia*, III,3," *Rivista di storia della Chiesa in Italia*, V (1951), 20, an article which skillfully exposes Dante's profound dislike of the domination of jurists in the Church.

[28] The expression *regnum ecclesiasticum* was very common in the thirteenth century; see, e.g., Alexander of Roes, *Memoriale*, cc.14,24,37,38, and *Notitia saeculi*, c.8, ed. H. Grundmann and H. Heimpel, *Die Schriften des Alexander von Roes*

while quoting Aquinas, could say: "Hence the Church compares with a political congregation of men, and the pope is like to a king in his realm on account of his plenitude of power."[29] To the extent, however, that the Church was interpreted as a polity like any other secular corporation, the notion *corpus mysticum* itself was charged with secular political contents. Above all, that originally liturgical notion, which formerly served to exalt the Church united in the Sacrament, began to be used in the hierarchical Church as a means to exalt the position of the emperor-like pope, "the chief Prince moving and regulating the whole Christian polity" (*primus princeps movens et regulans totam politiam Christianam*).[30] We now find all the well-known similes, metaphors, and analogies centered on the new *primum mobile*, the pope as vicar of Christ.

> Just as all the limbs in the body natural refer to the head, so do all the faithful in the mystical body *of the Church* refer to the head of the Church, the Roman Pontiff.[31]

The implications of the terminological changes become obvious: the pope could be the head of the "mystical body of the Church" as a corporation or polity or *regnum* more easily than head of the "mystical body of Christ." However, even the latter was not beyond reach. In order to prove that it made no difference whether

---

(Deutsches Mittelalter: Kritische Studientexte der MGH, IV, Weimar, 1949), pp.32, 46,66,78; see also Lubac, *Corpus mysticum*, 129, for James of Viterbo; also Scholz, *Publizistik*, 140f. See further, Scholz, *Streitschriften*, I,252, for *principatus christianus* (Anonymous); II,34 and 42, for *principatus ecclesiasticus* (Petrus de Lutra); II,456ff, 468,479 for *principatus papalis* and *apostolicus* (Ockham); also Scholz, *Wilhelm von Ockham als politischer Denker und sein 'Breviloquium de principatu tyrannico'* (Leipzig, 1944), 59ff, and passim; for *politia christiana*, see Scholz, *Streitschriften*, I,252ff, II,142f, and passim; Ladner, "Aspects," 412,n.34. See also Lubac, *Corpus mysticum*, 126,n.55, quoting the Roman Catechism, according to which the clergy's sacerdotal power (*potestas ordinis*) refers to the *corpus verum* (the eucharist), whereas the political power (*iurisdictionis potestas*) refers to the mystical body of Christ; both the body natural and the body mystical thus become the source of clerical *potestas*, but the mystical body is the source of jurisdictional power. See, for this doctrine, James of Viterbo, *De regimine christiano*, cc.4-5, ed. H.-X. Arquillière (Paris, 1926), 199f, 201.

29 Lucas de Penna, on *C*.11,58,7,n.8 (Lyon, 1582), p.563: "Unde et ecclesia comparatur congregationi hominum politicae et papa est quasi rex in regno propter plenitudinem potestatis" (a reference to Aquinas, *Summa theol.*, Suppl.III,q.XXVI,a.3); see, for the papal *plenitudo potestatis*, Ladner, "Concepts," 60ff,67,n.64.

30 See Scholz, *Streitschriften*, I,253, for the anonymous tractate *De potestate ecclesiae* (14th century).

31 Hermann of Schilditz, *Contra hereticos*, II,c.3, ed. Scholz, *Streitschriften*, II,143f.

the pope resided in Rome or in Avignon, since the pope was the Church,[32] Alvarus Pelagius exclaimed:

> The Church, which is the mystical body of Christ . . . and the community of Catholics . . . , is not defined by the walls [of Rome]. The mystical body of Christ is where the head is, that is, the pope (*Corpus Christi mysticum ibi est, ubi est caput, scilicet papa*).[33]

Ubi est fiscus, ibi est imperium was the twist given by Baldus to the ancient maxim "Rome is where the emperor is."[34] That Rome is where the pope is—"even were he secluded in a peasant's hut"— was a saying repeated over and over by the Canonists who linked also Jerusalem, Mount Sion, the *limina Apostolorum*, and the "common fatherland" to the person of the pope.[35] In a sacramental

---

[32] For the famous formula "summus pontifex qui tenet apicem ecclesie et qui potest dici ecclesia," see Aegidius Romanus, *De ecclesiastica potestate*, III,c.12, ed. Scholz (Weimar, 1929), 209; also Scholz, *Publizistik*, 60. The resistance against that identification began soon after 1300, and the decretalist Panormitanus (d. 1453) expresses his view perfectly clearly: "Caput et sponsus est ipse Episcopus [Christus]; papa autem est vicarius Episcopi, et non vere caput Ecclesiae." See Lubac, *Corpus mysticum*, 131,n.85.

[33] N. Jung, *Alvaro Pelayo* (L'Église et l'état au moyen âge, III; Paris, 1931), 150, n.2, quotes the passage, but omits the decisive second sentence. See Scholz, *Streitschriften*, II,506ff. One may be inclined to think of Ignatius, *Ad Smyrn.*, VIII,2, usually rendered "Where the bishop is, there is the Church" (e.g., H. Lietzmann, *Geschichte der alten Kirche* [Berlin, 1936], II,49). However, the text says "Where Christ is, there is the Catholic Church," and says about the bishop that "where he shall appear, there let the multitude be"—that is, the people shall gather where the bishop is.

[34] Baldus, on C.10,1,n.13, fol.232 (above, Ch.IV, n.276). For the origin of the maxim, see Herodian, I,6,5 (ἐκεῖ τε ἡ Ῥώμη ποτ' ἂν ὁ βασιλεὺς ᾖ), with interesting parallels quoted in the old edition of Herodian by T. G. Irmisch (1789), 1,209. See also *Paneg.lat.*, XI,12 (Mamertinus, *Genethl. Maxim.*), ed. W. Baehrens (1911), 285,2, and *Cambridge Ancient History*, XII,374,386. Further, Claudian, *In Rufinum*, II, 246f, ed. Birt, *MGH, Auct.ant.*, x,43: "quocumque loco Stilicho tentoria figat, haec patria est," which makes the military camp the soldier's fatherland; see Reinhard Höhn, "Der Soldat und das Vaterland während und nach dem Siebenjährigen Krieg," *Festschrift Ernst Heymann* (Weimar, 1940), 255, quoting from an anonymous tractate by S.B.N., *Die wahren Pflichten des Soldaten und insonderheit eines Edelmanns* (trans. from the French, 1753), p.12: "Der Ort wo der Feldherr sein Lager hat, muss Euer Vaterland seyn." See also Modoinus, *Ecloga*, 40f, *MGH, Poetae*, 1,386, referring to Charlemagne and Aachen: "Quo caput orbis erit, Roma vocitare licebit/ Forte locum . . ." Also Frederick II availed himself of that maxim; see Huillard-Bréholles, II,630 (June, 1226): ". . . ibi sit Alemanie curia, ubi persona nostra et principes imperii nostri consistunt." See *Erg.Bd.*, 41.

[35] See, e.g., Oldradus de Ponte, *Consilia*, LXII,n.3, fol.22ᵛ: ". . . ista intelligantur de ecclesia Romana universali, quae est ubicunque est papa." Hostiensis, *Summa aurea*, on X 1,8,n.3, col.155: ". . . quia non ubi Roma est, ibi Papa, sed econverso; locus enim non sanctificat hominem, sed homo locum." See, for the maxim *non locus sanctificat hominem*, etc., Hermann Kantorowicz, *Glossators*, 22. Johannes Andreae, *Novella Commentaria*, on c.4 X 2,24 (Venice, 1612), fol.185ᵛ: "limina enim

sense, it was rather usual to say that "where Christ is there is also Jordan," meaning, of course, that every baptismal font was "Jordan" with regard to Christ and with Christ being present.[36] The new twist produced by Alvarus Pelagius, however, carried the idea considerably further: not where the consecrated host is, but where the pope is, there the *corpus mysticum* was supposed to be present. It was a long way from the liturgy and the sacramental *corpus mysticum* to the mystical polity headed by the pope.

The curious definition of Alvarus Pelagius was matched by yet another terminological change which at least should be mentioned. When William of Ockham denied the pope the power to alienate Church property he merely repeated what scores of jurists had pointed out before him, though one of his arguments is of interest here. Ockham said the pope could not alienate these possessions because they did not belong to him personally, but belonged to "God and his mystical body which is the Church" (*Dei et corporis eius mystici quod est ecclesia*).[37] The Church as the mystical body of God, not of Christ, is a concept demonstrating the swiftness with which the *corpus mysticum* idea had been moving away from the original sacrificial sphere, from altar and Eucharist, so

apostolorum esse intelliguntur, ubi est papa." Cf. Jung, *Alvaro Pelayo*, 148,n.1: "Et quod ubicumque est papa, ibi est Ecclesia romana . . ." Baldus, on *D.*1,18,1,n.26, fol.44: ". . . puta ubi est palatium regis vel episcopi, sicut in regno regia civitas dicitur caput regni . . . Et in mensa, ubicumque est dominus, ibi caput; sicut ubi Papa, ibi Roma, etiam si esset in quodam tugurio rusticano reclusus." Baldus, on *D.*3,2,2,3,n.2, fol.164, brings a new note (important for the formula *rex et patria*; see below): "nota quod Roma et Imperator aequiparantur. Unde verum quod notat Inn[ocentius IV] ubi est Imperator, ibi est Roma, scilicet intellectualiter, quia idem iuris est de Imperatore et de urbe . . ." Baldus then can draw the conclusion (on *D.*5,1,2,3,n.1, fol.258ᵛ): ". . . Roma sit communis patria, et intelligo ubicunque est Papa vel Imperator." See also Baldus, on c.4 X 2,24,n.11, fol.249, quoting Innocent IV: "Dicit Innocentius quod ubi est Papa, ibi est Roma, Hierusalem et mons Sion, ibi et est communis patria." For Rome as the *communis patria*, see above, Ch.III, n.89, also below, p. 247; and for the connection of Rome with Jerusalem, see Tierney, *Cath. Hist. Rev.*, XXXVI, 428,n.57, quoting Hostiensis ("Urbs ista [Roma] altera Ierusalem intelligatur") and referring to the Norman Anonymous. The theory of Rome-Jerusalem, of course, is ancient Christian; it was important in Christian art (see, e.g., for the Presentation in Santa Maria Maggiore, A. Grabar, *L'empereur dans l'art byzantin* [Paris, 1936], 216ff), and it played later on a certain role also in legal literature; see, e.g., Oldradus de Ponte, *Consilia*, LXXXV,n.1, fol.32. It would be certainly rewarding to investigate systematically the transfer of the Jerusalem-Idea to Rome. See, for a few remarks, Williams, *Norman Anonymous*, 137ff.

[36] Ambrose, *Sermones*, XXXVIII,c.2, *PL*, XVII,702B: "Ubique enim nunc Christus, ibi quoque Jordanis est."

[37] Scholz, *Streitschriften*, II,428, where the expression occurs twice.

that a later jurist could easily define the Church as a corporation "representing a person which cannot be said ever to have lived, because that person is neither corporeal nor mortal, since it is God."[38] Admittedly, Ockham could have defended his diction, since the first and second persons of the Trinity no longer were distinguished as clearly in his time as they were in the earlier Middle Ages.[39] Nevertheless, *corpus mysticum Dei* has a false ring; it is an expression indicative of that new direction of which William of Ockham was, in so many respects, the exponent.

To summarize, the notion of *corpus mysticum*, designating originally the Sacrament of the Altar, served after the twelfth century to describe the body politic, or *corpus iuridicum*, of the Church, which does not exclude the lingering on of some of the earlier connotations. Moreover, the classical christological distinction of the Two Natures in Christ, still powerfully alive in the political theology of the Norman Anonymous around A.D. 1100, has all but completely disappeared from the orbit of political discussions and theories. It has been replaced by the corporational, non-christological concept of the Two Bodies of Christ: one, a body natural, individual, and personal (*corpus naturale, verum, personale*); the other, a super-individual body politic and collective, the *corpus mysticum*, interpreted also as a *persona mystica*. Whereas the *corpus verum*, through the agency of the dogma of transubstantiation and the institution of the feast of *Corpus Christi*, developed a life and a mysticism of its own, the *corpus mysticum* proper came to be less and less mystical as time passed on, and came to mean simply the Church as a body politic or, by transference, any body politic of the secular world.

---

[38] Gierke, *Gen.R.*, III,277,n.91, quoting Paulus de Castro (d.1439): "[ecclesia] universitas repraesentans personam quae nunquam potest dici vixisse, quia non est corporalis nec mortalis, ut est Deus." The jurist could not have made this remark had he thought of the Church as the mystical body of Christ of whom it could not be said that he never lived.

[39] In the bull *Unam sanctam*, e.g., Pope Boniface VIII, on the basis of I Cor. 11: 3, referred to the mystical body of the Church "cuius caput est Christus, Christi vero Deus." See also Aquinas, *Summa theol.*, III, q.VIII, art.1, ad 2. For the extreme reluctance of earlier centuries to style God the Father *caput ecclesiae*, see, e.g., Peter of Poitiers, *Sententiae*, IV,c.20, *PL*, CCXI,1215C, and, dependent on him, *Quaestiones Varsavienses trinitariae et christologicae*, ed. F. Stegmüller, in *Miscellanea Giovanni Mercati* (Studi e Testi, 122, Rome, 1946), II,303f, §§4 and 6.

2. *Corpus Reipublicae mysticum*

While the lofty idea of the Church as *corpus mysticum cuius caput Christus* was inflated with secular contents, corporational as well as legal, the secular state itself—starting, as it were, from the opposite end—strove for its own exaltation and quasi-religious glorification. The noble concept of the *corpus mysticum*, after having lost much of its transcendental meaning and having been politicized and, in many respects, secularized by the Church itself, easily fell prey to the world of thought of statesmen, jurists, and scholars who were developing new ideologies for the nascent territorial and secular states. Barbarossa, we recall, hallowed his empire by the glorifying title *sacrum imperium*—a perfectly legitimate para-ecclesiastical term which he borrowed from the vocabulary of Roman Law, and not from that of the Church. The efforts, however, to provide the state institutions with some religious aureole, as well as the adaptability and general usefulness of ecclesiastical thought and language, led the theorists of the secular state very soon to a more than superficial appropriation of the vocabularies not only of Roman Law, but also of Canon Law and Theology at large. The new territorial and quasi-national state, self-sufficient according to its claims and independent of the Church and the Papacy, quarried the wealth of ecclesiastical notions, which were so convenient to handle, and finally proceeded to assert itself by placing its own temporariness on a level with the sempiternity of the militant Church. In that process the idea of the *corpus mysticum*, as well as other corporational doctrines developed by the Church were to be of major importance.[40]

An early example of setting the state as a "body" over against the Church as a "body" emerged from the pamphlet literature of the Struggle of Investiture, when an imperial writer advocated *unum corpus reipublicae* to supplement *unum corpus ecclesiae*.[41] The antithesis reflects hardly more than the customary organological concept of both the state and the Church; nor does John of Salisbury's famous statement *res publica corpus quoddam* all by

[40] See Pollock and Maitland, *History*, 1,495, for some remarks on the influence which the *corpus mysticum* idea exercised on the growth of the law of corporations. Cf. Tierney, *Conciliar Theory*, 134ff.

[41] *De unitate ecclesiae*, in *MGH,LdL*, II,228,16, quoted by Ladner, "Aspects," 413,n.36. See also Hugh of Fleury, *De regia potestate*, I,3, *ibid.*, II,468,28ff: "rex in regni sui corpore."

itself imply a deviation from customary thought.[42] It was, however, a very different matter and a different aspect of the state as an organism when, in the·middle of the thirteenth century, Vincent of Beauvais, in order to designate the body politic of the state, used the term *corpus reipublicae mysticum*, "mystical body of the commonweal."[43] This was a clear case of borrowing from the wealth of ecclesiastical notions and of transferring to the secular commonweal some of the super-natural and transcendental values normally owned by the Church. An intention to raise the state beyond its purely physical existence, and to transcendentalize it, may be gathered perhaps from the *Mirror of Princes* of Vincent's contemporary, the Franciscan Gilbert of Tournai.[44] He visualized a perfect kingdom directed by the king as the vicar of Christ and guided by the ministers of the Church, and he, too, used in that connection the term *corpus mysticum*. But Gilbert of Tournai wanted his ideal kingdom to be a distinct entity *within* the traditional mystical body signifying the oneness of Christian society, whereas for Vincent of Beauvais the secular entity itself was a "mystical body."[45]

[42] *Policraticus*, v,c.2, ed. Webb, I,282ff. The organic doctrines certainly did not begin with John of Salisbury; they were fully developed, without then being original, in the works of contemporary jurists. See, e.g., Fitting, *Jur.Schr.*, 148,20 (above, n.19), the gloss on *princeps*: "Quasi primum caput, iudices enim capita sunt aliorum hominum, qui ab eis reguntur, ut membra a suis capitibus; sed princeps est caput aliorum iudicum et ab eo reguntur." There follows an explicit comparison of the dignities (*illustres, spectabiles*, etc.) with eyes, hands, chest, feet, etc., and also a comparison of the ecclesiastical dignities with the limbs of the human body. The organological metaphor, of course, is found also in Roman Law; see, e.g., *C.*9,8,5 (*Cod.Theod.*, 9,14,3): "virorum illustrium qui consiliis et consistorio nostro intersunt, senatorum etiam, nam ipsi pars corporis nostri sunt." This passage was quoted, time and time again (see below, Ch. VII,nos.341f), and was applied also to the papacy; see, e.g., Johannes Andreae, *Novella*, on c.4 X 2,24 (Venice, 1612), fol.184: "cum ipsi [cardinales] cum papa constituant ecclesiam Romanam, et sint pars corporis papae, ar.C. ad l.Jul.ma.l.quisquis (*C.*9,8,5)." See, in general, Nestle, "Menenius Agrippa" (above, n.6).

[43] *Speculum doctrinale*, VII,c.8, quoted by Gierke, *Gen.R.*, III,548,n.75; cf. Maitland, *Political Theories*, 131. I was unable to find that place, but the expression, no doubt, became popular in Vincent's time and surroundings; see, e.g., Berges, *Fürstenspiegel*, 195, n.1, and 306, §15. [Gierke erred: read *Spec.Doctr.* VII,c.15.]

[44] Gilbert of Tournai, *Eruditio regum et principum*, II,c.2, ed. A. de Poorter (Philosophes Belges, IX, Louvain, 1914), 45; Berges, *Fürstenspiegel*, 156.

[45] For reasons of convenience, the concept of "the state *within* the Church" has been called the "Carolingian tradition" by Ladner, "Plenitudo potestatis," 50f, who very skilfully points out (p.73) that this tradition began to evaporate in the 13th century and that from the thought of Aquinas, for whom the *regna* were natural in origin and character, all traces of the Carolingian tradition seem to be absent.

The notion of *corpus mysticum* signified, in the first place, the totality of Christian society in its organological aspects: a body composed of head and members. This interpretation remained valid throughout the later Middle Ages until early modern times, even after the notion had been applied, by transference, to smaller groups of society. In addition, however, *corpus mysticum* acquired certain legal connotations; it acquired a corporational character signifying a "fictitious" or "juristic" person. We may recall that already Aquinas had used, as an alternative of *corpus mysticum*, the term *persona mystica*, which hardly differed from the *persona ficta* of the jurists. In fact, it was chiefly among the lawyers, though not lawyers alone, that the organological interpretation was sided by or amalgamated with corporational contents, and that accordingly the notion of *corpus mysticum* was used synonymously with *corpus fictum, corpus imaginatum, corpus repraesentatum*, and the like—that is, as a description of the juristic person or corporation. The jurists, thereby, arrived, like the theologians, at a distinction between *corpus verum*—the tangible body of an individual person—and *corpus fictum*, the corporate collective which was intangible and existed only as a fiction of jurisprudence.[46] Hence, by analogy with theological usage as well as in contrast with natural persons, the jurists defined their fictitious persons not seldom as "mystical bodies." This term was applicable to every size and rank of *universitas* within the hierarchy of corporate communities of which mediaeval social philosophy, in a blending of Augustinian and Aristotelian definitions, distinguished five: household, neighborhood, city, kingdom, and universe.[47] Accordingly, a late mediaeval jurist, Antonius de Rosellis (b. 1386), enumerated, if with

[46] The transition from *corpus mysticum* to *universitas* in the legal sense is well illustrated by Oldradus de Ponte, *Consilia*, 204,n.1 (Lyon, 1550), 78ᵛ. The question was raised whether the Abbot of Cluny was the only head of the whole Order of the Cluniacs. Oldradus answers by pointing at the analogy with the mystical body: "Et quod unum tantum sit caput, prout probatur primo ex corporis mystici ad corporis veri similitudinem. Sicut enim in corpore naturali unum est caput, alias diceretur declinare ad monstrum ., . . ., sic et in corpore mystico. . . . Constat autem quod universitas et religio unum corpus repraesentat" (follows allegation of the *lex mortuo*; see below, Ch.vi,n.73). See Gierke, *Gen.R.*, iii,428, for the various expressions describing the juristic person as distinguished from the natural person. See also above, n.16, for the expression *corpus figuratum* as an equivalent of *corpus mysticum*. For *universitas* and *corpus mysticum*, see Tierney, *Conciliar Theories*, 134ff.

[47] For the problem, see Fritz Kern, *Humana Civilitas* (Leipzig, 1913), 11,n.1; Dante, *Monarchia*, 1,c.3.

slight alterations, five *corpora mystica* of human society—the *corpus mysticum* of each: village, city, province, kingdom, and world.[48] This was certainly a levelling down and a banalization of the originally very complex liturgical term. However, the notion of *corpus mysticum* was easily transferred to other secular units as well. Baldus, for example, defined *populus*, the people, as a mystical body. He held that a *populus* was not simply the sum of individuals of a community, but "men assembled into one mystical body" (*hominum collectio in unum corpus mysticum*), men forming *quoddam corpus intellectuale*, a body or corporation to be grasped only intellectually, since it was not a real or material body.[49] In a technical sense, Baldus' "mystical body of the people" appears plainly as an equivalent of "polity" or *universitas* or, in the language of Aquinas and Aristotle, of any *multitudo ordinata*.[50] Nevertheless, the designation *corpus mysticum* brought to the secular polity, as it were, a whiff of incense from another world.

There was yet another notion which became popular during the thirteenth century, the notion of "body politic," which is inseparable from both the age of early corporational doctrines and of the revival of Aristotle. Before long, the term "mystical body" became applicable to any *corpus morale et politicum* in the Aristotelian sense. It cannot be ventured here to assess Aristotle's influence on late-mediaeval political language, or even to ask what it meant that henceforth, owing to Aristotle, the state not only was interpreted as a "body politic," but also was qualified as a "body moral" or "ethical." The state or, for that matter, any other political aggregate, was understood as the result of natural reason. It was an institution which had its moral ends in itself and had its own

---

[48] Antonius de Rosellis, *Monarchia sive Tractatus de potestate imperatoris et papae*, ii,c.6, ed. Goldast, *Monarchia* (Frankfurt, 1668), i,312: "Nam sicut est in uno corpore naturali, ita est in pluribus mysticis corporibus [that the monarchy is the best form of government] . . . Et idem est in aliis mysticis corporibus universitatum, quia melius se habent cum per unum reguntur. Sunt enim secundum Philosophum quinque communitates . . . [cf. Gierke, *Gen.R.*, iii,545, n.64]." See, for the author, Karla Eckermann, *Studien zur Geschichte des monarchischen Gedankens im 15. Jahrhundert* (Abh. zur mittleren und neueren Geschichte, lxxiii [Berlin-Grunewald, 1933]).

[49] For Baldus, see Gierke, *Gen.R.*, iii,428,n.37 and 431f; also 433,n.61; see below, Ch.viii,n.70.

[50] Aquinas, *Summa theol.*, iii,q.viii,a.1,ad 2: "corpus . . . aliqua multitudo ordinata."

ethical code. Jurists and political writers gained a new possibility to compare the state as a *corpus morale et politicum* with, or to set it over against, the *corpus mysticum et spirituale* of the Church.[51]

After Aquinas had ecclesiasticized the Philosopher, there remained no difficulty in combining Aristotelian concepts with ecclesiastical thought and terminology. Godfrey of Fontaines, a Belgian philosopher of the late thirteenth century, for example, succeeded in integrating very neatly the *corpus mysticum* into the Aristotelian scheme.[52] To him the "mystical body" appeared not as a supra-natural foundation, but as a gift of nature. His major premise was that "everyone is [by nature] part of a social community, and thereby also a member of some mystical body." That is, man is "by nature" a social animal; as an *animal sociale*, however, man is "by nature"—not "by grace"—also part of some mystical body, some social collective or aggregate, which Dante, a little while later, would easily define as "mankind" or *humana civilitas*, whereas others might define it, as need be, in the sense of *populus, civitas, regnum*, or *patria*, or as any other social community and corporation, the ends of which were "moral" *per se*. A new halo descended from the works of Aristotle upon the corporate organism of human society, a halo of morals and ethics different from that of the ecclesiological *corpus mysticum*, yet by no means incompatible with it; in fact, *corpus mysticum* and *corpus morale et*

[51] Aristotle, *Polit.*, III,9ff (1280a-1282b), and Aquinas, *In libros Politicorum Aristotelis*, III, lect.VII and VIII, ed. Raymundus M. Spiazzi (Turin and Rome, 1951), 141ff. For the moral character of the state according to Aristotle, see also Max Hamburger, *Morals and Law: The Growth of Aristotle's Legal Theory* (New Haven, 1951), esp. 177ff. The essence of the state as a *corpus morale* consists, of course, in the fact that its ends aim at some good, actually "the greatest good and the good which is most pursued; for the good in the sphere of politics is justice." Aquinas, in his *Prooemium* to the Aristotelian *Politics* (§6, ed. Spiazzi, p.2). stressed that the *scientia politica* was according to customary classification a *scientia moralis*. Aristotle, though of course not a "corporationalist" in the later sense, has nevertheless supported corporational interpretations by his doctrine holding that the city—and, for that matter, every whole—was prior to its parts, and that neither foot nor hand would exist were there not a whole body, a doctrine which was grist to the mills of the organologists and which Aquinas emphasized also very strongly (*In Polit. Arist.*, I,1, §38f, ed. Spiazzi, 11f).

[52] Godfrey of Fontaines, *Quaestiones ordinariae*, 1,2,5, ed. Odon Lottin (Philosophes Belges, XIV, Louvain, 1937), 89; cf. G. de Lagarde, "La philosophie sociale d'Henri de Gand et de Godefroid de Fontaines," *L'Organisation corporative du moyen âge à la fin de l'ancien régime*, VII (Receuil de travaux d'histoire et de philologie, 3me série, XVIII; Louvain, 1943), 64.

politicum became almost interchangeable notions, and they were lined up with the same ease with which Dante assembled the terrestrial paradise and the celestial paradise on one denominator as the two goals of mankind.

This assertion will be borne out by the jurists who, especially when discussing the inalienability of fiscal property, fell to the metaphor of the ruler's marriage to his realm. This metaphor, though not unknown in Antiquity,[53] will not easily be found in the earlier Middle Ages. It is true, of course, that ever since Carolingian times, the mediaeval Prince received at his coronation, together with other symbols and insignia, a ring. The ecclesiastical writers, however, were careful to point out that this ring was conferred only as a *signaculum fidei* and to distinguish it from the episcopal ring by which the bishop, at his ordination, became the *sponsus*, the groom and husband of his church, to which he was married, a simile on which the canonists sometimes expanded at great length.[54] The secular marriage metaphor, however, became rather popular in the later Middle Ages when, under the impact of juristic analogies and corporational doctrines, the image of the Prince's marriage to his *corpus mysticum*—that is, to the *corpus mysticum* of his state—appeared to be constitutionally meaningful.

It would be difficult to tell when and where or by whom the canonistic metaphor was first transferred to secular legal-political thought.[55] It may have been fairly common around 1300 when,

[53] See below, n.59.

[54] For a brief survey of the history of the ring in connection with the imperial coronations, see Eichmann, *Kaiserkrönung*, II,94ff (also Index, s.v. "Ring"). The significance of the episcopal ring was widely discussed during the Struggle of Investiture; see the numerous tractates and poems *De anulo et baculo*, in *MGH,LdL*, II,508ff; III,720ff,723ff,726ff. The ritual of the "Bestowal of the Ring" at episcopal consecrations differed sometimes very little from the corresponding ritual at coronations: the episcopal ring likewise was called *fidei signaculum*, and the marriage formula (*quatenus sponsam . . . custodias*) was not always included at the ordinations; see, e.g., Andrieu, *Pontifical romain*, 1,48 and 149. See below, nos.55 and 61, for the canonistic marriage metaphor.

[55] See Mochi Onory, *Fonti canonistiche*, 151,n.1, for excerpts from Huguccio's gloss on c.10,D.63, v. 'subscripta relatio,' the complete text of which (from Clm.10247,fol.69rb-va), together with references to later canonists, I owe to the kindness of Dr. Robert L. Benson. Without referring specifically to D.50,17,30 ("Nuptias non concubitus, sed consensus facit") he compares a bishop's election to a matrimonial consent: "Item electio dicitur vinculum, quod ex mutuo consensu, scilicet eligentium et electi, contrahitur inter eos matrimonium spirituale; ut ille iam dicatur sponsus istius ecclesie vel istorum clericorum et hec ecclesia sponsa ipsius." The same idea is repeated in the *Glos.ord.* (Johannes Teutonicus), on c.10,D.63, v.

for example, Cynus of Pistoia produced it in a more or less casual fashion in his commentary on Justinian's *Code*. While discussing the extent of power accorded to an emperor elect, he considered the Prince's election on the part of the *respublica* and his acceptance of the election as a kind of contract or mutual consent similar to the one upon which matrimony was based, and then briefly expanded on that comparison which obviously impressed him because he thought it was striking.

> And the comparison between the corporeal matrimony and the intellectual one is good: for just as the husband is called the defender of his wife . . . so is the emperor the defender of that *respublica*.[56]

Cynus, whose arguments were repeated almost verbatim by Albericus de Rosate,[57] wrote his commentaries on the *Code* between 1312 and 1314. In those years others as well availed themselves of that comparison. In 1312, for example, one of the Italian jurists

---

'relatio,' and in the *Apparatus 'Ius naturale'* (Kuttner, *Repertorium*, 67ff), on the same canon, v. '*subscripta*' (Paris, Bibl.nat.MS.lat.15393, fol.49), where Huguccio is quoted: "et secundum Ug(uccionem) ex electione et electi consensu legitimo." See also a decretal of Innocent III (c.2 X 1,7; Friedberg, II,97): ". . . non debeat in dubium revocari, quin post electionem et confirmationem canonicam inter personas eligentium et electi coniugium sit spirituale contractum." Finally Bernard of Pavia, *Summa decretalium*, 1,4,5, ed. E. A. T. Laspeyres, *Bernardi Papiensis Faventini episcopi Summa Decretalium* (Regensburg, 1860), p.8: ". . . dum approbat [electus] de se factam electionem, ecclesiae sponsus efficitur propter mutuum consensum." Both Huguccio and the *Apparatus 'Ius naturale'* parallel the bishop's election with that of the emperor and see, for Huguccio, Mochi Onory, *loc.cit.*; the *Apparatus* says quite succinctly: "et sicut principes imperatorem dicuntur facere, et ita clerici prelatum electione," whereby the preceding clause mentions the "matrimonium inter episcopum et ecclesiam contractum." Hence it may be said that sooner or later the matrimonial idea was almost bound to be transferred to the Prince and the *respublica*. See next note.

56 Cynus, on *C.*7,37,3,n.5 (Frankfurt, 1578), fol.446rb: "quia ex electione Imperatoris et acceptione electionis Reipublicae iam praepositus negari non potest et eum ius consecutum esse, sicut consensu mutuo fit matrimonium . . . Et bona est comparatio illius corporalis matrimonii ad istud intellectuale: quia sicut maritus defensor uxoris dicitur . . . , ita et Imperator Reipublicae . . ." The allegations of Cynus refer exclusively to Civil Law; it is obvious nevertheless that his arguments follow those of the canonists, though it is noteworthy that the *matrimonium spirituale* of the canonists has been transformed into a *matrimonium intellectuale*. I was unable to ascertain whether perhaps one of Cynus' teachers, Jacobus de Ravanis (Révigny) or Petrus de Bellapertica (Belleperche), had used the marriage metaphor before.

57 Albericus de Rosate, on *C.*7,37,3,n.12 (*Venice*, 1585), fol.107va: "quia sicut matrimonium consensu perficitur . . . [*D.*50,17,30], sic ex mutuo consensu eligentium et electi ius plenum consequitur Imperator . . . Nota ergo quod ex quo res administrat, et est bona argumentatio matrimonii carnalis ad istud intellectuale, quia sicut maritus est defensor uxoris . . . [*Inst.* 4,4,2], ita Imperator Reipublicae . . ."

in the surroundings of Emperor Henry VII found it suitable to compare the emperor's coronation to a marriage rite.[58] None, however, was so explicit about this comparison or carried it to such an extreme as Lucas de Penna, the Neapolitan jurist, who wrote his commentary on the *Tres Libri*, the last three books of the *Code*, around the middle of the fourteenth century.

Lucas de Penna commented on a law concerning "Occupation of Desert Land" (*C*.11,58,7), excepting, however, lands belonging to the fisc and the princely patrimony. He started his arguments with a quotation from Lucan's *Pharsalia*, where Cato was styled "father to the City [of Rome] and the City's husband."[59] From this opening, the jurist made his way to the apostolic lesson of the Matrimonial Mass, which gave him a chance to discuss a fundamental law of the state on the basis of Ephesians 5. To Lucas de Penna, the Prince was plainly the *maritus reipublicae* whose wedlock with the state appeared as a *matrimonium morale et politicum*. Based on this premise, Lucas then could argue by analogy.

> There is contracted a moral and political marriage between the Prince and the *respublica*. Also, just as there is contracted a spiritual and divine marriage between a church and its prelate, so is there contracted a temporal and terrestrial marriage between the Prince and the state. And just as the church is in the prelate, and the prelate in the church . . . , so is the Prince in the state, and the state in the Prince.[60]

[58] See the Memorandum of John Branchazolus, *legum doctor* of Pavia, ed. Edmund E. Stengel, *Nova Alemanniae* (Berlin, 1921), I,No.90,ii,§6, p.50. For another vague comparison of that kind, see Ullmann, *Lucas de Penna*, 176,n.1, who, however, does not seem to have evaluated the interesting passages referred to in the notes following below.

[59] Lucas de Penna, on *C*.11,58,7,n.8, p.563: "Item princeps si verum dicere vel agnoscere volumus . . . , est maritus reipublicae iuxta illud Lucani . . ." There follows the quotation from Lucan, *Pharsalia*, II,388: *urbi pater urbique maritus*. For the history of the Roman *pater* title, see the admirable essay of Alföldi, "Die Geburt der kaiserlichen Bildsymbolik," *Museum Helveticum*, IX (1952), 204-243; X (1953), 103-124; XI (1954), 133-169. The title *urbi maritus* is not too rare either; see, e.g., Servius, XI,472, who, like Priscian, quotes Lucan. See, however, Aristophanes, *Aves*, 1706ff, where βασίλεια is called the bride of Alcibiades. Lucas de Penna actually may have elaborated on Cynus whose writings he used abundantly. See, for the following paragraphs, also my paper on "Mysteries of State," *Harvard Theological Review*, XLVIII (1955), 76ff.

[60] Lucas de Penna, *loc.cit.*: "Inter principem et rempublicam matrimonium morale contrahitur et politicum. Item, sicut inter ecclesiam et praelatum matrimonium spirituale contrahitur et divinum . . . , ita inter principem et rempublicam matrimonium temporale contrahitur et terrenum; et sicut ecclesia est in praelato et praelatus in ecclesia . . . , ita princeps in republica et respublica in principe." There follows the passage quoted above, n.29. The simile of the Prince's marriage

We notice that the jurist availed himself of the very old metaphor of the mystical marriage contracted between the bishop and his see in order to interpret the new relations between Prince and state.[61] Actually, Lucas de Penna quoted verbatim a passage from Gratian's *Decretum*: "The Bishop is in the Church, and the Church in the Bishop."[62] What the history of this formula implied remains to be seen;[63] but it is not too difficult to recognize whence the Tudor lawyers derived their maxims, when they explained that "the king in his body politic is incorporated with his subjects, and they with him."[64]

To illustrate his argument, Lucas de Penna quoted Seneca addressing Nero: "You are the soul of the *respublica*, and the *respublica* is your body."[65] He achieved the same effects, however, by continuing his political exegesis of Ephesians 5, and applying

---

to the *respublica* has been carried by Lucas de Penna to far greater detail than it seemed necessary to indicate here. In that respect, however, he had a predecessor in Huguccio (above, n.55) who not only compared the election to the matrimonial *consensus*, but considered the consent to the election on the part of the ecclesiastical superior synonymous with the consummation of the marriage, or else the ordination with the *concubitus* ("Sicut enim in matrimonio carnali precedit matrimonium in desponsatione per verba de presenti, et postea sequitur carnalis commixtio, sic et hic in mutuo consensu precedit matrimonium spirituale et postea sequitur quasi carnalis commixtio, cum iam ecclesiam disponit et ordinat"). And even for the case that the bishop should be debarred temporarily from his office or otherwise suspended Huguccio found a matrimonial simile: "Idem est in marito et uxore tempore menstrui vel partus vel dierum quadragesimalium . . ."

[61] The metaphor, of course, goes back to Eph. 5: 25 ("sicut et Christus dilexit ecclesiam"), which is basic also for the nuptial mass. The early Christian marriage rings, therefore, displayed on the bezel the marriage of Christ to the Church; see O. M. Dalton, *Catalogue of Early Christian Antiquities and Objects from the Christian East . . . of the British Museum* (London, 1901), 130 and 131; there are many more specimens, a particularly beautiful one in the Dumbarton Oaks Research Library and Collection, at Washington, D.C. The bishop's marriage to his see is mentioned in the rite of the episcopal ordination; see above, n.54. See further the decretal of Innocent III, c.2 X 1,7, ed. Friedberg, II,97. Pope Clement II, who refused to divorce himself from his bishopric Bamberg, alluded to this marriage in most telling words (Clement II, *Ep.*, VIII, *PL*, CXLII,588B); contrariwise, the abdication of Pope Celestine V was interpreted, especially by the adversaries of his successor Pope Boniface VIII, as an uncanonical "divorce" from the universal Church to which the pope was married; see, e.g., P. Dupuy, *Histoire du différend d'entre Pape Boniface VIII et Philippe le Bel* (Paris, 1655), 453ff, and passim; Burdach, *Rienzo*, 52f.

[62] See c.7,C.VII,qu.1, ed. Friedberg, I,568f.

[63] See below, Ch.VII, nos.399-409.

[64] See above, Ch.I,n.13; Bacon, *Post-nati*, 667.

[65] Seneca, *De clementia*, I,5,1: ". . . tu animus rei publicae tuae es, illa corpus tuum." Lucas de Penna, *loc.cit.*, n.8, p.564. The passage is quoted, in the same connection, also by Andreas of Isernia, *Prooemium in Lib.aug.*, ed. Cervone, p.xxvi.

to the Prince the versicle: "The man is the head of the wife, and the wife the body of the man." And logically, or analogically, he concluded: "After the same fashion, the Prince is the head of the realm, and the realm the body of the Prince."[66] The corporational tenet, however, was formulated even more succinctly, as he continued:

> And just as men are joined together spiritually in the spiritual body, the head of which is Christ . . . , so are men joined together morally and politically in the *respublica*, which is a body the head of which is the Prince."[67]

We may record again the Aristotelian undertone. Above all, however, we envisage here that bold equation by which "the Prince, who is the head of the mystical body of the state" (as Enea Silvio later phrased it[68]), was compared with Christ, the head of the mystical body of the Church. Lucas de Penna, by his *quid pro quo* method, thus arrived at an equiparation not only of Prince and bishop as the grooms of realm and diocese, but also of Prince and Christ. In fact, the jurist made the parallel with Christ poignantly clear, when he added:

> Just as Christ joined to himself an alien-born as his spouse, the Church of Gentiles . . . , so has the Prince joined to himself as his *sponsa* the state, which is not his. . . .[69]

Thus, the venerable image of *sponsus* and *sponsa*, Christ and his Church, was transferred from the spiritual to the secular and adapted to the jurist's need for defining the relations between

[66] Lucas de Penna, *loc.cit.*: ". . . item, sicut vir est caput uxoris, uxor vero corpus viri [Eph. 5: 23] . . . , ita princeps caput reipublicae, et res publica eius corpus." Lucas de Penna adds: *secundum Plutarchum*, meaning Pseudo-Plutarch, quoted by John of Salisbury, *Policraticus*, v,1ff (above, Ch.iv,n.20), whom the mediaeval jurists alleged very frequently; see Ullmann, "The Influence of John of Salisbury on Medieval Italian Jurists," *EHR*, lix (1944), 387,n.4.

[67] Lucas de Penna, *loc.cit.*: "Item, sicut membra coniunguntur in humano corpore carnaliter, et homines spirituali corpori spiritualiter coniunguntur, cui corpori Christus est caput . . . , sic moraliter et politice homines coniunguntur reipublicae quae corpus est: cuius caput est princeps . . ."

[68] Enea Silvio Piccolomini, *De ortu et auctoritate imperii Romani*, ed. Gerhard Kallen, *Aeneas Silvius Piccolomini als Publizist* (Stuttgart, 1939), 82, lines 418ff; see below, n.212.

[69] Lucas de Penna, *loc.cit.*: "Amplius sicut Christus alienigenam, id est, gentilem ecclesiam sibi copulavit uxorem . . . , sic et princeps rempublicam quae, quantum ad dominium, sua non est, cum ad principatum assumitur, sponsam sibi coniungit . . ." Lucas de Penna here refers to c.un.,C.xxxv,qu.i, ed. Friedberg, i,1263 (Gratian's commentary on Augustine, *Civ.Dei*, xv,c.16).

Prince and state—a state which, as a mystical or political body, was an entity in its own right, independent of the king and endowed with property which was not that of the king. What Lucas de Penna aimed at when enlarging on the Prince's *matrimonium morale et politicum*, was to illustrate a fundamental law: the inalienability of fiscal property.[70] Very appropriately, therefore, he interpreted the fisc as the dowry of the bridal *respublica*, and explained that a husband was entitled only to *use* the property of his wife, but not to alienate it. He further paralleled the vows, exchanged by groom and bride at their marriage, to the oaths taken at their consecration by king and bishop, by which both dignitaries promised not to alienate property belonging to the fisc and to the church respectively.[71]

It is perhaps of minor importance here to recall that Aristotle compared matrimony to a "political" government, whereas he claimed that the power a man had over his children resembled a "regal" government. Lucas de Penna may or may not have thought of this particular passage;[72] his debt to Aristotle, at any rate, should not be minimized. The real importance of Lucas de Penna's juristic analogies and equiparations has to be sought elsewhere. His model for the relations between Prince and state was—on the

[70] See below, Ch.VII, on "Inalienability."

[71] Lucas de Penna, *loc.cit.*, n.9, p.564: "Nam aequiparantur quantum ad hoc etiam iuramentum super his praestitum de alienatione facta non revocando episcopus et rex. Ita et principi alienatio rerum fiscalium, quae in patrimonio imperii et reipublicae sunt et separate consistunt a privato patrimonio suo, iuste noscitur interdicta. Ita et fortius non potest princeps fiscalem rem alienare quae plus est in bonis reipublicae quam actio iniuriarum in bonis ecclesiae. . . . Nam et fiscus est pars reipublicae. . . ." On this basis, Lucas de Penna then identified the fisc with the *dos* of the *respublica*. Naturally, the *patrimonium Petri* figures as the *dos* of the papal *sponsa*, the Roman Church; see, e.g., Oldradus de Ponte, *Consilia*, LXXXV, n.1 (Lyon, 1550), fol.28ᵛ, who admonishes the pope in Avignon "ut sanctitas vestra revertatur ad sponsam . . . et reparet suum patrimonium et suam dotem, quae multipliciter est collapsa." See, for the problem of the *dos* in the spiritual marriage of Christ to the Church, Aquinas, *Summa theol.*, Suppl.III,qu.XCV, art.1 and 3; the difficulties of assessing the *dos* were particularly great because, as Aquinas points out (art.1, ad 2), "pater sponsi (scilicet Christi) est sola persona Patris; pater autem sponsae est tota Trinitas"; also, because owing to the oneness with the "mystical body," Christ "nominat se etiam sponsam, et non solum sponsum" (art.3, ad 3).

[72] Aristotle, *Polit.*, 1259a; Aquinas, *In Polit. Arist.*, I, lect.x, §152, ed. Spiazzi, 47f: "Vir principatur mulieri politico principatu, id est sicut aliquis, qui eligitur in rectorem, civitati praeest." In addition, Aristotle discusses the despotic and paternal governments. Perhaps Lucas de Penna, *loc.cit.*, had this passage in mind, when he added: "Praelatus quoque et vir non nisi per electionem assumitur, sicut et princeps."

basis of Gratian's *Decretum*—the bishop in his relations to his church, patterned after the model of Christ in his relations to the universal Church. The Church as the supra-individual collective body of Christ, of which he was both the head and the husband, found its exact parallel in the state as the supra-individual collective body of the Prince, of which he was both the head and the husband—"The Prince is the head of the realm, and the realm the body of the Prince." In other words, the jurist transferred to the Prince and the state the most important social, organic, and corporational elements normally serving to explain the relations between Christ and the Church—that is, Christ as the groom of the Church, as the head of the mystical body, and as the mystical body itself.

Strange though this kind of political theology may appear to us, it was not the result of a personal whim of Lucas de Penna. The analogy of the *corpus mysticum* served to clarify the relations between the estates of the body politic and their king, and the marriage metaphor served to describe the peculiar nature of the fisc. Hence, comparisons of that kind were not restricted to Lucas de Penna, though it must be admitted that his arguments exercised a surprisingly great influence in later times, especially in sixteenth-century France, where both the *corpus mysticum* analogy and the metaphor of the king's marriage to his realm were linked with the fundamental laws of the kingdom of France.

The comparison of the state with a *corpus mysticum* had deep roots in France. It fell in with the mysticism of French kingship, which reached its first growth in and after the times of Charles V, and at the same time it counterbalanced the royal mysticism by a mysticism of the estates. Jean Gerson (1363-1429), the Chancellor of the University of Paris, for example, spoke with some regularity about the *corpus mysticum* of France whenever he discussed the organic structure of the realm as it appeared in the three estates. He reverted to a customary argument and declared that just as in the natural body all members exposed themselves to protect the head, so were in the "mystical body" all subjects held to defend their lord;[73] he warned the people that each be content

[73] Carl Schäfer, *Die Staatslehre des Johannes Gerson* (Cologne diss., 1935), 55,n.86, quoting *Vivat rex*, in Gerson, *Opera omnia*, ed. Ellies du Pin (Antwerp,

with his status, for otherwise *l'ordre du corps mystique de la chose publique seroit tout subverti*;[74] on the other hand, he demanded that taxes for the protection of the king and the realm should be distributed evenly per *totum corpus mysticum*;[75] and it was likewise in connection with the three estates, when, in one of his letters about the education of the Dauphin, he lets the young Prince meditate: "Thou hast those of the first estate [the chivalry] as the very strong arm to defend thy mystical body, which is the royal polity"—an identification of the Prince with the body politic or mystic which was by no means the rule, but which led Gerson promptly to attribute to the king, not as yet two bodies, but at least two lives, one "natural" and the other "civil or political."[76]

Jean de Terre Rouge, a French jurist (ca. 1418-19), a vigorous defender of the Dauphin's (Charles VII's) right to succeed to the French throne, and an ardent constitutionalist, mentioned the *corpus mysticum* of France likewise in connection with the estates. He argued that the succession to the throne was established by ancient custom and was introduced by the consent of the three estates "and of the whole civic or mystical body of the realm." He pointed out that the royal or secular dignities of the realm were not privately owned but public, because they belonged "to the whole civic or mystical body of the realm" just as did the ecclesi-

---

1706), IV,597B/C: "Secundum quod per naturalem instinctum omnia membra in uno solo corpore sese exponunt pro capitis salute, pariformiter esse debent in corpore mystico verorum subditorum ad suum dominum."

[74] Schäfer, 58,n.101, quoting the oration of 1413, *Rex in sempiternum vive*, in *Opera*, IV,676.

[75] Schäfer, 53,n.77, quoting *Vivat rex*, in *Opera*, IV,616C/D: "Postquam necessarium est ad protectionem et vitae civilis, regis et regni nutritionem et conservationem accipere et levare subsidia, id in bona aequalitate aut aequitate per totum corpus mysticum fieri debet."

[76] *Opusculum de meditacionibus quas princeps debet habere*, c.2, ed. Antoine Thomas, *Jean de Gerson et l'éducation des Dauphins de France* (Paris, 1930), 37: "Habes illos de primo statu tanquam brachia fortissima ad corpus tuum misticum, quod est regalis policia, defendendum." Gerson renders here, as it were, a soliloquy of the Dauphin. For the king's "two lives," see Gerson, *Vivat rex*, II, prol., in *Opera*, IV,592: "De secunda Regis vita verba faciemus, civili videlicet et politica, que status regalis dicitur aut dignitas. Estque eo melior sola vita corporali, quo ipsa vita diuturnior per legitimam successionem." See also *Vivat rex*, I,consid.iv, in: *Opera*, IV,591: "Pater post naturalem, aut civilem, mortem in filii sui adhuc vivit persona" (the "civil death" of the king would take place, e.g., in the case of an abdication or of mental incapability, which was true in 1405, when Gerson wrote his tractate, since Charles VI was insane). Actually Gerson seems to add a third or spiritual life; for in the *salutatio* of the tractate he exclaims: "Vivat [rex] corporaliter, vivat politice et civiliter, vivat spiritualiter et indesinenter."

astical dignities which belonged to the churches; therefore, the king could not make arbitrary dispositions about the succession to the throne.[77] Claude de Seyssel, a jurist in the administration under Louis XII, availed himself of words similar to those of Jean Gerson when he warned that, unless the subjects of every estate were content with their lot, the result might be "the ruin of the monarchy and the dissolution of this mystical body."[78] And at the end of the sixteenth century, Guy Coquille, a jurist going his own ways, stated in so many words that the king as the head and the three estates as the members "together form the body politic and mystic" of the realm.[79]

Here as elsewhere we find that in the organological concept of "body politic and mystic" the constitutional forces remained alive which limited the royal absolutism. This became manifest when, in 1489, the Parlement of Paris, France's supreme Law Court, remonstrated against the pretensions of the King's Council under Charles VIII. The Parlement, a body headed by the king and composed of the Twelve Peers, the Chancellor, the four Presidents of Parlement, a few officers and councillors, and of a hundred other members (allegedly after the model of the Roman Senate), objected to interference and proclaimed itself "un *corps mystique* meslé de gens ecclésiastiques et lais . . . representans la personne du roy," because this highest court of the kingdom was "the sovereign Justice of the Realm of France, and the true throne,

[77] Jean de Terre Rouge, *Tractatus de iure futuri successoris legitimi in regiis hereditatibus*, I, art.1, conclusio 24, published as an Appendix of François Hotman, *Consilia* (Arras, 1586), p.34: "Consuetudo . . . fuit et est introducta ex consensu trium statuum et totius corporis civilis sive mystici regni [follow allegations from the *Decretum*, including c.24, D.xciii: "exercitus imperatorem faciat," rendered by Terre Rouge: "exercitus populi facit *regem*, sive imperatorem"] . . . Praeterea dignitates regiae sunt totius corporis civilis sive mystici regni: sicut dignitates ecclesiasticae sunt ecclesiarum." See, for Terre Rouge, A. Lemaire, *Les lois fondamentales de la monarchie française d'après des théoriciens de l'ancien régime* (Paris thesis, 1907), 58; J. M. Potter, "The Development and Significance of the Salic Law of the French," *EHR*, LII (1937), 244; Church, *Constitutional Thought*, 29, n.20; also Hartung, "Krone," 29,n.3; Jean Comte de Pange, *Le roi très chrétien* (Paris, 1949), 427f.

[78] Church, *Constitutional Thought*, 34,n.36.

[79] Guy Coquille, *Les oeuvres* (Paris, 1666), I,323, quoted by Church, 278, n.16: "Car le Roy est le Chef, et le peuple des Trois Ordres sont les membres, et tous ensemble sont le corps politique et mystique. . . ." Coquille adheres to the customary organological interpretation: "Cette distinction des Trois Ordres au corps politique a correspondance à ce qui est du corps humain qui est composé de trois principales parties . . . qui sont le cerveau [Clergy], le coeur [Nobility] et le foye [Third Estate]."

authority, magnificence, and majesty of the king himself."[80] The idea was, of course, that the king and his council could not act against the Parlement, because this "mystical body" was representative of, or even identical with, the person of the king.

Likewise in the sense of limitation, the French jurists used the metaphor of the king's marriage to the realm; for this metaphor harbored another fundamental law of the country, the inalienability of the fisc. Here the French authors were largely under the influence, direct or indirect, of Lucas de Penna. His formulations were repeated verbatim by Charles de Grassaille, writing under Francis I, who styled the king the *maritus reipublicae* and talked about the *matrimonium morale et politicum* which the king contracted after the model of the prelate who wedded his church.[81] He as well as others—René Choppin, François Hotman, Pierre Grégoire, finally also Bodin—held that the king, when marrying the realm of France, received from the *respublica* the fiscal property as a dowry, and that this dowry was inalienable.[82] The jurists, however, were probably responsible even for an actual change in the coronation ceremonial of the French kings. Grassaille wrote his great work *On the Regalian Rights of France* in 1538.[83] On the

---

[80] The Remonstrance of 1489, to which Dr. R. E. Giesey kindly called my attention, was published by Édouard Maugis, *Histoire du Parlement de Paris* (Paris, 1913), I,374f.

[81] Charles de Grassaille, *Regalium Franciae libri duo*, I, ius xx (Paris, 1545), 217: "Rex dicitur maritus reipublicae. . . . Et dicitur esse matrimonium morale et politicum: sicut inter ecclesiam et Praelatum matrimonium spirituale contrahitur. . . . Et sicut vir est caput uxoris, uxor vero corpus viri . . . , ita Rex est caput reipublicae et respublica eius corpus." The whole passage stems from Lucas de Penna; see above, nos. 59 and 66. See, for Grassaille, Church, *Constitutional Thought*, 47ff, 57ff. It may be mentioned *obiter* that the combination of "moral and political" is found over and over again since the 13th century; see, e.g., Pierre Dubois, *De recuperatione Terrae Sanctae*, c.109, ed. Langlois (Paris, 1891), 96: "moraliter et politice loquendo" (following and preceding quotes from Aristotle).

[82] René Choppin, *De Domanio Franciae*, II,tit.1,n.2 (Paris, 1605), 203: Sicuti enim Lege Julia dos est a marito inalienabilis: ita Regium Coronae patrimonium individua Reipublicae dos" (see also below, n.83). François Hotman, *Francogallia*, c.IX,n.5 (Frankfurt, 1586), 66ff: "Est enim Domanium regium quasi dos regni," and "Par idemque esse ius Regium in suum Domanium quod est viri in dotem suae uxoris," quoting Lucas de Penna (*Francogallia* was first published in 1576, though without Chapter IX). See Lemaire, *Lois fondamentales*, 100, for the marriage metaphor, and 93,n.2, for the editions (also 99,n.2). Pierre Grégoire, *De Republica*, IX,1,11 (Lyon, 1609; first published in 1578), 267A: the Prince as *sponsus reipublicae* and the fisc as the *dos pro oneribus danda*. See, for Bodin (*De republica*, VI,2,n.641) and others, Vassalli, "Fisco," 198,nos.3-4, and 201.

[83] Above, n.81. It is most unlikely that Grassaille should have been the first to hark back to the formulations of Lucas de Penna, whose work was reprinted in

accession of Henry II of France, in 1547, we find, for the first time in a French Coronation Order, the almost juristic rubric before the Bestowal of the Ring, saying that by this ring "the king solemnly married his realm" (*le roy espousa solemnellement le royaume*).[84] The rubrics of the Order of 1594 were more explicit. They said that the king, on the day of his consecration, married his kingdom in order to be inseparably bound to his subjects that they may love each other mutually like husband and wife, and that the Bishop of Chartres presented to the king the ring *pour marque de ceste reciproque conjonction*.[85] This is the spirit of Cyprian and

---

France no less than six times during the 16th century, beginning with the edition of Paris, 1509; see Ullmann, *Lucas de Penna*, 14,n.2. Actually, Master Jacques Cappel, the king's advocate in the Parlement of Paris, may have availed himself of Lucas de Penna's metaphors in a *plaidoyé* of 1536, which is quoted by Pierre Dupuy, *Traitez touchants les droits du Roy* (Paris, 1655), 275: ". . . par les droits commun, divin et positif le sacré patrimoine de la Couronne et ancien domaine du Prince ne tombe au commerce des hommes, et n'est convenable à autre qu'au Roy qui est mari et époux politique de la chose publique, laquelle luy apporte à son Sacre et Couronnement ledit domaine en dot de sa Couronne, lequel dot les Rois à leur Sacre et Couronnement iurent solennellement ne iamais aliener pour quelque cause que ce soit, comme aussi il est inalienable." Cf. *Plaidoyez de feu maistre Jacques Cappel* (Paris, 1561), p. 11. It is easy to recognize the arguments of Lucas de Penna, and there is no need to assume that the passage could not have been written before the revision of the rubrics at the "Bestowal of the Ring" in the French coronation ceremonial (see nos. 84-85).

[84] Th. Godefroy, *Le Cérémonial de France* (Paris, 1619), 348. It is true that a "Benediction of the Ring," borrowed from the rite of episcopal ordinations, was introduced into the Coronation Order of Charles V; see *The Coronation Book of Charles V of France*, ed. E. S. Dewick (Bradshaw Society, xvi, London, 1899), 33 (cf. p.83). Schramm, *König von Frankreich*, I,238f (cf. II,117), holds that this borrowing from the episcopal rite, all by itself, would imply the king's marriage to the realm. However, the decisive words of the episcopal "Bestowal of the Ring" (*sponsam Dei . . . illibate custodias*) are lacking; moreover, the jurists had used the image at a far earlier date, and in the French *Ordines* of the Coronation the metaphor is first found in 1547. That the prayer at the Bestowal of the Ring in the episcopal ordination has also its history is a matter which is of no concern here. See above, n.54.

[85] Godefroy, *Cérémonial*, 661: "ANNEAU ROYAL: Parce qu'au jour du Sacre le Roy espousa solennellement son Royaume, et fut comme par le doux, gracieux, et amiable lien de mariage inseparablement uny avec ses subjects, pour mutuellement s'entraimer ainsi que sont les epoux, luy fut par le dit Evesque de Chartres presenté un anneau, pour marque de ceste reciproque conjonction." The rubric after the prayer says that the same bishop "mit le dit anneau, duquel le Roy espousoit son Royaume, au quatriesme doigt de sa main dextre, dont procede certaine veine attouchant au coeur." See, for the last remark concerning the ring finger, Gratian's *Decretum*, c.7,C.xxx,qu.5, ed. Friedberg, I,1106. Allusions to this marriage ritual are found frequently in later times; see, e.g., *Recueil des anciens lois françaises*, ed. Isambert, Taillandier, and Decrusy (Paris, 1829), xv,328, No.191, where Henry IV, in his edict (of 1607) concerning the reunion to the Crown of his private patrimony of Navarre, says about his predecessor kings that "ils ont

Gratian's *Decretum* in its twisted version—the realm is in the king, and the king in the realm; the subjects are incorporated in the king, and the king in the subjects.[86] Little wonder then that the doctrine of the *corpus mysticum* of the Church, married to its divine *sponsus*, came full circle, when one of the jurists, René Choppin, went so far as to say that "the king is the mystical spouse of the *respublica*."[87]

In mediaeval England, the marriage metaphor seems to have been all but non-existent, though in the speech to his first Parliament (1603) James I said:

> "What God hath conjoined then, let no man separate." I am the husband, and all the whole island is my lawful wife; I am the head, and it is my body; I am the shepherd, and it is my flock.[88]

With the *corpus mysticum* tenet, however, England was indeed very familiar. After all, England's greatest jurist of the Lancastrian period, Sir John Fortescue, talked without hesitation about the "mystical body" of the realm. In an important chapter of his *De laudibus legum Angliae*, in which he rendered the essence of his political doctrines, Fortescue discussed the origin of kingdoms ruled "politically"—that is, according to Aristotelian terminology, ruled by the whole body politic of the realm—as opposed to kingdoms such as France, which were ruled "regally"—that is, by the king alone.[89] If a people, wrote he, wishes to establish itself as a

---

contracté avec leur couronne (!) une espèce de *mariage* communément appellé *saint et politique*." [See Addenda, below, p. 568.]

86 See above, nos.60,64-66.

87 Choppin, *De Domanio Franciae* (above, n.82), III, tit.5, n.6, p.449: "Rex, curator *Reipublicae* ac *mysticus* . . . ipsius *coniunx*." The doctrine came the full circle also the other way round when jurists conceded to the pope fiscal and other rights in the States of the Church because they considered him *huius reipublicae temporalis maritum*, although in other respects he was, spiritually, the *vir Ecclesiae* anyhow; cf. Vassalli, "Fisco," 209, quoting Cardinal de Luca.

88 *Parliamentary History of England* (London, 1806), I,930.

89 Fortescue, *De laudibus*, c.XIII, ed. Chrimes, 30,17; see also Chrimes' remark (p.156): "This chapter is the most famous in all Fortescue's writings." Fortescue, of course, is quite proficient in the jurists' method of "equiparating" secular and ecclesiastical institutions; see, e.g., *op.cit.*, c.VIII, ed. Chrimes, 22, where he sets against the *misteria ecclesie* the *misteria legis Anglie* and warns the Prince against trying to *legis sacramenta scrutare*, which is the business of professional jurists only trained in legal science (cf. cc.III and VII, pp.6ff,18f). This is the very argument which so greatly displeased King James I when Coke, in 1608, referred to it; see Coke, *Reports*, XII,63ff (Case of Prohibitions).

kingdom or any other body politic, it will have to set up one man for the government of the whole body, a king. This necessity Fortescue tried to evidence by harking back to the customary expedient, the analogy between the social and the human body:

> Just as the physical body grows out of the embryo, regulated by one head, so does there issue from the people the kingdom, which exists as a *corpus mysticum* governed by one man as head.

On another occasion Fortescue compared the functions of the heart and the nerves of the natural body to the structural system of the body politic. While identifying the nerves of the body with the laws of the state, he explained:

> The Law by which a *cetus hominum* is made into a *populus* resembles the nerves of the physical body; for just as the body is held together by the nerves, so is the *corpus mysticum* [of the people] joined together and united into one by the Law.[90]

Fortescue apparently visualized the *corpus mysticum* as the last stage of perfection of a human society which began as a simple multitude (*cetus*) of men, acquired then the status of a "people," finally culminated in the development of a "mystical body" of the realm, a body incomplete without a head, the king.

Fortescue's usage of the term *corpus mysticum* in political matters was not exceptional. At the opening of the Parliament of 1430, Master William of Lyndwood, Doctor of Laws and Professor of Divinity at Oxford, later Bishop of St. Davids and well known for his *Provinciale* of Canterbury, delivered after the sermon the usual keynote speech. He expounded the organic oneness of the realm, and compared it to that of the human body and its limbs and, with regard to the unanimity of the will and of mutual love, to a *corpus mysticum*.[91] Both lawyers, Lyndwood and Fortescue, used

[90] *De laudibus*, c.XII, ed. Chrimes, 28. For the stages *cetus, populus, corpus*, ultimately derived from Aristotle, see Vincent of Beauvais, *Speculum doctrinale*, VII,c.7 (Venice, 1494), fol.91ʳ.

[91] *Rot. Parl.*, IV,367: the speaker "causam summonitionis eiusdem Parliamenti ... egregie declaravit." This was common procedure: "Post praedicationem debet cancellarius Angliae . . . vel alius idoneus, honestus, et facundus justiciarius vel clericus . . . pronuntiare causas parliamenti, primo in genere, et postea in specie." See *Modus Tenendi Parliamentum*, in Stubbs, *Select Charters*, 503. Lyndwood observed that scheme; he spoke on I Chron. 22: 10: "Firmabitur solium regni eius." He then discussed a *triplex unio* of the realm: "unam . . . collectivam, ut in rerum mobilium congerie et congregatione; alteram . . . constitutivam, ut in corpore humano diversorum membrorum annexione; et tertiam consentaneam, ut in cuiuslibet

the terms *corpus politicum* and *corpus mysticum* promiscuously and without clear distinction. This is true also of another parliamentary preacher of that century, John Russell, Bishop of Lincoln and Chancellor of England. In his sermon at the opening of Parliament in 1483, he discussed the body politic of England composed of the three estates with the "sovereign Lord, the King," being its head. Referring to the *locus classicus* of I Corinthians 12: 12,[92] he compared the natural body in which every limb has its proper function, with the body politic of the realm: "So ys hyt yn the mistik or politike body of the congregation of the peuple."[93] In another draft of his sermon he repeated the phrase concerning the "mystical or political body" of the people,[94] and occasionally remarked that this "grete publick body of Englonde [ys] but that and there where the Kyng ys hym self, hys court and hys counselle."[95]

We recognize a similarity with imperial and papal language: the empire is where the emperor is; and the *corpus mysticum* where the pope is. We are reminded, however, also of the French constitutionalists, the *Remonstrance* of 1489 or the assertion of Guy Coquille; for Bishop John Russell significantly specified the word "King" by adding "his court and his council."[96] That is to say, the body politic, mystic, or public of England was defined not by the king or head alone, but by the king together with council and parliament. This concept of a "composite" body, and therewith of "composite" authority, was not quite new by that time.[97] As early as 1365, a justice of Edward III opined that "Parliament represents the body of the whole realm."[98] Though

corporis mistici unanima voluntate et dilectione." For William of Lyndwood, see Maitland, *Roman Canon Law in the Church of England* (London, 1898); Arthur Ogle, *The Canon Law in Mediaeval England* (London, 1912).

[92] See above, n.6.

[93] Chrimes, *Ideas*, 180, has re-edited the sermon, first published by John Gough Nichols, *Grants from the Crown during the Reign of Edward the Fifth* (Camden Society, LX, London, 1854), p.li.

[94] Chrimes, *Ideas*, 185; Nichols, *Grants*, p.lviii.

[95] Chrimes, *Ideas*, 175, also 332, n.6; Nichols, *Grants*, p.xlvi.

[96] See above, nos.34f, and, for the French doctrines, nos. 79f.

[97] B. Wilkinson, "The 'Political Revolution' of the Thirteenth and Fourteenth Centuries in England," *Speculum*, XXIV (1949), 502-509, has carefully felt his way through the constitutionally truly "dark centuries." In fact, what he calls the "composite" sovereignty seems to be inseparable from that "organic unity of the state" (p.504, n.8) the perseverance of which prevented England from succumbing to the "abstract state" concepts that developed on the Continent.

[98] *Year Books*, 39 Edward III, f.7a, quoted by Maitland, *Sel.Ess.*, 107; see also

this view should not, retrospectively, be considered an inveterate rule of English constitutionalism, it is nevertheless true that indications of this concept may be found a bit everywhere.[99] Related ideas may have guided, for example, a philosopher of the rank of Walter Burley, who in his Commentary on Aristotle's *Politics* (around 1338) deviated from the official interpretation by Aquinas and Peter of Auvergne only to insert a sentence about the "multitude composed of the King, the powerful and the wise" (so to speak, the king with lords and commons) summoned to Parliament "for the dispatch of hard business," and about the fact that they "rule together in the king and with the king," *sicut hodie patet de rege Anglorum*—"as it appears today with regard to the king [Edward III] of the English."[100]

It all amounts eventually to Fortescue's famous definition of England as a *dominium regale et politicum*, describing a kind of government in which not the king alone but king and polity together bore the responsibility for the commonweal. Fortescue borrowed his famous formula, which in its turn was an effluence of Aristotelian political thought, from the continuation of Aquinas' unfinished tractate *De regimine principum*. The continuator, Tolomeo of Lucca, found the prototypes of that form of government in imperial Rome (which "holds the center between a political and regal government"—*medium tenet inter politicum*

McIlwain, *Constitutionalism*, 89, n.32; Wilkinson, *op.cit.*, 504, nos.14-15. According to the *Modus*, ed. Stubbs, *Select Charters*, 503, the king is "caput, principium, et finis parliamenti," and therewith alone constitutes the *primus gradus* of Parliament (the *Modus* distinguishes six ranks).

[99] One might think of *Fleta*, II,c.2: "habet enim rex curiam suam in consilio suo in parliamentis suis." With Wilkinson (*op.cit.*, 504, n.13), I too would hesitate to take those words to imply "the king and the magnates exercising sovereignty in the state." Important new points of view have been put forth by Gaines Post, "The Two Laws and the Statute of York," *Speculum*, XXIX (1954), 417-432.

[100] S. Harrison Thomson, "Walter Burley's Commentary on the *Politics* of Aristotle," *Mélanges Auguste Pelzer* (Louvain, 1947), 577: "et adhuc in regno multitudo constituta ex rege et proceribus et sapientibus regni quodammodo principatur. Itaque tantum vel magis principatur huiusmodi multitudo quam rex solus, et propter hoc rex convocat parliamentum pro arduis negociis expediendis." And later, while producing the customary Aristotelian arguments, Burley alluded to Edward III: "In optima enim policia . . . quilibet diligit gradum suum et contentus est, et quilibet vult singularem honorem, regit, et videtur sibi *quod in rege et cum rege conregnat*, et propter intimam dileccionem civium ad regem est intima concordia inter cives, et est regnum fortissimum sicut hodie patet de rege Anglorum. . . ." For the passage quoted by Thomson, compare Aquinas, *In Polit. Arist.*, §473, ed. Spiazzi, p.167.

et regale) and in the government of Israel's Judges whose rule was supported by God himself as their king. Fortescue, especially in his earliest writings, ventured to prove that this ideal *dominium regale et politicum* had been actualized a third time, that is, in England. Hence England fell in with the hallowed models of Israel and Rome. The English king, in contrast to the French king who ruled only "regally," appeared to Fortescue definitely polity-centered. Vice versa, however, the polity itself, or the mystical body of the realm, could not exist without its royal head.[101]

The English form of government by the whole body politic led to an apparently unique fashion of analogizing secular and ecclesiastical institutions. We are used to a semi-theological mysticism with regard to the Prince and the interpretation of his functions, but are perplexed to find in England similar features with regard to Parliament. Before the close of Parliament in 1401, the Speaker of the Commons saw fit to compare the body politic of the realm with the Trinity: the king, the Lords spiritual and temporal, and the Commons jointly formed a trinity in unity and unity in trinity. On the same occasion the Speaker compared the procedures of Parliament with the celebration of a mass: the reading of the Epistle and the expounding of the Bible at the opening of Parliament resembled the initial prayers and ceremonies preceding the holy action; the king's promise to protect the Church and observe the laws compared with the sacrifice of the mass;[102] finally, the adjournment of Parliament had its analogy in the *Ite, missa est*, the dismissal, and the *Deo gratias*, which concluded the holy action.[103] Although those comparisons do not mean very much all by themselves, they nevertheless reflect the intellectual climate and show to what extent political thought in the "high Gothic" age gravitated towards mysticizing the body politic of the realm.

[101] For the problem of Fortescue and Aquinas, see, in addition to A. Passerin d'Entrèves, "San Tommaso d'Aquino e la costituzione inglese nell' opera di Sir John Fortescue," *Atti della R. Accademia di Torino,* LXII (1927), 261-285, the fundamental study by Felix Gilbert, "Sir John Fortescue's 'Dominium regale et politicum,' " *Mediaevalia et Humanistica,* II (1943), 88-97, esp. 91ff, where the literature on the subject has been discussed.

[102] For the connection of Law and sacrifice, see above, Ch. IV, nos.91-92.

[103] *Rot.Parl.,* III,459, §32 (comparison with Trinity), and 466, §47 (comparison with Mass); Chrimes, *Ideas,* 68f. Parliamentary comparisons are sometimes picturesque. Bishop Henry of Winchester, e.g., compared in his parliamentary sermon of 1425 the king's councillors with elephants because they should be "sine felle, inflexibilis, et immensae memoriae." *Rot.Parl.,* IV,261.

Moreover, the analogy of king, lords, and commons with the Trinity may be taken as an additional evidence that a relatively clear idea about the "composite" nature of authority existed, and that in England not the king alone, but the king jointly with lords and commons formed the "mystical body" of the realm.[104]

That the king alone should have represented that "mystical body" appears unlikely in mediaeval England, even though Sir Edward Coke in 1608 made a marginal note to that effect: he referred to the Year Books of Edward IV where (said he) the king's "body politic" was styled *corpus mysticum*. This contention is not quite correct, since the Year Book does not refer to the king but to an abbot.[105] The passage shows nevertheless how far advanced corporate concepts were in England by the end of the fifteenth century. However, despite a smattering of strictly corporational interpretations—"The parliament of the king and the lords and the commons are a corporation," declared Chief Justice Fineux in 1522[106]—the old organological concept distinguishing between head and limbs still prevailed, and the king was merely the head in which the mystical or political body of the realm culminated. In that sense, Henry VIII, in 1542, addressed his council:

> We be informed by our judges that we at no time stand so highly in our estate royal as in the time of Parliament, wherein we as head and you as members are conjoined and knit together in one body politic.[107]

That is the same spirit in which earlier, in 1533, the preamble of the *Act in Restraint of Appeals* had been phrased, when Henry VIII declared that according to the most ancient authorities the realm of England was an empire,

> governed by one supreme head and king, and having the dignity and royal estate of the imperial crown of the same, unto whom a body politic, compact of all sorts and degrees of people, divided in terms and by names of spirituality and temporalty, be bounden....[108]

104 See, on that point, Chrimes, *Ideas*, 116, also 332, n.6.

105 See Coke, *Rep.*, VII,10a (*Calvin's Case*), referring to 21 Edward IV, f.38b. See below, Ch.VII,n.312.

106 Quoted by Maitland, *Sel.Ess.*, 107.

107 See, for that famous passage, *Letters and Papers of Henry VIII*, vol.XII, p.iv, n.3, and p.107, No.221; cf. A. F. Pollard, *The Evolution of Parliament* (London, 1926), 231.

108 *Statutes of the Realm*, III,427f; Stephenson and Marcham, *Sources of English Constitutional History*, 304, No.74B; Maitland, *Sel.Ess.*, 107f. Coke, *The 4th Part of*

We still recognize the old organological doctrine which had proved useful long before when it served Philip IV of France, in his struggle against Pope Boniface VIII, to bring the whole "Gallican Church" part and parcel into the French *patria* headed by the king. It now served Henry VIII to incorporate the *Anglicana Ecclesia*, so to speak, the genuine *corpus mysticum* of his "empire," into the *corpus politicum* of England, of which he as king was the head.[109] The fusion of bodies politic and spiritual was absolute and complete, and the resulting confusion was sensed very strongly by Cardinal Pole, who in a pamphlet addressed himself to Henry VIII, saying:

> Your whole reasoning comes to the conclusion that you consider the Church a *corpus politicum*. . . . Great as the distance is between heaven and earth, so great is also the distance between the civil power and the ecclesiastical, and so great the difference between this body of the Church, which is the body of Christ, and that, which is a body politic and merely human.[110]

Here the fronts have been curiously reversed. Instead of treating the state as a *corpus mysticum* Henry treated the Church as a simple *corpus politicum* and therefore as part and parcel of the realm of England. Contrariwise, Cardinal Pole tried in vain to restore the supra-political character of the Church and to undo the

---

the *Institutes of the Laws of England*, c.74 (London, 1809), 341, adduces that Act in order to prove that England was, and at all times has been, an "empire." For the problem, see A. O. Meyer, "Der Kaisertitel der Stuarts," *QF*, x (1907), 231ff, who starts with the imperial title of Henry VIII (for some additions, see E. E. Stengel, "Kaisertitel und Suveränitätsidee," *DA*, III [1939], 46), but without exhausting in any respect a most promising subject which still demands a thorough and systematic investigation.

109 See below, pp. 250ff, for Philip IV. The discussion about the realm's "body politic" (see Chrimes, *Ideas*, 304, 332f, nos.6-8) was greatly intensified under Henry VIII; see, e.g., Richard Sampson, *Oratio qua docet, hortatur, admonet omnes etc.* (London, 1533), fol.B^v (pagination according to a microfilm of that rare pamphlet in the University of California Library, at Berkeley): "Quis nescit totum regnum unum esse politicum corpus, singulos homines eiusdem corporis membra esse? Ubi nam est huius corporis caput? Estne aliud quam rex?" Cf. A. Passerin d'Entrèves, "La teoria del diritto e della politica in Inghilterra all' inizio dell' età moderna," *R. Università di Torino: Memorie dell' Istituto Giuridico* (Ser.II, No.IV, 1929), 27, n.15.

110 "Tota tua ratio concludit te Ecclesiam existimare corpus politicum esse. . . . Quantum enim distat caelum a terra, tantum inter civilem potestatem et ecclesiasticam interest: tantum hoc corpus Ecclesiae quod est corpus Christi, ab illo, quod est politicum et mere humanum, differt." Cardinal Pole, *Ad Enricum VIII . . . pro ecclesiasticae unitatis defensione*, in Juan T. Rocaberti, *Bibliotheca maxima pontificia* (Rome, 1698), XVIII,204, quoted after d'Entrèves, *op.cit.*, 27, n.15.

process of secularization which the *corpus Ecclesiae mysticum* had succumbed to ever since the thirteenth century.

That the corporational doctrines *could* result in an identification of the whole body politic with the head alone has been shown by papal writers who claimed that the mystical body of the Church was where the pope was.[111] The later French identification of the body politic with the monarch, to which Jean de Terre Rouge and other constitutionalists still objected,[112] would likewise suggest that the head could engulf the body, although legistic concepts—*Princeps est imperium, est fiscus,* said Baldus[113]—were probably more important in France. It is quite likely that also in England under Henry VIII the Cyprianic formula of the *Decretum* and of the Italian jurists began to gather volume, implying now by a new twist that all Englishmen were incorporated in the king, and that the king's personal acts and deeds were those of a body politic absorbed by its monarchical head. But even while resorting to those formulae, the English jurists, as in the case *Willion v. Berkley,* still distinguished between head and members, when they said:

> the other [Body] is a Body politic, and the Members thereof are his Subjects, and he and his Subjects together compose the Corporation . . . and he is incorporated with them and they with him, and he is the Head and they are the Members, and he has the sole Government of them. . . .[114]

All by itself, however, the corporational doctrine, so long as it was primarily organologic, did not necessarily result in that complete identification of the limbs with the head, nor did it actually in mediaeval England. One could accept the precise words of the Bishop of Lincoln when he declared that England's body politic or mystic was where king and council and parliament were; but one

---

111 Above, n.33. See also Gierke, *Gen.R.*, III,596,n.214.

112 For Terre Rouge, see above, n.77. Church, *Constitutional Thought*, has excellently brought to the fore the struggle between constitutional and absolutist ideas in sixteenth-century France, and one sometimes wonders to what extent the persuasive antitheses of Fortescue were valid in his time.

113 Baldus, on *Cod.* 10,1, rubr.,nos.12,13,18; Gierke, *Gen.R.*, III,596, n.216; also Gierke, *Johannes Althusius*, 137, n.47. The essence of *l'état c'est moi* (cf. Fritz Hartung, "L'État c'est moi," *Historische Zeitschrift*, CLXIX [1949], 1ff) may be traced very far back, as Victor Ehrenberg, "Origins of Democracy," *Historia*, I (1950), 519, has pointed out recently ("Thou art the state, thou the people" in Aeschylos' *Suppliants*, 370ff), though the profound differences of the general climate are probably more worth stressing than the similarities of diction.

114 Maitland, *Sel.Ess.*, 108; Plowden, *Reports*, 233a; above, Ch.I, n.13.

carefully refrained, as in the case of Richard II, from allowing the body to be swallowed by the head, just as on another occasion protests were voiced against the severance of the limbs from the head.[115] Perhaps Fortescue's definition of England as a true *dominium regale et politicum* remained the most accurate description, the one which preserved its value even though it was temporarily obscured. That magic formula, so much more important in English political thought than among the scholastic philosophers from whom it hailed, implied that head and body depended mutually on each other and that as the king was supreme in some respects, so was the polity in others. It will not be inappropriate here to recall Fortescue's contemporary, Nicholas Cusanus, who, in his *Concordantia catholica,* said that only so far as the Prince recognized himself "the creature of all his subjects collectively, did he become the father of the individual citizens,"[116] a concept later reduced to the more lapidary formula *Princeps maior singulis, minor universis,* "The Prince is more than the individual citizens, but less than their totality."[117] Fortescue seems to have cherished similar ideas when he developed his doctrine about an England both regal and political. His king was both above and below the body politic of the realm, just as the thirteenth-century king was both above and under the Law.[118]

Late mediaeval kingship, from whatever point of view it be considered, had become polity-centered after the crisis of the thirteenth century. The continuity, first guaranteed by Christ, then by the Law, was now guaranteed by the *corpus mysticum* of the realm which, so to speak, never died, but was "eternal" like the *corpus mysticum* of the Church. Once the idea of a political community endowed with a "mystical" character had been articu-

---

[115] Above, n.95. See the exclamation in the *Gesta Edwardi* of the canon of Bridlington (*Chronicles of the Reigns of Edward I and II,* ed. Stubbs, II,70): "Mira res! ecce qualiter membra a capite se disjungunt quando fit consideratio per magnates in parliamento, regis assensu minime requisito" (referring to the action against the Despensers in 1321). See Wilkinson, "The Coronation Oath of Edward II and the Statute of York," *Speculum,* XIX (1944), 460,n.4.

[116] Gierke, *Gen.R.,* III,590; *Johannes Althusius,* 126.

[117] Gierke, *Johannes Althusius,* 144, quoted by d'Entrèves, "La teoria," 36,n.27; see also Holdsworth, *History of English Law,* IV,213, and his reference to Hooker's *Ecclesiastical Polity,* I, §2,7.

[118] Unless I am mistaken, Professor McIlwain, *Constitutionalism,* 89f, indicates precisely this change, when confronting Fortescue with Bracton.

lated by the Church, the secular state was almost forced to follow the lead—to respond by establishing an antitype. This view does not detract from the complexity of other stimuli which were perhaps even more effective: Aristotelian doctrines, Roman and Canon Law theories, the political, social, and economic development at large during the later Middle Ages. But those stimuli seem to have worked in the same direction: towards making the polity co-eternal with the Church and bringing the polity—with or without a king—to the center of the political discussion.

However that may be, the corporational problem of the later Middle Ages began to eclipse the preponderance of the legal problem and the "tyranny of the Law" of the preceding period. This does not imply that the king's relation to the Law had become an irrelevant question, but that it was absorbed by, and included in, the far broader problem of the king's relation to a polity which itself could claim to be the Law and which, by its inherent dynamics, quickly developed its own ethical and semi-religious code—apart from the Church.

3. Pro patria mori

PATRIA RELIGIOUS AND LEGAL

Neither from the idea of polity-centered kingship nor from that of the state as *corpus morale, politicum, mysticum* can there easily be separated another notion which came to new life independently of, though simultaneously with, the organological and corporational doctrines: the *regnum* as *patria*, as an object of political devotion and semi-religious emotion.[119]

Patria, in classical Antiquity so often the aggregate of all the political, religious, ethical, and moral values for which a man might care to live and die, was an almost obsolete political entity

---

[119] For the general problem, see Halvdan Koht, "The Dawn of Nationalism in Europe," *AHR*, LII (1947), 265-280, as well as my paper *"Pro patria mori," AHR*, LVI (1951), 472-492, where the subject has been treated from a somewhat different angle and on a narrower basis, though occasionally with fuller documentation. In the meantime, Gaines Post, "Two Notes on Nationalism in the Middle Ages: 1. *Pugna pro patria*," *Traditio*, IX (1953), 281ff, has published an excellent study in which he, most gratifyingly, supplements my paper by reviewing the legal material on *patria* of which I had not been aware and which I badly neglected. I received his study only after the present book had been concluded, and I could barely do more than to integrate, in a last revision, some of the wealth of his material and some of his suggestive results.

in the earlier Middle Ages.[120] During the feudal age, when personal bonds between lord and vassal determined political life and prevailed over most other political ties, the ancient idea of *patria* had all but completely faded away or disintegrated. This does not imply that the word *patria* vanished entirely from the vocabulary of mediaeval Latin. Though hardly applicable to the actual conditions of life and badly fitting the political reality, the term will be found quite frequently in the works of mediaeval poets and scholars who drew their inspiration from Vergil and Horace and other classical authors.[121]

The word *patria* existed also in the daily language. In a narrow and purely local sense it referred to the native hamlet, village, township, or province, designating, like the French *pays* or the German *Heimat*, the home or birthplace of a man;[122] and in that sense it was used, for example, in English legal language: *per patriam se defendere* was a means of defense by which the defendant submitted to the judgment of the community in which he lived.[123] *Literati*, to be sure, might continue to extol a man's death *pro patria*; but death for that narrow local unit, which the word *patria* actually described, had—beyond the natural defense

[120] See "*Pro patria mori*," 474,n.8; further Louis Krattinger, *Der Begriff des Vaterlandes im republikanischen Rom* (Diss. Zürich, 1944), a useful discussion of the problem showing that Italy began to be *patria* only in the times of Cicero and Caesar (p.59) and that the *imperium* was not called *patria* in the classical period (p.69), whereas the *res publica* as well as the city of Rome were *patria* without restriction. This is borne out also by the mediaeval jurists, who, as Post, "Two Notes," 286,n.22, has shown, distinguished between the home-town as *minor patria* and Rome as *communis patria*. See below, nos.165ff.

[121] A few remarks in "*Pro patria mori*," 477,n.16. The poets and *literati*, when describing the heroes of classical Antiquity, used *patria* over and over again; see, e.g., Walter of Châtillon, *Alexandreis*, III,313 (ed. F. A. W. Mueldner, Leipzig, 1863), in his description of the battle of Issus: "Pro domino patriaque mori dum posset honeste. . . ." Also *ibid.*, II,355: "Pro patria stare et patriae titulis et honore/ Invigilare decet. . . ." More interesting is Wipo, who uses *patria* consistently in the sense of the classical tradition, without ever defining it; see his *Gesta Chuonradi*, prol., ed. Bresslau (*MGH, SS.r.germ.*), p.7,20, where he mentions as his *causa scribendi* the fact *quod proderit patriae*; see also p.9,14, and passim (cf. Index, 123, s.v. *patria*).

[122] Du Cange, in his *Glossarium* (s.v. *patria*), refers exclusively to the local meaning. See also Ernest Perrot, *Les institutions publiques et privées de l'ancienne France jusqu'en 1789* (Paris, 1935), 400f: "Le mot même de *patria* . . . n'avait jusqu'alors qu'une valeur géographique avec le sens restreint de 'région.'" See also Koht, "Dawn of Nationalism," 266f,n.6; Post, "Two Notes," for the often very indefinite usage of *patria*.

[123] For the English trial *per patriam*, to which Professor Joseph R. Strayer kindly called my attention, see Pollock and Maitland, *English Law*, II,620f,624,627.

of house and home—no political consequences: wanting, with few exceptions,[124] the broader politico-philosophical background it would have appeared as a private rather than a public sacrifice. Wars, after all, were normally not fought by the citizens, but by an army composed of feudal vassals and knights summoned to defend their lord and his political aims or personal interests. A liegeman's death for his personal lord, of course, rated high as a sacrifice for loyalty, and the mediaeval sagas abundantly glorified victims of *fidelitas* and of *fides*. But those warriors offered themselves up *pro domino*, not *pro patria*, and it only illustrates the general shift of the center of political life, when jurists in the early thirteenth century pointed out "that the duty to defend the *patria* was higher than the feudal obligations of vassal to lord."[125]

There was nevertheless one domain in which the idiom *patria* retained, as it were, its full original meaning and its former emotional values, if only by transference and in a transcendentalized form: in the language of the Church. The Christian, according to the teaching of the early Church and the Fathers, had become the citizen of a city in another world. His true *patria* was the Kingdom of Heaven, the celestial city of Jerusalem. The final return to that spiritual and eternal "fatherland" was, according to the Apostolic Epistles, the natural desire of the Christian soul peregrinating on earth. It was not simply a poetic metaphor, but a word spoken in the spirit of the Epistle to the Hebrews (11: 13-14), when, in the exequies, the priest entreated God that the holy angels be ordered to receive the soul of the defunct and to conduct it *ad patriam Paradisi*. The community of the blessed and saints was, after all, the civic assembly of the celestial *patria* which the soul desired to join. For the sake of that *communis patria* in heaven the martyrs had shed their blood. The Christian martyr, therefore, who had offered himself up for the invisible polity and had died for his divine Lord *pro fide*, was to remain—actually until the

124 We may think, e.g., of Anglo-Saxon England during the Norman invasions, and of similar events. One great exception, of course, was formed by the Italian cities which never quite lost the character of ancient city-states; the identification of *Italia* with *patria* is of a later date; above, n.120, and, for a good suggestion, Post, "Two Notes," 292. See also the survey, unfortunately very incomplete, of Hans Haimar Jacobs, "Studien zur Geschichte des Vaterlandsgedankens in Renaissance und Reformation," *Die Welt als Geschichte*, XII (1952), 85-105.

125 See Post, "Two Notes," 288,n.13, quoting Johannes Teutonicus (on c.18, C.XXII,q.5) and others.

twentieth century—the genuine model of civic self-sacrifice.[126] Christian doctrine, by transferring the political notion of *polis* to the other world and by expanding it at the same time to a *regnum coelorum*, not only faithfully stored and preserved the political ideas of the ancient world, as so often it did, but also prepared new ideas for the time when the secular world began to recover its former peculiar values.

From the outset, therefore, one should at least consider the possibility whether—before the full impact of legal and humanistic doctrines became effective—the new territorial concept of *patria* did not perhaps develop as a re-secularized offshoot of the Christian tradition and whether the new patriotism did not thrive also on ethical values transferred back from the *patria* in heaven to the polities on earth. In fact, some changes pertinent to this problem occurred in the wake of the crusades. After the pattern of the crusading taxes "for the defense (or needs) of the Holy Land" (*pro defensione* [*necessitate*] *Terrae Sanctae*), taxes were introduced by the Western kingdoms "for the defense (or needs) of the realm" (*pro defensione* [*necessitate*] *regni*). What was good for the *regnum Christi regis*, Jerusalem and the Holy Land, was good also for the *regnum regis Siciliae, Angliae*, or *Francorum*. If a special and extraordinary taxation was justifiable in the case of an emergency of Jerusalem, it seemed justifiable too—especially in the age of the purely political and secular crusades of the thirteenth century—to meet the emergencies of the territorial kingdoms in the same fashion.[127] By the middle of the thirteenth century, however, and especially in France, we find an emotional

126 For the "political" aspect of the heavenly world as *patria*, see, above all, Augustine, *De civ. Dei*, v,c.16. See, in general, Karl Ludwig Schmidt, *Die Polis in Kirche und Welt* (Rektoratsprogramm der Universität Basel, 1939); Hans Bietenhard, *Die himmlische Welt im Urchristentum und Spätjudentum* (Tübingen, 1951), 192-204. The quasi-political concept of celestial Jerusalem has been made a focal point in the works of Erik Peterson, now united in his *Theologische Traktate* (Munich, 1951), esp. 165ff: "Zeuge der Wahrheit"; 323ff: "Von den Engeln," and passim. Heaven as the *communis patria* of the Christians compares with the κοινὴ πατρίς which in ancient times had designated the nether-world; see Plutarch, *Moralia*, 113C; also "Pro patria mori," 475f, and *ibid.*, 472f, for the 20th-century controversy between Cardinals Mercier and Billot.

127 For the problem in general, see Joseph R. Strayer, "Defense of the Realm and Royal Power in France," *Studi in Onore di Gino Luzzatto* (Milan, 1949), 289ff; Helene Wieruszowski, *Vom Imperium zum nationalen Königtum* (Historische Zeitschrift, Beiheft 30, Munich and Berlin, 1933), 168ff and passim; also "Pro patria mori," 478f, and below, n.129.

element integrated into the prosaic business of taxation: taxes then were often imposed *ad defensionem (tuitionem) patriae* or, as Philip IV of France phrased it, *ad defensionem natalis patriae*, "for the defense of the native fatherland."[128]

This new terminology was not the result of some shrewd inventiveness on the part of French nationalists, but an application of legal language to national ends. The word *patria* was found in Canon Law, and it was indeed very frequent in Roman Law. The glossators were prompted to comment on it and to use it freely. When discussing the notion of *bellum iustum*, the "just war," the Canonists, ever since the late twelfth century, pointed out that war was justified, in case of "inevitable and urgent necessity," for the defense of the *patria* as well as for the defense of the faith and the Church, and they repeatedly exemplified such *necessitas* by referring to the wars which the Oriental Christians waged against the infidel in the Holy Land.[129] They concurred with the Civilians who held that in a case of emergency the emperor was entitled to levy new taxes for the defense of the *patria* and who followed the model of the Digests when talking about the "sweet" or "sweetest fatherland."[130] The jurists originally spoke of *patria* in general terms without specifying what the term meant, and it will be shown presently how they gradually came to express themselves with greater precision. There can be no doubt, however, that in the case of France in the age of Philip the Fair the word *patria* had actually come to mean the whole realm, and that by

[128] Strayer, "Defense," 292,n.7, quotes, for the year 1265, a case *ad tuitionem patrie senescallie Carcassonensis* where doubtless a limited military service for the protection of the seneschal of Carcassonne was demanded; however, that seneschalsy together with that of Beaucaire had belonged, since 1229, to the King of France directly (see F. Kern, *Die Anfänge der französischen Ausdehnungspolitik* [Tübingen, 1910], 319) so that in this case the local *patria* was also directly connected with the Crown of France. In 1302 (August 29), King Philip IV wrote to the clergy of the bailiwick of Bourges concerning subventions "ad defensionem natalis patrie pro qua reverenda patrum antiquitas pugnare precepit, eius curam liberorum preferens caritati." See *"Pro patria mori,"* 479,n.26; also Wieruszowski, *Vom Imperium*, 173,n.107. The letter of Philip IV is modelled after *D*.49,15,19,7 ("disciplina castrorum antiquior fuit parentibus Romanis quam caritas liberorum"), a passage occasionally quoted by the jurists; see, e.g., Petrus de Ancharano, *Consilia*, ccciii,n.4 (Venice, 1574), fol.162. Cf. Post, "Two Notes," 287, n.28, and 290, n.42.

[129] Post, "Two Notes," 282ff. For the fight against the infidel as the prototype of the just war, see also below, nos.155ff, the opinion of Henry of Ghent.

[130] Post, "Two Notes," 285ff. Cf. *D*.32,1,101, where the Greek words τῇ γλυκυτάτῃ μου πατρίδι are rendered *patriae meae suavissimae* or (in the *Glos.ord.*) *dulcissimae*; cf. Post, 286,n.22, and passim.

this time the territorial—perhaps we may even say national— monarchy of France was strong enough and sufficiently advanced to proclaim itself as the *communis patria* of all its subjects and to demand extraordinary services in the name of the fatherland.[131]

In England, such terminology developed in approximately the same period in literature as well as in legal language.[132] Bracton, drawing from legal material of the first half of the century, used the word *patria* as a matter of course. He distinguished, for example, between services due to the feudal lord and services pertaining to the king *ad patriae defensionem et hostium depressionem*, a distinction reflecting also the frequent dilemma between feudal and public obligations.[133] Again, in connection with *Essoign*—that is, valid "excuses" for failure to appear in court—Bracton declared that a proper excuse was service with the king's army *ad defensionem patriae*, but also recognized, as an alternative excuse for the normal *servitium regis*, the *servitium regis aeterni* overseas—a fact which demonstrates once more that the defense of the *Terra sancta* and the defense of the *patria* were in juristic language as well as in court on the same level.[134]

Perhaps here is the place to recall that in France the "holy soil" of the *Terra Sancta* overseas and the "holy soil" of *la dulce France* were not at all incompatible and incomparable notions, and that both were equally filled with emotional values. The kingdom of France, *Francia*, whose very name suggested to her children that she was the Land of the Free (*franci*), was considered the home of a new chosen people.[135] Pliny, on one occasion, had praised

---

[131] See below, nos.165ff, for the *communis patria*.

[132] The English material on *patria* has as yet been neither collected nor sifted, but there is every reason to assume that the word was used in the twelfth century for designating the whole territory of the island monarchy (see below, nos.145ff, for Geoffrey of Monmouth).

[133] Bracton, fol.35b, ed. Woodbine, II,113 and 114. For the priority of the *patria* over the feudal lord, see Post, "Two Notes," 283,n.13; 288,nos.34ff; see also Andreas of Isernia, on *Feud.* II,6 (*De forma fidelitatis*), n.1, fol.90ᵛ: The vassal is obliged to support his lord "etiam contra filium vel patrem [see below, n.161] . . . non tamen erit [obligatus] contra seipsum vel *contra patriam* . . . , quia plus tenetur patriae quam filiis" (with more material in the gloss, v. *patriae*).

[134] Bracton, fol.336b, Woodbine, IV,71: "Si autem ex causa necessaria et utili ut rei publicae causa, ita quod profectus sit in exercitum cum domino rege *ad defensionem patriae* per praeceptum domini regis, cum ad hoc obligatus sit, excusatur. . . ." See also fol.339, Woodbine, IV,76: "Item de ultra mare excusatur quis per essonium de servitio regis aeterni sicut de Terra Sancta. . . ."

[135] For *Franci = liberi*, see, e.g., Alexander of Roes, *Memoriale*, c.17, ed. H. Grundmann and H. Heimpel (Deutsches Mittelalter: Kritische Studientexte der *MGH*,

Italy as "a land sacred to the gods" (*Haec est Italia dis sacra*).[186] Now France appeared like a *Francia Deo sacra*, a *regnum benedictum a Deo*,[187] which God embraced with special love, which Christ honored with the prerogative of a special eminence, in which the Holy Spirit dwelled, and for whose sacred soil it was worth while and even sweet to make the supreme sacrifice. To defend and protect the soil of France, therefore, would have semi-religious connotations comparable to the defense and protection of the sacred soil of the Holy Land itself.[188]

To grant some religious glorification to the knight who sacrificed his life in the service of the Church and for the cause of God, had become customary even before the crusades.[139] Through the crusades, however, the possibility of acquiring that glorification was expanded from the chivalry to the broad masses, and the privilege of becoming a soldier-martyr was extended to classes which normally would not have engaged in fighting at all. A crusader

---

iv; Weimar, 1949), p.38, 13, and passim; also the sermon of William of Sauqueville, ed. Hellmut Kämpf, *Pierre Dubois*, 112f; further, the anonymous sermon, published by Leclercq (below, n.176), p.170f, lines 103ff; also Schramm, *Frankreich*, 1,138, for Pseudo-Turpin; Berges, *Fürstenspiegel*, 76f. For the French as a new chosen people, see a letter of Pope Clement V, the first Avignon pontiff: "regnum Francie in peculiarem populum electum a Domino in executione mandatorum celestium specialis honoris et gratie titulis insignitur." *Registrum Clementis V Papae*, No. 7501, quoted by Kämpf, *Pierre Dubois*, 99.

[186] Pliny, *Naturalis historia*, III, xx, 138.

[187] Innocent III, in his decretal *Novit*: c.13 X 2,1, ed. Friedberg, II,242; cf. Post, "Blessed Lady Spain," *Speculum*, XXIX (1954), 203,n.28.

[188] See, e.g., Richier, *La vie de Saint-Remi*, ed. W. N. Bolderston (London, 1912), line 61: "Molt fait dieus aperte monstrance / D'especial amour a France"; or line 114: "A bien Dieus [en] France eslargie / La grace dou Saint Esperite." Some material has been collected by Kämpf, *Pierre Dubois*, 91, 99, and passim; Wieruszowski, *Vom Imperium*, 147f, n.26; Schramm, *Frankreich*, 1,228f. The legists—Flotte, Plaisians, Nogaret, Dubois—repeated the theme of France's election incessantly, and the royalist Dominican William of Sauqueville, harping on the *Franci = liberi* formula, claimed that "proprie loquendo nullum regnum debet vocari regnum Francie nisi solum regnum Christi et beatorum." The sermon of the Dominican, together with others by the same author, has been transcribed from Paris, Bibl.Nat.MS lat.16495, fols.98-100v, and discussed by my former pupil Miss Hildegard Coester, *Der Königskult in Frankreich um 1300 im Spiegel der Dominikanerpredigten* (Thesis [Staatsexamens-Arbeit] Frankfurt, 1935-36, typescript), p.VIII; similar phrases are found in the sermon edited by Kämpf, *op.cit.*, 113. We may recall here also the epithets in praise of Paris, in Jean de Jandun's *Tractatus de laudibus Parisius*, in: *Paris et ses historiens aux XIVe et XVe siècles*, ed. Le Roux de Lincy and L. M. Tisserand (Paris, 1857), 32-79 (*instar triumphantis Jerusalem, locus sanctus*, etc.). All that was not restricted to France, as Post (above, n.137) has shown for Spain; but it was practiced in France more consistently in that period.

[139] This is one of the leading themes of the excellent study by Erdmann, *Kreuzzugsgedanke*.

who battled against the infidels for the Christian faith and died for the cause of the Holy Land in the service of Christ the King, was entitled, according to common belief, to expect his immediate entry into the celestial Paradise and, as a reward for his self-sacrifice, the crown of martyrdom in the life hereafter.

> He that embarks to the Holy Land,
> He that dies in this campaign,
> Shall enter into heaven's bliss
> And with the saints there shall he dwell.[140]

Whether the confidence in other-worldly reward, as reflected by the crusaders' song, was dogmatically sound or rather a misunderstanding of papal decrees (which granted crusaders not remission of sins, but remission of such punishments as the discipline of the Church might have imposed) made little difference then, nor shall it make any difference here. Belief in the crusader's assumption to paradise was shared by everyone; and it was still shared by Dante: he met his ancestor Cacciaguida, slain in the Second Crusade, in the heaven of Mars where the martyrs and champions of God had their place, and made him speak: "I come from martyrdom unto this peace" (*Venni dal martiro a questa pace*).[141]

In a similar fashion, to be sure, the death of a liegeman for his feudal lord might be glamorized, especially in a battle for the Christian faith. At a council in Limoges, in 1031, where a truce of God was discussed, the vassal of a duke was told: "For your lord you have to accept death . . . and for this loyalty you will become a martyr of God."[142] That is, the vassal offering himself up for his lord who defended a holy cause, compared with a Christian martyr who gave himself up for his divine Lord and master, for Christ. Accordingly, the Frankish warriors in the *Song of Roland* were told by Archbishop Turpin of Reims:

---

[140] "Illuc quicumque tenderit,/ Mortuus ibi fuerit,/ Caeli bona receperit,/ Et cum sanctis permanserit." See Dreves, *Analecta Hymnica*, XLVb, 78, No.96; Erdmann, *Kreuzzugsgedanke*, 248.

[141] For the "remission of sins," see Erdmann, *op.cit.*, 316f, also 294, and passim. The confusion was general, even among Canonists; cf. *Summa Parisiensis*, on c.14,C.XVI,q.3, ed. Terence P. McLaughlin, Toronto, 1952, 184: ". . . ad resistendum Saracenis Christianos hortatur ecclesia eosque quae profecti defensione moriuntur a peccatis absolvit." For Cacciaguida, see *Paradiso*, XV,148.

[142] *PL*, CXLII,1400B: "Debueras pro seniore tuo mortem suscipere . . . et martyr Dei pro tali fide fieres." Cf. Bloch, *Rois thaumaturges*, 244, n.3.

For our king we have to die.
Help to sustain the Christian faith . . .
I shall absolve you, heal your souls.
If so you die, you shall be holy martyrs
Obtaining seats high up in paradise.[143]

Since the warriors in the saga of Charlemagne were fighting the
Saracens in Spain, they rated as crusaders and enjoyed the privileges by which, in the times of the poet, crusaders were normally
distinguished.[144] However, the death of those "French" crusaders
waging war against the Saracens was at the same time a death for
the supreme lord, for Charlemagne, *li empereres Carles de France
dulce*, a fact which, for a French reader in the twelfth century,
gave to the martyrdom of the slain unfailingly also a national
flavor.

With due reserve it may be said that, what the *Song of Roland*
meant to the French, Geoffrey of Monmouth's *History of the Kings
of Britain* meant to the English. To Geoffrey of Monmouth *patria*
designated clearly the "monarchy of the whole island" (*totius
insulae monarchia*) which King Arthur, after having obtained it
by right of inheritance,[145] had to defend against the infidel: Saxons,
Scots, and Picts. Once, when the Saxons made an inroad on the
British *patria*, King Arthur assembled his army and addressed his
soldiers briefly to praise his own faithfulness as opposed to the
faithlessness of the Saxons who had disregarded the truce. The
main harangue, however, was again made by a bishop, Saint
Dubrick of Caerleon, who admonished the soldiers to be valiant
defenders of *pietas et patria*[146] for the sake of their fellow-citizens.

[143] *La Chanson de Roland*, lines 1128-1135, ed. J. Bédier (Paris, 1931), 96;
Leonardo Olschki, *Der ideale Mittelpunkt Frankreichs* (Heidelberg, 1913), 14ff;
see also Franz Cumont, *Lux perpetua* (Paris, 1949), 445.

[144] Concerning Charlemagne himself, Jocundus, *Translatio S. Servatii, MGH,SS.*,
XII,93 (written around 1088), says: "Karolus mori pro patria, mori pro ecclesia non
timuit. Ideo terram circuit universam et quos Deo repugnare invenit, impugnabat"
(I am indebted to Professor M. Cherniavsky for calling my attention to this place).
See, in general, Robert Folz, *Le Souvenir et la Légende de Charlemagne dans
l'Empire germanique médiéval* (Paris, 1950), 137f.

[145] Geoffrey of Monmouth, *Historia Regum Britanniae*, IX, c.1, ed. Jacob Hammer
(Mediaeval Academy of America Publications, No. 57 [Cambridge, 1951]), 152,7:
"Dubricius ergo, calamitatem patriae dolens, associatis sibi episcopis, Arthurum
regni diademate insignivit." *Ibid.*, line 17: ". . . cum [Arthurus] totius insulae
monarchiam debuerat hereditario iure obtinere."

[146] *Hist.Reg.Brit.*, IX,c.2, Hammer, 154,80: "[Saxones] patriam usque ad Sabrinum
mare depopulant." For Arthur's allocution, *ibid.*, lines 88ff; see lines 95f, for *pietas*

Fight for your *patria* and suffer even death for her if such should overwhelm you. Death itself is Victory and is a means of saving the soul. For whoever suffers death for his brothers, offers himself a living host to God, and unambiguously he follows Christ who for his brothers deigned to lay down his life [I John 3: 16]. If, therefore, one of you be overcome by death in this war, let that death be atonement for, and absolution of, all his sins. . . .[147]

The speech of the Bishop of Caerleon, like that of Archbishop Turpin of Reims in the *Song of Roland*, was perhaps patterned after sermons of crusade preachers, except that the spiritual rewards—absolution and salvation of the soul—as promised to the victims of the "holy wars" were conferred here on the martyrs dying for their patria. That the Welsh warriors of King Arthur died for the Christian faith as well, since they were battling the Saxon pagans, and that they died also for their lord and king, is perfectly true. Nevertheless, the death *pro fide*—for faith and fealty—is eclipsed by, or included in, the idea that they died *pro patria*, that is, *pro totius insulae monarchia*. Moreover, their death was interpreted as a self-sacrifice *pro fratribus*, and the author compared it with the self-sacrifice of Christ for his brothers.[148] Therewith the death *pro patria* appeared as a work of *caritas* rather than of *fides*, although the latter should not be excluded.

The note of "brotherly love" was occasionally struck before, in connection with the crusades. Pope Urban II, for example, in a letter to the Spaniards defending Tarragona against the Saracens, declared that

none who shall be killed in this campaign for the love of God *and his brothers* shall doubt that he will find remission of his sins and the eternal beatitude according to the mercy of God.[149]

---

et patria, two inseparable notions in ancient Roman thought which Aquinas (*Summa theol.*, II-II, qu.101,art.1 and 3) neatly linked together again.

[147] *Ibid.*, 154,97-104: "Pugnate pro patria (see below, n.159), et mortem, si supervenerit, ultro pro eadem patimini. Ipsa enim victoria est et animae remedium. Quicumque enim pro confratribus suis mortem inierit, vivam hostiam se praestat Deo Christumque insequi non ambigitur, qui pro fratribus suis animam suam dignatus est ponere. Si aliquis igitur vestrum in hoc bello mortem subierit, sit mors illa sibi omnium delictorum suorum paenitentia et absolutio. . . ." I am most grateful to the late Professor Jacob Hammer for calling my attention to this interesting passage.

[148] The scriptural passage I John 3: 16, was repeatedly adduced to draw a comparison between the victim *pro patria (fratribus)* and Christ; see, e.g., below, n.157.

[149] Paul Kehr, *Papsturkunden in Spanien, I: Katalanien* (Abh. Göttingen, N.F., XVIII:2, Berlin, 1926) 287f, No.23: "In qua videlicet expeditione si quis pro Dei et

And a little later, Ivo of Chartres assembled in his fundamental works, *Decretum* and *Panormia*, relevant sections from the Fathers and from papal letters in which celestial reward was promised to those dying "for the truth of faith, the salvation of the *patria*, and the defense of Christians"—sections which soon passed on to Gratian's *Decretum* and exercised permanent influence.[150]

It was, however, only in the thirteenth century that the Christian virtue of *caritas* became unmistakably political, and that it was utilized more persistently than hitherto and activated to sanctify and justify, ethically and morally, the death for the political "fatherland."

> *Amor patriae in radice charitatis fundatur*—Love for the fatherland is founded in the root of a charity which puts, not the private things before those common, but the common things before the private. . . . Deservedly the virtue of charity precedes all other virtues because the merit of any virtue depends upon that of charity. Therefore the *amor patriae* deserves a rank of honor above all other virtues.

Therewith a theological standard of *amor patriae* was authoritatively established; for these words passed for the opinion of Thomas Aquinas even though they were actually written by Tolomeo of Lucca, the continuator of Aquinas' *De regimine principum*.[151] In his discussion about *patria*, Tolomeo of Lucca followed, by and large, Saint Augustine's reflections on the superiority of the fatherland in heaven over that on earth; but he quoted also Cicero saying that parents and children, relatives and household members may be dear to us, but that "the fatherland embraced *caritate* all those relations." With Cicero he exclaimed: "What good citizen would hesitate to welcome death if it were profitable for the *patria*?"[152] Those were arguments and quota-

---

fratrum suorum dilectione occuberit, peccatorum profecto suorum indulgentiam et eterne vite consortium in venturum se ex clementissima Dei nostri miseratione non dubitet." Cf. Erdmann, *Kreuzzugsgedanke*, 294.

150 Cf. "*Pro patria mori*," 481f, nos.34-36; Erdmann, *op.cit.*, 248; Post, "Two Notes," 282, for the places in the *Decretum* of Gratian.

151 Thomas Aquinas, *De regimine principum*, III,c.4, ed. Joseph Mathis (Rome and Turin, 1948), 41. Tolomeo quoted the Roman examples, with the same references to Augustine (*De civ. Dei*, V,c.12-19), also in his *Determinatio compendiosa*, c.21, ed. Mario Krammer, 1909 (*MGH, Fontes iuris Germanici antiqui*), 42f. See Theodore Silverstein, "On the Genesis of *De Monarchia*, II, v," *Speculum*, XIII (1938), 326ff, and, in general, Hélène Pétré, *Caritas* (Louvain, 1948), 35ff.

152 Cicero, *De off.*, 1,57, a passage quoted frequently.

tions which the lawyers customarily produced,[153] and Tolomeo himself was well versed in handling at least Canon Law.

The whole problem of *patria*, stimulated not only by the Two Laws but also by intensified study and practical-political interpretation of Aristotle, was more lively discussed in the age after Aquinas than ever before in the Middle Ages. Aquinas himself touched upon the problem quite frequently. He too demanded that the virtuous citizen expose himself to the danger of death for the conservation of the commonweal, and he held that the virtue of *pietas*, often hardly distinguishable from *caritas*, was the power animating devotion and reverence to both parents and *patria*.[154] Later in the century, Henry of Ghent, the *Doctor solemnis* teaching at Paris, came to discuss related problems.[155] Taking as his starting point the Christian retreat from Acre and the fall of this city in 1291, he dealt with the question under what circumstances a soldier should either sacrifice his life or turn his back and flee. Henry strongly rejected any self-sacrifice for selfish reasons (vainglory, rashness, injustice, and others) and made it clear that flight and self-preservation might often be more valuable and commendable—except in the case of a priest who was not allowed to flee if his presence were demanded for the salvation of souls or the care of the sick.[156]

[153] Post, "Two Notes," 287,n.28, and passim.

[154] *Summa theol.*, I,qu.60,art.5, resp.: "Est enim virtuosi civis ut se exponat mortis periculo pro totius reipublicae conservatione." See above, n.147, for another passage on *patria*, and also the good commentary on the notion *patria* according to Aquinas, in *Die Deutsche Thomas-Ausgabe* (Heidelberg, 1943), xx,343ff. Usually, however, Aquinas means "Heaven" or "Paradise" when talking about *patria*; see, e.g., *Summa theol.*, II-II,qu.83,art.11; III,qu.8,art.3, etc.

[155] Henry of Ghent, *Quodlibeta*, xv, qu.16 (Paris, 1518 [*Quodlibeta Magistri Henrici Goethals a Gandavo*]), fols.594ff (Dr. Schafer Williams kindly provided me with photocopies). The argument, inspired ultimately by Cicero, *De off.*, 1,83, is: "Quod ·miles praevolans in exercitum hostium non facit opus magnanimitatis." See Paul de Lagarde, "La philosophie sociale d'Henri de Gand et de Godefroid de Fontaines" (above, n.52), 80ff, through whose article my attention was called to this *Quodlibet*.

[156] Henry discusses, fol.596, those who take a stand while the others flee: "Hoc licitum est eis, et tunc alii tenentur cum eis contra hostes stare et esse parati aut cum aliis hostes devincere aut simul mori cum illis; aut si sint aliqui inter illos qui tenentur eis ministrare spiritualia, fugere non possunt." Also the preceding passages (fol.595ᵛ) bring a discussion *de fuga praelatorum*. Henry finds it difficult to decide "si licitum sit fugere bellum, quod contra patriam aut patrias leges attentatum est ab hostibus legis et fidei christianae. Et censeo in hac materia idem de fuga praelatorum maiorum et minorum, et principum superiorum et inferiorum . . . quia sicut praelati tenentur ministrare populo in spiritualibus ad fomentum et

On the other hand, however, Henry praised the magnanimity of a soldier's sacrifice if dictated by love. He quoted the Song of Solomon (8: 6)—"For love is strong as death"—to demonstrate that a soldier's sacrifice for his friends was a work of charity and of faith. He defended the *bellum iustum*, the just war for the protection of the *patria* and the *spiritualia*. To give emphasis to his arguments, Henry quoted maxims from ancient authors. He quoted Vegetius; he quoted Cicero to the effect that none should love himself and his own life more than the *respublica*; he held with Plato (as transmitted by Cicero's *De officiis*) that man is not born for himself alone; and he accepted Cicero's religion: *Patria mihi vita mea carior est*, "The fatherland is dearer to me than my life." Despite those gleanings from Antiquity, Henry of Ghent centered on the traditional Christian arguments. Death in defense of the fatherland appeared, also to him, chiefly as a work of *caritas*, and Henry gave, as it were, the final blessing to *pro patria mori* by comparing—like Geoffrey of Monmouth—the sacrifice of a citizen for his brothers, and for his community, to the supreme sacrifice which Christ made for the salvation of man, and of mankind.[157] Thus it happened that in the thirteenth century the crown of martyrdom began to descend on the war victims of the secular state.

---

conservationem vitae eorum spiritualis, sic principes ministrare tenentur eidem in temporalibus ad fomentum et conservationem vitae eorum temporalis." Henry of Ghent, in his attitude toward the duties of clerics, is of course in full agreement with the teaching of scholasticism; cf. Aquinas, *Summa theol.*, II-II, qu.185, art.4 and 5; also the remark by Post, "Public Law," 48. He is, in general, also in agreement with the teaching of Canon Law; cf. Stephan Kuttner, *Kanonistische Schuldlehre von Gratian bis auf die Dekretalen Gregors IX.* (Studi e Testi, 64; Vatican City, 1935), 254f; also A. M. Stickler, "Sacerdotium et Regnum nei decretisti e primi decretalisti," *Salesianum*, XV (1953), 591, on c.19,C.XXIII,q.8 (fighting of prelates having *regalia*).

157 Fol.596, Henry quotes, with regard to those who could flee but prefer to take a last stand (*aut pariter vivant aut pariter moriantur*), the passage I John 3: 16 (above, n.148): "Hinc maxime probatur illa charitas quam Johannes apostolus commendat dicens: 'Sicut pro nobis Christus animam suam posuit, sic et nos debemus animas nostras pro fratribus ponere.'" For the passages from Cicero and others, see fols.595v and 596. A fourteenth-century canonist, Petrus de Ancharano, *Consilia*, CCLXXXI,n.9 (Venice, 1574), fol.148, quotes also the passage I John 3: 16, and parallels the *militia armata* (knighthood) and the *militia coelestis* (clergy). It is, said the jurist, becoming for a cleric "et mortem etiam non fugere tanquam miles Christi, qui animam suam posuit pro ovibus suis. nam et miles armatae militiae obligatur iuramento mortem non vitare pro Republica, ut l.fi.ff. ex qui. cau.ma. [C.2,53 (54),5? The allegation is faulty], quanto magis ad hoc adstringitur miles coelestis militiae pro Ecclesiae unitate."

In the arguments of Henry of Ghent the humanistic note is audible. It is even stronger with Dante to whom those giving their lives for the salvation of the *patria*, like the Roman Decii, appeared as "most sacred victims," bringing "that ineffable sacrifice" (*illud inenarrabile sacrificium*)[158] of which Cato was praised as the exemplary offeror. *Pugna pro patria*, "Fight for the fatherland," was supposedly Cato's device, for so it was found in the *Distichs* falsely ascribed to him.[159] Both *literati* and lawyers liked to refer to this maxim, apply it, expound it, and thereby ethicize the idea of *patria* after the model of the suicidal pagan.

With patriotic ethics, of course, Roman Law abounded. The lawyers could not fail to come across that passage in the *Institutes* where it is stated that those who "fell [in battle] for the *respublica* are understood to live forever *per gloriam*," and to gloss on this passage in which eternal fame or glory so conspicuously takes the place of eternal beatitude or is paired with it. Nor could they fail to come across that law in the *Digest*, formulated by a Roman jurisprudent of the times of Hadrian, which said that for the sake of the *patria* a son might kill his father, and a father his son.[160] The mediaeval jurists, when interpreting this law, pointed out that an action normally considered parricide was a praiseworthy deed when committed in the name of *patria*, though only when committed in self-defense.[161] They did not revel in the idea of patriotic massacre as occasionally humanists did—for example Coluccio Salutati, who exclaimed:

Thou knowest not how sweet is the *amor patriae*: if such would be expedient for the fatherland's protection or enlargement [*sic!*], it would seem neither burdensome and difficult nor a crime to thrust the axe into one's father's head, to crush one's brothers, to deliver from the womb of one's wife the premature child with the sword.[162]

---

158 *De monarchia*, II,5,15, and the important study on that chapter by Silverstein (above, n.151).

159 W. J. Chase, *The Distichs of Cato* (Madison, 1922), 12; and for the whole problem, of course, Post's note on *Pugna pro patria* ("Two Notes," 281ff).

160 *Inst.*1,25,prol.; *D.*11,7,35; cf. Post, *op.cit.*, 287.

161 See, for Accursius' gloss on that law, Post, 287,n.25, and, for the canonists, 283,n.10. See also below, nos.163 and 178, for Lucas de Penna and Nogaret. The argument, of course, was repeated over and over again. See, e.g., Durandus, *Speculum iuris*, IV, part. iii, §2, n.32 (Venice, 1602), III,321: "Nam pro defensione patriae licitum est patrem interficere."

162 Salutati, *Ep.*, I,10, ed. F. Novati, *Epistolario di Coluccio Salutati* (Rome, 1891), I,28,22ff: ". . . ignoras quam sit dulcis amor patriae: si pro illa tutanda augendave

This type of scholarly blood-lust and overheated desk patriotism was, on the whole, not to the taste of the more soberly thinking jurists, who would have contradicted Salutati on almost every point.[163] However, horrors justified by the names of God or *patria* are as old as they are new. Baldus could maintain that a soldier killing an enemy for the sake of the *patria* performed no less than an *opus divinum*, bringing a sacrifice to the Creator. And this was done in the name of *caritas*—no longer, to be sure, the evangelical virtue of Charity as an expression of active brotherly love, but its secularized counterpart: a *publica caritas*, as Baldus called it, for the protection of the *naturalis patria*.[164]

Secularization had other facets as well. It is true, crusaders fighting for the Holy Land and warriors fighting *pro patria* were on equal terms; but the standards of the Holy Land were transferable to secular kingdoms only to a limited extent. Other standards were provided by Rome; for what held good for Rome, the capital of the world, was to hold good also for the budding national monarchies: Roman imperial ideologies were transferred, and became applicable, to the kingdoms of France and Sicily, England and Spain.

The *Digest* distinguished between two *patriae*: a man's individual city in which he lived—*patria sua* or *propria*—and the City of Rome, the *communis patria*. That is to say, every individual had his own local fatherland, but all subjects of the empire recog-

---

expediret, non videretur molestum nec grave vel facinus paterno capiti securim iniicere, fratres obterere, per uxoris uterum ferro abortum educere." Cf. A. von Martin, *Coluccio Salutati und das humanistische Lebensideal* (Leipzig and Berlin, 1916), 126, who claims that those pagan (?) views were corrected by Salutati in his later years.

163 There is no dissent among the jurists that war may not be waged *pro patria augenda*; cf. Kuttner, *Schuldlehre*, 255; also above, p. 243, for Henry of Ghent; Post, 282,n.9. Lucas de Penna, on *C*.10,31[32],35,n.2 (Lyon, 1582), p.162, has a remark concerning a warrior's wife: "Et pro patria filius in patrem, et pater in filium, ac vir in uxorem insurgere debent." His allegations are *D*.11,7,35, and a decretal of Celestine III (c.1 X 3,33, ed. Friedberg, 11,587), which of course are perfectly sober and lack any similarity to Salutati's theory.

164 Baldus, *Consilia*, 111,264,n.1, fol.74ᵛ: "Qui fervore *publicae charitati*[s] pro tutela naturalis patriae accensus cruentissimum eiusdem patriae hostem occidit, non dicitur fratricida, sed pugnans pro patria nuncupatur opus divinum faciens plenum laudis, si quidem convenit hostiles beluas mactare, et fit sacrificium creatori. . . ." Andreas of Isernia, on *Feud*. 11,24,n.7 ("Quae sit prima causa"), fol.126r-ᵛ, has a full discussion (too long to be quoted here) on *publica charitas*, spiced with Stoic quotations, esp. Seneca.

nized Rome as their "common fatherland."[165] The notion of Rome
as the *communis patria* changed its meaning rapidly. The Canonist
of the early thirteenth century may have thought of the Rome of
the Apostles as the *communis patria*, or of the Church as the
virtual embodiment of the *imperium Romanum*, or of neither,
when he contradicted the *Digest*: "Today that is not so, for not
all are under the emperor, but under the Church."[166] The legists
used the cypher of Rome as the *communis patria* for other purposes: they transferred it to the individual monarchies. That the
capital city, for example, Paris, could be equated with the *communis patria* because Paris—France's Rome, as it were, just as
Avignon became the Church's Rome—was "the more common and
excellent city of the kingdom of France," was only one aspect of
that development.[167] It was of far greater momentum that the city
concept of *patria* now yielded to a kingdom or monarchy concept
of *patria*. The kingdom of France itself, the territorial monarchy
as represented by the king or Crown, took the place of Rome when
contrasted with a man's local *patria*: now France became the
communis patria of all Frenchmen. "Just as Rome is the *communis
patria*, so is the Crown of the realm the *communis patria*," wrote
a French jurist around 1270, when summing up the opinions of
the *doctores legum*. The idea of Rome's sovereignty passed on to
the national monarchies and with it the idea of loyalty to Rome
and to the universal empire.[168] In other words, the loyalty to the
new limited territorial *patria*, the common fatherland of all subjects of the Crown, replaced the supra-national bonds of a fictitious
universal Empire. In agreement with Law, one admitted that a
just war could be declared and waged only by the Prince, but

---

[165] *D*.48,22,7,15; cf. Post, *op.cit.*, 286,n.22. See *D*.50,1,33, and Post, 291, n.45, for
Rome as *communis nostra patria* (see above, n.126, for Plutarch's related expression).
For the origins of that concept (Cicero, *De lege agraria*, 2, 86), see Tierney, *Conciliar
Theory*, 140,n.1.

[166] See the Decretist who composed the *Apparatus* "Ecce vicit leo" (1202-1210),
quoted by Post, 301,n.22: "Odie tamen non fit, quia non sunt omnes sub imperatore,
sed ecclesia. . . ."

[167] See Post, 291, nos.45,46, and 293,n.54, quoting Pierre de Belleperche. The same
was true with regard to Avignon. See Baldus, on *D*.5,1,2,3,n.1, fol.258ᵛ (Rome is
where pope or emperor reside; above, n.35): ". . . tamen ibi [Rome] non possunt
conveniri legati . . . et hoc est notandum pro clericis, quia vadunt Avinionem, an
possint ibi conveniri, quia non habent alium iudicem quam Papam . . ."

[168] Post, 290, quoting Jacques de Révigny (n.44): ". . . quia Roma est communis
patria, sic corona regni est communis patria, quia caput." See above, n.35.

added "unless it be so that the *patria* has no superior,"[169] and from the premise or fact that "today the empire is in pieces," one concluded that every Prince *est in patria sua imperator*.[170] It is evident that the equation of Rome as *communis patria* with the national kingdom as *communis patria* falls in with the general trends of that age—with the new theories concerning kings not recognizing a superior and kings being emperors in their realms.[171] And to this cluster of ideas there belongs also the code of patriotic ethics which then was built up and remained conventional until the present: "Justice it is to defend the *patria* and the brothers,"[172] for the cause of the fatherland would always be the just cause; "virtue demands to live for the *patria* and procreate children for the *patria*";[173] or "we must love the Prince and the *respublica* more than our father,"[174] and similar maxims.

It would be wrong to overhear in this symphony of theology, scholastic philosophy, and law the voice of humanism, or to underestimate the influence of classical literature on the development of Western *patria* ideologies. Nothing would be easier than to extract many relevant passages from the writings of Petrarch, Boccaccio, Salutati, Bruni, and others, and to show how the secularized Christian notions of *martyr* and *caritas* henceforth were sided by the classical notions of *heros* and *amor (patriae)*. But it would be superfluous to spread out more material here just to prove what is self-evident: that humanism had some easily recognizable effects on the cult of *patria* and on national self-glorification, and that the final heroization of the warrior who died for the fatherland was an achievement of the humanists. There is no doubt but that the Roman *amor patriae*—resuscitated, cultivated,

---

169 See Heydte, *Geburtsstunde des souveränen Staates*, 73, who quotes "Ulrich von Strassburg, *Summa theologiae*, VI,3, Cod.Vat.lat."

170 See Philip of Leyden, *De cura reipublicae*, Tabula tract., rubr. VII,105, ed. Fruin and Molhuysen, p.421: "Quomodo intelligitur 'scissum est imperium hodie' et 'quilibet est in patria sua imperator'?" The summary refers to *Casus* IX,28 (p.54), where, however, the word *patria* is not repeated.

171 This, of course, did not escape Post, 292f, whose second note (296ff) deals with the "Rex imperator" theory in particular.

172 Lucas de Penna, on C.10,70,4,n.7, p.345: "Idem iustitia est patriam et socios defendere."

173 Lucas de Penna, on C.10,31[32],35,n.2, p.162: "Pertinet autem ad virtutis officium, et vivere patriae et propter patriam filios procreare."

174 Andreas of Isernia, on *Feud.*II,24 ("Quae sit prima causa"), n.21, fol.131: "Ante omnia, principem et rempublicam plus quam patrem diligere debemus."

and glorified so passionately by the humanists—has moulded the modern secular mind.[175]

The humanistic influence, however, became effective only after, and not before, the idea of *patria* had taken shape and had been ethicized by both theology and jurisprudence. The original quasi-religious aspect of death *pro patria* as a "martyrdom" clearly derived from the teaching of the Church, from the adaptation of ecclesiastical forms to the secular bodies politic. This source was tapped persistently, especially in France where the leading politicians began to deploy the forces of religious sentiment systematically and make them subservient to the undisguised political goals of the new *corpus mysticum*, the national territorial monarchy. It is of great interest to note how unimportant and almost absent (if we except Roman Law and Aristotle) was the humanistic influence during the first great outbreak of a compact patriotism which followed in the wake of the "crusades" launched by King Philip IV against Pope Boniface VIII and the Knights Templar.

This struggle shows, for the first time, the new patriotism at work. All the—more or less casual—arguments which theologians and jurists had previously put forth to justify on religious and legal grounds the devotion to and death for any *patria*, were on this occasion, so to speak, drawn together and summed up and placed as a coherent system and consistent ideology in the service of a clearly defined *patria*: the national monarchy of France. It is not intended here to rehash well known details of a well known process. An interesting document, however, which came to light only in recent years, may demonstrate how the currents coming from many wells could flow together, and may illustrate at the same time some new factors relevant to the present investigation.

PATRIOTIC PROPAGANDA

In 1302, after the bull *Unam Sanctam* had been hurled against the secular governments at large, and against France in particular, after Philip IV had summoned the first Parliament of the three estates of France to bolster his position against the pope by a public manifestation from the whole kingdom, and after the king,

---

[175] See Jacobs, "Vaterlandsgedanken" (above, n.124); for Petrarch, H. W. Eppelsheimer, *Petrarca* (Bonn, 1926), 137ff, 203ff; for Salutati, above, n.162.

in his disastrous campaign against the craftsmen and peasants of Flanders, had suffered the terrific defeat at Courtrai (July 11, 1302), an unknown French cleric delivered a sermon on the departure to war of a royal army. The sermon may have been designed to intensify the political propaganda which the king was then releasing. Philip ordered prayers throughout the country; he made, in a somewhat modern fashion, a general appeal to the *amor patriae* of all his subjects; he raised new funds for the continuation of the war, and asked subventions from all, including the clergy, "for the defense of the native fatherland."[176] That the term *patria* then did not mean the native hamlet, village, or province, but meant the whole kingdom of France, is not only implied, but this time also stated *expressis verbis* by one of the outstanding legal councilors of the Crown, William of Nogaret. He repeatedly declared that he, Nogaret, like everyone else, was ready to defend, together with the Catholic faith and unity of the Church, "his king and his fatherland, the realm of France," and that he himself as a knight was willing to die to defend *patriam meam regnum Franciae*,[177] explaining on one occasion—like other jurists—that in defense of the fatherland it was a merit rather than a crime if a man killed his own father.[178] Without going to these extremes,

176 Dom Jean Leclercq, "Un sermon prononcé pendant la guerre de Flandre sous Philippe le Bel," *Revue du moyen âge latin*, I (1945), 165-172. The sermon, as noticed by Leclercq, 165, n.2, also 176, n.8, is closely related to sermons of William of Sauqueville (see Kämpf and Miss Coester; above, nos.135, 138). It should be compared, however, also with ideas of the official propaganda and of speeches made by Nogaret and other legists. For the French propaganda action, see Leclercq, 166,n.6; also above, n.128.

177 The phrase turns up time and again in Nogaret's "self-defenses" in matters concerning the attempt on Boniface VIII at Anagni, and in his protests against that pope. See, e.g., Robert Holtzmann, *Wilhelm von Nogaret* (Freiburg, 1898), 268 (Beilage IX,3): ". . . uror et estuor in immensum etenim pro fidei catholice defensione, pro sancte matris ecclesie unitate servanda scismatisque vitando periculo . . . , nihilominus pro defensione domini mei regis ac patrie, regni Francorum." See also Nogaret's plea to Benedict XI in 1303 (next note); further, Dupuy, *Histoire du différend*, 310, §25 ("pro defensione quoque salutis dicti domini mei patriaeque meae, regni Franciae"); similarly p.312, §37, and 585, where Pope Clement V quotes these words (". . . dictus Guillelmus de debito fidelitatis erat astrictus dominum suum Regem praedictum defendere . . . nec non et patriam suam regni Franciae"). See also Strayer, "Defense," 294, n.6 (I am indebted to Professor Strayer for additional information).

178 Dupuy, *Histoire du différend*, 309, §20 (Nogaret's plea to Benedict XI): "Item cum quisque teneatur patriam suam defendere, pro qua defensione si patrem occidat, meritum habet nec poenam mereretur [see above, nos.16off], nedum mihi licebat, sed necessitas incumbebat patriam meam, regnum Franciae . . . defendere et pro ipsa defensione exponere vitam meam."

the French bishops, following the doctrines of the canonists, were nevertheless bound to admit in a letter to the Holy See that the ecclesiastical privileges and immunities had to be suspended when all the forces of France were mobilized *ad defensionem regni et patriae*.[179] Actually another great French jurist, William Durandus, Bishop of Mende, had discussed in his *Speculum iuris*, some twenty years earlier, the extraordinary steps a king was entitled to take *pro defensione patriae et coronae*—a not uncommon juxtaposition of "fatherland" and "Crown" which naturally made *patria* synonymous with the whole kingdom or body politic over which the "Crown" or its bearer ruled.[180]

Within this general propaganda action—uniting the king, the legists and the reluctant bishops—the sermon of the unknown French cleric of 1302 has its place.[181] He preached on I Maccabees 3: 19-22:

> *They* march against us in the plenty of pride and lawlessness. . . . *We*, however, will fight for our souls and laws; and the Lord himself will crush them before our faces.

It was a suitable text for a patriotic proclamation and it had been selected by others before, a text which would lend itself probably in any century as an ideal motto for justifying any war in a self-righteous fashion.[182]

[179] Dupuy, *Histoire du différend*, 26, the letter of the Archbishop of Reims to Boniface VIII (1297), which begins: "In hac terrestri patria Ecclesiam militantem constituens providentia conditoris . . ." Thereafter the writer turns to the narrower secular *patria*, the Kingdom of France, where the king and magnates "cum omnes tum singulos incolas dicti regni ad defensionem regni et patriae . . . vocare praetendunt." Cf. Wieruszowski, *Vom Imperium*, 173; and, for the canonists on taxation of the clergy in a case of necessity, Post, 284f, nos.16-18.

[180] See Durandus, *Speculum iuris*, IV,part.iii,§2,n.31 (above, n.161): In the case of war with a foreign power, the allegiance to one's own king precedes that to a baron, "nam vocati sunt [tenentes] ad maius tribunal . . . Et hoc verum est. nam Rex, qui habet administrationem regni, vocat eos pro communi bono, scilicet pro defensione patriae et coronae. unde sibi iure gentium obedire tenentur . . ." Hartung, "Die Krone," 21,n.2, hesitated to accept this quotation which Perrot, *Institutions publiques*, 400f, had cited without locating it. Phrases such as *pro corona regni defendenda*, however, were anything but rare in that period; see, for an example of 1197, Strayer, "Defense," 292,n.4; also my article "*Pro patria mori*," 483,n.40; and above, n.168.

[181] See Leclercq, "Sermon," 166.

[182] Leclercq, "Sermon," 169,12-26. Henry of Ghent (above, n.155), *Quodlibeta*, xv,qu.16,fol.595 (last line), regrets that the Acconites did not resist the infidel by placing their confidence in I Macc. 3: 19f; he adds that, had they confided in those words, they might have thought also of Psalm 115: 15: "Pretiosa in conspectu domini mors sanctorum eius." In other words, the Acconites, if killed, would have become martyrs and saints.

To prove the righteousness of the French and the just cause they were fighting for, the preacher started by exalting the saintly character of the *nobiles et sancti reges Francorum*. The French kings, said he, were saints (1) for the perfect purity of the blood royal which was holy because purity itself was a kind of holiness (*puritas quae est sanctitas quaedam*), (2) for their protection of holiness with regard to the Church, (3) for their spreading of holiness by siring new saints, that is, holy kings, and (4) for their working of miracles. These arguments were current and ever repeated in the years of nascent dynasticism in France when the king's *sancti praedecessores* were invoked with the same ease with which in the Hohenstaufen circles the emperor's *divi praedecessores* were remembered.[183] That the French *reges christianissimi* were the hereditary special protectors of the Church was an ancient claim which, for obvious reasons, had to be reiterated in a campaign pretending to protect the Church and the true faith against the pope. The royal miracle of healing scrofula, the "king's evil," was a popular topic of preachers and orators to prove the French king's general superiority over other kings and his spiritual sovereignty within his realm.[184] Only the claim saying that the

[183] See, e.g., for the answer of the masters of theology at the University of Paris (March 25, 1308), Georges Lizerand, *Le dossier de l'affaire des Templiers* (Paris, 1923), 62: ". . . vos sanctorum predecessorum vestrorum mores laudabiles imitantes." Cf. Jean de Paris, *De potestate regia et papali*, c.xxi, ed. Leclercq, 246,22: "Tenuerunt . . . regnum Franciae reges sancti." The sermons of William of Sauqueville (above, n.138) are full of those ideas. See also Schramm, *Frankreich*, I,228; Bloch, *Rois thaumaturges*, 244,n.1, and passim; Kämpf, *Pierre Dubois*, 59; Wieruszowski, *Vom Imperium*, 145ff. The dynastic intention of the preacher is obvious when he says (Leclercq, 169, 15): "aliis enim sanguinibus foedatis per spurios et spurias, sanguis regum Franciae purissimus remanet, cum a Priamo primo eorum rege usque ad istum, reges scilicet XLVIII, nunquam spurius est exortus." For the *divus* titles of the Hohenstaufen, see *Erg.Bd.*, 222f. To be sure, the *sanctus* titles, including *sanctus Fridericus*, are not missing in the Hohenstaufen surroundings; cf. *Erg.Bd.*, 209; also Nicholas of Bari, in his encomium for Frederick II, ed. Kloos, in DA, XI (1954), 169ff, uses almost exclusively saintly metaphors ("Hec est virga de radice Iesse, id est de avo flos") and apostrophes ("Ave, domine imperator, gracia Dei plene, dominus tecum"). Vice versa, the expression *divina et regia domus Franciae* is found also, at least in Italy; see, e.g., Luigi Colini-Baldeschi, "Rolandino Passagerii e Niccolò III," *Studi e memorie per la storia dell'Università di Bologna*, VIII (1924), 181f, referring to A.D. 1277.

[184] Leclercq, "Sermon," 169,24: "Quarto sanctitatem declarant, cum hi soli reges vivi miracula operentur et ab illa infirmitate curent." Concerning the miracle of healing and the French political propaganda under Philip IV, see Bloch, *Rois thaumaturges*, 110, n.1, for Nogaret and Plaisians; 116, n.3, for the royal surgeon Henry of Mondeville (comparison of Christ the Surgeon with the French king); 129f, n.1, for the *Quaestio in utramque partem* (containing also a comparison with

sancti reges Francorum also "begot holy kings" seems to carry slightly further than usual some essentially familiar ideas of that age; it may have been inspired by Vergil, who called the young Trojan Ascanius, Aeneas' son, a "son of gods and sire of gods to be"—a verse which had been effective in Antiquity and which now was applied, not unsuitably, to the French dynasts who, according to popular sagas, could claim Trojan origin and trace their descent from King Priam.[185]

From the holiness of the dynasty the preacher could easily make the deduction *a fortiori* that the cause of "holy kings" could not be but the cause of Justice herself. Naturally, the Flemings were fighting for an unjust cause, since the French were fighting for the just one—*cum autem nos bellemus pro iustitia, illi pro iniustitia.* The wicked Flemings were almost to be congratulated, though, because through a war carried against them by a king who was a saint, they had a fair chance to be, as it were, "liberated" from their injustice. Better to be conquered by the holy king of France than by some wicked philosophy of life or by Evil itself— an idea, reflecting the doctrines of scholastic philosophy, which conveniently put the Flemings in the position of political and moral "infidels" and made the war a crusade for justice.[186]

Moreover, the preacher asserted that the king's peace—the necessary corollary of the King's justice—was the peace not only of the kingdom of France but also of the Church and of Learning, Virtue, Justice, and that the peace of the realm would permit the concentration of forces for the sake of the Holy Land. To

---

Christ. Plaisians has been suggested as author of this tractate; in fact, the words *aperta miracula* of the *Quaestio* are found also in the *Memorandum* of Plaisians); 130, for the historians; 131, for William of Sauqueville. See also Kämpf, *Pierre Dubois,* 34,38,98.

[185] Leclercq, "Sermon," 169,21: ". . . sanctitatem generant, cum generent sanctos reges." See Vergil, *Aeneis,* IX,642: "dis genite et geniture deos." See also Seneca, *Consolatio ad Marcum,* XV,1: "Caesares qui dis geniti deosque genituri dicuntur"; and the inscription *CIL,* III, 710 (Diocletian and Maximian): "diis geniti et deorum creatores." See Alföldi, "Insignien," 84,n.2, for additional places. The preacher himself had previously referred to the French kings' descent from Priam (above, n.183), which makes the adaptation of the Vergil line not unlikely; see, for the French Trojan legend, Leclercq, "Sermon," 167,n.12; also 170,91-102.

[186] Leclercq, "Sermon," 170,78ff, and 172,163ff: "Summa enim victoria est ut, vitiis debellatis, secundum rationem homo vivat, quia si ipsi [Flamengi] volunt ab injustitia vinci, orabimus ut a potestate et exercitu regio devincantur. Melius est enim eis a rege vinci quam a malo et in injustitia perdurare." For the underlying scholastic doctrine, see Harry Gmür, *Thomas von Aquino und der Krieg* (Leipzig and Berlin, 1933), 7f and 46.

stress the cultural and educational mission of France had become a fad, at once aggressive and politically important, in an age in which France was generally, even by foreigners, given credit for having almost monopolized the *studium*, just as Italy harbored the *sacerdotium* and Germany the *imperium*.[187] Also, to make the plight of the Holy Land a lever for foreign and home policy was a stratagem used incessantly by France in the second half of the thirteenth century, and by others as well.[188] Finally, the oneness of French issues and Church issues, always strongly emphasized, was a most effective means of political propaganda in the days of Philip the Fair: *Pax regis, pax vestra; salus regis, salus vestra*[189] was the key-note for nationalizing the clergy and gallicanizing the Church of France. Hence, it was not difficult for the preacher to draw his conclusion straightforwardly:

> He that carries war against the king [of France], works against the whole Church, against the Catholic doctrine, against Holiness and Justice, and against the Holy Land.[190]

[187] Leclercq, "Sermon," 170,63ff: "Pax regis est pax regni; pax regni est pax ecclesiae, scientiae, virtutis et iustitiae, et est acquisitio Terrae Sanctae." For the *translatio studii* from Athens and Rome to Paris, see the interesting study by Herbert Grundmann, "Sacerdotium-Regnum-Studium," *Archiv für Kulturgeschichte*, XXXIV (1951), 5-22, who, without exhausting the subject, analyses the trichotomy upon which the tractates of Alexander of Roes hinge; see, above all, *Notitia seculi*, c.12 ("sacerdotium, regnum et studium una esset ecclesia"), ed. Grundmann and Heimpel, 84; also *Memoriale*, c.25, p.48: ". . . ut sicut Romani tamquam seniores sacerdotio, sic Germani vel Franci tamquam iuniores imperio, et ita Francigene vel Gallici tamquam perspicatiores scientiarum studio ditarentur," whereby the triad *seniores-iuniores-perspicatiores* represents not the author's independent phrasing, but a formula going back to Priscian, *Institutiones grammaticae*, 1,1 ("grammatica ars . . . cuius auctores, quanto sunt iuniores, tanto perspicaciores"). Alexander of Roes thus falls in with the catchword of the idea of progress in the 12th and 13th centuries. For the *studium* in French political propaganda, see also Scholz, *Publizistik*, 427ff; Kern, *Ausdehnungspolitik*, 51ff; Kämpf, *Pierre Dubois*, 97ff.

[188] It is sufficient here to recall the connections between the crusading idea and the various efforts to secure the imperial crown for the French dynasty; see, e.g., the *Memorandum* of Charles of Anjou (1273), inserted in a relation of French ambassadors to the Holy See, in *MGH, Const.*, III, No.618, pp.587f; or the *Memoriale* of Pierre Dubois (1308), *ibid.*, IV, No.245, pp.208ff, where, closely akin to his suggestions in the *De recuperatione terre sancte* (ed. Ch.-V. Langlois [Collection des textes, IX], Paris, 1891), the crusade serves as a pretext for developing a full program for French world conquest.

[189] *Disputatio inter clericum et militem*, in: Melchior Goldast, *Monarchia Romani imperii* (Hannover, 1611-13), 1,16, quoted by Baethgen, in: *ZfRG, kan.Abt.*, XXIV (1935), 380 (review of Wieruszowski, *Vom Imperium*). See above, n.187, for a similar remark in Leclercq, "Sermon," 170,63ff.

[190] Leclercq, "Sermon," 170,65ff: "Igitur qui contra regem invehitur, laborat contra totam ecclesiam, contra doctrinam catholicam, contra sanctitatem et iustitiam et Terram Sanctam."

Here a general equation of anything with everything has been achieved: war for the king, war for France, war for justice, war for culture and education, war for the Church, war for the Christian faith—all these were interrelated, interdependent arguments placed on the same general denominator. We can hardly be surprised when we find another preacher of those years proclaiming that "properly speaking, no kingdom should be called *regnum Franciae* except the Kingdom of Christ and the blessed," thus projecting the holy realm of this world into the other world as the model of the *regnum coelorum*.[191] Already we seem to hear the iron-clad maid of Domremy saying: "Those who wage war against the holy realm of France, wage war against King Jesus."[192]

Even that bulky freight of moral-political ideas interspersed with religious values was not beyond enlargement, for the preacher was capable of integrating yet another argument. As might be expected he demanded from his compatriots readiness to suffer death, if necessary, for the holy king of France. He demanded such willingness not on the grounds of the old feudal ties between lord and vassal, but on the grounds of "natural reason" and of the organological concept of the state.[193] Natural reason, argued the preacher,

[191] See the sermon of William of Sauqueville on the text *Et erunt signa in sole et luna* (Luke 21: 25), in which he compares the two banners of the king of France—the lilies and the red oriflamme—with the two *adventus* of Christ, that is, the Incarnation and the Second Coming: "Proprie loquendo nullum regnum debet vocari regnum Francie nisi solum regnum Christi et beatorum: *Sola illa que sursum est, Jerusalem libera est* (Gal. 4: 26). Omne regnum mundanum est regnum servorum. Merito summus pontifex maior in regno mundo vocat se servum servorum Dei. Modo rex Francorum Christus in duplo adventu suo usus est et utetur duplici vexillo. Vexillum enim adventus Christi fuit depictum cum floribus liliorum. Signum enim adventus sui primi fuit flos vel lilium virginitatis. . . . Set vexillum adventus secundi, quando veniet contra adversarios ad peccatores debellandum, erit totum coloris sanguinei. . . . Primum vexillum non indicabit furorem sed pacem et mansuetudinem regis [Francie]. . . . Sed secundum vexillum sanguineum ab eo indicabit furorem regium, quod non erit ita audax, qui non tremat totus." See Coester, *Königskult in Frankreich* (above, n.138), p.viii; Bibl.Nat.MS lat.16495, fol.99ᵛ.

[192] "Tous ceulx qui guerroient au dit saint royaume de France guerroient contre le roy Jhesus. . . ." Cf. Jules Quicherat, *Procès de condamnation et de réhabilitation de Jeanne d'Arc* (Paris, 1841-49), v,126.

[193] The *ratio naturalis* pervades all the documents of that period; see, e.g., Wieruszowski, *Vom Imperium*, 173, n.107, 186, n.146; 198, n.183, quoting places such as Philip's decree of embargo on money, weapons, horses, etc. (1296), which the king introduced because *naturalis ratio suggerit et aequitas persuadet* (Dupuy, *Histoire du différend*, 13); or Nogaret's self-defense of 1304 in which he asserts (*ibid.*, 243f) that every Christian, even a private person, should be held, by the authority of divine and human Laws, to resist failings of the spiritual and secular powers: *et si nulla lex hoc exprimeret, satis hoc ratio naturalis ostendit.* Passages

dictates that all limbs of the body not only be directed by the head and serve it, but also be willing to expose themselves for the head. The head of the realm is the king. Therefore, any part of the realm that assails the king, assails the head and ventures to destroy the whole body and finally himself.[194] To fight for the body politic of France meant, at the same time, to fight for the cause of justice as represented by the holy king. Consequently, to those killed on the battlefield for that just cause, spiritual rewards were promised such as would be granted to the crusader.

> Since the most noble kind of death is the agony for justice, there is no doubt but that those who die for the justice of the king and of the kingdom [of France] shall be crowned by God as martyrs.[195]

In other words, death on the battlefield for the political *corpus mysticum* headed by a king who was a saint and therefore a champion of Justice, became officially "martyrdom." It equaled the self-sacrifice of the canonized martyrs for the *corpus mysticum* of the Church, the head of which was Christ. The "agony for justice," exemplified by Christ, was the price paid for the national martyr's

---

such as these could be multiplied on end. This *ratio naturalis* is related to, though not quite identical with, the *ratio prepotens* (above, Ch.iv,n.54) of Frederick II; the latter derived from Roman Law and was almost a personification, whereas the former betrays the influence of scholastic and Aristotelian thought.

[194] Leclercq, "Sermon," 169,52ff: "Hoc dictat ratio naturalis, cum dictat quod omnia membra dirigantur a capite, subserviant capiti et pro capite se exponant, et ideo membrum quod contra caput inveheretur, niteretur totum corpus destruere et per consequens seipsum. Caput autem regni rex est, et ideo quaecumque pars regni contra regem invehitur, merito est punienda." The argument of self-destruction is frequently found in that connection; see Dupuy, *Histoire du différend*, 21f (below, n.200); Dubois, *Summa*, ed. Kämpf, 53,29 (Kämpf, *Pierre Dubois*, 72,n.16): "Qui contra rempublicam vadit, se ipsum impugnat." Vice versa, it could be said that "qui se ipsum impugnat, contra rempublicam vadit," that is, with regard to suicide which was treason.

[195] Leclercq, "Sermon," 170,87ff: "Cum enim nobilissimum moriendi genus sit agonizare pro iustitia (Ecclus. 4: 33), non dubium quin isti qui pro iustitia regis et regni moriuntur, a Deo ut martyres coronentur." See Nogaret's self-defense of 1304 (Dupuy, *Histoire du différend*, 250, §60): ". . . concludit dictus Guillielmus se in praemissis bono zelo Dei et fidei ac defensionis Ecclesiae sanctae Dei, et specialiter sui domini Regis et regni Franciae . . . ac legitime processisse, agonizando pro iustitia, pro Romana Ecclesia, pro Republica . . . ac pro sua patria dicti regni ac pro suo domino Rege Franciae. . . ." The enumeration of faith, Church, justice, realm, fatherland, king is common to both the Sermon and Nogaret's self-defense; the phrase *agonizare pro iustitia*, though going back to Ecclus. 4: 33, is very specific. The verb itself means "to struggle" or "fight," mainly, however (according to Du Cange, *Glossarium*, s.v. *agonizare*), in a religious sense; that is, "to suffer agony," especially with regard to Christ and the martyrs. The notion has been transferred here to the *patria*.

crown and palm branch, even though "justice" meant, purely and simply, anything that was expedient, according to natural reason, for the body politic of France and its head, the holy king. In the garb of justice the idea of "reason of state" began to betray itself.[196]

In all this, as throughout his sermon, the preacher echoed only thoughts which others, too, had expressed, including the king and his councillors. *Quisque teneatur patriam suam defendere*, "Everyone shall be held to defend his fatherland," declared William of Nogaret,[197] a statement which certainly agreed with legal opinion and with the customs of France around 1300. Ever since the battle of Bouvines in 1214, the armed contingents of citizens formed part of the royal armies. In addition to the third estate, however, the clergy too ranged as "limbs" of the national body politic of France, and like ordinary citizens they had to contribute at least financially to the burden of defending the French *patria* and with it the Gallican *corpus mysticum*.[198] Philip himself threatened to confiscate, in 1302, the possessions of those refusing to observe the king's orders of embargo and thus to contribute to the defense of the realm, because those "deserters of the fatherland's defense" were not worthy to enjoy proceeds and returns resulting from the efforts of all and from the burdens shouldered by others.[199] The organic-corporational concept, looming in back of King Philip's decree, was actually asserted with greatest precision in a pamphlet of 1296, pretending to be an answer to a papal letter in connection with the taxation of the clergy. The pamphlet itself was appar-

---

[196] That the expression *ratio status*, which Henry of Ghent uses on one occasion, may be understood as "an anticipation of 'reason of state,'" has been pointed out by Post, "Statute of York," 421,n.16, who adds, however, that *status* meant the common welfare, and not the personified state.

[197] Above, n.178.

[198] Above, n.179.

[199] See the king's decree of embargo of 1302 (Dupuy, *Histoire du différend*, 87): ". . . dignum est enim et competens, ut defensionis patriae desertores bonorum habitatione priventur et excludantur a fructu, qui onera recusant debita supportare, et nihilominus transgressor huius extra gratiam nostram positus, et indignationem illa prorsus se nostrum et regni noverit inimicum." Those exporting money, weapons, horses, etc. thus forfeited their possessions and were threatened with the "king's indignation" and loss of the "king's grace." For the interesting history of those sanctions, which, by that time, had completely eclipsed the spiritual sanctions, whereas the imperialized papacy of the eleventh century introduced the notion of *indignatio papae*, see Rudolf Köstler, *Huldentzug als Strafe* (Kirchenrechtliche Abhandlungen, LXII; Stuttgart, 1910); also Joachim Studtmann, "Die Pönformel der mittelalterlichen Urkunden," *AUF*, XII (1932), 302,320f,324ff, and passim.

ently composed by one of the royal legists, probably Peter Flotte, who bluntly declared:

> Depraved is the part that does not conform with its whole, and useless and quasi paralytic a limb that refuses to support its own body; layman or cleric, nobleman or man of low birth, whoever refuses to come to the support of his head and his body, that is, the lord king and the kingdom [of France], and lastly of himself, proves to be a non-conforming part and a useless and quasi paralytic limb.[200]

The royal legist thus stigmatized "non-conformance with the body politic of France" as an offense almost of *laesa maiestas* of which, according to this interpretation, the Roman Pontiff had tried to make the Gallican clergy guilty. To parry those efforts, the French jurist drastically called upon the organic nature of the French kingdom. The Gallican clergy, which together with the French laity formed the "Gallican Church," was exhibited as an integral part of the body of *patria*—limbs of the French body politic, no matter what in other respects the clerics' place may have been within the mystical body of the universal Church. By thus levelling the Gallican clerics to the status of French nationals the author succeeded in transcending, at least politically, the dualism of clergy and laity, not by the *corpus mysticum* of the Church, but by the mystical *corpus politicum* of the French *patria*.[201] The *corpus mysticum patriae* was set over against the *corpus mysticum ecclesiae*.[202]

200 See the pamphlet *Antequam essent clerici* (Dupuy, *Histoire du différend*, 21f): "Et quia turpis est pars, quae suo non congruit universo, et membrum inutile et quasi paralyticum, quod corpori suo subsidium ferre recusat, quicumque, sive clerici sive laici sive nobiles sive ignobiles, qui capiti suo vel corpori, hoc est domino regi et regno, imo etiam sibimet auxilium ferre recusant, semetipsos partes incongruas et membra inutilia et quasi paralytica esse demonstrant. Unde si a talibus pro rata sua subventionum auxilia requiruntur, non exactiones vel extorsiones vel gravamina dici debent, sed potius capiti et corpori et membris debita subsidia." See above, n.194.

201 See, for *Antequam essent clerici*, Scholz, *Publizistik*, 359ff; also, Wieruszowski, *Vom Imperium*, 183f, who rightly emphasizes that the author of the pamphlet energetically brushed aside the curial doctrine that tried to identify the Church body with the hierarchy ("non solum est ex clericis, sed etiam ex laicis"). See also Kurt Schleyer, *Anfänge des Gallikanismus im 13. Jahrhundert* (Historische Studien, 314; Berlin, 1937), 91f.

202 The ecclesiastical *corpus mysticum* doctrine was quoted very often by the French legists to demonstrate that the *ecclesia Gallicana* was one of the most important members of that body; see, e.g., Dupuy, *Histoire du différend*, 243f, 585f, and passim. On the other hand, the assaults of Pope Boniface VIII were often rejected with an organological argument ("qui tangit aurem hominis, totum hominem tetigisse videtur"); cf. Dupuy, *Histoire du différend*, 309, §19, Nogaret's plea

REX ET PATRIA

William of Nogaret asserted more than once that he was ready to die *pro rege et patria*. He was, on one occasion, even more specific when he said that "by his oath of fealty he was astricted to defend his Lord the King . . . as well as his *patria*, the kingdom of France."[203] What Nogaret meant is obvious: as a *miles*, a knight, he was bound to defend his feudal lord, and as a member of the body politic of France he, like every other Frenchman, was obliged to defend this very body, the *patria*. That being a Christian he was held also to defend the Church was repeated by Nogaret over and over again; but this point is less relevant here. The formula *pro rege et patria*, "for king and fatherland," survived until modern times; normally it would not have been felt—in the twentieth century as little as in the thirteenth—that in fact two different strata overlapped and two different obligations coincided: one feudal, and the other public. After all, the feudal lord was, at the same time, the head of the body politic, and what difference did it make whether a man offered his life to the "head" or to the "limbs" or to the "head and limbs" together? It would be difficult to tell where exactly the line of separation should be drawn— and yet, the possibility of a conflict of obligations was certainly not precluded.[204]

Things had a slightly different aspect from the point of view of the king. He could fight and die *pro patria*, but not *pro rege*, for himself. He might, in that case, die for the dynasty, for the succession to the throne; or for the "Crown" and the "Royal Dignity," provided that he should choose to fight at all. That the mediaeval king himself went to battle and brandished his sword was a matter of course, at least in the West. This ideal of a fighting king was,

---

to Pope Benedict XI and its various repetitions. Philip IV, at the Parliament of Tours, in 1308, said: ". . . qui sumus unum corpus regnaturi cum eo [sc. Domino Salvatore] pariter" (Lizerand, *Dossier*, 104; also 184, for a similar utterance of Plaisians); these passages, however, do not refer to the king's oneness with the body of Christ, as Wieruszowski, *Vom Imperium*, 147, and others seem to assume, but to the future oneness of all Christians with Christ.

203 Above, n.177.

204 The formula *pro rege et patria*, which survived in the Prussian army (*Für König und Vaterland*) until the recent past, brought about conflicting obligations in 1918, when the officers felt free to serve the *res publica* only after the flight of William II to Holland, when their "feudal" oaths of loyalty became obsolete. A similar situation arose in 1945, when the personal oath bound them against the *patria*.

on the whole, unquestioned in the thirteenth century. In 1283, the kings of Naples and Sicily, Charles of Anjou and Peter of Aragon, were ready to carry out their political differences by means of a duel.[205] The jurists claimed that the man waging war for the common good of the realm, was also the one most worthy of the crown of the kingdom.[206] The French people, in 1308, took it for granted that their king would lead his army to war *sus le peril de votre vie*.[207] It would be easy to add scores of similar utterances picked at random from the writings of the humanists.[208] Nor is there any lack of fighting warrior kings in the annals of the later Middle Ages or the Renaissance. Actually, one of the philosophically most interesting discussions about a king's obligation to offer his life *pro patria*, which combined traditional arguments of the thirteenth and fourteenth centuries with humanistic ideals, came from the pen of a late-mediaeval author, Enea Silvio Piccolomini, later Pope Pius II.

This learned humanist dedicated to the Habsburg emperor Frederick III, in 1446, a tractate the title of which—*De ortu et auctoritate imperii Romani*—betrays its descent from the political literature of the preceding century.[209] In this pamphlet, Enea Silvio discussed among other topics wars and emergencies of the state. In traditional fashion he claimed that in case of a *necessitas* of the commonweal the Prince was entitled to take away the private property even of meritorious citizens. The Prince, said he, may demand *ad usum publicum* even the life of a citizen, "since we are not born for ourselves alone."[210] He reminded the emperor

---

[205] The source material for this duel of kings has last been summed up by Johannes Haller, *Das Papsttum: Idee und Wirklichkeit* (Stuttgart, 1953), V,341f. Cf. A. Nitschke, in *DA*, XII (1956), 184.

[206] Post, *op.cit.*, 284,n.15.   [207] Lizerand, *Dossier*, 88.

[208] See, for an early example, Gerbert of Reims, *Ep.* 183 (to Otto III), ed. J. Havet, *Lettres de Gerbert* (Paris, 1889), 168: "Et quaenam certe maior in principe gloria . . . quam . . . seipsum pro patria, pro religione, pro suorum reique publicae salute maximis periculis opponere."

[209] Aeneas Silvius Piccolomini, *De ortu et auctoritate imperii Romani*, ed. R. Wolkan, *Der Briefwechsel des Eneas Silvius Piccolomini* (Fontes rerum Austriacarum, LXVII [Vienna, 1912]), 8ff; ed. Gerhard Kallen, *Aeneas Silvius Piccolomini als Publizist* (Stuttgart, 1939), 52ff.

[210] *De ortu*, ed. Wolkan, 18; ed. Kallen, 80,383ff: ". . . nempe liberum est imperatori, non solum homini nequam sed etiam viro bono ac de re publica bene merito, proprium agrum, proprias domos propriasque possessiones auferre, si rei publicae necessitas id expostulat." For the principle *Necessitas non habet legem*, see c.11, *De consecr.*, D.1, ed. Friedberg, I,1297; Post, "Public Law," 56. For the maxim *non nobis solum nati sumus*, see Cicero, *De off.*, I,22 (quoting Plato).

of illustrious men and women who for the sake of a community, a crew, a people, had been sacrificed, and recalled in that connection Jonas and Arion, the Roman Curtius and the Greek Iphigeneia: *Expedit enim unum hominem mori pro populo,* "It is proper that one man should die for the people."[211] The influence of the Renaissance is reflected by the motley assemblage of classical and biblical figures. But then Enea Silvio turned back again into more traditional lanes, and argued:

> It should not appear too hard if we say that for the benefit of the whole body a foot or hand, which in the commonweal are the citizens, must be amputated, since *the Prince himself, the head of the mystical body of the respublica, is held to sacrifice his life* whenever the commonweal demands it.[212]

We notice that the "mystical body of the Church the head of which is Christ," has been replaced—as in the writings of the jurists—by the "mystical body of the *respublica* the head of which is the Prince." And Enea Silvio—like Lucas de Penna before him—left no doubt what parallel he had in mind: he added that Christ sacrificed himself even though he—like the emperor—was a "Prince," the *princeps et rector* of the Church which he headed.[213] Enea Silvio mentioned both the sacrifice of the members—foot or hand—and the sacrifice of the head. The ordinary citizen offering himself up for the commonweal became, no doubt, a martyr whose *caritas* imitated that of Christ. But the sacrifice of the Prince for his *corpus mysticum*—the secular state—compared with the sacrifice of Christ more directly and on a different level: both offered their lives not only as members but also as the heads of their mystical bodies.

Here, at any rate, the parallelism of spiritual *corpus mysticum* and secular *corpus mysticum*, of the mystical body's divine head and its princely head, of self-sacrifice for the heavenly transcen-

---

211 *De ortu,* ed. Wolkan, 18f; Kallen, 82,403ff.

212 *De ortu,* ed. Wolkan, 19; Kallen, 82,418ff: "Turpis enim est omnis pars, que suo toto non convenit et semper minus malum tolerandum est, ut evitetur maius; nec grave videri debet, si pro salute corporis pedem vel manum, ut sunt in re publica cives, dicimus resecandam, cum princeps, qui caput est mystici rei publicae corporis, cum salus communis expostulat, vitam ponere teneatur. . . ."

213 *Ibid.:* "Imitandus est enim Christus Jesus, qui . . . ipse quoque, cum esset caput ecclesiae, princeps et rector, ut nobis mortem demeret, voluntariam mortem subivit." See, for similar comparisons, above, nos. 147 (Geoffrey of Monmouth), and 157 (Henry of Ghent).

dental community and self-sacrifice for the terrestrial—moral and political—community has come to a certain conclusion. The mutual loyalty between lord and vassal as prescribed by feudal custom was not the issue here: the sacrifice of the Prince was just as polity-centered as that of Christ himself.

In the politico-legal discussions of the citizen's sacrifice *pro patria* as well as in the patriotic propaganda campaign launched by Philip IV of France around A.D. 1300, it was naturally the members of the body politic who were required to expose themselves in defense of king and country. About the royal head and his duty to offer himself up for the body politic, the legists were less eloquent. Apparently they took it for granted that the king would take upon himself the same burdens and dangers as his subjects. It is, therefore, most surprising that one of the French jurists, Pierre Dubois, expressed quite explicitly the opposite opinion. He declared that in case of war the king should not expose himself or even join his army. The king, wrote Dubois, was to remain "in his native land and indulge in the procreation of children, their education and instruction, and in the preparation of armies—*ad honorem Dei.*"[214] That is to say, whereas the ordinary citizen was expected and even obliged to sacrifice fortune and life for the *patria*, the head of the body politic was not expected to bring the same sacrifice but supposed to submit to another patriotic occupation after the model, as Dubois added, of some Roman emperors and of the Khans of the Tartars "who rested quietly in the middle of their kingdom" while sending their generals out to wage war.[215] With Pierre Dubois, apparently, the expediency of the realm rated higher than the divine model.

Pierre Dubois may have been rather crude in his formulation; but the idea itself which he expressed, was not original. In fact, a new ideal of kingship is found sporadically in the later Middle

---

214 Dubois, *Summaria brevis*, ed. Kämpf, 19,21ff: ". . . remanentes in terra vestra natali liberorum procreacioni, eorum educacioni, instruccioni, exercituum preparacioni vacando—ad honorem Dei. . . ." See also Dubois' *De recuperatione*, cc.119ff, ed. Langlois, 111ff, where this doctrine is discussed at full length. Cf. Kämpf, *Pierre Dubois*, 70.

215 *Ibid.*: "Si quis arguat iste modus regendi est alias inauditus . . . , respondeo: ymmo legitur nonnullos Romanos imperatores sic quamplura mundi regna et climata gubernasse. Audivi quendam qui cum Tartaris conversatus fuerat, recitare quod rex terre eorum quiescens circa medium regni sui sic mittit ad singulas partes eius pugnans per alios, cum necessitas hoc exposcit."

Ages: the Prince who did not himself fight, but stayed at home while generals fought his wars. It may be that the model of Justinian (domineering, as it was, in the age of the jurists) was authoritative also in this respect[216]—was not he perhaps one of the "Roman emperors" Pierre Dubois had in mind? Nor is it impossible that the Pseudo-Aristotelian tractate *De mundo*, which was twice translated into Latin during the thirteenth century, bears some responsibility for that new vision of kingship. In this work, the Persian Great King was depicted as an antitype of God: "invisible to all" he resides in his palace at Susa or Ekbatana; "he sees all and hears all" in his seclusion, because by means of a clever intelligence system he is speedily informed about every event in his far-flung empire; he acts through his officers, for it would be unseemly for the king to be in person everywhere, and more dignified and venerable anyhow to reside, like God, in the remoteness of the supreme region and yet to be the cause of everything wholesome "by the power extending from the king through the whole world."[217] Some reflection of this, so to speak, "celestial Versailles" and this rational type of rulership perhaps is found in the philosophical romance called *Sidrach*, which was popular reading in the thirteenth century. The wise Sidrach, asked by his interlocutor, a fabulous king of the Levant, whether the king should go to battle, gave the advice that the king himself should not fight, but stay in the rear of his army; for "if the army is lost and the king escapes, he can recover another army; but if the king is lost, all is lost."[218] We cannot tell whether Pierre Dubois

---

[216] We may think also of many another Byzantine emperor; between Theodosius I and Heraclius no emperor had gone to war personally; see G. Ostrogorsky, *Geschichte des byzantinischen Staates* (Munich, 1940), 60.

[217] Ps.-Aristotle, *De mundo*, 398a-b, ed. W. L. Lorimer (Paris, 1933), 83ff; for the two Latin versions, see Lorimer, *The Text Tradition of Pseudo-Aristotle 'De mundo'* (St. Andrews University Publications, XVIII, 1924), 76ff, and his final edition in: *Aristoteles latinus* (Rome, 1951), XI:1-2, pp.42 and 70; see also my sketch "Invocatio nominis imperatoris," 46f, nos.41ff.

[218] *Roman de Sidrach*, c.333, edited (the Italian version of the 14th century) by Adolfo Bartoli, *Il Libro di Sidrach* (Bologna, 1868), 355f; see, for an abstract, preceded by an excellent introduction, Ch.-V. Langlois, *La connaissance de la nature et du monde au moyen âge* (Paris, 1911), 180ff and 251. Sidrach is not at all "heroic." When, however, he says "Mieux vaut un bon fuir que mauvaise demorée," he is not cynical, but simply conforms with the scholastics who defended flight as well as resistance (see above, nos.155ff, for Henry of Ghent). The king, says Sidrach, should never be found in battle, only in the rearguard of his army. "Si l'ost est perdu et le seignor eschape, il recoverra .i. autre ost; et se il est perdu, tout est perdu." Those are the places apparently referred to by Heydte, *Geburtsstunde des*

was influenced by the *Sidrach.* However, the idea of the "non-fighting king" gradually gained ground, though Froissart still mentions it as a somewhat paradoxical fact that King Charles V of France, *estans en ses cambres et en ses deduis,* reconquered everything his predecessors—*la teste armée et l'espée en la main*—had lost on the battle-field.[219]

A king not exposing himself to the dangers of war implicitly demanded from his subjects a unilateral sacrifice. This idea of unilateral sacrifice for the head by the members of the body politic was carried to extremes on the scholastic side of the fence. Augustinus Triumphus, admittedly a radical curialist (d. 1328), discussed in his work *On the Supreme Ecclesiastical Power* also various legal aspects of the problem of appeal from the pope: Could a person appeal from the pope to God? Was not an appeal from the pope to God an appeal against God? Was there an appeal to the College of Cardinals? To a General Council? The author rejected an appeal to a General Council on the ground that God approved of his creation as "very good" (Genesis 1: 31) chiefly in view of the order of things; and "of the whole ecclesiastical order the leader and head was the pope." He then argued:

> Just as this order would be overthrown by an appeal [to a General Council], so would this good be brought to naught, because the good of an army would be non-existent were it not for the good of the general; and the good of the Church would be non-existent were it not for the good of the pope. The good of the general is superior to that of the whole army, and the good of the pope superior to that of the whole Church.[220]

---

souveränen Staates, 329f, n.31 (who quotes "Cod.franc. 24395 der Nationalbibliothek in Paris," without either folio or chapter of this voluminous work). See also, for a similar attitude, the "Mirror of Princes," written for King Konradin by Peter of Prece (ca. 1266-1267), ed. Kloos, "Petrus de Prece und Konradin," *QFIAB,* xxxiv (1954), 107, §14, and 108.

[219] Froissart, *Chroniques,* ii,c.87, ed. Gaston Raynaud (Paris, 1894), ix,127; see also Christine de Pisan, *Le livre des fais et bonnes meurs du sage roy Charles V,* ed. S. Solente (Paris, 1936), 131, who mentions the fact that Charles V was highly successful in his campaigns *non obstant n'y alast en personne.* Cf. Heydte, *op.cit.,* 334,n.42. Charles V, by the way, owned several copies of *Sidrach*; see Langlois, *op.cit.,* 180,n.1.

[220] Augustinus de Ancona, *De summa potestate ecclesiastica,* i, qu.vi, ad 6 (Augsburg, Johannes Schüssler, 1483), fol.66r-v (the title usually given is *Summa de potestate ecclesiastica*; but the incunabulum of the Library of Congress, which Dr. Schafer Williams kindly inspected for me, has a different title). The author discusses various possibilities of appealing from the pope ("Primo: Utrum a papa possit appellari ad Deum. Secundo: Utrum a papa appellare ad Deum sit appellare

Here the head, so to speak, has devoured the whole mystical body. What mattered was not the *corpus Ecclesiae*, but the *caput Ecclesiae*, as though life itself or the continuity of life rested in the head alone, and not in head and members together.

It is plausible to assume that some problem of continuity vested in the "head" was behind the curious statements of both Pierre Dubois and Augustinus Triumphus. In the case of Dubois it was obviously the continuity of the dynasty which, for the sake of the whole body politic, appeared more important than the king's exposure to the contingencies of warfare. In the case of Augustinus Triumphus the problem of continuity is more difficult to disentangle. His strange statement was caused by a misinterpreted and misapplied passage of the *Metaphysics*, where Aristotle investigated the nature of the "good": did the good consist, immanently, in the orderly arrangement of the parts forming the whole, or did it exist, transcendentally, as something separate and independent beyond the whole? Aristotle decided that the good existed probably in both senses as illustrated, for example, by an army.

> For the efficiency of any army consists partly in its own order, and partly in the general; chiefly, however, in the latter, because the general does not depend upon the order, but the order depends upon him.[221]

Aristotle, of course, was far from saying that the whole army may "go to the dogs" for the good of the general. But it is evident also that his simile could easily be interpreted in a hierarchical and teleological sense. This had been the tendency already of Aquinas, who, however, made it perfectly clear that the "general" himself was not the goal: the order of the army was "for the fulfilment of the good of the general" only insofar as it served "the fulfilment

---

contra Deum," etc.). The sixth question is "Utrum a papa possit appellari ad concilium generale," to which he remarks: ". . . Vidit deus cuncta que fecerat, et erant valde bona. Omnia a deo producta bona quidem erant in se; sed valde bona propter ordinem quem ad invicem retinent, cum ergo totius ecclesiastici ordinis dux et caput sit ipse papa; sicut per appellationem tolleretur talis ordo, ita tolleretur tale bonum, quia cum bonum exercitus non sit nisi propter bonum ducis, et bonum ecclesie non nisi propter bonum pape. Maius bonum est bonum ducis quam totius exercitus; et bonum pape maius quam totius ecclesie." Cf. G. de Lagarde, "Individualisme et corporatisme au moyen âge," *L'Organisation corporative du moyen âge à la fin de l'ancien régime* (Recueil de travaux d'histoire et de philologie, 2me sér., XLIV; Louvain, 1937), II,42,n.3. See also Gierke, *Gen.R.*, III,596,n.214.

[221] Aristotle, *Metaph.*, 1075a,12-17 (XII,10,1-2); see, for the Latin version, Thomas Aquinas, *In Metaph.*, ed. Cathala and Spiazzi (Turin, 1950), 611, §1102f.

of the general's desire to achieve victory."[222] And on another occasion he made it clear once more that the "general" was himself just as little a goal in itself as a mediating angel, since the ultimate good was none but God.[223]

Augustinus Triumphus seems to have faltered at this very point: despite the warnings of Aquinas, he obviously mistook the *vicarius Christi* for the One whose vicar the pope was, thus conveying the impression that the pope (or Aquinas' "angel") was the ultimate—

[222] Aquinas, *In Metaph.*, §§2627ff, ed. Cathala and Spiazzi, p.612; see, especially, §2630: "Sicut videmus in exercitu: nam bonum exercitus est et in ipso ordine exercitus et in duce qui exercitui praesidet: sed magis est bonum exercitus in duce quam in ordine: quia finis potior est in bonitate his quae sunt ad finem: ordo autem exercitus est propter bonum ducis adimplendum, scilicet ducis voluntatem in victoriae consecutionem; non autem, e converso, bonum ducis est propter bonum ordinis." In the next paragraph (2631), Aquinas makes the order of the universe refer to the *primum movens*: "Ita etiam bonum separatum, quod est primum movens, est melius bonum bono ordinis, quod est in universo. Totus enim ordo universi est propter primum moventem. . . ." Augustinus Triumphus, therefore, made simply the equation: *primum movens = papa*; also, he left *bonum* vague and undefined ("the good *in* the general" as opposed to "the good *of* the general"). Dante, who quotes the passage in *Monarchia*, 1,6,2, follows Aquinas (cf. *Convivio*, IV,4,5). See next note.

[223] Aquinas mentions the passage several times; see, e.g., *Summa theol.*, I, qu.103,art.2,ad 3: ". . . finis quidem universi est aliquod bonum in ipso existens, scilicet ordo ipsius universi; hoc autem bonum non est ultimus finis, sed ordinatur ad ducem, ut dicitur in XII. Metaphys." Aquinas simply paraphrases Aristotle, but since he says that the order of the army is ordered "towards the general," he is far from holding that the whole army is of little value as compared with the general. He is more outspoken in his answer to a proposition (*Summa theol.*, I-II, qu.5,art.6), where the Aristotelian general compares with an angel: "Videtur quod homo possit fieri beatus per actionem alicuius superioris creaturae, scilicet Angeli. Cum enim duplex ordo inveniatur in rebus—unus partium universi ad invicem, alius totius universi ad bonum quod est extra universum—primus ordo ordinatur ad secundum sicut ad finem [!], ut dicitur XII. Metaphys.: sicut ordo partium exercitus ad invicem est propter ordinem totius exercitus ad ducem. . . ." Hence, the proposition takes, like Augustinus Triumphus, the general, or angel, as the *finis*. Aquinas answers very logically that to the art of the helmsman, who is in command of the ship, there pertains that use of the ship for which the ship itself was built, just as in his commentary on the *Metaphysics* he said that the final goal of an army's order is victory through the craft of the general. And therefore he can easily conclude: "Sic igitur in ordine universi homo quidem adiuvatur ab angelis ad consequendum ultimum finem. . . ; sed ipsum ultimum finem consequitur per ipsum primum agentem qui est Deus." The metaphors of Aquinas make it sufficiently clear how nonsensical it would be, e.g., to say "the good of the helmsman is superior to the good of the whole ship." On the other hand, however, a curialist such as Augustinus Triumphus could easily derive from the phrase *propter bonum ducis* the far-reaching statement that "the good of the pope is superior to that of the whole Church," which, to say the least, is liable to be misunderstood and to appear both un-Aristotelian and un-Christian—not to mention that it proves nothing with regard to an appeal from the pope to a General Council. The problem, however, is involved, and no more could be done here than to indicate how Augustinus Triumphus could have arrived at his astounding statement.

and therewith eternal—good of the visible Church. The continuity, in his case, will have to be sought in the *supremum bonum*, falsely or rightly believed to be actualized in the pope and therefore justifying the unilateral sacrifice of the limbs for the head, be he angel or pope or general. In other words, a martyrdom for the head alone was indeed justified so long as the *caput corporis mystici* was Christ himself who was not simply a mortal man but also the immortal and eternal sharer of the throne of God: he was, as Aquinas said,[224] the head of the Church *secundum omne tempus*, whereas the pope, an ordinary mortal man, was head of the (visible) Church *secundum determinatum tempus* only, having no claim to that eternity or continuity which distinguished the eternal head of an eternal *corpus mysticum*.

There was, no doubt, some impasse in the organological doctrines: they may have suggested a continuity of the bodies politic or mystic, but not a continuity of the head alone; and yet it was quite customary to say that, just as in the natural body, every member was bound to protect the head.[225] This impasse should be kept in mind, since precisely by this flaw we may be led to the core of the matter and to the essence of the problem whose nature will be recognized more clearly once the results of our investigation are garnered.

At the beginning of this chapter (p. 199) the question was raised whether interrelations were effective between the *corpus mysticum* of the Church and the new secular polities. This question now may be answered in the affirmative: the idea of the *corpus mysticum* was undeniably transferred and applied to the political entities, no matter whether the ecclesiological designation itself was used or whether one preferred more specific equivalents such as the Aristotelian *corpus morale et politicum* or the more emotional *patria*. There were many strands which made up the new pattern: theological, legal, philosophical, humanistic; and the transfer of the Rome or Empire ideologies to the territorial monarchies was hardly less momentous than the applications of religious thought. In the earlier phase, however, the main contents of the veneration of *patria* were derived from a world of thought which was religious in a broad sense; and the mainspring

---

[224] *Summa theol.*, III, qu.8,art.6 (resp.).   [225] See, e.g., above, n.194.

of this devotion was that at a certain moment in history the state appeared as a *corpus mysticum* comparable to the Church. Hence, *pro patria mori*, death for the sake of that mystico-political body, made sense; it became meaningful, as it was considered equal in value and consequence to the death for the Christian faith, for the Church, or for the Holy Land. If indeed every Christian "who lives in the body of the Church is held to rise in defense of that body," it was a straight and simple conclusion to maintain that every Frenchman who lived in the body of France, was held to rise in defense of that national body.[226] By analogy, therefore, death for the body politic or the *patria* was viewed in a truly religious perspective and was understood religiously even without classical heroization and the later amplifier of the humanistic tuba. It was a sacrifice all the more worthy to offer because it was made for the sake of a body moral and politic which cherished its own eternal values and had achieved its moral and ethical autonomy alongside of the *corpus mysticum* of the Church.

Far more difficult it is to answer the question raised simultaneously: whether or not the concept of the *duplex corpus Christi*, the "two bodies of Christ," had any bearing upon the idea of the "king's two bodies." The tenet of the two bodies (not "natures") of Christ—his bodies natural and mystical, or individual and collective—hinged of course on the organic-corporational concept of the Church. While the Church as *corpus Christi* was a notion going back to St. Paul, the Church as *corpus Christi mysticum* was a concept of a more recent date which attained its legalistic connotations in the course of the thirteenth century. Did the idea of doubleness—"One body of Christ which is he himself, and another body of which he is the head"[227]—find its equivalent in the secular sphere when the *corpus reipublicae mysticum* came into being?

At first glance we might be tempted to look here for the solution of the whole problem of the king's two bodies. The analogies built up by jurists and philosophers were indeed numerous: the Prince, being the head of the mystical body of the state and sometimes even that body itself, paralleled Christ who was both the head of the mystical body of the Church and that body itself; also,

---

[226] Dupuy, *Histoire du différend*, 243f, §§26,27,29; cf.586, and passim. Not only kings and knights, but every Christian had to rise as a member of the *corpus Ecclesiae* for the protection and conservation of the Church.

[227] Gregory of Bergamo, *De veritate*, c.18, ed. Hurter, 75f; see above, n.15.

just as Christ laid down his life for his corporate body, so was the Prince supposed to sacrifice his life for the commonweal. We may recall also the persistence of those analogies: the suicide committed an act of felony not only because he acted against Nature and God, but also (as the Tudor jurists pointed out) against the king "in that hereby he [the King] has lost a subject, and he being the Head has lost one of his mystic members."[228] *Obiter* it may be mentioned that according to the *Nicomachean Ethics* the suicide did not wrong himself or any other person, but he wronged the *polis*, the commonweal—in Christian language: the *corpus mysticum*, or its head.[229] It would be probably not too difficult to assemble more material which might make the parallelism of the spiritual head of the *corpus mysticum* and the secular head of the *corpus politicum* even more striking. Why, then, should we not deduce from the *duplex corpus Christi* the *duplex corpus regis*, and let the whole problem remain at that?

On further thought, however, it will appear less likely that the organic concept of the commonweal, though otherwise highly effective, led *per se* to a theory of the "king's two bodies" or, for that matter, to the secular equivalent of the "two bodies" of Christ. To begin with, our sources do not support that suggestion: nowhere do we find, merely on the basis of the organic concept of the state, the idea expressed that the king as the head of the body politic has two bodies.[230] Nor is there any reason why he

---

[228] Above, Ch.I, n.21.

[229] *Eth. Nicom.*, 1138a,9ff (v,15); see, for the Latin version, Aquinas, *In Ethic. ad Nicom.*, ed. Spiazzi (Turin, 1949), 300, §§781ff, and also Aquinas' commentary, 301, §1094: "Sed considerandum est cui iniustum facit. Facit enim iniustum civitati quam privat uno cive, sive non facit iniustum sibiipsi." Cf. R. Hirzel, "Der Selbstmord," *Archiv für Religionswissenschaft*, xi (1908), 271; Hamburger, *Morals and Law*, 8of. According to Roman Law (*D*.48,21,3), confiscation of property and disinheritance of the heirs followed a suicide, provided that the act was committed to escape punishment for some crime; otherwise suicide was not punishable. In England, suicide was considered an act of felony (*felo de se*) and punishable, although Bracton was inclined to follow Roman Law practice; see Güterbock, 170; Pollock and Maitland, ii,488. Between the concept of the state as a "body politic" and the interpretation of suicide as an act of "felony" there is a connection which, however, is still in need of further clarification; see above, n.194 (who rises against the Prince and the body politic commits suicide); also "Pro patria mori," 491,n.62.

[230] Baldus, of course, distinguished between a *persona personalis* and a *persona idealis*, and other jurists attributed to a judge a *duplex persona* (see below, Ch.vii, nos.275,397,422); but in all those cases, the organic concept has been eclipsed by the corporation theory. Seneca, *Ep*.85,35, talks about the two persons of a helmsman (*Duas personas habet gubernator*) because he is both passenger and master

should. King Philip IV of France was the head of the body politic of France as a natural man, and like every French citizen he was merely one part, though the most prominent part, of that body. Canon Law, it is true, made a clear distinction between the bishop and the chapter: each was said to represent a *corpus separatum*, even though in other respects bishop and chapter together formed one body of which the bishop was the head.[231] But this tenet presupposes other than organological doctrines, and the theorists of the secular state do not seem to have recognized the head of the commonweal as a *corpus separatum*; they were, on the contrary, most reluctant to separate the limbs from the head, or vice versa, and the idea of the organic unity of head and limbs was too strong to allow a separation of one from the other.[232] That the king could appear in two different capacities—that is, as feudal overlord and as head of the whole body politic—has been pointed out before: death *pro rege et patria* would suggest this double aspect of royal authority. But this doubleness had no analogy in the natural and mystical bodies of Christ. For what would it have meant, or what would have been gained, had one coined an analogous formula saying: "There is one body of the king which is he himself, and another body of which he is the head?" It would have been a definition without consequence or obligation, amounting to nothing.

Another possible argument may be disposed of quickly: the state as a *persona ficta*, an abstract personification beyond its members. It is true, the Church was occasionally defined by Aquinas as a *persona mystica*.[233] Would that questionable term entitle us to understand accordingly also the state as a *persona politica et moralis?* The term does not seem to occur; for the state, around 1300, was not a "fictitious person" but an organic or organological whole. It did not exist apart from its members, nor was the "state" some superior being *per se* beyond its head and members or beyond moral values and the Law.[234] To put it succinctly, the *regnum* or *patria* was not "personified"—it was

---

of a vessel; but this passage, though known, apparently was referred to only by very late jurists; see Vassalli, "Fisco," 205ff.

[231] Gierke, *Gen.R.*, III,266ff; see also Post, "Two Laws," 425,n.35.

[232] Wilkinson, in *Speculum*, XIX (1944), 460,n.4; above, n.115.

[233] Above, n.24.

[234] Cf. Post, "Public Law," 45f; "Two Laws," 422.

"bodified." Mainly because the state could be conceived of as a "body," could there be constructed the analogy with the mystical body of the Church. The parallel hinged, as it were, upon the word *corpus*, and not on the word *persona*, just as the theologians reflected on the *duplex corpus Christi*, and not on the *duplex persona Christi*—which would have been Nestorianism anyhow. In like fashion, the Tudor lawyers argued about the "king's two bodies," and not about the "king's two persons"—even though they might slip occasionally. The terminology itself should prevent us from lightheartedly discarding the old organic oneness of head and limbs in the body politic and from rashly replacing it by the abstraction of a personified state.[235]

Our laborious quest for the interrelations between the *corpora mystica* of Church and state will nevertheless have been not quite futile once we change our question. Instead of asking for features transferred from the spiritual to the secular, we should ask: In what respect did the concept of the "two bodies of Christ" fail to be transferable or even indirectly applicable to the head of the mystical body of the state? Where is the flaw in the analogy?

The answer will be simple enough once we recognize that perhaps the chief problem involved is a problem of Time. The head of the mystical body of the Church was eternal, since Christ was both God and man. His own eternity, therefore, bestowed upon his mystical body likewise the value of eternity or rather timelessness. Contrariwise, the king as the head of the body politic was a common mortal: he could die, and did die, and was not eternal at all. That is to say, before the king could represent (as in the language of Tudor jurists) that strange being which, like the angels, was immortal, invisible, ubiquitous, never under age, never sick, and never senile, he had either to stop being a simple

---

[235] For the notion of "State," see Post, "Two Laws," 420ff,n.8. Aquinas' Commentary on Aristotle's *Politics* should be considered in that connection. He uses *status* in a descriptive fashion without any connotation of abstractness, e.g., §§393-398, ed. Spiazzi, 139f, where *status popularis* (Democracy), *status paucorum* (Oligarchy), *status optimatum* (Aristocracy) are mentioned time and time again. See also §414, p.147, where Peter of Auvergne (Aquinas' continuator) brings those various *status* into line with the *regnum*, though• always with reference to the form of government. In other words, *status* has not the meaning of "well being" (*bonus status regni, ecclesiae*, etc.), nor, of course, of "estates" (though that notion then became current too), nor of state in the abstract. It means "government," the *status publicus* of the community which—later on, admittedly—came to mean "State."

mortal or to acquire somehow a value of immortality: the eternity which Christ, in the language of theology, owned "by nature," had to accrue to the king from another source. Without some *character aeternitatis* he could not have his *character angelicus*, and without some inherent value of eternity he could not have "two bodies" or have a super-body distinct from his natural mortal body.

Admittedly, Grace as well as Justice and Law remained eternity-values not easily to be discarded, and they were co-operative at building up the continuity of the new monarchies; for the idea of rulership "by the Grace of God" gained new life in the dynastic ideologies, and the continuity of a Justice "which never dies" played a major part with regard to the continuity of the Crown. But the value of immortality or continuity upon which the new polity-centered rulership would thrive, was vested in the *universitas* "which never dies," in the perpetuity of an immortal people, polity, or *patria*, from which the individual king might easily be separated, but not the Dynasty, the Crown, and the Royal Dignity.

CHAPTER VI

ON CONTINUITY AND CORPORATIONS

1. Continuity

UNDOUBTEDLY the concept of the "king's two bodies" camouflaged a problem of continuity. This was less evident, or perhaps only more concealed, in the earlier Middle Ages. But the truly essential point became manifest as well as articulate when, as a result of the reception of the Aristotelian doctrine of the "eternity of the world" and its more radical Averroist interpretation, the question of perpetual continuity itself became a philosophic problem of the first order.

The revival of the doctrine of the eternity of the world, which captivated Western minds after the middle of the thirteenth century,[1] coincided with analogous, if independent, tendencies towards "continuity" in the constitutional and legal-political spheres. For it would be a mistake to assume that the new philosophic tenet produced, caused, or created a new belief in the perpetual continuity of political bodies. Facts of chronology would preclude such a hypothesis anyhow, because the development towards continuity in the fields of law and politics was already in full swing before an influence of the new philosophy could have been effective. Practice, as usual, preceded theory; but existing practice made the minds all the more receptive for a new theory. However, simultaneity does not imply causality, and all that can be said is that the philosophy defending the infinite continuum of Time made its appearance as a concomitant of related trends in other fields; further, that the ground was peculiarly well prepared to receive a doctrine which confirmed and justified what one thought or did anyhow, and thereby intensified and accelerated existing conditions; finally, that both strands—the philosophic-scholastic theory and the politico-legal practice—together decisively influenced the general pattern of Western social and political thought in its formative period.

---

[1] Frederick II had already asked Ibn Sabin for the proofs of the eternity of the world; see *Erg.Bd.*, 102,152.

For all those restrictions it would be nevertheless inexcusable to ignore the impact of the new trends in philosophy, because such neglect would whittle down our capability of understanding more profoundly the corresponding phenomena in other sectors of thought—constitutional, legal, or political. The heated arguments between philosophers and theologians about meaning and effects of an infinite continuity contributed, to say the least, to the articulation of some phenomena which previously had been difficult to express, or had not been expressed at all because they had not penetrated the conscious mind. Now, in the wake of the Aristotelian revival, the Averroist extremists, the moderate Aristotelians, and the anti-Aristotelians had each to produce their reasons for and against an eternity of the world. The very fact that the definition of continuity, duration, perpetuity, sempiternity, eternity, and related notions formed, over and over again, a matter for discussion and argument seems telling enough: it reveals to the historian that something formerly stable and settled had become unstable and unsettled—or even questionable—and that some serious change was taking place within the realm of Time, and in man's relation to Time.

Whereas the philosophic aspects of that change have been studied frequently and are known well enough, the historical inferences of that new attitude toward Time, difficult to substantiate as they are, have hardly been investigated.[2] However, a new approach to Time and a new conception of the nature of Time must be considered not only as a philosophical but also as a historical factor of great moment. The new valuation of Time, which then broke to the surface, actually became one of the most powerful agencies by which Western thought, at the end of the Middle Ages, was transformed and energized; and apparently it still holds sway with unabated vigor over modern thought. After all (to mention only one item), the optimistic philosophy of unlimited progress, which the generations preceding the two World Wars

---

[2] See, however, Hans Baron, "A Sociological Interpretation of the Early Renaissance in Florence," *South Atlantic Quarterly*, XXXVIII (1939), 436ff, who called attention to the opposite trend of revaluating Time: the preciousness of Time. There may be other historians who dropped occasional remarks on that subject; on the whole, however, it is surprising how rarely the element of Time has been considered as a decisive historical factor in the innumerable studies on the genesis of the modern state and of modern economy.

saw fit to cherish, had its roots and premises in those intellectual changes which stirred the thirteenth century—stirred it no less profoundly than the combats between empire and papacy, or between spiritual and secular powers at large.

AEVUM

The great crisis in man's approach to Time, while previously latent, came to a head when the doctrine of the uncreatedness and infinite continuity of the world was recovered from Aristotelian philosophy. This tenet dealt an all but mortal blow to the supremacy of the traditional Augustinian concepts of Time and Eternity. Time, under the influence of Saint Augustine's teaching, had enjoyed a bad rather than a good reputation. Time, *tempus*, was the exponent of transitoriness; it signified the frailty of this present world and all things temporal, and bore the stigma of the perishable. Time, rigorously severed from Eternity, was of inferior rank. For whereas the Eternity of God was conceived of as a Now-and-Ever without Time, the fugitive Time showed all the weakness of the evanescent moment. As Saint Augustine pointed out in one of the most famous passages of the *Confessions*,[3] Time—like sun and moon, plant, beast, and man—was created. It was created, not before, but together with the transitory world as a short span which, like a blind alley, was doomed to meet an abrupt end at any given moment, just as the whole created world might be overtaken at any hour by the Last Events. Time was finite. It covered no more than the hours from Creation to the Last Day, and words such as *temporalis* and *saecularis*, indicating the, so to speak, moral degradation of Time, were burdened to express the brevity of an only relatively important life of this world and the nearness of death in it.

The validity of the Augustinian teaching on Time and Eternity

---

[3] Augustine, *Confessions*, XI. The literature on Christianity and Time is next to infinite, and the flood has been swelling constantly during the last years; see, e.g., J. Baudry, *Le problème de l'Origine et de l'Eternité du Monde* (Paris, 1931); Jean Guitton, *Le temps et l'éternité selon Plotin et saint Augustin* (Paris, 1933); Oscar Cullman, *Christus und die Zeit* (Zollikon-Zürich, 1948); Henri Marrou, *L'Ambivalence du temps de l'histoire chez saint Augustin* (Montreal, 1950); and, for a brief bibliographic survey of more recent publications, Paul Henry, "The Christian Philosophy of History," *Theological Studies*, XIII (1952), 419ff. In general, see the useful study of Frank Herbert Brabant, *Time and Eternity in Christian Thought* (Bampton Lectures, 1936; London, 1937).

was broadly attacked, together with the most fundamental premises of the Christian faith, by the Averroists who carried Aristotelianism to sweeping conclusions; but even a moderate Aristotelian such as Aquinas had to admit at least the potentiality of a world without beginning.[4] In the long lists of *errores condemnati* which Church authorities drafted to curb the Averroist plague, the tenet of the "eternity of the world" played a major part. The Church proclaimed it an error to maintain that motion had no beginning; that Time was eternal; that heaven was not created; that there would be no resurrection of the dead; that corruption and generation followed each other successively without a beginning or end; that there was no such thing as a first man, and that there would never be a last man; that there always was and ever will be a human race and a generation of man from man, and many similar or related maxims.[5] All those condemned errors pointed in the same direction: they all asserted that there was neither Creation nor Last Day, that by corruption and generation the dispositions of the world might change but that the present world itself was permanent by the laws of nature, and that Time was infinite, a continuum of successive moments rolling forth perpetually from endlessness to endlessness.[6] *Tempus*, the

[4] See the famous passage in *Summa theol.*, I,qu.46, art.2: "Respondeo dicendum, quod mundum non semper fuisse, sola fide tenetur, et demonstrative probari non potest."

[5] Best known is the long list of 219 errors drafted by Bishop Stephen Tempier of Paris (1277) and published by H. Denifle, *Chartularium Universitatis Parisiensis* (Paris, 1889), I,544ff; but there were many other lists published as well; see J. Koch, "Philosophische und theologische Irrtumslisten von 1270-1329," *Mélanges Mandonnet* (Paris, 1930), II,305-329. Those lists were, in fact, the best propaganda for Averroism insofar as they condensed most difficult problems into easily conceivable slogans. No bibliography on Averroism will be required here; but Martin Grabmann's *Der lateinische Averroismus des 13. Jahrhunderts und seine Stellung zur christlichen Weltanschauung* (Sitz.Ber., Munich, 1931, No.2), his *Studien über den Einfluss der aristotelischen Philosophie auf die mittelalterlichen Theorien über das Verhältnis von Kirche und Staat* (Sitz.Ber., Munich, 1934, No.2), as well as the studies collected in his *Mittelalterliches Geistesleben* (esp. vol. II [Munich, 1936]) may just be mentioned as a landmark of scholarship on mediaeval Aristotelianism during the last decades. Attention, however, should be called to the recently discovered tractate of Boethius of Dacia, ed. Géza Sajó, *Un traité recemment découvert de Boèce de Dacie "De mundi aeternitate," texte inédit avec une introduction critique* (Budapest, 1954).

[6] By rejecting the Aristotelian tenets concerning the infinity of Time and the impossibility of a spatial void, Bishop Tempier most curiously was compelled to defend the possibility of a plurality of worlds; see Alexander Koyré, "La vide et l'espace infini au XIVe siècle," *Archives d'histoire doctrinale et littéraire du moyen âge*, XXIV (1949), 45-91. The problem of primordial matter was discussed in the

limited span of terrestrial Time, thereby lost its ephemeral frailty and limitation, and its character also changed morally: Time no longer appeared predominantly as the symbol of caducity, of Death; Time, to the Averroists, became a vivifying element, a symbol of endless duration, of Life.

To be sure, not the individual life was immortal; but immortal was the life of the genera and species which the mortal individual represented. Time now became the symbol of the eternal continuity and immortality of the great collective called the human race, of the species of man, of the seminal powers, of the forces of germination. It gained, through its connection with ideas of religious and scientific progress,[7] an ethical value when one recognized that "the daughter of Time was Truth."[8] Finally, the unlimited continuity of the human race itself bestowed a new meaning on many things. It made meaningful, for example, the craving after worldly fame, the *perpetuandi nominis desiderium*, which increasingly became a decisive impulse for human actions. Perhaps this trail, too, was first trodden by the jurists: "Notice that the dead lives through glory," says an Accursian gloss, while in another connection the glossator held that those who fell in battle for the *respublica* as well as those killed in tournaments lived forever in

twelfth century in a scholarly fashion; see Heinrich Flatten, "Die *primordialis materia* in der Schule von Chartres," *Archiv für Geschichte der Philosophie*, XL (1931), 58-65.

[7] The problem of progress in the thirteenth century will be discussed separately on a broader basis and in another connection. For the religious aspect of the problem, which is inseparable from the doctrines of Joachim of Fiore and the Spiritualists, see most conveniently Ernst Benz, *Ecclesia spiritualis* (Stuttgart, 1934), 265ff, and passim; the ever increasing literature on Joachim (see Herbert Grundmann, *Neue Forschungen über Joachim von Fiore* [Marburg, 1950]) rarely fails to consider also the idea of progress as an implication of Spiritualist doctrines. The scientific idea of progress, stimulated very strongly by Priscian, *Institutiones grammaticae*, I,1 (see above, Ch.v, n.187), has been briefly discussed by R. Klibansky, "Standing on the Shoulders of Giants," *Isis*, XXVI (1936), 147f; cf. G. Sarton, "Query n.53," *Isis*, XXIV (1935-6), 107ff; J. de Ghellinck, "Nani et gigantes," *Bulletin Du Cange*, XVIII (1945), 25-29. The best source on that subject, however, has passed almost unnoticed; that is, the philosophical reflections of the jurists.

[8] The phrase comes down from Gellius, *Noctes Atticae*, XII,11,7. For the earlier history of this maxim, often represented in Renaissance art and found also in Erasmus' *Adagia*, see the remarks of F. Saxl, "Veritas filia Temporis," *Philosophy and History: Essays Presented to Ernst Cassirer* (Oxford, 1936), 200, n.1. For the pre-Renaissance period the material has not yet been investigated; but it was probably again the jurists who equated Time and Truth; see, e.g., Baldus, on *D.1,3,32*, n.88, fol.23, discussing the validity of unwritten customary Law, that is, of custom "of which human memory is not to the contrary," to which he remarks: *tempus loco veritatis est.*

fame and glory.[9] Other jurists wrote, and Frederick II, their pupil, built, for the perpetual fame of their names.[10] The new continuity of Time did not create, but it intensified, the desire for the perpetuation of a man's fame and name. Fame, after all, made sense only if this world and if mankind were believed to be, in one way or another, permanent and immortal; and if Time was Life, and not Death. We may consider, perhaps, "immortal fame" in this world as the equivalent of or secular substitute for the immortal beatitude of the other world, and Dante consequently was implored by the lost souls in Inferno to keep alive their memory and their fame on earth in order to compensate for the forfeited, and often even despised, eternal beatitude of the soul.[11]

It would be tempting to understand the infinite duration of the

[9] See *Post*, "Two Notes," 286,n.24. The essential place of reference is *Inst*.1,25,pr. (above, Ch.v,n.160) to which the *Glos.ord.*, v. *per gloriam vivere*, says: "Nota, mortuum vivere per gloriam," with an allegation of *D*.9,2,7,4 (no punishment if "in publico certamine alius alium occiderit . . . , quia gloriae causa et virtutis, non iniuriae gratia videtur damnum datum"), to which the *Glos.ord.*, v. *gloriae causa*, remarks: "Per gloriam quis occiditur, ut hic [the one killed *in publico certamine*, interpreted as tournament]: et ideo post per gloriam vivere potest, licet sic mortuus dicatur." Also *Glos.ord.*, on *D*.3,2,25, v. *ceciderit*: "Qui per gloriam vivere intelligitur," with allegation of *Inst*.1,25,pr.

[10] Placentinus, *Summa in Tres Libros*, prooem., ed. Savigny, *Geschichte des Römischen Rechts im Mittelalter* (2nd ed., Heidelberg, 1850), IV,245: "Secundo, credidi multum expedire mihi ad memoriam meique nominis famam in perpetuum conservandam. . . ." See also the prooemium of the *Margarita super Feudis* (late 13th century) of Dulius Gambarini: ". . . cunctos literatoriae scientiae amatores expedit dare operam studio indefesso ut sua in evum memoria relinquatur"; cf. Jean Acher, "Notes sur le droit savant au moyen âge," *Nouvelle revue historique de droit français et étranger*, XXX (1906), 125. See also Angelo de Ubaldis, on *D*.1,1,1,n.2 (Venice, 1630), fol.3ʳ (v. *perpetui*): "Vel dic quarto quod Justinianus est perpetuus perpetuitate memoriae . . . [C.1,3,23]." The same jurist (*loc.cit.*, v. *Itaque procul dubio*, n.7, fol.2ᵛ) draws also an interesting parallel with saints: "Memoria no[ta]: post mortem quis salvatur in sua memoria. Item no[ta] quare omni anno celebrantur festa Sanctorum." For Frederick II, see Huillard-Bréholles, v,907, the reconstruction of an aqueduct *ad laudem et gloriam nostri nominis*; see also the places quoted *Erg.Bd.*, 181. See also Dante, *Monarchia*, I,1: "ut palmam . . . in meam gloriam adipiscar." Or Andreas of Isernia, *In usus feudorum*, prooem.,n.11, fol.1ᵛ, quoting Seneca: *immortalis est ingenii memoria*.

[11] *Inferno*, XIII,53 (Petrus de Vinea): ". . . tua fama rinfreschi/ Nel mondo su . . ." Also *Inferno*, VI,88f; XVI,85; XXXI,127; cf. Burckhardt, *The Civilization of the Renaissance in Italy*, trans. by S. G. C. Middlemore (Vienna, n.d.), 307, nos.285-287. It is, of course, perfectly logical that *per perpetuam gloriam vivere* is desired by those in *Inferno*, since only the *Inferno* is of perpetual duration (Purgatory ends and Paradise is timeless), an idea expressed by the inscription of the Gate of Hell (*Inf.*, III,7f:

Dinanzi a me non fur cose create
Se non eterne, ed io eterno duro.

See below, n.15.

Aristotelian uncreated "world without end" likewise in terms of some secularized Eternity. But if we were to proceed on that assumption, the difficult question arises immediately: What kind of Eternity was it that was secularized and became immanent in this world? It was certainly not the Eternity of the Divine Being which Augustine had set against the short span of created Time allotted to this world and to mankind. For the *aeternitas* of God was timeless; it was a static Eternity without motion, and without past or future; it was, as Augustine called it, "a Now ever standing still" (*nunc semper stans*), or, as Dante put it, "the point at which all times are present."[12] This was certainly not the continuously flowing mutable Time of permanently successive moments which the Averroists had in mind and defended.

The answer comes from scholastic philosophy. A readiness on the part of theologians and scholastic philosophers to revise the Augustinian dualism of Time and Eternity and to embark on the problem of an unlimited continuity which was neither *tempus* nor *aeternitas*, may be noticed as far back as the twelfth century. The revival of Pseudo-Dionysius, John the Scot, the theological writings of Boethius, and the reception of the works of Avicenna by the school of Gilbert de la Porrée produced, so it has been said, "a powerful whiff of dynamism."[13] It led, among other things, to the revival of the notion of *aevum* ("eon"), a category of endless infinite Time which Saint Augustine's forcefully simplifying dualism had not really accounted for. Something comparable to a great intellectual clearing began, since it now became the task of scholastic philosophers to distinguish between the various categories of Time. It was not too difficult to explain the difference between *aeternitas* and *aevum*. Eternity, of course, was God's timeless and motionless Now-and-Ever, knowing neither past nor future. *Aevum*, however, was a kind of infiniteness and duration which had motion and therefore past and future, a sempiternity which according to all authorities was endless. There was differ-

---

12 *Paradiso*, XVII,18.

13 See M. H. Vicaire, "Les Porrétains et l'Avicennisme avant 1215," *Revue des sciences philosophiques et théologiques*, XXVI (1937), 449-482 (p.455: "un souffle dynamique puissant"); R. de Vaux, *Notes et textes sur l'Avicennisme latin aux confins des XIIe et XIIIe siècles* (Bibliothèque Thomiste, XX [Paris, 1934]); also J. M. Parent, *La doctrine de la création dans l'école de Chartres* (Publications de l'Institut d'études médiévales d'Ottawa, VIII [Paris and Ottawa, 1938]).

ence of opinion though, whether that sempiternity, which was created, was created before Time or together with Time; that is to say, whether *aevum* was infinite only in view of the future or also in view of the past. Whatever the correct answer may be, the fact remains that a third category had been worked into the former dualism of Eternity and Time, the *aevum*, which had a share in both Eternity and Time and which Aquinas later defined very accurately as something "placed in the middle between *aeternitas* and *tempus*."[14]

Hence, scholastic philosophy had to distinguish between three categories: *aeternitas, aevum,* and *tempus.* But which belonged to whom? The distribution of *aeternitas* and *tempus* was self-evident. The timeless Now-and-Ever was identical with God alone; and the finite created Time of this world, lasting from Creation to the Last Day, belonged to man. And *aevum?* The answer must have been likewise self-evident to an age which began to discover the intellectual joy and stimulus emanating from angelological investigations: *aevum,* of course, belonged to the angels and celestial Intelligences, the "eviternal" beings which were placed between God and man. The angels, like man, were created; but man's transitory *tempus* could not be theirs, since angels were eternal beings, bodiless, immortal, and outlasting the Last Day. On the other hand, being created they could not be coeternal with the Creator. It was, so to speak, true that the angels by their permanent vision of the divine glory participated, like the souls of the blessed, in the timeless Eternity of God. But the immortal spirits had a share also in terrestrial Time, not only because they could appear to men within Time, but also because they were created

---

14 For *aevum,* see the survey by A. Michel, "Eternité," *Dictionnaire de théologie catholique,* v:1, col.919. In general, Brabant, *Time and Eternity,* 74ff. Of course, the philosophers did not always interpret *aevum* in the same way; see F. Beemelmans, *Zeit und Ewigkeit nach Thomas von Aquino* (Beiträge zur Geschichte der Philosophie im Mittelalter, xvii,1; Münster, 1914), 52ff; E. Gilson, *The Philosophy of St. Bonaventura* (New York, 1938), 26off; C. R. S. Harris, *Duns Scotus* (Oxford, 1927), ii,141ff; Gilson, *Jean Duns Scot* (Études de philosophie médiévale, xlii [Paris, 1952]), 401ff. The notion of *aevum* was certainly not unknown in the earlier Middle Ages; in 799, Alcuin defined it on the whole correctly (*MGH, Epp.* iv,263ff, No.163). Philosophically and theologically, however, *aevum* gained new impetus by its integration into the angelologies of scholasticism. For the infinity of Time with regard either to past and future or to future alone, see Ambrose, *Hexaemeron,* i,1,3, *PL,* xiv,135, who connects those differing concepts with Aristotle and Plato respectively; cf. Richard McKeon, "Aristotelianism in Western Christianity," in *Environmental Factors in Christian History* (Chicago, 1939), 224, n.68.

and therefore had, after their peculiar angelic fashion, a Before and an After. *Aevum* (in fact a far more complicated notion than can be demonstrated here), bridged the chasm between timeless Eternity and finite Time. If God in his Eternity was the Immutable beyond and without Time, and if man in his *tempus* was the Mutable within a mutable and changing finite Time, then the angels were the Immutable within a changing, though infinite, *aevum*.[15]

To summarize this brief excursus into meta-history, there existed indeed an otherworldly equivalent of the changing and infinite Time which the Averroists claimed for this present world: the *aevum* of the angels in heaven. This fact is less surprising than it may seem once we realize that the celestial Intelligences— Spirits without a material body—were the created Ideas or Prototypes of God. They were the transcendentalized Christian descendents, not really of the Platonic Ideas which had an independent status, but of the Aristotelian εἴδη, the immanent actualizations of the separate types. The revival of the Aristotelian "eternity of the world," which presupposed and resulted in the immortality of the genera and separate species, was therefore indeed a "secularization" of the angelic *aevum*: an infinite continuum of Time was, so to say, transferred from heaven to earth and recovered by man. It was the secularization of the Christian concept of continuity perhaps even more than the classical belief in the circular motion of an infinite time, which the Averroists likewise endorsed, but which was one of the least acceptable of their theses. Public opinion quickly discarded this theorem implying a periodical recurrence of events, and replaced the circular continuity by the conventional linear continuity characteristic of Christian thought in general—and probably also of the angelic *aevum*.[16]

---

[15] See Brabant, *Time and Eternity*, 77. I am fully aware of the fact that *aevum* has many other aspects as well, and that the Time continuum of the angels is a most involved problem, discussed over and over again by the scholastic philosophers in their *Quodlibet* literature and elsewhere. That Hell belonged to *aevum* is suggested by Aquinas, *Quodlibet*, v,7, ed. P. Glorieux, *La littérature quodlibétique de 1260 à 1320* (Bibliothèque Thomiste, v. [Kain, 1925]), 1,281: *Utrum Lucifer sit subiectum aevi?* See, above, n.11, for Dante, in whose system the three categories are represented: to the Paradise belongs *aeternitas*, to the Purgatory *tempus*, and to Hell *aevum*. It would be senseless, of course, should the sinners be made to suffer in timelessness, since in that case there would not be an infinite succession of punishment and pain.

[16] For the doctrine of eternal recurrence in periodical circles, see, in Bishop

According to the teaching of Aquinas, every angel represented a species: the immateriality of the angels did not allow the individuation of the species in matter, in a plurality of material individuals.[17] Little wonder then that finally the personified collectives of the jurists, which were juristically immortal species, displayed all the features otherwise attributed to angels; for the legal "fictitious persons" were, in fact, pure actualizations and thus appeared like the next of kin of the angelic fictions. In the center of the corporational doctrines of the jurists were the collective abstractions, or immortal and immutable species, in comparison with which the mortal, and ever replaceable, individual components appeared of lesser importance and in many respects negligible. The de-individualized fictitious persons of the lawyers, therefore, necessarily resembled the angels, and the jurists themselves recognized that there was some similarity between their abstractions and the angelic beings.[18] In this respect, then, it may

---

Tempier's list of errors, No.6 (Denifle, *Chartularium*, 544). Whether the angelic *aevum* was always linear continuity or whether it was also simultaneity (changes without a succession of moments; see Beemelmans, *Zeit und Ewigkeit nach Thomas von Aquino*, 44f), is a different matter; it certainly had nothing to do with the cycles of 36,000 years which the Averroists defended.

[17] It was against the angelic coincidence of species with individual, as defended by Aquinas, that Duns Scotus polemicized; see Gilson, *Jean Duns Scot*, 399ff, and, in general, F. Ueberweg and M. Baumgartner, *Grundriss der Geschichte der Philosophie der patristischen und scholastischen Zeit* (10th ed., Berlin, 1915), 498 and 580.

[18] An Accursian gloss shows the familiarity of the glossators with the scholastic distinctions; see *Glos.ord.*, on *D*.8,2,33 ("ut in perpetuum idem paries aeternus esset"—a perpetual easement for the upkeep of an eternal wall of a building), v. '*aeternus*': "id est sempiternus. nam aeternum dicitur, quod semper fuit et est: ut Deus. sempiternum dicitur, quod incepit et non desinet: ut anima et angelus et haec servitus." Shortly thereafter Odofredus, on *D*.8,2,33 (Lyon, 1550), fol.263r, implied that "nihil in hoc seculo potest esse perpetuum nisi per surrogationem," and later glossators on that law, Bartolus (fol.222) or Baldus (fol.311), simply state that *perpetuatio fit per successionem sive subrogationem*. More eloquent is Angelus de Ubaldis, on *D*.8,2,33,rubr. (Venice, 1580), fol.185v. He states: "Nota sub sole nihil possibile est [esse] aeternum, fit tantum aeternitas per successionem seu subrogationem, et ita est casus hic." With the *Glos.ord.* of Accursius, he distinguishes between "eternal" and "sempiternal," but feeling uneasy about the "equiparation" of *servitus* with *anima* and *angelus* and about some similarities with the Aristotelian doctrine of the Eternity of the World, he argues against Accursius: "Sed quod dicit glossa 'et haec servitus,' non dicit bene referendo ad extra predicta, quia impossibile est aliquid esse sub sole sine fine, et ideo mundus habebit finem *secundum fidem*, licet princeps philosophorum fuerit in opinione contraria motus rationibus naturalibus." The notions of "eternal" and "sempiternal" were nevertheless often enough confused. For example, Innocent IV's sentence against Frederick II at Lyon (1245) was published in the *Liber Sextus* (c.2 VI 2,14; ed. Friedberg, II,1008) under the correct

be said that the political and legal world of thought of the later Middle Ages began to be populated by immaterial angelic bodies, large and small: they were invisible, ageless, sempiternal, immortal, and sometimes even ubiquitous; and they were endowed with a *corpus intellectuale* or *mysticum* which could stand any comparison with the "spiritual bodies" of the celestial beings.

Undeniably the problem of Time and Continuity was close to the center of discussions carried on by both scholastic and secular philosophers. To maintain that the problem of Time had the effects of an activating intellectual undertow throughout the later Middle Ages and the Renaissance would probably be an understatement. Man's new attitude in his relation to Time affected almost every sector of life. The world, of course, did not turn "Averroist" as a result of the teaching of a Siger of Brabant, Boethius of Dacia, and other masters in the faculty of arts at the University of Paris: the world remained Christian. Nevertheless, what had been epidemic in the thirteenth century became endemic in the fourteenth and fifteenth: one did not accept the infinite continuity of a "World without End," but accepted a quasi-infinite continuity; one did not believe in the uncreatedness of the world and its endlessness, but one began to act as though it were endless; one presupposed continuities where continuity had been neither noticed nor visualized before; and one was ready to modify, revise, and repress, though not to abandon, the traditional feelings about limitations in Time and about the transitoriness of human institutions and actions.[19]

This, we may take it, marked the new approach to Life and to Time of the intellectual sector of society. One had not invented a new notion of Time, but accepted Time's other aspect. Only in so far as another aspect of Time—its continuity and practical infiniteness—was emphasized, where previously the emphasis was laid on Time's transitoriness, was there a change of man's sense of the nature of Time. "If you want to govern for thousands and

---

heading: *Ad memoriam sempiternam.* Durandus, however, establishing a general rule concerning the passing of sentences, refers to it wrongly (*Speculum iuris,* II, part.iii,§6,n.7, vol.II,790), when he says: "Sententia enim fertur *ad aeternam rei memoriam,* ut legitur . . . [c.2 VI 2,14] in superscriptione." See below, Ch.VII,n.6.

[19] G. de Lagarde, *La naissance etc., II: Marsile de Padoue* (Paris, 1948), 79 and 85ff, remarks correctly: "L'Averroïsme est moins une doctrine qu'une attitude." See also Leclercq, *Jean de Paris,* 75.

thousands of years," ran a Sienese inscription referring to the images of classical and Christian heroes and virtues, "you who are ruling look upon these."[20] The change implied a revaluation of Time rather than some total revolution, a dialectical shift from Time's fragility to its ever-flowing, vivifying dynamism.

PERPETUA NECESSITAS

No matter whether the Aristotelian and Averroist doctrines of a "World without End" were accepted, rejected, or modified, the debate itself left its unmistakable and easily traceable imprints on the thinking of the generations to come. Independently, however, the practical needs of kingdoms and communities led to the fiction of a quasi-infinite continuity of public institutions—a continuity, to be sure, of a far less philosophical pattern. The maxim of the inalienability of the royal demesne as well as the idea of an impersonal fisc "which never dies"[21] stand out as landmarks of a new concept of institutional continuity inspired chiefly, it seems, by the two Laws, Roman and Canon. The factor of Time, however, started to permeate also in other respects the daily technique of public, financial, and legal administration—a phenomenon worth being rapidly outlined here by means of a few illustrative examples.

Public taxation, in the earlier Middle Ages, was always extraordinary and always *ad hoc*, for taxes fell due not on the return of a certain date, but on the return of a certain event. The feudal aids were due for ransom of the lord, knighting of his eldest son, dowry of his eldest daughter, and, haltingly since the twelfth century, for the defense of the realm in the case of a public emergency, the *casus necessitatis*. Those four cases referred each to an event: the first three were linked to the private and personal life of the lord, whereas the fourth case was, so to say, public and supra-personal, referring chiefly to *regnum* and *patria*.[22] Ransom, knighting, and dowry were unrepeatable instances; an "emergency of the realm," however, could be proclaimed, technically, year after year, at least until the Prince met with the resistance of his

---

[20] Theodor E. Mommsen, "Petrarch and the Decoration of the Sala Virorum Illustrium in Padua," *Art Bulletin*, XXXIV (1952), 114.

[21] Above, Chapter IV, nos.267, 292.

[22] See Post, "Two Laws," 420ff. See also above, Chapter V, n.127, for the connection with crusading taxes; in general, A. Gottlob, *Die päpstlichen Kreuzzugssteuern des dreizehnten Jahrhunderts* (Heiligenstadt, 1892).

drained subjects. As is well known, the fourth case, the *necessitas regis et regni*, eventually flung the gates open to permanent, annual taxation dependent not upon an event, but upon Time. Frederick II, for example, in the last phase of his struggle against the Roman pontiffs, proclaimed almost regularly at the beginning of every year in beautifully phrased and almost apologetic manifestoes the *dira et dura necessitas* of the empire only to impose a new *collecta* on his Sicilian subjects, the clergy included.[23] So did Charles of Anjou, later; so did Philip the Fair of France, and others. Indeed, the fiction of an unrepeatable event, of a singular emergency, and of the extraordinary character of the taxation still was maintained, and it would be maintained for some time to come; but the old fiction was to yield to a new fiction, and what remained was routine: an undisguised annual recurrence of financial requests.

[23] See, for Sicily, *Erg.Bd.*, 193, 243. Most revealing, though hardly evaluated, is a letter of Pope Martin IV, written to Charles of Anjou after the Sicilian Vespers and dealing with the *collecta* as an ordinary tax; cf. *Les registres du Pape Martin IV*, ed. Olivier-Martin (Paris, 1913), 225, No.488; see also *Les registres du Pape Honorius IV*, ed. M. Prou (Paris, 1886), 75, No.96,§§3-7. Concerning the pre-Angevin history of the *collecta* Pope Martin IV asserted that "de modo subventionum et collectarum, que in regno Sicilie tempore clare memorie Guillelmi regis Sicilie solvebantur, . . . nichil aliud potuit inveniri, nisi quod antiquorum habet relatio, quod quondam Fridericus Romanorum imperator *tempore quo de ultramarinis partibus rediit, primo subventiones et collectas ordinarias in regno imposuit supradicto*, et quod ante predictum tempus collecte et subventiones tantum fiebant, cum rex Sicilie pro defensione ipsius regni defensionem faciebat, ac in coronatione regis ipsius, necnon et quando filius eius suscipiebat cingulum militare, ac ipsius filia nuptui tradebatur." This became the common opinion; for the papal verdict, unfavorable to Frederick II, was repeated very often, even in later times; see, e.g., Paris de Puteo (d.1493), *De Syndicatu*, I,2,n.59 (Lyon, 1548), fol.8: "nam Federicus fuit depositus ab imperio, quia collectas in regno imposuit. . . ." For the oppressiveness, see E. Sthamer, *Bruchstücke mittelalterlicher Enqueten aus Unteritalien* (Abh. preuss. Akad., 1933, No.2; Berlin, 1933), 13, the quotation from Saba Malaspina, III,c.16, in Muratori, *Scriptores*, VIII,831f. The value of the papal statement should be sought in the fact that the Holy See noticed quite precisely that a taxation *ad hoc* had been changed into "ordinary taxation." The date of this change, however, is certainly not correct, because it is hardly true that Frederick II introduced annual taxation as early as 1230, nor is it permissible to intimate that the introduction of annual *collectae* depended on "Oriental" influences. What exercised influence was Roman Law (see below, n.34) which, we are told, prompted Barbarossa at Roncaglia, in 1158, to try to exact from the Italian cities an annual imperial tribute. Cf. Rahewin, *Gesta*, IV,c.7, ed. Hofmeister, *MGH,SS.r. Germ.* (3rd ed., 1912), 240: The emperor demanded "nec de terra tantum, verum etiam de suis propriis capitibus *census annui redditionem*." Also *Ligurinus*, VIII,v.574, ed. C. G. Dümge, Heidelberg, 1812: "capitolium *certo sub tempore* censum." Barbarossa's intentions, however, never materialized. See also P. W. Finsterwalder, "Die Gesetze des Reichstages von Roncalia vom 11. November 1158," *ZfRG*, germ.Abt., LI (1931), 59ff.

It is true, of course, that the scholastic doctrines concerning taxation strictly denied the right of the state to any annual or even periodically recurrent taxation.[24] However, by the *casus necessitatis*, which also the Church acknowledged, a new principle was set.[25] It was set for the permanent annual taxation such as finally became the recognized right of the sovereign state in order to meet the needs of the polity. By the fourteenth century, or even in the thirteenth, the pretense of an *ad hoc* taxation was occasionally dropped, and the fictitiously extraordinary became the overtly ordinary: public taxation, at least in many parts of the Continent, became synonymous with annual taxation. In other words, taxation, formerly linked to an unrepeatable event, now was linked to the calendar, to the eternally rolling wheel of Time. The state had become permanent, and permanent were its emergencies and needs, its *necessitas*.

The notion of *necessitas*, thereby, acquired another, in fact, a completely new meaning. As a ground for taxation, the *casus necessitatis* originally referred to emergencies arising chiefly from without: defense of the *patria* against a hostile inroad, a war against political or religious enemies, also against rebels, against heretics, even against the spiritual power. Around 1300, however, the notion of *necessitas* began to be focused also upon the ordinary and (so to speak) budgetary needs of administration; and to meet these administrative needs the governments arrived at the new fiction of a *perpetua necessitas*, implying (not unlike the modern tenets of "perpetual revolution") the perpetuation of something that, by definition, indicated an exception, some singular condition or some momentary deviation from the rule.

The perpetuation of *necessitas*, of course, was noticed also by

[24] For the scholastic and theological doctrines on taxation, see Paul Kehl, *Die Steuer in der Lehre der Theologen des Mittelalters* (Volkswirtschaftliche Studien, 17, Berlin, 1927), 74ff and passim. It is true that in France, after 1314, the estates had the right to grant a special tallage; but the assumption began to develop later on that the tallage had been granted perpetually. Cf. Holtzmann, *Französische Verfassungsgeschichte*, 408. In England, of course, every general subvention to the king had to be granted by Parliament.

[25] Langlois, "Philippe III," in: Lavisse, *Histoire de France* (Paris, 1901), III:2, 250f: "Le principe était posé." See, for France, the numerous studies of Carl Stephenson, above all "Les 'aides' des villes françaises au XIIe et XIIIe siècle," *Moyen âge*, 2e sér., XXIV (1922), 274-328, and "La taille dans les villes d'Allemagne," *ibid.*, XXV (1925), 1-43; further, Joseph R. Strayer and C. H. Taylor, *Studies in Early French Taxation* (Cambridge, Mass., 1939).

contemporaries, and a jurist of the early fourteenth century, Oldradus de Ponte (d. 1335), provides us with all the clues we may desire. In one of his legal opinions, dealing with the taxability of certain noblemen with regard to an annual tallage, Oldradus distinguished between the ancient singular necessity and the new perpetual necessity. The question posed to the legal expert is described in the title, as follows:

> Is a person, that is held to contribute to taxes imposed for the sake of [public] utility or necessity, held also to pay taxes imposed for the sake of an *habitual* necessity, though [this be] not an *actual* necessity?[26]

The distinction made here between an habitual, that is, perpetual need (*necessitas in habitu*) and an actual emergency (*necessitas in actu*) is telling enough all by itself. Oldradus, of course, was fully aware of the fact that formerly the imposition of a direct tax for the sake of "public and common utility and necessity" was understood as an exception, an extraordinary taxation (*indictio extraordinaria*). He knows also that the reason (a case of necessity) for imposing a tallage as well as the king's regalian right of imposing the emergency tribute agreed with old feudal custom, and he is honest enough to admit that "the imposition of an annual tallage is a new action: and in this respect the taxes are called ordinary (*indictio ordinaria*)."[27] However, ordinary and extraordinary taxes served the same idea: to meet a *necessitas*. Only, *necessitas* itself had in each case a different point of reference; and this too has been clarified by Oldradus.

The question laid before the jurist was whether certain noblemen could claim tax exemption if the King of France demanded annually a tallage "for the public and common utility and neces-

---

[26] Oldradus de Ponte, *Consilia*, 98 (Venice, 1621), fol.39: "Contribuere si unus tenetur ad munera, quae fiunt causa utilitatis vel necessitatis, tenetur praestare munera, quae fiunt causa necessitatis in habitu, licet non in actu." It is not certain, of course, whether this summary is by the author himself or by a later editor. However, the distinction between *necessitas in actu* and *necessitas in habitu* covers precisely what Oldradus discusses in his *Consilium*.

[27] *Ibid.*, n.4: ". . . quod, si contingat aliquam talliam indici quae fiet gratia publicae et communis utilitatis et necessitatis et cetera, quasi de futuris et extraordinariis indictionibus intellexerit. Sed huic respondetur. . . . Licet enim talliam indicendi causa et regalia sint antiqui actus: tamen indictionis omni anno est novus: et hoc respectu ordinariae praestationis indictiones appella[n]tur. Extraordinariae vero superindicta. . . ." See, for the distinction between ordinary and extraordinary taxations, also above, nos.23f.

sity." There was no doubt, declared Oldradus, that the tallage served public utility and necessity and that the King of France was entitled to impose a tallage, for "he has imperial rights and he owns, by his imperial privilege, all that pertains to imperial service."[28] The jurist then turned to the evidence proving that in other respects the noblemen actually paid annual taxes which indeed served to meet some "habitual need." And in that connection he discussed two ancient feudal obligations—*alberga* and *cavalcata*—which despite their original *ad hoc* character had likewise been converted into annual taxes and which the noblemen would not hesitate to pay "when the king, or his procurator, announced these contributions annually."[29] He discussed, in the first place, the *alberga* or *droit de gîte*, meaning the obligation of quartering the feudal lord or king when he visited a district or province to hold court and hear the complaints of the people against their lords.[30] In former days, explained Oldradus, this obligation was due only when the suzerain visited the district in his proper person.

> Today this [obligation] is paid annually in money. . . . For no one itinerates through the province to administer justice to the inferior grades against their lords: for there are judges in every single place, who do that very thing [administer justice], and they receive *de publico* a salary from the king. . . . Therefore, since such display of justice is in itself a public utility and necessity, it seems that also the noblemen . . . should be held to contribute, because [this taxation] is truly for the utility and the need of the province.[31]

28 *Ibid.*, rubr.2: "Quaeritur modo, si talliae, quas indicet rex seu eius curia, reputentur fieri gratia publicae utilitatis et necessitatis. Et est sciendum quod rex habet in dictis communitatibus et provincia iura imperialia et quae pertinent ad imperiale servitium ex privilegio imperiali." This "privilege," of course, does not refer to an emperor's charter, but to the king's imperial privilege as *imperator in regno suo*. Oldradus does not say *expressis verbis* that he is talking about the King of France; but since he lived in Avignon and styled the ruler *dominus rex noster*, he could not easily have referred to another king. Also, the fact that noblemen were supposed to contribute to the tallage, seems to hint that the *consilium* referred to Southern France; see Holtzmann, *Französische Verfassungsgeschichte*, 263f.

29 *Ibid.*: "Item rex, seu eius procurator, bis in anno annuatim indicit in dicto castro duo munera: unum quod vocatur alberga, aliud cavalcata."

30 *Ibid.*: "Alberga praestatur ista ratione: quia solebant communes provinciae ire ad castra et audiebant querelas hominum de dominis suis: tunc homines solvebant expensas et illud vocatur alberga."

31 *Ibid.*, n.1: "Quae [alberga] hodie solvitur in pecunia annuatim . . . licet hodie nullus circumeat provinciam inferioribus de dominis suis iustitiam ministrando: quia tamen sunt iudices in singulis locis, qui hoc ipsum faciunt et de publico salarium a rege recipiunt. . . . Unde cum exhibitio talis iustitiae habeat in se

In addition to the change—clearly outlined by Oldradus—from an *ad hoc* obligation to a permanent and ordinary taxation, it is evident that the meaning of *necessitas* has shifted from an outer emergency to an inner administrative need, that this inner need has been perpetualized, and that the perpetual administration of justice required an annual emergency tribute just as a singular emergency contribution was required for the defense of *patria*. But even the defense of *patria* was now perpetualized. There was, in the fourteenth century, as yet no permanent professional army of an individual government, although the companies of mercenary knights then roaming about Italy represented, so to speak, independent armies in permanence. There was, nevertheless, permanent taxation for military purposes. The *cavalcata* or *chevauchée*, originally the feudal obligation of performing military service, came to mean the commutation of this service into a fine or scutage paid annually. Oldradus de Ponte saw again the essential point.

> Even though the army might not be summoned in every year, it is nevertheless advisable to look ahead that there be money in the treasury to pay the soldiers if [or when] an army be raised. . . . For, the purpose of an army is the public good.[32]

Oldradus, while conveying to us some foretaste of the approaching mentality of mercantilism, again demonstrates that a *necessitas in actu* has been commuted into a perpetual *necessitas in habitu* in order to meet potential needs in the future.[33] Annual taxation, at any rate, was rationalized by perpetuation of public needs, by a *perpetua necessitas* belonging either to the present as in the case of

---

publicam utilitatem et necessitatem, . . . videtur quod huiusmodi expensas nobiles, de quibus quaeritur, contribuere teneantur: quia verum est propter provinciae utilitatem et necessitatem." See, for the annual payment of the *droit de gîte* already in the 13th century, Holtzmann, *Französische Verfassungsgeschichte*, 257.

32 *Ibid.*, n.1: "Cavalcata est pro exercitu regis: quae quamvis non fiat, solvitur in pecunia annuatim." *Ibid.*, n.3: "Et idem videtur de secunda [i.e. cavalcata] dicendum: licet enim non semper fiat exercitus, expedit uti provisione, ut cum locus fuerit, in aerario sit pecunia, ex qua militibus satisfiat. . . . Finis autem exercitus est ad bonum publicum. . . ." See above, Ch.v,n.222.

33 Oldradus (*ibid.*, nos.3-4) points out that those military general taxes had been customary in the Roman Empire and that Christ himself recommended the payment of the tribute: "Christus tributa Caesari monet reddi, quia per bella necessario militi stipendia praebentur [c.4, C.xxiii, q.1, ed. Friedberg, 1,893], et ab huiusmodi contributione nullus excipitur. Si enim censum filius Dei solvit, quis tu tantus es qui non putas esse solvendum [c.28, C.xi, q.1, ed. Friedberg, 1,634]?"

legal administration or to the future as in the case of military preparation.

The distinction between extraordinary and ordinary needs applies also to diplomatic communication. Mediaeval embassies always served momentary needs; they were despatched *ad hoc* for a special purpose—to present a message or a gift, offer friendship or terminate it, or any other purpose—and the envoys would always return to their lords when their negotiations had come to an end. Those embassies were always "extraordinary" delegations entrusted with a special order and serving a special purpose. The usage of keeping ambassadors at other courts for longer periods, not to mention permanently, was unknown in the Middle Ages, and the credit is usually given to fifteenth-century Venice for having inaugurated modern diplomacy. That, however, is not quite correct. Kings began to keep so-called *procuratores*, legally trained envoys, almost permanently at the papal court—from the time of Gregory IX (1227-41) onward—to take care of legal business in Rome where law-suits pended often for many years. Again, a principle was set. For around 1300, as the *Acta Aragonensia* have clearly revealed, kings began to appoint permanent representatives also to important secular courts where not legal but political business had to be observed. Moreover, the credentials of those ambassadors, formerly describing perhaps the special nature of the diplomatic business, now were not rarely drawn up for a specific time rather than for a specified singular purpose. Once more we notice a tendency to link an institution—the ambassadorial office—to Time.[34]

We may think also of the custom to record all administrative

---

[34] R. von Heckel, "Das Aufkommen der ständigen Prokuratoren an der päpstlichen Kurie," *Miscellanea Fr. Ehrle* (Rome, 1924), II,315ff; Hermann Grauert, "Magister Heinrich der Poet," *Abh.bayer.Akad.*, XXVII (1912), 230ff; H. Finke, *Acta Aragonensia* (Berlin and Leipzig, 1908), I, pp.cxxiiiff; Gaines Post, "Plena potestas and Consent in Medieval Assemblies," *Traditio*, I (1943), 364ff. Frederick II, at least, had a *nuntius consuetus* accredited to England; see the author's "Petrus de Vinea in England," 65, n.81; for other appointments mentioning the continuity or time at large, see *Calendar of Patent Rolls 1232-1247*, pp.11, 32, 147 (Simon de Steland); Finke, *op.cit.*, cxxxviiif and cxxxii; Luis Weckmann, "Les origines des missions diplomatiques permanentes," *Revue générale de Droit International Public* (1952, No.2), pp.17ff. See also Garrett Mattingly, "The First Resident Embassies: Mediaeval Italian Origins of Modern Diplomacy," *Speculum*, XII (1937), 423-439, who (p.427) mentions as the first instance of permanent representation an envoy of Ludovico Gonzaga of Mantua at the court of Milan (1375), but fails to consider the evidence of the *Acta Aragonensia*.

acts in permanent registers which, by their technical division into annual rolls or books, were linked indeed to the calendar and to Time.[35] Nor would it be too difficult to add other examples illustrating a peculiar continuity of the administrative apparatus of the new monarchies and of governments at large. However, all that had to be said here was that practical needs produced institutional changes presupposing, as it were, the fiction of an endless continuity of the bodies politic. And while it cannot be claimed that any particular philosophy caused the new governmental practice, it cannot easily be denied that existing techniques of government found support, and were quickened in their development, by philosophic thought and legal theories which worked their way into administrative practice from many sides.

2. Fictio Figura Veritatis

IMPERIUM SEMPER EST

The climax of the eschatological mission of the *Ecclesia militans* was its disappearance on the Day of Judgment, the day when it merged with the *Ecclesia triumphans*. It was, therefore, a matter of dogma and faith to believe that the Church militant was to last until the end of Time. This belief in the continuity of the Church until the Last Day, however, not only had effects on spiritual matters, but also influenced quite profane issues of ecclesiastical administration and law. A canon (c. 70) of the Fourth Council of Toledo (633) became rather important in this respect; for the Council decreed that freedmen of the Church and their descendants could never be dismissed from the clientage of the Church because their patron, the Church, "never dies,"—*nunquam moritur*.[36] This sentence, after having passed through various canonical

---

[35] On the registers and their introduction by the secular states, see R. von Heckel, "Das päpstliche und sizilische Registerwesen," *ArchUF*, I (1908), 445ff, and passim; H. Bresslau, *Handbuch der Urkundenlehre* (2nd ed., Leipzig, 1912), I, 103ff; also F. Kern, "Recht und Verfassung im Mittelalter," *HZ*, cxx (1919), 34ff, and *ibid.*, cxv (1916), 496ff, translated by S. B. Chrimes in *Kingship and Law in the Middle Ages* (Oxford, 1948), 149ff.

[36] See c.65,C.xii,q.2, ed. Friedberg, 1,708: "Liberti ecclesiae, quia numquam eorum moritur patrona, a patrocinio ecclesiae numquam discedant. . . ." See Friedberg, *loc.cit.*, n.734, for the transmission of c.70, Toledo IV, in canonical collections. The *Glossa ordinaria*, v. *moritur*, refers simply to the parallel from St. Augustine (see next note); but the passage is quoted frequently; see, e.g., *Glos.ord.* on c.24,D.LIV (Friedberg, 1,214), v. *fuerint*: "quia eorum [libertorum] domina, scilicet ecclesia, nunquam moritur, ut 12.q.2.liberti." Cf. Gierke, *Gen.R.*, iii,277,n.93.

collections, found its way finally into Gratian's *Decretum* where it was supported by a passage from Saint Augustine, inserted into a letter of Pope Pelagius, saying that "it cannot be that there be no Church"—*ecclesia nulla esse non potest.*[37] Thus, the dogmatic sempiternity of the Church militant found its juristic equivalent in the maxim *Ecclesia nunquam moritur,* "the Church never dies."

Sempiternity was attributed also to the Roman Empire. The belief in the continuity of the empire *in finem saeculi* was as common in the Middle Ages and as much an established fact as was the late-antique belief in the "eternity" of the city of Rome; and the struggle against Antichrist, expected to take place just before the End, bestowed upon the Christian empire an eschatological function related to that of the militant Church.[38] The belief in the sempiternity of the Roman Empire, to be sure, was not a matter of dogma. It rested, for one thing, on Jerome's identification of Daniel's vision of the Four World Monarchies the last of which, that of the Romans, was to continue till the end of the world; and the late-mediaeval jurists occasionally found it convenient to recall the popular argument.[39] This argument was not defeated by a

[37] See c.33, C.xxiv, q.1, ed. Friedberg, I,978f.

[38] Baldus, *Consilia*, I,328,n.8, fol.103: "[imperium] quod debet durare usque in finem huius saeculi." The eternity of Rome was denied by Augustine insofar as the fall of Rome was supposed to signify the end of the world; but the old belief survived; see Theodor E. Mommsen, "St. Augustine and the Christian Idea of Progress," *Journal of the History of Ideas*, xII (1951), 351; also J. Straub, "Christliche Geschichtsapologetik in der Krisis des römischen Reiches," *Historia*, I (1950), 52ff, and, for the idea in general, esp. in the Middle Ages, F. Kampers, *Die deutsche Kaiseridee in Prophetie und Sage* (Munich, 1896). The basis of the whole speculation was II Thess. 2: 1-8, quoted already by Tertullian, *Apol.*, xxxII,1, in connection with the prayer for the emperor and the Roman Empire; see Ladner, "Aspects," 419,n.55, on the later interpretation of the Pauline epistle. The belief in the duration of the Empire, of course, was alive also in Byzantium; see, e.g., Endre von Ivanka, "Der Fall Konstantinopels und das byzantinische Geschichtsdenken," *Jahrbuch der Österreichischen Byzantinischen Gesellschaft*, III (1954), 19ff.

[39] For the doctrine of the four empires, see C. Trieber, "Die Idee der vier Weltreiche," *Hermes*, xxvII (1892), 321-342; F. Kampers, "Die Idee von der Ablösung der Weltreiche," *Hist.Jhb.*, xIx (1898), 423ff; and, for the most recent literature, Mommsen, "St. Augustine," 350,nos.5-6; also Schramm, *Kaiser, Rom und Renovatio*, I,244f. Interesting is Otto of Freising, *Chronica*, v, prol., ed. Hofmeister, 226f, who connects the idea of the four empires with that of "progress" as represented by Priscian, *Inst.gram.*, I,1 (above, Chapter v,n.187); see also Joseph Schmidlin, *Die geschichtsphilosophische und kirchenpolitische Weltanschauung Ottos von Freising* (Freiburg, 1906), 28ff. For the jurists, see, e.g., Bartolus, on *Ad reprimenda* (Edict of Emperor Henry VII, in *MGH, Const.*, IV,965, No.929), n.8, v. *totius orbis*, in Bartolus, *Consilia, quaestiones et tractatus* (Venice, 1567), fol.115ᵛ, also in *Corp.Iur.Civ.*, IV,124, where the Edict is among the *Extravagantes* of mediaeval emperors appended to the *Libri feudorum*. Bartolus, referring to Daniel 2: 39-40, talks about "Nabuchodonosor rex

thesis, popularized by Tolomeo of Lucca, the continuator of Aquinas' tractate on Princely Government, and saying that the fourth monarchy had been followed by a fifth, the monarchy of Christ, "the true lord and monarch of the world," whose first vicar was, if unwittingly, the Emperor Augustus.[40] This new version played occasionally a role in legal thought, too. "With the coming of Christ, the empire of the Romans began to be the empire of Christ," wrote Bartolus, and therefore "it is true if we maintain that everything belongs to the Roman Empire, which now is the Empire of Christ."[41] Though Bartolus merely wished to prove the universal jurisdiction of the emperor or rather the fact that "the

---

qui tunc erat universalis imperator," and finally develops the full doctrine of the four (or five) empires (see note 41). Also Baldus, *Consilia*, 1,328,n.8, fol.103: ". . . et hoc apparet in mutatione quatuor principalium regnorum."

[40] Aquinas, *De regimine principum*, III,12-13, ed. Mathis, 53ff: ". . . sed nos quintam [monarchiam] possumus addere (c.12)." The *principatus* of Christ began immediately on the day of his birth (c.14), and the census paid to Augustus universally (Luke 2: 1) was "non sine mysterio, quia ille natus erat, qui verus erat mundi Dominus et Monarcha, cuius vices gerebat Augustus, licet non intelligens, sed nutu Dei . . . (c.13)." Cf. Woolf, *Bartolus*, 318ff; Ladner, "Aspects," 419, n.55.

[41] Bartolus, on *Ad reprimenda*, n.8, v. *totius orbis* (above, n.39): "Quarto fuit imperium Romanorum. Ultimo adveniente Christo istud Romanorum imperium incepit esse Christi imperium, et ideo apud Christi vicarium est uterque gladius, scilicet spiritualis et temporalis. . . . Dic ergo quod ante Christum imperium Romanorum dependebat ab eo [principe] solo et imperator recte dicebatur quod dominus mundi esset et quod omnia sua sunt. Post Christum vero imperium est apud Christum et eius vicarium et transfertur per papam in principem saecularem [reference to the Decretal *Venerabilem*: c.34 X 1,6]. Unde sic dicimus omnia sunt imperii Romani, quod nunc est Christi, verum est, si referamus ad personam Christi. . . ." It was customary to discuss the doctrine of the Two Swords in connection with the Decretal *Venerabilem*; see Post, "Unpublished Glosses on the *translatio imperii* and the Two Swords," *AKKR*, CXVII (1937), 408,410f, and, above all, the unwieldy mass of excellent studies by A. M. Stickler on the Two Swords, enumerated in his article "Sacerdozio e Regno nelle nuove ricerche," in *Sacerdozio e Regno da Gregorio VII a Bonifacio VIII* (Miscellanea Historiae Pontificiae, XVIII; Rome, 1954), 3,n.3; the posthumously edited study of Wilhelm Levison, "Die mittelalterliche Lehre von den beiden Schwertern," *DA*, IX (1951), 14-42, does not consider the Bartolus passage, whereas Joseph Lecler, "L'Argument des deux glaives," *Recherches de science religieuse*, XXII (1932), 171, quotes the passage, but does not comment on it. It was customary also, in connection with the Two Swords, to point out that historically the empire preceded the papacy: "Ante enim fuit imperator quam papa, ante imperium quam papatus" (see, e.g., Stickler, "Der Schwerterbegriff bei Huguccio," *Ephemerides Juris Canonici*, III [1947], 211, n.3; the argument is repeated, over and over again; cf. Friedrich Kempf, *Papsttum und Kaisertum bei Innocenz III*. [Miscellanea Historiae Pontificiae, XIX; Rome, 1954], 212f, nos.48ff), that therefore originally all power was in the hands of the emperor, but that after the advent of Christ the imperial and pontifical powers were separated, because only Christ himself had both powers. Bartolus, of course, followed that doctrine, but he preferred to connect it with that of Tolomeo of Lucca.

whole world's regularity rests in the emperor,"[42] there followed nevertheless the obvious conclusion that the terrestrial Roman Empire of Christ would last until the End.[43] Tenets such as these, however, supported and were supported by the Justinian Law itself which asserted that the empire was founded by God directly;[44] that the empire was "forever";[45] and that, therefore, as Andreas of Isernia put it, "the Church does not die and is forever, like the Empire."[46]

This transcendentally-founded continuity of the Roman Empire was buttressed by an argument in favor of an immanent continuity. The *lex regia*, it will be recalled, established—at least according to the defenders of popular sovereignty—the imprescriptible right of the Roman people to confer the *imperium* and all power on the Prince. If, however, Rome and the empire were "forever," it followed *a fortiori* that the Roman *populus* likewise was "forever," no matter who may have been substituted for the original *populus Romanus* or played its part at a given moment: there always would be men, women, and children living in Rome and in the empire and representing the Roman people. The interpreters of Roman Law specifically recognized the principle of "identity despite changes" or "within changes."[47] Already the Accursian *Glossa ordinaria* acknowledged this principle when

---

[42] Bartolus, *loc.cit.*, continues: ". . . verum est si referamus ad personam Christi. Si vero referamus ad personam imperatoris saecularis, non proprie dicitur, quod omnia sunt sua vel sub sua iurisdictione. . . . In hac ergo constitutione [sc. imperatoris Henrici VII], si se retulit ad imperium vel si se retulit ad personam suam: locutus est caute. Non enim dicit [imperator] quod totius orbis iurisdictio sit sua, sed quod totius orbis regularitas in eo requiescit." Bartolus borrowed the word *regularitas* from Henry's constitution itself: ". . . Romanum imperium, in cuius tranquillitate totius orbis regularitas requiescit" (*MGH, Const.*, IV,965,25). The idea is similar to that of Dante, *Monarchia*, I,14,7: ". . . humanum genus secundum sua communia, que omnibus competunt, ab eo [imperatore] regatur et communi regula gubernetur ad pacem: quam quidem regulam sive legem particulares principes ab eo recipere debent. . . ."

[43] Bartolus, *loc.cit.*: ". . . cuius [Christi] regnum non dissipabitur, de quo prophetavit Daniel in dicto c.9 [in fact, c.7], ubi haec omnia imperia describuntur expresse."

[44] *Nov.*73, pr.1: "Quia igitur imperium propterea deus de coelo constituit. . . ." In Gratian's *Decretum*, c.11,D.XCVI, ed. Friedberg, I,341, a similar idea is expressed, and the decretists (v. *divinitus*) referred sometimes to *Nov.*73; see Kempf, *Innocenz III.*, 212,n.49.

[45] *Nov.*6, epil.: " (Licentiam damus) nobis et ad imperium quod semper est. . . ."

[46] Andreas de Isernia, on *Feud.* I,13 (*De alienatione feudi*), n.3, fol.49ᵛ: "nam ecclesia non moritur et semper est, sicut imperium."

[47] For the principle, see Gierke, *Gen.R.*, III, 277, n.92; cf. 364, nos.41-43, and 430, n.46; also, for the Romans, 571f.

defending the identity and continuity of a law court even though individual judges may have been replaced by others.

> For just as the [present] people of Bologna is the same that was a hundred years ago, even though all be dead now who then were quick, so must also the tribunal be the same if three or two judges have died and been replaced by substitutes. Likewise, [with regard to a legion], even though all soldiers may be dead and replaced by others, it is still the same legion. Also, with regard to a ship, even if the ship has been partly rebuilt, and even if every single plank may have been replaced, it is nonetheless always the same ship.[48]

It was, in fact, the continuity and invariability of "forms" which the glossator defended.[49] Baldus, glossing that gloss, was quite explicit on that point: "Notice, that where the form of a thing does not change, the thing itself is said not to change." And in an additional example Baldus explained that an interdict of the Church, imposed on a community, even though all the individuals who had caused the interdict may have died, could nevertheless remain valid for a hundred years or more "because the people does not die"—*quia populus non moritur.*[50]

[48] *Glos.ord.*, on *D*.5,1,76, v. *proponebatur*: "Primum est, quia sicut idem dicitur populus Bononiensis qui erat ante-C-annos retro, licet omnes mortui sint qui tunc erant, ita debet etiam esse [idem iudicium] tribus vel duobus iudicibus mortuis, et aliis subrogatis. Secundum est, quod licet omnes milites moriantur et alii sint subrogati, eadem est legio. Tertium est in navi, quia licet particularatim fuit refecta, licet omnis tabula nova fuerit, nihilominus est eadem navis." The glossator, Vivianus Tuscus of Bologna, a contemporary of Accursius (cf. Savigny, v,339f), adds laconically: "quia . . . non idem esset homo hodie qui fuit ante annum." (See below, n.50.) For repetitions of those images, cf. Gierke, *Gen.R.*, iii,365,n.42, to whose collection there might be added Bracton, fol.374b, ed. Woodbine, iv,175: "In collegiis et capitulis semper idem corpus manet, quamvis successive omnes moriantur et alii loco ipsorum substituantur, sicut dici poterit de gregibus ovium, ubi semper idem grex, quamvis omnes oves sive capita successive decedant." The source of all those examples (*populus, legio, navis, grex*) is *D*.41,3,30,rubr., and they descended, through the agency of the Roman jurist Pomponius writing under Severus Alexander, ultimately from Greek philosophy; see, on this law, the study of Alexander Philipsborn, "Der Begriff der juristischen Person im römischen Recht," *ZfRG*, rom.Abt., LXXI (1954), 41-70.

[49] The "form" itself remains identical and, though existing as form only compositely with matter, it is yet independent of the variability of the component matter. See, e.g., Aquinas, *Summa theol.*, 1,q.9,a.1,ad 3: "Ad tertium dicendum, quod formae dicuntur invariabiles, quia non possunt esse subiectum variationis; subiiciuntur tamen variationi, in quantum subiectum *secundum eas* variatur."

[50] Baldus, on *D*.5,1,76,n.4, fol.270: "Quarto, nota quod ubi non mutatur forma rei, non dicitur mutari res." He then quotes the example of the interdict which may last a hundred years or more, "quia *populus non moritur*, licet sint mortui illi qui praestiterunt causam interdicto." The principle has been formulated by Paulus de Castro (d.1441), who opined, likewise on *D*.5,1,76: "quod stante identitate

For the sake of that immanent continuity of a *populus qui non moritur* the transcendental legitimation of continuity had not necessarily to be discarded. One combined the two "continuities"—that from above and that from below—with the result that the conferring of the *imperium* on a Prince became jointly a work of the eternal God and the sempiternal people. The briefest formula for that cooperation of God and people was perhaps the one introduced by John of Paris and repeated by him several times: *populo faciente et Deo inspirante*, "the people acts and God inspires." John of Paris, who wrote his tractate around 1303, bolstered his statement by a reference to Averroes' commentary on the *Nicomachean Ethics* where it is said that the king's government "accords with nature" if he, or the dynasty, is constituted by the free will of the people.[51] In other words, through the people electing him the king governed "by nature," whereas the election itself of the specific individual, or the royal house, was effected by God as a *causa remota* and inspired "by grace."[52] The cooperation of God and people, however, had been established long before

---

formae, licet in substantia contingat mutatio, intelligitur eadem res," which would be true also with regard to the metabolism of the human body (above, n.48); quoted by Gierke, *Gen.R.*, III,430,n.46.

[51] John of Paris, *De potestate regia et papali*, c.19, ed. Leclercq, 235: "populo seu exercitu [see, on *exercitus*, the literature quoted by Leclercq, 95, n.1; also Mochi Onory, *Fonti canonistiche*, 68, 87 (n.1), 238, 253; Kempf, *Innocenz III.*, 214,n.55] faciente et Deo inspirante quia a Deo est [imperator]." Here (235,13) is also the reference to Averroes' paraphrase of the Nicomachean Ethics, saying "quod rex est a populi voluntate, sed cum est rex, ut dominetur, est *naturale*." See on that passage, also F. v. Bezold, *Aus Mittelalter und Renaissance* (Munich and Berlin, 1918), 22; Scholz, *Publizistik*, 331f. John of Paris expressed the same idea also in c.10, Leclercq, 199,23: "Potestas regia [non] . . . est a papa sed a Deo et a populo regem eligente in persona *vel in domo*," an important passage because here the dynastic element comes into the picture. Moreover, not only the royal power derives from God directly without the mediatorship of the pope, but the same is true with regard to the prelates (199, 35): "Sed potestas prelatorum non est a Deo mediante papa, sed immediate, et a populo eligente vel consentiente." See also 22, 5: "nam populus facit regem et exercitus imperatorem"; or 226, 15: "[potestas regia] cum sit a Deo et a populo consentiente et eligente." Leclercq, 73-76, is probably correct when describing the "Averroism" of John of Paris as an *averroisme théocratique*, for that doctrine had many shades.

[52] John of Paris, of course, was in no way exceptional (see below, nos.53f) but rather an exponent of the trends of his time. It is quite revealing, however, to find that fourteenth-century jurists frequently referred to John of Paris, sometimes together with "Dantes de Florentia . . . [qui] pulchre tractat . . . de necessitate monarchiae." Cf. Nardi, "Nota alla 'Monarchia,'" *Studi Danteschi*, XXVI (1942), 100-107; also, for the revival of John's doctrine in the *Songe du Vergier*; cf. Lemaire, *Lois fondamentales*, 46ff; Schramm, *König von Frankreich*, I,244, II,120.

John of Paris. Accursius, glossing the words "God has established the empire from heaven," added lapidarily: "or rather the Roman people from earth—*immo populus Romanus de terra.*" And he added the further explanation: "God has constituted the empire by his permission, and the people [have constituted it] by the dispensation of God; or else you might say: God constituted the empire by his authority; the people, by ministry."[53] Accursius thus recognized the transcendental foundation of the empire and preserved it by making the people ministers of the divine will. Another solution, distinguishing—as the canonists did—the emperor from the empire, was proffered by Cynus of Pistoia, who ruled: "Nor is it absurd that the empire should be derived from God and the people: the emperor is from the people, but the empire is called divine from God."[54] In that case, the supra-personal body politic of the empire was from God, whereas the personal Prince as individual was nominated by the people which itself was sempiternal. But whatever the interpretations may have been like, the co-agency of an eternal God and a sempiternal people made the cooperation of the Church as superfluous as it had been in the fourth and fifth centuries: the Church was practically frozen

[53] *Glos.ord.* on *Nov.*73, pr.1, v. *De caelo*: "Immo populus Rom. de terra, ut Inst. de iure naturali.§.sed et quod principi [*Inst.*1,2,6: *lex regia*], que est contra. Sed Deus constituit permittendo, et populus, Dei dispositione. Vel dic, Deus constituit auctoritate, populus ministerio." The teaching of the canonists moved along similar lines, since they too had to combine v. *divinitus* in c.11, D.XCVI (above, n.44), with the *lex regia*. See, e.g., Post, "Unpublished Glosses," 414, for Silvester Hispanus (?), who claimed the *imperium a Deo*, but distinguished (as many others did) between *iurisdictio* and its *executio*, between *imperium* and *imperator*, who likewise referred to the *lex regia*, and who then declared: "Sed dic, quod aliud est ipsa iurisdictio per se inspecta, que a deo processit, et aliud quod ipsius iurisdictionis executionem consequatur aliquis per populum . . . ; nam populus per electionem facit imperatorem, sed non imperium, sicut cardinales per electionem preferunt aliquem sibi ad iurisdictionem, que a deo data est, exercendam." The distinction between *iurisdictio* and *gubernaculum*, so strongly emphasized by McIlwain, *Constitutionalism,* 75ff (above, Chapter IV, n.177), belongs to this general compound of problems. For related places, see Kempf, *Innocenz III.,* 213f, nos.52ff, 244f, nos.32ff; cf. 210,n.42. See also below, Ch.VII,n.25.

[54] "Nec est absurdum quod sit a Deo et a populo. Imperator est a populo, sed imperium dicitur divinum a Deo." Cf. Theseider, *L'Idea imperiale,* 262. See also Ullmann, *Lucas de Penna,* 175,n.1, for a similar statement of Cynus on another occasion. Further, Andreas of Isernia, on *Feud.* II,52 (*De prohib. feudi alien.*), rubr., fol.231ᵛ: "Imperium quidem a Deo est: ideo dicitur divina gratia." Otto of Freising, *Chronica,* IV, prol., ed. Hofmeister, 182,15, asks *quo iure* the rulers exercise power, and answers: "ex ordinatione Dei et electione populi." For some opinions of canonists, see above, n.53, and below, Ch.VII,n.25; and, for other related utterances, Gierke, *Gen.R.,* III,570,n.140.

out, as the continuity was achieved para-ecclesiastically by the powers of God and the people or "nature."[55]

The *lex regia*, manifesting the inalienable rights of the people and thus proclaiming the perpetuity of the *maiestas populi Romani*, was not restricted to Rome alone, although the Romans served as the prototype of the perpetuity of a people. That fundamental law, of course, was universally applicable to the conditions of any *regnum* and every people, and it actually did appear in the legal writings of all European countries. The transfer, however, of the idea of the people's perpetual majesty from the Romans to the nations and communities of Europe in general—we may recall Marsiglio of Padua's *Defensor pacis*—was defined quite explicitly by Baldus, who said:

> The commonweal [i.e. any commonweal] has its majesty *after the example of the Roman people*, provided that the commonweal be free [i.e. having no superior] and have the right to create a king.[56]

By implication, therefore, any *regnum* and every people was legally granted the continuity of the Roman people and the perpetuity of its *maiestas*. We recognize that well known "cascading" from the empire to the *regna* and *civitates*, epitomized precisely and powerfully by the slogans *Rex imperator in regno suo* and *Civitas sibi princeps*.

Nevertheless, the perpetuity of kingdoms and communities "having no superior" rested on more than the transfer and secularization of the empire idea. The doctrine of the perpetual identity of forms despite changes, which had been used by the earlier glossators without the support of Aristotelian notions, was not rarely strengthened in the writings of the post-glossators by Aristotelian maxims. Baldus, for example, when discussing the emperor of former days as the lord of "provinces" which by now had become independent kingdoms, remarked:

[55] That the empire, like every kingdom, had been placed "auf eine vom Papst an sich unabhängige Grundlage," has been recognized also by Kempf, *Innocenz III.*, 226f. On the other hand, Pope Innocent IV's famous formulation: "papa habet imperium a Deo, imperator a populo" (Gierke, *Gen.R.*, III,570, n.142), rendered the emperor a completely profane power severed from God—unless consecrated by the Church. However, the devaluation of the imperial and royal consecrations, resulting from very many and often quite heterogeneous developments and trends of thought (see below, Chapter VII:1), is closely connected also with the prominence of the people. See Innocent IV, *Apparatus*, on c.1 X 1,7,n.2 (Lyon, 1578), fol.57ᵛ.

[56] Baldus, *Consilia*, III,159,n.6, fol.46: ". . . nam ipsa respublica maiestatem habet ad instar populi Romani, cum libera sit et ius habeat creandi regem."

Now, however, the dispositions of the world have changed, as says Aristotle in *De caelo et mundo,* not in the sense that the *world* will generate and corrupt, but its *dispositions*: and there is nothing imperishable under the sun. The cause of corruption namely is, all by itself, Time . . . ; and although the empire is forever . . . , it nevertheless does not remain in the same status because it dwells in continuous motion. . . .[57]

Baldus, to say the least, assumed a relatively permanent duration of the world which lasted "forever" although its dispositions changed and were subject to corruption and generation. In this case, Baldus applied the doctrine of permanent duration to the *imperium quod semper est;* but he used the same argument also with regard to commonwealth and fisc in general when he said that "they cannot die," that both were "something eternal and perpetual with regard to their essence, even though the dispositions change frequently."[58] His formulations were even slightly bolder when talking about the perpetuity of kingdoms and peoples.

A realm contains not only the material territory, but also the peoples of the realm because those peoples collectively are the realm. . . . And the totality or commonweal of the realm does not die, because a commonweal continues to exist even after the kings have been driven away. For the commonweal cannot die [*non enim potest res-publica mori*]; and for that reason it is said [*D.2,3,4*] that the "commonweal has no heir" because in itself it lives for ever, as says Aristotle: "The world does not die, but the dispositions of the world die and change and are altered and do not persevere in the same quality."[59]

---

[57] Baldus, *Consilia,* 1,328,n.8, fol.103: "Nunc autem dispositiones mundi mutatae sunt, ut ait Aristoteles in *coeli et mundi,* non utique mundus generabitur et corrumpetur, sed dispositiones ipsius: et nihil perpetuum sub sole. Corruptionis enim causa per se est tempus, iv.*Physicorum.* Licet imperium semper sit, in Auth. quomodo oportet episc.§.fi. [*Nov.* 6,epil.; supra, n.45], tamen non in eodem statu permanet, quia in continuo motu et perplexa tribulatione insistit, et hoc apparet in mutatione quatuor principalium regnorum. . . ." The reference to Aristotle is *De caelo et mundo,* 1,280a, 19-23: οὐκ ἂν ὁ κόσμος γίγνοιτο καὶ φθείροιτο, ἀλλ' αἱ διαθέσεις αὐτοῦ. For the Latin text (quoted verbatim by Baldus) and Aquinas' interpretation, see Thomas Aquinas, *In Aristotelis libros de Caelo et Mundo,* 1, lect.23, ed. Spiazzi (Turin and Rome, 1952), 110 and 112. See further, Aristotle, *Physics,* iv,12,221b,1: φθορᾶς γὰρ αἴτιος καθ' αὑτὸν μᾶλλον ὁ χρόνος; also 221a,30ff: καὶ γηράσκοι πάνθ' ὑπὸ τοῦ χρόνου.

[58] Baldus, *Consilia,* 1,271,n.3, fol.81ᵛ (see above, Chapter iv, n.292): "respublica et fiscus sint quid eternum et perpetuum quantum ad essentiam, licet dispositiones saepe mutentur."

[59] Baldus, *Consilia,* iii,159,nos.3,5, fol.45ᵛ: "Nam regnum continet in se non

We are confronted with a new version of the problem of a "double truth." There is no reason to doubt that Baldus, in perfect honesty, would not have hesitated in the confessional to admit the createdness, and deny the eternity, of the world. Juristically, however, he needed the heuristic hypothesis of some infinite perpetuity, and it is easy to see how useful Aristotelian notions were to him and how useful to the lawyers in general who, on grounds totally different from those of the philosophers, defended the perpetuity of bodies politic and immortality of fictitious persons. For the same reasons the doctrine of the immortality and continuity of the genera and species was almost indispensable, since it was most convenient for the jurists to identify the immortal bodies corporate and other collectives with species. A law in the *Digest* recognized clearly the danger of making a *municipium* the usufructor of property because any collective usufructor had the tendency to usufruct "perpetually." When glossing that law, Odofredus remarked that "a *municipium* cannot easily perish except on the day of Last Judgment," because "genera cannot perish"—*genera perire non possunt.*[60] Odofredus, who died in 1265, hardly meant to refer to Aristotle. Baldus, however, in his gloss on the instrument of the Peace of Constance of 1183, used a philosophically more refined language when he wrote "that something which is universal cannot perish by death, just as man in his species does not die."[61] In short, by the fourteenth century the Aristotelian

---

solum territorium materiale, sed etiam ipsas gentes regni, quia ipsi populi collective regnum sunt. . . . Et etiam [non moritur] universitas seu respublica ipsius regni, quae etiam exactis regibus perseverat. Non enim potest respublica mori, et hac ratione dicitur, quod respublica non habet heredem, quia semper vivit in semetipsa . . . , sicut dicit Aristoteles: mundus non moritur, sed dispositiones mundi moriuntur, et mutantur, et alternantur, et non perseverant in eadem qualitate." See above, n.57, and also Aristotle, *Meteorologica*, I,14,352b, with Aquinas' commentary, ed. Spiazzi, 459f; also for the Latin text.

[60] See *D.*7,1,56 and, for Odofredus, Gierke, *Gen.R.*, III,365,n.43. Roman Law, by restricting the usufruct of a city to 100 years in order to avoid perpetuation ("Periculum enim esse videbatur ne [usufructus] perpetuus fieret"), anticipated, as it were, the anxieties of Henry VIII; for that king made the unpleasant discovery that trusts of lands in favor of corporations—guilds, fraternities, communities, and others—formed a great danger and a threat of perpetual alienation, because from them "there groweth to the King . . . the same like losses and inconveniences . . . as in case where lands be alienated into *mortmain.*" Cf. Maitland, *Sel.Ess.*, 214.

[61] Baldus, *Liber de pace Constantiae* (following after the *Libri feudorum* and the imperial *Extravagantes* of the *Corpus iuris civilis* [Venice, 1584] IV, App.159ff), v. *Nos Romanorum*, p.161C: the Emperor [Frederick I] "vult istam pacem esse perpetuam, id est, quamdiu fides servetur . . . vel per praesentem mundi aetatem,

tenets concerning perpetuity were deeply ingrained in legal thought. Little wonder then that Padua and the jurists at large—mostly, it seems, by popular misconception—were notorious and ill-famed for their "Averroism."[62]

To summarize, the continuity of the people and the state derived from many sources, and in general it may be said that theory followed existing practice. Without depending on any broader philosophical outlooks the administrative technique of the state developed its own patterns of continuity. Theory, however, was effective in other respects. The *lex regia* asserted the perpetuity of the Roman people,[63] and by transferring that claim from the Romans to others as well, the perpetuity of any and every people was, so to speak, legally confirmed. Finally, the Aristotelian and Averroist doctrines brought about a consciousness of "natural" perpetuity

---

et futuram et sine praefinitione temporis, quia Imperator facit hanc pacem nomine sedis, non nomine proprio tantum: et imperium non moritur . . ." (for *nomine proprio*, on the basis of c.14 X 1, 29, see below, Chapter VII, nos.232ff). Then, towards the end of the same long gloss (162D), Baldus states: "Item quia quod universale est non potest morte perire, sicut homo in genere non moritur."

[62] Grabmann, *Mittelalterliches Geistesleben* (Munich, 1936), II,239ff, and 261ff, in fact discovered two Averroist teachers at Bologna in the early fourteenth century, Taddeo da Parma and Angelo d'Arezzo, both professors of philosophy in the faculty of arts at Bologna, and concluded (270f) that the first cell of academic Averroism in Italy must be sought at the ancient stronghold of juristic studies, at Bologna itself, before it spread to Padua (also p.240f). For the problem and the latest publications on the subject, see Charles J. Ermatinger, "Averroism in Early Fourteenth Century Bologna," *Mediaeval Studies*, XVI (1954), 35-56. Petrarch, too, in his fight against the Averroists (cf. Grabmann, 240, n.4; Eppelsheimer, *Petrarca*, 194,n.6; P. O. Kristeller, "Petrarch's Averroists," *Bibl. d'Humanisme et Renaissance*, XIV [1952], 59-65), lashes at the jurists at Padua. However, Petrarch's extreme irritability against scholastic philosophers, theologians, jurists, physicians, and non-humanists in general is well known, and his readiness to call anyone disagreeing with him an "Averroist" has its equivalent in modern habits. Petrarch's testimony, therefore, is of doubtful value. Without denying the possibility that Averroism had adherents also among the lawyers (and Grabmann's findings would support such a suggestion), it nevertheless seems to me that the jurists, when developing and overdoing their corporational doctrines, may often have been mistaken for and erroneously labelled "Averroists" simply because those doctrines recalled the tabooed tenets. This is true with regard to the eternity of the world and of species, of which the jurists themselves were quite conscious (see above n.18, for Angelus de Ubaldis); it is true also with regard to the unity of the intellect (see below, Ch. VIII, n.71); and it would be easy also to extract the dogma of double truth from their writings: what is true philosophically may not be true juristically (see above, p.282; also Bartolus, on *D.*,48,19,16,10 [below, nos.64,89]; Gierke, *Gen.R.*, III,365f). Hence, we should be careful with generalizations concerning "the Averroist jurists." Not every person using the terms "subconsciousness" or "complex" is philosophically a Freudian or Jungian.

[63] See above, nos. 53f.

in a philosophic sense, whereby the tenet concerning the eternity of the genera and species proved particularly useful to the lawyers who for purely juristic reasons defended the continuity of collective bodies and the immortality of juristic universals and species.

UNIVERSITAS NON MORITUR

Though probably rewarding, it would be nevertheless complicated and tiresome to try to build up a concordance of scholastic and juristic thought, or to hazard a decision as to whether the philosophic notions which the jurists used rather indiscriminately for defining their legal abstractions (forms, species, genera, universals, and their like), reflected any clearly determinable school concepts, nominalistic or other, as has occasionally been suggested.[64] There is no doubt, however, but that the jurists borrowed abundantly from the vocabulary of scholastic philosophy, that they moved freely in the borderlands of theology, philosophy, and jurisprudence, and applied, more or less eclectically, the scholastic matrix to express their own ideas. According to language and content, for example, the jurists' "fictitious" or "intellectual" persons are hardly distinguishable from the Universals which the nominalists liked to call *fictiones intellectuales*.[65] Moreover, the doctrine of the perpetual "identity despite change" of a community— Bologna, for instance—might be taken to refer to the *eidos* of Bologna, which was distinct from the material city at any given moment and detached from both the citizens living at present within Bologna's walls and the bricks forming at present those very walls. We might also consider the great ease with which the philosophers following Duns Scotus formed abstract notions such as *Socratitas* to designate the principle of individuation by which the generic "man" became the individual Socrates. Though hardly depending upon the Scotists, the jurists nevertheless created something comparable. For between the generic *communitas* or

[64] It is probably correct if Gierke, *Gen.R.*, iii,281,365f,425f, and passim, indicates the affinity with nominalistic tenets; but as Gierke himself points out (365f), the juristic notions do not exactly coincide with the scholastic notions, and Bartolus (on *D.*,48,19,16,10, n.3, fol.228ᵛ), when referring to the *philosophi et canonistae*, makes it perfectly clear that a juristic "fiction" is not identical with a philosophic "notion."

[65] Überweg-Baumgartner, 579, 601; also 322.

universitas on the one hand, and the individual and material community of Bologna composed of mutable citizens and perishable buildings on the other hand, there arose a third entity different from both, an entity which was immaterial and invariable, though not devoid of individuation, which existed (as it were) in some perpetual *aevum*, and which appropriately might have been called *Bononitas* or "Bolognity," had the lawyers not preferred to talk about the corporate *universitas*—that is, the juristic person or personified community—of Bologna. Nevertheless, that corporate, if incorporeal, *Bononitas* represented, like the angels, species and individuation at the same time.[66]

It might be mentioned parenthetically that the personifications of communities, cities, and kingdoms created by juristic speculation were not simply a revival of those toponymic personifications of classical Antiquity which had lingered on in the miniatures of Carolingian, Ottonian, and even later manuscripts.[67] In fact, the juristic personifications of cities and countries were not at all identical with their august predecessors of classical cults. The classical city goddesses, adorned with mural crown or halo, still belonged, in a broad sense, to the stratum of ancient anthropomorphism: they were the *genius* of a city and they could claim immortality and perpetuality simply because they were goddesses. The personifications of the jurists, however, were philosophical fictions belonging to the realm of speculation. The cities, instead of receiving, like Antique city goddesses at their epiphanies, a

---

[66] For the *Socratitas*, see Harris, *Duns Scotus*, II,20,n.3: "Et sicut Socratitas quae formaliter constituit Socratem, nusquam est extra Socratem, sic illa hominis essentia quae Socratitatem sustinet in Socrate, nunquam est nisi in Socrate, vel quae est in aliqui alio individuorum." What Scotus seems to mean (see Harris, *loc.cit.*) is the "collection" of the concrete material object and of the universal in the "image" or "intelligible species." See, e.g., Baldus, on c.3 X 1,31,n.14 (*In Decretalia*, fol.126), and his definition of *universitas*: "Omnis universitas dicitur corpus, quia compositum et aggregatum, ubi corpora sunt tanquam materia; dicitur autem forma, id est, formalis status [see above, n.49]. . . . Est igitur collegium imago quaedam quae magis intellectu quam sensu percipitur [D.41,3,30; 4,2,9,1; c.53 X 5,39]." Or see, for the intermediate stratum between the genus and the concrete individual, Baldus, on c.3 X 2,12,n.15 (*In Decretalia*, fol.178): "Est autem universale quod non distinguitur in species dialectico modo assumptas, sed in res. Generale autem est id, quod habet species sub se. . . ." In other words, the *universale* and *universitas* is, in legal philosophy, itself a species ranging above the things in which it individualizes, but ranging below the *generale* which itself is divisible into species. It must be left, however, to the specialist to analyze the juristic terminology and to compare it to that of scholastic philosophy.

[67] See above, Chapter III, n.88.

visible body, were actually deprived of their visible body and were granted by legal thought only an invisible one. This invisible body, to be sure, was immortal and perpetual; yet it was immortal, not because it was the body of a goddess, but precisely because it was invisible—the body of an immaterial being. Hence the lawyers were far from reviving classical "anthropomorphic" personifications; they created instead, in full agreement with the mediaeval scheme of thinking, what may be called "angelomorphic" personifications. In other words, legal corporations compared structurally with Christian angels rather than with pagan goddesses.

In his gloss on the Peace of Constance, Baldus called a city "something universal that cannot perish by death," and he compared that "universal" with the genus or species of man which does not die either.[68] It is possible that the term "something universal" (quoddam universale) evoked associations with the likewise immortal Universals of philosophic speech; but what the term universale really meant in legal language was quite unambiguous: it was synonymous with the technical term universitas deriving from Roman Law, the corporational collective at large which the early glossators defined as "a conjunct or collection in one body of a plurality of persons."[69] On that basis, Bartolus could maintain that "the whole world is some kind of universitas," not to mention kingdoms and cities.[70] Baldus could define a populus as "a collection of men in one mystical body,"[71] or call a regnum "something total which both in persons and things contains its parts integrally,"[72] or talk briefly about "some universal person."[73] For to interpret a collective bluntly as a "person" was suggested

[68] Baldus, De pace Const., p.162D (above, n.61).

[69] Gierke, Gen.R., III,193f.

[70] Bartolus, on D.6,1,1,3, fol.204: "[The emperor is lord of the world] Nec obstat quod alii sunt domini particulariter, quia mundus est universitas quaedam; unde potest quis habere dictam universitatem, licet singulae res non sint suae." Cf. Woolf, Bartolus, 22,n.3; cf.123f, for the three kinds of universitates.

[71] Baldus, on C.7,53,5,n.11, fol. 73ᵛ: "[populus] debet intelligi de hominibus collective assumptis. . . . Unde populus proprie non dicitur homines, sed hominum collectio in unum corpus mysticum, et abstractive assumptum, cuius significatio est inventa per intellectum." Cf. Gierke, Gen.R., III,432.

[72] Baldus, Consilia, I,333,n.1, fol.105: "regnum quoddam totum suas partes integraliter continens tam in personis quam in rebus, sicut omne nomen collectivum populorum et territorii."

[73] Baldus, on C.6,26,2, n.2, fol.80ᵛ: "Est et quaedam persona universalis . . . ut populus [lex mortuo: D.46,1,22; cf. next note], et haec persona similiter loco unius habetur, et individuum corpus reputatur."

by Roman Law itself, which, in the frequently quoted *lex mortuo*
(D.46,1,22), called a municipality, law court, or guild—under certain conditions even an inheritance—"a person."[74]

The underlying general idea was hardly different when Andreas
of Isernia compared the *patria* to an ecclesiastical *collegium*.[75] For
even before the civilians made their deductions and personified
the *universitas*, the canonists had applied the legal notion of *universitas* to the various ecclesiastical *collegia*—chapters, congregations, and others—as well as to the whole Church. Being the *universitas fidelium* according to oldest definitions, the universal
Church was also legally *universitas* without restriction; and
through the fusion with the organological concept of *corpus
mysticum* on the one hand, and the anthropomorphic designations
of the Church as *mater* or *sponsa* on the other, the temptation
to personify the ecclesiastical collective also juristically may have
been present at an early date.[76] In any event, the general tendency
to treat the various ecclesiastical *collegia* as though they were real
persons who could be punished and excommunicated must have
been far advanced when Innocent IV found it necessary to define
unambiguously the character of those collective "persons." At the
Council of Lyon, in 1245, he forbade the excommunication of an
universitas or *collegium*, and later interpreted his action and
justified it on the grounds that *universitates* such as a chapter, a
people, a tribe, were "names of Law" only and not of persons, and
that names cannot be subject to excommunication. He pointed

[74] D.46,1,22: ". . . quia hereditas personae vice fungitur, sicuti municipium et
decuria et societas."
[75] Andreas of Isernia, on *Feud.* II,52 (*De prohib. feudi alien. Loth.*), n.1, fol.232:
"Princeps est pater patriae, dicit Seneca primo de clementia [1,14,2]. ergo illorum,
qui sunt in patria, idest subditorum. sicut arguit ipse [Seneca] secundo *de ira*
[2,31,7]: 'nefas est nocere patriae, ergo civi quoque.' non enim est patria, nisi
homines agentes in ea: sicut Ecclesia possidet et collegium, idest clerici et illi qui
sunt in collegio. . . ." Although Andreas of Isernia admits that *patria* is nothing
but the human beings acting in it, he nevertheless defends the corporate character
of *patria* and its citizens, and fights against the atomization of this body; see his
remarks on *Feud.* II,27 (*De pace tenenda*), n.9, fol.162r-v, where he argues against
Seneca's opinion (*De ira, loc.cit.*) "quod unus homo de patria est pars patriae,"
and declares: "Hoc iuristae non recipiunt, nisi quando universitas redigitur ad
unum [D.34,7,2; see below, n.96] . . . Dividere ergo patriam in tot partes quot
homines habet, concisio est, non divisio." Andreas reproduces probably the doctrine
of his fellow countryman Roffred of Benevento, who declared that "universitas est
quoddam individuum, unde partes non habet," since according to Aristotle an individual is indivisible; see Gierke, *Gen.R.*, III,204; also below, n.89.
[76] Gierke, *Gen.R.*, III,248,253,278, and passim.

out that an *universitas* was a person without a body, a pure *nomen intellectuale* and thing incorporeal which, as later canonists were quick to point out, could not be condemned because it was lacking a soul, nor be decapitated because it was lacking a body.[77] The personified *universitas*, therefore, was only an imaginary "represented person" (*persona repraesentata*) or a "fictitious person" (*persona ficta*).

Although Innocent's epochal statement[78] about the *universitas* as a fictitious person was actually made in a negative sense, the definition itself created or articulated something very positive: the possibility of treating every *universitas* (that is, every plurality of men collected in one body) as a juristic person, of distinguishing that juristic person clearly from every natural person endowed with body and soul, and yet of treating a plurality of individuals juristically as one person. That this corporate person was fictitious detracted nothing from its value, especially its heuristic value; besides, the word fiction itself was not necessarily derogatory. In a descriptive sense, it will be recalled, the nominalists styled the Universals *fictiones intellectuales*.[79] Aquinas, actually following Augustine, could define "fiction" in a signally positive sense as *figura veritatis*.[80] And Baldus, elaborating glosses of Accursius and Bartolus, finally declared, with a slight twist of an Aristotelian tenet: "*Fiction imitates nature. Therefore, fiction has a place only where truth can have a place.*"[81]

[77] *Ibid.*, 280ff. See Innocent, *Apparatus*, on c.57 X 2,20 (later equalling c.2 VI 2,19), n.5, fol.176ᵛ ("cum collegium in causa universitatis fingatur una persona"); c.53[52] X 5,39,nos.1-3, fol.364; and (same title) c.64,n.3 (Innocent's own decretal *Romana Ecclesia*, later equalling c.5 VI 5,11), fol.367ᵛ. The relevant passages of Innocent's next to inaccessible *Apparatus* have most gratifyingly been made accessible by I. Th. Eschmann, O.P., "Studies on the Notion of Society in St. Thomas Aquinas, 1. St. Thomas and the Decretal of Innocent IV *Romana Ecclesia: Ceterum*," *Mediaeval Studies*, VIII (1946), 1-42, esp.8ff,29ff.

[78] That Innocent's definition had certain antecedents has been noticed by Gierke himself; see, e.g., *Gen.R.*, III,204.

[79] See above, n.65.

[80] *Summa theol.*, III,q.55,a.4,ad 1, quoting Augustine, *De quaestionibus Evangelistarum*, II,c.51, PL, XXXV,1362: "non omne quod fingimus, mendacium est; . . . cum autem fictio nostra refertur in aliquam significationem, non est mendacium, sed aliqua *figura veritatis*. Alioquin omnia quae a sapientibus et sanctis viris, vel etiam ab ipso Domino, figurate dicta sunt, mendacia deputabuntur."

[81] Baldus, on *D.*17,2,3,n.2, fol.120ᵛ: "Nam ex hoc dicto glossae [sc. glos. ord.] nota quod ibi demum habet locum fictio, ubi est possibile quod habeat locum veritas." Baldus then refers to a passage in the law of adoption (*D.*1,7,16; see also *Inst.*1,11,4) "ubi textus dicit quod fictio imitatur naturam," and, in summarizing, says: "Fictio

What matters here, however, is merely the problem of continuity. It is significant that it was precisely this problem which prompted Innocent IV to decide most emphatically that the *universitas* was an intellectual person which cannot die, and not a real person. Hence, an excommunication which was extended to a whole body corporate, instead of being reserved for guilty individuals, would finally affect also innocent men joining the *universitas* as substitute members (*subrogati*) at a later date.[82]

---

ergo imitatur naturam. Ergo fictio habet locum, ubi potest habere locum veritas."
The law of adoption, to which he refers, says: "Adoptio enim in his personis locum
habet in quibus etiam natura potest habere." In his own gloss on *D*.1,7,16, fol.38ᵛ,
Baldus (now quoting, in fact, Aristotle, *Physics*, II,2, 194a21) states: "*Ars naturam
imitatur* inquantum potest," to which he makes an *additio*: "Nota quod fictio
naturae rationem atque stylum imitatur." See also Bartolus, on *D*.17,2,3, fol.139,
as well as *Glos.ord.* on that law, v. *nominibus*. Rather interesting is Oldradus de
Ponte, *Consilia*, LXXIV,n.1 (Lyon, 1550), fol.27ʳᵃ, who proves that alchemy is permissible: "Cum ergo ars imitetur naturam (*D*.1,7,16), non videntur isti alchimistae
peccare. . . ." See also *Consilia*, XCIV, n.8, fol.33ʳ: "sic in natura videmus quod
ars imitatur (*Inst*.1,11,4)." Also Cynus, on *C*.7,37,3,n.5, fol.446ʳᵃ, demands that
"civiles actus naturam habeant imitari."
Obviously, the juristic formula *Fictio imitatur naturam* has to be considered in
connection with the whole cluster of notions such as *ars simia naturae*, *ars simia
veri*, and the Aristotelian *ars naturam imitatur*, catchwords so meaningful in
Renaissance art and culture at large; see, for the problem, Ernst Robert Curtius,
Europäische Literatur und lateinisches Mittelalter (Bern, 1948), 524f; H. W. Janson,
Apes and Ape Lore in the Middle Ages and the Renaissance (Studies of the Warburg Institute, XX, London, 1952), 287ff. "Aping" was not only used in a derogatory
sense as in Dante, *Inf.*, XXIX,139 (the forger Capocchio confesses: *fui di natura
buona scimia*); Dante himself calls art (*Inf.*, XI,105) "as it were, the grand-child of
God," because according to Aristotle "art mimics nature," and John of Jandun
styles himself "the ape of Aristotle and Averroes" (Grabmann, *Mittelalterliches
Geistesleben*, II,239). Concerning "fiction" we might recall Petrarch's definition of
the *officium poetae*: to disclose and glorify the truth of things woven into a decorous
cloud of fiction ("veritatem rerum decora velut figmentorum nube contextam");
see Attilio Hortis, *Scritti inediti di Francesco Petrarca* (Trieste, 1874), 33,n.1;
Burdach, *Rienzo*, 509f; and, for the dependency of Macrobius (*Saturnalia*, 5,17,5;
see also the scholion on Horace, *Ad Pisones*, 119), E. H. Wilkins, "The Coronation
of Petrarch," *Speculum*, XVIII (1943), 175. The jurists not only fell in with the
literary and artistic theories, but may have had even the function of pathfinders,
since they embarked on that theory—derived from the Roman laws of adoption—
much earlier than others. At any rate, the hitherto apparently unnoticed strand
should not be neglected.
⁸² In his decretal, published at the Council of Lyon (c.5 VI 5,11, ed. Friedberg,
II,1095), Innocent IV declared it his intention to make the endangering of souls impossible "quod exinde sequi posset, quum nonnumquam contingeret innoxios huiusmodi sententia irretiri." The commentator of the decretal was in that case Innocent
IV himself whose opinion has been discussed by Gierke, *Gen.R.*, III,280ff. The
Glossa ordinaria on the *Liber Sextus*, composed by Johannes Andrea, indeed emphasizes (on c.5 VI 5,11, rubr.) that in the case of the excommunication of a *collegium*
"illi qui erunt postea subrogati, debent se tenere pro excommunicatis." The problem of the *subrogati*, however, seems to have been an afterthought; for the decretal

It was a simple application to the future of the customary doctrine of "identity despite changes," which more often referred to the past; and the later jurists argued accordingly:

> The *universitas* is the same today which it will be a hundred years hence. . . . If, therefore, we would say that an *universitas* can fall delinquent, the children, infants, women, and their likes would be included, which would be absurd; and for these reasons Innocent concluded that an *universitas* cannot be excommunicated.[83]

The implications are obvious: the *universitas* thrives on succession; it is defined by the successiveness of its members; and owing to its successive self-regeneration the *universitas* does not die and is perpetual—as Bartolus said: "Nothing in this world can be perpetual . . . except by way of substitution."[84]

On a far broader scale, and in a completely different connection, Thomas Aquinas came to define the problem of successiveness within the *corpus mysticum*. He started by distinguishing between the mystical body of Christ and man's natural body. In the human body, says Aquinas, the members are present "all at once" whereas to the mystical body the limbs accrue gradually in permanent succession "from the beginning of the world [Adam, of course, belonged to the ecclesiastical *corpus mysticum*] till the end of the world." Therefore that mystical body embraces not only those actually in the fold but also those who potentially might join the fold now or in the future—that is, it extends to both the as yet unborn future generations of Christians and the as yet unbaptized pagans, Jews, or Mohammedans, since the mystical body of Christ, that is, the Church, grows not only by nature but also by grace.[85] What Aquinas said was certainly not new; but his neat

---

itself thinks only of the members composing the *collegium* at that time among whom there might be innocent men. See n.84.

[83] See, e.g., Petrus de Ancharano (c.1330-1416), on c.53 X 5,39,n.8 (*In quinque Decretalium libros facundissima Commentaria*, Bologna, 1631), p.231: "Item, eadem est universitas hodie, quae erit usque ad centum annos, ut l.proponebatur.ff.de iud. [*D*.5,1,76]. Si ergo diceremus universitatem posse delinquere, includerentur isti [pueri, infantes, mulieres, et similes], quod esset absurdum. et ex his rationibus concludit In[nocentius] quod universitas non possit excommunicari." These arguments, of course, were repeated over and over again.

[84] See above, n.18, for Bartolus, on *D*.8,2,33,n.1, fol.222.

[85] *Summa theol.*, III,q.8,a.3, concl.: ". . . haec est differentia inter corpus hominis naturale et corpus Ecclesiae mysticum, quod membra corporis naturalis sunt omnia simul, membra autem corporis mystici non sunt omnia simul, neque quantum ad *esse naturae*, quia corpus Ecclesiae constituitur ex hominibus qui fuerunt a principio

formulation made it very clear that the *corpus mysticum* was composed not only of those living simultaneously in the ecclesiastical *oikumene* and within a universal Space, but that it encompassed also all members past and future, actual and potential, who followed each other successively in a universal Time. That is to say, not only the plurality of men living together in a community formed a "mystical body," but the corporate plurality was achieved also in view of the successiveness of its members.

The principle expressed in Aquinas' definition of the *corpus mysticum* of the universal Church was applicable, with slight variations, to any *corpus mysticum*, to any *universitas* large or small, ecclesiastical or secular. The canonists stressed time and time again that the church of this or that place or country remained the same church even if all its members were dead and replaced by others; or, that the *collegium* or chapter of a cathedral was "today the same as it was a hundred years ago although the persons were not the same."[86] With this chorus Bracton fell in: "Though abbot or prior, monks or canons successively die, the house will remain in eternity."[87] The *Glossa ordinaria*, we recall, made the same statement about the identity of Bologna a hundred years ago with the present Bologna and, implicitly, with any future Bologna.[88] Bartolus argued that the same was true with regard to the *universitas scholarium*, the University.[89] Other civilians held that every *popu-*

---

mundi usque ad finem ipsius, neque etiam quantum ad *esse gratiae*. . . . Sic igitur membra corporis mystici accipiuntur non solum secundum quod sunt in actu, sed etiam secundum quod in potentia. . . ." This definition was often repeated; see, e.g., James of Viterbo, *De regimine Christiano*, c.3, ed. H.-X. Arquillière, *Le plus ancient traité de l'Église* (Paris, 1926), 110.

86 See, e.g., Gierke, *Gen.R.*, III,277,n.92.

87 Bracton, fol.374b, ed. Woodbine, IV,175: "Et ideo si abbas vel prior, monachi vel canonici successive obierint, domus in aeternum permanebit."

88 See above, n.48.

89 Bartolus, on *D*.48,19,16,10 v. *nonnunquam*, fol.228ᵛ, makes it the main argument against the nominalists claiming "quod totum non differt realiter a suis partibus," and that accordingly "nil aliud est universitas scholarium quam scholares." He argues instead (like Andreas of Isernia before him; see above, n.75) that "universitas representat unam personam, quae est aliud a scholaribus seu ab hominibus universitatis [reference to *lex mortuo D.*46,1,22], quod apparet: quia recedentibus omnibus istis scholaribus et aliis redeuntibus, eadem tamen universitas est. Item mortuis omnibus de populo et aliis subrogatis, idem est populus." The corporational aspect of the *totum* would have been admitted by the *philosophi et canonistae* whom Bartolus contradicts, though he admitted their "philosophical truth"; but Bartolus makes the element of succession and identity the axis of his argument—that is, he makes Time the essence of the "juristic truth," of the *fictio iuris* which he defends.

lus or *universitas* "was the same as it had been a thousand years ago because the successors represent the same *universitas*."[90] It is true, of course, that minor communities could not claim—like the *corpus mysticum* of the universal Church—their identity ever since the creation of the world; but they could claim their identity within Time ever since their own creation or foundation, and thence onward to the end of the world or any other practically unlimited time. Baldus, for example, styled the Roman empire "that great *universitas* which encompasses in itself all the faithful of the empire both of the present age and of successive posterity," and of course he included implicitly also the past.[91] The empire, perhaps, could claim like the Church a universality also regarding Space: ". . . that every soul be subjected to the Roman Prince," as Emperor Henry VII proclaimed.[92] But the universality of the minor corporate bodies was restricted to the universality of Time, as far back as it went in each individual case.

In other words, the essential feature of all corporate bodies was not that they were "a plurality of persons collected in one body" at the present moment, but that they were that "plurality" in succession, braced by Time and through the medium of Time. It would be wrong, therefore, to consider the corporational *universitas* merely as the *simul cohabitantes*, those living together at the same moment;[93] for they would resemble, in Aquinas' language, only the physical body of man whose members were present "all at once," but they would not form the genuine *corpus mysticum* such as Aquinas had defined it. The plurality in succession, therefore, or the plurality in Time was the essential factor knitting the *universitas* into continuity and making it immortal.

[90] Gierke, *Gen.R.*, III,365,n.41, quoting Albericus de Rosate (+ 1354): "populus, id est universitas cuiusque civitatis et loci, . . . idem qui fuit retro mille annis, quia successores representant eandem universitatem."

[91] Baldus, *De pace Const.*, p.161A, v. *universitas*, speaks "de ista magna universitate (see above, n.70), quae omnes fideles imperii in se complectitur tam praesentis aetatis quam successivae posteritatis. . . ." See above, n.84.

[92] Henry VII, in the edict *Ad reprimenda* (above, n.41), also *MGH, Const.*, IV,965,No.929: ". . . divina praecepta quibus iubetur quod omnis anima Romano principi sit subiecta." Cf. the bull *Unam Sanctam*: "Subesse Romano pontifici omni humanae creaturae declaramus . . . omnino esse de necessitate salutis." Mirbt, *Quellen*, 211, No.372.

[93] This was the opinion of the early glossators who tried to define the *collegium* by distinguishing between *simul cohabitantes* and *non cohabitantes*; that is, they tried to find the essence of the *collegium* within Space, and not with regard to Time, and thereby missed the essential point. See Gierke, *Gen.R.*, III,193.

We now recognize the flaw in the purely organological concept of state which regarded "head and limbs" mainly as they were represented at a given moment, but without projecting beyond the Now into Past and Future. The purely organological state became "corporate" only *ad hoc*, it was "quasi-corporate for some purposes of jurisdiction, taxation and administration,"[94] or in a moment of national emergency and effervescing patriotism, but it was not corporate in the sense of that perpetual continuity characteristic of the *universitas*. That is to say, the organological concept all by itself—John of Salisbury's analogy of the state with a human body—had not yet consciously integrated the factor of unlimited Time, which was absorbed only when the state organism became a "body" in the juristic sense: an *universitas* which "never dies." It is not surprising, therefore, that the organological analogy, important as it was as an initial step during the age of transition, gradually became philosophically dispensable because it was superseded by the corporational concept of *universitas* which embraces "head and limbs" also in succession.

It shall not be denied, however, that notions such as *patria* or *corpus morale et politicum* contained by implication also the element of continuity in Time; but this conclusion was not drawn before the fourteenth century nor was it rationalized that a mystical body, such as that of the French *patria*, encompassed not only all the Frenchmen living at present, but also all those having lived in the past and going to live in the future. It naturally took some time before the findings of the jurists—the identity in succession and the legal immortality of the corporation—began to sink in and to be combined with the idea of the state as an ever-living organism or with the emotional concept of *patria*. And expressions of national flavor such as *La France éternelle*, "immortal France," and others belonged definitely to a later period.

To say it once more, the most significant feature of the personified collectives and corporate bodies was that they projected into past and future, that they preserved their identity despite changes, and that therefore they were legally immortal.[95] The detachment

[94] Post, "Quod omnes tangit," 223, whose remarks about England are valid also for the Continent in that period.

[95] Ke Chin Wang, "The Corporate Entity Concept (or Fiction Theory) in the Year Book Period," *LQR*, LVIII (1942), 500,n.13, and 504,n.37, stresses in his stimulating study the point that "continuity is not an essential test of the Fiction Theory."

of the corporate *universitas* from its individual components resulted in the relative insignificance of these mortal components who at any given moment constituted the collective; they were unimportant as compared to the immortal body politic itself which survived its constituents, and could survive even its own physical destruction.[96] But granted that the *universitas* and the ever-changing limbs of the body corporate constituted an immortal entity, what about the "head" of the body politic which, after all, was a mortal individual man?

If the factors Time, Perpetuity, or Identity despite Change formed a decisive feature of the bodies corporate, and if further the present constituents of a body corporate were of relative unimportance as compared to the immortal *universitas* as such, then it might not appear too difficult to isolate, as it were, those decisive features and to arrive at a new construction: the corporation existing exclusively in Time and by succession. Normally the "plurality of persons" needed to form a collective body was constituted both ways: as it were, "horizontally" by those living simultaneously, and "vertically" by those living successively. Once, however, the principle was found that "plurality" or "totality" (*totum quoddam*) was—contrary, or even diametrically opposed, to the purely organological concept—not restricted to Space, but could unfold successively in Time, one could discard conceptually the plurality in Space altogether. That is to say, one constructed a corporate person, a kind of *persona mystica*, which was a collective only and exclusively with regard to Time, since the plurality of its members was made up only and exclusively by succession; and thus one arrived at a one-man corporation and fictitious person of which the long file of predecessors and the long file of future or potential successors represented, together with the present incumbent, that "plurality of persons" which normally would be made up by a multitude of individuals living simultaneously. That is, one constructed a body corporate whose members were echeloned longitudinally so that its cross-section at

---

While admitting that there may be fiction theories not involved with "continuity," I should say nevertheless that the *universitas* as a fictitious person is essentially a body having continuity.

[96] A very popular and much discussed argument, often based on D.3,4,7,2 (above, n.75); see Gierke, *Gen.R.*, III,236f,350 (nos.337ff), 411f (nos.240ff), 497f.

any given moment revealed one instead of many members—a mystical person by perpetual devolution whose mortal and temporary incumbent was of relatively minor importance as compared to the immortal body corporate by succession which he represented.[97]

This curious concept solved, as it were, the difficult problem of the perpetuity of the "head" of the body politic. It is on that basis and with that corporational plurality by succession in mind that we have to approach the problem of the King "who never dies."

[97] This is not identical with the one-man corporation achieved "by devolution," that is, when all members but one have passed away; see above, n.75, and Gierke, as quoted in the preceding note. See also Baldus, on c.36 X 1,6,n.8 (*In Decretales*, fol.79), speaking of a *collegium* or *universitas* which has been reduced to one person: ". . . verum est quod in uno non residet [universitas] primitive . . . , sed devolutive sic, quia pro pluribus habetur qui in plurium ius succedit, vel plures representat."

CHAPTER VII

THE KING NEVER DIES

BY INTERPRETING the People as an *universitas* "which never dies" the jurisprudents had arrived at the concept of a perpetuity of both the whole body politic (head and members together) and the constituent members alone. The perpetuity, however, of the "head" alone was of equally great importance, since the head would usually appear as the responsible part and its absence might render the body corporate incomplete or incapable of action. The perpetuation of the head, therefore, created a new set of problems and led to new fictions.

In the case of the ecclesiastical *collegia* the solution was as old as it was—at least, theoretically—simple: on the death of a prelate or other dignitary the property of the individual church as well as the dignity of prelate or abbot were said to lapse either to the hierarchical superior or to the Church universal or to the head of the Church, that is, to Christ or the vicar of Christ.[1] In the last analysis, therefore, Christ would have functioned during the interval, so to speak, as *interrex*. This was how Innocent IV saw the problem: "Possession and property [of a church . . . remain] with Christ who lives in eternity, or with the Church—universal or individual—which never dies and is never non-existent."[2] In other words, Church property lapsed to some perpetual entity—either to the eternal head of the Church or to the immortal and "never non-existent" Church itself.

Within the realm of practical Law and legal procedure, however, things were more difficult than in theory: it was not feasible that the divine incumbent of a vacant dignity (or his vicar on earth) should be summoned, or be held responsible, or be penalized. Hence practical difficulties arose concerning the continuity of the head of a corporate body. Not only did the legists and canonists run into trouble resulting in solutions such as the concept of the *corpora separata* whereby the head, the members, and head and members together each formed a separate body and corporate

---

[1] Gierke, *Gen.R.*, III,250,n.18, also 293 and passim.

[2] *Ibid.*, 351, n.340. Cf. Innocent, *Apparatus*, on c.4 X 2,12,n.4, fol. 145ᵛ. The ownership of Christ, or of saints, had a legal basis in C.1,2,25.

unit,[3] but also the Common Law jurists found the problem of the continuity of the head difficult to solve and often perplexing. The English *Year Books*, especially in the fifteenth century, reflect very clearly the predicaments of the royal judges who were quite willing to accept the corporational doctrine and terminology with regard to the incorporated members, but were far less willing to conceive also of a corporational character of the "head alone." Chief Justice Brian, for example, in a case of the City of Norwich heard in 1482, produced the argument: "If the mayor dies, the corporation becomes incomplete; and until the community appoints another mayor the corporation is incapacitated."[4] The death of the mayor thus created an interregnum, which rendered the body politic of Norwich incomplete and unfit for legal action *qua* corporation. On the other hand, a great jurist such as Littleton, as well as some of his colleagues on the bench, felt very strongly that there was a fundamental structural difference between the body corporate and its head. When, on one occasion, a plaintiff talked about a chapter or commonalty "and its successors," Justice Choke, supported by Littleton, declared quite correctly:

> The chapter can have no predecessor or successor, because the chapter is perpetual, and every one is in being, and cannot die, any more than a convent or commonalty; thus the chapter which was, and the chapter which is existing at present, are the same chapter, and not different: thus the same chapter cannot be a predecessor of itself, for a thing cannot be predecessor or successor to itself.[5]

Contrariwise, the judges very naturally all agreed that a dean or mayor, being a mere individual, could and did have predecessors and successors. That is, they were very far from admitting the identity of predecessor and successor, or from applying to those officers, for example, the *aeternitas* which Roman Law attributed to the *princeps* and which Bartolus appropriately corrected by interpreting it as "the sempiternity of the emperor which, with regard to his office, ought not have an end."[6] In other words, while

---

[3] *Ibid.*, 267f; above, Ch.v, n.231.

[4] Wang, "Corporate Entity," *LQR*, LIX (1943), 73, n.8 (21 Edw.IV).

[5] Wang, 76, n.16 (39 Hen.VI).

[6] Bartolus, on *C*.11,9,2,n.1 (Lyon, 1555), fol.37ᵛ: "Opinio quod Princeps non sit aeternus, quia omne elementum est corruptibile: ut l.eum debere.ff.de ser.urb. predi. [= *D*.8,2,33; cf. above, Ch.vi, n.18]. Solutio: improprie dicitur aeternus: tamen imperator respectu officii, quod non debet habere finem, potest dici sempiternus."

one adopted very willingly and without hesitation the content and terminology of the romano-canonical doctrines concerning the *universitas* "which never dies,"[7] one felt very clearly that the head could and did die, but realized also that the continuity of the "complete" corporation depended on the continuity of the head as well, a continuity vested successively in single persons.

It is obvious that a similar incompleteness with resulting incapacitation of the whole body politic of the *regnum* would have been almost intolerable. Interregna, whether long or short, had been a danger even in earlier times; they fitted badly into an age which had developed a relatively complicated machinery of state administration, as was the case in the later Middle Ages. It is noteworthy that the remedies introduced to neutralize the dangers of interregna and to secure the continuity of the royal head began to take shape far earlier in practice than in theory. The theories concerning the king's dynastic continuity, for example, served rather to explain and articulate existing customs than to create new ones, although admittedly it would often be difficult to decide accurately at what stage a developing practice may have been influenced also by the doctrines of jurists.

The perpetuity of the head of the realm and the concept of a *rex qui nunquam moritur*, a "king that never dies," depended mainly on the interplay of three factors: the perpetuity of the Dynasty, the corporate character of the Crown, and the immortality of the royal Dignity. Those three factors coincided vaguely with the uninterrupted line of royal bodies natural, with the permanency of the body politic represented by the head together with the members, and with the immortality of the office, that

---

[7] Bracton, it should be stressed, had a sounder perception of the essence of the corporation, its head and its members; see fol.374b, Woodbine, IV,175: "Et unde talis abbas praedecessor fuit seisitus in dominico suo et cetera, non fiat narratio de abbate in abbatem vel priore in priorem, nec de abbatibus vel prioribus mediis fiat mentio, quia in collegiis et capitulis semper idem corpus manet quamvis omnes successive moriantur et alii loco ipsorum substituantur, sicut dici poterit de gregibus ovium, ubi semper idem grex quamvis omnes oves sive capita successive discedant [Bracton evidently reproduces the metaphors of *D.*41,3,30, and of the *Glos.ord.* on that law, v. *singulae res*; see above, Ch.VI, n.48] nec succedit aliquis eorum alteri iure successionis ita quod ius descendat hereditarie ab uno usque ad alium, quia semper ius pertinet ad ecclesiam et cum ecclesia remanet, secundum quod videri poterit in cartis religiosorum de feoffamento, ubi manifeste videri poterit quod donatio facta est primo et principaliter deo et ecclesiae tali, et secundario monachis vel canonicis ibidem deo servientibus. Et ideo si abbas vel prior, monachi vel canonici successive obierint, domus in aeternum permanebit."

is, of the head alone. It has to be stressed, however, that those three components were not always clearly distinguished; they were often interchangeably referred to, and the lack of clarity and discrimination concerning the point of reference was particularly great in late mediaeval England where finally the jurists arrived at the strange solutions reflected by Plowden.

1. Dynastic Continuity

In his report on *Calvin's Case*, Sir Edward Coke, in 1609, discussed the manner in which the English crown descended to a new king. He pointed out that the king held the kingdom of England "by birth-right inherent" and that the title was by descent from the blood royal, "without any essential ceremony or act to be done *ex post facto*: for coronation is but a royal ornament and solemnization of the royal descent, but no part of the title." Coke even launched a vehement attack against two "Seminary Priests" who had dared to divulge the opinion that the king before his coronation "was no complete and absolute king" and that therefore ("observe their damnable and damned consequent") one might commit any act of violence against an as yet uncrowned king without being charged for treason. "But it was clearly resolved by all the Judges of England that . . . coronation was but a royal ornament and outward solemnization of the descent."[8]

Not to mention the seminary priests' dubious concept of the nature of treason and of the rights at large of any bishop, pope, or king before the consecration,[9] their theory of interregnum covering the time between a king's accession and his coronation was at any rate considerably out of date in the England of James I. Their argument must have appeared like some quaint remnant from a distant past, and the two seminarists appear to us like late descendants of the Englishmen of 1135 or 1272 who were said to have indulged in robberies and other disturbances because allegedly on the king's death the king's peace ceased to exist—or of those people of Pavia who, on the death of Emperor Henry II, destroyed the imperial castle because they claimed that there was no longer

---

8 Coke, *Reports*, 7th Part, vol. IV, fol.10a, 11.

9 The substance and limitation of powers exercised between election and consecration have been investigated by Robert L. Benson, "Notes on a Canonistic Theory of the Episcopal, Papal and Imperial Offices," a study as yet unpublished.

an emperor who owned it.[10] Probably, however, the two priests had in mind little more than to recall the former legal importance of the king's consecration at the hands of the clergy; for indeed the legal or constitutional value of that ritual action had been decreasing for many centuries.

That the view held by the two seminarists was not the one generally accepted by the English clergy at that time goes without saying. Coke easily assembled a string of precedents refuting the dangerous doctrine of those clerics. He might as well have alleged the words of Archbishop Cranmer, who, when addressing King Edward VI on his coronation in 1547, explained that kings

> be God's Anointed, not in respect of the oil which the bishop useth, but in consideration of their power which is ordained . . . and of their persons, which are elected of God and indued with the gifts of his Spirit for the better ruling and guiding of this people. The oil, if added, is but a ceremony: if it be wanting, that king is yet a perfect monarch notwithstanding, and God's Anointed as well as if he was inoiled.[11]

Archbishop Cranmer's words do not merely betray the spirit of the Reformation in England with its general aversion to all sorts of ritualistic "inoiling"; they sum up ideas which had been developing ever since the twelfth and thirteenth centuries and which reflected both the legal devaluation of the ecclesiastical coronations and the victory of dynastic succession.

The devaluation of the late mediaeval anointments of kings— notwithstanding an actual increase of mysticism connected with the performance itself—descended chiefly from two sources: one hierocratic and the other juristic.

[10] For the well known events, see Stubbs, *Select Charters*, 115 and 439. Powicke, *Henry III*, II,588ff, explains the nature of the riots of 1272 as "noisy demonstrations" of "tumultuous Londoners" in connection with a mayor's election, but does not seem to accept the constitutional aspect; Pollock and Maitland, *History*, I,521f, on the other hand, have stressed rather strongly the interregna in order to prove that the king "can die." For the parallel case in Pavia, see Wipo, *Gesta Chuonradi*, c.7, ed. Bresslau, 30. That "the period between accession and coronation was not one during which royal rights could be invaded with impunity," has been pointed out, for the time of the accession of Edward II, by H. G. Richardson, "The English Coronation Oath," *Speculum*, XXIV (1949), 63, n.92.

[11] Schramm, *English Coronation*, 139. For similar views, see also Figgis, *Divine Right*, 122f.

What had originally been a sacrament comparable to the sacraments of baptism and ordination had been reduced by the spiritual power itself to a considerably lower rank in order to enhance all the more efficiently the sublimity and uniqueness of the ordination to priestly offices.[12] The long development was epitomized by the decretal of Innocent III "On Holy Unction" in which the pope carefully separated the formerly interrelated and interlocked offices of king and bishop as outlined, for example, by the Norman Anonymous.[13] Pope Innocent III granted to the bishops the anointment with chrism and on the head, but denied emphatically the same privilege to the Prince. His arguments are interesting not only on account of the lowering of liturgical ceremonial, but also because they reveal a complete reversal of the former idea of Christ-like and Christ-centered kingship. For the very essence of royal or imperial *christomimesis* was in jeopardy when Innocent argued that chrism and head anointment were withheld from the Prince *because* Christ, the Head of the Church, had received the head anointment from the Holy Spirit. That is to say, in order to stress the *dissimilarity* with the anointment of Christ the anointment of the Prince was removed from the head to arms and shoulders, and it was performed, not with holy chrism, but with lesser oil.

> On the head of the bishop, however, the sacramental pouring has been retained because in his [episcopal] office, he, the bishop, represents the person of the Head [i.e. of Christ]. There is a difference between the anointments of bishop and Prince: for the bishop's head

[12] The original connection prevailing between coronation anointings and baptismal anointings has been stressed recently by Jean de Pange, "Doutes sur la certitude de cette opinion que le sacre de Pépin est la première époque du sacre des rois de France," *Mélanges d'histoire du moyen âge Louis Halphen* (Paris, 1951), 557-564; see also the same author's book *Le roi très chrétien* (Paris, 1949) and the review by Schramm, *ZfRG*, kan.Abt. xxxvii (1951), 395f. De Pange's discovery, however, is not as new as his reviewer believes; see, e.g., Thomas Michels, "Die Akklamation in der Taufliturgie," *Jahrbuch für Liturgiewissenschaft*, viii (1928), 76-85; Williams, *Norman Anonymous*, 79, 144, passim; see also Erdmann, *Ideenwelt*, 71f, who rightly warns against taking for a debasement what in fact was often only a different rite. Philipp Hofmeister, *Die heiligen Öle in der morgen- und abendländischen Kirche* (Das östliche Christentum, N.F., vi-vii [Würzburg, 1948]), yields little for the present purpose. See, however, Eichmann, *Die Kaiserkrönung*, i,145ff (with n.26), and 206. I shall deal with the subject in a forthcoming study on "Coronation and Epiphany"; see my brief remark in *Laudes regiae*, 142.

[13] See above, Ch.iii, n.30, and passim.

is *consecrated* with chrism, whereas the arm of the Prince is *soothed* with oil. Let it be shown how great is the difference between the authority of the bishop and the power of the Prince.[14]

The liturgically inferior rank of the ruler's anointment is obvious: it was restricted to a slightly sublimated exorcism and to a sealing against evil spirits.[15] According to the hierocratic doctrine the royal unction no longer conferred the Holy Spirit, although the Coronation Orders still preserved that idea and canonists still pondered whether or not the emperor was a *persona ecclesiastica*.[16] Above all, however, the Prince was expressly refused a Christlike representation or the character of a *christus Domini*.[17] As so often, the Roman

[14] See c.un. X 1,15, ed. Friedberg, II,131ff: "Sed ubi Iesus Nazarenus . . . unctus est oleo pietatis prae consortibus suis, qui secundum Apostolum est caput Ecclesiae, quae est corpus ipsius, principis unctio a capite ad brachium est translata: ut princeps extunc non ungatur in capite, sed in brachio. . . . In capite vero pontificis sacramentalis est delibutio conservata, quia personam capitis in pontificali officio repraesentat. Refert autem inter pontificis et principis unctionem; quia caput pontificis chrismate consecratur, brachium vero principis oleo delinitur, ut ostendatur quanta sit differentia inter auctoritatem pontificis et principis potestatem." For an analysis of that passage, see Eichmann, *Kaiserkrönung*, I,147f. The section of the decretal dealing with the royal anointments has been rarely glossed, though it was not ineffective. Hostiensis, e.g., follows the decretal when he explains (*Summa aurea*, on X 1,15,n.11, col.214): "Effectus unctionis regalis est, ut augeatur ei gratia ad officium, quod ei committitur exercendum . . . et honorabilior habeatur." In another connection, he says that technically the word *consecrare* was not even applicable to the imperial coronation; see K. G. Hugelmann, "Die Wirkungen der Kaiserweihe nach dem Sachsenspiegel," *ZfRG*, kan.Abt., IX (1919), 34, whose study assembles much of the later canonistic material.

[15] The difference of oils probably did not imply an intentional debasement in early times (Erdmann, *Ideenwelt*, 71f); some rites may have followed more closely the baptismal procedure (blessed oil), others that of confirmation (chrism). The meaning of the oils can be conveniently gathered from the answers to Charlemagne's questionnaire on baptism; see, e.g., the brief explanation of Leidrad, *De sacram. bapt.*, c.VII, *PL*, XCIX,863f: oil is used to exorcize the devil, water to clean from sin, chrism for the illumination by the grace of the Holy Spirit. See also the answer published by Wilmart, "Une catéchèse baptismale du IXe siècle," *Rev. bénéd.*, LVII (1947), 199, §11, where the effects of the lesser oil are described *ut undique muniatur*. The same phrase is used by Alcuin, *Ep.*, CXXXVII, *MGH, Epp.*, IV,214f (cf. *Ep.* CXXXIV, 202f): "Pectus quoque eodem perungitur oleo, ut signo sanctae crucis diabolo claudatur ingressus; signantur et scapulae ut undique muniatur." Contrariwise, the anointment with chrism is explained in the following fashion: "Tunc sacro chrismate caput perungitur et mystico tegitur velamine, ut intelligat se diadema regni et sacerdotii dignitatem portare" (according to I Peter 2: 9; Rom. 12: 1). See also F. Wiegand, *Erzbischof Odilbert von Mailand über die Taufe* (Leipzig, 1899), 33f, §§13 and 17.

[16] See Kempf, *Innocenz III.*, 127,n.52, who has collected interesting material on that point; also Mochi Onory, *Fonti canonistiche*, 90,n.1, 112,n.1, 117,n.1.

[17] See above, n.14, where Innocent III clearly implies the *christomimesis* on the part of the bishop while denying it to the emperor. Accordingly Tolomeo of Lucca, *Determinatio*, c.25, ed. Krammer, 47,29, declares: "Hoc autem non invenitur de imperatore aliquo, quod sit vicarius Christi."

pontiff appears here as the chief promoter of precisely that "secularism" which in other respects the Holy See tended to fight. Somewhat contemptuously Pope John XXII could allow King Edward II to repeat his anointment if the king so desired, because anyhow "it left no imprint on the soul," that is, it had no sacramental value.[18]

The decretal—in its section referring to the Prince—is important chiefly because it reflects the general change of mind of which Pope Innocent III was not the initiator but indeed the most prominent spokesman. Outside of Rome the papal decree exercised little, if any, influence.[19] It affected in no way the coronation rites observed, for example, in England and France: Hostiensis had to admit that in those countries the chrismation of the king's head was continued according to tradition and custom,[20] and the mystico-liturgical elaborations of the French ceremonial reached their peak long after the Innocentian era.[21] The ritualistic lowering of the value of consecration would have had little importance beyond the coronation liturgy of Rome had not, at approximately the same time, canonists and legists started to reduce the value of coronations in the legal-constitutional sphere as well.

The Innocentian decree was an effluence of the extreme hiero-

---

[18] J. W. Legg, *English Coronation Records* (Westminster, 1901), No.X, p.72: ". . . regalis [unctio] in anima quicquid non imprimit. . . ." See also Kern, *Gottesgnadentum*, 114; Bloch, *Rois thaumaturges*, 238ff; Schramm, *English Coronation*, 131f.

[19] The Innocentian Coronation Order—probably first used in 1209, at the coronation of Emperor Otto IV—shows very distinctly the influence of the new course; see Eichmann, *Kaiserkrönung*, I,253ff, esp. 266ff; also my remarks in *Laudes regiae*, 144ff.

[20] Hostiensis, *Summa aurea*, on X 1,15,n.8, col.213: "Sed et consuetudo antiqua circa hoc observatur: nam supradictorum regum Franciae et Angliae capita inunguntur." The same was true apparently in Naples, since Charles II of Anjou was granted the privilege of an anointment "sicut inunguntur reges Francie"; see L. H. Labande, "Le cérémonial romain de Jacques Cajétain," *Biblioth. de l'école des chartes*, LIV (1893), 72.

[21] See, in general, Kern, *Gottesgnadentum*, 114ff; Schramm, *Frankreich*, I,148ff, 157, for France and the new exaltation of the royal anointments due to the "celestial balm" added to the chrism; further Schramm, *English Coronation*, 126ff, who believes that in England the chrism was temporarily replaced by lesser oil, though the head anointing was not abolished; there is, however, reason to believe that the liturgico-technical accuracy of sources mentioning *oleum sanctum* instead of *chrisma* is overrated, and Schramm himself ("Krönung in Deutschland," 253) interprets Widukind's mention of *oleum sanctum* in the sense of chrism. It stands to reason that the belief in the sacramental power of the coronations continued; Cynus of Pistoia, e.g., claims that the consecration bestowed upon the Prince *spiritualia dona, gratiam spiritus sancti* (Hugelmann, "Kaiserweihe," 30,n.2), and so did others.

cratic views current at the papal *curia* ever since the days of the Reform Papacy. The canonists, however, who came to think of coronations as a matter of lesser importance were not the representatives of the hierocratic wing, that is, of those defending the theory that all power ultimately culminated in or derived from one man: the pontiff and his pontifical plenitude. On the contrary, the hierocratic canonists favored the imperial consecration because they held that only at his unction did the emperor receive the power of the material sword from the pontiff.[22] The other group of canonists, however, the "dualists," who favored a balance of the two universal powers, held that the imperial power (wrongly identified with the "material sword")[23] derived from God alone—through the act of election. The customary argument of these "dualistic" canonists of the twelfth and early thirteenth centuries was that emperors existed before there were pontiffs and that the emperors in former days had full power even without a consecration, because all power was from God anyhow.[24] They referred to the *lex regia* and pointed out that through the very election by the princes or the people, or by both princes and people, the emperor-elect obtained the full power of the sword and of administration because by that act princes and people had conferred all the rights on the new Prince.[25] They therefore concluded quite

[22] The whole problem of the "Two Swords" ("Num imperator gladium habeat a papa?") has been re-investigated by A. M. Stickler in a great number of papers which were not always easily accessible to me (I am indebted to Professor G. B. Ladner for allowing me to use the offprints which were at his disposal); they are enumerated in his article "Sacerdozio e regno nelle nuove ricerche attorno ai secoli XII e XIII nei decretisti e decretalisti fino alle decretali di Gregorio IX," *Miscellanea Historiae Pontificiae*, XVIII (1954), 3,n.3; see also his latest paper "Imperator vicarius Papae," *MIÖG*, LXII (1954), 165-212. For an excellent discussion of these papers, which urgently demand a synthesis on the part of the author, see Brian Tierney, "Some Recent Works on the Political Theories of the Mediaeval Canonists," *Traditio*, X (1954), 609ff. The whole problem has been brought into focus by Kempf, *Innocenz III.*, 204ff (for the "hierocrats"), and 212ff (for the "dualists").

[23] Stickler, "De ecclesiae potestate coactiva materiali apud magistrum Gratianum," *Salesianum*, IV (1942), 2-23, 97-119, shows that Gratian had in mind the spiritual and physical coercion belonging to the Church, and not the spiritual and secular powers; see Tierney, *op.cit.*, 610; Kempf, *op.cit.*, 187ff.

[24] "Ante enim erant imperatores quam summi pontifices et tunc habebant potestatem, quia omnis potestas a Deo est." This argument (or its equivalents) was repeated over and over again; see Stickler, "Sacerdotium et Regnum nei decretisti e primi decretalisti," *Salesianum*, XV (1953), 605 (*Quaestiones Orielenses*, s.XII ex.), 610 (*Quaestiones* of Bazianus, s.XII ex.), 611 (Richard of Mores, s.XII ex.); see, for additional places (Simon of Bisignano, Huguccio, and several *Summae*), Kempf, *op.cit.*, 212ff, nos.48,50,51; also Hugelmann, "Kaiserweihe," 23.

[25] *Quaestiones Orielenses* (Stickler, *op.cit.*, 605): "Nos vero dicimus quod a Deo hanc potestatem habet imperator . . . Nam ante potest uti gladio quam ab apostolico inungatur. Ex electione enim populi (Bazianus: 'principum' [Stickler, 610])

logically that the imperial power did not derive from the pope; that the Prince was *verus imperator* even before he was confirmed—meaning here: consecrated—by the pope, and that at his unction in Rome the Prince received only the papal confirmation together with the imperial title.[26]

It is true, of course, that very often the opinions of "hierocrats" and "dualists" overlapped and that there were numerous modifications of the general scheme. Moreover, the canonists made many subtle and often highly important distinctions concerning the extent of actual power which the elect was entitled to exercise before his consecration, and naturally they visualized as a pattern of the *imperator electus* the "bishop elect" whose powers before the consecration were restricted, whereas the "pope elect" exercised practically full power from the moment of his election, especially if he ascended as an ordained bishop.[27] But while theories and analogies were to remain fluid for a long time to come, there crystallized nevertheless the doctrine that the Prince's exercise of imperial rights and adminstrative functions did not really depend upon his Roman coronation. And since this opinion finally was popularized also by Johannes Teutonicus' ordinary Gloss on the *Decretum*,[28] the new theory could not fail to make the jurists at large conscious of the problem.

---

hoc sibi licet, qui ei et in eum omne ius transfert. Tamen confirmatur ei ab apostolico tempore inunctionis." See also Huguccio (quoted by Kempf, 213,n.50): "Ego autem credo quod imperator potestatem gladii et dignitatem imperialem habet non ab apostolico, sed a principibus et populo per electionem. . . ." Cf. Stickler, "Der Schwerterbegriff bei Huguccio," *Ephemerides iuris canonici*, III (1947), 201-242.

[26] The jurists do not have in mind the papal *confirmatio* following after the election and preceding the consecration of exempt bishops and other ecclesiastical dignitaries; see Kempf, *Innocenz III.*, 106ff. The words *confirmare* and *inungere* are almost interchangeable; see, e.g., Oldradus de Ponte, *Consilia*, CLXXX, n.19, fol.75ᵛ: "quid est enim approbare, inungere, et consecrare nisi confirmare?" See also Kempf, 123ff, 215 (n.58), 245ff. For *verus imperator*, see note 28.

[27] One of the more important distinctions was that between *administratio* (owned by the emperor immediately and directly from God) and *auctoritas* (conferred upon the emperor at his consecration by the pope) introduced by Rufinus, on c.1, D.XXII, v. *terreni simul*, ed. H. Singer, *Die Summa Decretorum des Magister Rufinus* (Paderborn, 1902), 47; cf. Kempf, *op.cit.*, 208ff. Benson (above, n.9) has investigated the pre-consecrational rights of bishop and pope in their relationship to the pre-coronational rights of the emperor. See below, nos. 32 and 40.

[28] *Glos.ord.*, on c.24, D.XCIII, v. *imperatorem*: "ex sola enim electione principum dico eum verum imperatorem antequam a papa confirmetur. Arg[umentum] hic, licet non appelletur." Johannes Teutonicus (see, for his authorship, Hugelmann, "Kaiserweihe," 18ff) repeats verbatim the *Glossa palatina* (ca.1210-1215); cf. Stickler, "Sacerdotium et regnum," 589, and Kuttner, *Repertorium*, 81f, who first recognized the interrelations between the *Glossa palatina* and Teutonicus' *Glos.ord.* (see *ZfRG*, kan.Abt., XXI[1932], 141-189).

Such consciousness is not yet found in a famous gloss of Accursius. In full agreement with the older tradition according to which a ruler's reign and regnal years began with the date of his consecration, Accursius held *quod non valet privilegium principis ante coronationem,* "that the Prince's privileges are not valid before his coronation."[29] The idea embedded in this gloss died hard—not only on account of the authority of Accursius, but because it fitted the purposes of certain political groups. During the great Interregnum of the empire after the death of Frederick II, when Roman coronations were suspended for more than 60 years (1250-1312), cities and princes in the non-German parts of the empire—Burgundy and Italy—came forth with the theory that outside of Germany the emperor elect, the *rex Romanorum,* lacked executive and jurisdictional power before he was crowned emperor in Rome. This, of course, was but a flimsy excuse to elude the imperial overlordship in general; but since that theory played politically into the hands of Charles of Anjou, the most powerful man in Italy during the decisive years of the Interregnum, there was a strong group of powers inclined to back up the Accursian gloss to the letter and to forestall, at the same time, an imperial coronation altogether.[30]

At this juncture, the jurists at large began to occupy themselves with the very complex problem of the pre-coronation rights of the Prince. "Secular laws do not scorn imitation of the holy canons," remarked an early decretist[31]—and indeed not only can-

---

[29] *Glos.ord.,* on *C.*7,37,3, v. *infulas.* Another gloss of Accursius was, to say the least, misleading; on *C.*3,12,6,5, v. *vel ortus,* he remarks: "idest coronatus." The *dies imperii* or *ortus imperii,* which the Emperors Valentinian, Theodosius, and Arcadius ordered celebrated, were their days of accession and election; an ecclesiastical coronation was as yet unknown. Accursius, however, reflected the mediaeval custom according to which the regnal years were counted from the day of the coronation, and not from the day of election or accession. In this sense the Accursian gloss was understood, e.g., by Oldradus de Ponte, *Consilia,* CLXXX, n.7, fol.74ᵛ: "sed imperator in coronatione dicitur oriri et sic incipere esse [follows reference to the Accursius gloss]: ergo ante hoc non operatur, quae ad imperationem pertinent." Also Durandus, *Speculum iuris,* II, partic.I, De rescripti praesentatione, §9,n.18 (Venice, 1602), 424: "Et dies coronationis dicitur ortus Imperii . . ." Albericus de Rosate, on *C.*7,37,3,n.12, fol.107ᵛ (see also nos.3 and 13) repeats Oldrado's statements verbatim, but argues against him, thus supporting Cynus (on the same law).

[30] F. Kern, "Die Reichsgewalt des deutschen Königs nach dem Interregnum," *HZ,* CVI (1911), 39-95. Charles of Anjou had certainly different views with regard to the pre-coronational powers of the French king; see below, n.47.

[31] "Seculi leges non dedignantur sacros canones imitari," a paraphrase of *Nov.* 83,1 (cf. *Nov.*131,1), found, e.g., in the *Glossa palatina,* on c.7 (add.), C.II,q.3, v.

onists, but also legists and feudists followed the lead of Johannes Teutonicus' gloss on the *Decretum*. Chiefly for practical reasons Durandus opined that the Prince enjoyed full powers before his consecration because otherwise the donations to the Holy See made by Rudolf of Habsburg would be invalid,[32] while Oldradus de Ponte discussed in great detail all arguments for and against the pre-coronational powers of the emperor.[33] Perhaps it was Oldradus' teacher, Jacobus de Arena (d. 1296 or before), who started among the civilians the more general discussion of the involved principle when, during the Interregnum, the issue reached a state of actuality; and his opinion, favoring the Prince's pre-coronational powers, was cited and supported by the Ghibelline Cynus of Pistoia, who drew the conclusion that "the one elected by the people through the *lex regia*" enjoyed the full sovereign rights and powers even without coronation.[34] Eventually, however, the doctrine of the "dualistic" canonists had the effects of a rallying cry for those defending the maxim "the king is emperor in his realm" as well as for the anti-curialists. Andreas of Isernia, at the court of Naples, declared: "Certainly the emperors before being crowned in Rome are kings, and as kings they have *maiestas* and *fiscus*, and many were Kings of Germany or of the Romans, who were not crowned emperors at all."[35] Clearly, the Neapolitan jurist aimed at demonstrating that "emperor and king were on equal terms" and that the emperor, in fact, was simply "king in his empire" and did not differ essentially from the King of Naples and other rulers whose rights derived from the *lex regia*

---

cum leges seculi, quoted by Stickler, "Sacerdotium et regnum," 589, and later often repeated; see, e.g., Hostiensis, *Summa aurea*, prooem., n.11, col.7.

[32] Durandus, *loc.cit.* (above, n.29), who interestingly parallels emperor and pope: "Imperator enim ex sola Principum electione etiam ante confirmationem aliquam verus est Imperator et consequitur ius administrandi . . . sicut et Papa ex sola electione consequitur plenam potestatem regendi et temporalia administrandi . . ." There follows an enumeration of actions which the pope can perform only "postquam ordines et insignia recepit." Cf. Hugelmann, "Kaiserweihe," 29,n.1; also below, n.46, where the same argument was applied to Constantine and his donation, and n.41, for the imperial constitution *Licet iuris*.

[33] Oldradus de Ponte, *Consilia*, CLXXX, fol.74ᵛ-75ᵛ.

[34] Cf. Hugelmann, "Kaiserweihe," 29, n.2, for both Jacobus de Arena and Cynus of Pistoia; see also Ullmann, *Lucas de Penna*, 177,n.1.

[35] Andreas of Isernia, *prooemium* of his Gloss on *Lib. aug.*, ed. Cervone, p.xxvi, §*Sed certe*: "Sed certe antequam coronentur Romae Imperatores sunt Reges, et habent majestatem, et fiscum, et multi fuerunt Reges Alemanniae, et Romanorum, qui non fuerunt incoronati Imperatores."

and from their title alone.[36] Lucas de Penna, likewise a Neapolitan, may have thought of Andreas of Isernia, on whom so often he relied, when mentioning "some jurisprudents" who claimed that the ruler has "the plenitude of power by his [dynastically or electorally transmitted] title alone, from God alone, and in God's place on earth; and he can do anything without [ecclesiastical] examination, blessing, or coronation."[37] On the other hand, the tendency was anti-hierocratic when John of Paris bluntly declared that kings were kings without anointment and that in many Christian countries anointments of kings were not practiced at all.[38] Definitely anti-curial were the Sicilian jurists of King Frederick III of Sicily who, in 1312, argued that the emperor had his full powers by his election alone;[39] nor were the Italian jurists who gave counsel to the emperors Henry VII and Louis of Bavaria less anti-curial when they argued along similar lines.[40] Finally, that

[36] Andreas of Isernia, *loc.cit.* (preceding paragraph): "quod Imperator et Rex pari passu sunt." See also Andreas, on *Feud.* 1,1,n.8, fol.9ᵛ: ". . . postquam est Rex Romanorum, consecratur per Papam . . . Ex sola electione habet administrationem sine consecratione . . . Inde Imperator dicitur Rex . . . Et lex regia fuit quae transtulit in principem omne ius . . . Idem de Rege Siciliae et aliis, qui cum Imperio nihil habent facere: quorum quilibet est Monarcha in suo regno. . . ."

[37] Lucas de Penna, on *C.*10,74,n.12 (quoted by Ullmann, *Lucas de Penna*, 176, n.3), mentions some lawyers who held that the ruler "ex solo nomine a solo Deo et vice Dei in terris plenitudinem potestatis habere ac sine ulla examinatione, benedictione et coronatione omnia posse." Lucas de Penna himself did not share this view.

[38] John of Paris, *De potestate*, c.18, ed. Leclercq, 229,11f. In order to demonstrate the superfluousness of ecclesiastical coronations, John refers to Spain: *ut patet in regibus Hispanorum.* This is correct in so far as Portugal never introduced a coronation; Navarre introduced coronation and unction only after 1257 (Schramm, "Der König von Navarra," *ZfRG*, germ.Abt., LXVIII[1951], 147f); Castile abandoned, in 1157, its coronation ritual, though resuming it in the thirteenth century (Schramm, "Das kastilische Königtum und Kaisertum während der Reconquista," *Festschrift für Gerhard Ritter* [Tübingen, 1950], 115ff); and Aragon, having introduced the ceremony in 1204, observed a peculiar ritual—at least after the accession of Pedro II in 1276—in that the king not only invested himself with all the royal insignia, but also crowned himself with his own hands, "ninguna persona ni larcebispe, ni infant, ni ninguna persona otra de cualquiere condicion que sea" being allowed to touch the diadem (Schramm, "Die Krönung im katalanisch-aragonesischen Königreich," *Homenatge a Antoni Rubió i Lluch* [Barcelona, 1936], III,8f).

[39] *MGH, Const.*, IV, No.1248, p.1311,40: "Romano principi sola electio eius omnem tribuit potestatem." Cf. Rudolf Most, "Der Reichsgedanke des Lupold von Bebenburg," *DA*, IV (1941), 467,n.2, for the later influence of the Memorandum.

[40] See, for the Doctors of Law Johannes Branchazolus and Ugolino da Celle, E. E. Stengel, *Nova Alemanniae* (Berlin, 1921), 50, No. 90, §6; 73, No.123, §5; cf. Most, "Lupold," 468, n.1; 470, n.3. Even stronger is a later declaration (Stengel, 402), where the author claims that "iste corone sunt quedam sollempnitates adinvente per ecclesiam, nomina non res impendentes" (at the same time a good example for the influence of Nominalism on juristic thought). See below, nos.42,46 for the coronation as a mere solemnity; also above, n.8.

theory triumphed at Rhense, in 1338, when the German princes elector decreed—and when, a little later, in the Constitution *Licet iuris*, Louis of Bavaria declared—that the emperor's power and dignity derived directly from God alone and that the one legally elected by the princes had all the imperial powers, rights, and privileges by his election alone and without any papal approval or confirmation.[41] This chorus was joined by the philosophers— William of Ockham, Marsiglio of Padua, and others—who held that the rights claimed and assumed by the Roman Pontiff nullified the importance of the electoral act and that solemnities such as coronations conferred no authority whatever, but only signified that such authority was owned and had been conferred already.[42]

The official legislation of the empire in 1338 settled the issue for all practical purposes—also among the lawyers. Bartolus, it is true, did not come out with a clear statement.[43] Baldus, making some contradictory statements, operated skilfully with the old distinctions—introduced as early as the twelfth century by Rufinus—of "general administration" and "plenitude of power" and declared that the emperor before his coronation enjoyed only the "general administration," a compound of powers which long before the German princes had occasionally called the *imperatura*.[44] However, the gloss of Johannes Teutonicus exercised its influence also

---

[41] For the passages, see Mirbt, *Quellen*, 223, Nos.383,384 (the wording of the Teutonicus gloss is clearly recognizable); in general, E. E. Stengel, *Avignon und Rhens* (Weimar, 1930); also Most, "Lupold," 466ff; Heinrich Mitteis, *Die deutsche Königswahl: Ihre Rechtsgrundlagen bis zur Goldenen Bulle* (2nd ed., Brünn, Munich, and Vienna, 1944), 216ff. The power exercised by the emperor elect before the coronation was compared to that of the pope elect before his coronation, since the pope received "omnia iura pontificis ex electione"—at least, according to Cynus; see Hugelmann, "Kaiserweihe," 30 (note); Ullmann, *Lucas de Penna*, 177f, also (n.3) for the effects of the imperial decree at the papal court. Cf. Durandus, above, n.32.

[42] For Marsiglio, see *Defensor pacis*, II, c.26, §§4-5, ed. R. Scholz (*MGH, Fontes iuris germanici antiqui*, 1932), 490f: "Non enim conferunt huiusmodi solempnitates auctoritatem, sed habitam vel collatam significant." For Ockham, see Most, "Lupold," 470, n.5, 471, n.3; Schramm, *Frankreich*, I,243, and 227, for John of Jandun.

[43] Woolf, *Bartolus*, 31f.

[44] Baldus, on C.7,37,3, additio, fol.28ᵛ: "ante coronationem non habet plenitudinem potestatis, licet habeat generalem administrationem." See, for these and similar distinctions, above, n.27; also Ullmann, *op.cit.*, 178. Cf. Mitteis, *Königswahl*, 120ff, for *imperatura*. Coinages of that kind must have been rather common; Cynus (quoted by Hugelmann, "Kaiserweihe," 30, note) mentions *Imperatoriam (iurisdictionem)*; Oldradus de Ponte (above, n.29) uses *imperatio*, though not in the sense of the German princes, but rather as Dante talks about the *imperiatus (De monarchia*, III,12). These coinages show that one wished to avoid the ambiguity of the word *imperium*.

on these later jurists. Baldus, though referring occasionally also to the "Archidiaconus" (Guido de Baysio),[45] depended in fact on the Teutonicus gloss, and expanded it, when he stressed the purely "ornamental" character of the Roman coronation: he opined that the Roman coronation added nothing but some "lustre and an increase of honor," whereas the true essence of imperial authority derived from the concord reached at the election alone.[46] It was by drawing from one of those jurists that finally the English experts—Cranmer, Coke, and others—produced the opinion that the coronation was "but a royal ornament and outward solemnization of the descent" and that the king had all the gifts of the Holy Spirit even without being "inoiled."

It would be difficult to tell with some degree of accuracy whether or to what extent the lively discussion which was carried on during the Interregnum by canonists and legists about the emperor's pre-coronational rights, may have influenced the political decisions of the European kingdoms. We may assume, however, that the legal theories were at least subsidiarily effective when the two great Western monarchies, France and England, ventured to put into practice what later jurisprudents would have taken almost for granted: to sever the beginning of a king's reign and his exercise of full power from his ecclesiastical consecration. When Saint Louis died in Africa in 1270, Philip III, himself then present on the shores of Tunis and guided by Charles of Anjou, immediately assumed full power. Without waiting for his coronation, which had to be postponed anyhow until after his return to France, Philip III became king of France with all his rights and privileges. Accordingly he began to date his regnal years, contrary to all custom, from the day of his accession, and not from that of his consecration.[47] Similar was the procedure in England

[45] Baldus, on prooem. ("Rex pacificus") X 1,n.5, *In Decretales*, fol.5: "Rex Romanorum statim, cum electus est, habet imperium plene formatum authoritate potestatis, licet coronam expectet, ut not. Archidia. xciii. distin. capit. legimus (c.24,D.XCIII)."

[46] Baldus, on c.33 X 2,24,n.6, *In Decretales*, fol.261v: "Coronatio in imperatore non addit nisi coruscationem et honoris augmentum (above nos.40,42), sed veram essentiam ex sola electione concordi. Hoc patet in Constantino, qui coronavit papam, non autem fuit coronatus a papa, tamen ei donavit maxima et meliora, et ecclesia in parte utitur illa donatione, ergo valuit. Ex hoc sequitur quod administratio potest praecedere coronationem et sequi." See also above, n.32.

[47] Schramm, *Frankreich*, 1,226f; in general, Kern, *Gottesgnadentum*, 308f.

in 1272. When Henry III died, his son Edward I, then absent in the Holy Land, began to rule with a king's full authority and power on the day of his accession, which was the day of his father's burial. Edward did not have to wait until his coronation, which was consummated only in 1274, to assume full power; he, too, began to count his regnal years, contrary to the hitherto valid practice in England, from the day of his accession.[48] Thus, for practical reasons, and by coincidence almost simultaneously, both Philip III and Edward I put the teaching of the jurists into practice, who held that the full government began with the day of a ruler's accession: *et incipiunt anni imperii.*[49]

Both France and England thus succeeded in abolishing the "little interregnum" arising between the king's accession and his coronation, just as finally the decree of Rhense and the constitution *Licet iuris* did away with that interval in the empire. The coronation ceremonial, of course, was not abandoned; but for all its late-mediaeval exuberance, the crowded symbolism and courtly-religious pomp of the pageantry, the live essence of liturgical kingship evaporated, and the prevalence of secular considerations—political and legal—deprived that ritual of most of its former constitutional values. The new king's government was legalized by God and the people alone, *populo faciente et Deo inspirante.* The Church, as Marsiglio of Padua said, had merely to "signify." It had to testify that the new king was the right king and was orthodox. However, it still remained a task of the Church to solemnize the important coronation oath.[50] Moreover, as an occasion for the display of courtly pomp and splendor, to which the newly founded dynastic Orders of Knighthood contributed their punctilio, the coronations gained some new momentum.[51]

[48] Pollock and Maitland, *History*, I,521f; Stubbs, *Select Charters*, 438ff; also Schramm, *English Coronation*, 166f.

[49] Oldradus de Ponte, *Consilia*, CLXXX, n.6, fol.74ᵛ, discussing the opinion of others according to whom the emperor elect derived from his election alone the rights of a *verus imperator*: "Et ut nomen [rex Romanorum] indicat, ex tunc videtur romanorum praepositus rebus. Si sic, ex tunc est verus imperator, et incipiunt anni imperii." Cf. Theseider, *L'Idea imperiale*, 264 (where the senseless *utitur [vr̄]* should be replaced by *videtur*).

[50] The king swore his oath on one occasion only, that is, on his coronation; see Richardson, "Coronation Oath," 62f, n.91; also Schramm, *English Coronation*, 204ff, for the changes involved, and my study "Inalienability," *Speculum*, XXIX (1954), 488-502, for the introduction of the non-alienation clause which increased the constitutional importance of the coronation oath.

[51] See the concise account of Schramm, *English Coronation*, 90ff.

Finally, the crownings served, as Sir Edward Coke said, "the solemnization of the royal descent," that is, as a medium for the quasireligious enhancement of the dynasty and for the manifestation of a dynasty-bound divine right.

Not by any special act or decree, but *de facto*, both France in 1270 and England in 1272 recognized that the succession to the throne was the birthright of the eldest son: on the death—or burial[52]—of the ruling monarch the son or legitimate heir became king automatically. Nor could there be an interruption in the succession: legally testator and heir were considered one person, and this view—supported by philosophical maxims—was transferred from Private to Public Law.[53] Hence, the continuity of the king "body natural" was secured, when the two Western monarchies did away not only with the "little interregnum" between accession and coronation, but also eliminated, once and for all, the possibility of a "great interregnum" which might occur between the death of a king and the election of his successor. "Time runneth not against the King"—it did not run against the dynasty either.

Henceforth, the king's true legitimation was dynastical, independent of approval or consecration on the part of the Church and independent also of election by the people. "The royal power," wrote John of Paris, "is from God and from the people electing the king in his person or in his house, *in persona vel in domo*."[54] Once the choice of the dynasty had been made by the people, election was in abeyance: the royal birth itself manifested the Prince's election to kingship, his election by God and divine providence. That a person succeeded to the throne of his ancestors by hereditary right was something "which can be done by none except God." This was the opinion of an eleventh-century author; it was epitomized later by Bracton in the oft-quoted maxim "Only

---

[52] The burial took place on the fourth day after King Henry III's death; after 1308, however, there was an interval of only one day, until the sixteenth century abolished this honorary last-day rule of the dead monarch; see Schramm, *op.cit.*, 166f. Baldus, on c.36 X 1,6,n.3, *In Decretales*, fol. 79, recommends an interval of at least three days with regard to the coronation of the new king: "Quod rege mortuo filius eius non debet de honestate coronari nisi post triduum, quia post tres dies Christus resurrexit a mortuis."

[53] See below, nos.6off, and 78ff.

[54] John of Paris, *De potestate*, c.10, ed. Leclercq. 119,23; see above, Ch.vi, n.51, and, Kern, *Gottesgnadentum*, 47ff.

God can make an heir,"[55] suggesting that the very birth of an heir resembled a "judgment of God."[56] Hence, Archbishop Cranmer could finally maintain, when demonstrating that "inoilings" were dispensable, that in their persons God's Anointed "are elected of God and indued with the gifts of His Spirit."[57] The Holy Spirit, which in former days was manifested by the voting of the electors, while his gifts were conferred by the anointment, now was seated in the royal blood itself, as it were, *natura et gratia*, by nature and by grace—indeed, "by nature" as well; for the royal blood now appeared as a somewhat mysterious fluid.

'He that cometh from heaven is above all' (John 3:31), that is, he that descends from imperial stock is more noble than all.[58]

The eulogist thus praising Frederick II merely echoed opinions current at the imperial court, and Frederick himself extolled the nobility of the imperial race and of the royal races at large.[59] Moreover, in Frederick's surroundings one began to combine the dynastic idea with philosophical doctrines implying a belief in certain royal qualities and potencies dwelling in the blood of kings and creating, so to speak, a royal species of man. In a letter to Frederick's young son, King Conrad IV, for example, the writer said:

So much more are Princes who lack knowledge stained and blemished than private persons, as the nobility of the [royal] blood is distinguished by the infusion of a subtle and noble soul which makes Princes before other men susceptible to teaching.[60]

[55] See the tractate *De unitate Ecclesiae* (c. A.D. 1090), c.13, *MGH,LdL*, II,204,32: ". . . qui pro patribus suis successit in regnum iure hereditario, quod fieri non posset nisi a Deo." Cf. Kern, *Gottesgnadentum*, 245, n.449, for additional places. Bracton, fol.62b, ed. Woodbine, II,184: "Nec potest aliquis sibi facere heredem, quia solus deus heredem facit." Cf. Figgis, *Divine Right*, 36; Kern, *op.cit.*, 48,n.90.

[56] See Figgis, *Divine Right*, 36.

[57] See above, n.11.

[58] Nicholas of Bari, ed. Kloos, in *DA*, XI (1954), 170,4: "qui de celo venit, super omnes est, id est, qui de imperiali semine descendit, cunctis nobilior est."

[59] See *Erg.Bd.* 221ff, esp. King Manfred's manifesto to the Romans, of 1265; *MGH, Const.*, II, No.424, pp.559ff.

[60] Huillard-Bréholles, *Hist. dipl.*, v,274f: "Immo tanto se maiori nota notabiles faciunt principes inscii quam privati, quanto *nobilitas sanguinis per infusionem subtilis et nobilis anime* facit ipsos esse pre ceteris susceptibiles discipline." The whole letter is of great interest, and though it may be a school exercise only, it yet reflects concepts of the blood royal apparently common in a period so strongly influenced by tenets of Aristotelian-Stoic anthropology. Dubois (below, n.64) uses similar phrases, and the doctrines of absolutism later on work with the same argument: "[Le sang Royal] est d'estoffe et qualité trop plus noble et auguste, que celui

It is not quite clear what doctrine the writer of these lines may have had in mind or from what sources he drew. It is not simply the Aristotelian anthropology, the doctrine of generation and hereditism according to which there is a power active in the male seed deriving from the soul of the begetter and impressing itself on the son;[61] nor is it the Stoic doctrine of the "seminal principles" of the *genus humanum* in general;[62] the idea of a specially refined soul, "subtle and noble," and infused in the blood of princes is reminiscent rather of the Hermetic tenet concerning the creation of the souls of kings, but it seems doubtful that this doctrine was known at that time.[63]

---

des autres hommes." Cf. Church, *Constitutional Thought*, 317,n.36, quoting Charles Loyseau, *Traité des ordres et simples dignitez*, VII,n.92, in his *Oeuvres* (Lyon, 1701), 47.

[61] The passages relevant to Aristotle's generationism and spermatology, though particularly numerous in *De generatione animalium*, are yet widely scattered; see Harold Cherniss, *Aristotle's Criticism of Plato and the Academy* (Baltimore, 1944), 470f. The whole problem has recently been dealt with by Erna Lesky, *Die Zeugungs- und Vererbungslehren der Antike und ihr Nachwirken* (Akademie d. Wissenschaften und der Literatur: Abh. d. Geistes- und Sozialwiss. Kl., 1950, No.19, Mainz, 1951); see 125ff (1349ff), for Aristotle, and esp. 146ff (1370ff), for A.'s doctrine of hereditism. See also A. Mitterer, *Die Zeugung der Organismen, insbesondere des Menschen, nach dem Weltbild des hl. Thomas von Aquin und der der Gegenwart* (Vienna, 1947). Aquinas' doctrine holding that "virtus activa quae est in semine, est quaedam impressio derivata ab anima generantis" (*Summa theol.*, I,q.119,art.1,resp.2, also I,q.118,art.1,ad 3; cf. Lesky, 135 and 137, for Aristotle's view), was influential also on juristic thought; see, e.g., Jean de Terre Rouge, *De iure futuri successoris*, Tract.I, art.2, concl.1, p.35: ". . . nam secundum Philosophum in semine hominis est quaedam vis impressiva, activa, derivata ab anima generantis et a suis remotis parentibus. Et sic est identitas particularis naturae patris et filii. . . ." For the tenet of the identity of father and son, see below, nos.258ff.

[62] See, for the Aristotelian-Stoic doctrine of the *rationes seminales* as transmitted by Augustine and Macrobius, Hans Meyer, *Geschichte der Lehre von den Keimkräften von der Stoa bis zum Ausgang der Patristik* (Bonn, 1914), esp.184ff; cf. Lesky, *op.cit.* 164ff (1388ff); also 172f (1396f), for Philo, *Legatio ad Gaium*, c.8,55, where the "seminal logoi" are said to have predisposed Caligula for rulership; cf. Harry A. Wolfson, *Philo* (Cambridge, Mass., 1948), 1,342f.

[63] *Kore kosmou*, frg.XXIV, ed. W. Scott, *Hermetica* (Oxford, 1924), 1,494ff; ed. A. D. Nock and A.-J. Festugière, *Corpus Hermeticum* (Paris, 1954), IV,52ff; see also Delatte, *Traités de la royauté*, 154ff, for the connections with the "Pythagorean" theories on kingship. Of the *Corpus Hermeticum* there was at least one tractate known in the school of Chartres, the *Asclepius*; see Theodore Silverstein, "The Fabulous Cosmogony of Bernardus Silvestris," *Modern Philology*, XLVI (1948), 109ff; Robert B. Woolsey, "Bernard Silvester and the Hermetic Asclepius," *Traditio*, VI (1948), 340-344; also Manitius, *Lateinische Literatur*, III,199 and 262. *Kore kosmou*, however, or, for that matter, Stobaeus' *Florilegium*, can have been hardly accessible in the 13th century. Loyseau, *loc.cit.* (above, n.60), refers to Plato and Aristotle in that connection: "veu que Platon au 3. de sa *Republ.* a dit, que ceux, qui sont nays pour commander, sont composez d'autre metail, que les autres. Et Aristote a dit encor plus à propos, que les Roys sont d'un genre moyen entre Dieu et le peuple."

However that may be, a peculiar kind of scientific mysticism—irrational and material at the same time—seized upon the budding idea of dynastic legitimism. Pierre Dubois assembled astrological and climatological arguments to prove the natural and physical preeminence of the French royal race not only above that of common people but also above that of other dynasts.[64] In the same period, the French theories justifying the dynastic principle produced truly exquisite structures of dynastic scholasticism: a dynasty that had returned to the blood of Charlemagne, saintly kings siring new saintly kings, a race promoted by Christ from the very beginnings of the Christian faith, a most holy royal house to which God had granted a heavenly oil for the anointment of its kings, and certainly a royal stock endowed with miraculous gifts the like of which not even the Church could claim.[65] Although similarly exalted elaborations of mystic endowments of the royal house by grace and by nature were hardly found in England at that period, the hereditary right to the crown on the part of the eldest son became nevertheless deeply engrained as an "indefeasible right" and an incontestable, if unwritten, law of the realm.[66]

See Plato, *Rep.*, III,415Aff; but it is not clear to what passage of Aristotle the author refers; see, however, Goodenough, *Politics of Philo*, 98, for similar places.

[64] Scholz, *Publizistik*, 411,n.137; Kämpf, *Pierre Dubois*, 95,n.7; also 70. It remained the standard practice of absolutism to enhance the royal blood "en l'excellence duquel on ne doit imaginer aucune souilleure ni corruption, ains au contraire ce sang Royal purifie et ennoblit tout autre sang avec lequel il se mesle." Charles Loyseau, *loc.cit.* (above, n.60), a passage which should be compared with Leclercq, "Sermon," 169,15 (above, Ch.V, n.183). For England, see, e.g., Bacon, *Post-nati*, 667: ". . . that his [the king's] blood shall never be corrupted . . ."

[65] Above, Ch.v,nos.183-185. For the return to the Carolingian race, see Karl Ferdinand Werner, "Die Legitimät der Kapetinger und die Entstehung des 'Reditus regni Francorum ad stirpem Karoli'," *Die Welt als Geschichte*, XII (1952), 203-225, who shows that the slogan, though introduced already by Stephen of Marchiennes (ca.1196), became effective only through Vincent of Beauvais (after 1244); cf. Kern, *Ausdehnungspolitik*, 23. The French claims were adopted by the Anjous of Naples. See, e.g., Charles II of Anjou, in the announcement of his coronation: "Inter regales autem prosapias, Christianitatis caractere insignitas, ab ipsis fidei Christiane primordiis idem altissimi filius stirpem regiam inclite domus Francie altis provexit radicibus et provectam gubernare non desinit in gloria et honore" (Paris, Bibl.Nat., MS lat.8567, fol.20v). These and similar arguments are found over and over again. See, e.g., Terre Rouge, *De iure futuri successoris*, Tract.I, art.1, concl.15, p.31: "Nam legimus domum regiam Franciae sanctissimam Deum de oleo suo . . . prae aliis regibus . . . decorasse."

[66] See Chrimes, *Ideas*, 22ff, who shows, however, that the problem still was fluid in late mediaeval England; also Figgis, *Divine Right*, 81ff; for the popular opinions and their legal background, see the sketch by Keeton, *Shakespeare and his Legal Problems*, 109ff ("The Title to the Crown in the Histories").

What matters here is the principle of continuity. In the earlier Middle Ages, apparently following the lead of the Church, the continuity of a realm during an interregnum had been sometimes preserved by a fiction: Christ stepped into the gap as *interrex* and secured, through his own eternity, the continuity of kingship. The ancient formula of dating documents *regnante Christo*, descending from the times of the persecutions,[67] often serving as a mere formula of devotion,[68] then applied by Pope Hadrian I to indicate his refusal of further recognition to the iconoclast Byzantine emperor,[69] was occasionally used in times of an interregnum for the dating of documents when a king's regnal years were not available. The sometimes very specific formulae speak for themselves:

> Burgundy lacking a king, while our Lord Jesus Christ rules here and everywhere. . . .

[67] Arnold Ehrhardt, "Das *corpus Christi* und die Korporationen im spätrömischen Recht," *ZfRG*, rom.Abt., LXXI (1954), 34,n.27 (see also his *The Apostolic Succession* [London, 1953], 41f), stresses the politically revolutionary character of the datings in the Acts of Martyrs and gives as an example *Martyrium Irenaei Syrmiensis*: "sub Diocletiano imperatore, agente Probo praeside, regnante Domino nostro Jesu Christo." The antithesis "Diocletiano imperatore—regnante Domino" is obvious; it is even stronger through the additional *vero* in the *Acta Cypriani*: "sub Valeriano et Gallieno imperatoribus, regnante vero Domino . . ."; or by an additional κατὰ δὲ ἡμᾶς βασιλεύοντος τοῦ κυρίου ἡμῶν (*Pionius*,c.23), or ἐν οὐρανοῖς δὲ βασιλεύοντος κτλ. (*Dasius*,c.12), or βασιλεύοντος εἰς αἰῶνας (*Agape, Irene*, and others, c.7); ed. Rudolf Knopf, *Ausgewählte Märtyrer-Akten* (2nd ed., Tübingen, 1929), 71, 86, 92, and passim. It is very plausible that the formula originated as Dr. Ehrhardt seems to suggest, in the Acts of the Martyrs and in a spirit of opposition against the imperial dating. This kind of dating was used also, relatively early, for political purposes (below, n.69); see, e.g., the inscription of 641 from Hauran, in Arab-occupied Syria, in which the meaningless imperial years of Constantinople were replaced by κυρίου Ἰησοῦ Χριστοῦ βασιλεύοντος; Philippe Le Bas and W. H. Waddington, *Voyage archéologique: Explication des inscriptions grecques et latines recueillies en Grèce et en Asie Mineure* (Paris, 1888ff), Partie 6, *Syrie*, p.552, No.2413a, quoted by Milton V. Anastos, "Political Theory in the Lives of the Slavic Saints Constantine and Methodius," *Harvard Slavic Studies*, II (1954), 31f.

[68] The formula was anything but rare; it appears very frequently in the *invocatio* of Anglo-Saxon documents; see, e.g., W. de Gray Birch, *Cartularium Saxonicum* (London, 1885-93), I,7,No.3; 45,No.25; 47,No.27; III,623,No.1303, and passim, for invocations such as "Regnante imperpetuum domino nostro . . ." and similar phrasings, sometimes replaced or supplemented by a *labarum*, which has the same meaning; see, for the scribes, Richard Drögereit, "Gab es eine angelsächsische Königskanzlei?" *ArchUF*, XIII (1935), 370,391,397.

[69] For Hadrian I, see Schramm, *Die Anerkennung Karls des Grossen als Kaiser* (Munich, 1952), 11f (also *HZ*, CLXXII, 1952); cf. A. Menzer, "Die Jahresmerkmale in den Datierungen der Papsturkunden bis zum Ausgang des 11. Jahrhunderts," *Römische Quartalschrift*, XL (1932), 62f. Schramm is correct when he calls the lengthy formula (it includes God the Father and the Holy Spirit) "liturgical." The model, however, should be sought in the datings of the Acts of Martyrs and in expedients such as the inscription from Hauran; see above, n.67.

In the first year after the death of King Rudolf, while Christ rules hoping for a king. . . .

While Christ rules expecting a king. . . .[70]

That is to say, while no king rules, Christ rules. The true government devolved upon the God, and the realm escheated to the divine Lord paramount until a new king was invested.

This seemingly strange idea to which, for the last time, the Florentine Republic resorted in 1528,[71] had its dangers. For the escheat of the realm to Christ became politically a threatening reality when the pope began to claim for himself the rights of the transcendental *interrex* and to assume as *vicarius Christi* a position of overlord over secular dominion in times of an interregnum. As usual it began with the empire. Already under Gregory VII we find, after the excommunication of Henry IV, documents which show the date: *Domno nostro papa Gregorio Romanum imperium tenente*.[72] Innocent III, then, somewhat casually claimed imperial rights in the empire during a vacancy; Innocent IV drew the hierocratic conclusion that the empire returned to its true lord on earth, the vicar of Christ, and at the same time he vaguely expanded that claim, *regnis vacantibus*, to other kingdoms as well; finally Hostiensis tied together the remaining loose ends and firmly established the theory of the pope's interregnal vicariate.[73] In the fourteenth century, the theory was

[70] The character of an interregnal formula may have been ambiguous in the case of Hadrian I; but it was unequivocal in the case of Pope John VIII who, during the vacancy of the empire after the death of Louis II and before the coronation of Charles the Bald in 875, used the formula: *regnante imperatore domno Iesu Christo*; see Bresslau, *Urkundenlehre*, I, 837; Menzer, *op.cit.*, 63. See, in general, Kern, *Gottesgnadentum*, 7,n.12, and 30,n.59. For the forms mentioned here ("Burgundia rege carente, Domino nostro J.Ch. hic et ubique regnante . . . ; Anno primo quod obiit Radulfus rex, Christo regnante, regem sperante . . . ; Christo regnante regem expectante . . ."), see U. Chevalier, *Cartulaire de Saint-André-le-Bas de Vienne* (Lyon, 1869), 268ff; Ph. Lauer, *Le règne de Louis VII d'Outre-mer* (Paris, 1900), 15,n.1. The formula *Regnante domino nostro* etc. was used also during a vacancy of the Holy See; cf. Gregory VII, *Reg.*, I,1, ed. Caspar, p.1,n.2; see also above, n.2.

[71] Cecil Roth, *The Last Florentine Republic* (London, 1925), 76f,82f, sums up the material, though without clearly distinguishing the various formulae.

[72] *Cartulaire de l'abbaye de Saint Bernard de Romans* (Romans, 1898), I,203ff, Nos.168,188; cf. *Laudes regiae*, 140,n.93. The idea is found, though with reference to the end of the Roman Empire on the Last Day, in Tolomeo of Lucca's *Determinatio*, c.25, ed. Krammer, 49: "Deinde redit [imperium] ad verum dominum, qui contulerat, scilicet Christum, cuius vices summus pontifex gerit."

[73] For the whole problem, see F. Baethgen, "Der Anspruch des Papsttums auf das Reichsvikariat," *ZfRG*, kan.Abt., X (1920), 172-268; and, for Innocent IV and Hostiensis, especially 178ff, 182f; also Carlyle, *Political Theory*, V,322,n.1; Ullmann, *Lucas*

applied for political expediency even to dominions which the Holy See only *regarded* as vacant, but which in fact had their ordinary rulers. Hence, the vicariate of the empire of Edward III, which Louis of Bavaria had conferred upon the English king, was objected to by Pope Benedict XII because it encroached upon the rights of the papacy.[74]

These and similar papal claims naturally lost their very foundation in kingdoms in which, as a result of the continuity of dynastic succession, interregna ceased to exist altogether. The king's reign began with the demise of the predecessor or, as in England after 1308, on the day after the predecessor's death.[75] Henceforth the hereditary succession suffered theoretically no interruption so that, for reasons of dynastic continuity, it might be claimed that the king body natural "never died": the dynasty, the "house," resembled a supra-individual entity comparable to an *universitas* "which never died." At any rate, the pious fiction of the Christ-centered age concerning the divine *interrex* who safeguarded the continuity of government in times of an interregnum, had become superannuated owing to the continuity by dynastic succession. This, at least, was true with regard to the natural body of the head of the body politic. The continuity, however, of the complete body politic—head and members together—was preserved by another fiction, that of the sempiternity of the Crown.

2. The Crown as Fiction

CORONA VISIBILIS ET INVISIBILIS

In ancient times, writes Baldus, when the Roman Empire was in its prime, one used to say that the emperor, whose "material and visible" crown consisted of a diadem, had his "invisible" Crown imposed by God.[76] What was valid for the elective dignity

---

de Penna, 172,n.9, for some objections against that theory on the part of Lucas de Penna. Also Ullmann, *Medieval Papalism*, 188,n.5, for Cynus' repudiation of the papal vicariate of the empire.

[74] Baethgen, "Reichsvikariat," 262,n.2, for Edward III. The papacy, throughout the reign of Louis of Bavaria, considered the empire vacant and consequently assumed vicarial power.

[75] Schramm, *English Coronation*, 166f; *König von Frankreich*, I,226f.

[76] Baldus, *Consilia*, III,159,n.2,fol.45ᵛ: "Et tale Regnum [sc. the elective Regnum Romanorum] a Deo hominibus mittitur (*C.*,1,17,1; *Nov.*,6, in pr.; *Nov.*,73, in pr.1; *Nov.*,113,1; *Nov.*,105). Et dicebatur antiquitus, dum Romanum Imperium erat in flore, quod corona Imperialis invisibilis imponebatur a Deo, materialis vero et visi-

of the Roman emperor, was valid also for the hereditary dignity of a king. Baldus likewise distinguished two crowns in the monarchies in which—according to the Law of the Realm, and not according to Roman Law—the son succeeded the father by birthright.

> [With regard to the succession of the] son I do not consider an interval of time; for the *Crown* descends on him in continuity, albeit that the *exterior crown* demands an imposition of the hand and the solemnity of offices.[77]

What Baldus wishes to express is clear enough. There was a visible, material, exterior gold circle or diadem with which the Prince was vested and adorned at his coronation; and there was an invisible and immaterial Crown—encompassing all the royal rights and privileges indispensable for the government of the body politic—which was perpetual and descended either from God directly or by the dynastic right of inheritance. And of this invisible Crown it may well be said: *Corona non moritur.*

To corroborate the sempiternity of the invisible Crown and the continuity without incision of dynastic succession Baldus applied, in agreement with the customary practice of jurists, an argument of Private Law to the sphere of Public Law. He quoted from the

---

bilis erat ipsa Imperialis infula (*C.*,7,37,3,5)." The passage is quoted verbatim by Matthaeus de Afflictis, on *Lib.aug.*, 1,7,n.32,fol.52ᵛ, to corroborate the maxim "quod rex in regno dicitur lex animata." It would be difficult to tell whether Baldus had some specific ancient author in mind (*dicebatur*), because his juristic allegations do not really bear out the theory of the two crowns. Nicholas of Bari, in his praise of Frederick II, refers to Exodus 25: 25, when he says: "In tabernaculo federis erant due corone auree, una quarum dicebatur aurea, altera aureola, sed aureola superposita auree preminebat, sic dignitas istius [imperatoris] omni preminet dignitati." The difference between the visible, material crown of the emperor and the "invisible" diadem placed on his head by the hand of God was, of course, very much alive in Byzantine art; see, e.g., André Grabar, "Un médaillon en or provenant de Mersine en Cilicie," *Dumbarton Oaks Papers*, VI (1951),34ff, who discusses a medallion (sixth century, but of a design carrying us back to the post-Constantinian era) showing in addition to the diadem which the emperor actually wears, the "invisible" Crown which the *dextera Dei* extends from heaven, not to mention the insignia of the *torques* which the personified Sun bestows upon him. We may recall that the radiate crown, though displayed time and again on imperial coins, was not an insignia actually worn by the emperor.

77 Baldus, on c.36 X 1,6,n.3, *In Decretales*, fol.79: "Quod rege mortuo filius eius non debet de honestate coronari nisi post triduum . . . ; ego in filio non facio temporis distinctionem, quia corona continuitive descendit in ipsum . . . licet corona exterior requirat manus impositionem et officiorum celebritatem." The doctrine "Filius succedit patri in regno iure regni, non iure Romano" is standard; see, e.g., Baldus on c.24 X 1,6,n.2, fol.78.

law of inheritance in Justinian's *Institutes*: "And immediately on the death of the father, ownership, so to say, is continued"—a passage on which the Accursian Gloss commented: "Father and son are one according to the fiction of Law."[78] The "oneness" of father and son, and therewith the very complex idea of identity of predecessor and successor, thus had roots also in the law of inheritance: the dying king and the new king became one with regard to the invisible and perpetual Crown which represented the substance of the inheritance. This, to be sure, was a concept drawing very close to identifying the dynasty technically with a "corporation by succession" in which successor and predecessor appeared as the same person with regard to the personified office or dignity.[79] On the other hand, however, it was an old conceptual property of juristic thought to personify the inheritance; that is, to treat the estate, as it passed from the testator to the heir, as a person.[80] Hence, there were juristically several possibilities to personify the immaterial and invisible Crown, especially if its perpetuity was linked to that of a hereditary monarchy, to the dynastical continuity without break or incision and, as it were, without change of person—despite a change of the mortal ruling individuals.

For all these refinements of late-mediaeval jurisprudence, the concept of the immaterial Crown originated in strata not at all, or only vaguely, related to legal thought. It may not always be quite easy for us to decide whether an author referred to the visible crown or to the invisible Crown. In his long poem glorifying Reims and St. Rémi, its first bishop, a French poet of the thirteenth century, Richier, naturally came to discuss one of the *cimelia* of the cathedral treasure—the vial containing the holy balm by the infusion of which the kings of France prevailed over all other anointed who had to purchase their coronation ointments "in the

---

[78] *Inst.*,3,1,3: "Et statim morte parentis quasi continuatur dominium." See *Glos.ord.*, v. *quasi*: "Hoc ideo, quia in corporalibus dicitur proprie continuatio, sed dominium est incorporale. . . . Dic ergo improprie fieri continuationem: quia inter diversa, non inter eadem fieri debet: *sed pater et filius unum fictione iuris sunt.*" The other relevant place is *D*.28,2,11. See, for this theory, above, n.61, and below, nos.258ff,265ff.

[79] See above, Ch.vi, n.97.

[80] *D*.46,1,22 (the famous *lex mortuo*): ". . . quia hereditas personae vice fungitur, sicuti municipium et decuria et societas." Cf. Gierke, *Gen.R.*, iii,362, and passim; above, Ch.vi, n.74.

drugstore."[81] That celestial balm, declared Richier, had been sent from high heaven *por la corone deffendre*; God himself had sanctified "king, crown, and realm"; finally, the French were bound to love the crown more than the most precious relic, because those killed in defense of the Crown would be saved in the life thereafter.[82]

We obviously cannot be quite certain whether the poet was talking about the material crown of the French kings, which actually contained a thorn from the Crown of Thorns and therefore indeed was also a holy relic,[83] or had in mind the immaterial Crown of France, the political Crown in the abstract. It seems, however, that in this case material and immaterial crowns were merged into one another; and the borderline between the visible object of worship and the invisible idea was as hazy here as it was, for example, with regard to the Crown of Hungary which was at once the visible holy relic of St. Stephen, Hungary's first Christian king, and the invisible symbol and lord paramount of the Hungarian monarchy.[84] Since the French poet mentioned

[81] Richier, *La vie de Saint Remi*, vv.8140ff, ed. W. N. Bolderston, London, 1912, 335:

> Et molt li doit bien sovenir
> Qu'en toutes autres regions
> Covient les rois · lor ontions
> Acheter en la mercerie. . . .

Cf. Bloch, *Rois thaumaturges*, 229; Schramm, *Frankreich*, 150, 239.

[82] See Richier, 117ff:

> Saint Remi · cui Dieus envoia
> l'oile · dont il saintefia
> le roi · la corone · le regne . . .

> 73ff: C'est por la corone deffendre
> Dont Dieus fist l'oncïon descendre
> Dou ciel . . .

> 45ff: Et ce doit donner remenbrance
> As François d'anmer la coronne . . .
> Et qui por si juste occoison
> Morroit comme por li garder,
> Au droit Dieu dire et esgarder
> Croi je qu'il devroit estre saus,
> S'il n'estoit en creance faus. . . .

Cf. Bolderston, 43,40f; Bloch, *Rois thaumaturges*, 244.

[83] Schramm, *Frankreich*, 209.

[84] For Hungary, see Hartung, "Die Krone," 35ff; see also Josef Karpat, "Die Lehre von der hlg. Krone Ungarns im Lichte des Schrifttums," *Jahrbuch für Geschichte Osteuropas*, VI (1941), 1-54; also Joseph Holub, "Quod omnes tangit. . . ," *Revue historique de droit français et étranger*, XXIX (1951), 97-102; and, for the archeological material, P. J. Kelleher, *The Holy Crown of Hungary* (Papers and

the "Crown" together with anointment, we might be inclined to identify it with the golden crown placed on the head of the anointed king; however, the "defense of the Crown" and the celestial reward for the "martyrs of the Crown" would put the insignia in the place of the French *patria*. But did it really make a very great difference whether a man exposed himself and suffered death for the tangible relic of the *corpus mysticum* of faith, or for the intangible symbol of the *corpus mysticum* of the realm, since both were one? The indefiniteness itself of the symbol may have been its greatest value, and haziness the true strength of the symbolic abstraction.[85]

It was by coincidence only that the Chapter of the cathedral of Reims, the coronation cathedral of the French kings, received in 1197 a letter from King Philip II asking the canons, who owed him no service, to lend him military support *tam pro capite nostro, tam pro corona regni defendenda*, "for the defense of our head as well as of the Crown of the realm."[86] The antithesis of *caput nostrum* and *corona regni* hardly warrants speculation as to whether reference was being made to the immaterial Crown or to the material crown on the king's head: in either case it would have been the Crown as a symbol of the whole realm. It is easier to make an unambiguous decision when we turn to the answer of the canons of Reims on a later occasion. For then they admitted that they owed military service to the king "for the defense of Crown and realm."[87] The canons, in that case, simply availed themselves of a standard phrase which can be traced back at least to Suger of St.-Denis who, in 1150, assured King Louis VII of the loyalty which the magnates owed "to realm and Crown."[88] Here, as well as in a great number of charters where

---

Monographs of the American Academy in Rome, XIII; Rome, 1951). The Hungarian material deserves more consideration than given here; see below, n.144. A collection of papers by various authors on the Crown, chiefly in Eastern Europe, is about to be published: *Corona Regni—Die Krone als Symbol*, ed. Manfred Hellmann (Darmstadt, Wissenschaftliche Buchgesellschaft).

[85] See William H. Dunham, Jr., "The Crown Imperial," *Parliamentary Affairs*, VI (1953), 201f: ". . . the vagueness of its meaning enabled the term [Crown] to perform a fruitful function." I am much obliged to Professor Dunham, at Yale University, for valuable information.

[86] Strayer, "Defense of the Realm," 292,n.4, quoting H. F. Delaborde, *Recueil des actes de Philippe Auguste* (Paris, 1916-1943), II, 47.

[87] Strayer, *op.cit.*, 292, n.5.

[88] Hartung, "Die Krone," 20,n.3; Bouquet, *Recueil des historiens*, XV,522.

"Crown" was used in a fiscal sense,[89] there cannot be the slightest doubt but that "Crown" indicated something more general than the gold rim adorning the king's head.

The difficulties of definition should not be exaggerated. Suger as well as the canons of Reims obviously used the term "Crown" as something not quite identical with "realm," if closely related to it. On the other hand, "Crown" was not quite identical with "king" either: Philip II clearly distinguished between his physical head and the "Crown of the realm" adorning that head. In other words, "Crown" was distinct from both *rex* and *regnum*. It was something different from king and realm although not separated from either; and it was something that king and realm had in common although it was not quite identical with either. The argument of rhetorical redundancy should not be made: in both cases ("head and Crown" and "realm and Crown") something was to be expressed that apparently would not have been covered by either king alone or kingdom alone. The solution, however, may lie close by. In the phrase "head and Crown" the word Crown served to add something to the purely physical body of the king and to emphasize that more than the king's "body natural" was meant; and in the phrase "realm and Crown" the word Crown served to eliminate the purely geographic-territorial aspect of *regnum*[90] and to emphasize unambiguously the political character of *regnum* which included also the emotional value of *patria*— "the Crown of the kingdom is the common *patria*" was the opinion of jurists quoted by Jacques de Révigny, whose contemporary, William Durand, justified the king's extraordinary measures "for the defense of *patria* and Crown."[91] Briefly, as opposed to the pure *physis* of the king and to the pure *physis* of the territory, the word "Crown," when added, indicated the political *metaphysis* in which both *rex* and *regnum* shared, or the body politic (to which both

[89] Hartung, 20,n.4.

[90] Cf. H. G. Richardson, "The English Coronation Oath," *Speculum*, XXIV (1949), 50: "The fact that *regnum*, like our word 'kingdom' can mean not only the sovereignty of a king but also a country under the rule of a king, makes it a word to be avoided. There is not the same ambiguity about *corona*." While agreeing with Mr. Richardson concerning his distinction between the "country" and its "sovereignty," I would not say that the words *regnum* and *corona* are "virtually synonymous," although some of the content of *regnum* indeed is covered by *corona*; but *corona* has also meanings which do not coincide with *regnum*.

[91] See above, Ch. v, nos.168 and 180.

belonged) in its sovereign rights. It may be helpful also to recall the perhaps decisive factor: the value of perpetuity inherent in the Crown. For the Crown, by its perpetuity, was superior to the physical *rex* as it was superior to the geographical *regnum* while, at the same time, it was on a par with the continuity of the dynasty and the sempiternity of the body politic.

THE FISCAL CROWN

If really it was in the times of Abbot Suger, around 1150 or a little earlier, that the idea of the "invisible" Crown was introduced into the political terminology of France, the French and English developments had a fairly even start. Our evidence in England sends us back to the time of Henry I. From the onset, however, it should be mentioned that "Crown" in England had hardly that "patriotic" touch—not, at least, in official documents— which was so characteristic of all that Suger of St.-Denis did or said. "Crown," in England, belonged in the first place to the sphere of administration and law. In Henry I's Charter for the City of London, of 1130 or 1133, the word occurs in the phrase *placita coronae*, "pleas of the Crown."[92] It appears there as something quite common and was not restricted, as the Pipe Roll shows, to the London Charter alone although for some time the expression *placita regis*, "pleas of the king," may be found as an alternative.[93] Henry's Pipe Roll mentions even a custodian of the pleas of the Crown;[94] and although we customarily let the office of the "Coroner" (*custos placitorum coronae, coronator*) take its official start in 1194 with the so-called *Iter* (more explicitly the *Forma procedendi in placitis Coronae Regis*),[95] there is no doubt but that the office itself goes back to an earlier date.[96]

[92] By far the most interesting and the fullest study on the notion of Crown is Hartung, "Die Krone," where the problem is treated on the basis of comparative constitutional history; see pp.6-19 for a rich, though purposely not exhaustive, collection of English material. See, for the later period, Dunham, "Crown Imperial" (above, n.85). The problem, of course, has been recognized before; see Pollock and Maitland, *History*, I,511ff; McIlwain, *Political Thought*, 379ff. For the charter of Henry I, see Stubbs, *Select Charters*, 129; Liebermann, *Gesetze*, I,525, also II,560, s.v. "Kronprozess," I,b, *kinehelme*.

[93] *Leges Henrici* (whatever their date may be), 7,3;52;60,3; Liebermann, I,553, 573,581.

[94] Charles Gross, *Select Cases from the Coroners' Rolls* (Selden Society, IX. London, 1896), xvff, esp. xvii.

[95] Stubbs, *Select Charters*, 252ff.

[96] Gross, *Coroners' Rolls*. xvff; Pollock and Maitland, *History*, I,534,n.2.

Simultaneously we find "Crown" used in a more fiscal sense and referring to the royal demesne. In 1155, the year after his accession, Henry II revoked towns, castles, and manors *quae ad coronam pertinebant*,[97] and at Northampton, in 1176, he advised his itinerant justices to look after all the rights and things "pertaining to the Lord King and his Crown" (*spectantes ad dominum regem et coronam eius*).[98] It would not be justified to take that phrase simply as a pleonasm. To be sure, to Henry II himself it may have made little, if any, practical difference whether things belonged to him by right of the king or by right of the Crown. Sometimes the first, sometimes the latter may have been more advantageous to him. However, by building up a royal demesne as an administrative entity which was set apart from lands falling in with the feudal dependencies, Henry II certainly laid the foundation to the *fiscus* which, clearly by the thirteenth century, "has been separated, as something for the common utility, from the person of the king."[99] Moreover, by categorizing the royal demesne as an entity pertaining to the Crown, Henry II, no matter whether intentionally or not, prompted the officials to distinguish on their part more carefully than before between rights of the Crown and rights of the king.[100] In the *Dialogue of the Exchequer*, a semi-official treatise written in 1177, we find the distinction between tenants-in-chief who hold "what pertains to the Crown" and those "who hold from the king a knight's fee not by right of the royal Crown but by that of some barony."[101] The distinction between what pertains *ad coronam* and what may be held *de rege* was not new all by itself. Substantially the difference between *terra regni* and *terra regis* goes back to Anglo-Saxon times when occasionally the king could even charter, or "book," land to himself, though being probably quite unaware of the highly complicated constitutional and legal premises which a

---

[97] Stubbs, *Const.Hist.*, I,488,n.1; Hartung, "Die Krone," 6,n.2.

[98] Stubbs, *Select Charters*, 180, §7.

[99] Post, "Public Law," 49f, and "Two Laws," 423. For the fisc in general, see above, Chapter IV. The word itself is found in the twelfth century; see Stubbs, *Select Charters*, 152,232, passim; *Dialogus de Scaccario*, II,c.10, ed. Charles Johnson (London and New York, 1950), 97.

[100] Hoyt, *Demesne*, 124, stresses the simultaneous growth of "royal demesne" and "impersonal crown," a distinction which one would look for in vain in and after the age of the Conquest; *ibid.*, 50f.

[101] *Dialogus de Scaccario*, II,c.10, ed. Johnson, 96, cf.14; Stubbs, *Select Charters*, 231f; Hartung, "Die Krone," 7.

transaction of that kind implied.[102] Nevertheless, *terra regni* has now become something pertaining *ad coronam*, and therewith the notion Crown has been set over against the king.

Towards the end of the twelfth century distinctions between Crown and king began to be rationalized under the influence of legal thought. Pleas in which the king was plaintiff, had been listed in the earlier sets of law.[103] Glanvill, however, opened his tractate *On the Laws and Customs of the Realm of England* with the words: *Ad coronam domini regis pertinent ista*, and then—though rather deficient in his section on Criminal Law which Bracton later treated extensively[104]—referred to the *leges*, the laws of Justinian, in order to discuss the crime of *laesa maiestas*.[105] He referred also to purprestures, fines for encroachment on royal lands, as something pertaining *ad coronam* because things public—utilities such as public roads, public waters, or public squares—were involved, just as pledges pertained *ad coronam* if public peace was affected.[106] "Crown" in Glanvill's treatise was not simply synonymous with king: Crown referred to the public sphere and to common utility. How carefully words were chosen, notwithstanding innumerable inconsistencies then and later, may be gathered from the writs to the courts spiritual which Glanvill quotes: invariably they are treated as pleas pertaining, not to the Crown alone, but to the Crown *and* the royal Dignity, *ad coronam et dignitatem meam pertinent.*[107] This is not a haphazard formulation; for although the formula will be used more and more frequently and generally in the thirteenth century, we find that also Bracton, whenever dealings with ecclesiastical courts were at stake, invariably referred to both the Crown and the royal Dignity. It was apparently a "must" to quote both Crown and royal Dignity in cases entangled with ecclesiastical matters, whereas it was a "may" on other occasions.[108] Nothing, however, would be more wrong than

---

[102] Maitland, *Domesday Book and Beyond* (Cambridge, 1897), 254,n.1; F. M. Stenton, *Anglo-Saxon England* (Oxford, 1943), 304.

[103] Liebermann, *Gesetze*, 556 (*Leges Henrici*, §§10-11).

[104] Bracton, fols.115b-155b, ed. Woodbine, II,327ff.

[105] Glanvill, *De legibus et consuetudinibus regni Angliae*, I,1-2, ed. Woodbine (New Haven, 1932), 42.

[106] Glanvill, IX, 11, and x,5, Woodbine, 132,136.

[107] Glanvill, IV,13 (advowson), X,1 (debts of laymen), XIII,21 (lay fees), Woodbine 82f,133,156.

[108] Above, Ch.IV,n.300. It is true, of course, that *corona et dignitas*, sometimes

to claim rhetorical tautology on the part of the chancery which issued the writs. For while there could be no doubt that all pleas concerning the competency of either courts Christian or courts secular were *a priori* pleas of the Crown, since they affected the public sphere, the chancery apparently held that those cases affected also the king's office or dignity as king, his sovereignty or "royalty." It was perhaps as though the papal chancery distinguished between *sancta sedes* and *papatus*.

In other respects the orbits of Crown and king were certainly not always marked out as clearly and consistently as we might desire, and in documents of a "mixed character"—as, for example, the *Iter*—we find feudal rights interspersed with regalian rights, whereas on other occasions things pertaining "casually" to the king are treated alongside those pertaining "permanently" to the Crown.[109] Bracton, whose mind was already far more polity-centered and who was quite familiar with corporate concepts,[110] has clarified admirably the difficult problem of what served the king and what belonged for the sake of public utility and the whole polity inalienably to the Crown.[111] The revocation of alienated property and rights of the Crown had been started, we recall, by Henry II immediately after his accession. Henry, after the confused and damaging reign of King Stephen, would have been the last to be ignorant of what "alienation" meant. Yet, the legal terminology was limping behind the administrative practice, and notions such as "prescription" or "inalienability," still in a formative stage during his reign, were not yet applied as readily as in a later period.

That the principle of non-alienation was clearly formulated in England, and was claimed as a fundamental law of government, belonged to the time around 1200. Shortly after the turn of the century, an anonymous Londoner composed a legal treatise, known as the *Leges Anglorum*, parts of which were inserted or interpolated in the third version of the so-called Laws of Edward the Confessor.[112] The work reflects some knowledge of Law, but it

---

corona, dignitas, et regnum, occur quite frequently also in other connections; but writs concerning the courts spiritual seem to add the word *dignitas* throughout.

[109] Hoyt, *Demesne,* 188, concerning casual and permanent demesnial rights.

[110] Bracton, fol.374b, Woodbine, IV,175; see above, n.7.

[111] Above, Ch.IV, nos.252,298.

[112] Liebermann, *Gesetze,* I,635; for the whole problem of the treatise and the

reflects above all the glamorous ideals of the Arthurian legend in connection with which Geoffrey of Monmouth so often conjured the idea of the "monarchy of the whole Island" which was obtained by right hereditary and was held together with all its appurtenances beyond the seas by the diadem of Constantine.[113] That anonymous author made it his fancy to talk incessantly about the "Crown of Britain." He claimed that "by right of the excellency of the Crown, [Britain] ought to be called Empire rather than kingdom," and that the Crown had vast and inalienable rights: "The universal and total land and the isles pertain to the Crown," including even Norway, because on the basis of the Arthurian legend "Norway had been confirmed for ever to the Crown of Britain."[114] Here the Crown begins to coincide with the ideas of kingdom and nation, presaging also those of emperor-like sovereignty and imperial aims, with the *rex-imperator* theory.[115] The true importance of this author, however, has to be sought in the passage in which he imputes that Edward the Confessor had sworn an oath to restore all the rights, dignities, and lands which his predecessors "have alienated from the Crown of the realm," and to recognize it as his duty "to observe and defend all the dignities, rights, and liberties of the Crown of this realm in their wholeness."[116]

---

interpolations, see his *Über die Leges Anglorum* (Halle, 1894) and *Über die Leges Edwardi Confessoris* (Halle, 1896). See, further, H. G. Richardson, "The English Coronation Oath," *Speculum*, XXIV (1949), 44-75, esp. 61ff, also his "Studies in Bracton," *Traditio*, VI (1948), 75ff; Schramm, *English Coronation*, 196ff.

[113] Geoffrey, *Historia*, is full of that terminology; see, e.g., IX,1 ("iure hereditario" and "totius insulae monarchia"); IX,7 (conquest of Norway; diadem [also v,17]); XI,4-5 (empire overseas), ed. Hammer, 152,159,103,190, passim. See Liebermann, *Gesetze*, I,659, also *Über die Leges Anglorum*, 5, and, for Arthur, 22, §15: Aethelstan ruling over an England "usque ad metas Arthuri quas corone regni Britannie constituit et imposuit." The extent to which Edward I was under the spell of the Arthurian legend has been pointed out by Roger S. Loomis, "Edward I, Arthurian Enthusiast," *Speculum*, XXVIII (1953), 114-127.

[114] Liebermann, *Gesetze*, I,635: "Universa vero terra et tota, et insule omnes usque Norwegiam et usque Daciam pertinent ad coronam regni eius et sunt de appendiciis et dignitate regis." Cf. 660: To Arthur "confirmata fuit [a papa et a curia Romana] Norwegia imperpetuum corone Britannie." Cf. Liebermann, *Leges Anglorum*, 6: "De iure potius appellari debet excellentia corone [Britannie] imperium quam regnum."

[115] For the influence of the Arthurian Legend on practical politics, e.g., the English claims to Scotland, see Loomis, *op.cit.*, 122, the letter to Boniface VIII of 1301; in general also Laura Keeler, *Geoffrey of Monmouth and the Late Latin Chroniclers* (Univ. of California Publications in History, XVII,1 [Berkeley and Los Angeles, 1946]).

[116] For the oath, see Liebermann, *Gesetze*, I,635 (11,1A,2); also I,640 (13,1A),

INALIENABILITY

Therewith the idea of an impersonal Crown, representing the fundamental rights and claims of the country, began to affect and shape constitutional matters whose importance eclipsed that of myth, law, or fisc. An oath—and that would be a coronation oath—containing, as suggested by the author of the *Leges Anglorum*, some special clause in which the king promised not to alienate rights and possessions of the Crown and to recover what had been lost, was unknown in the English coronation rite around 1200. But whether such an oath was something altogether unknown in that period, is a very different matter. In fact, there is reason to believe that the customary tripartite oath which, with slight variations, had survived from Anglo-Saxon times and which Bracton still quoted as valid, may indeed have been augmented by a fourth clause concerning non-alienation and that this fourth clause was added in 1216 at the coronation of Henry III, even though such an additional clause has not been codified.[117] Pope Gregory IX, at any rate, referred twice to an oath which, he said, Henry III had taken, *ut moris est,* at his coronation and in which the king had sworn to maintain the rights of his realm and to revoke what had been alienated.[118] That such an additional oath existed be-

where it is said that the Confessor himself "servavit sacramentum in quantum potuit; noluit sacramenti sui fieri transgressor." For the influence of the legend of Edward the Confessor on Edward II, see Richardson, in: *Bulletin of the Institute of Historical Research*, xvi (1938), 7 and 10; and in: *Transactions of the Royal Historical Society*, 4th Ser., xxiii (1941), 149f; his findings defeat the thesis of Schramm, *English Coronation*, 206 (also *ArchUF*, xv[1938], 350), according to which the *rex Edwardus* in the Oath of Edward II referred to Edward I.

[117] McIlwain, *Political Thought*, 379: "It is a curious fact calling for further investigation, that in no surviving contemporary form . . . is there to be found any provision touching the inalienability of regalian rights." Numerous efforts have since been made to solve the question of the "fourth clause." Richardson, "Coronation Oath," *Speculum*, xxiv (above, n.112), has come closest to a solution (for reasons of simplicity I shall refer exclusively to his study in the following pages). See further B. Wilkinson, "The Coronation Oath of Edward II and the Statute of York," *Speculum*, xix (1944), 445-469, who is inclined (448ff) to disregard altogether the numerous references to an additional oath; Schramm, *English Coronation*, 203, does not believe that a change was made (that is, a clause added) in 1274, at the coronation of Edward I, and does not take any earlier addition into consideration. The useful study of Peter N. Riesenberg, *Inalienability of Sovereignty in Medieval Political Thought* (Columbia Studies in the Social Sciences 591; New York, 1956), was published too late to be used here.

[118] For the letters of Gregory IX, see W. Shirley, *Royal and other Historical Letters of the Reign of Henry III* (London, 1862, Rolls Series), I,551; Rymer, *Foedera*, I:1, 229, and for the correct date (July 1), Potthast, 9952; Richardson, "Coronation Oath," 51,nos.43,44; also below, nos.144,145.

comes certainty under Edward I; the king himself mentioned at least eight times that by the oath taken at his coronation he was "astricted" to conserve the rights of the Crown—but again that additional clause did not go on record.[119]

Whereas English sources yield no more than indirect evidence of an additional promise concerning inalienability, Canon Law practice offers us a clue or, at least, some better understanding of what papal and royal letters referred to. Without going into full detail, it will be sufficient to summarize here a technical and circumstantial discussion printed elsewhere.[120]

Under the influence of Feudal Law, which began to spread in the States of the Church during the eleventh century,[121] and under the impact of the well-known imperializing tendencies which transformed the Church administration into a centralized papal monarchy, the ancient oath of office taken by bishops as prescribed by the *Liber Diurnus* was replaced by a new form.[122] It has been observed that after the Church Reform of the eleventh century the old *professio fidei* changed into a *iuramentum fidelitatis*, and that this change affected also the secular sphere: the king's coronation *promissio* was gradually transformed into a coronation *iuramentum*.[123] Whereas the old formularies of the *Liber Diurnus* demanded from the bishop assurances mainly in matters of faith and of devotion to the papal head of the Church, the new oath

---

[119] Richardson, 49f, nos.31-39.

[120] Kantorowicz, "Inalienability," *Speculum*, XXIX (1954), 488-502.

[121] Karl Jordan, "Das Eindringen des Lehenswesens in das Rechtsleben der römischen Kurie," *ArchUF*, XII (1931), 13-110, esp. 44ff.

[122] The history of the episcopal oaths has been efficiently studied by Th. Gottlob, *Der kirchliche Amtseid der Bischöfe* (Kanonistische Studien und Texte, IX, Bonn, 1936), a book which may be consulted throughout even when not mentioned in the footnotes. For the early oaths, see forms 73,74,75,76 of the *Liber Diurnus*, ed. Th. vonSickel (Vienna, 1889), 69ff; *PL*, CV,67ff; Gottlob, Append., 170ff, reprints the forms; cf. 11ff, for an analysis.

[123] This connection has been brought to light by Marcel David, *Le serment du sacre du IXe au XVe siècle* (Strasbourg, 1951); first published in *Revue du moyen-âge latin*, VI (1950) (after which the study is quoted here); see esp. 168ff, for the general changes and the fact that until the twelfth century, only coronation *promissiones*, and not *iuramenta*, were known. In most countries the change took place during the twelfth century. In England, however, a swearing at least to the coronation charters was practiced ever since the accession of Henry I, and a swearing to the coronation *promissio*, since 1189. For the change of the Roman coronation oaths, see Eduard Eichmann, "Die römischen Eide der deutschen Könige," *ZfRG*, kan.Abt., VI (1918), 154-196, whose study strikingly illustrates the parallel developments of imperial and episcopal forms of oaths.

was rather an administrative oath of office and fealty in which the word "faith" no longer had a place.[124]

The oldest known form of the new oath goes back to 1073. It is the oath which, at his consecration, Archbishop Wibert of Ravenna swore to Pope Alexander II, since the three North-Italian archbishops (Ravenna, Milan, Aquileia) were consecrated by the pope himself.[125] The oath contained seven clauses of which the last three referred exclusively to certain episcopal duties: reception of papal legates, appearance at synods, and annual visits to the *limina Apostolorum*.[126] The first four, however, were moulded after the feudal oath of fealty, expounded as early as 1020 by Fulbert of Chartres in a letter which later was included in both the *Decretum* of Gratian and the *Libri feudorum*; the earliest extant form of the feudal oath seems to be that of Robert Guiscard swearing fealty to Pope Nicholas II, in 1059.[127] The bishop, according to the new oath, swore fealty to St. Peter, the Church, and the pope, including the successor popes; he foreswore acts of treason, promised secrecy in counsel, and swore to defend the *papatus Romanus* and the *regalia sancti Petri*. Although the new episcopal oath implied neither vassalage nor tenure—with regard to the *spiritualia* this would have been simony[128]—the general influence of feudal thought is quite evident. In one respect, however, the oaths imposed by the Holy See showed a remarkable deviation from feudal norms: the defense of the personal lord, the pope, has been supplemented by a defense of the impersonal *papatus Romanus*, a coinage hardly older than that of *regalia Petri*.[129]

The oath of Wibert of Ravenna became the "standard form" which, with appropriate changes, was to serve many other pur-

124 Cf. Kantorowicz, "Inalienability," 491,n.22.

125 Gottlob, 20ff,44f.

126 For the form of Wibert's oath, see Deusdedit, *Collectio canonum*, v,423, ed. Wolf von Glanvell (Paderborn, 1905), I,599; *Liber censuum*, No.148, ed. Fabre-Duchesne, I,417; Gottlob, Append., 176f; also Gregory VII, *Reg.*,I,3, ed. Caspar, 6,n.3. See also "Inalienability," 492,n.25.

127 See Fulbert, *Epistolae*, 58, *PL*, CLXI,229CD; for Gratian, see c.18, C.XXII, q.5, ed. Friedberg, 1,887 (with n.157); *Libri feudorum*, II,6; and for Guiscard's oath, Deusdedit, *Coll. can.*, III,c.285, ed. Glanvell, 393f; *Liber censuum*, No.163, ed. Fabre-Duchesne, I,422; and, for the repetition of the oath in 1080, Gregory VII, *Reg.*, VIII,1a, ed. Caspar, 514. See also my notes in "Inalienability," 492f.

128 See "Inalienability," 493, n.29.

129 See above, Ch.IV,n.293; also "Inalienability," 492,n.26.

poses as well.[130] It was included, with a few insignificant changes, in the *Liber Extra* of Pope Gregory IX, in 1234, and therewith became the official Law of the Church.[131] It still contained no more than seven clauses. What surprises us, then, is to find, around 1200, scattered evidence for an additional clause. For example, in a decretal of Pope Celestine III (1191-98), originally a letter addressed to the Archbishop William of Ravenna, the archbishop was reminded of his "oath of fealty" by which "he was held to alienate nothing from the Holy See."[132] Similarly, Pope Innocent III, Celestine's successor, reminded the Archbishop of Milan in a letter which likewise became a decretal, that the archbishop was "held 'astricted' by his oath not to reinfeudate anew without previous consultation with the pope."[133]

The parallel with England is striking: in England, an official oath of only three clauses, and nonetheless the mention of a non-alienation clause; in Rome, an official oath of seven clauses, yet likewise the mention of some additional non-alienation clause. We are, however, more fortunate with regard to Rome than we are with regard to England, since forms containing the "eighth clause" actually are known. They begin to make their appearance by the time of Pope Gregory IX, and the earliest form so far known refers by chance to Archbishop Edmund Abingdon of Canterbury, consecrated in 1234.[134] In that eighth clause, which was simply tacked on to the seventh clause of the standard oath, the archbishop swore that he would not sell, give away, pawn,

---

[130] It was, with minor variations, the oath taken by all sorts of papal dependents: by the papal vice-chancellor and the papal notaries (M. Tangl, *Die päpstlichen Kanzleiordnungen von 1200-1500* [Innsbruck, 1894], 33ff, Nos.1 and 3), by the Roman Senator, by the community of Tibur, by papal feudatories (*Liber censuum*, Nos. 59,144,67, ed. Fabre-Duchesne, 313,415,341; see F. Baethgen, "Die Promissio Albrechts I. für Bonifaz VIII.," *Aus Politik und Geschichte: Gedächtnisschrift für Georg von Below* [Berlin, 1928], 81ff). Basically the same form is reflected by the oath of the Archimandrite Onofrius of San Salvatore to his metropolitan, the Archbishop of Messina (ca.1158-1165); see Hugo Buchthal, "A School of Miniature Painting in Norman Sicily," *Late Classical and Mediaeval Studies in Honor of Albert Mathias Friend, Jr.* (Princeton, 1955), 338. The form was used also (at least clauses 1-4) for the feudal oath of King John; see below, n.142.

[131] Cf. c.4 X 2,24, ed. Friedberg, II,360.

[132] Cf. c.8 X 3,13, ed. Friedberg, II,514 (Jaffé-Löwenfeld, 17049): ". . . cum ex sacramento fidelitatis tenearis Apostolicae Sedi nihil alienare."

[133] Cf. c.2 X 3,20, ed. Friedberg, II,525 (Potthast, 3525): ". . . iuramento tenearis astrictus non infeudare de novo, Romano pontifice inconsulto."

[134] *Liber censuum*, No.198, Fabre-Duchesne, p.449 (cf. *ibid.*, Nos.198a-c), and Gottlob, 56f.

re-infeudate, or otherwise alienate, "without having consulted the Roman pontiff," the property pertaining *ad mensam archiepiscopatus*, that is, pertaining to the "table possessions of the archbishopric," which served for the support of the archbishop and for a few other purposes.[135] To what extent the non-alienation clause was felt to be "additional" becomes strikingly clear when we turn to another form, referring to the Archbishop of Auch, Amanieu of Armagnac, who was ordained in Rome in 1263. Like the codex in which it has been transmitted, the form of the oath is somewhat archaic, reflecting usages of the twelfth century, that is, of the time of the decretal of Celestine III. Here we find the customary seven clauses of the standard oath, concluded (as prescribed in the *Liber Extra*) by the words "So help me God" (*Sic me deus adiuvet*), and then, following *after* that final corroboration and in no organic connection with the oath proper, there comes the non-alienation promise, which in this case referred not only to the mensal property of the see, but to all properties, possessions, and church valuables *que iuris sunt N. ecclesiae.* Moreover, the archbishop promised the revocation of all the rights and properties which had been alienated from his archbishopric.[136]

135 "Possessiones vero ad mensam mei archiepiscopatus pertinentes non vendam neque donabo neque inpingnorabo neque de novo infeudabo vel aliquo modo alienabo inconsulto Romano pontifice. Sic me Deus adiuvet et hec sancta evangelia." The phrase *inconsulto Romano pontifice* is the one already used by Innocent III; above, no.133. For the *mensa episcopalis*, see A. Pöschl, *Bischofsgut und mensa episcopalis* (Bonn, 1908-1911); also his "Bischöfliche Tafelgüter oder Urbare," *Zeitschrift des histor. Vereins für Steiermark*, XXVI (1931), 141-153.

136 I quote the oath (*Professio quam facit archiepiscopus domino pape*) beginning with the 7th clause:

Apostolorum limina singulis annis aut per me aut per meum nuntium visitabo, nisi eorum absolvar licentia.

             Sic me Deus adiuvet et hec sancta evangelia.

Predia, possessiones, ornamenta ecclesiastica, que iuris sunt N. ecclesie, nunquam alienabo, nec vendam, nec in pignora ponam, neque alicui sine communi consensu capituli vel potioris partis et sanioris consilii in beneficio vel feudo dabo. Que distracta sunt, vel in pignore posita, ut ad ius et proprietatem eiusdem N. revocentur ecclesie, fideliter laborabo.

The form, as yet unknown to Gottlob, was published by Michel Andrieu, *Le pontifical romain au moyen-âge* (Studi e testi, 86 [Vatican, 1940]), I,290f, also 51 (for the date and other circumstances). The MS (Vat.lat. 7114), though 13th century, reflects customs of the preceding century so that M. Andrieu could use it for reconstructing the "Roman Pontifical of the Twelfth Century." Also the Coronation Order *Ad ordinandum imperatorem secundum Occidentales* as well as the *laudes* in that Order are antiquated; see Erdmann, *Ideenwelt*, 72ff; Kantorowicz, *Laudes regiae*, 237f, and, for more details, "Inalienability," 495, n.43.

It appears that Canon Law provided for a standard episcopal oath of seven clauses, but that in some instances an eighth clause was appended, forswearing alienation and promising revocation of properties belonging to the see as such. At that point the glosses are of interest because they shed light on the procedure. Bernard of Parma, who composed the *Glossa ordinaria* on the *Liber Extra* around 1245,[137] remarked on the decretal of Celestine III: "Every bishop who is *immediately under the pope*, swears to him that he will not alienate property of the Church, nor give it anew in tenure."[138]

A century later, Baldus, glossing the standard oath of seven clauses of the Decretals, added, at the very end of his interpretation, a brief remark:

> The *Liber Extra* notes that the *exempti* have to swear also *(etiam)* that they will not alienate Church property without having consulted the pope [reference to the decretal of Innocent III].[139]

That is to say, the glossators indicate that certain bishops have to take an additional oath concerning non-alienation, although such an oath was not on record in the body of Canon Law. The group of bishops bound by that eighth clause were designated as *exempti* or *immediate sub papa*. Now, those who were *nullo medio* directly under the pope were, in the first place, the papal suffragans of the pope's own ecclesiastical province; second, the archbishops of Ravenna, Milan, and Aquileia heading the three North-Italian ecclesiastical provinces—within the *pomerium* of the papal power, as it were; third, certain exempt bishoprics such as Bamberg, Puy, the Corsican sees, and many others which, for one reason or the other, depended *nullo medio* on the Holy See. To

---

[137] Cf. A. van Hove, *Prolegomena* (2nd ed., Mechlin and Rome, 1945), 473f, but the date is conjectural.

[138] Cf. c.8 X 3,13, v. *sacramento*: "Nam quilibet episcopus qui immediate domino pape subest, iurat ei fidelitatem quod non alienabit bona ecclesie, nec in feudum dabit de novo, et idem iuramentum prestent alii episcopi suis metropolitanis." Gottlob, 65,n.108, holds that the glossator was inaccurate when talking about *bona ecclesiae* in general, and not specifically about the *possessiones mensae*; however, Gottlob was not familiar with the form cited above, n.136. For the oaths of suffragans to their metropolitans, which may be disregarded here, see Gottlob, 138-169; also p.183, for the late forms of that oath.

[139] Baldus, on c.4 X 2,24,n.14, *In Decretales*, fol.249: "Extra no. quod exempti debent iurare quod non alienabunt proprietates ecclesie Romano Pontifice inconsulto, de feu.c.2.de reb.ecc. non ali.ut super [c.2 X 3,20]." See, for Baldus' quotation, above, n.133.

these there were added, at the latest during the thirteenth century, most of the metropolitans and other recipients of the *pallium* who were likewise *nullo medio* under the pope, although not all of them had to swear to the eighth clause.[140] In other words, those who were, so to say, "tenants-in-chief" of the pope had to forswear alienation of the properties of their *episcopatus*.

The canonical procedure observed in Rome around 1200 perhaps clarifies the practice alluded to so frequently in England. To the traditional standard oath of three clauses, there was apparently added a non-alienation clause which was not legally codified. Its absence no longer needs to startle us, for the corresponding clause was absent also from the standard oath of the Decretals. Furthermore, the addition of the non-alienation clause to the English coronation procedure finds a plausible explanation: Cardinal Guala Bicchieri, who in 1216 administered as papal legate the oath to Henry III,[141] simply followed the practice known to him because observed, by that time, in Rome: *exempti*, who were *nullo medio* under the pope, swore not only the standard oath, but promised also, and additionally, not to alienate properties of their *episcopatus*. The impersonal *episcopatus*, of course, was sensibly replaced by the impersonal *corona*; but otherwise the English king and "tenant-in-chief" of the Holy See was treated— at least, with regard to the additional non-alienation oath—like the episcopal "tenants-in-chief," the *exempti*.

Side issues, important though they may be otherwise, will not be considered here. It would certainly be legitimate to raise the question whether the additional clause was appended to the

---

140 At the Roman Synod of 1078, Pope Gregory VII decreed concerning his suffragans: "Ut nulli episcopi predia ecclesie in beneficium tribuant sine consensu pape, si de sua sunt consecratione." Cf. *Reg.*, vi,5b,§30, ed. Caspar, 402,16; cf. Gottlob, 57. That, however, was a general decree, which as yet had nothing to do with the oath; consequently, the oath of Aquileia of the eleventh century still lacks the non-alienation clause; cf. Gregory VII, *Reg.*, vi,17a,4, ed. Caspar, 428f; Gottlob, 44. For the exempt bishoprics, see *Liber censuum*, 1,243,§xix, including the notes 247ff; also Gottlob, 64ff. For the form of Bishop Ekbert of Bamberg, see Raynald, *Annales ecclesiastici, ad a.*1206, §13. Gottlob, 57, assumes that the non-alienation clause was introduced for archbishops in general by the time of Gregory IX, but that it had been used previously for those sees which, for one reason or another, were in a particularly close relationship with the Holy See. Not all metropolitans took the non-alienation oath; it is lacking, e.g., in that of the primate of Bulgaria (Innocent III, *Reg.*, vii,11, *PL*, ccxv,295A), and whether it was included in that of the Latin patriarchs in the East (Gottlob, 55f), is doubtful.

141 Cf. Richardson, "Coronation Oath," 55 and 74.

coronation oath proper or rather to the oath of fealty sworn to the pope; or to ask whether King John, in 1213, took that non-alienation oath.[142] But those questions are not really relevant here: it could not have been before 1216 at any event that the canonistic oath promising to refrain from alienation of Crown property was connected with a coronation ceremonial. Relevant, however, is another point related to what perhaps may be termed "constitutional semantics," and most revealing with regard to constitutional development in general. A feudal oath had been adopted by the Church. It had been transformed into an episcopal oath at a time when the papal monarchy was in its formative stage. Owing to that appropriation by the Church, however, the feudal vassalitic oath had become an oath of office binding the bishop, not as a vassal, but as an "officer," and binding him not only to the pope but also to the abstract institution, the *papatus*, and to the bishop's own office, the *episcopatus*. Finally, that ecclesiastified, and now pseudo-feudal oath returned in a new guise to the secular state as an oath of office urging the king as well as his officers to protect an impersonal institution which "never dies," the Crown.

The canonistic influence on the concept of Crown was to continue in England. Four years after the coronation of Henry III, Pope Honorius III wrote, in 1220, to the Archbishop of Kalocsa. metropolitan of Southern Hungary, about certain alienations authorized by King Andrew II of Hungary. The king, wrote Honorius, had acted in prejudice of his realm and against his honor, and should be asked to revoke the alienations, since "at his coronation he [the King of Hungary] had sworn to maintain unimpaired the rights of his realm and the honor of his Crown."[143]

---

[142] For the feudal oath of King John, see Stubbs, *Select Charters*, 280f (where, however, *catholice* should be replaced by *canonice*; cf. "Inalienability," 494,n.34). The oath has the first four clauses in common with the standard episcopal oath, notwithstanding the insertion of a clause in which the king promises not to plot against the pope and to inform him of actions planned to the pope's damage: "Eorum [that is, pope and successor popes] damnum, si scivero, impediam et removere faciam si potero: alioquin quam citius potero, intimabo vel tali personae dicam quam eis credam pro certo dicturam." The sentence is taken from the ancient *Indiculum episcopi* of the *Liber diurnus*, Form 75 (*PL*, cv,72f), of which Innocent III availed himself on other occasions as well, e.g., for the oath of the Bulgarian primate (above, n.140). See also "Inalienability," 498,n.52, and below, n.159.

[143] Cf. c.33 X 2,24, ed. Friedberg, II,373 (Potthast, 6318): ". . . studeat revocare, quia quum teneatur et in sua coronatione iuraverit regni sui et honorem corone

This letter, too, passed into the *Liber Extra*, so that its basic ideas became binding Law of the Church. It is possible that King Andrew II of Hungary (1205-35) actually had taken a non-alienation oath at his coronation; in his "Golden Bull" of 1222, issued after many years of struggle with magnates and bishops, he made indeed a non-alienation promise of a specific kind, and the Holy See, in the following years, referred several times to Andrew's coronation oath.[144] But whether the Hungarian king had done so or not appears of minor importance as compared to the fact that apparently the Holy See then proceeded on the assumption that a non-alienation oath of some kind was customarily taken by a king at his coronation just as it was taken by a group of high-ranking princes of the Church at their consecration. In other words, in Rome the existence of certain royal obligations towards the impersonal Crown—analogous to the obligations of a bishop towards his See—was taken for granted at a time when that idea had as yet hardly penetrated secular political thought. "As is the custom," *ut moris est*, wrote Gregory IX, in 1235, to Henry III[145]— the custom, according to the assumption of the Holy See, probably

---

illibata servare, illicitum profecto fuit . . ." See Richardson, "Coronation Oath," 48, who has clearly recognized the influence of that decretal on a letter of Edward I (below, n.147). The letter of Honorius III was included in Canon Law as early as 1226; it is found in the *Compilatio Quinta* (*Comp.* v,15,3), ed. Friedberg, *Quinque compilationes antiquae* (Leipzig, 1882), 165.

[144] Professor Josef Deér, in Bern, kindly informs me that it is quite likely that Andrew II, in 1205, swore an oath similar to the one which the first Anjou king of Hungary, Charles I, took at his coronation in 1310. The backgrounds of the decretal of Honorius III are complicated, but there is some hope that Professor Deér himself may wish to discuss the matter of inalienability in Hungary. For the Hungarian "Golden Bull," see Werner Näf, *Herrschaftsverträge des Spätmittelalters* (Quellen zur Neueren Geschichte herausgegeben vom Historischen Seminar der Universität Bern, xvII; Bern, 1951), 9, §16: "Integros comitatus vel dignitates quascunque in praedia seu possessiones non conferemus perpetuo" (a place to which Professor Deér kindly called my attention). The content of the Honorian decretal of 1220 was substantially repeated by the same pope, in 1225, and by Pope Gregory IX, in 1233; cf. Potthast, 7443 (July 15) and 9080 (Jan. 31). See also next note.

[145] Gregory IX's letter of July 1, 1235 (see Rymer, *Foedera*, I:1,229), repeats sections of the Honorian decretal (e.g., "in praeiudicium regni et contra honorem tuum" or "illicitum profecto extitit"), which might explain why the pope thought a non-alienation oath was the general custom: "Cum igitur in coronatione tua iuraveris, *ut moris est*, iura, libertates et dignitates conservare regales." Strangely enough, the same phrase (as Richardson, "Coronation Oath," 51 and 54, indicates) is used in the declaration of Louis of France in 1215, in which the French prince asserts that King John "in coronatione sua solempniter, *prout moris est*, iurasset se iura et consuetudines ecclesie et regni Anglie conservaturum." Prince Louis knew, of course, perfectly well that such oath was not the *mos* of France at that time; see next note.

not only with regard to England and Hungary, but at large. Even if that assumption can easily be proved to have been substantially wrong—for example, with regard to France[146]—there is no reason to doubt that in England the papal legate Guala would have seen to it that the facts corresponded to the papal assumption as well as to curial practice in general. Thus, as a result of King John's surrender to the Holy See and of an objectively incorrect assumption on the part of the Holy See, the canonistic doctrine of "inalienability" had been formulated and had actually become the norm, much earlier in England than in most other countries.

If the influence of Canon Law may have been less prominent with regard to Henry III, there is no ambiguity whatever with regard to Edward I. By his time, the decretal of Honorius III, mentioning in so many words the inalienable rights of the Crown, began to be effective too. When Edward, ten months after his coronation, referred for the first time to his coronation oath, his clerk alleged verbatim the Honorian decretal saying that the king was obliged "to maintain unimpaired the rights of the realm."[147] To be sure, Edward I found it most convenient to refer to the non-alienation clause of his coronation oath in order both to refute papal claims in general and to seek papal support against the baronage, and therefore he asserted time and again that he was "astricted" by his oath to maintain the rights of the Crown, to protect the Crown against diminution, and to preserve the *status coronae*.[148] As late as 1307, the year of his death, Edward I mentioned his coronation oath and his duty to preserve the rights of the Crown.[149] A year later, and indeed somewhat unexpectedly,

---

[146] In France, the non-alienation clause was added as late as 1365; see Schramm, *Frankreich*, 1,237f (with nos. 1 and 7).

[147] *Parliamentary Writs*, 1,381f: ". . . et iureiurando in coronacione nostra prestito sumus astricti quod iura regni nostri servabimus illibata." See, for the wording, the decretal of Honorius III, above, n.143; Richardson, "Coronation Oath," 49. I find it difficult to follow Wilkinson, "Coronation Oath," *Speculum*, XIX (1944), 448ff, because it seems to me most unlikely that Edward I, only ten months after his coronation and at a time when every one concerned would have known what the king actually promised, should have tried to fabricate a story about a coronation promise which in fact he had not made.

[148] See above, n.133, for *iuramento astrictus* in Innocent's decretal; this, however, may have been or become a quite common technical term, the presence of which proves nothing. For Edward's other references to his oath, see Richardson, *op.cit.*, 49f.

[149] *Foedera*, 1,2,1011; Richardson, 50,n.39.

we find the decretal of Honorius III cited once more, this time in direct connection with the coronation oath of Edward II. For in the *Liber Regalis*, a liturgical book which may even have been used at the coronation of 1308, an additional note says: "Be it known that the king at his coronation has to swear to maintain unimpaired the rights of the Crown." We easily recognize the wording of the Honorian decretal; in fact, the scholarly annotator quoted explicitly and in a juristically correct form the *Liber Extra*.[150] Whether or not Edward II still took the same non-alienation oath, we cannot tell; the fourth clause, then actually added to his coronation oath, had a different intent, and his non-alienation promise has to be extracted from the reference to the Laws of the Confessor contained in the reshuffled first clause.[151] However, Edward II himself seems to have referred, on one occasion, to an "oath by which he had sworn to maintain the laws of the land and the estate of the Crown,"[152] and the note in the *Liber regalis* shows at any rate how deeply the idea of the king's nonalienation promise was engrained in the minds of the clergy—as deeply as certainly it was in the minds of fourteenth-century jurists. "Take note," wrote Baldus, "that all kings in the world have to swear at their coronation to conserve the rights of their realm and the honor of the Crown"—an assertion which undoubtedly was true in the latter half of the fourteenth century when Baldus wrote.[153] But the jurists noticed also the parallelism of royal and episcopal oaths. Already the *Glossa ordinaria* on the Honorian decretal indicates that the bishops too, and not only

<hr/>

[150] Richardson, in *Bulletin of the Institute of Historical Research*, XIV (1938), 11, was aware of the importance of the annotation: "Sciendum quod rex in coronacione sua iurare debet iura regni sui illibata servare, Extra de iureiurando, intellecto etc. [c.33 X 2,24]." The place has been misunderstood by Wilkinson, "Coronation Oath," *Speculum*, XIX (1944), 450,n.1, although Schramm, in *ArchUF*, XVI (1939), 284, had already clearly recognized the allegation to the *Liber Extra*.

[151] Lodge and Thornton, *Documents*, 10f,n.3. Richardson, "Coronation Oath," 6off, has very ingeniously demonstrated that the non-alienation promise was actually embedded in the first clause of the oath of Edward II; that is, in the reference to the Laws of Edward the Confessor, including the interpolation from the *Leges Anglorum*; see above, n.116.

[152] Johannes de Trokelow, *Annales*, ed. H. T. Riley (Rolls Series; London, 1866), 109: ". . . iuramentum quod de legibus terrae et statu coronae manutenendis fecerat . . ." Professor Robert S. Hoyt kindly called this place to my attention.

[153] Baldus, on c.33 X 2,24, n.3, *In Decretales*, fol.261v: "Nota quod omnes reges mundi in sua coronatione debent iurare iura regni sua conservare et honorem coronae."

the kings, have to promise not to alienate.[154] Lucas de Penna, writing in the fifties of the fourteenth century, holds that bishops and kings are "equiparate" with regard to their oaths concerning alienation.[155] And his contemporary Petrus de Ancharano says quite straightforwardly: "The king, at the time of his coronation, swears not to alienate the things of his kingdom; similarly, the bishops swear [not to alienate] the rights of their bishopric."[156]

By that time—that is, in the late fourteenth century or early fifteenth—the non-alienation clause finally went on record in England, if in a spurious form: it emerged in a formulary based upon the coronation oath of Edward II to which there was added the non-alienation promise demanded by the *Leges Anglorum*. Since this curious oath appeared in print in a fifteenth-century Book of Statutes, it eventually achieved official recognition.[157] However that may be, the influence of Canon Law—in England as well as elsewhere—on the development and articulation of the idea of inalienability, and thereby of the notion of "Crown" as something distinct from the person of the king, appears as an established and hardly disputable fact.[158]

CROWN AND UNIVERSITAS

The canonistic influence was not confined to the oath *of* the king; it affected also the oath *to* the king. In the course of his negotiations with King John, Pope Innocent III gave the assurance that Archbishop Langton with his diocesans would promise the king, by oath and in writing, not to permit anyone to plot or

---

[154] Cf. c.33 X 2,24, v. *Regni sui*: "Sic et episcopi iurant in sua coronatione, quod iura sui episcopatus non alienabunt . . ."

[155] See above, Ch.v, n.71.

[156] Petrus de Ancharano, on c.33 X 2,24,n.1, *In quinque Decretalium libros commentaria* (Bologna, 1581), fol.291: "Rex iurat tempore suae coronationis non alienare res regni sui. Similiter episcopi iurant sui episcopatus iura."

[157] Schramm, "Ordines-Studien III," *ArchUF*, xv (1938), 363f; *English Coronation*, 196ff; Liebermann, *Gesetze*, 1,365, n.c.

[158] The references to the Honorian decretal *Intellecto* are innumerable; see, e.g., Oldradus de Ponte, *Consilia*, xcv,n.1, fol.37ᵛ: ". . . cum per tales donationes et alienationes diminuantur iura regni quod esset contra iuramentum quod praestitit in principio sui regiminis. argumentum Extra de iureiurando intellecto." Also Andreas of Isernia, on *Feud.* I,1,n.10,fol.10: ". . . dummodo infeudationes suae non diminuant honorem et Regis et Coronae, extra de iureiurando intellecto. nisi donet Ecclesiae, ut fecit Constantinus . . ." That is to say, around 1300 the assumption prevailed also among the jurists that kings in general took a non-alienation oath in agreement with the Decretal of Honorius III.

attempt "against his [the king's] person or against the Crown."[159] The phrase "king and Crown," it is true, had been used repeatedly in earlier times. But the papal version *contra personam vel coronam*, distinguishing between person and institution, is much more specific: it shows how the pope understood and interpreted "king and Crown" and it blots out every possibility of taking the two words as meaning tautologically the same thing. Unmistakably the pope has discriminated between person and Crown. We may assume that, when in the course of the thirteenth century, English bishops continued to take an oath "to king and Crown,"[160] the difference between the personal king and the impersonal institution was felt no less clearly than by Pope Innocent III. At any rate, we recognize that the notion of Crown, introduced in England during the twelfth century mainly in fiscal and legal matters, began to gain new momentum under the impact of Canon Law concepts and to assume constitutional connotations which it did not have before.

[159] *PL*, CCXVI,774D; Rymer, *Foedera*, I:1,109); Potthast, 4392. The passage (Mr. Robert L. Benson kindly called my attention to it) is interesting. The pope informed King John that the bishops "praestabunt . . . *iuratoriam et litteratoriam cautionem* quod ipsi ne per se nec per alios contra personam vel coronam tuam aliquid attentabunt, te illis praedictam securitatem et pacem illibatam servante." *Cautio iuratoria* is a technical term: it is the strengthening of an already existing obligation by an oath. In this case, the *cautio* was *litteratoria* as well, that is, the obligation was sworn to and given in writing. This was the custom with episcopal oaths; see, e.g., the *Cautio episcopi* of the *Liber diurnus*, Form 74 (*PL*, CV,68-72; Gottlob, 8f,nos.31f, also 21f). For the procedure of taking that oath, see Andrieu, *Pontifical romain*, I,47f, and, for bishops consecrated in Rome, III,392,n.33. In that sense, apparently, already young King Henry's oath, in 1170, was a *cautio*; cf. Rymer, *Foedera*, I:1,26; Richardson, "Coronation Oath," 47,n.17. The episcopal *cautio* as a promise to refrain from plotting against king and Crown, referred to by Innocent III, has its equivalent in the promise of King John to the Holy See (above, n.142), which depended on the *Liber diurnus*, Form 75 (*PL*, CV,72f), where the bishop promises "quodlibet agi cognovero, minime consentire, sed in quantum virtus suffragaverit, obviare et . . . modis quibus potuero, nuntiabo etc." Now, in that old *Diurnus* form, which goes back to the 7th, probably however to the 5th century (Gottlob, 12, with n.44), the promise is made with regard to *respublica* and *princeps*; these distinctions were later cancelled and eventually replaced by *papa* and *papatus*, until finally the original version was, so to speak, reinstated by transference and by the application to *persona regis* and *corona* (whereby *corona* may still have a more "personal" touch than *respublica*).

[160] In the case of *William of Valence v. Bishop Godfrey of Worcester*, which was heard in 1294 before the King's Council, the plaintiff claimed that the bishop had acted *contra sacramentum suum regi et corone sue prestitum*; cf. *Cases before the King's Council, 1243-1482*, ed. I. S. Leadam and J. F. Baldwin (Selden Society, XXXV; Cambridge, 1918), 6. However, the oath form published in *Statutes of the Realm*, I,249, does not refer to the Crown.

At the demand of Pope Innocent, only the bishops swore to protect the Crown. However, the other members representing the governing part of the body politic soon followed; that is, the king's officers and the feudal lords. Matthew Paris, who in his writings often alludes to the Crown, tells us that in 1240 the king's clerk in custody of the seal, Master Simon the Norman, himself a papal chaplain and frequent envoy to Rome, refused to seal a charter because he found that its content was contrary to the interest of the Crown (*contra coronam*), and it has been suggested that perhaps he had sworn not only to give good counsel, but also to refrain from any act reducing the Crown.[161] A formulary of an oath of office to that effect has been preserved, if of a later period: in the councillors' oath of 1307 the members of the king's council were held to swear that they would "keep and maintain, safeguard and restore the rights of the king and the Crown"; further, that they would "support the Crown to the best of their ability and in loyal fashion"; and also that they would not take part in court or council *ou le Roy se decreste de chose qe a la Corone appent.*[162] As in the case of Simon the Norman the assumption obviously did exist that the king could deprive the Crown and that the councillors were obliged to protect the Crown even against the king. King and Crown no longer were the same thing.

Moreover, letters of King Edward I and the magnates to the Holy See betray that the magnates also took an oath "in defense of the royal dignity and the Crown"; and if we can trust those letters in respect of the wording of the oath, the magnates may even have availed themselves of canonistic models when they declared that "by the bonds of their oath they were astricted to preserve and defend the rights of the Crown."[163] Admittedly, it may have had little practical significance that, in 1258, the revolutionary "Commonalty of England" swore at Oxford mutual support to each other, though "saving faith to the king and the Crown."[164] Yet, on closer inspection of the few documents referred to here, we recognize that even without that Oxford oath, or rather despite it, it

---

[161] Matthew Paris, *Historia Anglorum,* ed. Madden (Rolls Series), II,440; for Simon's career and the whole affair, see Powicke, *King Henry III and the Lord Edward* (Oxford, 1947), II,772ff, esp. 781f.

[162] Lodge and Thornton, *Documents,* 53, No. 1. See below, n.174.

[163] See Richardson, "Coronation Oath," 50f, who adds quite a number of places concerning the oath of the lords.

[164] Stubbs, *Select Charters,* 379: "salve la fei le rei e de la corune."

normally was the "community of the realm" that swore to the Crown, since king, councillors, officials, and lords spiritual and secular took consonantly the same oath to maintain the rights of the Crown; and they together and with the king as their head, after all, represented and were the "community of the realm," the *universitas.* Equally, and using similar terms, they all were constrained to protect the Crown as something superior to all of them and as something they all had in common. In the Crown, therefore, and by the oath to the Crown, the "Commonalty of England" united—at least, the responsible portion of the realm.

This, then, may provide us with the background needed to appreciate that most instructive letter which Edward I, in 1275, wrote to Pope Gregory X on matters of England's feudal tribute to Rome. Indeed, the letter is quite remarkable. Its strict observation of the *cursus* is not the only thing suggesting the dictation of one of the learned Italians who then served with King Edward as advisers or clerks—Francis Accursius, for example, or Stephen of San Giorgio.[165] It is also the legalistic touch of the document which reveals the trained jurist and his language. The decretal of Honorius III was alleged verbatim to support the rights of the Crown; the Crown itself is solemnly called the "Diadem"; and the king's oath, normally *iuramentum* or *sacramentum,* is called no less solemnly *iusiurandum,* apparently in allusion to the legal title *De iureiurando* under which the Honorian decretal had found its place in the *Liber Extra.* As so often in later years, the king asserted that by his oath he was "astricted" to maintain "unimpaired" the rights of the Crown. After that, however, there follows an interesting twist of the romano-canonical maxim *Quod omnes tangit* upon which, as we know, the idea of community representation hinged.[166] For the king declared that by his oath

165 See G. L. Haskins and E. H. Kantorowicz, "A Diplomatic Mission of Francis Accursius," *EHR,* LVIII (1943), 424ff and 424,n.4, for Stephen of San Giorgio. See for this South-Italian clerk, also Robert Weiss, "Cinque lettere inedite del Card. Benedetto Caetani (Bonifacio VIII)," *Rivista di storia della Chiesa in Italia,* III (1949), 157-164, esp. 162ff; further A. J. Taylor, "The Death of Llywelyn ap Gruffydd," *The Bulletin of the Board of Celtic Studies,* XV (1953), 207-209. The rich material on Stephen of San Giorgio and on the intellectual relations of Edward I with the South has as yet not been sifted. See, for the time being, my paper "The Prologue to *Fleta* and the School of Petrus de Vinea," *Speculum,* XXXII (1957), n.29.

166 For the principle (cf. *C.*5,59,5,2), see Gaines Post, "Quod omnes tangit," *Traditio,* IV,197-252. Antonio Marongiu, *L'Istituto parlamentare in Italia dalle origini al 1500* (Rome, 1949), 65-78, has devoted a chapter to that maxim, but

he was bound also "to do nothing that touches the Diadem of this realm without having resorted to the counsel of prelates and magnates."[167] If the diocesans often promised not to alienate without the common counsel of their chapter, we now find King Edward asserting that he could not alienate tribute money to Rome without having consulted with his prelates and magnates. That is to say, matters concerning the *episcopatus* or the *corona* involved the whole body corporate or politic; they could not be decided high-handedly by the bishop alone or the king alone. The whole body, as represented by bishop and chapter, or by the king as head and the lords spiritual and temporal as limbs, had to approve actions of importance to all. Hence, "what touches the Diadem, shall be considered and approved by all concerned," by the body politic in its highest representatives. Clearly and authoritatively, it has been stated here by Edward I that the Crown was not the king—or, at least, not the king alone. It was something that touched all and, therefore, was "public," and no less public than waters, highways, or *fiscus*. It served the common utility and thus was superior to both the king and the lords spiritual and secular including—a little later—the commons as well.

Hence, the preservation of the *status coronae* amounted to preserving the *status regni*. The Crown, therefore, was not something apart from the body politic and its individually changing constituents. This was pointed out explicitly two generations later, in 1337, when the Bishop of Exeter, John of Grandisson, declared that "the substance of the nature of the Crown is found chiefly in the person of the king as head and of the peers as members."[168]

---

has since withdrawn his suggestion according to which the formulary of summons of Edward I might have been inspired by Rudolph of Habsburg's summons for the Diet of Nürnberg, in 1274 (*MGH, Const.*, III,50, No. 56); see Marongiu, "Note federiciane," *Studi Medievali*, XVIII (1952), 306ff, where he calls attention to Frederick II's summons for a Diet to be held in Verona, in 1244; cf. *MGH,Const.*, II,333, No. 244: "Porro cum imperii principes nobilia membra sint corporis nostri, in quibus imperialis sedis iungitur potestas . . . , presenciam omnium tenemur instantius evocare, ut quod tangit omnes ab omnibus approbetur." For the princes as *membra corporis imperatoris*, see C.9,8,5, and above, Ch.v,n.42; also below, n.342.

167 ". . . nec aliquid quod diadema tangat regni eiusdem absque ipsorum [prelatorum et procerum] requisito consilio faciemus." *Parliamentary Writs*, I,381f; Richardson, *op.cit.*, 49.

168 "La substance de la nature de la corone est principaument en la persone le roi, come teste, et en les piers de la terre, come membres, qi tenent de lui par certeyn homage." *Register of John de Grandisson*, ed. F. C. Hingeston-Randolph (London, 1894-99), II,840, quoted by Richardson, "The English Coronation Oath," *Transactions of the Royal Historical Society*, 4th Ser., XXIII (1941), 148,n.2.

The composite character and corporate aspect of the Crown could not have been expressed more poignantly than by linking it to the old image of head and limbs describing the *corpus politicum* or *mysticum* of the realm. A century later, in 1436, the Bishop of Bath and Wells repeated in a parliamentary sermon a similar idea in a more allegorical guise. To him the Crown was the symbol of both polity and sovereignty:

> In the figure of the Crown, the rule and polity of the realm are presented; for in the gold, the rule of the Community is noted, and in the flowers of the Crown, raised and adorned with jewels, the Honor and Office of the King or Prince is designated.[169]

In those years, a poet gave a more detailed description of the components of the Crown:

> What doth a kynges crowne signifye,
> Whan stones and floures on sercle is bent?
> Lordis, comouns, and clergye
> To be all at on assent . . .
> The leste lyge-man, with body and rent,
> He is a parcel of the crowne.[170]

There can be no doubt that in the later Middle Ages the idea was current that in the Crown the whole body politic was present—from king to lords and commons and down to the least liege-man. This did not preclude different interpretations on other occasions: the *universitas* might be represented by Parliament or even by the king as King.[171] What matters here, however, is the possibility of attributing a corporate character to the Crown. In this respect indeed the Crown and the "mystical body of the realm" were comparable entities. Neither one nor the other existed all by itself "in the abstract" and separate from the constituents, the difference being chiefly that "Crown" emphasized more the prerogative and sovereign rights resting in those responsible for the whole community, whereas *corpus mysticum* seemed to stress more the corporate nature and the continuity of the whole people. But the two interrelated notions should probably not be separated at all, and English lawyers, as we recall, had a strong aversion to recog-

---

[169] Chrimes, *Const.Ideas*, 14,n.1, quoting *Rot.Parl.*, iv,495; cf. Dunham, "Crown Imperial," 201.

[170] *Political and Other Poems*, ed. J. Kail (Early English Text Society, Orig. Series, cxxiv; London, 1904), 51, quoted by Chrimes, *loc.cit.*; cf. Dunham, *loc.cit.*

[171] Dunham, *op.cit.*, 203f.

nizing a corporation when it was incomplete and therefore juristically incapacitated. What Justice Fineux said in 1522, namely
that "a corporation was an aggregate of head and body: not a head
by itself, nor a body by itself," was essentially valid in earlier
times as well, even with regard to the Diadem "that touches all."[172]
For the Crown would have been incomplete without both the
king as the head and the magnates as the limbs, since only both
together, supplemented by the parliamentary knights and burgesses, formed the body corporate of the Crown which, in modern
language, meant Sovereignty. And in that sense, indeed, the king
could be said to be "the head, the beginning and end of
Parliament."[173]

Edward I, in 1275, had not defined the notion of Crown; but
from the description he gave of the nature and functions of the
Crown there leads a direct line to the exclusively English concept of Sovereignty, the King in Council in Parliament.

THE KING AND THE CROWN

No theory, it seems, had any chance to prevail in England,
which attempted to isolate the Crown as something set apart from
its components. That attempt was made nevertheless; and the
temptation to set up the Crown as something disconnected from
the king must have been great at a time when it had become
customary to point out that king and Crown were not simply
the same thing. But not being the same thing did not yet imply
a breaking-apart nor the playing-off of one against the other. That,
however, was the danger which arose when the magnates, in their
effort to remove Edward II's favorite and to restrict the king,
came forth with their well-known Declaration of 1308, in which
they proclaimed:

> Homage and oath of allegiance are more by reason of the Crown
> than by reason of the king's person, and are more bound to the
> Crown than to the person. And that appears from the fact that,
> before the estate of the Crown has passed by descent, no allegiance
> is due to the person. Wherefore, if it happen that the king is not
> guided by reason in regard to the estate of the Crown, his lieges,

[172] See Maitland, *Sel.Ess.*, 79, for Justice Fineux.
[173] *Modus Tenendi Parliamentum*: "Rex est caput, principium, et finis parliamenti, et ita non habet parem in suo gradu, et ita ex rege solus est primus
gradus . . ." Cf. Stubbs, *Select Charters*, 503, § "De Gradibus Parium."

by the oath sworn to the Crown, are justly bound to lead the king back to reason and repair the estate of the Crown, or else their oath would be violated. . . .

Proceeding from this premise, the magnates then drew the conclusion that "when the king cares not to remedy an error and remove that which is harmful for the Crown and obnoxious for the people," the error must be removed by coercion.[174] Apparently the barons were prepared to face a desperate alternative: to choose between Crown and king. That, however, was a false alternative from the outset, because the Crown without the king was incomplete and incapacitated. "For," said Sir Francis Bacon later when referring to that Declaration, "it is one thing to make things distinct, another thing to make them separable, *aliud est distinctio, aliud separatio*"; and he added with great emphasis that the king's person and the Crown were "inseparable, though distinct."[175] The barons seem to have had in mind something which perhaps would have been feasible had the Crown been simply identical with the king, and had it not been—even by that time—a corporate entity composed, as the barons implied, of both the king and the magnates. The barons may have wished to express a distinction between the king as King and the king as a private person; but what they actually did was to set the king as King—and not only his private person—over against the corporate Crown, and thus, for the sake of the Crown, they were

---

[174] "Homagium et sacramentum ligiantiae potius sunt et vehementius ligant ratione coronae quam personae regis, quod inde liquet quia, antequam status coronae descendatur, nulla ligiancia respicit personam nec debetur; unde, si rex aliquo casu erga statum coronae rationabiliter non se gerit, ligii sui per sacramentum factum coronae regem reducere et coronae statum emendare juste obligantur, alioquin sacramentum praestitum violatur. . . . Quocirca propter sacramentum observandum, quando rex errorem corrigere vel amovere non curat, quod coronae dampnosum et populo nocivum est, iudicatum est quod error per asperitatem amoveatur, eo quod pei sacramentum praestitum se obligavit regere populum, et ligii sui populum protegere secundum legem cum regis auxilio sunt astricti." *Gesta Edwardi de Carnarvan* (Rolls Series, London, 1883), 33f; Lodge and Thornton, *Documents*, 11, No.4; J. C. Davies, *The Baronial Opposition to Edward II* (Cambridge, 1918), 24ff; Richardson, "Coronation Oath," 66f, who doubts the authenticity, but admits the wide circulation, of that proclamation. For the oath referred to in the proclamation, see above, n.162.

[175] For the rejection of the theory, see Lodge and Thornton, *Documents*, 18f, No.7. Bacon, *Post-nati*, 669f, makes more than one good remark on "the poison of the opinion and assertion of Spenser," though he probably overestimated the magnates when he said that "their blood did rise to hear that opinion, that subjection is owing to the crown rather than to the person of the king."

ready to throw overboard even the king as King. For that reason, their otherwise very interesting political philosophy had no future and fell indeed, as has been said, "on peculiarly barren ground." For all practical purposes this theory was soon forgotten, especially after the barons themselves repudiated it; but it was remembered in the Courts of Law, by Coke and Bacon above all, as something perilous and poisonous which cried out for vehement rejection.[176]

And yet, the distinction between the king as King and the king as a private individual was not at all unknown by that time. It would be easy enough to refer to canonical practice once more in order to show the distinction made between office and incumbent.[177] Since, however, Hugh Despenser the Younger, who was held responsible for the political theory of the magnates, embarked upon a new "philosophy," it is fair to turn to philosophical evidence. Unfortunately, we have no information whatever about the sources from which the younger Despenser may have drawn his inspiration. Christopher Marlowe spoke, presumably, in general terms when he made his Edward II address the elder Despenser:

> Make triall now of that philosophie,
> That in our famous nurseries of artes
> Thou suckedst from Plato, and from Aristotle.[178]

However, it would not be altogether impossible that by some channel, directly or indirectly, Aristotle's *Politics*, including its thomistic commentary, exercised some influence—and was misunderstood.[179] Peter of Auvergne, the continuator of Aquinas'

[176] Bacon's doctrine of the inseparability of king and Crown conformed with that of Coke who, in *Calvin's Case* (Coke, *Reports*, Part VII, vol.IV,11f), unqualifiedly identified the Crown with the king's "politic capacity"; he, too, held that the theory of the magnates in 1308 "inferred execrable and detestable consequences."

[177] Gierke, *Gen.R.*, III,331f; for a related problem raised by Drogheda, see Post, "Quod omnes tangit," 217f; see also *Year Books, 5 Edward II*, Y.B. Ser., XI (Selden Society, XXXI; London, 1915), 66, Chief Justice Brabanzon remarking: "The Bishop has two estates, to wit, the estate of a patron and the estate of ordinary, and they say that the Bishop gave his vicarage in right of his church, and not as an ordinary." For a similar statement under Edward I (*Archbishop of York* v. *Bishop of Durham*) see Davies, *Baronial Opposition*, 22,n.6.

[178] Christopher Marlowe, *The troublesome raigne and lamentable death of Edward the second, King of England*, lines 1884ff.

[179] The continuation of Aquinas' Commentary on the *Politics* was written by Peter of Auvergne, a few years before or after 1300; there is no reason why that work should not have been known in England in 1308. The commentary of Walter Burley, though not written before 1338, follows Peter of Auvergne verbatim; cf.

commentary (though the whole commentary passed under the name of Thomas Aquinas), discussed in great detail a section of the Third Book of the *Politics* in which Aristotle stated that a Prince had in his officers and friends many eyes and ears and hands and feet, but that those men had really the function of co-rulers.[180] The commentator's remarks on that passage are important enough to justify their rendering in full. He wrote:

> Princes make those [men] co-rulers who are *their* friends as well as those of the principate. For if they [the co-rulers] were not friends of both, but only of one, as for instance the principate, they would not care about the good of the Prince, but only about the principate. Contrariwise, if they would not love the principate, but only the Prince, they would not care for the good of the principate. Therefore the co-rulers have to take care of the good of both the Prince and the principate. . .

The commentator then elaborates the point. He avoids a split between the principate and the Prince by demonstrating that the men who were received as co-rulers on behalf of the Prince were in fact received at the same time on behalf of the principate, because the good of the Prince was directed toward the good of the principate. That statement, however, the commentator did not consider valid without qualification. For, writes he,

> only he that loves the prince as Prince, loves the principate. For he that rules may be considered in two ways: either according to his being Prince, or according to his being an individual man. If you love him according to his being Prince, you love the principate, and by obtaining the good of one, you obtain the good of the other. If, however, you love the Prince because he is this or that man, you do not necessarily love the principate: and then you obtain the good of this or that individual without obtaining the good of the principate.[181]

S. Harrison Thomson, "Walter Burley's Commentary on the *Politics* of Aristotle," *Mélanges Auguste Pelzer* (Louvain, 1947), 558f, and, for the passage in question, 571f.

[180] *Politics*,III,16,13,1287b, makes the distinction between φίλοι κἀκείνου [τοῦ μονάρχου] καὶ τῆς ἀρχῆς, to which W. L. Newman, *The Politics* (Oxford, 1887), III,301f, adduces a number of interesting parallels from antiquity.

[181] See Aquinas, *In Polit.Arist.*, §520, ed. Spiazzi, 182: "Faciunt autem comprincipes illos, qui sunt amici sui et principatus; quia si non essent amici utriusque, sed alterius, sicut principatus, non curarent de bono principis, sed principatus. Iterum, si non diligerent principatum, sed principem, non curarent de bono principatus. Oportet autem comprincipantes curare de bono principis et principatus . . . Et est intelligendum circa id quod dictum est, quod assumit princeps sibi comprincipantes amicos sui et principatus, quod ratio principis sumitur a ratione

It is easy to recognize the difference between the baronial theory and the theory of the commentator on Aristotle's *Politics*. The commentator arrived at a distinction of the two capacities of the ruler, the Prince as Prince and the Prince as a private individual, whereby the princely capacity and the principate remained concentric. The barons, however, operated only with an antithesis of principate and Prince, which made those two entities, as it were, eccentric. It was the shortcoming of their doctrine that they divorced the Prince as Prince from the principate, or the *K*ing from the Crown, instead of separating only the individual man from his office, the *status regis*. What they were about to do was to divorce, not the person from the *status regis*, but the *status regis* from the *status coronae*.[182] And in that, they failed, as they played off alternately the "person of the king" and the "King" against the "Crown." Their main deficiency was perhaps lack of clarity, and their distinctions, useful though they may have been otherwise, were hardly applicable to their oath of fealty: their tenet minimizing the importance of personal allegiance amounted to an encroachment upon the authority of the king as King. This the barons themselves later branded as treasonable, and it made the chronicler cry out: "What a strange thing! See how the members divorce themselves from the head."[183] Edward II found a willing Parliament when, in 1322, he revoked the ordinances of the magnates, whereby he correctly upheld the distinction between *status regni* and *status coronae*—though bringing both entities as well as the "royal power" back on one denominator—and treated them as something which was the concern of the whole *universitas*, the famous "commonalty of the realm."[184]

---

principatus; et ideo bonum principis est in ordine ad principatus bonum: et ideo qui diligit principem secundum quod princeps est, diligit principatum. Sed ille qui principatur, duobus modis potest considerari: vel secundum quod princeps, vel secundum quod homo talis; et ideo potest aliquis diligere ipsum, vel secundum quod princeps, vel secundum quod talis homo. Si diligat ipsum secundum quod princeps, diligit principatum; et procurando bona unius, procurat bona alterius. Si diligat ipsum secundum quod talis vel talis, non oportet quod diligat principatum: et tunc procurat secundum quod talis vel talis, non procurando de bono principatus."

[182] The terms *status regis, status coronae*, of course, are equivalent to *bonus status regis, bonus status coronae*, or, in Aristotelian language, to *bonum regis, bonum coronae*. The meaning coincides largely with both welfare and utility of the public sphere; see Post, "Public Law," 47f, and, more explicitly, "Two Laws," esp. 425ff.

[183] Above, Ch.v,n.115.

[184] Lodge and Thornton, *Documents*, 128f,No.4.

The distinction between king and Crown, to be sure, never ceased to exist, and kings could easily be accused of having "blemished the Crown." The affair of Richard II and the charges against him abound in "crimes against the Crown." Richard himself, in 1398, the year before his fall, proclaimed in his extension of the Law of Treason that every attempt against the king's physical person was a crime of "high treason against the Crown."[185] Vice versa, when a year later the same king was charged with having jeopardized "the freedom of the Crown of England," of having squandered the property of the Crown, and of having disinherited the Crown, he was also accused of having acted on those occasions merely *ad sui nominis ostentationem et pompam et vanam gloriam,* "for reason of personal ostentation and pomp and vainglory"—certainly an effort on the part of his accusers to single out the king's private person as distinct from his office and his official capacity.[186] But the lords appellant of 1388 were very careful to avoid the mistake of the lords ordainer of 1308, for when banding together they made an express reservation concerning their "allegiance to our lord the king and the prerogative of his Crown."[187]

Hence, a distinction was made, time and again, between the estate of the king and the estate of the Crown. But the attempt to exclude adherence to the personal king for the sake of adherence to the impersonal Crown was not repeated. Instead, the doctrine of capacities gained ground steadily, albeit slowly. An early effort in that direction was abortive when a royal counsellor claimed that Edward I as a king was "of another estate than he was when he made a grant [as a prince]"; for the grantee, an earl, immediately retorted: "He is one and the same person that he was when

---

[185] Lodge and Thornton, *Documents,* 26,No.18.

[186] *Ibid.,* 25,No.16, for the king's demand to safeguard "les Libertees de sa dite Corone." For the freedom proper of the Crown, see, however, the Statute of *Praemunire,* of 1393 (*ibid.,* 312,No.23): "et ensy la Corone Dengleterre qad este si frank de tout temps . . . serroit submuys a Pape." In 1399, however, the king himself was charged (in almost the same words as had been used in *Praemunire*) with having submitted the Crown to the pope "quamvis Corona regni Angliae et Iura eiusdem Coronae . . . fuerint ab omni tempore retroacto adeo libera quo Dominus Summus Pontifex . . . [non] se intromittere debeat de eisdem"; *Rot.Parl.,* III,419,§27; for other charges concerning the Crown, see *ibid.,* 417,§18; 419,§32; 420,§41. In general, see Hartung, "Die Krone," 16ff.

[187] *Rot.Parl.,* III,244,§13: "Sauvant toute foitz vostre ligeance envers nostre Seigneur le Roy et la Prerogative de sa Corone"; cf. Hartung, "Die Krone," 17,n.2.

he made the gift."[188] The capacities were more clearly developed in the case of the Duchy of Lancaster which Henry IV refused to merge with the property of the Crown and kept as his private possession. That action, which became a *cause célèbre* and prompted the judges in the days of Plowden to make their most subtle distinctions concerning the king's two bodies, led the royal judges as early as 1405 to formulate clearly the difference between things *que appertaine al Corone* and those belonging to the king *come auter person*,[189] the latter a good anticipation of what was to be called in Tudor times the king's "body natural." Under Henry V, Parliament decided that the king could leave his property by will but could not bequeath his kingdom[190]—an old maxim, to be sure, and in fact only a reformulation of the old non-alienation clause. The problem itself, in the thirteenth and fourteenth centuries, had been widely discussed by the jurists in connection with the Donation of Constantine and the admissibility of granting away half of the empire to the papacy; and it had been discussed also by English lawyers in connection with King John's subjection of the kingdom to the Holy See and the admissibility of that action.[191] In the law courts, cases turned up in which the king's personal actions, or actions by his prerogative, came into conflict with the interests of the Crown and therefore with those of the community of the realm.[192] And under Henry VII the jurists recognized that the king might be seized of land in right of the Crown.[193]

A move of exceptional interest in the direction of distinguishing between the capacities of the king was the *De facto Act* of 1495, under Henry VII. When, in the course of the dynastic struggles between York and Lancaster, King Henry VI succeeded

---

[188] Pollock and Maitland, *History*, I,524; Davies, *Baronial Opposition*, 23,n.4.

[189] Chrimes, *Ideas*, 35,n.2, and 352, No.11.

[190] K. Pickthorn, *Early Tudor Government: Henry VII* (Cambridge, 1934), 140,n.1.

[191] Laehr, *Konstantinische Schenkung*, 98ff,128ff, and passim, whose material, however, could be considerably broadened; see, e.g., Nardi, "La *Donatio Constantini* e Dante," *Studi Danteschi*, XXVI (1942), 47-95; Ullmann, *Mediaeval Papalism*, 107ff, 163ff; Schramm, *English Coronation*, 197ff; see, for Wiclif and England, also Laehr, "Die Konstantinische Schenkung in der abendländischen Literatur des ausgehenden Mittelalters," *QF*, XXIII (1931-32), 140ff,146.

[192] Plucknett, "Lancastrian Constitution," 175ff, for the case of the Abbot of Waltham; Pickthorn, *Henry VII*, 159; above, Ch.IV, n.253.

[193] Pickthorn, *Henry VII*, 157f.

in "readepting" the royal power, if only for six months, King
Edward IV was considered a usurper and was consistently referred to in court and elsewhere as the *nuper de facto rex Angliae,*
"the late *de facto* King of England." Vice versa, after Edward's
return, the Lancastrian Henry VI appeared as the usurper and *de
facto* king in contradistinction to the *de jure* ruling Yorkist.[194] It
is significant also that the courts in that period talked about "the
king's demise" not in the sense of the king's death, but of his
departure from power, thereby indicating, exactly as Plowden
later reported, "a Separation of the two Bodies [in] that the Body
politic is conveyed over from the Body natural, now dead *or
removed* from the Dignity royal, to another Body natural."[195]
It was the purpose of the *De facto Act* to wipe out all the potentially unpleasant consequences from the aftermath of the civil
wars. The Act recognized that no subject "should loose or forfeit
any thing for doyng their true dutie and service of allegiance"
by going either with one or the other anti-king. That is to say,
true and faithful adherence to the "body politic" or "king as
King" could not lead to attainder even if "the King and Sovereign
Lord of this land for the time being" to whom a subject had adhered and with whom he had served, was later defeated or otherwise disabled of the Crown.[196] The Act thus acknowledged in

[194] *Year Books of Edward IV: 10 Edward IV and 49 Henry VI, A.D. 1470,* ed.
N. Neilson (Selden Society, XLVII, London, 1931), 115,117,118,126, and passim, for
the title, sometimes (p.168) reduced to *nuper rex;* see also Introduction, xiif,xiv,xxix.
For another distinction (*le Roy que fuit* and *Le Roy que ore est*), see a Year Book
case of 1465 (the outlawry of John Paston), in Lodge and Thornton, *Documents,*
37,No.29.

[195] *Year Books of Edward IV* (above, no.194), 114: *en temps lautre roy* a law suit
was started, but *fuit mys saunz iour par demys le roy,* said Littleton; see also 115,
119,135f,146,168; see also Lodge and Thornton, *Documents,* 37, and above, Ch.I,n.13.
That the king's "death" was replaced by the king's *demise* seems to belong to the
fifteenth century. The early fourteenth-century king apparently still died; see, e.g.,
Year Books, 1 and 2 Edward II, Y.B. Ser. 1 (Selden Society, XVII, London, 1903),
5,10,17,98: *le Roy morust.* In 1388, however, a plea was said to have gone without
day *par demys le Roy* (sc. Edward III); cf. *Year Books of Richard II, 12 Rich.II,
A.D. 1388-1389* (Ames Foundation, Cambridge, Mass., 1914), VI,98.

[196] *Statutes of the Realm,* II,568, where it is called unreasonable, "that the seid
subgettis going with their sovereign lord in Werres attending upon him in his
persone or being in other places by his commandement," should be attainted. The
Act had its antecedents because immediately on the accession of Henry Tudor, who
himself was an attainted person, a court decided that *eo facto* that Henry "prist
sur luy le Roial dignite estre roy, tout ce fuit void" and that it afforded no special
Act to reverse his attainder; see Chrimes, *Ideas,* 51 and 378f; above, Ch.I,n.9, for
the idea that the "Body politic" wipes out any deficiencies of the king. Cf. Pick-

retrospect the former coexistence of two anti-kings or, as we may say, two "Bodies natural," but the existence of only one Crown, one "Body politic," adherence to which in any form could not be made punishable even though the subject may have chosen the "wrong incarnation," the king who was defeated. It was certainly a wiser principle than the more usual slaughter of adherents of the defeated party, a principle for which precedents might have been found in the history of the papacy a century earlier when two or even three anti-popes mutually excommunicated each other and each other's henchmen.[197]

THE CROWN A MINOR

The Crown, it is true, could hardly be severed from the king as King. Despite that inseparability, however, it was not quite identical with the King either. It remained possible, for example, to personify the Crown which, representing something that touched all, stood in many respects for the whole body politic; and consequently it became possible, too, to ascribe to the king as King a definite function and a moderately well-defined role with regard to the Crown.

Among the many charges repeatedly brought against Richard II was also the one that he had acted "in prejudice of the people and in disherison of the Crown of England."[198] Disherison, of course, was a notion applicable only to a person, natural or corporate. The charge was not a new coinage. Already Henry III had applied it when he blamed his son Edward for having disinherited the

---

thorn, *Henry VII*, 151ff; Holdsworth, *History of English Law*, III,468,n.5, and IV,500.

[197] According to Johannes Andreae, *Glos.ord.*, on c.un., *Clement.*, II,9, v. *reges*, Pope Innocent III (in connection with the dispute about the empire in 1198) supposedly decided "quod inconcussa consuetudo imperii . . . hoc habet, quod duobus electis in discordia, *uterque administrat ut rex* et omnem imperii iurisdictionem exercet: quod, declarat ibi Papa, locum habere donec per Papam alterius electio fuerit approbata; aut reprobata." Cf. Hugelmann, "Kaiserweihe," 27; Kempf, *Innocenz III.*, 125,n.49. The co-existence of two *de facto* kings is openly acknowledged in this case, while the finding of the *de iure* king is left to the pope.

[198] Parliament, in 1386, complained of royal grants "en desheritison de la Corone" (*Rot.Parl.*, III,216); and again in 1388 (III,230,Art.v); the Statute of *Praemunire*, in 1393, complains that the papal demands were "en overte desheritance de la dite corone et destruccion de regalie nostre dit seigneur le Roi" (Lodge and Thornton, *Documents*, 312); in 1399, the king was charged with having acted "in magnum preiudicium Populi et exheredacionem Corone Regni" (*Rot.Parl.*, III,420,§41); Hartung, "Die Krone," 16ff.

Crown by alienating the Isle of Oléron; Edward I himself applied it whenever it suited his purposes; and during the struggles about the Crown under Edward II, the magnates reproached their king more than once for having acted in "disherison of the Crown."[199]

The metaphor itself, meaning hardly more than "deprivation," deserves our attention. It derived obviously from the Law of Inheritance, where it meant that a person was deprived, for one reason or another, from his legal rights as heir to a possession.[200] We may recall also that the Law of Inheritance was closely connected with the perpetuality and continuous descent of the Crown: just as the *dominium* passed on from the father to the son without the interruption of any intervening period of time, so did the Crown descend without any interval to the new king.[201] To be sure, the Crown, being something that concerned all, was not a private but a public inheritance: "Kings are heirs, not of kings, but of the kingdom," as a Tudor author phrased it, and French constitutionalists such as Terre Rouge were at pains of pointing out that the heir to the Crown was, properly speaking, not at all the heir of his predecessor, for he was only heir with regard to the administration of things which were not his, since they were public.[202] The crime, therefore, of disinheriting the

---

[199] For Oléron, see Rymer, *Foedera*, I,1,374: ". . . posset . . . exhereditationis periculum imminere." Cf. Hartung, "Die Krone," 10. For Edward I, see, e.g., his letter to Pope Nicholas IV (Rymer, I,2,740), in which the king declared he would avoid "exheredationem nostram quae statum coronae nostrae contingit." For Edward II, see the Declaration of 1308 (Lodge and Thornton, 11) where the magnates complain that Gaveston *coronam exheredavit*; in the Ordinances of 1311 (§23) they claim that Lady de Vescy had exercised influence "a damage et deshonour du roi et apert desheriteson de la corone" (also §20, with reference to Gaveston; *Statutes of the Realm*, I,162), after the barons, in their Articles of 1310, had accused the king of "desheritaunce et deshonour de vous et de vostre roial poer, et desheritaunce et vostre corone"; *Annales Londinienses* (*Chronicles of the Reigns of Edward I and Edward II*, vol.I), 168. Cf. Hartung, "Die Krone," 12ff, who quoted practically all the places here mentioned.

[200] Bracton, of course, discussed the legal aspects of *exheredatio*; see, e.g., fols. 8of, Woodbine, II,233f. For certain peculiarities of the English Law of Inheritance as compared with Roman and Canon Laws, see Güterbock, *Bracton*, 125ff; Holdsworth, *History of English Law*, III,74f. That, however, is not the question here.

[201] Above, nos. 53ff.

[202] McIlwain, *Political Thought*, 382,n.4, quoting Adam Blackwood. The same idea (i.e., the public, and not private, nature of inherited kingship) was expressed by Fortescue; cf. Chrimes *Ideas*, 10ff. For France, where the problem was often discussed in connection with the Salic Law, see Church, *Constitutional Thought*, 28f; also Lemaire, *Lois fondamentales*, 55ff; J. M. Potter, "The Development and Significance of the Salic Law of the French," *EHR*, LII (1937), 235-253.

Crown was not simply a matter of ordinary deprivation; it meant, in legal language, the deprivation of a minor.

A law of the Emperors Diocletian and Maximianus declared that the *respublica* was used to apply to itself the right of minors and therefore could implore the remedy of "reinstatement into the former legal position" (*restitutio in integrum*); and the glossators explained that in this respect commonweal and Church were on the same level.[203] However, the Roman jurist Labeo, writing in the times of Augustus, declared a certain edict to be pertinent to "madmen, children, and cities."[204] The *tertium comparationis* of this seemingly weird scramble was that all three were unable to manage their own affairs except through a curator who had to be a sane, adult, and natural person. When, in the course of the thirteenth century, the corporational doctrines were developed, the notion of "city," *civitas*, was logically transferred to any *universitas* or any body corporate, and it became a stock-in-trade expression to say that the *universitas* was ever an infant and under age because it needed a curator. In that sense, the canonists developed a detailed doctrine according to which the bishop figured as tutor or guardian of his church, whereby the Church—being "equiparated" with the *respublica*—figured also as a minor.[205] Therewith the body corporate, which was ever under age, came to enjoy all the privileges of a minor person: no prescription ran against a minor; property and fortune of the ward could not be alienated or diminished by the guardian or, for that matter, by any other person; and the guardian was responsible for the unimpaired preservation of his pupil's property, which, being "inalienable," was specially protected against dolose and

---

[203] C.2,54,4: "Res publica minorum iure uti solet ideoque auxilium restitutionis implorare potest." See *Glos.ord.* on this law, v. *solet*: "Sicut enim minores sunt sub curatoribus, sic et respublica sub administratoribus . . . sic et in ecclesia cum reipublicae parificetur." Accordingly, Hostiensis, *Summa aurea*, on X 1,41,n.4, col. 414 (quoting Guilelmus Naso, an early decretalist, writing ca. 1234): "ecclesia fungitur iure minoris, nam comparatur reipublicae." This, of course, was also the source of the parliamentary sermon of John Russel, Bishop of Lincoln, in 1483, who repeatedly emphasized that *res publica fungitur iure minoris* when describing the "mistik or politike body" of England. See Chrimes, *Const.Ideas*, 180 (n.1) and 187; cf. above, Ch.v,nos.93f. The corporational theme must have been rather popular, since the preacher at the next Parliament (the first one held under Henry VII, in 1485) discussed in his sermon the story of Menenius Agrippa; cf. *Rot.Parl.*, VI,267.

[204] D.4,6,22,2: "Quod edictum etiam ad furiosos et infantes et civitates pertinere Labeo ait." Cf. Gierke, *Gen.R.*, III,99,n.223, also 157,no.102.

[205] Gierke, *Gen.R.*, III,332,n.274, and above, n.203.

fraudulent actions by the *in integrum restitutio*, the restitution of a thing to its former condition or the revocation of all lost property to its original status. Certain difficulties arising from that doctrine, when, for example, jurists amusingly argued that the Church was a *sponsa* and therefore could not be under age, were of no importance.[206] It was admitted also that the relation of a bishop to his church differed in some aspects from that of a tutor to his pupil because, for example, the bishop—or his episcopal dignity—was a perpetual tutor and enjoyed the usufruct of his pupil's property perpetually, whereas the ordinary tutor's office was limited in time (until the coming of age of the minor) and excluded usufruct.[207] All that, however, could not prevent the general acceptance of the rule that a juristic person or corporation was privileged and treated like a person under age.

Those tenets were common knowledge in England as they were elsewhere. Bracton dealt with that question very expertly:

> Since the Church is in the place of a minor, it acquires and retains [property] through its rector like a minor through his tutor. And although the rector may die, the church does not forfeit its claim . . . any more so than a minor if his guardian dies.[208]

"Here we have," says Maitland, "a juristic person, the church, with a natural person as its guardian, and with a patron and ordinary to check that guardian in his administrative acts, for some things the rector cannot do without the consent of patron and ordinary."[209] Noteworthy is a case of 1294—coming up before the court at a considerably later date, in the first year of Edward II—because here the connection with disinheritance becomes quite obvious. The court argued that

> a church, being always within age, takes the place of a minor; and it is not consonant with the law that persons within age should suffer

206 Gierke, *ibid.*, n.272; also Hostiensis, *Summa aurea*, col.414 (above, n.203).

207 Gierke, *ibid.*, 256,n.40, refers in the first place to *Glos.ord.*, on c.3,C.5,q.3, v. *quia episcopus*: "Nulla est enim comparatio inter tutores et praelatos, quia tutor est temporalis, praelatus est perpetuus; tutor non utitur bonis pupilli, sicut praelatus bonis ecclesiae; tutela est onus, sed praelatura est honor etc."

208 Bracton, fol.226b, Woodbine, III,177: "Et cum ecclesia fungatur vice minoris, acquiritur per rectorem et retinet per eundem, sicut minor per tutorem. Et quamvis moriatur rector, non tamen cadit ecclesia a seisina sua de aliquo, de quo rector seisitus moritur, nomine ecclesiae suae, non magis quam minor si custos suus moriatur et pervenerit in alterius custodiam: et per hoc non mutatur status minoris."

209 Pollock and Maitland, *History*, I,504; cf.503,n.2.

disherison by the negligence of their guardians, or should be prevented from action if they wished to speak up concerning those things which through their guardians have been perpetrated in disherison of themselves who are within age.[210]

In other words, the negligence of a guardian may not lead to disherison of the pupil, and the negligence of the rector of a church may not lead to disherison of his church. On the contrary, the minor (that is, the church) is to have its day in the king's court in order to get the disherison revoked.

By that time, however, the doctrine concerning the eternal minority of Church and *respublica* was transferred to the Crown: it was fused with the complex idea of inalienability of Crown rights or Crown property and with the maxim *Nullum tempus currit contra regem*. In the last decade of the thirteenth century cases came up in court in which the "disherison of the Crown" was discussed;[211] and a little later we find the vocabulary for the minority of corporations, customary in romano-canonical procedure, applied to king and Crown. This was true especially in cases of *Quare impedit* in which the Crown claimed advowson over a church. In the case *King v. Latimer* (10 Edward II), the official Record of the Case expounds:

> [The king] presented to the aforementioned church his aforementioned clerk Robert as of the right of his Crown which is always, so to say, in the age of a minor and against which in this case no time runs. . . .[212]

[210] *Placitorum abbreviatio*, 304 (Norfolk), 1 Edward II: "Set quia ecclesia que semper est infra etatem, fungitur vice minoris, nec est iuri consonum quod infra etatem existentes per negligentiam custodum suorum exhereditacionem paciantur, seu ab accione repellantur, si loqui voluerint de hiis que per custodes suos ad ipsorum infra etatem exhereditacionem minus rite facta fuerunt, quin potius ad ipsam revocandam audiantur in curia Regis et ad hoc admittantur ex consilio curiae, dictum est predicto Adam etc." Cf. *Year Books, 22 Edward I* (London, 1873, Rolls Series), 33: "le Eglise est deinz age"; see Pollock and Maitland, *History*, I,503,n.2. See also *Year Books, 10 Edward II, 1316-17*, Y.B. Ser., XXI (Selden Society, LIV, 1935), 197: [Serjeant Toudeby] ". . . kar ele [seint Eglise] doit de resoun estre deinz age touz jurs en mayn de gardeyne." The guardian of the Church universal was, of course, the pope. See, e.g., Baldus, on *D.,4,4,39,n.45,fol.234*[v]: "Ecclesia sine papa nihil agit, ideo oportet [quod] per alium regatur, sicut et regitur minor."

[211] *Select Cases in the King's Council*, pp.iixf.

[212] *Year Books, 10 Edward II, 1316-17*, 46 (Record of the case): "J(ohannes) Rex ad predictam ecclesiam presentavit predictum Robertum clericum suum ut de iure corone sue que semper est quasi minoris etatis et cui in casu nullum tempus currit etc." This is the case found also in *Placitorum abbreviatio*, 339 (15 Edward II), which Pollock and Maitland, *History*, I,525,n.2, refer to. For the writ *Quare impedit*, see Holdsworth, *History of English Law*, III,661,No.ii.

In the same year, Justice Scrope of Common Pleas argued, in *King v. Prior of Worksop*, that the title to a church derived from King John, the ruling king's great-grandfather,

> and we have said how he was seised of this advowson as of the right of his Crown, and no right can outweigh the right of his Crown against our lord the king, for it is always within age and cannot lose in court. . . .[213]

Justice Scrope, however, was not always consistent in his arguments, for in the *Latimer* case, where the official Record clearly talks about the nonage of the *Crown*, Scrope said:

> And the king has spoken of the right of his Crown also, whereas on such a right no time runs against the king because *he* [the king] is always within age, wherefore we ask judgment for our lord the king. . . .[214]

Here, as well as on other occasions, the difference between Crown and king is blurred: the judges, perhaps misled by the fiscal maxim "No time runs against the king," wrongly attributed minority to the king where obviously they meant the Crown. That lack of precision was noticed by the justices themselves; for when, in the case of the *Prior of Worksop*, Justice Scrope slipped and talked about the nonage of the *king*, Serjeant Toudeby interfered with a noteworthy epigrammatic remark: "The king is only guardian of the Crown."[215] That perfectly correct insight into the matter, however, did not prevent Toudeby, at a later hearing of the same case, from falling into the same trap and likewise talking about the *king* "who is always within age and against whom therefore time does not run." Whereupon Chief Justice Bereford of Common Pleas interjected: "If the king were always within age,

---

[213] *Ibid.*, 74: ". . . et avoms dit coment y fut seisi de cel avouson cum du dreit de sa Coroune. ou nul dreit sur dreit de sa Coroune ne pust a nostre seignur le Roi qe touz jurs est deinz age et ne put perdre en curt."

[214] *Ibid.*, 45: ". . . et le Roy ad parlé du droit et de sa Coroune. ou nul temps de teu dreit encurt au Roi pur ceo q'il est toz jurs deynz age." See also Justice Scrope (*ibid.*, 75): ". . . et le Roy est touz jours deinz age issint qe encountre ly nul temps ne court quaunt a maintener l'estat de sa Coroune . . ."

[215] *Ibid.*, 74: "le Roy n'est qe gardein de la Coroune." It was almost proverbial with the jurists to say: "Rex debet esse *tutor regni*, non depopulator nec dilapidator." See, e.g., Baldus, on the decretal of Honorius III (c.33 X 2,24), *Decretales*, fol.261. In other respects, the king was the "Patron paramount" (*Soverein Patroun*) of all churches in his country; *Year Books*, 17 *Edward III* (Rolls Series, 1901), pp.l-lii, and 538,No.396.

no deed which he makes, would bind him according to what you say; of which the contrary is true. . . ."[216]

The quibbling of the jurists sheds light on many details. We learn that the Crown, like a church, was treated as a corporation and that in this respect *corona* was coordinated with *ecclesia*; for perpetual nonage expresses unambiguously corporative character.[217] Moreover, we find that by implication the judges attributed, if inadvertently, to the king likewise a corporative character when they declared that he, the king, was always under age. At that, Justice Bereford correctly took offense: the acts of a minor had only limited validity, if any validity at all. In fact, the grants made by a king during his minority needed confirmation when the king came of age. This was true under Henry III, and it was still true under Henry VI, although in the meantime, during the minority of Edward III, some "peers and sages of the realm" asserted that the king's nonage would not defeat the King's gifts.[218] That opinion, of course, was a step in the direction of the more concise and rationalized legal tenets of the Tudor jurists who held that the king as King and as body politic was *never* under age nor sick nor senile. Hence, from the same corporational premises there could originate two diametrically opposed opinions: a king *ever* under age versus a king *never* under age. In either case, of course, the intention was to emphasize the exceptional position of the king and his rights, that is, the perpetuity which he shared with the Crown. But whereas the Tudor lawyers arrived more or less at a fusion of the King body politic with the perfections of the Crown—Bacon talks about "the body politic of the Crown," though he continues: "That the king in law shall never be said to be within age"[219]—their mediaeval predecessors arrived at a

---

[216] *Ibid.*, 198, for Bereford: "Si le Roi fut tut temps deinz age, nul fet q'il fet li liereit a vostre dit. *cuius contrarium est verum etc.*" See also *Year Books, 5 Edward II, 1311*, Y.B. Ser. x (Selden Society, LXIII, 1944), 167, where Toudeby likewise says that "the king is always within age etc., and in different places he can change his title to the same property." Bereford occasionally opined that "le roy est sur la ley," and in that he was sided by Toudeby ("et pur ceo est il [the king] sanz piere et passe tote la ley"); cf. *Year Books, 8 Edward II, 1314-15*, Y.B. Ser. XVII (Selden Society, XLI, 1924), 74-75. How difficult it was for English lawyers to distinguish between the king's capacities has been stressed by G. O. Sayles, *Select Cases in the Court of King's Bench under Edward I* (Selden Society, LVIII, 1939), III,xliiif.

[217] Maitland, *Sel.Ess.*, 106.

[218] Holdsworth, *History of English Law*, III,464.

[219] Bacon, *Post-nati*, 668; above, Ch.I,n.9.

confusion of the king's as yet undivided capacities with a corporational Crown. The arguments of the judges around 1300 appear strangely illogical when, furthermore, we think of the argument of Serjeant Toudeby who, in full agreement with the teaching of canonists and legists, stated that "the king was only the guardian of the Crown."[220] For to the perpetual minor, the Crown, there belonged a perpetual adult as guardian, a king who, like the Crown, never died, was never under age, never sick and never senile. In that respect, finally, Justice Bereford was perfectly sound in his judgment when he stated that if the *king* were a perpetual minor, he, the king, could not be held responsible for what he was doing, which certainly was contrary to the facts. Above all, however, the minority theory was defeated by the king's duties as "guardian of the Crown," since a guardian by definition had to be of age.

It is quite obvious that the judges around 1300 found it extremely difficult to coordinate with the king's office and person the relatively new theory concerning a corporation's perpetual minority, which insouciantly they transferred from the *respublica* and Church to the Crown. While most likely they would never have ventured to maintain that a bishop was "always under age," since it was easy to distinguish between the bishop and the bishopric, the undefined and hazy notion of "Crown," which in so many respects coincided with the king's power and dignity, led them astray. The judges under Edward II thus arrived at a confusion similar to that of the magnates of 1308, who, as it were, severed the infant Crown from its adult guardian, whereas they really intended to sever an individual from his guardianship. The judges were certainly mistaken when they applied the corporational nonage theory to the Crown which itself was a composite body encompassing the king as head and the lords spiritual and secular as limbs. By confusing the king with the Crown, however, and by attributing now to the king, if by mistake only, the corporational character of a perpetual minor, those jurists were about to create a genuine corporation sole: the nonage king. Had they continued in that illogical vein, they should have arrived at creating some other king to be the guardian of the fictitious non-

---

[220] See above, n.215; also, for the king as administrator of the fisc, above, Ch.IV, n.310.

age king, and so forth in eternal regress. Reason, however, prevailed: the court pointed out that the king was "only the guardian of the Crown," and the whole argument concerning the minority of the Crown soon disappeared from legal discussions. Nevertheless, we notice how easily one might arrive at the conclusion that the king was a corporation all by himself. Verily, "the corporation of the Crown utterly differeth from all other corporations within the realm."[221]

At this juncture we should probably recall the idea of dynastic continuity implying the hereditary descent of the Crown and thereby also the dynasty's hereditary guardianship of the Crown. That dynastic point of view was mentioned incidentally by Edward II when, shortly after his accession and before his coronation, he wrote to a cardinal:

> Since we are ruling in the hereditary kingdom of England, one thing should be weighed above all with foresight and careful consideration, how . . . the rights . . . of our Crown and royal dignity may be preserved without diminution.[222]

In other words, in its individual ruling exponent the dynasty as such was the perpetual guardian of a perpetual Crown, or, more correctly, the perpetual head of a body of guardians whose limbs were then the peers. It did not pass unnoticed that by its continuity the dynasty differed from the customary heads of corporations whose office was not hereditary. None but the king was entitled to talk about his royal power and royal estate "and his *heirs* thereto."[223] In the case of a normal corporate body, however, one began to grow conscious of the word "heirs," and by the fourteenth century the jurists would correctly replace the word "heirs" by "successors,"[224] a distinction which later on gave Bacon a good opportunity to deny altogether the applicability of ecclesiastico-corporational parallels to the Crown.

[221] Bacon, *Post-nati*, 667.

[222] Rymer, *Foedera*, ii,2,21f; Richardson, "Coronation Oath," 62,n.91.

[223] See, e.g., the Statute of York; Lodge and Thornton, *Documents*, 129, No.4. Vice versa the king's predecessors were called his "ancestors"; see, e.g., Sayles, *Select Cases* (Selden Society, lvii, 1938), ii,p.lxi, n.1: "The act of the king or his ancestors ought not to be judged without consulting him." See also *Year Books, 17 Edward III* (ed. Pike; Rolls Series, 1901), Introd., pp.l-li, concerning advowson of churches founded "by the king's ancestors."

[224] Those observations have been made by L. O. Pike, in the Introduction to his edition of *Year Books, 16 Edward III* (Rolls Series, 1896), i,xlivf, also lxxxivf; cf. Holdsworth, iii,483.

For no man can shew me in all corporations of England, of what nature soever, whether they consist of one person, or of many, or whether they be temporal or ecclesiastical—not any one takes to him or his heirs, but all to him and his successors. . . . For the king takes to him and his heirs in the manner of a natural body, and the word "successor" is but superfluous: and where it is used, it is ever duly placed after the word "heirs": the king, his heirs and successors.[225]

It was indeed the amalgamation of the dynastic continuity of the natural body with the perpetuality of the Crown as a political body in the person of the ruling king which accounts for many ambiguities and inconsistencies in late-mediaeval English political theory.

To summarize, we find ourselves involved in a tangle of intersecting, overlapping, and contradictory strands of political thought all of which somehow converge in the notion of Crown. The Crown was the owner of inalienable fiscal property; the Crown defended inalienable rights "which touched all"; and legal disputes arising therefrom as well as criminal cases and actions in which the courts Christian were involved, were treated invariably as pleas of the Crown. The Crown, as the embodiment of all sovereign rights—within the realm and without—of the whole body politic, was superior to *all* its individual members, including the king, though not separated from them. In many respects the Crown would coincide with the king as the head of the body politic, and it certainly coincided with him dynastically, since the Crown descended on the king by right hereditary. At the same time, however, the Crown appeared also as a composite body, an aggregate of the king and those responsible for maintaining the inalienable rights of the Crown and the kingdom. As a perpetual minor, the Crown itself had corporational character—with the king as its guardian, though again not with the king alone, but with that composite body of king and magnates who together were said to be, or to represent, the Crown. There were indeed innumerable aspects of that notion of Crown, which people then applied so thoughtlessly and easily to all sorts of capacities and competences, and it would hardly be justified to blame judges or magnates or the kings themselves for their failure to define clearly

[225] Bacon, *Post-nati*, 668.

and unambiguously what the Crown was. Crown, after all, was then a live conception, and owing to its lifelike complexity it resisted all efforts to grasp its essence in unambiguous terms: what appeared as correct from one angle, was felt to be wrong from another.

What can be said is, as Sir Francis Bacon put it, that king and Crown were "inseparable, though distinct."[226] Also another thing seems to emerge quite clearly: that the Crown was rarely "personified" but very often "bodified." Comparable to the *corpus mysticum*, the Crown was and remained a complex body, a body politic which was not separated from either its royal constituent as the head nor from those co-responsible for the *status coronae* as limbs. Who those limbs were depended upon the occasion: they were sometimes the councillors, sometimes the magnates, and sometimes the Lords together with the Commons in Parliament. The surprisingly long survival in England of the mediaeval organological concept of government was sanctioned by the existence of the representative body of Parliament in which the *corpus morale et politicum* of the kingdom really lived and became visible. To be sure, the Crown was individually ever present in the king; but the Crown could become also quasi-corporate *ad hoc*, for some purpose of taxation or jurisdiction or administration,[227] and corporately it became visible when actually the king wore the insignia (as Henry VIII said) "in the time of Parliament, wherein we as head and you as members are conjoined and knit together in one body politic."

At any rate, the Crown in late mediaeval England was not the fictitious person which the continental "State" became during and after the sixteenth century, a personification in its own right which was not only above its members, but also divorced from them. This step, apparently, was not taken in mediaeval England. For all that, however, fiction or traits of fictitiousness came into the picture also in England when the Tudor lawyers began to distinguish between the king's body natural and the king's body politic, and began to identify the latter, which bore all the features and attributes of an "angel" or other supernatural being, with the "body politic of the Crown"—not wholly perhaps, but

---

[226] *Ibid.*, 670.
[227] Cf. Post, "Quod omnes tangit," 223,nos.125f.

to a large extent. Those features of a highly abstract nature originated, in their entirety, in Canon Law and Roman Law where they served to characterize the only one-man corporation which the two Laws had constructed and which they described as *Dignitas.* The English lawyers adopted the essence of that notion and, while making little use of the notion as such in the sense of a fictitious person, they ingeniously adapted all its characteristics to existing English conditions and transferred all its ingredients to the most prominent office, that of the king, and to this office's symbol, the Crown.

3. Dignitas non moritur

A continuity of the king's natural body—or of individual kings acting in hereditary succession as "guardians of the Crown"—was vouched for by the dynastic idea. The perpetuity of the sovereign rights of the whole body politic, of which the king was the head, was understood to be resting in the Crown, hazy though this notion may have been. Both principles—that of continuous succession of individuals and that of corporate perpetuity of the collective—seem to have coincided in a third notion without which the speculations about a king's "two bodies" would remain almost incomprehensible: the *Dignitas.*

It will be recalled that ever since the twelfth century the custom arose to emphasize in some groups of writs (especially those concerned with the courts Christian, but others as well) that certain legal cases pertained *ad coronam et dignitatem regis.*[228] Moreover, kings not rarely were charged—we may think of Edward II or Richard II—with having "blemished and prejudiced the Crown and the royal Dignity and the heirs Kings of England."[229] It would be a mistake, though, to understand the word Dignity only in its moral or ethical qualifications, that is, as something contrary to an "undignified" conduct—although this connotation was by no means absent. Likewise, it would be a mistake to assume that the terms Crown and Dignity were coterminous and exchangeable, or simply redundant, even though,

---

228 Above, nos.107f.

229 See, e.g., *Rot.Parl.*, III,360, the cancellation (in 1397) of the judgment against the Despensers which was said to have been "emblemissement et prejudice de sa corone et sa dignitee royale et de ses heires roys d'Engleterre." See Hartung, "Krone," 17f; also 18,n.4.

more often than not, they were lacking precision and were applied thoughtlessly and confusingly. The Crown, as we have tried to explain, was something that referred chiefly to the sovereignty of the whole collective body of the realm, so that the preservation of the integrity of the Crown became a matter "that touches all." The Dignity, however, differed from the Crown. It referred chiefly to the singularity of the royal office, to the sovereignty vested in the king by the people, and resting individually in the king alone. This, to be sure, did not imply that the royal Dignity was something that touched the king alone and did *not* touch all. Since the king's Dignity, together with his prerogative rights, had to be maintained and respected for the sake of the whole realm, the Dignity too was of a public, and not merely private, nature. It was as little a private matter as the *officium regis*, with which it largely coincided.

Officium and *Dignitas*, however, were not precisely the same thing either, and the distinction between the two notions sometimes caused trouble. The jurists—Bartolus, for example, or Baldus—pointed out most correctly that a person might have the Dignity of Senator or Proconsul, or have the Dignity of a *super-illustris*, *illustris*, *spectabilis*, or *clarissimus*, and yet be without Office. Bartolus, therefore, held that, strictly speaking, we would have to say "that the Office itself was not a Dignity, but had a Dignity attached (*habet dignitatem annexam*)."[230] For all the correctness of these distinctions, the jurists at large had yet to succumb to the terminology which the Church and Canon Law had been developing at least since the thirteenth century. For according to canonical usage it was, so far as the notions were distinguished at all,[231] the *Dignitas* rather than the *Officium*

[230] Bartolus, on *C.*12,1,rubr.,n.38, fol.53ᵛ: "proprie enim loquendo aliud est officium, aliud dignitas," and *ibid.*, n.44: "vere enim officium ipsum non est dignitas, sed habet dignitatem annexam." Baldus, on c.8 X 1,2,n.9, *In Decretales*, fol.19: "Dignitas est in habendo officium et in illud exequendo. Et nota quod de iure civili sunt quatuor dignitates tantum proprie loquendo, scilicet superillustris, illustris," etc.

[231] The canonists seemed to be quite ready to identify *officium* and *dignitas*; see, e.g., Johannes Andreae, on c.28 X 3,5,n.13, *Novella*, fol.35: "Sciendum est quod dignitas et personatus et officium videntur synonima." His reference is Innocent IV, *Apparatus*, on the same decretal, nos.6-7 (Lyon, 1578), fol.237, who makes a certain restriction with regard to *personatus*, "quia *personae* ecclesiarum dicuntur in Anglia, quae praesunt ecclesiis" (that is, *parsons*). See, for the connection of "parson-person" with the Corporation sole, Maitland, *Sel.Essays*, 87.

which became the subject of those legal speculations from which the *Dignitas* finally emerged as a corporate entity.

PHOENIX

As usual, it was on the basis of an individual and very concrete case that the canonistic theory reached its full growth. Under the pontificate of Pope Alexander III, the abbots of Leicester and Winchester served as delegate judges. When Winchester died, Leicester waited for the election of a new abbot and then resumed his work together with the successor, the newly-elected Abbot of Winchester. The pope approved of that substitution because, he explained, the power of delegate judge had originally been conferred on *The Abbot of Winchester*, mentioning only the place name, but without mentioning an individual name; the commission, therefore, carried over automatically to the new abbot, Winchester's successor.[232] Though the practice itself may have been observed long before, it was nevertheless Pope Alexander III—himself an outstanding jurist—who rationalized the existing practice and formulated a legal principle, the implications of which the jurisprudents were quick to grasp and expand upon. The author of an *Ordo iudiciarius*, a book on canonical procedure, of the beginning of the thirteenth century stressed the difference between a delegation made with the mention of a proper name and one omitting the proper name; that is, in technical language, the difference between a delegation *facta personae* and one *facta dignitati*.[233] At the same time, a canonist, Damasus (ca. 1215), in a gloss on Pope Alexander's decretal, produced the decisive phrase: *Dignitas nunquam perit*, "The Dignity never perishes, although individuals die every day."[234] When included in the *Liber Extra* of Gregory IX, the decretal—known as *Quoniam abbas*—received the succinct heading: "A delegation made to the Dignity without expressing a proper name, passes

232 See c.14 X 1,29, ed. Friedberg, II,162: ". . . quia sub expressis nominibus locorum et non personarum commissio literarum a nobis emanavit."

233 [Damasus], *De ordine judiciario*, c.42, ed. Agathon Wunderlich, *Anecdota quae processum civilem spectant* (Göttingen, 1841), 84: "Item de persona ad personam, puta, si scribatur abbati Sancti Proculi, nomine proprio non expresso, extenditur ad eius successorem" (see also c.43). Gierke, *Gen.R.*, III,271,n.73; also Kuttner, *Repertorium*, 428,n.3, who (with H. Kantorowicz) doubts that Damasus was the author of the *Ordo iudiciarius*, although it was written ca. 1215.

234 Damasus, on c.14 X 1,29 (quoted by Gierke, *loc.cit.*): ". . . quia dignitas nunquam perit, individua vero quotidie pereunt."

on to the successor."[235] Finally, the *Glossa ordinaria*, composed around 1245 by Bernard of Parma, while paraphrasing that heading, gave also the clear reason for the existing practice: ". . . because predecessor and successor are understood as one person, since the Dignity does not die."[236] The fiction of the identity of the persons of predecessor and successor had been formulated in those very years also by Pope Innocent IV in his *Apparatus* on the Decretals, and it remained the stock phrase of the glossators and post-glossators for generations to come.[237]

Dignitas non moritur, "the Dignity does not die"—this, of course, was a principle which referred not only to the appointee but also to the dignitary making the appointment. For the delegating sovereign, the Pope, could make the delegation likewise in two ways: he could let it originate either from his person, in which case the delegation would terminate on the pope's death; or from the Dignity of the Holy See, in which case the delegation of power would be binding to the succeeding pope as well, *quia Sedes ipsa non moritur*, "because the [Holy] See itself does not die." Through Pope Boniface VIII this maxim—though quite current before—became authoritative because he inserted it into a decretal of his *Liber Sextus*, saying that a benefice given to a prelate on the part of the Holy See, unless revoked, "will last perpetually because the Holy See does not die."[238] In this case, it is the perpetuity of the Dignity of the Holy See which makes the renewal of grants unnecessary because, says the glossator of the *Liber Sextus*, "the incumbent of the papacy or Dignity may die, but the *papatus, dignitas*, or *imperium* is forever."[239]

---

[235] Friedberg, II,162: "Delegatio facta dignitati non expresso nomine proprio transit ad successorem."

[236] *Glos.ord.*, on c.14 X 1,29, v. *substitutum*: ". . . quia [praedecessor et successor] pro una persona intelliguntur: quia dignitas non moritur."

[237] Innocent, *Apparatus*, on c.28 X 1,6, n.5, fol.39, refers to *Quoniam abbas* when he says: "finguntur enim eaedem personae cum praedecessoribus (not substituted canons though, because they do not succeed to a Dignity)." Cf. Gierke, *Gen.R.*, III,272,n.77; see above, Ch.VI,n.97.

[238] See c.5 VI 1,3, Friedberg, II,939: "Tunc enim, quia sedes ipsa non moritur, durabit [beneplacitum] perpetuo, nisi a successore fuerit revocata [sc. gratia]."

[239] Johannes Andreae, *Novella*, on c.5 VI 1,3,n.5 (quoted by Gierke, *Gen.R.*, III,271,n.73): "tenens papatum vel dignitatem est corruptibilis, papatus tamen, dignitas vel imperium semper est." See also *Glos.ord.* (Johannes Andreae), on that decretal, vv. *Apostolice sedis* and *non moritur*. The whole doctrine, of course, deepened the split between office and office-holder, and the imperial chancery was not slow at recognizing the advantages for anti-papal propaganda offered by the decretal *Quoniam abbas*. It is clearly with reference to this decretal that (pre-

Once the principle was established that a Dignity never dies, the jurists could not fail to notice that certain similarities prevailed between the *Dignitas quae non moritur* and a corporation, an *universitas quae non moritur*. By maintaining the fictitious oneness of the predecessors with potential successors, all of whom were present and incorporated in the actual incumbent of the Dignity, the jurists constructed a fictitious person, a "corporation by succession" composed of all those vested successively with that particular Dignity—a fiction which makes us think of the witches in Shakespeare's *Macbeth* (IV,i,112ff), who conjure up that uncanny ghostly procession of Macbeth's predecessor kings whose last one bears the "glass" showing the long file of successors. By this fiction, at any rate, the plurality of persons necessary to make up a corporation was achieved—a plurality, that is, which did not expand within a given Space, but was determined exclusively by Time.[240] This was doubtless the prevailing theory until early modern times.[241]

Perhaps no less profound an aspect of the nature of that corporation by succession was produced by a philosophic afterthought. When commenting on the decretal *Quoniam abbas*, Bernard of Parma, the composer of the ordinary Gloss, very ingeniously

---

sumably) Petrus de Vinea writes (*MGH, Const.*, II,297,23ff): "non in contemptu papalis officii vel apostolice dignitatis . . . set persone prevaricationem arguimus." See Brian Tierney, *Foundations of Conciliar Theory* (Cambridge, 1955), 87,n.4, who in general stresses the competence of Petrus de Vinea with regard to Canon Law.

[240] See above, pp. 312f, and below, n.241. For the corporation by succession, see Gierke, *Gen.R.*, III,271f. Dr. R. Walzer, in Oxford, kindly called my attention to a passage in Al-Fārābī's *Model State* in which somewhat similar ideas are expressed: "The kings of the excellent state, who succeed each other at different times, one after the other, are all like one soul (!) as if they were one king, who remains the same all the time." See Al-Fārābī, *Idées des habitants de la cité vertueuse*, trans. by R. P. Jaussen, Youssef Karam, and J. Chlala (Publications de l'Institut français d'archéologie orientale: Textes et traductions d'auteurs orientaux, IX [Cairo, 1949]), 87. The idea of the Arabian author may be styled a qualitative monopsychism: if all kings are equally excellent, an individuation makes no sense because they are all like one king; and this would be true (as the author points out in the same chapter) not only with regard to Time—that is, to successive kings living at different times—but also with regard to Space, to all excellent kings living in various places at the same time. In the case of *Dignitas*, however, the unifying qualitative element is in the *Dignitas* itself rather than in the individual incumbents, who are "dignitaries" regardless of their personal merits. On the other hand, it would be difficult to identify without qualification the *Dignitas* with the Soul. At any rate, the parallel is interesting enough to be recorded here.

[241] Gierke, *Gen.R.*, IV,30, where the definition is found (n.32): "universitas . . . ratione plurium de futuro saltem."

introduced, or merely borrowed, a metaphor both curious and striking. He said that a Dignity—as, for example: Abbot of Winchester—was not the proper name of a person, but only singled a person out; it designated "a singular, like the *Phoenix*, and [was] likewise an appellative."[242] This parallel between Dignity and the fabulous bird of Classical and Christian myths may strike us as rather abstruse; later glossators, however, such as Johannes Andreae and Baldus, not only accepted that simile but drew from it some rather enlightening conclusions.

We have to remember that the mythical bird was indeed an extraordinary creature: there was always only one Phoenix alive at a time, who, after having lived his cycle of many years—500 or more—set his nest ablaze, fanned the fire with his wings, and perished in the flames, while from the glowing cinders the new Phoenix arose.[243] The lore of that bird, contradictory in many respects, is of minor importance here. In pagan as well as in Christian art the Phoenix usually signified the idea of immortality, of *perpetuitas* and *aevum* (αἰών).[244] The "self-begott'n bird," however, exemplified also virginity[245] and it served further as a symbol

---

[242] See *Glos.ord.*, on c.14 X 1,29, v. *substitutum*: "[hoc nomen: abbas talis loci] non est proprium nomen, sed singulare, ut phoenix, et appellativum similiter." It is possible, of course, that Bernard of Parma borrowed the metaphor from another author; but it was he, after all, who incorporated it into the ordinary Gloss and therefore made it widely known.

[243] The modern literature on the Phoenix, insufficiently rendered by H. Leclercq, "Phénix," *DACL*, XIV:1 (1939), 682-691, is considerable. See the thesis of Mary Cletus Fitzpatrick, *Lactantii De Ave Phoenice* (University of Pennsylvania thesis, Philadelphia, 1933), with a good bibliography; also E. Rapisarda, *L'Ave Fenice di L. Cecilio Firmiano Lattanzio* (Raccolta di studi di letteratura cristiana antica, 4, 1946), 10,n.1. The most important study is by Jean Hubaux and Maxime Leroy, *Le mythe du Phénix* (Bibl. de la faculté de philosophie et lettres de l'université de Liège, LXXXII [Liège and Paris, 1939]), who reprint a great number of relevant texts; for some important remarks on that study, see A.-J. Festugière, "Le symbole du Phénix et le mysticism hermétique," *Monuments Piot*, XXXVIII (1941), 147-151; further Paul Perdrizet, "La tunique liturgique historiée de Saqqara," *Mon. Piot*, XXXIV (1934), 110ff, for the representation of a Phoenix on a liturgical garment; and Jean Lassus, "La mosaïque du Phénix provenant des fouilles d'Antioche," *Mon. Piot*, XXXVI (1936), 81-122; see further Carl-Martin Edsman, *Ignis divinus* (Lund, 1949), 178-203, and Henri Stern, *Le calendrier de 354* (Institut français d'archéologie de Beyrouth, LV [Paris, 1953]), 146f. For the later Middle Ages, see Burdach, *Rienzo*, 83ff, and passim.

[244] Hubaux-Leroy, 38f; Stern, 145f; Festugière, 149f.

[245] Below, nos.251ff. The virginal bird suitingly became an emblem of the virgin queen, Elizabeth; see Yates, "Queen Elizabeth as Astraea," 37,55f,62,74,79, with pls. 17g,18b. Virginity, of course, was not all that the Phoenix signified in Elizabethan state symbolism; for the bird was also a paragon of royalty on account of its uniqueness or singularity, and by the sixteenth century it served for more than one reason as a royal emblem; see, e.g., Henry Green, *Shakespeare and the Emblem Writers*, 380ff.

of the resurrection of Christ, and of Christians in general.[246] To the resurrection motif Johannes Andreae actually alluded in his lengthy Phoenix gloss.[247] This, however, was only a side issue; for juristically the singleness and uniqueness of the bird appeared to be of greater importance. Baldus, at any rate, when epitomizing the arguments about the decretal *Quoniam abbas*, availed himself of that aspect of the symbol, which allowed him to draw the accurate philosophic conclusion: "The Phoenix is a unique and most singular bird in which the whole kind *(genus)* is conserved in the individual."[248] Evidently, Baldus had a clear analogy in mind. To him the Phoenix represented one of the rare cases in which the individual was at once the whole existing species so that indeed species and individual coincided. The species, of course, was immortal; the individual, mortal. The imaginary bird[249] therefore disclosed a duality: it was at once Phoenix and

246 This, of course, was the standard interpretation on the part of Christian authors; see Fitzpatrick, 24ff,n.67; Lassus, 108ff, and others. Of great influence was, as might be expected, *Physiologus*, c.IX: "Est aliud volatile quod dicitur phoenix; huius figuram gerit dominus noster Iesus Christus, qui dicit in evangelio suo: Potestatem habeo ponendi animam meam et iterum sumendi eam (John 10: 18)." See *Physiologus latinus*, ed. F. J. Carmody (Paris, 1939), 20f; also Hubaux-Leroy, pp.xxxiiff, esp. xxxv: Φοίνιξ . . . τὴν τοῦ Κυρίου τριήμερον ταφὴν καὶ ἀνάστασιν ὑπογράφων. See also next note.

247 Johannes Andreae, on c.14 X 1,29,nos.30f, *Novella*,fols.206ᵛ-207: "[et ibi, Phenix] fertur esse avis ex qua mortua nascitur alia, et non invenitur nisi una . . ." He then reproduces the narration of St. Ambrose, *Hexaemeron*, v,23, *PL*,XIV,253, and says: "et ex hoc invehit ibi Ambrosius contra illos, qui non credunt resurrectionem." There follows the story of St. Cecilia who "ad exemplum phenicis convertit beatum Maximum et eo postmodum decollato pro fide, in eius tumulo fecit sculpi phenicem, cuius exemplo animatus Christianus fieri et Christi martyr esse promeruit." Cf. *Vita et martyrium S. Caeciliae*, c.21, ed. L. Surius, *Historiae seu vitae Sanctorum* (Turin, 1879), XI (Nov.22), 651; also Paolo Aringhi, *Roma subterranea novissima* (Rome, 1651), II,451. He then refers to Isidore of Seville, *Ethymol.*, XII,7,22, and concludes his long gloss with the story about the appearance of a Phoenix in the time of St. Peter under the emperor Claudius, a story which ultimately may go back to Tacitus, *Ann.*, VI,28. To this catalogue of authorities, Baldus then adds Seneca, *Epist.*, XLII,1, and Albertus Magnus, *De proprietatibus rerum*, XII,15.

248 Baldus, on c.14 X 1,29,n.3, *In Decretales*, fol.107, quotes the Gloss (above, n.242), and adds: "Est autem phoenix avis unica singularissima, in qua totum genus servatur in individuo."

249 Whether Baldus believed in the bird or not, is irrelevant, since he and the other jurists used it merely as a metaphor. Frederick II actually refused to believe the Phoenix story as narrated by Pliny (cf. his *De arte venandi*, II,c.2, trans. C. A. Wood and F. M. Fyfe, *The Art of Falconry* [Stanford University, California, 1943], 109), nevertheless, he was one of the first mediaeval princes to be compared to that unique bird; see Nicholas of Bari, ed. Kloos, in *DA*, XI,170,§5: "Magnus est dignitate honoris . . . Ipse est sol in firmamento mundi . . . Ipse est cui flectitur omne genu . . . Unus est et secundum non habet, fenix pulcherrima pennis aureis decorata."

Phoenix-kind, mortal as an individual, though immortal too, because it was the whole kind. It was at once individual and collective, because the whole species reproduced no more than a single specimen at a time.

This queer ornithological dualism had not passed unnoticed by pagan and Christian mythographers. Quite the contrary, they never failed to indicate it. They interpreted the Phoenix, since he engendered himself, as ἀρρετόθηλυς, a creature having two sexes, a hermaphrodite.[250] Lactantius apostrophed him "female or male or neither or both," for the Phoenix entered into no compacts with Venus: he sired himself by his death.

> He is son to himself, is his own father, and his own heir.
> He is his own nurse, and is ever a foster-child to himself.
> He is himself, yet not himself, who is the same, yet not the same.[251]

Claudian described the bird in similar terms: the rise of the new-born Phoenix from the ashes was caused by neither conception nor semen; he is his own father and his own son with none to create him: "He who was father, leaps forth now the same as son, and succeeds as a new one. . . ." Claudian stresses the "twin-life" (*gemina vita*) of the Phoenix, separated only by the pyre, but claims that the borderline between those two lives is hardly discernible—*O felix heresque tui*, "Oh happy one and heir to thyself."[252] That the bird was always the same and "heir to its own body" was emphasized, a third time, by Ambrose.[253] On the

---

[250] Festugière, in *Mon. Piot*, xxxviii,148f; Hubaux-Leroy, 7, 12f. See also above, Ch. I,n.8.

[251] Lactantius, *Carmen de ave Phoenice*, 163ff:

> Femina seu mas sit seu neutrum seu sit utrumque,
> Felix quae Veneris foedera nulla colit . . .
> Ipsa sibi proles, suus est pater et suus heres,
> Nutrix ipsa sui, semper alumna sibi.
> Est eadem sed non eadem, quae est ipsa nec ipsa est. . . .

The text is that revised by Hubaux-Leroy, p.xv, which deviates in some instances from the edition of Samuel Brandt, in *CSEL*, xxvii (1893), 146f.

[252] Claudian, *Phoenix*, 23f,69ff,101, ed. Hubaux-Leroy, xxiff:

> Hic neque concepto fetu nec semine surgit,
> Sed pater est prolesque sui nulloque creante . . .
> Qui fuerat genitor, natus nunc prosilit idem
> Succeditque novus: geminae confinia vitae
> Exiguo medius discrimine separat ignis . . .
> O felix heresque tui. . . .

[253] Ambrose, *Expositio in Ps. CXVIII*, c.13, ed. Petschenig (*CSEL*, LXII), 428,19: ". . . et sui heres corporis et cineris sui factus."

other hand, Tertullian remarked that the Phoenix's dying day was also his birthday, "another, yet the same."[254] The coincidence of dying day and birthday, finally, was stressed also by Zeno of Verona, who however added that the Phoenix was "his own genus, his own end, his own beginning."[255] But already Ovid had said that whereas "other birds originate from others of their genus," there is one bird, the Phoenix, which renews itself and reseeds itself.[256]

The ancient mythographers and apologetics thus clearly recognized that some kind of duality was an essential feature of the Phoenix; but when expanding on that duality, they thought chiefly of the bird's androgynous character, and this concept, in its turn, had the backing of Orphic and Hermetic doctrines—relations interesting by themselves, though hardly relevant here.[257] It is relevant, however, to understand how the mediaeval jurists resuscitated, as it were, the tenets of ancient mysticism by their speculative fiction theory and how they made the lore of many hues of the fabulous Phoenix useful and applicable to legal thought.

If, according to Lactantius, Claudian, and Ambrose, the Phoenix was "heir to himself," it will be appropriate to recall the importance which the law of inheritance had for the corporational doctrines in general. We have to recall, in the first place, the gloss on the *Institutes*: "Father and son are one according to the fiction of law."[258] But there were other passages as well suggesting the

---

254 Tertullian, *De resurrectione carnis*, 13, *PL*,II,857B: "semetipsum lubenter funerans renovat, natali fine decedens atque succedens; iterum phoenix, ut iam nemo; iterum ipse, qui non iam, alius idem."

255 Zeno of Verona, *Tract.*, 1,16,9, *PL*, XI,381AB: ". . . ipsa [avis] est sibi uterque sexus, . . . ipsa genus, ipsa finis, ipsa principium, . . . mors natalicius dies, . . . non alia, sed quamvis melior alia, tamen prior ipsa." We should remember that the *natalicium* of saints and martyrs was the day of their death, and not their natural birthday.

256 Ovid., *Metam.*, xv,391f:

Haec tamen ex aliis generis primordia ducunt:
Una est, quae reparet seque ipsa reseminet, ales . . .

257 See Festugière, *op.cit.*, 149f, for αὐτόγονος, αὐτοπάτωρ, and other epithets; also for the *aevum* as represented by the Phoenix.

258 *Glos.ord.*, on *Inst.*3,1,3, v. *quasi*; see above, n.78. Cf. Giovanni Bortolucci, "La *Hereditas* come *Universitas*: Il dogma della successione nella personalità giuridica del defunto," *Atti del Congresso internazionale di Diritto Romano*, Section Rome, I (Pavia, 1934), 431-448, who summarizes the legal material and demonstrates strikingly that the theory descended, in the last analysis, from Plato and Greek philosophy in general.

oneness of father and son. When Frederick II, in a charter for his son Conrad, said that "by the benefice of an innate grace [the son] is held to be one person [with the father],"[259] he—or the responsible clerk—may have had Justinian's *Code* in mind where it is said that "father and son are understood to be by nature almost the same person."[260] Moreover, a similar remark was found in the *Decretum*.[261] In these cases, the fiction of law was actually supported by the philosophers—Aristotle and, in his wake, Aquinas—according to whose biogenetic doctrines the "form" ($\epsilon\tilde{\iota}\delta o\varsigma$) of the begetter and the begotten were the same owing to the seed's active power, which derived from the soul of the father and impressed itself upon the son.[262] Legal and philosophical doctrines then were combined with other arguments which were supposed to prove that a king's first-born son was even more than other sons the equal of his ruling father because he was, while the father still was living, one with the father in the royal Dignity. Again the jurists could refer to the *Decretum* where the king's son was called *rex iuvenis*[263] and where the prerogatives of the first-born were enumerated, for instance, the privilege of sitting at the right hand of the father.[264] An ardent

[259] Böhmer, *Acta imperii selecta*, I,265, No.301 (a.1233): ". . . [pure dilectionis obtentu] qua pater filium, sicut innate beneficio gratie una persona censetur . . ." For a fuller discussion of the theory and its application under Frederick II, especially in connection with the Kaiser-saga, see my paper "Zu den Rechtsgrundlagen der Kaisersage," *DA*, XIII (1957) 115-150.

[260] C.6,26,11: "Natura pater et filius eadem esse persona pene intelliguntur." The jurists referred also to *Glos.ord.*, on D.50,16,220, v. *Quam filii*: ". . . plus diligit filium pater, quam filius patrem. Sed quare hoc est? . . . nam cum quaelibet res conservationem sui desideret, et videat pater suam naturam in filio conservari . . ." Further to D.28,2,11: "[heredes] etiam vivo patre quodammodo domini existimantur" (referred to, e.g., by Petrus de Ancharano, *Consilia*, LXXXII,n.2, fol.40).

[261] See c.8,C.I,q.4, ed. Friedberg, I.419: ". . . unus erat cum illo," an idea often repeated by later canonists; see, e.g., *Glos.ord.*, on *Extravag. Joannis XXII*, III ('Execrabilis'), v. *sublimitatem eorum*: ". . . cum eadem persona fingatur esse [pater et filius]."

[262] Cf. Lesky, *Zeugungs- und Vererbungslehren* (above, n.61), 139, cf.134ff, 143ff, also 148ff; A. Mitterer, "Mann und Weib nach dem biologischen Weltbild des hl. Thomas und dem der Gegenwart," *ZfKT*, LVII (1933), 491-556, esp. 515 ("omne agens agit simile sibi"). See also above, n.258.

[263] See c.42,C.XXIV,q.1, ed. Friedberg, I,983; also Andreas of Isernia, *Usus feud.*, praelud.,n.33, fol.4v: "Filius talium regum dicitur rex etiam vivo patre" (with reference to the *Decretum*). Also Albericus de Rosate, on D.28,2,11,n.2, fol.101v, refers to the *Decretum* ("propter . . . spem succedendi filius Regis dicitur Rex, et sic de aliis dignitatibus"), but he stresses also the fact that, though the sons are "domini rerum patris, . . . non tamen possunt alienare nec de eis aliquid facere invito patre."

[264] *Glos.ord.*, on c.8,C.VII,q.1, v. *primatus*: "ius ergo primogeniturae (ut dicunt

defender of primogeniture such as Jean de Terre Rouge then could demonstrate that between a first-born son (*primogenitus*) and an only-begotten son (*unigenitus*) there sometimes was hardly a difference and that the one sitting at the right hand of the father was "one and the same in species and nature."²⁶⁵ In other words, he could build up almost a theology of primogeniture by using arguments of Aristotle and Aquinas, the *Code*, the *Institutes*, and the *Decretum*, and referring also to Alexander III's decretal *Quoniam abbas*, which had become a cornerstone of the doctrine of the oneness of predecessor and successor with regard to the Dignity.²⁶⁶

With all that, the lore of the Phoenix tied in smoothly, since it stressed almost without exception the personal identity of the dead Phoenix with his living successor; and other popular legal maxims strengthened that comparison. *Mortuus aperit oculos viventis*, "The dead opens the eyes of the living," said a proverb quoted by Baldus in order to show that one born unfree could become a freedman on the death of his master,²⁶⁷ and the proverb was quoted—with reference to Baldus—later by a French jurist,

[cf. Deuteronomy 21:17]) est dignitas talis: quia primogeniti prae aliis in festis sacrificia offerebant, et quod sedebant ad dexteram patris et quia cibos duplicatos recipiebant."

265 Terre Rouge, Tract.1,art.2,concl.10, p.40, points out that Christ was called by Luke (2: 7) the *primogenitus* "et tamen nullus fuit inde genitus," whereas Solomon (Prov. 4: 3) styled himself *unigenitus* although he was preceded by a brother who died (II Kings 12: 15-24). See further, *ibid.*, concl.1, p.35: ". . . quod pater et filius, licet distinguantur, supposito tamen unum idem sunt specie et natura nedum communi (quia uterque homo est), sed etiam in natura particulari patris . . ." Cf. concl.2: "Filiatio enim nihil aliud est, quam illa identitas particularis naturae praesens penetrans in filium [reference to *D.*50,16,220, v. *Quam filii*; see above, n.260] . . . Et pro hac consuetudine facit dictum Apostoli: 'Si filius, ergo heres' [Rom. 8: 17; Gal. 4: 7]." Cf. concl.3: ". . . quod filius vivente patre est secundum naturam dominus cum patre rerum patris. Probatur conclusio: nam ex quo . . . est eiusdem naturae cum patre, et idem cum patre vivente: ergo dominus cum patre . . . Pro hac conclusione facit etiam quod scribitur in Evangelio: 'Omnia quaecunque habet Pater, mea sunt' [Joh. 16: 15] . . . Et Luc.15 [:31]: 'Fili tu semper mecum es: scilicet per identitatem paternae naturae. Et omnia mea tua sunt . . .'" Cf. p.39 (concl.4): ". . . sedere autem a dextris patris, nihil aliud est, secundum Augustinum, quam conregnare patri: sicut ille qui considet regi ad dexteram, assidet ei in regnando et iudicando . . ." The Augustine place referred to must be an interpretation of Psalm 109, though it is not found in the *Enarratio in Ps. CIX.*

266 For Terre Rouge's reference to *Quoniam abbas*, see concl.2, p.35; for his references to Aristotle and Aquinas, see concl.1, and above, n.61; the legal passages, of course, were quoted over and over again.

267 Baldus, on *C.*7,15,3,n.2, fol.12.

André Tiraqueau, in order to elucidate the famous maxim of French law of inheritance, *Le mort saisit le vif*, "The dead seizes [with regard to the inheritance] the living."[268] Not unfittingly, therefore, was the successor to the French throne occasionally called *Le petit Phénix*.[269]

At any rate, the Phoenix metaphor fitted not badly to illustrate the nature of the *Dignitas quae non moritur*: the *Dignitas* of abbot, bishop, pope, or king appeared as a Phoenix-like *species* which coincided with the individual because it reproduced no more than one individuation at a time, the incumbent. Moreover, the Phoenix was, so to speak, a "natural" one-individual corporation, and thus there arose from the ashes of the Phoenix metaphor the prototype of that spectre called the "Corporation sole" which was at once immortal species and mortal individuation, collective *corpus politicum* and individual *corpus naturale*. What Maitland has said about the origins of that fiction of English Law—its connection with the parson, the patron, and the *Eigenkirche*—remains valid throughout.[270] We notice, however, that other factors—factors more philosophical than practical—deserve consideration as well. The Phoenix metaphor of the Italian jurists allows us perhaps to comprehend more fully, because in a different scheme of reference, the nature of that strange "Body corporate" which never dies, is never under age, never senile, never sick, and is without sex,[271] and therein resembles "the holy sprites and angels."[272] A frame of mind working with notions such as androgyny and self-

---

[268] André Tiraqueau (Tiraquella), *Le mort saisit le vif*, declar.3 (in Tiraquella, *Tractatus varii*, Frankfurt, 1574), IV,70. Tiraqueau mentions also the oneness of father and son; see, e.g., *De iure primogenitorum*, q.40,n.31, vol.I,p.453: "patrem et filium censeri unam et eandem personam etc." He denies, however, that the maxim *Le mort saisit le vif* (below, n.319) applies to *successio . . . nomine dignitatis; ibid.*, declar. v,73.

[269] Cf. A. Valladier, *Parennes royales* (Paris, 1611), 15, referring to Henry IV's son Louis XIII, a place kindly mentioned to me by Dr. Ralph E. Giesey.

[270] See Maitland, *Sel.Essays*, 73ff, for the parson as a prototype of the corporation sole; see also below, n. 308. Actually, Johannes Andreae mentions as an English peculiarity the fact that parochial priests were called "persons"; cf. *Novella*, on c.28 X 3,5,n.13, fol.35 (cf. above, n. 231), where he discusses the synonymity of *dignitas* and *personatus: "fere* ideo dictum est, quia in Anglia rectores parochialium dicuntur personae" (with a reference to c.6 X 3,7, ed. Friedberg, II,485). This is not a pun ("parson-person"), since "parson" actually derives from *persona*; see, for Innocent IV, above, n.231.

[271] See above, Ch.III,n.93, for queens bearing the title "king." Where the succession of females to the throne was barred, as in France, or later the so-called Salic Law dominated, the king's "Body corporate" could probably not claim sexlessness.

[272] See above, Ch.I,n.3.

reproduction could attribute similar features also to the Phoenix: Rabbinic tradition, for example, ascribed to the bird immortality because it refused to share in Eve's sin by tasting of the forbidden fruit, and therewith preserved its paradisean state of innocence— indeed, "sex perishes for perpetual bodies."[273] On the other hand, a frame of mind trained by scholastic philosophy might argue that it was the privilege or under-privilege, at any rate the pe- culiarity, of angels to be at once species and individual, since those sempiternal beings (lacking matter, though not individua- tion) did not reproduce their kind, but remained each, as a species, a single individual, though not in succession.[274] This may account for certain features which apparently Angels, Phoenices, and Bodies corporate had in common.

The concept of a *Dignitas* in which species and individual coincided, naturally brought into focus two different aspects of the dignitary himself—his "dual personality." Pope or bishop were not corporate *per se*: they became corporate as the sole representatives of their species only insofar as something supra- individual and perpetual was attached to them, namely the *Digni- tas quae non moritur*. How that attachment was explained by the jurists remains to be seen. Here it may just be mentioned that the jurists actually did arrive at a distinction of two personalities in the dignitary. It sounds very simple and straightforward when Cynus of Pistoia writes: "A bishop has two personalities, one so far as he is a bishop, and another so far as he is [the individual] Peter or Martin."[275] What Cynus puts forth is, in fact, conven-

---

[273] See Fitzpatrick, *Lactantii De ave Phoenice*, 16,n.5. The verse "Sexus perpetuis corporibus perit" (see for similar statements above, Ch.III,n.93) is found in *Obitus Baebiani*, v.60, ed. W. Brandes, "Studien zur christlich-lateinischen Poesie," *Wiener Studien*, XII (1890), 283. This 4th-century poem has nothing directly to do with the Phoenix, since it tells the story of Baebianus' resurrection from the dead and visit to heaven; but it was inspired also by Lactantius' *Phoenix*; see Brandt's edition of Lactantius and his notes on lines 2 and 164 (*CSEL*, XXVII, 135 and 146), as well as Rapisarda, *Fenice*, 40 and 86.

[274] Above, Ch.VI,nos.17-18.

[275] Gierke, *Gen.R.*, III,363,n.34, quotes several passages from Cynus, who dis- tinguished also in the judge a *duplex persona*, one public and the other private. The distinction is important, and its importance was recognized already by the 12th-century jurists in connection with the problem of conscience in court; that is, the question whether a judge was to try a case exclusively on the ground of the evidence produced in court or also on the ground of private knowledge he may have happened to obtain: "aliud facit aliquis in eo quod iudex est, aliud in eo quod homo est," says the ordinary Gloss on the *Decretum* (c.4,C.III,qu.7, v. *Audit*),

tional: it is merely another application—so to speak, the reverse side—of the canonistic distinction between a delegation *facta personae* and one *facta dignitati*, which had been expounded over and over again in connection with the decretal *Quoniam abbas*. His remark is nevertheless valuable because it shows that emphasis could easily be shifted from the dual aspect of the delegation of power onto the dual personality of the delegating as well as the delegated dignitary, and finally onto every office-holder both spiritual and secular. Hence, from the canonistic theory new political theories began to spread out, as the secular Dignities likewise were interpreted as corporate and immortal entities.

The immortality of the Holy See as a *Dignitas quae non moritur* was based on a rational juristic fiction. That, however, did not prevent the canon lawyers from lapsing into irrational thought and interpreting the perpetuity of the *Sancta Sedes* also transcendentally along traditional lines. Johannes Andreae, for example, when glossing the phrase *Sedes ipsa non moritur* of Pope Boniface's decretal, declared: "For it cannot be that there be no See, since the Lord has prayed for it."[276] That is to say, the sempiternity of the Holy See here appears as an effluence of the divine power and of the sempiternity of the Church whose domination knows no vacancy *quia Christus non moritur*, "because Christ does not die."[277] Contrariwise, the empire, we recall, was understood to be sempiternal for similar metaphysical reasons: it was the fourth world monarchy which was to last until the end; it had been constituted from high heaven by God himself; and the Justinian Law attributed to it sempiternity (*imperium semper*

---

and a maxim attributed to Christ reads: "non nisi per allegata iudex iudicet." See, for the problem, Max Radin, "The Conscience of the Court," *Law Quarterly Review*, XLVIII (1932), 506-20; Hermann Kantorowicz, *Glossators*, 21; Ullmann, *Lucas de Penna*, 126ff, also 130, where Lucas blames Pilate for having judged only on the basis of evidence, and not in accordance with his knowledge and his conscience.

[276] See *Glos.ord.*, on c.5 VI 1,3, v. *moritur*: "non enim potest esse nulla [sedes] ... quia dominus pro ea oravit." Cf. c.33,C.XXIV,q.1; above, Ch.VI,nos.36-37.

[277] "Licet moriatur praelatus et omnes clerici in ecclesia, dominium illorum non vacat, quia Christus non moritur, nec potest ecclesia deficere." Johannes Andreae, *Novella*, on c.4 X 2,12,n.5, quoted by Pierre Gillet, *La personnalité juridique en droit ecclésiastique* (Malines, 1927), 178. Andreae depended upon Innocent IV, on c.4 X 2,12,n.4 (Lyon, 1578), fol.145ᵛ: ". . . quantumcunque moriatur praelatus et omnes clerici, ecclesiae tamen proprietas et possessio remanet penes Christum, qui vivit in aeternum, vel penes universalem, vel singularem ecclesiam, quae nunquam moritur."

est).[278] It is noteworthy, however, that those arguments now were supplemented, or even superseded, by the new legal theory concerning the immortality of the Dignity. Thus Godfrey of Trani, when glossing (ca. 1241-43) the decretal *Quoniam abbas*, could reverse the argument, and say: "Since the Dignity does not perish on the death of the incumbent, therefore the *imperium* is perpetual."[279] And later authors declared straightforwardly that the phrase *imperium semper est* referred to the *Dignitas*.[280] This is a secularization of old ideas: the perpetuity of the empire no longer derived from God and the divine dispensation, but from the fictitious, if immortal, personage called *Dignitas*, from a Dignity created by the policy of man and conferred upon the Prince or present office-holder by a likewise immortal polity, by an *universitas quae nunquam moritur*.[281] It is manifest that the value of perpetuity no longer centered primarily in the Deity, nor in the immortal idea of Justice, nor in the Law, but rather in the *universitas* and the *Dignitas* each of which was immortal.

Naturally the civilians referred in the first place to the *imperium* when expounding their theories, just as papacy and episcopate would have been the first thought of canonists who explained the nature of *Dignitas*. By that time, however, almost everything that was valid with regard to the empire was valid also with regard to the kingdoms. Baldus, for example, when discussing—along the lines of *Quoniam abbas* and of Boniface's decretal[282]—the binding power of contracts and obligations, first chose the tradi-

---

278 Above, Ch.vi, nos. 38ff,41ff.

279 Godfrey of Trani, *Summa super decretalibus*, on c.14 X 1,29,n.29, quoted by Gierke, *Gen.R.*, iii,271,n.73: "Quia dignitas non perit decedente persona, unde imperium in perpetuum est."

280 For the interpretation of *imperium* in the sense of *dignitas* in the 16th and 17th centuries, see Gierke, *Gen.R.*, iv,240,n.124. The idea of perpetuation is rather strongly formulated by Albericus de Rosate, on *D.5,1,76,n.1* (Venice, 1584), fol.304ᵛ: "Sedes apostolica non moritur, sed semper durat in persona successoris . . . , et dignitas imperialis semper durat . . . et idem in qualibet dignitate, quia perpetuatur in persona successorum . . . [allegation of *Quoniam abbas*], fiscus etiam perpetuo durat locuplex . . ." Angelus de Ubaldis, on *D.5,1,76,n.2* (Venice, 1580), fol. 136, considers the insignia of a *societas*, such as *baculus* or *vexillum*, substantial with regard to the perpetuity: "quod licet mutentur caporales magnae societatis, et uni detur baculus et alteri vexillum, ut est moris, tamen adhuc durat eadem societas."

281 See below, nos.284ff, 295.

282 Those two decretals, above all *Quoniam abbas*, are quoted over and over again by Baldus; see e.g., *Consilia*, iii,121,n.6,fol.34; iii,159,n.4,fol.45ᵛ; iii,217,n.3, fol.63ᵛ, etc.

tional examples of emperor and pontiff: "The emperor in his person may die, but the Dignity itself, or the *imperium*, is immortal, just as the supreme pontiff dies, whereas the supreme pontificate does not die." But while pointing out that things proceeding from the person were personal matters whereas those proceeding from the Dignity were "perennial and eternal," Baldus switched as a matter of course from the *imperium* to the *regnum*, and from the emperor to the emperor-like king, "who in his realm holds the supreme principate, because he does not recognize a superior."[283] Contracts of kings, too, when made *sub nomine Dignitatis*, bind the successor:

> And in the contracts of kings it is expressed on whose part [person or Dignity] they are [made]; and they pass on to the successor in the kingdom if they are quoted in the name of the Dignity. . . . Nor is this surprising, because in the kingdom there has to be considered [not only] the Dignity which does not die, but also the *universitas* or *respublica* of the kingdom, which continues steadfastly even when kings have been expelled: for the *respublica* cannot die; and therefore one says that the *respublica* has no heir, because she always lives in herself.[284]

It is a minor point only when we notice that the whole canonistic doctrine of *Dignitas* has been transferred to kings—to be sure, not for the first time. It is, however, a point of major interest to find that in Baldus' reflections two distinct factors determine the responsibilities of kings: the immortality of *Dignitas* as well as the immortality of *universitas*; and that accordingly the Prince

---

[283] Baldus, *Consilia*, III,159,n.3, fol.45ᵛ: "Imperator in persona mori potest: sed ipsa dignitas, seu Imperium, immortalis est, sicut et summus Pontifex moritur, sed summus Pontificatus non moritur, et ideo quae procedunt a persona, et non a sede, personalia sunt, si a successiva voluntate dependent . . .Quaedam vero procedunt a sede: et ista sunt perennia et aeterna, donec superveniat casus extinctivus, seu terminus vitae ipsius concessionis. Huiusmodi sunt contractus Regum, qui contrahunt nomine suo et Regni, seu gentis suae." *Ibid.*, n.4: "Rex, qui in Regno suo tenet principalissimum principatum: quia non cognoscit superiorem, est totum continens, et potest contrahere nomine suo, et totius terrae, et populorum suorum. Habet enim plenissimam potestatem . . . Unde is qui contraxit sub nomine dignitatis, obligat successores." The whole paragraph is extremely interesting. See next note.

[284] *Ibid.*, nos.4-5: "Et in contractibus regum est expressum, quod partium sunt, et transeunt ad successores in Regno, si celebrati sunt nomine dignitatis . . . Nec mirum, quia in Regno considerari debet dignitas, quae non moritur; et etiam universitas, seu respublica ipsius Regni, quae etiam exactis Regibus perseverat. Non enim potest respublica mori. Et hac ratione dicitur, quod respublica non habet haeredem: quia semper vivit in semetipsa." Cf. above, Ch.VI,n.59.

was said to act by virtue of both the Dignity and the *respublica*,[285] that is, of two entities credited to be sempiternal. We can hardly avoid recalling the political concepts of earlier jurists, epitomized, for example, by John of Paris, who held that the king depended on God and the people, *populo faciente et Deo inspirante*.[286] In Baldus' political scheme, however, the notion of *populus* was changed into the legalistic *universitas quae non potest mori*; at the same time, *Deus* was fittingly replaced by the likewise legalistic *Dignitas quae non potest mori*. How closely interrelated God and Dignity actually were may be gathered from Baldus' gloss on the coronation oath of kings and emperors by which they promised not to alienate the possessions of the Crown: "Hence, the emperor . . . is under no obligation to man, though he is obligated to God and his Dignity which is perpetual."[287] We should probably recall the juxtaposition of *Deus* and *Fiscus* to understand that *Dignitas*, owing to its perpetuity, became, just as *Fiscus*, comparable to God or was "equiparated" with God. And it is also apposite to think of Bracton's famous words saying that "the king must be, not under man, but under God and the Law,"[288] in order to be aware of the shift from Law-centered to Polity- and Corporation-centered kingship.

The placing side by side of God and Dignity will require further attention.[289] What matters here is the incessant repetition of the catchword saying that the royal Dignity does not die, or, as Baldus occasionally put it, ". . . the Dignity is something regal . . . , and the regal quality does not die even if the individual [king] dies."[290] Pursuantly, Matthaeus de Afflictis, while

---

285 Below, n.295.

286 See above, Ch.VI,nos.51-54; Ch.VII,nos.25ff.

287 "Unde imperator rei suae potest dare legem quam vult et non obligatur homini, sed Deo et dignitati suae, quae perpetua est." Baldus, on c.33 X 2,24,n.5 (the decretal of Honorius III; above, nos.143f,147,150), *In Decretales*, fol. 261ᵛ.

288 Bracton, fol.5b, ed. Woodbine, II,33: "Ipse autem rex non debet esse sub homine, sed sub Deo et sub lege, quia lex facit regem." See also above, Ch.IV,n.298.

289 See below, n.423.

290 Baldus, on *C*.6,51,1,6a,n.4, fol.180ᵛ: "Vel ibi non est novum feudum, quia dignitas est quid regale, cum feudum regni sit concessum omnibus regibus, et qualitas regia non moritur, licet individuum moriatur." On the other hand, a diminution of actual power did not affect the immortality of the *Dignitas* itself. See, e.g., Albericus of Rosate, on *D.const.Omnem* (=*prima const.* or *prooemium*), rubr.,n.8 (Venice, 1585), fol.3ᵛ. While disapproving of the Donation of Constantine (he actually quotes approvingly Dante, *Inf.*, XIX,115ff), he does not accept all the reasons put forth against its validity: "Non obstat quod dignitas imperialis sit

referring to Baldus, declared in a gloss on the Sicilian Constitutions: "The royal Dignity never dies."[291] There were, of course, slight variations of the theme. Baldus himself said occasionally: *Regia maiestas non moritur,* "The royal Majesty does not die."[292] And he, too, arrived at distinguishing two persons in the king: a *persona personalis,* "which is the soul in the substance of man," that is the individual king; and a *persona idealis,* "which is the Dignity."[293] Here, then, Dignity—the *persona idealis*—is clearly personified. *Dignitas* is, like *Iustitia,* an "ideal" person having an independent existence even in the case of a vacancy, though otherwise she is inseparably attached to the ruler, so long as he lives or rules; she is attached to him as his permanent companion—not unlike an ancient deity, god or goddess, which appears on coins as *comes Augusti.*[294]

The duality resting in the king was the theme of Baldus on yet another occasion. When discussing the king's obligation to observe contracts made in the names of *Dignitas* and *respublica,* he explained that, "intellectually speaking," the predecessor king, who contracted the obligation, was not dead because neither his *Dignitas* nor the *respublica,* in whose names he acted, were dead.

> For it is true to say that the *respublica* does nothing by itself, whereas he who rules the *respublica,* acts in virtue of the *respublica* and of the Dignity conferred on him by that very *respublica.* Moreover, two things concur in the king: the person and the signification [i.e. the Dignity]. And that signification, which is something appealing to the intellect, miraculously perseveres forever, though not corporeally: for let the king be deficient with regard to his flesh, he nevertheless functions holding the place of *two* persons.[295]

---

perpetua et non moriatur: quia per talem donationem non est mortua nec eius potestas in aliis locis non donatis ecclesiae."

[291] Mattheus de Afflictis, on *Lib.aug.,* II,35,n.23, vol.II,fol.77: "Quae dignitas regia nunquam moritur."

[292] Baldus, on c.7 X 1,2,n.78, *In Decretales,* fol.18: ". . . quia ibi iuramentum fuit praestitum a dignitate dignitati. Nam regia maiestas non moritur."

[293] Baldus, *Consilia,* III,217,n.3, fol.63ᵛ: "[persona] personalis, quae est anima in substantia hominis, et non persona idealis, quae est dignitas."

[294] See A. D. Nock, "The Emperor's Divine *Comes,*" *Journal of Roman Studies,* XXXVII (1947), 102ff. The *comes* idea was not alien to Frederick II, not only with regard to *Iustitia,* but also to the *Fortuna Augusti;* cf. Franz Kampers, "Die *Fortuna Caesarea* Kaiser Friedrichs II," *Hist. Jahrb.,* XLVIII (1928), 208ff.

[295] Baldus, *Cons.,* III,159,n.5, fol.45ᵛ: "Unde cum intellectu loquendo, non est mortua hic persona concedens . . . Nam verum est dicere, quod respublica nihil per se agit, tamen qui regit rem publicam, agit in virtute reipublicae et dignitatis sibi collatae ab ipsa republica. Porro duo concurrunt in rege: persona et signifi-

In other words, the *K*ing survives the *k*ing, and in that sense Baldus then could declare that, while there is no will in a corpse, the dead Prince "seems to will even after his death"—as *Dignitas*, of course.[296]

However that may be, it is easy to recognize now to what extent the simple canonistic doctrine concerning the "Abbot of Winchester" and his Dignity influenced legal thought in general, especially after that theory had been transferred, in the course of the fourteenth century, to the secular sphere, to emperors and kings. In the much admired arguments of Baldus,[297] whose scholastic accent is unmistakable, we believe we hear already the Tudor jurists putting forth their arguments about the king's "two Bodies."

CORPORATIONAL SYMPTOMS IN ENGLAND

There is hardly a phrase or metaphor in the picturesque speeches transmitted by Plowden which could not be traced back to some antecedents in the legal writings of the thirteenth and fourteenth centuries, even though it would often be cumbersome to demonstrate how exactly one or the other detail found its way to the English legal language. It is perfectly true that in most cases in which the word *Dignitas* was used together with the word *Corona*, a corporational character of Dignity was *not* intended; nor can any intention of that kind be read into the texts. For all that, however, the doctrines of the Italian canonists left some traces in England, even at an early date. William of Drogheda, writing around 1239 on the procedure in ecclesiastical courts, was fully aware of the difference whether an abbot signed with his own seal or with that of his convent.[298] In the Year Books under

catio. Et ipsa significatio, quae est quoddam intellectuale, semper est perseverans enigmatice: licet non corporaliter: nam licet Rex deficiat, quid ad rumbum, nempe loco duarum personarum Rex fungitur, ut ff. de his, qui. ut ind. l. tutorum [D.34,9,22: 'Discreta sunt enim iura, quamvis plura in eandem personam devenerint, aliud tutoris, aliud legatarii']."

[296] Baldus, on *C.*10,1,rubr.,n.16, fol.232ᵛ: ". . . et velle videtur [imperator] etiam post mortem, quia etiam post mortem suam verba contulisse videtur . . ." See below, n.349.

[297] The *Repertorium in Consilia*, p.82 (forming vol. VI of Baldus, *Cons.*), s.v. "rex," refers to *Cons.*, III,159, and says: "Hic vide multa pulchra de dignitate regali." Also Gierke, *Gen.R.*, IV,239, admires, with reference to that *Consilium*, Baldus' *unübertreffliche Schärfe*.

[298] Post, "Quod omnes tangit," 217ff.

Edward II, in which we find much talk about the king's Dignity without ever suggesting corporational aspects, we find nevertheless a perfectly clear knowledge of the canonistic significance of *Dignitas*. In the case against the Prior of Kirkham, which was heard in 1313, Justice Inge referred, time and time again, to *Dignitas* in the sense of the canonists:

> Abbot and Prior are names of Dignity: and in virtue of the Dignity the right that was in the predecessor will so wholly vest itself in the person of the successor after his creation that none other than he can defend the rights of his Church.

Justice Inge, tacitly referring to *Quoniam abbas*, played up the fact that "the present Prior [of Kirkham] comes to the court as Prior," and that he had been summoned "by his name of Dignity." Emphatically Inge finally exclaimed: "And so let men learn to [be wary how to] bring a writ against a Prior by his name of Dignity."[299]

These quotations show that English jurists around 1300 were very familiar with the idea of Dignity in the legalistic sense, as well as with the idea of the virtual identity of predecessor and successor—at least with regard to ecclesiastical persons. Justice Inge indeed pointed out that the personality of an abbot "or other man of Dignity" was not "as it is with secular persons"[300]—an indication, it seems, that the idea of the continuous personality was as yet not commonly transferred to secular office, but was more or less restricted to spiritual dignitaries. It may well have taken some time before the secular dignitaries, too, were drawn into the magic circle of corporational doctrines. Nevertheless, by the fifteenth century the main distinctions were carried over to

---

[299] *Year Books, 6-7 Edward II (1313)*, Y.B. Ser., xv (Selden Society, xxxvi), 175, 177,178,182; cf. Holdsworth, iii,472,n.4. Whereas in this case the corporational substratum is evident, the mentions of the royal Dignity are lacking any corporational connotations; see, e.g., *Year Books, 5 Edward II (1311)*, Y.B. Ser., x (Selden Society, LXIII, 1944), 122f. Bracton's usage of *Dignitas* does not suggest corporational meaning either. It seems that the notion *status regis* or *status regalis*, either alone or in connection with *dignitas*, took over the functions which in canonistic doctrines and in those of the Italian jurists were vested in the abstract *Dignitas*. This, at least, would be suggested by Jean Gerson (above, Ch.v,n.76), when he talks about the king's "second life," the "vita civilis et politica, que *status regalis* dicitur aut *dignitas*." All those notions should be studied far more thoroughly than has hitherto been the case, though a good start has been made by Post (see, e.g., "Two Laws," 432ff).

[300] *Year Books, 6-7 Edward II*, 181.

the secular sphere as well, as, for example, in a lawsuit under Edward IV when the judges pointed out that a mayor contracted an obligation, not as mayor, but *par son propre nosme.*[301]

Under Edward IV, of course, corporational modes of thinking reached in England a state of full consciousness, and they were displayed most curiously by the king himself in the case of the Duchy of Lancaster.[302] The Duchy, as is commonly known, had been the private possession of the House of Lancaster, and the Lancastrian kings held it by hereditary right. On his accession in 1399, Henry IV ordained with the consent of Parliament that all the lands of the Duchy of Lancaster were to be governed and treated by the king "as though we would never have achieved the height of royal Dignity," since those lands had come to him, Henry of Lancaster, personally by right hereditary "before God called us to the Estate and Dignity royal."[303] A private property, disconnected from the Crown—so the Duchy was and remained under Henry V and Henry VI; it was held, as Plowden later reported, by the Lancastrians in their Body natural.[304] When, in 1461, the Yorkist Edward IV seized power, the status of the Duchy changed. Shortly after his accession, Edward IV had his Lancastrian predecessor convicted and attainted of high treason, a verdict resulting in the forfeiture of all the former sovereign's possessions and titles, including the private possession of the Duchy of Lancaster. Edward IV himself had no title to the Duchy except in right of the Crown, since it had been confiscated for treason committed against the Crown.[305] Yet Edward apparently did not intend to abandon all the advantages which a *Hausmacht* brought to the king's power and purse. To overcome those difficulties, the king or his legal advisers contrived a startling device: they "incorporated" the confiscated Duchy. By Act of Parliament it was decreed, on March 4, 1461, that the manors, castles, lord-

---

301 Maitland, *Sel.Essays,* 226,n.1.

302 Robert Somerville, *History of the Duchy of Lancaster* (London, 1953), 231ff, barely renders the content of the Act of Incorporation. On the whole, the strange action taken by Edward IV seems not to have attracted in modern times the attention it undoubtedly deserves.

303 William Hardy, *The Charters of the Duchy of Lancaster* (London, 1845), 99f,102.

304 See Plowden, *Reports,* 200b, and passim; also Chrimes, *Const. Ideas,* 352f (*App.* n.11), for the opinions of the judges under Henry IV.

305 The fullest discussion of the case is still found in Plowden's *Reports,* 212b-223; for Edward IV, see 219a.

ships, towns, and other possessions, with their appurtenances in the Duchy, henceforth

> make, and from the seid fourth day of Marche be, the seid Duchie of Lancastre corporat, and be called THE DUCHIE OF LANCASTRE.

Moreover, Parliament granted Edward IV the right to keep those lands

> by the same name of Duchie, from all other his enheritauncez separate . . . to him and to his heires Kyngs of Englond perpetually.[306]

The Duchy, now corporate, was to become, as a corporation, parcel of the Crown without being merged with other Crown property. That is to say, in order to preserve the former extent of the Duchy, with all its rights and appurtenances unimpaired, and also to keep it *en bloc* apart from other Crown property and place it under special administration, it was converted by Act of Parliament into a juristic person. THE DUCHY OF LANCASTER (one is inclined to add: LTD. or INC.) was to have a status exempt from central government and belong as a corporation to the Crown, whereby the king as King, and not the king privately, was to be hereditarily the head—or, as it were, "Director"—of that legal corporation, to whom the proceedings from that corporation accrued as though he were the private owner—to be sure, only by right of the Crown.[307]

Thus entered corporational thought into constitutional practice on the highest level. To conceive of a realm, a shire, a duchy, or even a fee, metaphorically in terms of a corporation (*universitas*), or a juristic person, was anything but unusual in the speech of the jurists; but the actual incorporation of a whole duchy by means of an Act of Parliament was something unique in mediaeval practice. We may consider that step perhaps a forerunner of the later incorporation of whole ecclesiastical dioceses, or of provinces of the spiritual orders, in those countries in which, owing to the separation of State and Church, the Churches form private corpo-

---

[306] For the Charter, see W. Hardy, *op.cit.*, 282 (English text), 323f (Latin text). The words spelt out in capitals in the quotation are in capitals in the Latin text: ". . . dictus ducatus Lancastriae corporatus, et DUCATUS LANCASTRIAE nominentur [sc. castra, maneria, et cet.]."

[307] In Plowden, 220b, the distinctions are put forth neatly: "The three [i.e. the Lancastrian kings] held it in their Body natural separate from the Crown, and the fourth [i.e. Edward IV] in his Body politic in right of the Crown, and separated in the Order and Government of the Crown, and not otherwise."

rations; this would be true, above all, in the United States where archbishops and bishops are—or were—recognized as "Corporations sole" and where, for example, the Benedictines are registered as *The Order of St. Benedict, Inc.*, while the Jesuit Provinces are incorporated statewise, e.g., as *The Society of Jesus of New England*, etc.[308] Here, then, secular corporational law had its retroactive effects on the status of the Church: in fact, the canonistic doctrine has run the full circle.

However that may be, by the latter half of the fifteenth century corporational ideologies had gained a firm footing in England, and apparently it was not unknown to the jurists what profits might be derived also in secular matters from corporational theories. The incorporation of Lancaster, in other respects perhaps without tangible effect,[309] left its indelible mark on legal thought insofar as it was in connection with the *Case of the Duchy of Lancaster*, argued in court in 1561, that the Tudor judges produced their most striking formulations concerning the king's "two Bodies." Since those formulations eventually passed into juristic textbooks and dictionaries such as those of Crompton, Kitchin, Cowell, and perhaps also of other authors around 1600; and since they were quoted by authorities such as Coke, Bacon, and later on by countless others, for instance Blackstone, they naturally penetrated quickly into political and popular parlance and were repeated over and over again.[310] Plowden, in his *Reports,* clearly demonstrates how lively and general was the interest in the principles involved in the Lancaster case, and how vivid were the discussions in the course of which distinctions between the "two

[308] Cases in which the United States recognized the Roman Catholic bishops and archbishops as "Corporations sole" are enumerated in *Corpus Juris* (New York, 1919), XIV,71,nos.73 and 78 (= 14 C.J. Corporations §38). In the new edition (*Corpus Juris Secundum*, XI,350 [Bishop]) it is said that the "Bishop has been regarded a corporation sole; but as the conception . . . seems to be passing out of the American Law, a Bishop is here no longer regarded as a corporation sole." A liturgical review, however, called *Orate Fratres*, is edited "by the Monks of St. John's Abbey, Collegeville, Minnesota (*The Order of St. Benedict, Inc.*)," and the American Jesuits are statewise incorporated; see, e.g., *Catalogus Provinciae Novae Angliae Societatis Jesu* (ineunte anno 1955), p.143.

[309] Somerville, *Lancaster*, 232.

[310] Richard Crompton, *L'Authoritie et Jurisdiction* (London, 1594), fols.134f; Joseph Kitchin, *Le Court Leete et Court Baron* (London, 1598), 1ᵛ; John Cowell, *The Interpreter* (Cambridge, 1607), s.vv. "King (Rex)" and "Prerogative." See, for Dr. Cowell, whose absolutist views were uncomfortable even to James I (cf. Godfrey Davies, *The Early Stuarts* [Oxford, 1952], 12), also the article by Chrimes, "Dr. John Cowell," *EHR*, LXIV (1949), 472ff. See, for Coke, Bacon, and Blackstone, above, Ch.I.

Bodies" were advanced. The coinages of the English judges were not lacking originality when they pointed out that the King's Body politic "contains his royal Estate and Dignity" or was "adorned and invested with the Estate and Dignity royal," even though the Italian jurists had fathered those ideas. The originality of the Tudor lawyers should be sought chiefly in the fact that they replaced the commonly used notion of *Dignitas* by the notion of "Body politic," and thereby were led to certain elaborations and conclusions which the civilians and canonists had not deemed it necessary to indulge in.

Fortunately, we are not deficient in early examples illustrating the replacement of *Dignitas* by *Corpus*. Maitland mentioned a case heard under Henry VII, in 1487, in the course of which Justice Vavasor argued that "every abbot is a body politic, because he cannot take anything except for the use of the house."[311] The argument itself is weak, but it discloses a parlance which must have been fairly common by that time. In fact, we find a similar utterance in an earlier case, heard under Edward IV, in 1482. Again an abbot was involved; Justice Fairfax, arguing in his favor, dropped a remark concerning "that mystical body of the abbot which never dies," since the office and the house continued in the successors of the abbot.[312] The judge's remark is interesting: the abbot is not mentioned as a member of the general *corpus mysticum* of either the Church or the realm, but as a mystical body *per se*, because he "never dies" and has "continuity." It is clear that the corporational notion of *Dignitas* was confused with the likewise corporational notion of *corpus mysticum*, or that the "mystical body" was fused with what otherwise was called "Dignity"—a fusion or confusion which was certainly not customary in Italian legal language. However, when we consider the influence which the "abbot" as a model exercised on legal and political thought in general, it will not be really surprising to find that in English secular practice the two notions were used almost synonymously also with regard to the king.

[311] Maitland, *Sel.Essays*, 83,n.2 (quoting *Y.B., 3 Henry VII*): ". . . chescun abbe est corps politike, car il ne poet rien prender forsque al use del meason."

[312] *Year Books, 21 Edward IV* (printed by Tottell, London, 1556-1572), fol.38b: ". . . pur ceo que cest misticall corps d'l abbe ne unque morust et le office et le meason continua a les successours en fee . . ." The case has been quoted by Coke, *Rep.*, VII,10a, *Calvin's Case* (not quite correctly: f.39b for 38b), and I am much obliged to Mr. H. G. Richardson for helping me to verify the quotation.

How the transition from the royal "Dignity" to the royal "Body politic" worked in legal arguments can be easily grasped from the case *Hill* v. *Grange*, which was heard in the Court of Common Pleas in 1556 and 1557, that is, about five years before the Lancaster case.[313] *Hill* v. *Grange*, a case of trespass, is itself of no interest here; but the trespassed land happened to have belonged originally to one of the monasteries dissolved by Henry VIII, and therewith the king came into the picture. The hearing, in certain sections, amounted to a rehearsal of the whole compound matter of *Quoniam abbas* and of the glosses on that decretal. The judges tried to find out whether King Henry VIII had acted as a person or as *Dignitas*, because in the latter case his actions would have bound his successors. Chief Justice Brook argued that statutes have commonly been "expounded to extend to a king's heirs and successors, to give them benefit or to bind them" even when the king's individual name was cited or referred to; he adduced *Magna Carta*, c. 17: "Common Pleas shall not follow *our* court,"[314] to prove that the word "our" did not refer to King John individually, but to the king as King; and finally, when summarizing, he said:

> And the reason is because *the King is a Body politic*, and when an act says "the king," or says "we," it is always spoken in the person of him as King, and *in his Dignity royal*, and therefore it *includes all those who enjoy his function*.[315]

Thereafter other justices—Staunford, Saunders, and Brown—took up the matter, likewise arguing that, although King Henry VIII was referred to by name, the reference was to him as King:

> And *King is a name of continuance, which shall always endure* as the head and the governor of the people, as the Law presumes . . . , and *in this the King never dies*.

For that reason, opined the judges, the king's death is in law not called death, but demise,

> because thereby he demises the kingdom to another, and lets another enjoy the functions, so that the *Dignity always continues*. . . . And

---

313 Plowden, *Reports*, 164ff.

314 Chief Justice Brook (Plowden, *Reports*, 175b) quotes "c.11" of *Magna Carta*; in fact, however, the reference is to *M.C.*, c.17 (King John), or c.12 (re-issue of 1216).

315 Plowden, *Reports*, 175b-176.

then when . . . the relation is to him as King, *he as King never dies, although his natural Body dies;* but *the King* in which name it has relation to him, *does ever continue,* and therefore . . . the word King shall extend [from Henry VIII] to King Edward VI [that is, to the successor]. . . . From whence we may see that where a thing is referred to a particular king *by the name of King,* in that case *it may extend to his heirs and successors.* . . .[316]

No commentary is needed to demonstrate to what extent the passages rendered here in italics for purposes of emphasis, were derived from arguments which the glossators and post-glossators had advanced long before: we recognize the catchword *Dignitas non moritur,* that is, the continuity of the *Dignitas* despite the death of the incumbent; the unity of predecessor and successor; the binding power of obligations made in the name of the Dignity; the importance of mentioning or omitting the "name"; and all the other implications which had been exploited for three centuries and more in connection with the decretal *Quoniam abbas,* or on similar occasions. Only in one respect did the English legal jargon deviate noticeably from the language of the glossators: the notion of Dignity, though mentioned by the English judges several times in its proper legal setting, was usually replaced by that of "Body politic." Here, at any rate, there is a striking parallel with the abbot's "mystical body which never dies."

Coke, when pleading in *Calvin's Case,* aptly remarked: "It is true that the King *in genere* dieth not, but, no question, *in individuo* he dieth."[317] We know those distinctions from the arguments of the Italian jurists, who, on the whole, were careful to point out that they were talking about the Prince *in genere,* about the *regia Dignitas* or *regia Maiestas,* when they said that a dignitary "never dies," and they refrained, very logically, from saying that "the King never dies." Perhaps Baldus went a little farther than others when he personified the *Dignitas* and said that the *persona idealis* never dies; but then that was, after all, only an "ideal person." The English lawyers, too, made it perfectly clear that not the king pure and simple was immortal, but that only as *King*—as "Dignity" or "Body politic"—he never died. Nevertheless, it was in the pleadings of the English lawyers that the phrase

---

[316] *Ibid.,* 177. See above, n.195.
[317] Coke, *Calvin's Case,* fol.10b.

"The King never dies" seems to have made its first appearance; and probably one could afford being a little careless, since the distinctions between the King's immortal Body politic and his mortal Body natural were so well established that misunderstandings were practically impossible. However that may be, where so much talk had been going on about immortal royal Dignities and Majesties, and where—as especially in France—the tendency was so strong to read into the individual living king features of a living *persona idealis*,[318] it was almost to be expected that one day, sooner or later, also the phrase *Le roi ne meurt jamais* would make its appearance.

LE ROY EST MORT . . .

Very little attention, if any, has been paid to the indisputable fact that the famous device *Le roi ne meurt jamais*, current in France since the sixteenth century,[319] descended in direct succession from the legal maxim *Dignitas non moritur*, and therefore ultimately from Pope Alexander's decretal *Quoniam abbas*. In other words, it represented merely another twist of the well-worn corporational doctrines of mediaeval canonists and civilians. That this quite unambiguous genealogy has so rarely been noticed may

[318] Church, *Constitutional Thought*, 94,n.41, 197,247ff. and passim.

[319] It would be difficult to tell when exactly the slogan first appears in France. Cf. Jean Bodin, *Les six livres de la république*, I,c.8 (Paris, 1583; first edition 1576), 160: "Car il est certain que le Roy ne meurt jamais, comme l'on dit, ains si tost que l'un est decedé, le plus proche masle de son estoc est saisi du Royaume et en possession d'iceluy au paravant qu'il soit couronné." This shows that by the time Bodin wrote (ca.1576) the maxim was well known (*comme l'on dit*). It is also interesting that Bodin raises the device *le mort saisit le vif* (above, n.268) from the sphere of private legal inheritance to the public sphere by replacing *le mort* by *le Royaume*: the kingdom itself seizes the heir to the throne. The same connection of *le Roy ne meurt jamais* with *le mort saisit le vif* is found in Charles Loyseau, *Cinq livres du droit des offices*, I,c.10,n.58 (Lyon, 1701; first published in 1610), 66, quoted by Church, *Const. Thought*, 319,n.44. By that time, of course, *le Roy ne meurt jamais* had become a religious dogma of the French nation, which, e.g., Bossuet, while still relying on the juristic doctrines, flamboyantly interprets in a new fashion: the image of God, visible in the king, cannot be but immortal; cf. Bossuet, *Oeuvres oratoires*, ed. J. Lebarq (Lille and Paris, 1892), IV,256ff ("Sur les devoirs des rois," a Palm Sunday Sermon delivered before the king, on April 2, 1662), who renders (p.262) an exposition of Psalm 81: 6, *Ego dixi: dii estis* (see my paper "Deus per naturam," 274,n.72): "Vous êtes des dieux . . . Mais ô dieux de chair et de sang, ô dieux de terre et de poussière, 'vous mourrez commes des hommes.' N'importe, vous êtes des dieux, encore que vous mouriez, et votre autorité ne meurt pas: cet esprit de royauté passe tout entier à vos successeurs . . . L'homme meurt, il est vrai, mais le roi, disons-nous, ne meurt jamais: l'image de Dieu est immortelle."

have been caused—at least, to some extent—by the fact that the legal maxim has far too often been combined, for deceivingly obvious reasons, with the cries heard at the burials of French kings in the Abbey of St.-Denis: *Le roi est mort! Vive le roi!*[320] Unduly, however, have those two slogans of legalistic and dynastic continuity been coupled together and finally confounded—for each has its own peculiar history. *Le roi ne meurt jamais* is dynastic only accidentally; *le pape, l'évêque, l'abbesse ne meurt jamais* would have been valid maxims even though in these cases dynastic dignity was not involved. Nor does the far-famed French device, which after all was daily bread in the jargon of English jurists of that time, appear in the burial ceremonial of French kings, since the funerary cries at St.-Denis originated in a totally different setting.[321]

By the Treaty of Troyes, in 1420, the sick King Charles VI of France and Queen Isabeau recognized King Henry V of England as the legitimate successor presumptive to the French throne; the English claims were acknowledged in northern France, including the city of Paris. Two years later, on August 31, 1422, Henry V died at Vincennes, leaving his French claims to his son Henry VI. While the dead king's body was being conveyed first to St.-Denis, thence via Rouen to London, King Charles VI of France died also, on October 21, 1422. The Duke of Bedford, in his capacity of Regent of France for the infant Henry VI of England, returned to Paris, on November 5th, where the *Conseil* seems to have awaited his arrival to make the arrangements for the funeral and to conduct the funerary rites.[322]

Other events, however, imperiled the English succession to the French throne. South of Paris, at Méhun-sur-Yèvre, the Dauphin

---

[320] See, e.g., Robert Holtzmann, *Französische Verfassungsgeschichte* (Munich and Berlin, 1910), 311; Schramm, *English Coronation*, 1, and *König von Frankreich*, I,260. Bloch, *Rois thaumaturges*, 218f, stresses mainly the dynastic aspect of the St.-Denis cries, which is important but not decisive. The two notions have been confused already by the French authors around 1600.

[321] Much, and sometimes most, of the following paragraphs are drawn from the forthcoming book of Ralph E. Giesey, *The Royal Funeral Ceremony in Renaissance France*, a thorough and comprehensive study (based upon his University of California Ph.D. dissertation, Berkeley, Cal., 1954), which I quote according to chapter and footnote numbers. I am greatly indebted to Dr. Giesey not only for allowing me to use his manuscript freely, but also for contributing additional relevant passages and for placing liberally at my disposal his own excerpts from hitherto unpublished material collected by him abroad.

[322] Giesey, *Royal Funeral*, Ch.vi,nos.87ff.

Charles VII was acclaimed by his officers with the cry *Vive le roi!* while the banner of France was hoisted.[323] The Duke of Bedford, therefore, was pressed to act quickly and efficiently to protect and proclaim the rights of his sovereign lord, King Henry VI of England. When Charles VI was entombed at St.-Denis, on November 11th—just four days after Henry V had been buried at Westminster Abbey—the ceremony was concluded by the customary short prayer for the deceased king: *"Priez pour l'ame de tres-excellent prince Charles VI, roy de France."* Then, after a short pause, a king-of-arms proclaimed the rights of the child Henry VI, and cried with loud voice: *"Vive Henry par la grace de Dieu roy de France et d'Angleterre!"* Whereupon the other heralds responded with the cry: *Vive le roy Henry!* to which the English added *Noël!*—"as if the Lord were descending from heaven," according to the French chronicler.[324]

Here, for the obvious purpose of forestalling the claims of the rival Dauphin and his party, the prayer for the dead king was coupled with the acclamation of the new king in the form in which normally it would be heard at royal coronations and on other occasions. Henceforth that procedure remained the custom in France: the prayer for the dead king was said and then, after a short silence "long enough to say a *Pater noster*,"[325] the acclamation of the new king followed. However, the prayer for the dead king as well as the proclamation of the new king were gradually reduced in length, until finally the brief impersonal cries, interrupted only by short ceremonial, were heard: *Le roi est mort! . . . Vive le roi!* This brief and depersonalized version seems to have made its first appearance at the interment of Louis XII, in 1515, whereas an intermediary formula—the short successive cries with the mention of the individual names of both the dead king and

---

[323] This ceremony is described in detail by Monstrelet, *Chroniques*, ed. Douët d'Arcq (Soc. de l'hist. de France, Paris, 1857-62), IV,310: "Sy fu lors levée une banière de France dedans la chapelle, et donc lesditz officiers commencèrent a cryer hault et cler par plusieurs fois Vive le Roy!" For the date (Oct. 30th instead of Oct. 24th), see Giesey, *op.cit.*, Ch.VIII,n.20f.

[324] The cries for Charles VI and Henry VI reported here are from the "original" version of the *Cérémonial de l'inhumation de Charles VI*, the oldest MS of which (Paris, BN.,fr.18674,fols.119f) is reproduced by Giesey, *Royal Funeral*, Appendix II. The cry "Noël" is reported, e.g., in *Chronique du Religieux de Saint-Denis*, ed. M. L. Bellaguet (Coll. des documents inédits, Paris, 1852), VI,496.

[325] Mathieu d'Escouchy, *Chroniques*, ed. G. du Fresne de Beaucourt (Soc. de l'hist. de France, Paris, 1863-64), II,443f. relating the funeral of Charles VII in 1461.

the new king—apparently was used before 1515.[326] This is all the more likely, since in 1509, on the death of Henry VII of England, the English funerary ceremonial observed that intermediary style. The stewards broke their staves, the vault was closed,

> and incontinent all the herauds did [take] of theire cotearmours and did hange them uppon the Rayles of the herse: crynge lamentably in French "The Noble kynge Henry the Seaventh is deade." And as soone as they had so done, everie heraud putt on his cotearmour againe and cryed with a loude voyce: "Vive Le noble Roy Henry le VIIIme," which is to say in englyshe tonge "God send the noble Kynge Henry the eight longe life."[327]

The English procedure which, in all likelihood, followed the example of the French ceremonial, suggests that the short succession of the two brief cries, though as yet with the invocations of the kings' names, actually was the French custom before 1509, a consideration which sends us back to the funeral of Charles VIII, in 1498.[328] The later omission of the individual names certainly brought into prominence the perpetuity of the *Dignitas* as such, severed from its impersonators; but it is impossible to tell whether this was intended or not. What matters here is that the cries "The king is dead! Long live the king!" which—with or without mention of proper names—powerfully demonstrated the perpetuity of kingship, were introduced in England at a time when in the Inns of Court the maxim saying that "the king as King never dies" was just about to be formulated.

A broad political idea has been given expression through the funerary ceremonial in lapidary terms and in a dramatic display. Nevertheless, the famous cries were neither the first nor the only

---

[326] It is commonly assumed that those cries were heard, in their shortest form, for the first time at the funeral of Francis I, in 1547; see, e.g., Bloch, *Rois thaumaturges*, 218f; Schramm, *Frankreich*, II,125 (= I,260,n.4). The depersonalized cries, however, are actually found already in a contemporary report of the funeral of Louis XII in 1515: *L'obsèque et enterrement du Roy* (Paris, 1515), reprinted in L. Cimber and F. Anjou, *Archives curieuses sur l'histoire de France* (Paris, 1835), Ier sér., II,69f. Cf. Giesey, *Royal Funeral*, Ch.VIII,nos.50f, for further detail.

[327] The relation is preserved in Brit.Mus., *Harley MS 3504*, fol.259^r-v (ancient 271), a copy of which Dr. Giesey kindly placed at my disposal.

[328] French, being the language of heraldry, cannot, of course, be taken as evidence of the French origin of the ceremony. The cries, however, are not found in the ceremonial of the interment of Edward IV, in 1483 (cf. Brit.Mus., *Egerton MS 2642*, fols.186^v-188^v), while they are almost verbatim the cries used in 1498 at the funeral of Charles VIII of France; cf. Jean de Saint-Gelais, *Chronique*, in Th. Godefroy, *Histoire de Louys XII* (Paris, 1622), 108; cf. Giesey, *op.cit.*, Ch.VIII,n.45.

utterance of the idea of immortal kingship within the framework of royal funerals.

Coins, or coin-like productions, of the sixteenth and seventeenth centuries displaying a Phoenix are not rare. The mythological bird was, for example, an emblem of Queen Elizabeth signifying her virginity as well as her singularity: SOLA PHOENIX is the inscription on some of her coins, and as UNICA PHOENIX she is celebrated in a medallion issued in the year of her demise, 1603 (fig. 22).[329] A different idea was expressed by a Phoenix medallion struck by English royalists in 1649, after the execution of Charles I. The obverse shows the profile head with the legend CAROLVS·I·D:G:MAG:BR:FR:ET·HI:REX. The reverse has the legend CAROLVS·II·D:G:MAG:BRIT:FRAN:ET·HIBER:REX; but instead of a portrait, it shows the Phoenix rising from his burning nest, and the inscription: EX·CINERIBVS (fig. 23). About the meaning of this memorial medal there can be no doubt; it was struck with the clear intention to assert against the Lord Protector and the Commonwealth the perpetuity of hereditary kingship and of the royal Dignity in general: the king's son rising as a Phoenix *ex cineribus*, from the ashes of his father—or, though less likely, from the shambles of the monarchy.[330] Even more telling is the design of a jetton for the French king, devised a few years earlier, in 1643, to announce the death of Louis XIII and the accession of Louis XIV (fig. 24). It shows the Phoenix in his mountain nest, illumined by the rays of the Sun. The inscription, borrowed from Vergil's Fourth Eclogue, reads: *Caelo demittitur alto*, "He is sent from high Heaven"—as dynasts were supposed to be ever since the thirteenth century.[331] The gist of the design, however, is given in an additional explanatory note, saying:

[329] Hawkins, *Medallic Illustrations*, Pl. VI,7,8,9; cf. VIII,17, and, for the medallion, J. D. Köhler, *Munz Belustigung* (Nürnberg, 1729ff), XXI,225ff. Cf. above, n.245.

[330] Hawkins, *op.cit.*, Pl.XXX,19. My reproduction (fig. 23) is of the copy in the Hunterian Museum at Glasgow, a cast of which was kindly provided by Mr. G. K. Jenkins, of the British Museum. The royal Phoenices were said to make England another Arabia, at least according to Ben Jonson, "A Speach presented unto King James on the Birth of the Prince," in *The Poems*, ed. B. H. Newdigate (Oxford, 1936), 281:

> Another Phoenix, though the first is dead,
> A second's flowne from his immortal bed,
> To make this our *Arabia* to be
> The nest of an eternal progeny.

[331] See above, n.58.

The Phoenix is born and soars from the cinders of his father by the influx sent to him from heaven and the sun. In the same way, the king is given to us miraculously from on high: and from his father's *lit funèbre* he soars to his own *lit de justice*.[332]

The metaphor was not badly chosen, for we have to recall that the French king made his first solemn appearance in the Court of Parlement as legislator and supreme judge—that is, held his first *lit de justice*—almost immediately after his accession, and sometimes even before his predecessor king was buried.[333] The richly decorated throne couch with its baldachin was said to be the place where "one sees *Lex et Rex* reposing under the canopy . . . , sees them together on that bed of Justice,"[334] and accordingly a medallion displaying the *lit de justice* (fig. 25) pro-

---

[332] Paris, *Bibl. Mazarine MS 4395*, fol.1ᵛ (I owe the photograph [fig. 24] to Dr. Giesey), contains a series of designs proposed for the royal jetton for New Year's day, 1644. The note on the Phoenix design reads:

Le Phoenix naist et s'eleve des Cendres de son pere par l'Influence qui luy est envoyée du Ciel et du Soleil. Ainsy le Roy nous a esté miraculeusement donné d'en-haut: Et du lict funèbre de son pere il s'eleve à son lict de Justice.

The Phoenix symbol was not infrequently used in the French court ceremonial of the 16th century. For example, the Order of the Holy Ghost, founded by Henry III in 1579, was originally to be called *Order of the Phoenix*, because, argued the courtiers, that bird was "the only creature of his kind, and without any paragon," and therein resembled the French king who "was the Phoenix of all kings in the world." See André Favin, *The Theater of Honour and Knighthood* (first published in 1620; English version, London, 1623), 416. Moreover, in 1600, at the *entrée* of Maria de' Medici into Avignon—she came as a bride to marry Henri IV—a triumphal arch was erected showing in a spandrel the Phoenix with the inscription addressing Maria: *O felix haeresque tui* (quotation from Claudian; see above, n.252), making allusion to the hope of an heir to the throne from the marriage, eventually *Le petit phénix* (above, n.269); cf. André Valladier, *Labyrinthe de l'Hercule Gaulois* (Avignon, 1601), 187 (cf. 200); cf. Giesey, *Royal Funeral*, Ch.x.

[333] Both Louis XIV and Louis XV, infants at the time of their accession, were carried to a *lit de justice* before their predecessors were buried; cf. Holtzmann, *Französische Verfassungsgeschichte*, 315. On the *lit de justice*, see Church, *Constitutional Thought*, 150ff; F. Funck-Brentano, *L'ancienne France: Le roi* (Paris, 1913), 158ff; see next note.

[334] Bernard de la Roche Flavin, *Treize livres des Parlemens de France*, IV,c.1 (Geneva, 1621), 353ff, gives the fullest description of the *lit de justice*; cf. §9, p.355: ". . . on void que *Rex et Lex* se reposent soubs le couvert [= ciel ou daix; cf. §3, p.353] de ceste sale . . . , on les void ensemblement en ce lict de Iustice . . ." Needless to say, Justice is considered by the author to be almost a French monopoly; cf. §15, p.356 (talking about the *main de Justice*, which is claimed to be an exclusively French attribute), "pource que la Iustice est nee avec la France, et a son droit hereditaire en la terre de France, comme il y a des pays qui sont doüés de choses rares, et qui ne peuvent venir ailleurs." India has odoriferous trees; Persia has pearls; only the North has amber. "Aussi il n'y a qu'une France, ou s'exercent les vrayes functions de la Iustice."

claims: *Hinc suprema lex,* "From here there emanates the supreme law."[335] The kingdom could not be left for ever so short a time without the continuity of Law and Justice which the king personified, and therefore the new Phoenix had to soar instantly and directly, without loss of time, "from his father's deathbed to his own bed of Justice." Once more, the notion of Justice was destined to have some bearings as a symbol of sempiternity.

At the king's funeral, the privilege of carrying the four corners of the mortuary pall fell to the four "Presidents of Parlement," that is, the four highest judges of the kingdom's supreme court. This custom can be traced back to the fourteenth century,[336] and the reason for this distinction is given unanimously by later authors, who explained

> that they [the presidents] represent his [the king's] person or the doing of Justice [in Parlement], which is the principal member of his Crown and by which he reigns and has sovereignty. . . .[337]

> that they, who represent in Parlement the person of the king and govern the sovereign Justice of the realm, should be closest to the body of the king. . . .[338]

The four presidents, however, were not only metaphorically *un vray pourtraict de Sa Majesté,* but also their regalia passed as

335 Claude-François Menestrier, *Histoire de Louis le Grand* (Paris, 1691), pl.28. The design is patterned after the paleo-Christian and pagan *Etimasia,* the empty throne of gods and rulers, later of Christ; it here is adapted for the legislating king: canopied, displaying on the seat the scepter and *main de justice,* showing on the back the emblem of the sun, and flanked by Justice and Faith. For another pattern of representation, the *lit de justice* at Vendôme, in 1458, see Le Comte Paul Durrieu, *Le Boccace de Munich* (Munich, 1909), 51ff, and pl. I. An idea closely related to the medallion of Louis XIV is expressed by the device of James I: *A Deo rex, a rege lex;* cf. Schliermann, "Sakralrecht des protestantischen Herrschers," 344.

336 See next note, referring to 1364. Giesey, *Royal Funeral,* Ch.v,nos.3ff, is inclined to believe that the privilege goes back to 1350 (burial of Philip VI), or possibly to 1328 (Charles IV).

337 "Et portèrent le corps dudit Roy les gens de son Parlement . . . pour ce que ilz representent sa personne ou fait de justice, qui est le principal membre de sa coronne, et par lequel il regne et a seigneurie." *Chroniques des règnes de Jean II et de Charles V,* ed. R. Delachenal (Société de l'histoire de France, 1910), I,343.

338 ". . . ilz qui en parlement representent la personne du roy et qui gouvernent la justice souveraine du royaume, soient au plus près du corps du roy." Cf. *Cérémonial de l'inhumation de Charles VI,* ed. Giesey, *Royal Funeral,* Appendix II; in the same passage the four presidents are described: "vestus de leurs manteaulx vermeils fourrez de menu vair."

le vray habit dont estoient vestues Leurs Majestez.[339] The costume of the justices consisted of a bright red robe trimmed with miniver and probably reflecting the royal purple, just as the cardinal's red tunic reflected an authority affiliated to the *cappa rubea* of the pope; it can likewise be traced back to the fourteenth century.[340] Moreover, as a special mark of distinction, the justices were entitled to wear three pendants of gold ribbon or silk attached to their shoulder, called sometimes *le bouton d'or*; there is reason to believe that this decoration derived from the three pendants of the royal (originally imperial) shoulder-clasp, the *fibula*, often mentioned by the mediaeval jurists as one of the four insignia of imperial majesty, the others being the purple, the scepter, and the diadem.[341] There can be little doubt that the red

[339] Funck-Brentano, *Le roi*, 151f, has collected a number of interesting remarks concerning the identity of the robes of the king and of the presidents, drawn chiefly from La Roche Flavin, *Parlemens*, x. cc.24-25, pp.792ff.

[340] See Giesey, *Royal Funeral*, Ch.v,nos.9,15, for a miniature of the funeral procession of Queen Jeanne de Bourbon (d.1378).

[341] For the *bouton d'or*, see La Roche Flavin, *Parlemens*, x,c.25, §12, p. 796; also Funck-Brentano, *Le roi*, 152,n.5. For the Roman imperial *fibula*, see, e.g., Richard Delbrück, *Consulardiptychen und verwandte Denkmäler* (Berlin, 1926-29), 40 (plainly visible in the Justinian mosaic at San Vitale in Ravenna). Cf., e.g., Lucas de Penna, on C.11,8,4,n.5 (Venice, 1582), 393: "quatuor sunt insignia regalia, scil. purpura, fibula aurea, sceptrum et diadema"; see also Lucas de Penna, on C.11,11,1, n.2, p.401; Matthaeus de Afflictis, on *Lib.aug.*, I,20 (21),n.1, fol.104ᵛ. Further Isidore of Seville, *Ethymol.*, xix,24,2, quoted, e.g., in *Graphia libellus*, c.5, ed. Schramm, *Kaiser, Rom und Renovatio*, II,95. De la Roche Flavin, *loc.cit.*, refers also to the Hellenistic and Biblical model, I Macc., 10: 89: "Et misit [rex] ei [Jonathae] fibulam auream, sicut consuetudo est dari cognatis regum" (also I Macc., 11: 58, and 14: 44). That is to say, Jonathan received the *fibula aurea* as *amicus regis* (συγγενὴς τοῦ βασιλέως), which was an official title designating a high-ranking member of the privy council; see John Crook, *Consilium Principis* (Cambridge, 1955), 21f. Now, the *consiliarii* of king or emperor were officially *amici regis* or *imperatoris*, a fact well known to the mediaeval jurists; see, e.g., Lucas de Penna, on C.12,16,rubr., n.1, p.706, who, *vice versa*, interprets John 15: 14f (Christ addressing the Apostles: *Vos autem dixi amicos*), almost constitutionally: *amici Christi* = privy councillors of Christ. Since the French presidents—just like the chancellor and two or three other high-ranking officials—were of course *consiliarii regis*, they received the badge apparently in their capacity of *amici regis*. This hypothesis perhaps finds support in *Graphia libellus*, c.21, ed. Schramm, II,104: at the investiture of a judge the emperor "convertat fibulam [manti] ad dextram partem," signifying that on the open right side of the mantle "lex ei debeat esse aperta." Cf. La Roche Flavin, *Parlemens*, x,c.25, §12, p.796, for the restriction of the *bouton d'or* to the right shoulder; see also, for a few remarks (not always correct) on the history of the insignia, J. Quicherat, *Histoire du costume en France* (Paris, 1877), 324. How and why the pendants of the *fibula* turned into three golden or red ribbons, can be gathered from Carolingian miniatures; see Schramm, *Kaiser und Könige in Bildern*, II, pl.17, also pls.9b,18a,28; cf. Deér, "Ein Doppelbildnis Karls des Grossen," *Forschungen zur Kunstgeschichte und christlichen Archäologie*, II(1953), 111.

robes as well as the *bouton d'or* were supposed to mirror royal insignia on a smaller scale. Not in vain were these high judges called *pars corporis principis*, "part of the king's body."[342]

This digression into the study of costumes was necessary to understand yet another privilege enjoyed by the justices. While at the royal funerals all the mourners and the whole *cortège* were clad in black or displayed signs of mourning, the pall-bearing Presidents of the Paris Parlement alone appeared in their bright red robes. They were *exempts de porter le dueil*, "exempt from wearing mourning," as an eye-witness of the funeral procession of Francis I (1547) explained, "because the Crown and Justice never die."[343] This exemption of the high judges from wearing mourning, first mentioned in 1422 in connection with the funeral of Charles VI, goes back to the fourteenth century as the miniatures disclose.[344] The explanation of this custom, however, was always the same.

> Aucuns avoient leur manteau rouge,
> En exemple et signifiance
> Que Justice jamais ne bouge
> Pour trespas du Roy, ne muance. . . .

writes Martial de Paris, describing the funeral of Charles VII, in 1461,[345] while Jean du Tillet, writing a century later, remarks

---

[342] Charles de Grassaille, *Regalium Franciae libri duo*, I, jus XII (Paris, 1545), 116: "Item illud magnum consilium dicitur proprie consistorium principis . . . et in corpore unde sumitur." Cf. Church, *Constitutional Thought*, 54. The terminology clearly derives from *C.9,8,5*, where the emperor styles his *consilium* the *consistorium*, and understands the senate as *pars corporis nostri*; see above, Ch.V, n.42; also Ch.IV,nos.188 and 195.

[343] Vieilleville, *Mémoires*, ed. J. Michaud, and P. Poujoulat, *Nouvelle collection des mémoires sur l'histoire de France* (Paris, 1836-39), IX,63: ". . . car les presidents et conseilleurs de la cour de Parlement l'environnoient [that is, the king's effigy; see below] de toutes partes, en leurs robbes rouges, exempts de porter le dueil, avec cette raison, que la couronne et la justice ne meurent jamais; de laquelle justice ils sont, soubs l'autorité des roys, premiers et souverains administrateurs." See below, n.376, for Vieilleville as onlooker in the suite of Henry II. Also De la Roche Flavin, *Parlemens*, XIII,c.88, §10, p.1181: "La Iustice, et mesmes l'authorité des Parlements est estimee tousiours durer en ce Royaume, soit le Roy mort, prins, ou absent. Et en signe de ce, les officiers des Parlements és obseques des Roys ne sont vestus de dueil, comme tous les autres, ains d'escarlate . . ."; cf. *ibid.*, §29, p.1186f, where the rubric says "Le Parlement en corps ne porter iamais dueil," and the text stresses once more: "Mais la Cour y assiste [aux obseques] en corps en robe rouge, et marche avec l'effigie du Roy, qui est dans un lict, comme accompagnant le Roy en son lict de iustice."

[344] See above, nos.338,340.

[345] Martial de Paris, dit d'Auvergne, *Les Vigilles de Charles VII*, in the edition of his *Les poésies* (Paris, 1724), II,170.

that it was the duty of the four Presidents to demonstrate by their colourful robes "that by the death of the king Justice does not cease."[346]

The underlying ideas are obvious, and they were obvious to the contemporaries, too. The justices in their costume mirroring that of the king himself displayed no signs of mourning because "Crown and Justice never die." They represented, and were part of the body of, a king who as King never died; and they were administrators of a Justice which likewise never died and whose ministry never suffered interruption. *Iustitia enim perpetua est et immortalis*, says the Book of Wisdom (1:15), and on the strength of that verse Baldus, using Aristotelian definitions, glorified Justice as a *habitus qui non moritur*, something divine and immortal like the soul.[347] The individual king may die; but the King who represents sovereign Justice and was represented by the supreme judges, was not dead; he continued his jurisdiction ceaselessly through the agency of his officers even though his natural body had passed away. *Parlamentum Franciae non servat ferias*, "The Parlement, the supreme court, of France does not observe holidays," ran a French legal maxim based on Roman Law.[348] Hence, the Presidents of Parlement showed by their red

---

[346] Jean du Tillet, *Recueil des Roys de France* (written ca. 1560, first published in 1578; Paris, 1618) 1,341: "Le principal office desquels [membres du Parlement] est bien administrer la justice . . . et faire cognoistre que par la mort desdits Rois elle ne cesse."

[347] Baldus, on D.1,1,1,n.2, fol.7r, and D.1,1,10,n.1, fol.15r; cf. Ullmann, "Baldus' Conception of Law," 390; above, Ch.iv,nos.70 and 159. The definition of Justice as *habitus*, stimulated by the words "Iustitia est constans et perpetua voluntas" (actually the opening words of the *Institutes*), was known to the glossators through Cicero, *De inventione rhetorica*, 11,53, but goes back to Aristotle.

[348] Grassaille, *Regalia Franciae*, I, ius xii, ad quartum (Paris, 1545), 120: ". . . quod parlamentum Franciae non servat ferias: imo ex consuetudine, omnibus diebus etiam feriatis (aliquibus exceptis) reddit ius . . . Ideo, de curia Franciae potest dici, quod de Romana dicit[ur] . . . , quod solennibus diebus solennes processus facit." See De la Roche Flavin, *Parlemens*, xiii,c.87, pp.1174ff, for the exceptions (including a king's funeral when *les Cours de Parlement assistent en corps*) which match, by and large, those enumerated in C.3,12,6 and 9. On that basis, already Frederick II ordered, *Lib.aug.*, 1,50 (52), that "iustitiarii . . . continue curias . . . regere debeant, causas audiant et decidant." See the glosses on that law by Andreas of Isernia, ed. Cervone, 108f, and by Matthaeus de Afflictis, 1,fol.195,n.3, who refer for that ideal of uninterrupted activity of the law courts to C.3,12,9. In France, that principle had been valid ever since the 13th century; see Durandus, *Speculum iuris*, ii, partic.I, "De Feriis," §1,n.10, p.506: ". . . quia nulla lex potest curiam Principis coarctare, quin possit quolibet tempore ius reddere, etiam diebus feriatis . . . Nam ipse est lex animata in terris . . . Et pro hoc potest excusari consuetudo curiae regis Franciae quo[d] tempore parlamentorum omni die ius reddit. . . ."

robes that the king's death did not affect Justice "who never dies." Those were ideas formulated long before by the mediaeval jurists, and the French Presidents of Parlement actually may have appeared, when acting as pall-bearers, like a *tableau vivant* illustrating Baldus' remark: "The power of ordinary jurisdiction lives even when in the meantime the emperor dies." It is true, added Baldus, that a corpse does not will, but the dead emperor, his *Dignitas*, "seems to will even after his death, because . . . everything pleases the Prince that is done by his judges even after his death, provided that they do not act against the Law."[349] How then could the justices wear mourning, since *their* King did not die?

Yet another feature connected with the burial rites deserves attention here. Charles VIII, in 1498, was entombed as customary at St.-Denis. Pierre d'Urfé, Master of the Horse, bore the sword of the realm at the funeral, and the First Chamberlain carried the banner of France. D'Urfé has left an account of the final burial scene: as the coffin slipped into the vault—that is, at the lament *Le Roy est mort!*—the stewards broke their batons and threw them into the tomb, while the heralds and sergeants-at-arms deposed their coats-of-arms and maces. The banner of France, however, just as the sword, was only dipped for a short moment, and at the cry *Vive le roy!* it was quickly raised again because, as d'Urfé explains, "the banner never dies," *car elle [la bannière] ne meurt jamais.*[350] Thus, the famous formula was transferred to the banner of France as well. In other words, insofar as the king as King was identifiable with "sovereign Justice" or with the "Banner of France" the funerary rites suggested indeed that "the King never dies."

EFFIGIES

With this symbolism of the *K*ing's survival despite the *k*ing's death there fell in one of the most startling features of royal

---

[349] Baldus, on *C.*,10,1,rubr.,n.16, fol.232ᵛ: ". . . quia non ex vi talis mandati fuit facta delegatio, sed ex vi ordinariae iurisdictionis, quae viget licet moriatur interim imperator . . . Et velle videtur [imperator] etiam post mortem, quia etiam post mortem suam verba contulisse videtur: omnia enim placent principi quae per suos iudices etiam post mortem suam fiunt, nisi contra legem sint." See above, n.296.

[350] See Th. Godefroy, *Le cérémonial de France* (Paris, 1619), 39f, for the *Ordonnance* of Pierre d'Urfé ("L'Ordre tenu à l'enterrement du Roy Charles VIII, l'an 1498, par Messire Pierre d'Urfé, grand escuyer de France").

duplication contrived in modern times: the rites connected in France with the king's effigy.[351]

It is fortunate that, in this case, we are fairly accurately informed about the origins of the usage: it was borrowed from England where the display of effigies at royal funerals is on record since 1327.[352] On September 21st of that year, King Edward II died or was murdered (we do not know) at Berkeley Castle; some time later, his disemboweled and embalmed body, accompanied by an effigy, was taken to Gloucester and buried, on December 20th, in the abbey church of St. Peter. Was it the defaced appearance of the king which made the use of an image advisable? Had some profound changes taken place in Western burial customs? We might think, of course, of purely practical reasons, since the entombment of Edward II was delayed for three months (September 21 to December 20); however, the long delay of the burial cannot have been the only reason for replacing the body by the visible effigy: no effigy was used at the funeral of Edward I who was buried at Westminster almost four months after he died at Burgh-upon-the-Sands on the Solway (July 7 to October 28, 1307).

No matter how we may wish to explain the introduction of the effigy in 1327, with the funeral of Edward II there begins, to our knowledge, the custom of placing on top of the coffin the "roiall representation" or "personage," a figure or image *ad similitudinem regis*, which—made of wood or of leather padded with bombast and covered with plaster—was dressed in the coronation garments or, later on, in the parliamentary robe. The effigy displayed the insignia of sovereignty: on the head of the image (worked apparently since Henry VII after the death mask) there was the crown,

[351] On the effigies in connection with death masks and at large, see Ernst Benkard, *Das ewige Antlitz* (Berlin, 1927); English version by Margaret M. Green, *Undying Faces* (New York, 1929); W. H. Hope, "On the Funeral Effigies of the Kings and Queens of England," *Archaeologia*, LX:2 (1907), 518-565; E. Bickermann, "Die römische Kaiserapotheose," *Archiv für Religionswissenschaft*, XXVII (1929), Excursus, pp.32f; J. Schlosser, "Geschichte der Porträtbildnerei in Wachs," *Jahrbuch der kunsthistorischen Sammlungen des allerhöchsten Kaiserhauses* (Vienna), XXIX (1910), 195f; Giesey, *Royal Funeral*, Ch.VI. Andreas Pigler, "Portraying the Dead," *Acta historiae artium Academiae scientiarum Hungariae*, IV (1956), 1-75, quoted by Harald Keller, "Effigie," in *Reallexikon zur Deutschen Kunstgeschichte*, IV (1956), 743-749, was not yet accessible to me.

[352] See, in addition to Hope, "Funeral Effigies," 530f, also S. Moore, "Documents relating to the Death and Burial of King Edward II," *Archaeologia*, L:1 (1886), 215-226.

while the artificial hands held orb and scepter.[353] Wherever the circumstances were not to the contrary,[354] the effigies were henceforth used at the burials of royalty: enclosed in the coffin of lead, which itself was encased in a casket of wood, there rested the corpse of the king, his mortal and normally visible—though now invisible—body natural; whereas his normally invisible body politic was on this occasion visibly displayed by the effigy in its pompous regalia: a *persona ficta*—the effigy—impersonating a *persona ficta*—the *Dignitas*.

Ideas such as these, though perhaps not totally absent from the English funerary ceremonial either, became very pronounced in France once the usage of the effigy was introduced in that country in the course of the fateful year 1422. King Henry V of England, we recall, died at Vincennes. In agreement with English custom an effigy was prepared for display on the coffin—perhaps already in St.-Denis, and most certainly in Rouen.[355] When, a few weeks after the demise of Henry V, Charles VI of France also died, the Duke of Bedford, as mentioned before, was responsible, directly or indirectly, for arrangements for the French king's funeral. On Bedford's return to Paris on November 5th, or just before his return, order was given to prepare an effigy of Charles VI for his funeral on November 11th. The records of the funerary expenses show that this order was executed in considerable hurry.[356] That is to say, as a result of the peculiar circumstances of the year 1422, when simultaneously the Anglo-French and the native French kings died and were buried, the English custom of exhibiting the king's funerary effigy was transplanted to France.

Henceforth the royal effigy literally "played a rôle" in the funerary ceremonial of French kings. In fact, it played an independent rôle of its own, apart from the king's dead body. In 1538, a prominent French jurist, Charles de Grassaille, asserted that "the King of France has two good angels as guardians: one in

---

[353] Hope, "Funeral Effigies," 531.

[354] As, e.g., in the cases of Richard II, Henry VI, Edward V, and Richard III.

[355] For the display of the effigy in Rouen, see Monstrelet, IV,112f; for the rites at St.-Denis, the French chronicles do not mention an effigy specifically; see, however, the very detailed *Vita Henrici Quinti* (ed. T. Hearne, Oxford, 1727), 336f, which implies that an effigy was used from the outset; see Giesey, *Royal Funeral*, Ch.VI, nos.100f.

[356] See Giesey, Ch.VI,nos.96f, for details.

reason of his private person, and the other in reason of his royal Dignity."[357] Indeed, if the king according to Jean Gerson had "two lives," he could not have less than two angels to protect them; nor will it be too hazardous to conjecture that at the king's funeral the second angel hovered presumably around the effigy. At any rate, we notice that the distinction between a ruler's person and his Dignity, disseminated for centuries by Italian jurists, was not absent from French political thought either.[358] But whereas the nature of the Dignity was normally expounded in court and in council only, it was a peculiar knack of the French to make the *Dignitas* also visible and expose it to the eye in pageant and ceremonial. The King "himself is not the Dignity, but acts the person of the Dignity," said Pierre Grégoire, a French legist writing in the last quarter of the sixteenth century;[359] and he pursued that idea in a remarkable fashion. Crown and diadem, he remarked, were external accessories of a mortal human head, and the purple was an external accessory of a mortal human body which was exposed to disease and any freak of fortune; true, the regalia "have the divinity of the Dignity," but they do not deliver man of his human nature.[360] And in that connection, Grégoire arrived at an unexpected statement: "The Majesty of God appears in the Prince *externally*, for the utility of the subjects; but *internally* there remains what is human."[361] Grégoire, when relegating the "Majesty of God" to the external display of regalia,

357 Grassaille, *Regalia Franciae*, I, ius xx, p.210: "Item, Rex Franciae duos habet bonos angelos custodes: unum ratione suae privatae personae, alterum ratione dignitatis regalis."

358 For Jean Gerson, see above, Ch.v,n.76. See further Church, *Constitutional Thought*, 253,n.1, who quotes François Grimaudet distinguishing between the Prince as Prince and the individual Caesar; or René Choppin, *De domanio Franciae*, III,tit.5,n.6 (Basel, 1605), p.449: ". . . dignitati magis quam personae concessa." See also Pierre Grégoire, *De republica*, IX,c.1,n.11 (Lyon, 1609; first published in 1578), p.266C: all belongs to the Prince in times of an emergency "in qua principis dicuntur ut principis . . . , non principis privati." See, however, Church, *op.cit.*, 309, who emphasizes that by the end of the 16th century "the extreme absolutists reduced drastically the traditional significance . . . of the distinction between the king and the crown . . ."

359 Grégoire, *op.cit.*, VI,c.3,n.7: "Docendus est itaque princeps separatim prius se ipsum cognoscere, postea dignitatem quam gerit. Nam ipse non est dignitas: sed agit personam dignitatis." The whole chapter (pp.137ff) is devoted to the *Dignitas*.

360 Grégoire, *loc.cit.*, n.7 (quoted by Church, *op.cit.*, 248,n.12), also n.3: "Principum insignia . . . , quae habent dignitatis numen, non adimunt hominis naturam et quod humanum est . . ."

361 Grégoire, *loc.cit.*, n.1: "Maiestas Dei in principibus extra apparet in utilitatem subditorum, sed intus remanet quod humanum est."

no more sought to be paradoxical than did his contemporary across the Channel, Coke, who made the striking observation that the mortal king was God-made, but the immortal King, man-made.[362] However, the visibility of God in the regalia "for the utility of the subjects" makes us think of Thackeray's caricature (fig. 26) in which the great novelist pokes fun at Rigaud's famous painting of Louis XIV by juxtaposing the final pompous state portrait and its two components: the king's pitiful body natural and a dummy decorated with the regalia.[363] In fact, for the utility of the subjects, the Majesty might as well be vested externally in the funerary effigy by the means of which the king's person seemingly doubled: the two bodies, unquestionably united in the living king, were visibly segregated on the king's demise.

Actually, the importance of the king's effigy in the funerary rites of the sixteenth century soon matched or even eclipsed that of the dead body itself. Noticeable as early as 1498, at the funeral of Charles VIII, and fully developed in 1547, at the rites held for Francis I, the display of the effigy was connected successively with the new political ideas of that age, indicating, for example, that the royal Dignity never died and that in the image the dead king's jurisdiction continued until the day he was buried. Under the impact of those ideas—strengthened by influences deriving from the mediaeval *tableaux vivants*, the Italian *trionfi*, and the study as well as the application of classical texts—the ceremonial connected with the effigy began to be filled with new contents and to affect fundamentally the funerary mood itself: a new triumphal element came into the ceremony which was absent in earlier times.

Apart from other changes, that new mood led to the replacement of the simple bier on which in former days the corpse had been carried, by the triumphal "chariot d'armes" on which henceforth the effigy rode—at first on top of the coffin, later alone and separated from the corpse.[364] Hence, to the lugubrious aspects

---

[362] Coke, *Calvin's Case*, fol.10: ". . . one a natural body . . . , and this body is of the creation of Almighty God, and is subject to death . . . ; and the other is a politic body . . . framed by the policy of man . . . and in this capacity the King is esteemed to be immortal, invisible, not subject to death . . ."

[363] Marianna Jenkins, *The State Portrait* (Monographs on Archaeology and Fine Arts, III [New York, 1947]), fig.63, cf. p.46. See Thackeray, *Paris Sketch Book*, in the Charterhouse edition of the *Works of Thackeray* (London, 1901), xvi, facing p.313.

[364] While at the funerals of Charles VII (1461) and Charles VIII (1498) the

which formerly dominated the funerary ceremonial, a new triumphal element was added, which may not have been caused by the introduction of the effigy, but which certainly received from the introduction of the funerary image, and through it, new and unexpected impulses. It should be emphasized, however, that the new triumphal idea differed profoundly from that substratum of triumph which, of course, gave a certain tinge also to the mediaeval funeral rites; for that new concept of triumph did not mean to anticipate the king's future *conregnatio* with Christ in heaven, but to celebrate and display the dead king's *conregnatio* with the immortal royal *Dignitas* on earth of which the substance had passed on to the successor, but which still was visibly represented by the effigy of the deceased ruler.[365] For the last time, the dead king "acts the person of the Dignity." Moreover, the deceased king now approached the eternal Judge in heaven in a different attire: in the Middle Ages the king was buried with his crown and his regalia, or copies thereof; now, however, he was naked or in his winding sheet, and he came to heaven as a poor wretch, whereas the regalia were reserved for the effigy, the true bearer of royal glory and the symbol of a Dignity "which never dies."[366]

---

effigy was still lying on top of the coffin, a separation took place at the funeral of Louis XII. With Francis I's funeral (1547), the coffin in a black draped chariot went in the van of the procession, while the effigy, in full royal triumph, was carried near the rear, the position of honor. For the details of a complicated development, see Giesey, Ch.vii,n.42ff.

[365] This antithesis was felt apparently as early as the 1560's by Du Tillet, *Recueil des Roys de France* (ed. 1617), I,341, when he remarks that with Francis`I and Henry II "a commencé estre divisé le corps de l'effigie, et mis dedans le chariot d'armes, ou de parement, pour faire (comme est vray-semblable) l'effigie plus eminente: par ce moyen à l'effigie seule ont depuis esté rendues les honneurs appartenans au corps mis en arrière: combien que par la future resurrection il sera immortel." That is to say, the eminence of the image which receives on earth all the honors, is set over against the now decaying corpse which nevertheless will be the truly immortal body after the Day of Resurrection. For the *conregnatio* with Christ in the future life (a privilege of the Redeemed at large, but especially of kings), see the material collected by Schramm, "Herrscherbild," 222-224; also O. Treitinger, *Die oströmische Kaiser- und Reichsidee* (Jena, 1938), 155f.

[366] When the tombs of the French kings were opened during the Revolution, the skeletons of all the kings up to Charles VII were found in royal robes, and also enclosed were crown, scepter, hand of justice and ring (not always all of these items, but always some of them). Beginning with Charles VIII, however, the corpses were found to have been buried without any royal attire or insignia. Cf. A. Lenoir, *Musée des Monumens Français* (Paris, 1801), II,xcixff: "Notice historique sur les inhumations faictes en 1793 dans l'abbaye de Saint-Denis." The same account is in G. d'Heilly (pseud. for E. A. Poinsot), *Extraction des cercueils royaux à Saint-Denis en 1793* (Paris, 1868). See Giesey, *Royal Funeral*, Ch.vii,nos.14,15,34. [See Addenda, below, p.568.]

Byzantium, as the saying is, was liturgically bifocal: a "liturgy of the court" had been developed side by side with the normal liturgy of the Church. At the French funerary rites, another bifocality developed: one ritual of the Church, observed by the clergy for the misery of the naked or half-naked man *in* the coffin ("internally there remains what is human"), and another ritual of the state, celebrating through the effigy the immortal and regal Dignity exposed *on* the coffin ("externally there appears the Majesty of God"). The triumph of Death and the triumph over Death were shown side by side.

Only a few features of the ceremonial connected with the effigy shall be mentioned here to illustrate the continuous juxtaposition of the dead king's earthly remains and his undying Dignity, each of which alternately was given prominence. At the funeral of Francis I, the encoffined body in the flesh was exhibited for about ten days in the hall of the palace. Then the scenario changed: the coffin containing the corpse was placed in a small chamber while in the hall the lifelike effigy of the king, made by Francois Clouet, took its place and lay in state—the so-called "imperial" crown on its head, the hands folded, scepter and *main de justice* on pillows on either side of it (fig. 27).[367] No signs of mourning were visible in the colorfully decorated room in which cloth of gold,

[367] The picture shows not Francis I, but Henry IV on his *lit d'honneur* (cf. Benkard, *Undying Faces*, pl.I, facing p.18, with the notes on p.59), since Clouet's effigy of Francis is not preserved; however, from the extracts of accounts, published by L. Delaborde, *La renaissance des arts à la cour de France* (Paris, 1850), I,85-90, the makeup of the effigy of Francis I can be completely reconstructed; see Giesey, *Royal Funeral*, Ch.I,n.17f. For the "imperial" crown of the French kings, see the two fundamental studies by Josef Deér, "Die abendländische Kaiserkrone des Hochmittelalters," and "Der Ursprung der Kaiserkrone," *Schweizerische Beiträge zur allgemeinen Geschichte*, VII (1949), 53-86, and VIII (1950), 51-87; but the transition of that emblem to the kings of France and England (cf. Schramm, *König von Frankreich*, I,210) has as yet to be studied in detail, whereby interesting aspects may be gleaned from the French jurists. For the *lit d'honneur* of Francis I, see Giesey, who stresses the triumphal character. It is interesting to note in this connection that the so-called *Castrum doloris* (liturgically called also *tumba*) of the Prussian kings (Frederick William I and Frederick the Great) displayed the triumphal idea exclusively, as the picture published by Benkard (*Undying Faces*, pl.VI, and pp.34ff) shows clearly: a canopy of gold brocade vaulted the effigy *in* the show coffin; on the back of the canopy was the dead king's "State Portrait" (below, n.371), while a trumpet-blowing Victory or winged Genius (taking the place of the Roman *consecratio* eagle or of a Christian angel) ascended from the top of the canopy and carried as an *imago clipeata* the monogram flourish (which by that time had joined the heraldic emblems) of the dead king to heaven—a weird conglomeration of many symbols (excepting Christian symbols, which apparently did not fit the mood of an apotheosis).

gold lilies on blue ground, and other heraldic emblems dominated. On either side of the *lit d'honneur* were altars on which the clergy, almost incessantly, celebrated masses, and at the foot of the bed was a vessel with holy water for the visitors who came to asperse— that is, keep away the demons, not from the dead man's soul on its journey to heaven or from the flesh destined to return to dust, but from the Dignity in effigy which had its own guardian angel anyhow.[368]

During that period, the image (according to the description of Pierre du Chastel, which was repeated by Jean du Tillet) was attended as though the dummy were the living king himself:

> The table being set by the officers of the commissary; the service carried by the gentleman servants, bread-carrier, cup-bearer, and carver, with the usher marching before them and followed by the officer of the cupboard, who spread the table with the reverences and samplings that were customarily made. After the bread was broken and prepared, the meat and other courses were brought in. . . . The napkin was presented by the steward to the most digni- fied person present, to wipe the hands of the Seigneur [i.e., the king in effigy]. The table blessed by a Cardinal; the basins of water for washing the hands presented at the chair of the Seigneur, as if he had been living, and seated in it. The three courses of the meal were carried out with the same forms, ceremonies, and samplings as they were wont to do during the life of the Seigneur, without forgetting those of the wine, with the presentation of the cup at the places and hours that the Seigneur had been accustomed to drink, two times at each of his meals. . . .[369]

These services rendered to an image are as startling as is the active participation of the Cardinal and the clergy. To be sure, there were ritual services proffered to sacred images—anointing, censing, aspersing, laving.[370] And to transfer quasi-religious honors

---

[368] For the guardian angels, see above, n.357. For the meaning of the aspersion of the dead, see Ludwig Eisenhofer, *Handbuch der katholischen Liturgik* (Frei- burg, 1932), I,308. The aspersion of holy images at their dedication was common practice, just like the annual washing of some images; see, e.g., for the washing of the *Volto santo*, W. F. Volbach, "Il Cristo di Sutri e la venerazione del SS. Salvatore del Lazio," *Rendiconti della Pont. Accademia Romana di Archeologia*, XVII (1940-41), 97-126. See also below, n.370.

[369] Pierre du Chastel, *Le Trespas, Obseques et Enterrement de très hault, très puissant et très magnanime Francoys, par la grace de Dieu, Roy de France* (Paris, 1547), reprinted in Godefroy, *Cérémonial de France* (Paris, 1619), 280f; Jean du Tillet, *Recueil des roys de France* (Paris, 1618, first published 1578), follows Du Chastel very closely. Cf. Giesey, *Royal Funeral*, Ch.I,n.20.

[370] Hofmeister, *Heilige Öle*, 212f, for the anointings of holy images; see above, n.368, for lavings of images. Aspersion and censing of images, of course, was common usage.

from the holy images to the images of kings and princes would not have been quite foreign to a century in which the "State Portrait" just began to make its reappearance, in which images beautifying the divine cult appeared on one level—or were "equiparated"—with those "appertaining to Civile discipline," and in which the ground was laid for the later renewal of the antique custom of displaying the ruler's image in court rooms and council chambers and thereby signifying the king's ubiquity in court.[371]

The veneration of the funerary effigy of the French king, though trimmed with some ecclesiastical exterior, was not of ecclesiastical origin. In his *Roman Histories*, Herodian, when describing the apotheosis of Emperor Septimius Severus, described also a series of ceremonial services which were rendered to the effigy of the dead ruler: the effigy, treated like a sick man, lies on a bed; senators and matrons are lined up on either side; physicians pretend to feel the pulse of the image and give it their medical aid until, after seven days, the effigy "dies."[372] Herodian's *Histories*, and especially his chapter on Septimius Severus in the Latin translation of Angelo Poliziano, were not unknown in France around 1500. Moreover, in 1541, the first full version of Herodian in

---

[371] For the fluctuations between ruler image and holy image in the 16th century, see Jenkins, *State Portrait*, esp. p.6 (with n.39), for the English version of Lomazzo's *Trattato dell'arte*, published in 1598, rendering straightforwardly the words *culto divino* by "Civile discipline" and thus changing the reference point of images. See also Jacques de la Guesle and Joys Buysson, *Remonstrances faictes à Nantes en l'an MDXCIV en la presence du deffunct Henry IV* (Paris, 1610), 42, where Buysson, a French jurist of the Crown, says in his *Remonstrance* of 1594 quite plainly "que leurs [the kings'] statues estoient tenues comme sainctes" and attributes to them the right of asylum. What he refers to are, in fact, the laws collected in C.1,24 and 25, also 8,11,13. By glossing on those laws the jurists again prepared the way leading toward the modern valuation of the ruler images; see above Ch.iv,n.72, and, for the crime of lese majesty in case of the injuring of imperial statues and images, e.g., Lucas de Penna, on C.12,20,5,n.28, p.624b, and 11,40,4,n.3, p.446, though similar remarks may be gathered in great numbers. See also Nicolas Sanders, *A Treatise of the Images of Christ and His Saints* (Louvain, 1567), 109, quoted by Yates, "Elizabeth as Astraea," 77,n.3, who defended against John Jewel the images of Christ and the saints: Why, asked Sanders, if the images of Christ are to be destroyed, are the images of rulers to be respected? But "breake . . . if you dare the image of the Queenes Maiestie or the Armes of the realme." For the "holiness" of the "Armes of the realme," there is a line leading back to the French *garda regis*, symbolized ever since the 13th century by the king's coat-of-arms; cf. Kern, *Ausdehnungspolitik*, 40f, passim. The problem of holy images versus ruler images, of course, was ardently discussed in the period of Byzantine Iconoclasm; see the studies of Ladner, in *Mediaeval Studies*, ii(1940), 127-149, esp. 137ff, and in *Dumbarton Oaks Papers*, vii(1953), 1-34. I shall discuss the rather complex problem elsewhere.

[372] Herodian, *Hist.Rom.*, iv,2; cf. Bickermann, "Kaiserapotheose," 5f.

French—by Jehan Collin—was published in Paris, followed by a second edition in 1546, a year before the death and burial of Francis I.[373] Now, the French law clerk and historian Jean du Tillet, who himself attended the funeral of Francis I, preceded his description of the modern effigy ceremonial with a detailed account of Herodian's report on Septimius Severus, adding a few scattered passages from other ancient authors as well as Eusebius' report of the *post mortem* government of Constantine the Great.[374] Directly, or through the medium of Du Tillet, the classical authors began to exercise a considerable influence on the imagination of the French who were tempted to believe that the French custom had survived from ancient Rome.[375] But to what extent they influenced the French ceremonial itself is a different matter. For the stimuli emanating from the study of Antiquity—undeniable though they were in Renaissance France—should not be overestimated, since the French ceremonial had been developing the forms and rites of royal funerals quite independently: the effigy was introduced after the English model, and not after the Roman model, and it was only subsequently that the image ceremonial was perhaps enlarged and embellished also after the pattern of ancient Rome.

Moreover, the relation between the effigy and the legalistic Dignity "which never dies" led to the emphasis of certain features which were within the compass of contemporary jurists and political thinkers, but not within that of the Roman historians. When, for example, Francis I's successor, King Henry II of France, came to asperse the body of his father, it was not the body in effigy but the real corpse which finally replaced again the effigy lying in state. It seems that the new king could not come to visit the image

---

[373] See F. Saxl, "The Classical Inscription in Renaissance Art and Politics," *Warburg Journal*, IV (1940-41), 26 and 45, for Poliziano's translation of the Herodian chapter, and, for the French versions, Giesey, *Royal Funeral*, Ch.IX.

[374] Du Tillet, *Recueil*, I,336f, mentions, in addition to Herodian, IV,2, also Cassius Dio, LVI,34, and Eusebius, *Vita Const.*, IV,72. See, for the Constantinian funerary ceremonial and its peculiarities, A. Kaniuth, *Die Beisetzung Konstantins d.Gr.: Untersuchungen zur religiösen Haltung des Kaisers* (Breslauer historische Forschungen, 19 [Breslau, 1941]); P. Franchi de' Cavalieri, "I funerali ed il sepolcro di Constantino Magno," *Mélanges d'archéologie et d'histoire*, XXXV (1915), 205-261; and also Hubaux and Leroy, *Le mythe du Phénix*, 192ff. Cf. Giesey, *Royal Funeral*, Ch.IX.

[375] This, apparently, was the opinion of Du Tillet himself, and it became a common misunderstanding on the part of French humanists who believed in the survival of Roman customs.

because the image was treated as the live king in his Dignity. Apparently one of the two kings, either the demised or the living one (though *one* only), had to represent that immortal Dignity. From the fifteenth century onward the ceremonial involvements were such that, when both the corpse and the effigy were paraded in the great funerary procession, the successor king had to stay away altogether and leave the office of chief mourner to one of the princes of the royal blood: the new king could not at once wear mourning and not wear mourning; nor could he, at the same time, "act the person of the Dignity" and cede this privilege to the effigy of his deceased predecessor. Therefore, there was no other solution except staying away.[376]

The funerary procession itself demonstrated very clearly the concurrence of two heterogeneous ideas: the triumph of Death and the triumph over Death. There was the ecclesiastical ritual of the exequies and the general care attached to the dead king's body and soul; and there was the triumphal state ceremonial attached to the sempiternal glory symbolized by the effigy. This dichotomy was noticeable as early as 1498, at the funeral of Charles VIII. The procession conveying the corpse alone, without effigy, on a chariot from Amboise, where Charles died, to Paris

---

[376] Cf. Giesey, Ch.IV, passim, esp. 47f. Jacques de la Guesle, *Remonstrances* (see above, n.371), p.52, says: ". . . mesme la presence des Roys, doit estre accompagnee de joye, et de contentement; raison pour laquelle ils n'ont accoustumé se trouver aux obseques de leurs predecesseurs, ny encore le fils à celles du pere, n'estant convenable à leurs sacrees personnes s'entremettre des mortuaires." See also Du Tillet, I,337f. However, it was not only unsuitable for a king to show mourning, but also it would have been most awkward for the new king to appear in the presence of his predecessor's effigy, to which regal honors still adhered; see, e.g., Vieilleville, *Mémoires* (above, n.343), 62, who describes how the new king (Henry II) watched together with Vieilleville and the Marshal de St. André the funeral of Francis I—secretly and incognito: *y estant comme travesti*. The custom of staying away was fixed by Louis XII, at the funeral of Charles VIII in 1498. It is perhaps not amiss to recall in this connection the fact that the Byzantine emperor avoided also the wearing of mourning in the ordinary sense: whereas all others wore black, he alone wore white, later yellow, before he returned to purple garments; nor does the pope seem to wear mourning; cf. Treitinger, *Oströmische Kaiseridee*, 156,n.57. The underlying idea goes far back in the history of ceremonial: "He [the king] must separate himself from the human passions, and draw himself close to the gods ($\chi\omega\rho\iota\zeta\text{o}\nu\tau\alpha$ $\mu\grave{\epsilon}\nu$ $\grave{\epsilon}\alpha\upsilon\tau\grave{\text{o}}\nu$ $\grave{\alpha}\pi\grave{\text{o}}$ $\tau\hat{\omega}\nu$ $\grave{\alpha}\nu\theta\rho\omega\pi\acute{\iota}\nu\omega\nu$ $\pi\alpha\theta\acute{\epsilon}\omega\nu$, $\sigma\upsilon\nu\epsilon\gamma\gamma\acute{\iota}\zeta\text{o}\nu\tau\alpha$ $\delta\grave{\epsilon}$ $\tauο\hat{\iota}\varsigma$ $\theta\epsilonο\hat{\iota}\varsigma$)," wrote Diotogenes, author of a Hellenistic tractate *On Kingship*; cf. Goodenough, "Hellenistic Kingship," 72; Delatte, *Traités de la royauté*, 42f,269f; and for the problem in general, M. P. Charlesworth, "Imperial Deportment," *Journal of Roman Studies*, XXVII (1947), 34-38. That actually the Hellenistic tractates *On Kingship* were used in the 16th century for the interpretation of the French king's "absolutism" will be demonstrated on another occasion; see, however, below, Epilogue, nos. 12ff.

had the lugubrious appearance which one would expect: everything was draped in black, the banners were furled, the sword of the realm was sheathed, and the other emblems were kept covered. When, however, upon the entry into Paris, the effigy was placed on top of the coffin, the mood changed fundamentally: the naked sword now preceded the image adorned with the regalia and royal insignia; the unfurled Banner of France "which never dies" followed the effigy; likewise unfurled standards paraded alongside the coffin; clad in their regal scarlet robes, the four Presidents of Parlement (there services eventually were shifted from the corpse to the effigy) carried the four corners of the cloth of gold on which the figure rested—in short, the effigy representing the Dignity "which never dies" made its *Entrée* into Paris: a triumphal *Adventus* rather than a mourning procession.[377] Later on, when image and corpse were transported separately, it remained the custom to attach all the mournful elements to the naked body in the coffin and to assemble all the triumphal pageantry around the effigy, which alone was paraded under a canopy (fig. 29).[378] It was apparently in this intellectual climate that there originated the triumphal chariot for the dead, the modern funeral car, which until the beginning of the motorized age was used in practically all Western countries—or rather, it was reintroduced from classical models as interpreted by the taste of the Renaissance.[379] At the funeral of the Emperor Charles V, in 1559, the triumphal idea was carried so far that a float recalling the em-

[377] Cf. Giesey, Ch.v,n.90ff, where successive French royal funeral processions of the 15th and 16th centuries are reconstructed, showing the increasing pomp and display. The chivalrous elements may have been influenced by the sumptuous Burgundian processions of the 15th century, but the elements of triumph were decidedly in Italian neo-antique style, and come only after the French expeditions into Italy in 1494. In general on French Renaissance entrées, see J. Chartrou, *Les entrées solennelles et triomphales à la renaissance* (Paris, 1928).

[378] See above, n.365; also nos.359f, for Pierre Grégoire's distinction between Prince and regalia; for an illustration of the canopy over the effigy, separated from the wagon carrying the corpse, see *Pompe funerali fatte in Pariggi nella morte dell' invitissimo Henrico IIII Re di Francia et Navarra* (Francesco Vallegio et Catarin Doino D.D.D.), reproduced in Giesey, *Royal Funeral*, pls. XIV-XV. The woodcut (fig. 29) forms the frontispiece of a pamphlet on the funeral of Louis XII, *L'obsèque et enterrement du roy* [Paris, 1515].

[379] See, for a few good remarks on the subject, Leopold Ettlinger, "The Duke of Wellington's Funeral Car," *Warburg Journal*, III (1939-40), 254ff; also A. Alföldi, "Chars funéraires bacchiques dans les provinces occidentales de l'empire romain," *Antiquité classique*, VIII (1939), 347-359, and A. L. Abaecherli, "Fercula, Carpenta and Tensae in the Roman Procession," *Bolletino dell' assoziazione internazionale di studi mediterranei*, VI (1935-36), 1-11.

peror's victories paraded in the funeral procession—a blending of Renaissance *trionfi* and mediaeval *tableaux*.[380]

The juxtaposition of the lugubrious and the triumphal, the mourning for the dead king and the exaltation of the effigy, must have responded to some very general and very deep feeling of the late Middle Ages and the early Renaissance, since the sepulchral monuments of that age reflect similar ideas. From the times of Louis XII onward (d. 1515), the tomb monuments of the French kings at St.-Denis began to display the king or the royal couple as they were in life, kneeling in their regal attire before a *prie-Dieu* on top of the temple-like portico of the monument; within the portico, however, lay the dead king in his human misery, naked (except for a drapery) and his eyes closed.[381] That with the spreading of Renaissance ideas this nakedness tended to become a *nudité heroique* rather than a symbol of man's naked misery is a different matter: Caterina de' Medici, disgusted and horrified by a macabre naturalistic tomb effigy of her own self, commissioned a second tomb figure more to her taste which represented her as a reclining Venus.[382] Those, however, were not the ideas which had governed the "high Gothic" sentiments of the fifteenth century at the beginning of which that type of duplicated tomb monuments, or at least a certain type of dual representations of the dead, made its first appearance.

Without entering into any details of a complicated development in Western sepulchral art, it may at least be mentioned that in the late twelfth century the reclining effigy of the deceased—the *gisant*—began to replace the hitherto customary sculptured or incised plates which showed the dead standing in an upright position, no matter whether the plate itself was placed in the wall of a church or in the floor.[383] Moreover, double monu-

---

380 Ettlinger, *op.cit.*,255,n.1.

381 See the magnificent reproductions of the tombs at St.-Denis by Jean-François Noël and Pierre Jahen, *Les gisants* (Paris, 1949).

382 The macabre first model by Girolamo della Robbia (cf. A. Michel, *Histoire de l'art* [Paris, 1905-28], IV:2,670f, also P. Richer, *L'art et la médecine* [Paris, 1902], 514f and fig. 322) is now in the Louvre and therefore, ironically, far better known today than the Venus-like tomb effigy itself, which can be viewed in the abbey of St.-Denis only from a distance.

383 Professor Erwin Panofsky kindly pointed out to me that from the genuine *gisant* another kind of tomb figure has to be distinguished which might be called a *pseudo-gisant*. The latter is really an upright statue (known from the earlier

ments in which the deceased appeared both as a dead human being (though not as yet as a "corpse") and in the costume of his social rank in life are found sporadically during the late thirteenth and the fourteenth centuries.[384] Finally, a new feature was added. By the very end of the fourteenth century, the skeleton or cadaverous body began to appear in mediaeval art, a definitely late-mediaeval feature; we may recall, for example, that the first *Danse macabre*, the one in the cloisters of Saints Innocents in Paris, was executed under Charles VII, in 1425 or 1426.[385] By that time, however, this grim theme of high Gothic art was combined with the sepulchral representation of both the *gisant* and the (as yet rare) double representations of the dead. The result was a species of monuments showing the reclining dead as a putrefying skeleton-like corpse, whereas on some higher level, or superimposed on the tomb, the deceased would be seen pictured such as he had been during his life. The *gisant*, thereby, was often transformed into a kneeling, or sometimes sitting, figure.[386]

It is usually said that the first to have himself represented as a cadaverous corpse was a physician of Charles VI, Guillaume de Harcigny, who died in 1393 and was buried in the episcopal chapel at Laon; in fact, not too much will be lost if we forget about the

---

sculptured or incised tomb plates) laid horizontal: the drapery hangs stiffly down to the feet as on a standing figure, over the head there is often a sculptured niche, and the eyes are open. The genuine *gisant*, however, is truly a reposing figure; the eyes are closed, and the folds of the gown fall naturally to either side of the recumbent body. Probably the earliest tomb effigies of the genuine *gisant* pattern are those in the Abbey of Fontevrault of the Plantagenets Henry II and Richard I as well as their queens, and the Brunswick tombs of Henry the Lion and his wife, a daughter of Henry II of England. The *pseudo-gisant*, however, dominated (see, e.g., the tombs of the English bishops, figs. 30, 31), lasting in some places until the 16th century, although in the early 14th century the genuinely reposing *gisant* became more and more popular.

[384] For one of the earliest specimens—the tomb of Philip de Courtenay, pretender to the Latin Empire (d. 1283), at San Francesco in Assisi—see W. R. Valentiner, "The Master of the Tomb of Philippe de Courtenay in Assisi," *The Art Quarterly*, XIV (1951), 3-18.

[385] For the latest monograph on this subject, see James M. Clark, *The Dance of Death in the Middle Ages and the Renaissance* (Glasgow, 1950), who could not yet profit from Robert Eisler, "Danse Macabre," *Traditio*, VI (1948), 187-225, a study on the basis of which a few items in the brilliant chapter on "Das Bild des Todes" by J. Huizinga, *Herbst des Mittelalters* (3rd ed., Stuttgart, 1938), 193-213, may be revised.

[386] For the kneeling figure atop the reclining dead, see above, n.381; a seated statue of William the Silent in addition to the reclining sarcophagus figure (made between 1614 and 1621) is found in the Nieuwe Kerk at Delft.

slightly earlier tomb of Francis I de La Sarraz, in La Sarraz (Canton of Vaud), the horrors of which would spoil the appetite even of an inveterate ghoul.[387] There followed, within a decade after the Harcigny tomb, the now destroyed sepulchral monument, in Avignon, of Cardinal Lagrange, who died in 1402. The arrangement of this monument is complicated in many respects, and so is the reconstruction of details. One important feature of the composition, however, is indisputable: Lagrange was represented both as a naked, skeleton-like corpse and as a cardinal adorned with all the pomp and the regalia of his *Dignitas*.[388] A slightly different type of tomb architecture, or perhaps only a more condensed and more dialectical version of Lagrange's monument, became famous in the early sixteenth century through the mausoleum tombs, at Brou, of Philibert II of Savoy and his Duchess Margaret of Austria, although here the horror of death was mitigated.[389] But the pattern of those princely tomb figures was probably first developed in England.

Canterbury Cathedral harbors, as it should, the body of Archbishop Henry Chichele, Primate of England for 29 years—from 1414 to 1443. In 1424, ten years after his accession, Chichele began to build the tomb in which finally he was buried. Within the tomb, and barely screened by the Gothic trelliswork, the dead Henry Chichele's mortal body is exposed: naked, all skin and bones, the eyes gazing with a vacant stare, the pitiful corpse lying without a pillow on a linen sheet (fig. 30).[390] On the top of the tomb, however, magnificently attired, rests the *gisant*: Archbishop-Primate Henricus Cantuariensis in dalmatic, the pallium around his shoulders,

[387] For Harcigny, see C. R. Morey, *Mediaeval Art* (New York, 1942), 390. For the tomb of La Sarraz, see H. Reiners, *Burgundisch-alemannische Plastik* (Strasbourg, 1943), p.70 (with notes 99 and 100, on p.319) and figs. 86, 370; the date of this tomb, which in its nauseating repulsiveness is far from being "realistic," may be about 1370, as Professor Panofsky kindly pointed out to me.

[388] Eugène Müntz, "A travers le comtat Venaissin: Le mausolée du Cardinal de Lagrange à Avignon," *L'Ami des monuments et des arts*, IV (1890), 91-95,131-135, esp. 132; see also Mâle, *L'art religieux de la fin du moyen âge*, 431, fig. 194.

[389] For the tombs at Brou, see Victor de Mestral Combremont, *La sculpture à l'église de Brou* (Paris [191?]), pls.23,24,26,27.

[390] I am greatly indebted to Professor William A. Chaney, in Lawrence College, who first called my attention to this tomb, provided me with photographs, and gave me other valuable information. On Chichele, see the works of E. F. Jacob, and for the present purpose especially his essay on "Chichele and Canterbury," *Studies in Mediaeval History Presented to Frederick Maurice Powicke* (Oxford, 1948), 386-404.

the precious mitre on his head, the feet in pontifical shoes. His eyes are wide open, his hands folded in prayer. Nor is he in the miserable loneliness of the emaciated body below: angels are near the pillow on which his mitred head rests, and kneeling attendants near his feet join him in prayer.

The funerary ceremonial observed on his death has to be considered too. Chichele died in Lambeth from where his remains were transferred in solemn procession to Canterbury, escorted by scores of torchbearers and two hundred gentlemen on horseback with their retinues. Whereas in later times it was the custom to carry four banners of saints at the four corners of the coffin, the usage still prevailed in the fifteenth century to have instead the bishop's personal banner as well as the banner of his bishopric displayed by a gentleman mounted on a charger. One feature, in particular, attracts our attention: the coffin, shouldered on a bier, was topped by Chichele's effigy dressed in full pontificals and adorned with all the insignia of his office.[391] It is true, the display of a bishop's effigy fell in desuetude in sixteenth-century England; but it was the common custom in the fifteenth to parade at funerals the dead body of a high dignitary of the Church together with his image.[392] Hence, the sepulchral monument of Archbishop Chichele, showing the effigy on the top of the tomb and the corpse within the tomb, was the naturalistic reproduction of reality, rendering simply what was seen at the funerary procession: the effigy in regalia on top of the coffin which contained the almost naked corpse.

Since the parading of the effigy was the general usage at a bishop's funeral in fifteenth-century England, it might be expected to find more episcopal tombs worked during that period after

---

[391] Jacob, "Chichele and Canterbury," 388. For the banners displayed, see next note.

[392] Brit.Mus., *Egerton MS 2642*, fol.194 (I could avail myself of Dr. Giesey's MS copy), contains a *Note of the Manner of the Burieng of a Bysshop in old Tyme used*, of ca. 1560, which describes 15th-century customs no longer practiced:

The Corpse to bee Layed in th'aforesayd charre, and to have upon the corse a figure apparelled in a Bisshopps araye Mytred, and in his hand a Croyeser, and on his hands red gloves, and on his feet red shewes, and the said gloves to bee garnyshed with Rynges. The figure is not nowe used. And in tymes past a gentleman was wonte riding apon a goodly coursier trapped to beare a Banner of the Armes of the said Bishopp and of the Byshoppricke to be parte in palle. But now the usage is to have but the iiii banners of Saynts at the fower corners of the charet borne by fower gentlemen in morning habitts with hoods over theire faces.

the Canterbury pattern. There is, for example, in addition to the tomb of Bishop Richard Fleming (d. 1431), in Lincoln Cathedral, the monument of Bishop Beckington of Bath and Wells (d. 1465), which probably was finished in 1451, fourteen years before the bishop's death (fig. 31).[393] His monument is less sumptuous than Chichele's tomb at Canterbury, but again we recognize the strong contrasts: the naked corpse in the tomb and the effigy in full pontificals lying on top of the tomb. Nor was this fashion restricted to princes of the Church. John Fitzalan, 17th Earl of Arundel (d. 1435), was buried in a tomb showing the body in corruption below the effigy in glory (fig. 28); and King Edward IV decreed in his will (June 20, 1475) very circumstantially how he wanted to be buried in the Chapel of Saint George, at Windsor: his body was to be buried low in the ground, "and upon the same a stone to be laied and wrought with the figure of Dethe," and on the vault over the tomb there was to be "an Image of oure figure, which figure we will be of silver and gilte," or, may be, in copper.[394] In all those cases, one is tempted to say with the poet: "Of marble is the stone, and putried ther he lies."[395]

We may think, though, of other words as well when contemplating those tombs of powerful princes spiritual and secular. For the decrepit and decaying body natural in the tomb, now separated from the awe-inspiring body politic above it, appears like an illustration of the doctrine expounded over and over again by mediaeval jurists: *Tenens dignitatem est corruptibilis*, DIGNITAS *tamen semper est, non moritur*—"The incumbent of a

---

[393] For the tomb of Bishop Richard Fleming, see G. H. Cook, *Portrait of Lincoln Cathedral* (London, 1950), fig. 62, to which Professor Panofsky kindly called my attention; the tomb is dated by E. S. Prior and A. Gradner, *An Account of Mediaeval Figure-Sculpture in England* (Cambridge, 1912), 717, fig. 816, erroneously ca.1370; but, as Professor Panofsky and Mr. Francis Wormald, in London, inform me, the date of the tomb is ca.1430. For the Beckington tomb, see Lawrence Stone, *Sculpture in Britain: The Middle Ages* (Penguin Books: 1955), 213f. Professor W. A. Chaney was kind enough to provide me with a photograph and to give me additional information about date and some details. On Beckington, see the introduction to *Official Correspondence of Thomas Bekynton*, ed. George Williams (Rolls Series, 56:1; London, 1872); also W. F. Schirmer, *Der englische Frühhumanismus* (Leipzig, 1931), 66ff, with literature in n.35.

[394] I would have missed the Arundel tomb without the kind help of Mr. Francis Wormald, who not only mentioned it to me, but also provided me with the photo. See, for the will of Edward IV, W. H. St. John Hope, *Windsor Castle* (London, 1913), II,376; see also L. Stone, *Sculpture* (above, n.393), 213f.

[395] Hope, "Funeral Effigies," 529, quoting Robert of Bourn's translation of Bridlington's Chronicle.

Dignity may decay, the Dignity itself is nonetheless forever; it does not die."

Our rapid digression on funerary ceremonial, effigies, and sepulchral monuments, though not directly related to the rites observed for English kings, has nevertheless yielded at least one new aspect of the problem of the "two Bodies"—the human background. Never perhaps, except in those "late Gothic" centuries, was the Western mind so keenly conscious of the discrepancy between the transience of the flesh and the immortal splendor of a Dignity which that flesh was supposed to represent. We understand how it could happen that the juristic distinctions, though developing quite independently and in a totally different thought compartment, eventually fell in with some very general sentiments, and that the jurists' imaginative fictions met with certain feelings which in the age of the *Danses macabres*, where all Dignities danced with Death, must have been peculiarly close to the surface. The jurists, as it were, discovered the immortality of the Dignity; but by this very discovery they made the ephemeral nature of the mortal incumbent all the more tangible. We should not forget that the uncanny juxtaposition of a decaying corpse and an immortal Dignity as displayed by the sepulchral monuments, or the sharp dichotomy of the lugubrious funeral train surrounding the corpse and the triumphant float of an effigy-dummy wrapped in regalia, was fostered, after all, in the same ground, came from the same world of thought and sentiment, evolved in the same intellectual climate, in which the juridical tenets concerning the "King's two Bodies" achieved their final formulation. In both instances, there was a body mortal, God-made and therefore "subject to all Infirmities that come by Nature or Accident," set against another body, man-made and therefore immortal, which is "utterly void of Infancy and old Age and other Defects and Imbecilities."

In short, one revelled in strong contrasts of fictitious immortality and man's genuine mortality, contrasts which the Renaissance, through its insatiable desire to immortalize the individual by any contrivable *tour de force*, not only failed to mitigate, but rather intensified: there was a reverse side to the proud reconquest of a terrestrial *aevum*. At the same time, however, immortality—the decisive mark of divinity, but vulgarized by the artifice

436

of countless fictions—was about to lose its absolute, or even its imaginary, values: unless it manifested itself incessantly through new mortal incarnations, it practically ceased to be immortality. The *King* could not die, was not allowed to die, lest scores of fictions of immortality were to break down; and while *k*ings died, they were granted the comfort of being told that at least "as *K*ing" they "never died." The jurists themselves, who had done so much to build up the myths of fictitious and immortal personalities, rationalized the weakness of their creatures, and while elaborating their surgical distinctions between the immortal Dignity and its mortal incumbent and talking about two different bodies, they had to admit that their personified immortal Dignity was unable to act, to work, to will, or to decide without the debility of mortal men who bore the Dignity and yet would return to dust.[396]

Nevertheless, since life becomes transparent only against the background of death, and death against the background of life, the bone-rattling vitality of the late Middle Ages appears not devoid of some deeper wisdom. What one did was to build up a philosophy according to which a fictitious immortality became transparent through a real mortal man as its temporary incarnation, while mortal man became transparent through that new fictitious immortality which, being man-made as immortality always is, was neither that of life eternal in another world nor that of the godhead, but that of a very terrestrial political institution.

REX INSTRUMENTUM DIGNITATIS

It had been difficult enough to distinguish between man and his Dignity, and to separate one from the other. It was no less difficult to put them together again and to introduce theories which made it plausible that "one person sustains in the place of

---

396 See, e.g., Baldus, on *C.*7,61,3,n.1, fol.91ᵛ: ". . . sine quo dignitas nihil facit." Also Baldus, *Cons.*, III,121,n.6, fol.34: "quia dignitas sine persona nihil agit," with the additional remark "quia persona facit locum actui," that is, the person actualizes the potentialities resting in the Dignity. See further *Cons.*, III,159,n.5, fol.45ᵛ: "nam verum est dicere quod respublica nihil per se agit, tamen qui regit rem publicam agit in virtute reipublicae et dignitatis sibi collatae ab ipsa republica." Concerning different concepts of capability and incapability of a fictitious person to act or to will, see Gierke, *Gen.R.*, III,461ff. The English jurists, of course, made similar statements concerning the body politic which became capable of action only through the body natural.

two, one a real and the other a fictitious person,"[397] or that a king has "two bodies" though he has "but one person."[398] Once more it was theology as well as Canon Law which produced the similes by means of which the jurists could venture to explain the oneness of the two bodies—of the mortal in the immortal, and of the immortal in the mortal.

That the king as King was "incorporated with his subjects, and they with him,"[399] was a saying at which the jurists, despite the ominous word "incorporated," could have arrived easily from the relatively safe grounds of organological concepts or of the *corpus mysticum* doctrine in its secularized form; it meant that the king as the head and the subjects as the members together formed the body politic of the realm. It was a slightly different matter, however, when this "together" of a composite body— plausible within the limitations of the metaphor—was transferred from "head and members" to the head alone, and when that composite nature was reduced to the king alone, that is, to his "two Bodies." In the case of the Duchy of Lancaster, the jurists argued that the king's body natural was "neither divided by itself nor distinct from his office or the royal Dignity," but that they were

> a Body natural and a Body politic together indivisible; and [that] these two Bodies are incorporated in one Person, and make one Body and not divers, that is, the Body corporate in the Body natural, *et e contra* the Body natural in the Body corporate.[400]

Once this, so to say, monistic formula was coined, implying neither more nor less than the king's incorporation with himself, with his Dignity or his Body politic, it was naturally quoted by others as well—for example, by Francis Bacon:

> There is in the king not a Body natural alone, nor a Body politic alone, but a body natural and politic together: *corpus corporatum in corpore naturali, et corpus naturale in corpore corporato.*[401]

[397] Baldus, on c.3 X 2,19,n.5, *In Decret.*, fol.201ᵛ: "nota hic quod una persona sustinet vicem duarum, unam vere, alteram ficte, et quandoque utramque personam vere propter concursum officiorum." Cf. Gierke, *Gen.R.*, III,435,n.74, who mentions other similar places.

[398] Maitland, *Sel.Essays*, 110,n.4; see also Bacon, *Post-nati*, 667 (referring to Plowden, 285): ". . . not a body natural alone, nor a body politic alone, but a body natural and politic together." See also below, n.400: "two Bodies incorporated in one Person."

[399] See above, Ch.I,n.13, also n.5.

[400] Plowden, *Reports*, 213; see above, Ch.I,n.5.   [401] Bacon, *Post-nati*, 667.

It is easy to see how one arrived at that new formula: the "subjects plus King," being incorporated with each other and forming together the body politic of the realm, were replaced by the "King's Body politic" which now was incorporated with the "king's Body natural."

Actually, the very long history of a very old theological formula may well have culminated in this ultra-fanciful maxim of English jurists. In 1062, at the beginning of the Struggle of Investiture, Petrus Damiani, the purest mind of that revolutionary period, developed a program of mutual support and understanding to prevail between papacy and empire and, while summarizing his arguments, he demanded that henceforth there be found "the king in the Roman pontiff, and the Roman pontiff in the king."[402] This was a political utterance on an almost cosmic level suggesting that the two universal powers be incorporated with each other just as kingship and priesthood were one, and quasi "incorporated" with each other, in the divine model of both powers, in Christ. Petrus Damiani, of course, was not the source of the Elizabethan jurists, for his works were hardly within the compass of juridical thinking. Instead, we are sent back to the jurists. "The Prince is in the *respublica*, and the *respublica* is in the Prince," wrote, at the beginning of the sixteenth century, Matthaeus de Afflictis, an author incessantly quoted by the French jurisprudents;[403] and yet he repeated only what Lucas de Penna, in the fourteenth century, and Andreas of Isernia, around 1300, had said before: "Just as the Church is in the prelate, and the prelate is in the Church . . . , so is the Prince in the *respublica*, and the *respublica* in the Prince."[404] With this "equiparation" of prelate and Prince, Lucas de Penna indicated his source, to which Andreas of Isernia had already referred;[405] that is, to Gratian's *Decretum*, to

---

[402] Petrus Damiani, *Disceptatio synodalis*, in *MGH, LdL*, I,93,34ff: ". . . quatinus, sicut in uno mediatore Dei et hominum haec duo, regnum scilicet et sacerdotium, divino sunt conflata mysterio, ita sublimes istae duae personae tanta sibimet invicem unanimitate iungantur, et quodam mutuae caritatis glutino *et rex in Romano pontifice et Romanus pontifex inveniatur in rege* . . . ," a place to which Professor Theodor E. Mommsen kindly called my attention. See Fridolin Dressler, *Petrus Damiani: Leben und Werk* (Studia Anselmiana, xxxiv; Rome, 1954), 97,n.66.

[403] Matthaeus de Afflictis, on *Lib.aug.*, II,3,n.62, fol.11ᵛ: "quod princeps est in republica et respublica in principe" (quoting Lucas de Penna).

[404] See above, Ch.v,n.60.

[405] Andreas of Isernia, on *Feud.*, I,3,n.16 (*Qui success.ten.*), fol.21ᵛ: "Princeps et Respublica idem sint . . . Est princeps in Republica sicut caput, et Respublica in

a famous chapter in which it is said that "the bishop is in the Church, and the Church in the bishop."[406] Gratian, of course, and other canonical collections before him—such as that of Ivo of Chartres[407]—merely reproduced a famous letter of St. Cyprian, Bishop of Carthage in the third century, which has always been taken as a cornerstone of the doctrine of the "monarchic episcopate" and in which Cyprian declared: "The bishop is in the Church, and the Church in the bishop."[408] This form of inversion goes back to the Fourth Gospel (John 14:10): "I am in the Father, and the Father is in me," a verse to which (together with John 10:30) not only Andreas of Isernia referred, but also—very long before him, and in a most curious fashion—the staunchest fighter against Arianism, Athanasius of Alexandria. When defending the Pauline doctrine of Christ as the Image of God and, therewith, the divinity of the Son and his coequality with the Father, Athanasius resorted to the simile of the emperor's image, which he called "the idea (εἶδος) and form (μορφή) of the emperor," and said: "The image might well speak: 'I and the emperor are one, I am in him and he is in me.'"[409]

---

eo sicut in capite, ut dicitur de praelato in Ecclesia, et Ecclesia in praelato." Andreas of Isernia repeats that image in *Prooem. ad Lib.aug.*, ed. Cervone, p.xxvi, and carried the "equiparation" of Prince and prelate even further in his gloss on *Feud.*, II,56,n.81 (*Quae sunt regalia*), fol.306. The passage is interesting because Andreas in fact combines and twists two passages of the Fourth Gospel (John, 10:30, and 14:10)—just as Athanasius had done long before him (below, n.409). The jurist, however, does not refer to the Gospel but to the Decretum (c.7,C.VII,q.1; see next note) and to a decretal of Innocent III (c.19 X 5,40, where only the *Glos.ord.* on the *casus* and v. *et si capitulum* explain the reference). Moreover, in all three passages Andreas quotes Seneca, *De clementia*, 1,5,1—faithfully repeated by Lucas de Penna, on *C.*11,58,7,n.8, p.564 (see above, Ch.v,n.65).

[406] See c.7,C.VII,q.1, ed. Friedberg, I,568f.
[407] See Friedberg, I,568,n.106, for the earlier collections.
[408] Cyprian, *ep.*66,c.8, ed. Hartel (*CSEL*, III), II,733.
[409] Athanasius, *Oratio III contra Arianos*, c.5, PGr, XXVI,332A, quoted by Ladner, "The Concept of the Image," 8 and 24,n.31: εἴποι ἂν ἡ εἰκών· Ἐγὼ καὶ ὁ βασιλεὺς ἕν ἐσμεν. Ἐγὼ γὰρ ἐν ἐκείνῳ εἰμὶ κἀκεῖνος ἐν ἐμοί. See also Ladner for the later repetitions of that passage by John of Damascus and the Second Council of Nicaea (787). With that passage one may compare the London Magical Papyrus, ed. K. Preisendanz, *Die griechischen Zauberpapyri* (Leipzig and Berlin, 1928-31), II,47 (P.VIII,37ff): σὺ γὰρ ἐγὼ καὶ ἐγὼ σύ· τὸ σὸν ὄνομα ἐμὸν καὶ ἐμὸν σόν· ἐγὼ γάρ εἰμι τὸ εἰδωλόν σου. See also, for parallels, Preisendanz, II,123 (P.XIII,795ff). Wilfred L. Knox, *Some Hellenistic Elements in Primitive Christianity* (Schweich Lectures of the British Academy, 1942; London, 1944), 78,n.3, considers those passages "the nearest parallel to the Johannine language" (i.e., John 10: 30, and 14: 10); see also E. Norden, *Agnostos Theos* (Berlin, 1923), 305, for the language of John. All those parallels, however, do not contain the word ἐν (in), which is essential for the development from John 14: 10, to Cyprian, *ep.*66,c.8, and thence to the corporational doctrines of the later Middle Ages.

We now understand where in the last analysis the christological undercurrent in the jurists' language derived from. At any rate, when the English judges in the sixteenth century tried to conjoin again what they had separated, and declared that the body politic was incorporated with the body natural, and vice versa, they clearly applied theological and christological language as well as canonical thought to their fictions. Once more, as so often before, the bishop in his relation to his church served as a pattern for expounding the relation of the king to his kingdom as well as to his body politic. No doubt, St. Cyprian's coinage had been changed, but the original die and the die-sinker are still recognizable. Moreover, his doctrine of the monarchic episcopate did not fit badly as a model for the maturing absolutist monarchies in which the king became, in more than one respect, pontifical.[410]

The manner of speech which the English jurists sported suggests, however, yet another layer of theological thought. When those judges argued in court about the consolidation of the two bodies in one and thereby used phrases such as "together indivisible" or "two Bodies in one Person," they arrogated a set of distinctions found in the language of the Creed and normally reserved for christological definitions. To be sure, those lawyers were not talking about the king's "two Natures" but about his "two Bodies." However, we may recall that the theologians, ever since the twelfth century, explained that Christ had two bodies (one his individual natural body in the flesh, and the other his mystical collective body of which he was the head)[411] though indeed but one person. Arguments concerning the "two Bodies" thus became applicable to the "two Natures" as well, and vice versa, even though the two notions did not coincide completely. Now those arguments served, by transference, to explain the "two Bodies" of the king; and in that practice the English lawyers had their predecessors in the fourteenth century.

In one of his *Consilia*, Baldus, as we recall, distinguished between the "Majesty" and the "person in Majesty," and while discussing very elaborately the Majesty or Dignity as something distinct from the person of the individual king, he remarked:

Here we are aware of the Dignity as the principal, and of the person

---

[410] Concerning the "Pontificalism" of the absolute monarchs, see my remarks in "Mysteries of State," 67ff.

[411] See above, Ch.v,nos.14ff.

as the instrumental. Hence, the fundament of the [king's] acts is that very Dignity which is perpetual.[412]

Baldus must have considered the distinction between the *principalis* (the perpetual Dignity) and the *instrumentalis* (the mortal king) peculiarly useful, for he applied those notions in other places as well. But what did those notions really mean and whence did Baldus borrow them?

The question is interesting enough to justify a brief digression into Thomas Aquinas' teaching about the manhood of Christ. Through Aristotle, Aquinas became acquainted with the various meanings of *organon* or *instrumentum* and learned how to distinguish between the "conjoined instrument" (for example, the hand) and the "separate instrument" (for example, a hammer or axe). Moreover, Aquinas adopted also the distinction between the *instrumentum animatum* (a helmsman, for instance) and an *instrumentum inanimatum* (the rudder).[413] Mainly through the medium of John of Damascus, Aquinas then became acquainted with a tenet of the Greek Fathers according to which Christ with regard to his human nature, that is, the incarnate Christ, was the instrument of the Godhead, that is, the triune Deity as well as his own divine nature—*humanitas instrumentum divinitatis*.[414] Aquinas, by combining those two strands (and he seems to have been the first to do so consistently), naturally gained new aspects

[412] Baldus, *Consilia*, III,121,n.6, fol.34: "Ibi attendimus dignitatem tanquam principalem et personam tanquam instrumentalem. Unde fundamentum actus est ipsa dignitas quae est perpetua." In the same paragraph, Baldus makes also the distinction "quod persona sit causa immediata, dignitas autem sit causa remota," whereby it should be recalled that God is often said to act as the *causa remota*.

[413] The most famous passage is *Politics*, 1253b,27 to 1254a,1; see Aquinas' *Expositio in Polit.Arist.*, §§52-55, ed. Spiazzi, 15f: also 1255b,11-12, and §88, p.25. See also *De anima*, 432a,1-2, for the hand as the organ of organs, and *De partibus animalium*, 687a,19-21; further *Nicom.Ethics*, 1161b,4-5; *Endemian Ethics*, 1241b, 22-24; and the Ps.Arist. *Problemata*, 955b,23ff. I am greatly indebted to Professor Harold Cherniss for his help and advice in this matter. Tschipke (see next note), 143, seems to underestimate the Aristotelian influence on Aquinas in this particular case.

[414] The whole subject has been treated and thoroughly investigated by Theophil Tschipke, O.P., *Die Menschheit Christi als Heilsorgan der Gottheit unter besonderer Berücksichtigung der Lehre des Heiligen Thomas von Aquin* (Freiburger Theologische Studien, LV [Freiburg, 1940]); see also M. Grabmann, "Die Lehre des Erzbischofs und Augustinertheologen Jakob von Viterbo (†1307-8) vom Episkopat und Primat und ihre Beziehung zum Heiligen Thomas von Aquino," *Episcopus: Studien über das Bischofsamt . . . Kardinal von Faulhaber . . . dargebracht* (Regensburg, 1949), 190,n.10, for further literature on the subject; for Johannes Damascenus, see Tschipke, 115ff.

concerning the economy of salvation. He pointed out, for example, that

> the manhood of Christ is the instrument of the Godhead: not, however, as an inanimate instrument which itself acts in no way but is only acted on, but as an animated instrument [endowed] with a rational soul, which is so acted on that it also acts.[415]

That is to say, the incarnate Christ acts as the *instrumentum animatum* of the Deity, his own divinity included. Or else, Aquinas might distinguish three different grades: God was the *causa principalis*, Christ being a mortal man was the *instrumentum coniunctum*, whereas the sacraments of the Church appeared as *instrumenta separata*:

> The principal effecting cause of grace is God himself, to whom the manhood of Christ compares like a conjoined instrument, and the sacrament as a separate instrument.[416]

In a similar fashion, Aquinas then interpreted the bishop or priest as an *instrumentum coniunctum* of the mystical Body of Christ; but the bishop could appear also vicariously as an *instrumentum animatum* of the Deity, whereas the sacrament which he dispensed, appeared as the *instrumentum separatum*.[417] Aquinas himself transferred that metaphor also to his philosophical anthropology when he said that "insofar as the soul is the mover of the body, the body serves the soul as an instrument."[418] It seems that what matters chiefly here is not only the functional character of the manhood of Christ, but also the concept of the bishop who acts as the animate instrument of the Deity and, at the same time, as a conjoined instrument of the *corpus mysticum*.

Aquinas could not have foreseen to what extent his teaching might serve the purposes of the jurists when they enlarged upon

---

[415] Aquinas, *Summa theol.*, III,q.7,a.1,ad 3: "quod humanitas Christi est instrumentum divinitatis, non quidem sicut instrumentum inanimatum, quod nullo modo agit, sed solum agitur, sed tanquam instrumentum animatum anima rationali, quod ita agitur quod etiam agit.'"

[416] Aquinas, *Summa theol.*, III,q.62,a.5: "Principalis autem causa efficiens gratiae est ipse Deus, ad quem comparatur humanitas Christi sicut instrumentum coniunctum, sacramentum autem sicut instrumentum separatum." Aquinas introduces that passage by distinguishing between the various instruments: "Est autem duplex instrumentum: unum quidem separatum ut baculus, aliud autem coniunctum ut manus . . ."

[417] *Summa theol.*, III,q.64,a.8,ad 1: "instrumentum animatum sicut est minister."

[418] *Summa theol.*, III,q.8,a.2: "in quantum vero anima est motor corporis, corpus instrumentaliter servit animae" (with regard to soul and body of Christ).

their political doctrines concerning the *Dignitas*. It is, however, obvious what Baldus had in mind when he described the immortal Dignity as the "principal" and the mortal person of the individual ruler as the "instrumental," and declared at the same time that the Dignity, which was perpetual, was the fundament (the "mover") of the king's actions. Baldus was perhaps not the very first—and certainly not the last—to apply the notion of "instrumentality" to the relation between the king and the Dignity,[419] but he certainly applied it frequently and consistently. The question was raised whether a provincial governor asking the emperor for advice but finding that the emperor had died in the meantime, might expect an answer from the emperor's successor. Wrote Baldus in his opinion:

> I answer "Yes," because the [governor's] consultation concerned principally the Dignity which does not die, whereas the person is the instrument of that very Dignity without which the Dignity cannot act anything.[420]

Baldus' application of Thomistic teaching concerning the instrumentality of the incarnate Christ is even more obvious and direct on another occasion. When discussing the fact that two things concur in the king, the individual person and the Dignity—which is "something intellectual lasting forever miraculously, though not corporeally"[421]—he adds a brief commentary on the king and

---

[419] Oldradus de Ponte, *Consilia*, CLXXX,n.15, fol.67ᵛ (cf. Ullmann, *Lucas de Penna*, 174,n.7) holds that, though the empire "is from God as of the first cause," it still is the pope who as *vicarius Dei* promotes the emperor to the empire and therefore acts "tanquam causa secunda et quasi quoddam agens instrumentale" of the first cause. It may be doubted, however, that Oldradus had either Aquinas or Aristotle in mind. The vicar of God was in a very conventional fashion the minister and instrument of God, just as the king when styled the "finger of God" (cf. Luke 11: 20, and, e.g., the coronation *conductus* for Philip II of France, in 1223), was not considered the *instrumentum coniunctum* in a technical philosophic-scholastic sense; see, for the coronation hymn *Beata nobis gaudia*, Leo Schrade, "Political Compositions in French Music of the 12th and 13th Centuries," *Annales musicologiques*, I(1953), 28 and 56. Baldus, on the other hand, was certainly aware of the fact that he applied technical language; see, e.g., his remark on c.34 X 1,6,n.8, *In Decretales*, fol.78ʳ: "Ibi, 'manus,' dicit Aristoteles quod manus est organum organorum" (*De anima*, 432a,1-2). Without Aquinas, however, he could hardly have maintained that the king in the flesh was the instrument of the Dignity. For later repetitions of Baldus' arguments, see Gierke, *Gen.R.*, IV,239,n.122; also III,694,n.19.

[420] Baldus, on *C.*7,61,3,n.1, fol.91ᵛ: "Quaero si Praeses consuluit Principem et Princeps moritur, an debeat expectari responsum successoris? Respondeo sic, quia consultatio concernit principaliter dignitatem quae non moritur . . . licet persona sit organum ipsius dignitatis sine quo dignitas nil facit."

[421] See above, n.295.

his two persons, and says: "The king's person is the organ and instrument of that other person which is intellectual and public." And then he continues:

It is that intellectual and public person [sc. the *Dignitas*] which principally causes the actions; for the mind is turned more to action, or to the principal power, than to the instrumental power.[422]

We should probably recall that in Baldus' system of thought *Deus* and *Dignitas* were interrelated anyhow[423] so that there is no reason to be surprised how easily they could replace one another. The theological field of coordinates directing Baldus' arguments is obvious: Aquinas' *Divinitas* is replaced by the likewise "immortal" *Dignitas*, and the Humanity of Christ by the mortal king. The king, in former days often called *digitus Dei*,[424] was juristically the *digitus Dignitatis*, and whereas the bishop was said to be the "animate instrument" of the Deity, the king appeared as the animate instrument of a fictitious, and therefore immortal, person called Dignity. In other words: *Humanitas instrumentum Dignitatis*—the incarnate *k*ing the instrument of the *Dignity* or of the *K*ing. Not without some inner logic and some inner necessity have both separation and union of the "King's two Bodies" produced the dogma of a political Incarnation, a noetic incarnation of the *Dignitas* or of the Body politic, and therewith a new secularized version of the hypostatic union of the first and second persons, of *Dignitas* and *rex*.

Without doubt, it was from this general stratum that the English lawyers borrowed also the language which they applied so lavishly when arguing about the body natural and the body politic "together indivisible" or maintaining that there were "two bodies but only one person."[425] The theological, or even christo-

---

422 Baldus, *Consilia*, III,159,n.6, fol.45ᵛ: ". . . loco duarum personarum Rex fungitur . . . Et persona regis est organum et instrumentum illius personae intellectualis et publicae. Et illa persona intellectualis et publica est illa, quae principaliter fundat actus: quia magis attenditur actus, seu virtus principalis, quam virtus organica" (*organicus = instrumentalis*, just as *organum* equals *instrumentum*). Baldus, on c.9 X 2,14,n.3, fol.189, applies the same doctrine to hand and foot as instruments of the soul with regard to the act of taking possession of a thing: "et anima per se sine organo corporali [that is, without the hand as the *organum organorum* and without the foot as the *organum possidendi*] non potest incipere possidere per se."

423 See above, n.287.

424 For *rex digitus Dei*, see above, n.419.

425 See above, nos.398,400. Bacon, *Post-nati*, 657, says that "generally in corporations

logical, patterns by which they tried to make their intellectual creations comprehensible to themselves and to others, differed hardly from the world of thought of their Italian predecessors and from the juristic method of reasoning developed by the leading figures in that field. Maitland, therefore, was perfectly correct when he said that those English Crown jurists of the sixteenth century were building up "a creed of royalty which shall take no shame if set beside the Athanasian symbol." It was indeed a "royal Christology" which the jurists established, and which they were almost bound to establish once they started to interpret consistently the relation between the individual king and his immortal Dignity by means of the metaphor of the "two Bodies."

This expression itself remains startling even now after we have become familiar with its historical background. From factors historically given to all European nations and therefore common to all, it was nevertheless in England alone that there had been developed a consistent political, or legal, theory of the "King's two Bodies," just as the correlated notion of the "corporation sole" was a purely English device. It is true, of course, that the other European nations harboured in their constitutional thought kindred ideas; however, they were displayed in a different form. France, for example, though fully aware of the different manifestations of individual king and immortal Dignity, eventually interpreted the absolutist rulership in such a fashion that the distinctions between personal and supra-personal aspects were blurred or even eliminated; Hungary carried the distinction between the mystical Crown and a physical king to great refinement, but the material relic of the Crown of St. Stephen seems to have prevented the king from growing his own super-body; and in Germany, where constitutional conditions were most unclear and complicated anyhow, it finally was the personified State which engulfed the romano-canonical notion of Dignity, and it was the abstract State with which a German Prince had to accommodate

---

the natural body is but *suffulcimentum corporis corporati*, it is but as a stock to uphold and bear out the corporate body." Since, however, Bacon tries to prove the union of the Crowns of England and Scotland through the king's natural body, he has to attribute greater importance to the king in the flesh, because (p.665) "his natural person, which is *one*, has an operation upon both [Crowns]."

himself. At any rate, the theory of the "King's two Bodies" in all its complexity, and sometimes scurrilous consistency, was practically absent from the Continent; and even the Italians, who first developed the legal theory of two persons concurring in the Prince, did not pursue this concept consistently nor in all directions. Nowhere did the concept of the "King's two Bodies" pervade and dominate the juristic thinking so generally and so enduringly as in England, where, not to mention other aspects, that notion had also its important heuristic function in the period of transition from mediaeval to modern political thought.

Any effort to "explain" a historical phenomenon, even though one may hope to understand some factors by which it was conditioned and with which it was interrelated, remains a hopeless task because there are too many layers of life effective at the same time and actively concatenated as to permit any straightforward explanation; and to answer the question why certain potentialities actualized in one way and why they did not crystallize in another will necessarily be an undertaking of limited and doubtful value. It seems, however, that the notion of the "King's two Bodies" cannot be severed from the very early development and the lasting momentum of Parliament in English constitutional thought and practice. Parliament was, by representation, the living "body politic" of the realm. That is to say, the English Parliament was never a *persona ficta* or *persona repraesentata*, but always a very real *corpus repraesentans*. "Body politic of the realm," therefore, had in England far more than in any other European kingdom a uniquely concrete meaning, and there was no need to render it more comprehensible by making of it an artificial abstraction, by transforming that concrete political body of Parliament into a fictitious person, or by talking about the realm as a *persona politica* in the way in which Aquinas occasionally talked about head and members of the Church community as *persona mystica*.[426] In other words, owing to the absolute reality, concreteness, and plain visibility of England's "body politic" in this world; owing also to its very material existence and its ever recurrent self-manifestations when the king as the head and the lords, knights, and burgesses as members were constituted "in Parliament," the old organological metaphor of "head and limbs" survived in England sur-

[426] See above, Ch.v,n.24.

prisingly long. As a result, the notion "body politic of the realm" remained valid and preserved its concrete meaning at a time when in other countries that particular notion no longer was current.

On the other hand, the old *corpus mysticum* idea, with all its consequences and implications, continued to determine—especially after the Supremacy Act (1534)—some facets of the *corpus politicum* idea in England. It is comprehensible that especially in times of parliamentary weakness, when the king and council were quite obviously the mainspring of government, the notion of "body politic" was made to refer also to the king alone, to the *pars pro toto*. A certain terminological confusion existed certainly in the ecclesiastical sphere where the "mystical Body of Christ" and the "mystical Body of the Church" were used interchangeably; and the same "confusion of tongues," as Bacon called it, existed also in the secular sphere where notions such as Crown, kingdom, body politic of either the realm or the king as King were used interchangeably and often inefficiently distinguished.[427] In those ambiguities—increased by the fact that the king actually became the head of the mystical body of the *Ecclesia Anglicana*—the terminological peculiarity of stressing the two *bodies* of the king, and not, for example, the two *persons* (as was the custom of Italian jurists), may have its roots.

In a more technical sense it would appear that a fusion, and an indeed pardonable confusion, of Crown and Dignity was at the bottom of the legal fiction of the "King as Corporation" or as "Corporation sole." The Crown, we recall, was interpreted often enough in mediaeval England as a composite body made up of the parliamentary estates with the king as their head.[428] The same parliamentary estates together with the king formed, however, in other respects also the "body politic and mystical" of the realm— or, as the French called it, the "body civil and mystical."[429] Hence,

---

[427] See Bacon, *Post-nati*, 651: "Some say . . . to the Law, some to the crown, some to the kingdom, some to the body politic of the king: so there is a confusion of tongues amongst them, as it commonly cometh to pass in opinions that have their foundations in subtlety and imagination of man's wit, and not in the ground of nature."

[428] Above, nos.168ff. See, for the estates, Chrimes, *Constitutional Ideas*, 116ff, esp.123, the Parliamentary Sermon of Bishop Russel, in 1483, who identifies repeatedly the "politike body of Englonde" with the "iii estates as principalle membres undir oone hede."

[429] The identification of estates and king with the *corpus civile et mysticum* is found time and again as an expression of French constitutionalism; see, e.g., Jean

Crown and body politic of the realm frequently had their chief components in common. With this organic-corporational concept of Crown and body politic, however, there interfered the concept of Dignity, that is, of a "corporation by succession." Whereas the Crown could appear "corporate" because it encompassed all the members of the body politic living at the same time, the Dignity was a Phoenix-like one-man corporation encompassing in the present bearer of the Crown the whole *genus*, the past and future incumbents of the royal Dignity. What apparently happened was that the English jurists failed to make a clear-cut distinction between the corporate body of the Crown and the supra-individual personage of the Dignity, and instead equated each with the body politic—tempted perhaps by the current formula "Crown and Dignity royal." That is to say, they fused two different concepts of the current corporational doctrines: the organic and the successional. And from this fusion of a number of interrelated corporational concepts there originated, it seems, both the "King's body politic" and the king as a "corporation sole."

This assumption is not contrary to what Maitland put forth so ingeniously when he derived the English "corporation sole" from the model of the *persona*, the parson, who in his village church was the only priest and who, with regard to the landed property of his prebend, took the place of the corporate cathedral chapters or monastic communities in their relation to church property. It is certainly correct to say that the model of the parson had subsidiary effects in conceiving of the king as a corporation sole, and Maitland struck with his pun at the very root of the problem when he joked about the king who had been "parsonified." However, the common basis of both parson and king was probably the *Dignitas*, which, in the case of the king, was fused with the organic body politic whose head he was—comparable rather to abbots and bishops who were also both Dignities and heads of corporate bodies. Hence, it was said that every abbot was a "body politic," and when Coke referred to the "mystical body" of an abbot in

---

de Gerson, *De meditacionibus*, 37: "Habes illos de primo statu tanquam brachia fortissima ad corpus tuum misticum, quod est regalis policia, defendendum" (follow the other two estates). Also Terre Rouge, Coquille, and others make that identification; Church, *Constitutional Thought*, 29,n.20; 278,n.16, and passim. The expression *corpus politicum* is not completely absent (see, e.g., Church, 278,n.16), but *corpus civile* seems to prevail in France, whereas it is hardly found in England.

order to explain the meaning of the king's "body politic," he merely referred to another, though similar, confusion between *corpus mysticum* and *Dignitas*, which was current as early as the fifteenth century.[430] It appears that Blackstone was, after all, not quite wrong when he boasted that the idea of corporations, which he derived from the Romans, had been considerably refined and improved "according to the usual genius of the English nation," especially what concerns "sole corporations, consisting of one person only, of which the Roman lawyers had no notion."[431]

Legal speculation of the thirteenth and fourteenth centuries, for the sake of interpreting the nature of *Dignitas*, introduced a simile which, being individual and species at the same time, appeared as a prefiguration of the corporation sole: the mythical bird Phoenix. To what extent these characteristics had validity in theological thought as well is a question which shall not be raised here. However, it should not be forgotten that a genuine corporation sole has actually existed, even "historically," if we may say so. It existed in Adam, the first man, who being the then only existing man was at the same time individual and the totality of the then existing *genus humanum*. He was at once man and mankind. In order to recognize, however, some of the implications linked with the myth of Adam, we had best entrust ourselves to the guidance of Dante.

[430] See above, nos.311 and 312.
[431] Blackstone, *Commentaries*, I,c.18, p.469; above, Introd., n.7.

CHAPTER VIII

MAN-CENTERED KINGSHIP:
DANTE

CONCEPTIONS of kingship centering in the God-man, in the ideas of justice and law, in the corporate bodies of political collectives or institutional dignities, were developed, successively and alternately, with much overlap and much mutual borrowing, by theologians, jurists, and political philosophers. It remained to the poet to establish an image of kingship which was merely human and of which MAN, pure and simple, was the center and standard—MAN, to be sure, in all his relations to God and universe, to law, society, and city, to nature, knowledge, and faith. *Homo instrumentum humanitatis*—this twist of the theologico-legal maxim might well serve as a motto for penetrating into Dante's moral-political views, provided that the opalescent notion *humanitas* be perceived in all its numerous hues.

It has never been denied that Dante the political philosopher as well as Dante the poet assimilated to the full the political doctrines by which his century was moved. In fact, Dante held a key-position in the political and intellectual discussions around 1300, and if in a superficial manner he has often been labelled reactionary, it is simply the prevalence of the imperial idea in Dante's works— different though it was from that of the preceding centuries— which obscured the overwhelmingly unconventional features of his moral-political outlook.[1] Dante, of course, cannot easily be labelled at all. He was anything but a Thomist although he used the works of Aquinas constantly, nor was he an Averroist although he quoted the Commentator and gave Siger of Brabant a place in

[1] See Michele Barbi, "Nuovi problemi della critica dantesca: VI. L'ideale politico-religioso di Dante," *Studi danteschi*, XXIII (1938), 51. Only very few studies on Dante's political thought, to which I feel indebted and which may have influenced my formulations more often than would be indicated in the footnotes, shall be mentioned here. Fritz Kern, *Humana Civilitas* (Leipzig, 1913); Francesco Ercole, *Il pensiero politico di Dante* (Milan, 1927-28); Bruno Nardi, *Saggi di filosofia dantesca* (Milan, 1930); Étienne Gilson, *Dante et la philosophie* (Paris, 1939; Engl. trsl. by David Moore, *Dante the Philosopher*, New York, 1949 [quoted here]); A. P. d'-Entrèves, *Dante as a Political Thinker* (Oxford, 1952). Useful, so far as it goes, is the commentary in Gustavo Vinay's edition of the *Monarchia* (Florence, 1950). For reasons of convenience, however, the *Monarchia* will be quoted here according to the edition of E. Moore and Paget Toynbee, *Le opere di Dante Alighieri* (4th ed., Oxford, 1924), upon which the Dante Concordance is based.

Paradise next to St. Thomas.[2] Dante castigated the decretalists in the harshest terms; yet, the most recent studies on the political theories embedded in the glosses on Canon Law show clearly to what extent Dante followed traditional lines of canonistic thought.[3] His attitude toward Justinian and toward Roman Law in general, with which he must have familiarized himself, was certainly most affirming; about the jurists, however, he was acrimonious even though Cynus of Pistoia, the great luminary among the civilians of that age and a teacher of Bartolus, was his friend. But who would care in any event to label Dante, the judge of the dead and the quick, a jurist?[4] The difficulty with Dante is that he, who reproduced the general knowledge of his age on every page, gave every theorem which he reproduced a slant so new and so surpris-

[2] This point has been considerably clarified by Gilson, *Dante*, 153ff, 166ff, 211ff, and passim.

[3] For Dante's thrusts against the decretalists, see M. Maccarone, "Teologia e diritto canonico nella Monarchia, III,3," *Rivista di storia della Chiesa in Italia*, v (1951), 7-42; for Dante's siding with the moderate group of canonists, see below, nos. 15-17.

[4] On the jurists, see, e.g., *Monarchia*, II,11,71. Whether or not Dante studied Law, is quite uncertain; but, as has been pointed out correctly by Chiappelli, "Dante in rapporto etc.," 40 (see end of this note), Dante certainly studied the *ars dictandi*, and every student of that art acquired some legal knowledge. At any rate, he cited accurately Roman and Canon Laws, and used also (directly or indirectly) the *Glossa ordinaria* of Accursius. Nardi, *Dante e la cultura medievale* (2nd ed., Bari, 1949), 218-223, has shown one case in which Dante depended upon the Gloss. The same, however, is true in *Monarchia*, I,10,12: "par in parem non habet imperium." This legal maxim was based on *D.4,8,4*, and *D.36,1,13,4*, the gist of which the early glossators rendered in a form less lapidary than the one cited by Dante; see, e.g., Fitting, *Jurist. Schr.*, 149,7: "par non potest inperare pari legitime," or Azo (quoted, together with other places, by Schulz, "Kingship," 138f, cf. 149): "cum par pari imperare non posset." The form cited by Dante is found in a decretal of Innocent III; see c.20 X 1,6, ed. Friedberg, II,62: "quum non habet imperium par in parem." While it is not totally impossible that Dante (as assumed by Chiappelli, 18f) cited from the decretal, it is much more likely that his source was the Accursian *Gloss*, which quotes the maxim not only in connection with *D.36,1,13,4*, v. *imperium*, but also with *C.1,14,4*, v. *indicamus* ("quia par in parem non habet imperium"), the latter being the famous *lex digna*, which, e.g., Aquinas quoted (above Ch.IV,n.153; see also Jean-Marie Aubert, *Le droit romain dans l'oeuvre de Saint Thomas* [Paris, 1955], 84,n.2) and which Dante could not have failed to know. The maxim in the form of the *Glossa ordinaria* was repeated over and over again; see, e.g., Andreas of Isernia, on *Lib.aug.*, prooem., ed. Cervone, p.2 (§ *Econtra quod non*); and, which may be more important, Cynus' gloss on the *lex digna*, that is, on *C.1,14,4,n.7* (Frankfurt, 1578), fol.26. Dante's references to the two Laws have been summed up by Luigi Chiappelli, "Dante in rapporto alle fonti del diritto," *Archivio storico Italiano*, Ser.5, XLI (1908), 3-44, who may have overshot his goal, but was right as against Mario Chiaudano, "Dante e il diritto romano," *Giornale Dantesco*, XX (1912), 37-56, 94-119; see the supplementary note, *ibid.*, 202-206 ("Ancora su Dante e il diritto romano"). See also Francesco Ercole, *Il pensiero politico di Dante* (Milan, 1928), I,7-37 (Ch.1: "La cultura giuridica di Dante"), and D'Entrèves, 27f,104f.

ing that the evidence proving his dependency on other writings serves mainly to underscore the novelty of his own approach and his own solutions.[5] His stratagem was obvious enough, for the point of reference towards which he assembled and directed his material, or the denominator to which he reduced it, was rarely the institutional phenomenon itself; it was practically always the man behind the institution. And in that sense Dante's image of the Prince or Monarch—though composed of innumerable mosaic tesserae borrowed from theology and philosophy, from historical, political, and legal arguments all of which were within the current tradition—reflects a concept of Man-centered kingship and of a purely human *Dignitas* which without Dante would be lacking, and would have been lacking most certainly in that age.

The other great difficulty is that every Dante interpretation is bound to be fragmentary where Dante himself is complex. The visions of Dante the poet seem to interfere constantly with the logical arguments of Dante the political philosopher, even though in other respects those two modes of human approach to the realm of the mind were bound to support each other. Dante's hard-riding logic, though perfectly clear and perhaps even consistent within the whole of his work, was yet anything but linear, because every point on the line of his thought was cross-connected with countless other points on countless other lines. Any effort, therefore, to reproduce the thoughts of Dante the philosopher in a straightforward fashion will hardly escape the danger of falling flat and becoming trite simply because the complexity of the poet's views has been neglected. Moreover, there are pitfalls which concern none but the interpreter himself. Any deviation from the straight line of argument which the literary critic wishes to trace, will lead immediately onto the ocean of Dante speculation on which the interpreter will be lost like Dante's Ulysses after setting sail for his last voyage to the Unknown. Finally, the Dante expositor will be tempted far too often to read into Dante things which Dante neither said nor meant to say. The maxim *Che è fuori della coscienza del poeta a noi non può importare* holds good; it should be ever present to the interpreter's mind.[6]

[5] For an example of that kind, see my paper on "An 'Autobiography' of Guido Faba," *Mediaeval and Renaissance Studies*, I (1941-43), 261f.

[6] Michele Barbi, "Nuovi problemi," (above, n.1), 48 (cited by Gilson as the motto of his book on Dante), in his important essay on "L'ideale politico-religioso di Dante."

While admitting the dangers of both isolating a single strand of Dante's complex thought and reading into his work doctrines which, though perhaps impeccable all by themselves, could never have crossed his mind, it will be possible nevertheless to indicate a theme which illustrates Dante's mode of apportioning theological thought to the secular world and which is inextricably intertwined with the duality of his fundamental concepts of mankind and man, and of man's ultimate goals in this world and the other.

The distinction between person and office stands out clearly and sharply in Dante's work; in fact, it is found not at all rarely. We may think, for example, of Pope Boniface VIII as he appears in the *Divine Comedy*. To Dante, the Gaetani pope was plainly the "Prince of the new Pharisees," who regarded "neither the highest office nor the holy orders in himself" or in others; who cynically boasted: "The heaven I can shut and open, as thou knowest";[7] who is styled by an irate St. Peter a person

> Usurping on earth my place, my place, my place,
> Which in the presence of God's Son is vacant;[8]

who in the chasm of the Simonists is shown in that ridiculous position—head down in an earth-hole while legs and feet are fidgeting in the air[9]—and whom Beatrice, in her last words to Dante, once more remembers when she predicts that Pope Clement V will also be thrust into the earth tubes of Simon Magus and there push deeper down "him from Anagni."[10] And yet, in that very village of Anagni and in the moment when William of Nogaret and the agents of Philip IV dared lay their hands on Boniface to seize him, the same Pope Boniface appeared to Dante, in reverence of the papal office, as the true vicar of Christ, even as Christ himself:

> I see the fleur-de-lys enter Anagni
> And in his Vicar Christ made captive.
> A second time I see him mocked, I see
> The vinegar and gall renewed, I see
> Him slain between the living thieves.[11]

Dante, not being a Donatist, was far from denying or disregarding

[7] *Inf.*, XXVII,85ff. [8] *Par.*, XXVII,22f. [9] *Inf.*, XIX,52ff.
[10] *Par.*, XXX,147f. [11] *Purg.*, XX,86ff.

the effectiveness of the office even in a man whom he considered an unworthy incumbent. Dante had the lowest possible opinion of Benedetto Gaetani, but recognized without hesitation the vicariate of Christ in the pontifical robes which Boniface donned when facing Nogaret and the invaders. The individual pope and the papal Dignity, Benedetto Gaetani and Boniface VIII, were clearly distinguished and kept apart.

After a similar fashion Dante proceeded in the *Convivio*. The problem he tried to solve concerned the true nature of nobility and its definition. To this problem, widely discussed by the troubadours as well as at the imperial court, the Emperor Frederick II allegedly had contributed a statement.[12] The imperial definition (*antica ricchezza e be' costumi*), though inspired by Aristotle, displeased the poet, and in order to reject it Dante made a trenchant distinction between Frederick's authority as an emperor and his authority as a philosopher. True enough, according to the jurists the emperor as emperor was *philosophissimus* and *philosophiae plenus*,[13] and in Dante's general concept of the final ends of mankind it was quite indispensable that imperial and philosophic authorities should coincide and ultimately unite to lead mankind to the blessedness of the present life. Nevertheless, Dante denied that the emperor as emperor had any binding authority as a philosopher—even though it seemed worth Dante's while to take cognizance of the private opinion of so educated a man as Frederick II was in the poet's estimation.[14]

It would not be too difficult to extract from Dante's works a considerable number of passages illustrating the way in which

---

[12] *Convivio*, iv,3ff. See, for the problem at the imperial court, *Erg.Bd.*, 129f,152.

[13] Cf. *C.*6,35,11; *Nov.*22,19, and 60,1. Though the epithets referred to the Emperor Marcus Aurelius, they were customarily applied to the emperor in general; see, e.g., Bartholomeus of Capua, on *C.*5,4,23,5, v. *invictissimo* (ed. Meyers, *Iuris interpretes saeculi XIII.*, 196), where *philosophissimus* appears among the imperial titles; also Marinus de Caramanico, on *Lib.aug.*, II,31, ed. Cervone, 256; Albericus de Rosate included the expression in his *Dictionarium iuris tam civilis quam canonici*, v. *Imperator* (Venice, 1601), fol. 152ᵛ. Andreas of Isernia, on *Feud.* 1,3,n.16, fol. 21ᵛ, connects the epithet with the emperor's council ("Potest dici quod quia princeps multos habet in suo consilio peritos . . . et ideo dicitur Philosophiae plenus"), and Lucas de Penna, on *C.*10,35,n.24, p.214, while referring also to the council, defines the notion of philosophy: "Dicitur enim princeps Philosophiae, id est legalis scientiae, plenus . . . Omnia iura in scriniis sui pectoris censetur habere." Law, or Jurisprudence, of course, belonged to Philosophy, and more specifically, to Ethics.

[14] On the political doctrines of the *Convivio*, see Gilson, *Dante*, 142ff. Actually Dante, *Monarchia*, II,3,15, accepted Frederick's definition.

he distinguished between a Dignity and its human incumbent, and many a time the place assigned by him to a personage in the *Divine Comedy* might tacitly betray such distinctions. The principle of making such distinctions was in itself common enough in his time, and it is not a matter of major interest here to know that Dante too availed himself of it. He struck, however, a completely new chord when, on one occasion, he set over against the office not simply the individual officer, some "Titius" or "Petrus," but Man—Man as both the individual and the exponent of his species, or Man in the most emphatic sense of the word.

To the Third Book of the *Monarchy* Dante assigned the task of proving that the emperor derived his power from God directly, and not through papal mediation, and even less so from the pope as the ultimate source of imperial power. This problem had been broadly treated by the canonists ever since the twelfth century. A powerful group of hierocrats (more recently called the "monists") indeed defended the thesis that the emperor, occasionally styled in a restricted sense the "vicar of the pope," enjoyed only a delegated power, since in the last analysis all power rested with the spiritual head of the hierarchy who disposed of both the spiritual and the material swords.[15] It was against this radical group of canonists and political publicists that Dante raised his voice and thereby sided with the broadening opponent group of moderates, the so-called "dualists." Their most prominent spokesman had been, in the twelfth century, Huguccio of Pisa, and what they stood for was, in fact, the old Gelasian formula of mutual independence of pope and emperor: both powers derived from God directly, and therefore the emperor exercised his power "by his election alone," even before his Roman coronation. But, of course, there was general agreement that the emperor being a member of the Church depended in religious matters on the

---

[15] Above, Ch.VII,nos.22ff. Stickler, "Imperator vicarius Papae," *MIÖG*, LXII (1954), 165-212, has a good point when restricting the catchword of the emperor as *vicarius papae* to the coercive functions of the imperial power, at least according to earlier canonistic teaching; he is, however, equally correct when he stresses the perpetual, and inevitable, confusion of juristic and political elements in the arguments of later mediaeval authors as well as the great number of misunderstandings resulting from overcharged language and resisting reasoned solutions. At any rate, the hierocrats around 1300 were not misinterpreted canonists, but true hierocrats who brought the more carefully balanced system of earlier Canon Law necessarily into disrepute.

sacramental power of the pope, and, in some respects, depended on him even in temporal matters.[16] Dante, while on the whole accepting the teaching of the dualists,[17] carried those doctrines to ends of which their authors had never dreamt. In order to prove that his universal Monarch was free from papal jurisdiction, Dante had to build up a whole sector of the world which was independent not only of the pope, but also of the Church and, virtually, even of the Christian religion—a world sector actualized in the symbol of the "terrestrial paradise" which, it is true, served at the same time as a propylaeum of eternal bliss. Nevertheless, Dante's "terrestrial paradise" had its own autonomous and independent functions in juxtaposition with the celestial paradise.[18] Man—Dante argued—being composed of a corruptible body and an incorruptible soul, holds alone of all created beings an intermediary place, "comparable to the horizon which holds a middle place between the two hemispheres." As a result of that duality, man alone among all creatures was bound to attain to a duality of goals.

> Two ends have been set by Providence, that ineffable, before man to be contemplated by him: the blessedness, to wit, of this life, which consists in the exercise of man's proper power and is figured by the terrestrial paradise; and the blessedness of eternal life, which consists in the fruition of the divine aspect, to which his power may not

16 See above, Ch.vii,nos.24ff,28, and Kempf, *Innocenz III.*, 212ff.

17 See *Monarchia*, iii,16,102ff, where Dante clearly reproduces the opinion of the "dualists." Their tenet *Ex sola electione principum* (see above, Ch.vii,nos.28 and 32) served almost as a party-cry, and it is significant that Albericus de Rosate (d.1354) repeatedly referred in connection with that slogan to Dante (especially to *Monarchia*, iii) as a juristic authority; see, e.g., on *C.*1,1,n.20, fol.8; *C.*7,37,3,n.16, fol.108; cf. B. Nardi, "Note alla *Monarchia* (1. La *Monarchia* e Alberico da Rosciate)," *Studi Danteschi*, xxvi (1942), 99f,102, who (p.100) breaks off his long quotation just before Albericus continues: "Quod ex sola electione competat sibi administratio . . ." Another slogan ("Ante enim erant imperatores quam summi pontifices" [above, Ch.vii,n.24]) was referred to by Dante in *Monarchia*, iii,13,17ff, though in the guise of syllogisms. The opinion of Huguccio (Kempf, *op.cit.*, 221f): "Ergo neutrum pendet ex altero . . . quoad institutionem" was, of course, the gist of Dante's thesis, and even when Huguccio held that the emperor depended upon the pope "in spiritualibus et quodammodo in temporalibus," this was not incompatible with *Monarchia*, iii,16,126ff, either. There are, however, far more passages in the *Monarchia* reflecting the teachings of the dualists which, by Dante's times, had pervaded also the writings of the civilians, until these tenets became, in 1338, the official law of the empire.

18 About the "separatism" of Dante there can be no doubt; see, e.g., M. Barbi, "Nuovi problemi della critica dantesca (viii. Impero e Chiesa)," *Studi Danteschi*, xxvii (1942), 9-46, also xxiii (1938), 46ff; see also Nardi, "Dante e la filosofia," *ibid.*, xxv (1940), 25ff, and Gilson, *Dante*, 191ff, and *passim*.

ascend unless assisted by the divine light. And this blessedness is given to be understood by the celestial paradise.[19]

Those were, according to Dante, two utterly different goals of the human race. Therefore, ran his conclusion, the offices of pope and emperor, by whose direction mankind should be guided to its predestined ends, were assigned by Providence two completely different tasks and functions which were mutually independent. The two supreme offices, which Dante called somewhat abstractly *papatus* and *imperiatus*,[20] were in fact so different from one another that, taken all by themselves, they precluded comparison. If, however, they were to be compared none the less, they became comparable only after being reduced to their common origin. Had man remained in the state of innocence, both directives would have been superfluous; such as man was after the fall, he needed the remedies of the two offices.[21] Both *papatus* and *imperiatus*, therefore, were institutions established by God for the proper guidance of mankind; both derived from God and both ultimately referred to God. Hence, they became comparable only when reduced to God himself, "in whom all disposition is universally united," or perhaps to some substance inferior to God, some celestial prototype of office, "in which the Godhead appears in a more particularized form."[22] In other words, Dante excluded with regard to either office the possibility of a human intermediary, since both depended directly on God. Or, if intermediary there be, he would be an "angel," a celestial prototype of *papatus* and *imperiatus* respectively, "some substance inferior to God" from whose universality that particularized form descended.[23]

Pope and emperor, however, were to be measured not only by the standards of heaven—of God or angel—but they became comparable also when reduced to a standard valid on earth, the standard of Man.

---

[19] *Monarchia*, III,16,14ff, and 43ff.

[20] See above, Ch.VII,n.44.

[21] *Monarchia*, III,4,107ff.

[22] *Monarchia*, III,12,85ff.

[23] *Ibid.*, 93ff: "Et hoc erit vel ipse Deus, in quo respectus omnis universaliter unitur; vel aliqua substantia Deo inferior, in qua respectus superpositionis, per differentiam superpositionis, a simplici respectu descendens, particuletur." For the neo-platonic substratum, see Wolfram von den Steinen, *Dante: Die Monarchie*, Breslau, 1926, 118. Dante arrives at angelic or "proto-typical" personifications of *papatus* and *imperiatus* which in many respects resemble the *Dignitas* of the jurists.

It is one thing to be man and another to be pope; and just so, it is one thing to be man and another to be emperor.[24]

At a glance, this may appear like the customary dichotomy of *Dignitas* and individual dignitary. Dante, however, by a sudden twist, presented the conventional problem in a new philosophic perspective. For he wished "Man" to be understood not only generically, but also qualitatively: pope and emperor became comparable as men not merely because they belonged to the same species of mortal human beings, but because Man in his most elated form should determine the standard the two officers had in common.

For as men they have to be reduced to the best man (*optimus homo*), who is the standard of all others and, so to say, their Idea, whosoever he may be; to him, that is, who is in the highest degree One within his own kind.[25]

Dante, it is true, derived his notions from Aristotle. He himself quoted the *Nicomachean Ethics* and the *Metaphysics*, and the notion of the *optimus homo* was probably inspired also by the Aristotelian *Politics*.[26] What matters here, however, is how he applied the Aristotelian notions.

Dante arrived at two standards by which pope and emperor could be measured, the standards of "God or angel" and of "Man at his best." The offices (*papatus* and *imperiatus*), established by divine dispensation, were to be measured by the standard of God (or angel). The human incumbent of the office, however, was to be measured according to the standard of Man, that is, of him

---

[24] *Monarchia*, III,12,31ff: ". . . sciendum quod aliud est esse hominem, et aliud est esse Papam. Et eodem modo, aliud est esse hominem, aliud est esse Imperatorem." To Dante, just as to the jurists, the office had an independent existence, or was a *res* independent of the incumbents. See, e.g., *Monarchia*, III,7,41: "Auctoritas principalis non est principis nisi ad usum, quia nullus princeps seipsum auctorizare potest" (see above, Ch.IV,n.182, for Pseudo-Chrysostomus, *In Mattheum*: "nemo potest facere se ipsum regem"); also III,10,34: "officium deputatum Imperatori"; and *ibid.*, 73ff: "Praeterea omnis iurisdictio prior est suo iudice; iudex enim ad iurisdictionem ordinatur, et non e converso." The *imperium*, however, is a *iurisdictio*; therefore "ipsa [iurisdictio] est prior suo iudice, qui est Imperator."

[25] *Ibid.*, III,12,62ff: "Nam, prout sunt homines, habent reduci ad optimum hominem, qui est mensura aliorum et idea, ut ita dicam, quisquis ille sit, ad exsistentem maxime unum in genere suo."

[26] The places referred to are *Nicom.Eth.*, x,5,1176a16 (cf. Aquinas, *In Ethica Arist.*, §1466, and Commentary, §2062, ed. Spiazzi, pp.534ff), and *Metaph.*, IX,1, 1052b18. See also *Polit.*, III,11,8, and 12, 1287b20 and 1288a15ff and passim (cf. Aquinas, *In Pol.*, §378, and Commentary, §519, ed. Spiazzi, 178,182).

"who is in the highest degree One within his own kind" and the "Idea" of his kind, and who by his *humanitas* represented as well as encompassed most perfectly the *genus humanum*.[27] That is to say, pope and emperor, who were restricted by their functions to two different orbits and therefore were incomparable entities, became comparable nevertheless when they were referred to God and to Man. They should be measured by either divine or human standards, by either *deitas* or *humanitas*, standards relevant to office and officeholder respectively. But they should not be measured by totally irrelevant standards such as the similes of sun and moon, of the two swords, and other cobwebs or fancies so often spelt out to determine the extent of the papal power or of that of the emperor.[28] Dante thus transferred the age-old struggle about the superiority of either pope or emperor to a plane differing from the customary argumentations when he referred both powers to their absolute standards, those of *deitas* and *humanitas*, standards so closely interlocked with one another through the Incarnation that at times they became almost exchangeable.

The question might arise whether in Dante's general concept the capacity of "Being Man" (in the qualitative sense of being the "most One within his kind" and the "Idea of his kind") did not itself amount to an "office," the highly responsible office of Man towards mankind—an office equal in rank and responsibility and universality with *papatus* and *imperiatus* and adorned with a Dignity no less sempiternal than that of either the emperor or the pope: the Dignity of Man. Was it perhaps that he, who most perfectly represented the Idea of Man, thereby transcended his incidental individuality of "Petrus" or "Titius" and became the supra-individual representative of his species, the incumbent of a

---

[27] For "maxime unus in genere suo," see *Monarchia*, 1,15,1ff, where Dante builds up a "gradation" (*gradatim se habent*) of being, being one, and being good: "maxime enim ens maxime est unum, et maxime unum est maxime bonum," which leads to the conclusion: "Propter quod in omni genere rerum illud est optimum, quod est maxime unum." This gradation Dante now transfers to Man: he who is most one within his own kind, is the *optimus homo*, therefore also the Idea of his kind and its standard; he is, as it were, *humanitas* impersonated in both the qualitative and the quantitative senses.

[28] It is interesting to note that Albericus de Rosate, on *C.*7,37,3,n.19, fol.108rb, again makes his allegation to Dante in connection with those similes: "licet hoc [the Sun and Moon metaphor] communiter teneatur, tamen ipse Dantes negat verum esse quod in hoc figurentur sacerdotium et imperium. Et hoc probat in dicta quaestione per subtiles et probabiles rationes. Et idem dicit de duobus gladiis . . . negat enim predicta significare sacerdotium et imperium." Cf. *Monarchia*, III,4,12ff, and 9,2ff. See Nardi, "Note alla *Monarchia*," 103.

personal dignity in which the corporate and generic Dignity of Man became manifest? In fact, the assumption has been put forth that Dante's *optimus homo* not only was identical with the Aristotelian Sage, but also that this philosopher-sage represented, as though in a third orbit, a third *Dignitas* apart from and independent of that of the pope or the emperor.[29] Correct though this assumption may be in other respects,[30] the trichotomy of pope-emperor-philosopher does not fit the clear-cut duality of the *Monarchy* in which the standard of the *optimus homo* on earth ("whosoever he may be") and the standard of God or angel in heaven were in a state of equilibrium, which corresponded to the equilibrium of Dante's two paradises, terrestrial and celestial.[31]

[29] Gilson, *Dante*, 189ff.

[30] Cf. Burdach, *Rienzo*, 170ff, 501ff, on the "Apolline Empire"; Leonardo Olschki, *Dante "Poeta Veltro"* (Florence, 1953), who identifies the mission of the Veltro with that of the poet-philosopher.

[31] In his highly stimulating discussion of *Monarchia*, III,12, Gilson (*Dante*, 188ff) arrives at a trichotomy of orders (pope, emperor, philosopher) by identifying the *optimus homo* with the Aristotelian sage. That identification all by itself would be possible, though in that chapter Dante does not say so, nor does he suggest it. Moreover, Gilson having established the three orders of pope, emperor, and sage— all equal in rank—interprets the phrase *non potest dici, quod alterum subalternetur alteri* in such a way that it refers to all three orders: each of the three sovereign powers remains without a superior within his category. Although such a trichotomy was definitely within the range of 13th century thought as well as that of Dante himself, Gilson's interpretation fails to do justice to the leading idea of *Monarchia*, III,12. Apart from the fact that his interpretation meets with grammatical difficulties, because *alter* leaves only the choice of two, and not of three (see, e.g., with regard to papacy and empire: "Distincte enim sunt hae potestates *nec una pendet ex altera*," quoted by Kempf, *Innocenz III.*, 218,n.65, also 221,n.71), Gilson's coordination of the three orders under God is not convincing in other respects. He supports his argument by the following diagram (which has been simplified here):

Deus

| Optimus homo | Imperator | Papa |

But this is not at all what Dante says, who simply establishes two different reference points to which he relates pope and emperor (1) *qua* office and (2) *qua* man, as illustrated by the following diagram:

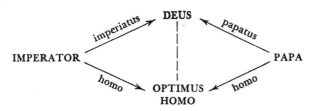

Moreover, the philosopher-sage cannot be conceived of as a third entity in the *Monarchy*, since this work was written to demonstrate that it was the task of the emperor to lead the *genus humanum* to its terrestrial intellectual or philosophic perfection. Hence, in the system of the *Monarchy* emperor and philosopher coincided; they were bound to coincide because otherwise the emperor would be wanting the ethical justification and moral qualification for his natural (that is, his purely human) task of guiding mankind by the proper usage of philosophic reason to its *natural* goal—just as the guidance to the *supra-natural* goal of the Christian formed the trust of the spiritual shepherd, the pope. In other words, Dante's whole scheme of duality postulated with regard to *humanitas* the figure, not of the Greek philosopher-sage, but of the Roman emperor-philosopher, just as it postulated the figure of the Roman pontiff with regard to *Christianitas*. After all, there were no more than two roads leading to no more than two goals of perfection, and these *due strade* were lit up by the two Roman Suns, emperor and pope:

> She, maker of the good world, Rome, was wont
> To having TWO SUNS which made plain to sight
> Both one road and the other, world and God.[32]

Whether or not the curious metaphor of the "Two Suns" was perhaps Dante's answer to those canonists who talked about "two emperors, one ecclesiastic and the other secular, who ruled the

---

Deus and *optimus homo* are the two entities to which both pope and emperor refer: their offices refer to God and their individualities to the "best man" (who may, or may not, be identical with the Aristotelian sage; the latter is likely, but it makes no difference with regard to what Dante wishes to express here). By transferring the *optimus homo* to the denominator of pope and emperor, Gilson deprives, as it were, both of their common human reference point and eliminates, at the same time, the tension between *Deus* and *optimus homo* which compares with that between office and man. In fact, the tension of this crucial chapter ties in with the general duality of human goals symbolized by Adam and Christ, the two paragons of perfection in the two paradises: Adam in the terrestrial paradise and Christ in the celestial.

[32] *Purg.*, XVI,106ff:

> Soleva Roma, che il buon mondo feo,
> due soli aver, che l'una e l'altra strada
> facean vedere, e del mondo e di Deo.

See, for the problem, my paper on "Dante's 'Two Suns,'" *Semitic and Oriental Studies in Honor of William Popper* (University of California Publications in Semitic Philology, XI [Berkeley and Los Angeles, 1951]), 217-231. The study of Michele Maccarone, "La teoria ierocratica e il canto XVI del Purgatorio," *Rivista di Storia della Chiesa in Italia*, IV (1950), 359-398, was then not known to me.

whole world," makes little difference here,[33] but his lines once more show the fundamental duality of human ends and human leadership.

It was, however, the major premise of the whole scheme of the *Monarchy* that Dante, inspired by Aristotle, attributed to the human community a moral-ethical goal which was "goal in itself," was para-ecclesiastical, and therefore independent of a Church which had its own goal. This duality of moral-ethical and ecclesiastical-spiritual values was rather common among the jurists of Dante's age who pointed out that the *universitas* was a *corpus morale et politicum*[34] which paralleled the *corpus mysticum* of the Church, or held with Dante that "just as the Church has its foundation, so has the empire; for the foundation of the Church is Christ . . . , but the foundation of the empire is human Law."[35] Dante, in order to justify the self-sufficiency and sovereignty of the *universitas generis humani*, appropriated, like the jurists, theological language and ecclesiastical thought for expressing his views concerning the secular body politic; and thereby he arrived at the construction of "a secularized imitation of the religious notion of the Church,"[36] while endowing his creation even with a blessedness of its own: the terrestrial paradise. The result was a duality of mutually independent corporate bodies, one "human-imperial" and the other "Christian-papal," both universal, each of which pursued its own ends and had its own goal of human perfection. That duality differed profoundly from the Thomistic system in which invariably the secular ends were subordinated to the spiritual, and it is only too comprehensible that the dantesque system immediately challenged a contemporary cleric, the Dominican Guido Vernani of Rimini, to launch a formidable attack against

---

[33] Cf. Stickler, "Imperator vicarius Papae," *MIöG*, LXII (1954), 200, n.66 (also Kempf, *Innocenz III.*, 211,n.47), quoting the *Summa Bambergensis*: ". . . infra xcvi di., duo, ibi dicitur, quod duo imperatores scl. ecclesiasticus et secularis, totum orbem regunt; verum, set per iura regunt." The allegation is c.10,D.xcvi, Friedberg, I,340, the famous Gelasian definition of pontifical *auctoritas* and regal *potestas*, beginning: "Duo sunt quippe, imperator auguste, quibus . . ." It seems that the author of the *Summa*, so to say, twisted the vocative *imperator* when he said *duo imperatores*.

[34] See above, Ch.v,nos.60,68,81; also Kantorowicz, "Mysteries of State," 81f.

[35] *Monarchia*, III,10,47ff: ". . . sicut Ecclesia suum habet fundamentum, sic et Imperium suum: nam Ecclesiae fundamentum Christus est . . . ; Imperii vero fundamentum ius humanum est." This passage was quoted in full by Albericus de Rosate, on *C*.7,37,7,n.30, fol.109; cf. Nardi, "Note alla *Monarchia*," 105.

[36] Gilson, *Dante*, 179f, also 166, and passim; d'Entrèves, *Dante*, 50.

the *Monarchy* and to declare that a political beatitude in this life as an ultimate end, attainable by the working of the moral or intellectual virtues alone, did not exist.[37] The duality, however, of corporate bodies marching (so to speak) *pari passu* towards different goals, was quite indispensable for Dante's vision of a self-sufficient world-monarchy not controlled by the pope. Dante's monarch was not simply a man of the sword and thereby the executive arm of the papacy; his monarch was necessarily a philosophic-intellectual power in its own right. For it was the emperor's chief responsibility, by means of natural reason and moral philosophy to which legal science belonged,[38] to guide the human mind to secular blessedness, just as the pope was charged by Providence to guide the Christian soul to supra-natural illumination.

A duality of goals does not necessarily imply a conflict of loyalties or even an antithesis. There is no antithesis of "human" versus "Christian" in the work of Dante, who wrote as a Christian and addressed himself to a Christian society, and who, in the last passage of the *Monarchy*, said clearly that "after a certain fashion (*quodammodo*) this mortal blessedness is ordained toward an immortal blessedness."[39] Nevertheless, the fact remains that Dante distinguished between a "human" perfection and a "Christian" perfection—two profoundly different aspects of man's possible felicity, even though these two actualizations of man's potentialities were ultimately destined to support, and not to antagonize or exclude, each other. For all that, however, the sphere of *Humanitas* was, in Dante's philosophic system, so radically set apart from that of *Christianitas*, and the autonomous rights of human society—though depending on the blessings of the Church—were so powerfully emphasized that indeed it is admissible to say that Dante has "abruptly and utterly shattered" the concept of the undisputed unity of the temporal in the spiritual.[40]

[37] Cf. Guido Vernani, *De reprobatione Monarchie composite a Dante*, ed. Thomas Käppeli O.P., "Der Dantegegner Guido Vernani O.P. von Rimini," *QF*, xxviii,123-146, see especially 126,14ff, 146,5ff and passim.

[38] Above, n.13. See Hermann Kantorowicz, *Glossators*, 37f.

[39] *Monarchia*, iii,16,132ff: ". . . quum mortalis ista felicitas quodammodo ad immortalem felicitatem ordinetur."

[40] See Gilson, *Dante*, 211ff, who rightly deals heavy blows to the so-called "Thomism" of Dante and recognizes the power of Dante's shattering political passion.

Dante's metaphysical surgery exceeded that of others who before him had separated the empire from the embrace of the Church, distinguished philosophic reason from theology, and questioned the oneness of the "intellectual soul" by appropriating, as it were, the intellect for the state and leaving the care of the soul to the Church. Dante did not turn *humanitas* against *Christianitas*, but thoroughly separated the one from the other; he took the "human" out of the Christian compound and isolated it as a value in its own right—perhaps Dante's most original accomplishment in the field of political theology.

The "separatism" of Dante led to the creation of different sociological strata. His *humana universitas* embraced not only Christians or members of the Roman Church, but was conceived of as the world community of all men, Christians and non-Christians alike. To be "man," and not to be "Christian," was the criterion for being a member of the human community of this world, which for the sake of universal peace, justice, liberty, and concord was to be guided by the philosopher-emperor to its secular self-actualization in the terrestrial paradise. And whereas great portions of men—Jews, Mohammedans, Pagans—did not belong to the mystical body of Christ, or belonged to it only potentially,[41] Dante's *humana civilitas* included all men: the pagan (Greek and Roman) heroes and wise men, as well as the Muslim Sultan Saladin and the Muslim philosophers Avicenna and Averroes. And Dante, while repeating a common argument, could maintain that the world had been at its best when mankind was guided by Divus Augustus, after all a pagan emperor, under whose reign

[41] See Aquinas, *Summa theol.*, III, q.8,art.3,resp.: "Quaedam tamen sunt [membra corporis mystici] in potentia, quae nunquam reducuntur ad actum." The question argued is *Utrum Christus sit caput omnium hominum*, which Aquinas answers in the affirmative, adding, however, "sed secundum diversos gradus." The hierocrats were less careful than Aquinas, but rather inclined to deduce from the potentiality (that is, the calling of the Church to universality) actual universal rights of the *vicarius Christi*, as, e.g., James of Viterbo (*De regimine christiano*, 1,4) or Aegidius Romanus (*De eccles. potestate*, III,2). Other authors, however, defended views similar to those of Dante. The author of the *Somnium viridarii* (*Songe du Verger*), e.g., says quite specifically: "Papa non est super paganos secundum apostolicas sanctiones, sed solummodo super Christianos," and draws the conclusion: "ergo [papa] non est dominus temporalis omnium." Cf. *Somnium viridarii*, II,35, ed. Goldast, *Monarchia* (Hanau, 1612-1614), I, p.154 (also II,174, ed. Goldast, p.175: "Romanus pontifex non praesit omnibus"). Cf. F. Merzbacher, "Das *Somnium viridarii* von 1376 als Spiegel des gallikanischen Kirchenrechts," *ZfRG*, kan.Abt., XLII (1956), 67,n.53.

Christ himself chose to become man, and, for that matter, a Roman citizen.[42]

According to the opinion of several canonists and papal political writers of the late thirteenth and early fourteenth centuries, there was "no rightful empire outside the Church," which implied that the pagan emperors did not hold the empire rightfully; and Guido Vernani, Dante's adversary, declared straightforwardly "that among the pagans there never was a true *respublica* nor was anyone ever a true emperor." That theory was not even refuted by Dante; it was almost reversed. Saint Paul had styled the moment of the incarnation of Christ the "fulness of the time" (Galatians 4: 4), an expression which referred to Christ exclusively. Dante, however, included Augustus, for he called "fulness of the time" that providential moment in which *both* Christ and Augustus were treading the ground of this earth "that there be no ministry of our bliss lacking its minister."[43] That is to say, only under the perfect

[42] *Monarchia*, 1,16,17ff, and, for the Roman citizenship of Christ, 11,12,44f; also *Purg.*, XXXII,102: "cive/ Di quella Roma onde Cristo è Romano." Dante is far more exuberant in his Augustus theology when he discusses the same problem in *Convivio*, IV,5,50ff: Not only heaven, but also the earth then appeared better disposed than ever before or after. "Nè'l mondo *non fu mai nè sarà* si perfettamente disposto, come allora che alla voce d'un solo principe del Roman popolo e commendatore fu ordinato . . . E però pace universale era per tutto, che *mai più non fu nè fia*: chè la nave della umana compagnia *dirittamente per dolce cammino a debito porto correa*." See, for the Pax Augusta, also *Par.*, VI,8of, and, for the Edict of Augustus (*de iustissimi principatus aula prodiisset edictum*), *Epistolae*, VII,64ff, also lines 14f for the application to Henry VII (*tu, Caesaris et Augusti successor*). Bartolus, who knew the *Monarchia* as well as Dante's poetry (cf. Woolf, *Bartolus*, 17,n.4, and 90f), flew the Augustus theology to the highest pitch when glossing on *D*.49,15,24,n.7, fol.261ᵛ: "Et forte, si quis diceret dominum Imperatorem non esse dominum et monarchum totius orbis, esset haereticus, quia dicerat contra determinationem Ecclesiae, contra textum sancti Evangelii, dum dicit *Exivit edictum a Caesare Augusto, ut describeret universus orbis*, ut habes Lucas II[:1]. Ita etiam recognovit Christus Imperatorem ut dominum." Bartolus' argument was often referred to or even verbatim repeated; see, e.g., Jason de Mayno, *Consilia*, III,70,n.3 (Venice, 1581), fol.119ᵛ. Others, however, attacked Bartolus vehemently; see Woolf, *Bartolus*, 25,n.2. For Dante, no doubt, Augustus belonged, like David and Solomon, among those redeemed at the Harrowing of Hell. To some extent, of course, Dante followed Orosius as well as Otto of Freising (*Chronica*, III,6); see, for the Orosian Augustus theology, in addition to Erik Peterson, "Der Monotheismus als politisches Problem," in his *Theologische Traktate* (Munich, 1951), 97ff, the study of Th. E. Mommsen, "Aponius and Orosius," *Late Classical and Mediaeval Studies in Honor of Albert Mathias Friend, Jr.* (Princeton, 1955), esp. 107ff, 110f, to whom I owe many valuable insights in the problem. See also below, n.43.

[43] See, for the maxim *extra ecclesiam non est imperium*, Gaines Post, "Some Unpublished Glosses," 408 (with reference to c.39 post, C.XXIV,q.1, ed. Friedberg, 1,982) and 411ff, where similar opinions are reviewed. See, for Guido Vernani, below, nos.80 and 82. Cf. Aegidius Romanus, *De eccles. potestate*, III,2, ed. Scholz,

emperor, Divus Augustus, was there the *perfecta monarchia*, the empire of the Romans, in a state of perfect peace; and in the "fulness of the time" the perfect imperial guide to mortal bliss was no more a Christian than Vergil, the poet of the empire, who finally was the guide of Dante himself to the paradise of this world. In other words, against those hierocrats who held that the pagans could never have had a *vera respublica* and a *verus imperator*, Dante maintained that the *perfecta monarchia*, such as it never existed either before or after, was found only under a pagan Prince, the most human Divus Augustus.

Perhaps the ambivalence of the word *humanitas* has to be taken into account, too. *Humanitas* meant, qualitatively, the truly human behavior; and it meant, quantitatively, the whole human race—two notions which in Dante's work were definitely interdependent and even might relate, theologically, to the human nature of Christ. In order to achieve the highest perfection of *humanitas*, qualitatively, all men had to contribute—each his share—to the whole body of man; and accordingly, the human race, or *humanitas* quantitatively, appeared to Dante like One Man, a single all-embracing community, a universal body corporate or "some totality" (*quoddam totum*) which the poet called *humana universitas* or *humana civilitas*. Whereas *universitas* was the customary legal-technical term for corporate bodies, *civilitas* (though not unknown in legal speech) had some additional overtones: man's universal citizenhood, his civic thinking, his human civility or perhaps even education.[44] At any rate, *humana civilitas* implied—beyond all practical problems of division of labor, demand of goods, and other necessities of the social animal—a uni-

---

153: ". . . apud infideles nec est proprie imperium neque regnum." The opposite point of view (similar to that of Bartolus; above, n.42) is found in the *Somnium viridarii*, I,179, ed. Goldast, 133f (esp. 134,10ff): ". . . certius notum est quod illi infideles erant veri imperatores . . . Nam de vero imperio seu regno illo infidelium habemus testimonium Christi" (references to Matth. 22: 21, and Luke 2: 1). Cf. *Monarchia* I,16,19ff: "Vere tempus et temporalia quaeque plena fuerunt, quia nullum nostrae felicitatis ministerium ministro vacavit." See also preceding note.

44 *Monarchia*, I,7,2ff, for *quoddam totum* and *universitas* (also I,3,31); for *civilitas*, see I,2,50ff, and passim. See, for *civilitas*, also Kern, *Humana Civilitas*, 33f; Nardi, *Saggi di filosofia dantesca*, 260; Ercole, *Il pensiero politico*, II,78ff, who points out (115ff) that both *ius gentium* and *ius civile* would refer to the *humana civilitas* as distinguished from the positive law of individual communities. See also the commentary of Vinay, on *Monarchia*, I,3,1, p.14,n.13. Baldus (and others as well) seems to use the word chiefly in the sense of "citizenship"; cf., e.g., *Consilia*, V,64,n.2, fol.19ᵛ, also IV,445,n.5, fol.101ᵛ.

versal community bound by natural as well as intellectual or educational ties, by a mental attitude which was that of a citizen of the world-polity. Dante did not in that connection avail himself of the term *corpus mysticum*, neither for the supra-natural community of the sons of Christ nor for the natural community of the sons of Adam; but if ever there existed a secular "mystical body," it existed in Dante's *humana civilitas*. For this universal community of man represented, as it were, the mystical body of the father of the human race, the *corpus mysticum Adae*, the head of which was the emperor charged by Dante with the task of leading mankind back to whence it came: the terrestrial paradise.

The way to the terrestrial paradise was marked by the intellectual or moral-political virtues; that is, by the classical-pagan cardinal virtues: Prudence, Fortitude, Temperance, and Justice. Now, scholastic philosophy distinguished between two sets of virtues: the four cardinal virtues, called technically *virtutes intellectuales* or *acquisitae*, which existed in man and were within his reach according to the conditions of his human nature and human reason; and the three theological virtues—Faith, Charity and Hope—which could be bestowed on man only by divine grace and, consequently, only on Christians, and which technically were known as *virtutes infusae* or *divinitus infusae*, "virtues infused by God" for the purpose of ordaining man to his supra-natural ends. Following in the wake of Augustinian arguments, the theologians of the twelfth and thirteenth centuries recognized only the *virtutes infusae* as authentic, as *verae virtutes* without restriction. They did not deny, of course, the existence of the acquired political or moral virtues; but they denied their *raison d'être* without their infused theological sisters, because they attributed to those purely human virtues no independent supra-natural merits, and therefore virtuous actions, performable even by a pagan or infidel, were in view of salvation without true consequence. It was Aquinas only who, under the pressure of Aristotle, broke away from that tradition and first attributed to the moral-political virtues their full and proper value *secundum rationem*: "An action of political virtue is *not* devoid of consequence, but is good by itself (*actus de se bonus*)." And he added: "and if [such action] were prompted by grace, it would be even meritorious."[45]

[45] This development has been excellently traced by O. Lottin OSB, "Les vertus

Dante, as usual, was the loyal, if undutiful, disciple of Aquinas. Nothing could be more acceptable to him than a tenet according to which an action of political virtue was *de se bonus*. It was, in fact, so acceptable to him that he could venture to isolate this independent value of the intellectual virtues and to set it over—equal in rank, though different in kind—against the supra-natural value of the *virtutes infusae*. At the same time, he clung to the distinction between humanly acquired and divinely infused virtues to which he referred in unambiguous terms.[46] But whereas Aquinas merely *distinguished* between intellectual and theological virtues, their functions and their ends, without disintegrating the functional unity of the total of seven virtues (which in their turn correspond with the seven vices), Dante broke the two sets of virtues apart. He combined them with his concept of the two paradises, consigning the intellectual virtues to the terrestrial paradise and the infused virtues to the celestial. In twelfth-century art the custom arose to represent so-called "Trees of Virtues and Vices"—diagrammatic representations of these two sets of human conduct—whereby the seven vices were sometimes superseded by a human figure inscribed *Vetus Adam* and the seven virtues by one inscribed *Novus Adam*, that is, Christ.[47] Dante perhaps would have suggested yet another division by allotting, not to the *Vetus Adam*, but to Adam in Paradise the four intellectual virtues, and accordingly to the *Novus Adam*, the three infused ones. He did not say so, but in his scheme of the two paradises it was appropriate to use the pagan-human virtues autonomously in order to provide his universal monarchy with an intellectual ultimate goal which did not depend on the means of grace of the Church. In other words, man, if properly guided, could attain to the terrestrial paradise of the first man through his own devices, through the

---

morales acquises sont-elles de vraies vertus? La réponse des théologiens de Pierre Abélard à saint Thomas d'Aquin," *Recherches de théologie ancienne et médiévale*, XX (1953), 13-39, who (p.38) quotes the decisive passage of Aquinas, *In II Sent.*, D.40,q.1.a.5. See also the continuation of Lottin's study, *ibid.*, XXI (1954), 101-129.

[46] *Monarchia*, III,16,53ff; cf. Aquinas, *Summa theol.*, I-II,qq.61-63, also q.65.

[47] A. Katzenellenbogen, *Allegories of the Virtues and Vices in Mediaeval Art* (London, 1939), 63ff, and pls.XL-XLI; also Herbert von Einem, *Der Mainzer Kopf mit der Binde* (Arbeitsgemeinschaft des Landes Nordrhein-Westfalen, Heft 37 [Cologne and Opladen, 1955]), 28,n.83, and figs.30-31. For the spreading of those representations in the 12th century, see also F. Saxl, "A Spiritual Encyclopaedia of the Later Middle Ages," *Warburg Journal*, V (1942), 107ff.

power of natural reason and of the four cardinal virtues alone. It is true, man *qua* Christian was in need of the assistance of the Church, of the virtues infused by God, and therefore also of papal guidance in order to achieve the eternal peace of celestial beatitude and ascend to the divine Light in the life thereafter. But man *qua* man did not need the support of the Church to arrive at a philosophic beatitude, at temporal peace, justice, liberty, and concord, which were within his own reach through the agency of the four intellectual virtues.

That fundamental idea was well understood not only by contemporaries such as Guido Vernani, who vehemently objected to Dante's interpretation,[48] but also by later scholars who interpreted Dante approvingly. In the Auditing Hall of the Collegio del Cambio in Perugia, for example, the walls are covered with famous frescoes which Perugino and his pupils executed according to the scholarly advice of a local humanist, Francesco Maturanzio. The central small wall, showing the human and the divine Christ (Nativity and Transfiguration), braces, as it were, the two long walls: one, displaying a theological scene—the Eternal God with cherubs and angels, prophets and sibyls—and the other displaying the four cardinal Virtues each of which is accompanied and symbolized by three men. The chief point of interest here is that the cortège attending the four Virtues—consisting of their twelve human concomitants or incarnations—is composed of pagan heroes and wise men, that is, of pagans exclusively, who under the conduct of the pagan human virtues balance the transcendental world visualized by prophets and sibyls.[49] Dante's ultimate responsibility for that composition, however, is evidenced by the fact that we find a solitary thirteenth figure, Cato Uticensis—for Dante (as shall be shown presently), the truest embodiment of all four civic virtues.[50]

---

[48] Vernani, *De reprobatione Monarchie*, on *Monarchia*, III,16, ed. Käppeli, 145f.

[49] See Lionello Venturi, *Il Perugino: Gli Affreschi del Collegio del Cambio*, a cura di Giovanni Carandente (Edizioni Radio Italiana, 1955), 28, for the humanist Francesco Maturanzio; see further pl. II: *Prudentia* and *Iustitia* with Fabius Maximus, Socrates, Numa Pompilius, Furius Camillus, Pittacus, Trajan; and pl. IV: *Fortitudo* and *Temperantia* with Lucius Sicinius, Leonidas, Horatius Cocles, Publius Scipio, Pericles, and Cincinnatus. My thanks go to Professor Erwin Panofsky, who not only called my attention to the problem, but also put at my disposal the publication quoted above.

[50] Venturi, *op.cit.*, pl.I; cf. *Purg.*, I.22ff,37ff, and below, nos.94ff.

However that may be, Dante, by separating the intellect from its former unity with the soul and separating the intellectual virtues from their unity with the divinely infused virtues, released the power of the now free intellect. He used it to bind into one, for the pursuit of this-worldly happiness, the human world-community composed of all men, Christians and non-Christians alike. To be sure, the universal Christian faith was common to all Christians; the human intellect, however, and human natural reason were common to all men. And whereas the salvation of the individual soul could apply only to those who believed in salvation through Christ, the purely intellectual perfection and philosophic self-redemption in the terrestrial paradise was within the grasp of all men—including the Scythians and Garamantes mentioned in the *Monarchy*.[51]

It is evident that Dante, in his ardent endeavor to prove the secular monarch's independence of the pope, "borrowed from the Church its ideal of universal Christendom and secularized it"[52]—secularized it by substituting the notion of "mankind" for "Christendom." His contemporaries, the so-called Averroistic philosophers at the University of Paris, advocated the philosopher's intellectual beatitude in this world more or less as the ultimate goal of the human *individual*.[53] Dante, however, though never taking terrestrial felicity for the ultimate goal, transferred much of their radicalized Aristotelian doctrine from the individual to the *universitas humana*, advocating a philosophic-intellectual beatitude in

[51] *Monarchia*, I,14,42ff.

[52] Gilson, *Dante*, 166. For a striking example, see, e.g., *Monarchia*, I,16,23, and esp. III,10,44, where the *inconsutilis tunica* of John 19:23, traditionally referring to the indivisible faith or indivisible Church (see, e.g., *Liber aug.*, I,1), has been transferred to the indivisible world empire.

[53] It is, for the present purpose, quite sufficient to glance at the list of *errores condemnati* of 1277, published by Denifle and others (see above, Ch.VI,n.5), in order to understand the meaning of Dante's stress on the *virtutes intellectuales*; see, e.g., Denifle, No. 144: "Quod omne bonum, quod homini possibile est, consistit in virtutibus intellectualibus"; or, Denifle, No. 157: "Quod homo ordinatus quantum ad intellectum et affectum, sicut potest sufficienter esse per virtutes intellectuales, et alias morales, de quibus loquitur Philosophus in *Ethicis*, est sufficienter dispositus ad felicitatem aeternam." Cf. Grabmann, *Der lateinische Averroismus*, 10f. The most prominent representative of that idea of philosophic beatitude was Boetius of Dacia, especially in his tractate *De summo bono sive de vita philosophi*, ed. Grabmann, *Mittelalterliches Geistesleben*, II,200-224. For the Aristotelian background in general, see the useful study of Harry V. Jaffa, *Thomism and Aristotelianism: A Study of the Commentary by Thomas Aquinas on the Nicomachean Ethics* (Chicago, 1952).

this world not only for the individual or the sum-total of individuals, but rather for the greater collective as such, the body corporate of Man. That body was supposed to be knit together by the united intellectual capacities of man; it took its justification from the intellectual oneness of the human race; and that oneness again made the oneness of monarchic-philosophic leadership imperative. Now, that combination of human oneness, intellectual oneness, and political oneness—directed towards the intellectual self-manifestation of the body of mankind as the natural goal on earth—prompted Dante to draw a very bold conclusion, logically perhaps unavoidable, but seemingly unorthodox. By analogy with man's individual body and intellect, Dante provided the body corporate of universal mankind with a Universal Intellect. Dante was not heedless of the fact that the "Unity of the Intellect" was taken to be one of the outstanding axioms of the Averroistic doctrine, for he himself quoted Averroes explicitly, when he argued:

> It is evident, then, that the specific potentiality of *humanitas* is a potentiality, or capacity, of the intellect. And because that potentiality cannot wholly and simultaneously (*tota simul*) be reduced to actuation by one man alone, or by one of the . . . particularized communities, the human race is necessarily a compound of many (*multitudo*) through whom the entire potentiality can become actuality.

And Dante added that Averroes, in his commentary on the Aristotelian *De anima*, agreed with this doctrine.[54] That is to say, only the whole body corporate of mankind was able to achieve what neither the individual nor a local corporate body could achieve: to allow *all* potentialities of the *total* human intellect to be actualized *semper* and *simul*, "at all times" and "all at the same time."[55] Hence, Dante concluded, the world-monarchy was needed to secure the perpetual actuation of the whole of *humanitas*, quantitatively and qualitatively. He visualized a huge political collective whose intellectual potentialities, through the agency of the four cardinal virtues, were guided to perfection by the Roman philosopher-monarch—admittedly a somewhat undefined and enig-

---

[54] *Monarchia*, I,3,63ff.

[55] *Monarchia*, I,3,66ff: "potentia ista per unum hominem . . . *tota simul* in actum reduci non potest . . . "; *ibid.*, 73f: "ut potentia *tota* . . . *semper* sub actu sit . . . "; I,4,3f: "actuare *semper totam* potentiam intellectus possibilis." See also Vernani, *De reprobatione*, ed. Käppeli, 127,19: "totius humani generis simul sumpti."

matic personality, but undoubtedly meant to be a mirror of the *virtutes politicae*, a man owning all and desiring nothing and therefore capable at all times of actuating Justice as well as the other virtues.[56]

One point, at least, demands further clarification. Strictly speaking, Dante did *not* say that an individual man could not possibly reach his own perfection or personal actuation. This assumption would have been in conflict with the teaching of the Church; it would have been refuted by Dante himself and tacitly by his pilgrimage to the terrestrial and celestial paradises, and would perhaps be belied even by the figure of Dante's world-monarch.[57] What Dante actually said was that the totality of human knowl-

---

[56] A detailed analysis of the figure of Dante's monarch (probably most rewarding, though rather difficult) is not intended here. Decisive is *Monarchia*, I,11, with its invocation of Vergil's *Fourth Eclogue*. Dante visualizes as a potentiality the return of the *Saturnia regna* (which he interprets as *optima tempora*) under the rule of *Iustitia* actualized by, or incarnated in, the *Monarcha*, who, so to speak, cannot avoid the exercise of true justice, because while possessing all, he lacks cupidity: "Remota cupiditate omnino, nihil iustitiae restat adversum." Were *Iustitia* actualized, then *Pax, Libertas, Concordia*, and all the rest would be actualized too. See, for the all-possessing monarch, I,11,81ff: "Sed Monarcha non habet quod possit optare; sua namque iurisdictio terminatur Oceano solum, quod non contingit principibus aliis, quorum principatus ad alios terminantur." Dante's source for the all-possessing Prince was mainly Aristotle; see Gilson, *Dante*, 176ff; Vinay (ed.), *Monarchia*, p.62,n.21. It should not be forgotten, however, that the jurists, especially the civilians, discussed that topic over and over again, granting to the Prince the possession of all *de iure*, though not *de facto*. They, too, broadened the basis of their argument philosophically, although their philosopher was not Aristotle, but Seneca and his ideal of the "Sage" who possesses everything "in the manner of a king" (*regio more*) and with whom the king is both contrasted and placed, as it were, on the same denominator (*De beneficiis*, VII,3ff). See, e.g., Andreas of Isernia, on *Feud.*, II,56,n.78 (*Quae sunt regalia*), fol.305ᵛ: ". . . et melius per Senecam, de benefi.§.iur.civili. [VII,4,2] 'omnia regis sunt etc.' et sequitur 'ad Regem potestas omnium pertinet, ad singulos proprietas'; et sequitur 'quemadmodum sub optimo Rege omnia Rex imperio possidet dominia' [VII,5,1], et hoc modo dicit infra 'Caesar omnia habet etc.' [VII,6,3]. Seneca fuit iurista optimus, ut patet illis qui legerunt eum . . ." See also Andreas of Isernia, *Prooem. ad Lib. aug.*, ed. Cervone, xxvii. The topic *Seneca iurista optimus* has as yet to be investigated. The Dantesque idea of the monarch "qui non habet quod possit optare" is generally that of the jurists; see, e.g., Baldus, on *C.*, prooem. ("*De novo Codice faciendo*"), rubr.n.14, fol.3ᵛ, who argues against applying to the emperor the word "*oportet*," "quia sibi [imperatori] nihil est necessarium; nam imperator libere agit ad similitudinem Dei, qui est agens omnino liberum . . ." This imperial philosophy is also represented in the surroundings of Frederick II; see, e.g., his letter to John Vatatzes (Huillard-Bréholles, VI,685). That Dante's vision does not agree with so-called "reality" should not, however, be interpreted as "un bel gioco dialettico" (Vinay, *loc.cit.*). What Dante outlines is not the *Monarcha* "body natural," but (so to speak) the perpetual *Monarcha* "body politic."

[57] See, for a few remarks on the problem in general, Vinay (ed.), *Monarchia*, 23ff,n.16 (on I,3); also below, nos.62f.

edge, the totality of that by which man became Man, or, briefly, the totality of *humanitas*, could become actuated only by the collective effort of the corporate body of mankind. The fact that this perfection of the human totality was a desirable task, and even a necessary one, is a different matter. Dante's intent perhaps may be conveniently gathered from a stanza in the *Comedy*:

> The human nature, when in its totality
> It sinned in its first seed, was parted both
> From its own dignities and from the paradise.[58]

That is, with regard to original sin the whole of mankind was like one body and one man, as Aquinas put it.[59] Against that totality of mankind which fell guilty potentially in the first man, Dante set the totality of mankind which potentially can regain "its own dignities" and paradise as well. It can achieve, by its own power and through the intellectual virtues, its own actuation in the terrestrial paradise whence Adam had been expelled, who, in the state of innocence, himself was the actuation of *humanitas* without restriction. Dante reversed, as it were, the potentialities: just as Adam potentially bore mankind and sin in his limbs, so did mankind in its totality bear Adam and his perfection, his *status subtilis* (if we may say so), in its limbs. What had fanned out from Adam—mankind—was reduced again corporately to Adam. For there is no doubt about it that Dante conceived of the *genus humanum* as though it were a single person, a single body corporate which, just like the *universitas* of the jurists, was "always" and "all at the same time" actuality. In comparison with that sempiternal *humana universitas* the intellectual powers of its individual constituents—mortal and ever changing as they were—could be but fragmentary, ephemeral, and imperfect just as in the case of any other corporate community. Hence, the status of perpetual actualization—normally a privilege of the celestial intelligences[60]—could

---

[58] *Paradiso*, vii,85ff:

> Vostra natura, quando peccò tota
> nel seme suo, da queste dignitadi,
> come da Paradiso fu remota.

[59] See below, n.72.

[60] *Monarchia*, i,3,55-62, Dante seems to mean that the sempiternal beings are perpetual actualization; but he contends that *esse* and *intelligere* coincided in the celestial intelligences, and thereby immediately met with the protest of Guido Vernani (*De reprobatione*, ed. Käppeli, 127,4) who branded this coincidence an *intolerabilis error*, because in God alone could there coincide *esse* and *intelligere*. See, for the passage, also Vinay, *Monarchia*, 22,n.15.

be achieved only by the whole corporation, the species of man, to which Dante attributed a single, if universal, intellect.

That Dante borrowed the notion of the "universal intellect" from Averroes, whom he quoted quite frankly, is evident; but it meant to Dante something different from Averroism. The Averroist dreamt of a separate world-intellect to be actualized in, or by, the philosopher, the *individual*; Dante, however, thought of the *collective*. He had in mind an immanent world-intellect which was not separate from its individual human constituents, though it transcended each one of them, and which could be actualized in its fulness only by an *universitas* acting as "one man," as a collective individual.[61] For all that, however, it is undeniable that Dante's concept could have an odor of heterodoxy, especially since Dante himself quoted, and certainly thought of, Averroes in that connection. In a superficial way, therefore, his adversary Guido Vernani was right when he branded the poet's philosophical tenet a *pessimus error*. But the *pessimus error* was not seated simply in the tenet of a collective intellect itself. Vernani—correctly from the conventional point of view—proceeded from the *anima intellectiva*, the intellectual soul, implying therefore the traditional unity of soul and intellect; and on that premise, Dante's collective intellect would have implied also a "collective soul," or world-soul, denying thereby to man the individual soul and the possibility of its individual perfection and redemption.[62] Dante, however, had separated, as it were, the intellect from the soul, and the *virtutes intellectuales* from the *virtutes infusae*; and perhaps, in an admittedly exaggerated fashion, one could advance the hypothesis that *qua* intellect Dante visualized a predominantly collective perfection, whereas *qua* soul he foresaw the traditional individual perfection.[63] All that, however, is beside the point here.

[61] Gilson, *Dante*, 169, is excellent on the difference between Averroistic individual perfection and Dante's collective perfection.

[62] See Vernani, *De reprobatione*, ed. Käppeli, 127f.

[63] See, for that distinction, M. Barbi, "Nuovi problemi, VIII: Impero e Chiesa," *Studi danteschi*, xxvi (1942), 13,n.1. It is more than doubtful, however, whether this distinction can be made: the goal of the *vita contemplativa* in this world is always the beatitude of the individual, whereas Dante, in the *Monarchia*, wishes to speak mainly about the *vita activa* or *politica* (cf.1,2,36ff), which is collective by definition. See, e.g., Jacobus de Pistorio, *Quaestio de felicitate*, ed. P. O. Kristeller (below, n.71), 462, lines 46off, who distinguishes between *ipsa felicitas* of the contemplating individual, *felicitas practica* of man as *pars multitudinis*, and perpetuation of the human race with regard to man as *pars universi*.

Far more relevant, it seems, was Dante's request that the universal intellect should be actuated *semper* and *simul*, that is, a demand of perpetuality which individually could not possibly be met—just as no individual citizen of Bologna could actuate the sempiternity of Bologna itself. At this juncture it becomes apparent that, more perhaps than with Averroes, Dante fell in with the corporational doctrines current in his time among jurists and philosophers.

Difficult though it was for the jurists to define accurately the culpability and responsibility of the *universitas*, there was at least some agreement about the fact that corporate bodies had neither a head nor a soul nor an intellect.[64] The corporation lacking a soul could therefore not be surrendered by excommunication to the hands of Satan or, lacking a head, be beheaded, whereas the problem of collective guilt (often interpreted as a secular parallel of the original sin with which the totality of mankind was charged) was as widely open to discussion in the thirteenth century as it is today.[65] It was hardly more than a playing with notions and words when occasionally a jurist declared that corporations, since they had by fiction a body, "could by the same fiction have a soul,"[66] which naturally had as little to do with "monopsychism"[67] as Dante's teaching had with the Averroistic

---

[64] See, for a few significant passages, Gierke, *Gen.R.*, III,363,n.36; cf.280f,282, n.112. That the whole world could be a "corporation" goes without saying; see, e.g., Bartolus, on *D.*6,1,1,3,n.2, fol.204 (above, Ch.VI,n.70): ". . . quia mundus est universitas quaedam." See, for Baldus, above, Ch.VI,n.91, and also Gierke, *Gen.R.*, III,356,n.8, 545,n.64.

[65] The problem of collective guilt (*peccatum multitudinis*), of international concern after 1945, has been treated in recent years quite frequently also from a scholastic-canonistic point of view and in connection with the *peccatum originale*; see, e.g., Franz König, "Kollektivschuld und Erbschuld," *Zeitschrift für katholische Theologie*, LXXII (1950), 40-65; Eschmann, "Studies in the Notion of Society" (above, Ch.VI,n.77), esp. 1-7, both with brief reviews of modern literature, and both showing convincingly the inapplicability of the modern notion of collective guilt to that of original sin. That does not exclude, however, that corporational doctrines were applicable to mankind with regard to the *peccatum originale*; see below, n.72.

[66] See Oldradus de Ponte, *Consilia*, LXV,n.7, fol.24ʳ, and the criticism of Gierke, *Gen.R.*, III,364f.

[67] Strangely enough, some jurists occasionally talked about the *anima mundi*. See, e.g., Azo, on *Inst.*2,2, fol.276ᵛ, ed. Maitland, *Azo and Bracton*, 130: "Forte et res incorporales sunt, quae in iure non existunt, ut genera et species, et calodaemones et cacodaemones, et animae hominum et *anima mundi*"—a passage repeated by Bracton, fol.10b, ed. Woodbine, II,48. The notion was well known in the school of Chartres; see, e.g., Theodore Silverstein, "The Fabulous Cosmogony of Bernardus Silvestris," *Modern Philology*, XLVI (1948-49), 114ff. Professor Silverstein was kind enough to point out to me that Azo borrowed all his exempla of incorporeal things

"Unity of the Intellect." On the other hand, however, the jurists of Dante's century claimed that the *universitas* was itself an indivisible Whole, "a kind of individual which therefore does not distinguish parts." When substituting for *universitas* the notion of *patria*, it became even more obvious that the Whole was an entity transcending the sum of its constituents, for (said Andreas of Isernia) "to divide *patria* into as many parts as she has inhabitants is a mutilation (*concisio*), and not a division (*divisio*)."[68] With Bartolus, the pupil of Cynus, it then became quite customary to argue that the "*universitas* represents one person which is different from the individuals composing it," for whereas the components change "the *universitas* itself remains the same."[69] And if finally Baldus styled the community "some universal person having the intellect of a single person, which nevertheless consists of many bodies,"[70] it becomes obvious that Dante's ways of thinking and arguing were closely related to those of the jurists. Technically, Baldus said exactly what Dante had said before him, although Baldus stopped at his definition of a corporational "single intellect" and did not build up that teleology of the human species which was the very essence of Dante's idea of a moral-political and pedagogical world-monarchy.

The conceptual collectivism of the Italian jurists was not Averroistic either, even though the lawyers were often accused of Averroistic inclinations.[71] It was no more Averroistic than the

---

from William of Conches, *De philosophia mundi*, ed. (under the name of Bede, *Elementa philosophiae*) in *PL*, xc,1127ff; see, for *calodaemones* and *cacodaemones*, 1131B, and, for the *anima mundi*, 1130CD. See, for the work of William of Conches, also Silverstein, "*Elementatum*: Its appearance among the Twelfth-Century Cosmogonists," *Mediaeval Studies*, xvi (1954), 157,n.6, and his most recent study "Hermann of Carinthia and Greek: A Problem in the 'New Science' of the Twelfth Century," *Medioevo e Rinascimento: Studi in onore di Bruno Nardi* (Florence, 1955), 693f. It is clear that Azo did not think of doctrines of monopsychism. Professor Silverstein's identification of the Azo text, however, is very valuable, because it shows that interrelations existed between the earlier glossators and the philosophers of Chartres; see, for another example, Hermann Kantorowicz, *Glossators*, 19f,n.10.

68 See above, Ch.vi,n.75, for Andreas of Isernia, and Gierke, *Gen.R.*, iii,204, for Roffred of Benevento.

69 Above, Ch.vi,n.89, for Bartolus on *D*.48,19,16,10.

70 Baldus, on *C*.6,26,2,n.2, fol.80v: "Est quaedam persona universalis, quae unius personae intellectum habet, tamen ex multis corporibus constat, ut populus . . . Et haec persona similiter loco unius habetur et individuum corpus reputatur . . ." Cf. Gierke, *Gen.R.*, iii,433,nos.61ff.

71 See above, Ch.vi,n.62, and add Paul Oskar Kristeller, "A Philosophical Treatise from Bologna Dedicated to Guido Cavalcanti: Magister Jacobus de Pistorio and his

"collectivism" represented by Thomas Aquinas when, in his *Summa Theologica*, he discussed the reasons of Adam's fall and its effects on mankind. For on that occasion Aquinas, too, advanced a corporational explanation of the guilt of mankind.

> We may say that all men born from Adam can be considered as *one* man (*possunt considerari ut unus homo*) in so far as they concur in the nature which they have received from the first man— just as in civil affairs all men of a community are reputed, so to say, as one body and the whole community as one man.[72]

"Mankind a corporation by the unity of the original sin, not by the unity of the intellect," so we might sum up the collectivism of Aquinas, thereby leaving undiscussed the curiosity that a collectivity by sin should be orthodox, and a collectivity by the intellect, to say the least, suspect of heterodoxy. It is evident, however, how closely interrelated the arguments of Dante, Aquinas, and the jurists were, and how narrow the margin was which separated corporational doctrines from pure collectivism.

That narrow margin was not always guarded by Remigio de' Girolami, Aquinas' pupil and Dante's teacher. Remigio's extreme and radical corporationalism had all but smothered the value of individual perfection. He, like Dante, operated with the Aristotelian doctrine of the actuation of the potential, and, by applying it to the political field, held that there was perfection only in the community, in the Whole.

> The Whole has more being than the part. The Whole, as a Whole, is existing in actuality, whereas the part, as part, has no being except in potentiality.[73]

'Questio de felicitate,' " *Medioevo e Rinascimento: Studi in onore di Bruno Nardi* (Florence, 1955), 427-463, a treatise revealing once more Dante's affinities to the non-Thomistic philosophers of his time.

[72] Aquinas, *Summa theol.*, I-II,q.81,a.1, resp.: "Et ideo alia via procedendum est, dicendo quod omnes homines qui nascuntur ex Adam, possunt considerari ut unus homo, in quantum conveniunt in natura quam a primo parente accipiunt secundum quod in civilibus omnes homines qui sunt unius communitatis, reputantur quasi unum corpus, et tota communitas quasi unus homo."

[73] Remigio de' Girolami's *Tractatus de bono communi* is known to me only through the long excerpts published by Richard Egenter, "Gemeinnutz vor Eigennutz: Die soziale Leitidee im *Tractatus de bono communi* des Fr. Remigius von Florenz († 1319)," *Scholastik*, IX (1934), 79-92. For the place quoted in the text, see 82,n.10: ". . . totum plus habet de entitate quam pars. Totum enim ut totum est existens actu, pars vero ut pars non habet esse nisi in potentia secundum Philosophum in 7 *Physic.*"

Therefore, the citizen must love the city more than himself, because the city is his only possible actuation: the Whole, the city, is more perfect than the individual and, being more perfect, it is more to the likeness of God.[74] Remigio overstressed that idea to such an extent that he denied the individual deprived of its city even the qualification of man:

> If Florence were destroyed, he, who was a Florentine citizen, no longer can be called a Florentine. . . . And if he no longer is a citizen, he no longer is man, because man by his nature is a civic animal.[75]

What Remigio produced was simply a caricature of Aristotle who had explained that a man asocial by *nature*, and not by *fortune*, was either less or more than man—a beast or a god.[76] However, Remigio, that curious thomistic proto-Hegelian,[77] was an extremist of anti-individualism: "being man" depended for him upon being a citizen because without a city the individual could not achieve perfection at all. True, Dante also admitted that man would be worse off on earth, were he not a citizen.[78] Remigio, however, had gone far beyond Dante; he was even ready to deny to the individual the eternal salvation of the soul should that prove necessary for the good of the city. To some extent Remigio finally

---

[74] Egenter, *op.cit.*, 84,n.11: "Unde [commune] . . . directe amatur, praeamatur autem post Deum propter similitudinem, quam habet ad Deum . . ." See also Egenter, 87,n.20. For the doctrine holding that the superior entity (commune or emperor) "is loved directly" and without intermediary, cf. *Monarchia*, I,11,111ff.

[75] Egenter, *op.cit.*, 82,n.10: "Unde destructa civitate remanet civis lapideus aut depictus, quia sc. caret virtute et operatione quam prius habebat, . . . ut qui erat civis Florentinus per destructionem Florentiae iam non sit Florentinus dicendus, sed potius flerentinus. Et si non est civis, non est homo, quia homo est naturaliter animal civile . . ." See G. de Lagarde, "Henri de Gand" (above, Ch.v,n.52), 88f, and "Individualisme et corporatisme" (above, Ch.v,n.220), 38f.

[76] Remigio actually quotes (in addition to the *Ethics*) Aristotles' *Politics*, I,1,1252b, to which Aquinas in his Commentary, §35, ed. Spiazzi, 11, remarks that those being "more than man" might have "naturam perfectiorem aliis hominibus communiter" and therefore could live self-sufficiently without the society of men "sicut fuit in Ioanne Baptista et beato Antonio heremita."

[77] See, e.g., Hegel's *Philosophie des Rechts*, §258: "Since the state is mind objectified, the individual has objectivity, truth, and ethical status only as one of the members of the state. The community as such is the true content and final aim."

[78] See the famous terzine in *Par.*, VIII,115ff:
> Ond' egli [Carlo Martello] ancora: "Or di', sarebbe il peggio
> per l'uomo in terra se non fosse cive?"
> "Si," rispos' io, "e qui ragion non cheggio."

See also the able discussion of that passage by D'Entrèves, *Dante*, 11ff, who, however, does not consider Remigio at all.

toned down his statement. He argued, however, that even the perfectly guiltless citizen should take upon himself his own eternal condemnation, if this would prevent his community from being eternally condemned to Hell; he should prefer being punished to being saved while his city was condemned. Apart from the fact that Remigio recognized a possibility of condemning to infernal punishment a fictitious person which had no soul, he carried his argument in every other respect to quite illicit extremes. For what he advocated was not a simple *pro patria mori*, that is, to suffer the *natural* death of the body for the community and expect the reward in heaven for a sacrifice on earth; Remigio advocated the *eternal* death of the soul, that is, the jeopardy of individual salvation and celestial beatitude, for the sake of the temporal fatherland.[79]

Dante, though lagging far behind his teacher's relentless corporationalism and anti-individualism, was nevertheless not uninfluenced by the general compound of ideas and ways of thinking of which Remigio was but an extreme exponent. Dante, too, carried Aristotelianism to (what seemed to him) the logical ends when he emphasized, time and time again, that the actuation of the total human intellect was a task which could be performed collectively only by the greatest of all possible communities, the *universitas generis humani* organized in the Roman world-monarchy—as it were, the body corporate of Man as distinguished from the body natural of each individual man. Into that scheme, however, Dante had to fit his world-monarch, whom the reader of the *Monarchy* could hardly avoid recognizing as an individual near to perfection and whose shadowy figure, as conjured by Dante, resembled the "body politic" of the world-monarch rather than his body natural. Not quite wrongly did Dante's adversary Guido Vernani describe that imaginary world-monarch as a Prince who (if the teaching of Aristotle be accepted) had to exceed all his subjects by virtue:

[79] Egenter, *op.cit.*, 89f,n.24. Remigio raises the question about a citizen's attitude in the case that "suum commune in inferno damnetur," and argues that "ex virtute amoris ordinati homo deberet potius ipsam [poenam] velle pati cum immunitate communis, quam quod commune suum ipsam [poenam] incurreret cum immunitate sui, inquantum est pars communis." That monstrosity, it is true, is subsequently somewhat alleviated by the fact that a guiltless person could not be condemned anyhow by divine Justice; also, Remigio leaves a few loopholes in the case that love of the city and love of God should come into conflict; see, on those points, Egenter, 89ff. [See Addenda, below, p.568.]

he "compares with all his subjects as the Whole compares with its parts."[80] That interpretation, in fact, comes close enough to the doctrine of the jurists—Andreas of Isernia and others—who held that "the Prince was in the *respublica*, and the *respublica* in the Prince."[81] But since in Dante's case the *respublica* was replaced by the *universitas humana* and thereby widened to its very limits, Guido Vernani could score once more when he concluded that "the [Dantesque] monarch of the whole human race must needs exceed in virtues and wisdom the whole human race." Vernani rejected Dante's thesis on the grounds that so perfect a human being could not possibly be found. He made, however, one reservation; for he declared that according to Dante's own philosophy there could be imaginable but one being in whom in fact the whole of *humanitas* was actuality: in Christ, the only true monarch of the world.[82]

Guido Vernani's conclusion was to the point. Moreover, it serves to demonstrate once more the fundamental duality[83] in

[80] Vernani, *De reprobatione*, ed. Käppeli, 128,11ff, first refers to Aristotle's *Politics*, III,17,1288a15, Latin version ed. Spiazzi, §386, with Aquinas' Commentary, §527f, pp.183ff, and then says: ". . . rex debet excellere et excedere in virtute totam multitudinem subditorum, et comparatur ad omnes subditos sicut totum comparatur ad partes." See *Monarchia*, I,6,1ff, where Dante applies to his monarch the Aristotelian maxim of the *duplex ordo*, including the comparison with the relations prevailing between army and general; above, Ch.v,nos.221ff.

[81] Kantorowicz, "Mysteries of State," 79f,nos.48 and 53; also above, Ch.v,nos.64ff.

[82] Vernani, ed. Käppeli, 128,13ff: "Monarcha ergo totius humani generis debet excedere in virtutibus et in prudentia totum genus humanum. Talem autem purum hominem impossibile fuit aliquando reperire. Unde secundum istam philosophicam rationem solus dominus Iesus Christus et nullus alius fuit verus monarcha." Vernani then refutes Dante's whole thesis of a monarchy based on *humanitas* as set against *Christianitas* by pointing out (*ibid.*, 128,n.4) "quod in infidelibus numquam fuit vera respublica nec aliquis verus imperator." See above, n.43.

[83] Dante's system of "dualities" and "juxtapositions" should not be mistaken for "dualism" of the Augustinian pattern. The latter places the immaterial compound of soul and intellect (*anima intellectiva*) over and against the material *corpus*. Dante, however, separating powerfully and consequently the intellect from the soul, in fact reverts again to the trichotomy of σῶμα, νοῦς, ψυχή of which residuals are found in the writings of St. Augustine as well as in the liturgies; see Erich Dinkler, *Die Anthropologie Augustins* (Stuttgart, 1934), 255-266, and, for the liturgies, F. E. Brightman, "Soul, Body, Spirit," *Journal of Theological Studies*, II (1901), 273f, to which there might be added the *Benedictio olei* of the *Gelasian Sacramentary*, ed. H. A. Wilson (Oxford, 1894), 70. See, for Antiquity, the important passage in Plutarch, *Moralia*, 943a ("The Face on the Moon," c.28), arguing against "the many" who fail to distinguish properly between soul and intellect, with the note of Harold Cherniss, in his edition of the tractate, in Loeb Classical Library; Plutarch, vol.XII, 197, note c. Hence, Dante's "heterodoxy" was not "Averroistic" (or it was Averroistic only incidentally), but resulted from the general trichotomy of his views.

Dante's thought in which every monopoly of *Christianitas* was obviated as well as supplemented by a counterpart belonging to *humanitas*. Undeniably, as Guido Vernani shows, the question thrust upon the reader of the *Monarchy* was to what extent Dante's world-monarch matched that image of the *optimus homo* who was "the most One in his kind" and who was "the Idea of his kind," that is, the "perfect man" in whom the whole of *humanitas* was actualized just as a kingdom was actualized in its king. Has there ever been such perfection in the individual? Has it ever happened that the whole community of universal mankind was epitomized in one man except in Christ? In the *Divine Comedy* Dante gives a fair answer to this question. Yes, such perfection did exist; for there have been two perfect beings, Adam and Christ.

> The human nature never was, nor shall it be,
> Such as it was in those two personages.[84]

Adam and Christ were perfect, no doubt: they descended from God himself, they were not burdened by original sin. They were, however, perfect also in a philosophic sense in so far as both were the actuation of all human potentialities and both epitomized, if in different ways, the totality of mankind: Adam, because at his creation and in the state of innocence he was the only man then living so that in this extraordinary case individual and species, man and mankind coincided; Christ, because he was at the same time God and man, and also because (said Dante) by the judge of the Roman emperor who had jurisdiction over the whole human race, it was "the whole human race that was punished in the flesh of Christ."[85] Moreover, both Adam and Christ were man in a peculiarly double fashion. The first man was, if successively, both the *Adam subtilis* of the state of innocence, immortal, "a little less

---

[84] *Paradiso*, XIII,86f:

> Chè l'umana natura mai non fue,
> Nè fia, qual fu in quelle due persone.

Non fue, nè fia is Dante's customary way of expressing what may be termed the moment of actuation; see, e.g., *Convivio*, IV,5,60ff; above,n.42.

[85] *Monarchia*, II,13 (11),40ff: ". . . et iudex ordinarius esse non poterat, nisi supra totum humanum genus iurisdictionem habens, quum totum humanum genus in carne illa Christi . . . puniretur." This is, of course, the traditional doctrine which, however, does not imply that by his incarnation Christ assumed the human nature in the sense of the human "species" and not in the sense of the human "individual." See, for this controversial point, Karl Holl, *Amphilochius von Ikonium* (Tübingen and Leipzig, 1904), 222ff.

only than the angels, crowned with glory and honor,"[86] and the *Adam mortalis* after having tasted the fruit of the tree of knowledge. Christ, according to scholastic teaching, assumed at his incarnation the nature of the *Adam subtilis* in so far as he was without guilt or sin, and assumed of his own free will an accident of the nature of the *Adam mortalis* in so far as he had the capability of suffering death.[87] Hence, the two actuations of mankind in a single individual are those in Adam and in Christ, lords of the terrestrial paradise and the celestial paradise respectively, paragons of perfection in this life and in the other life, and figures indicating once more the duality of Dante's philosophy concerning the "two ends which have been set by Providence, that ineffable, before man to be contemplated by him."

Every century of the Christian era had its own ideas about man's renovation, reformation, regeneration—in short, his moral as well as supra-natural rebirth; and these ideas varied considerably.[88] On certain basic points, however, the Christian writers agreed. On the one hand, it was the goal of every Christian, and of Christianity at large, to recover the original image of man such as it had been before the fall—created to the likeness of God "a little lower than the angels." On the other hand, every believer was potentially elected, owing to the Incarnation of the Son of God, to participate in the divine nature of Christ and thereby to re-establish in himself also the original integrity of human nature, that is, the very similitude with God which had been bestowed upon the first man on the day of his making. In other words, the image of the paradisian Adam was merged in that of Christ, the new Adam; and the original God-likeness of Adam in paradise was, by the

[86] See, in addition to *Monarchia*, I,4,14, also *Convivio*, IV,19,65, where the words of Ps. 8: 6 (also Hebr. 2: 7) are used to describe the actuation of human nobility based on virtue. The Psalter verse, of course, was quoted also in the Prooemium of the *Liber aug.*, where, however, very imperially the word "diadem" has been added: "honoris et gloriae *diademate* coronato . . ." See, for a similar change, *Monarchia*, II,9,39, where Cicero, *De officiis*, I,11,34: *imperii gloria*, has been changed into *imperii corona*.

[87] For the problem, see M. Landgraf, "Die Sterblichkeit Christi nach der Lehre der Frühscholastik," *Zeitschrift für katholische Theologie*, LXXIII (1951), 257-312.

[88] This is the subject of the forthcoming book of Gerhart B. Ladner, *Reform: The Influence of an Early Christian Idea on Mediaeval and Renaissance Civilization*, quoted by him in his preliminary study "Die mittelalterliche Reform-Idee und ihr Verhältnis zur Idee der Renaissance," *MIÖG*, LX (1952), 32-59.

support of divine grace, recovered through Christ. This new image of man was considered (for example, by Saint Augustine) superior to that of Adam before the fall.[89] There was no need for disintegrating what had been merged, or for taking the idea of a restitution of Adam's original image out of the general compound of Christian doctrines.

It was left to Dante to re-"humanize" the idea of a recovery of Adam's original nature and again to release the "human" from the Christian aggregate of thought.[90] For, as a consequence of his philosophy of dualities, or of his concept of perfection in both a terrestrial and a celestial paradise, it was probably unavoidable to "secularize" also the current Adam-theology and build up a doctrine of a purely *human* regeneration which was not identical with the doctrine of Christian regeneration—though the one did not need to contradict the other.

The first two parts of the *Divine Comedy*, Inferno and Purgatory, have clearly the function of demonstrating how Dante—that is, man in general or mankind impersonated in the poet—was led by philosophy and secular wisdom from a sinful state back to the *natura sincera e buona* of the first man before the fall. [91] To be sure, none but the Church was competent to prepare man for his future immortality, since as a remedy for the first transgression and the ensuing loss of corporeal immortality the Church administered the sacrament of spiritual rebirth, baptism. It is obvious that in one way or another some of the effects of the sacrament of baptism were to be fitted into Dante's concept of the terrestrial paradise where man was supposed to recover, not his eternal, but his temporal beatitude, his original human dignity, and his inner freedom from guilt. This state of temporal perfection, however, was to be achieved not by means of a sacramental and supra-natural act, but by man's own powers, by his natural

[89] See Ladner, *op.cit.*, 41ff, and also "St. Augustine's Conception of the Reformation of Man to the Image of God," *Augustinus Magister* (Congrès International Augustinien, Paris, 21-24 Septembre 1954, Communications; Paris, 1954), 867-878. See also Walter Dürig, *Imago. Ein Beitrag zur Terminologie und Theologie der römischen Liturgie* (Munich, 1952).

[90] In a very prominent place—in the prologue of the *Liber augustalis*—the image of Adam had been used before by Frederick II. See, in general, Burdach, *Rienzo*, 297ff,313ff, for the mysticism connected with Adam; also Georg Jellinek, *Adam in der Staatslehre* (Heidelberg, 1893), especially for the theories of Absolutism.

[91] *Par.*, VII,35f.

reason, and by the intellectual virtues. There is, of course, not the slightest reason for assuming that with regard to the effects of baptism Dante deviated in any respect from the common tradition. But since his idea of a return to the guiltless Adam in a terrestrial Eden was not at all within the scope of either the Church or the ecclesiastical sacrament or even the economy of salvation, the regeneration of man as visualized by Dante had to proceed necessarily para-ecclesiastically, though often in imitation of the procedures of the Church. Hence, as a consequence of his setting apart of *humanitas* from *Christianitas*, of *virtutes intellectuales* from *virtutes infusae*, terrestrial paradise from celestial paradise, Dante had to set apart also Adam from Christ and make the return to man's original image on earth independent of man's transcendental perfection in Christ by grace. In other words, Dante had to cleanse man from the *peccatum originale* in a non-sacramental fashion.[92]

According to Dante, it was in man's own power to recover the purity of the first man, to re-enter into the Garden of Eden, and finally return to the Tree of Knowledge and undo the effects of its fruits which had turned Adam's lordship to serfdom. In the *Comedy*, it was chiefly the pilgrimage through Purgatory which signified the purification of man in a philosophic, not in a theologico-sacramental, sense, and the result of this pilgrimage and purification paralleled in a way the effects of the sacrament of baptism: just as the neophyte, after his catechumenate, emerged from the baptismal font as one reborn and freed from original sin, so would Dante finally emerge from Purgatory as a new Adam-like being, "free, upright, and whole."[93] To be sure, there was also rebirth for Dante; but this rebirth was moral and ethical and not sacramental.

The purifying and regenerating power of moral philosophy and civic virtue was the theme which Dante struck in the first song of the Purgatory. The guardian watching the entrance of the Ante-Purgatory was a solitary old man, Cato Uticensis, the philosopher-hero who sacrificed his life, if suicidally, for political freedom, which in that case was almost identical with philosophic-

---

[92] See, in that connection, the diatribe of Guido Vernani, *De reprobatione*, ed. Käppeli, 137f, against *Monarchia*, II,13, where Dante tries to link the judgment of Pilate with the punishment for the sin of Adam.

[93] *Purg.*, XXVII,140.

intellectual freedom.[94] He was, for Dante, the impersonator of the four cardinal virtues: from Cato's features there shone forth "the rays of the four holy lights," the four stars which "never yet were seen save by the first people."[95] What Dante had in mind was, presumably, the Southern Cross belonging to the allegedly "unpeopled world behind the Sun," the southern hemisphere.[96] From the vantage-ground of the mount of Eden the four stars had been visible to Adam and Eve, but after the couple's fall they vanished from the sight of man. Dante, therefore, pretended to be the first living man to see again the cross of the four *virtutes intellectuales*, the lodestars of the intellectual catechumen for steering towards secular perfection and beatitude. Under this sign, or under the guidance of the "four fair ones" who imperially were "clad in purple,"[97] and whose light was reflected by Cato, Dante's secular catechumenate began. As in the Inferno, his guide was Vergil, the poet of the Roman empire, who at the bidding of the other pagan, Cato, cleansed his friend's face from the smoke and soot of Hell and girded Dante with the humble rushes, the only plant that still would grow in the waves of the buffeting sea—here a symbol of humility.[98]

In the mediaeval Church, the two rites of purification, baptism and reconciliation of the penitents, had in their preparatory stages many features in common. During the seven weeks from Lenten to Easter, penitential exercises, combined with ample ecclesiastical ceremonial, prepared the sinner for the reconciliation on Thursday in Holy Week; and during that same period, the catechumen was prepared by the so-called "scrutinies"—that is, liturgical actions and exorcisms combined with instructions—for his baptism on Saturday in Holy Week.[99] Neither the penitent

[94] For the Cato problem in general, see the literature quoted in the critical edition of Dante's *Convivio*, by G. Busnelli and G. Vandelli (Florence, 1937), II,55,n.4, esp. Francesco d'Ovidio, *Il Purgatorio e il suo preludio* (Milan, 1906), 33-147.

[95] *Purg.* I,23f,37f.

[96] Cf. *Inf.*, XXVI,117.

[97] *Purg.*, XXIX,130f ("quattro . . . in porpora vestite"), and XXXI,104 ("alla danza delle quattro belle").

[98] See Ferdinand Koenen, "Anklänge an das Busswesen der alten Kirche in Dantes Purgatorio," *Deutsches Dante-Jahrbuch*, VII (1923), 93, for Saint Elizabeth's interpretation of the rushes.

[99] Koenen, "Busswesen," 91-105, has collected the relevant passages. See, for the *scrutinia* in general, Eisenhofer. *Liturgik*, II,250ff, and, for greater detail, A. Dondeyne, "La discipline des scrutins dans l'église latine avant Charlemagne,"

nor the catechumen were admitted to the Mass of the Faithful, and both received during that period oral instruction in order to lead them, step by step, to their final illumination and purification. In Dante's Purgatory both penitential and baptismal rites have their place. They are intertwined, and on more than one occasion an interpretation in either the penitential or the baptismal sense would be admissible. It should not be forgotten, however, that Dante was not only a sinner to be reconciled with the Church, but that he was above all a man striving after both human perfection independent of the Church and supra-human perfection within the Church.

According to the rites of the early mediaeval Church, which survived in Northern Italy certainly until the eleventh century and perhaps (if we may trust Durandus) until the thirteenth, the entrance into catechumenate was followed by seven "scrutinies" designed to test the catechumen and to prepare him by degrees.[100] The scrutinies were distributed over the period of the seven weeks of Lent whereby the last scrutiny almost coincided with baptism itself.[101] It may be said that Dante's scrutinies in preparation for his intellectual baptism began when he entered into Purgatory proper, ready to start—in accordance with Cato's advice—his ascent of the Mount of Purgatory on whose summit the terrestrial paradise was located.[102]

To the gate of Purgatory Dante was borne by a dream. He dreamt that Jupiter's eagle snatched him like another Ganymede up to the fiery sphere of heaven where both the eagle and the poet seemed to go up in flames—a dream of purification through the imperial (that is, moral-philosophic) power which here compared also with the customary meaning of the eagle as a symbol of bap-

---

Revue d'histoire ecclésiastique, XXVIII (1932), 5-33, 751-787, as well as M. Andrieu, *Les Ordines Romani du haut moyen âge* (Louvain, 1948), II,382ff. A very elaborate ritual was observed in Northern Italy as late as the 11th and 12th centuries; see Dom C. Lambot, *Recueil d'Ordines du XIe siècle provenant de la Haute-Italie* (Henry Bradshaw Society, LXVII; London, 1928), xiiff.7ff.

[100] Martène, *De antiquis ecclesiae ritibus*, I,c.1,art.11,§4, quotes Durandus asserting that in Italy and in a few other churches the ceremonies of the scrutinies were observed even in the 13th century. See the preceding note.

[101] Eisenhofer, *Liturgik*, II,254. The last scrutiny took place on Saturday in Holy Week.

[102] *Purg.* I,107f.

tismal regeneration.[103] When Dante awoke he found himself at the gate of Purgatory where an angel, clad in the gray garb of penitence, was sitting on a step of diamond, his feet resting on the imperial porphyry of which the next lower step was made, usually interpreted as the step of Love. Like the penitent, but also like the catechumen who demands his first exorcisms and therewith admission to further purification, instruction, and final reception into the pale of the Church, Dante prostrated himself before the angel of penitence, smiting his breast and craving for his admission to Purgatory. The angel, yielding, unlocked the gate with the silver and golden keys of scrutiny and absolution and allowed Dante to enter, though not before having carved with the point of his sword on the poet's brow seven times the letter *P*.[104] The seven *P*'s marked the seven *peccata*—moral vices, not spiritual sins—of which Dante was to be freed, one by one, while ascending and perambulating the terraces of the Mount of Purgatory. They compare, however, also with the seven scrutinies[105] which the catechumen had to pass before, through baptism, he was freed of the last and impersonal sin as well, the *peccatum originale*. The last *P* was removed from Dante's forehead by an angel standing outside the wall of flames which, since the fall of man, surrounded the Garden of Eden and which alone now separated Dante from the beatitude of the terrestrial paradise.[106] Hence, the last "scrutiny" directly preceded Dante's crossing of the heavenly flames whose heat meant burning and lustration, but not death; and as a man cleansed and baptized by fire, the poet finally entered into the Garden of Eden whence Adam had been barred by the cherub with the flaming sword.[107]

To this point Vergil had served Dante as a guide; beyond the terrestrial paradise he no longer was competent, as he himself declared. Death, the punishment for man's transgression, was conquered by Christ only; his death and resurrection restored man's immortality in the eternal life. Man's *natura sincera e*

---

[103] *Purg.*, IX,19ff. For the eagle as a symbol of regeneration and resurrection, see *Physiologus latinus*, c.VIII, ed. F. J. Carmody (Paris, 1939), 19.

[104] *Purg.*, IX,94ff.

[105] See F. X. Kraus, *Dante* (Berlin, 1897), 424; also Temple Classics edition of *Purgatorio*, 115.

[106] *Purg.*, XXVII,7ff, the angel must have removed with his wing the last *P* before greeting the poets as "hallowed souls" and singing *Beati mundo corde*.

[107] *Ibid.*, 21 ("qui può esser tormento, ma non morte").

buona, however, was restored by human wisdom and intellectual virtue alone, and this original nature of man was worthy of being immortalized: it no longer could falter when directed by its own free will ("It were a fault not to act according to its prompting"),[108] and, like a *habitus*, man's true nature had become immutable. Hence, the consequences of original sin, so far as this meant the loss of the human dignity of the *Adam subtilis*, the loss of his natural judgment and of his inner and outer freedom, were undone when Dante crossed the flames; the curse of mankind was conquered, without the intervention of the Church and its sacraments, by the forces of intellect and supreme reason alone, forces symbolized by the pagan Vergil who, with regard to the individual Dante, took the place and the functions entrusted to the emperor with regard to the whole human race, the *humana civilitas*. But whereas the terrestrial paradise into which Dante entered was lacking that multitude of inhabitants of which the writer of the *Monarchy* had dreamt, because empire and papacy were negligent in their duties,[109] the individual Dante reached human perfection and his own actuation through Vergil, who finally will dismiss his pupil, now a true likeness of Adam before the fall.

One of the goals which Providence has set before man was reached. In the very last stanzas of the *Divine Comedy* it will be disclosed by Dante how man may reach his second goal and recognize his oneness with Christ: the vision of the features of Man's face, a dim reflex *della nostra effige*, faintly visible in outline only within the second circle of the Divine Light, which will allow Dante also to understand the mystery of the Incarnation.[110] But man's perfection in the triune God and in the eternal paradise was preceded by his perfection in the terrestrial paradise, the perfection in Adam. According to the rites of the Church, the return to the guiltless Adam in the state of innocence was achieved by baptism. And ever since the earliest times of the Church the baptismal unction was exposed in the sense which Peter gave it when addressing the converts (I Peter 2:9): "Ye are a chosen generation, a royal priesthood." Baptism was, spiritually, a conferment of royal and sacerdotal dignities on the neo-baptized.

---

[108] *Ibid.*, 140f.

[109] This may be deduced from *Purg.*, xxxii,100ff. See the preliminary note to this canto by P. H. Wicksteed, in the Temple Classics edition of the *Purgatorio*.

[110] *Par.*, xxxiii,130ff.

All of us are anointed into the kingship and priesthood of God by special grace (Ambrose).[111]

It is shown to the baptized, through the infusion of chrism, that unto them there has been conferred by God the royal and the sacerdotal dignities (Maximus of Turin).[112]

May the baptized understand that he bears the king's diadem and the dignity of priesthood (Carolingian).[113]

It would be easy to assemble any number of similar quotations from the works of mediaeval theologians and liturgiologists.[114] And perhaps we should also recall the fact that in the rites of practically all Oriental Churches the custom was (or still is) observed of crowning the neo-baptized with the baptismal crown, a ceremony logically followed by acclamations comparable to those offered at royal coronations and priestly ordinations.[115] Although the ceremony of baptismal crownings was not developed in the West, it was nevertheless not quite unknown: Durandus mentions for the province of Narbonne the custom of applying a red trimming *in modum coronae* to the cap of the chrisom, the white baptismal robe, which may hardly have differed from the red-

[111] Ambrose, *De mysteriis*, VI,30, *PL*, XVI,415B: "omnes enim in regnum Dei et in sacerdotium ungimur gratia speciali." See, for the following, Thomas Michels, "Die Akklamation in der Taufliturgie," *Jahrbuch für Liturgiewissenschaft*, VIII (1928), 76-85.

[112] Maximus of Turin, *De baptismo*, III, *PL*, LVII,777: ". . . per quod ostenditur baptizatis regalem et sacerdotalem conferri a Domino dignitatem."

[113] Pseudo-Amalar of Trier, *Epistola ad Karolum* (one of the numerous answers to Charlemagne's inquiry concerning baptism), ed. J. M. Hanssens, "Deux documents carolingiens sur le baptême," *Ephemerides Liturgicae*, XLI (1927), 80,7ff: "Tunc sacro crismate caput perungitur et mistico tegitur velamine ut intelligat se diadema regni et sacerdotii dignitatem portare." The text has been printed repeatedly; see, e.g., *PL*, XCVIII,939C; *MGH*, *Epp.*, IV,536,44, and *Epp.*, V,274,24; Morin, in *Rev. bénéd.*, XIII (1896), 291; Burn, in *Zeitschrift für Kirchengeschichte*, XXV (1904), 153. For the genuine Amalar, see *PL*, XCIX,898D: "ut intelligat baptizatus regale et sacerdotale ministerium accepisse, qui illius corpori adunatus est, qui Rex summus et Sacerdos est verus."

[114] See Michels, "Akklamation" (above, n.111), 79,n.9, for other places. For the later centuries, there may be added e.g., Ernaud de Bonneval, *Liber de cardinalibus operibus Christi*, c.VIII ("De unctione chrismatis"), *PL*, CLXXXIX,1654A: ". . . in quo mistum oleo balsamum regiae et sacerdotalis gloriae exprimit unitatem, quibus dignitatibus initiandis divinitus est unctio instituta." Aquinas, *De regimine principum*, I,14, ed. Joseph Mathis (Turin and Rome, 1948), 18: ". . . omnes Christi fideles, in quantum sunt membra eius, reges et sacerdotes dicuntur." John of Paris, *De potestate*, 18, ed. Leclercq, 228,27. See also L. Cerfaux, "Regale Sacerdotium," *Revue des sciences philosophiques et théologiques*, XXVIII (1939), 5.

[115] Michels, "Akklamation," 77ff. In the Coptic rite, quoted by Michels, the acclamation at the crowning promptly quotes Ps. 8: 6: "Gloria et honore coronasti eum."

trimmed *coiffe*, the linen cap for the protection of the holy oil, with which the head of the baptized was covered *quasi quadam mitra*.[116] At any rate, it was an opinion current throughout the Middle Ages and beyond[117] that baptism conferred on the neo-baptized the royal and the sacerdotal dignities to indicate that he had become—said Isidore of Seville—a member of the body of Christ, the King and High-Priest.[118]

Against the background of these simple facts it seems strange that the coronation of Dante at the hands of Vergil has been subject to so much guessing. It is true, of course, that the emperor in addition to his crown wore a mitre,[119] and that the pope in addition to his mitre wore a tiara-crown, and that Vergil may have crowned Dante either emperor or pope or both. Within the setting of the Twenty-seventh Canto of Purgatory, however, the primary meaning is obvious: in the moment when Dante re-enters into the terrestrial paradise like another Adam "crowned with glory and honor," he is "crowned and mitred" by Vergil. That is, the royal and sacerdotal dignities have been bestowed upon Dante just as on every newly baptized who through the sacrament of baptism was reborn in the original status of Adam and thereby potentially acquired immortality and eternal co-rulership with Christ in the kingdom of heaven.[120] Dante's coronation "with mitre and with crown," of course, was not sacramental; it was,

[116] Martène, *De antiquis Ecclesiae ritibus*, I,c.1,art.15,§7 (Rouen, 1700), I,141 and (Bassano, 1788), I,54: "Coronae neophytorum." He quotes Durandus, *Rationale*, VI,c.82 (cf. Michels, 85,n.23) to the effect that "hanc fuisse adhuc suo tempore ecclesiae Narbonensis consuetudinem, ut in candidae vestis baptizatorum superiori parte rubea vitta *in modum coronae* assueretur." See also *ibid.*, §6, where the Anonymous of Tours (*Chronicon S. Martini Turonensis auctore anonymo*) describes the chrisom: "Induitur deinde chrismali Neophytus, scilicet alba veste, quae instar cappae lineae caputium habet, quo caput *quasi quadam mitra* operitur et filo rubeo supersuitur."

[117] In the *Assertio Septem Sacramentorum or Defence of the Seven Sacraments*, ed. Louis O'Donovan and prefaced by James Cardinal Gibbons (New York, 1908), 422f, Henry VIII argued against Luther and pointed out, while citing I Peter 2: 9, that if all Christians are priests as Luther asserts, then "in a word all Christians are Kings in the same manner that they are Priests." Professor George H. Williams kindly called my attention to this passage.

[118] Isidore, *De officiis ecclesiasticis*, II,26,*PL*, LXXXIII,824A: "Omnis ecclesia unctione chrismatis consecratur pro eo quod membrum est aeterni regis et sacerdotis. Ergo quia genus sacerdotale et regale sumus, ideo post lavacrum ungimur . . ." Cf. Michels, "Akklamation," 80,n.9. See above, n.114.

[119] Schramm, *Herrschaftszeichen und Staatssymbolik* (Stuttgart, 1954), I,68ff, and 88,n.2.

[120] Cf. Aquinas, *Summa theol.*, III,q.69,a.7; see also a.5 and a.6.

naturā, non gratiā, an intellectual and moral "baptism by transference," prepared ever since Dante became a "catechumen," see-
ing again the Four Stars and prostrating himself—"reverent my
knees and brow"—before the suicide pagan, Cato.[121] In other
words, Dante achieved his "baptism" into *humanitas* in a para-
sacramental and para-ecclesiastical fashion, with Cato acting as
the sponsor, and with the prophet Vergil as his Baptist—a Baptist,
though, who this time unlocked to man not the heavens, but
the paradise of Man.

Whereas Dante's investiture with crown and mitre seems to
demand no further explanation, there remain other problems
which need some commentary. The baptismal rites of the Church
appeared as the conferment of royal and sacerdotal dignities because the neo-baptized became a "member of Christ the eternal
King and Priest." Through the intellectual baptism administered
by Vergil, however, Dante became a member, not of the *corpus
mysticum Christi quod est ecclesia,* but of the *corpus mysticum
Adae quod est humanitas.* Dante was baptized into the likeness
of Adam, the purely human model of man's perfection and actualization. But the divine model of man's perfection, Christ, was not
absent either; he was, most significantly, integrated into the
terrestrial paradise when Beatrice, with the first words she addressed to Dante after his slumber in Eden, conjured—and in the
same breath transcendentalized—the image of the Incarnate in
his human-political capacity of a Roman citizen.

> Here shalt thou be short time a forester;
>   Thou shalt be everlastingly with me
>   A burgher of that Rome whence Christ is Roman.[122]

The replacement of transcendental Jerusalem by a transcendental-
ized Rome; the transfiguration of the purely human capacity of
Christ as a Roman citizen and thereby a member of the body of
Adam; the promise to Dante of his future co-citizenship with
Christ as a fellow-Roman after having been crowned by the
Roman Vergil a fellow-citizen and co-ruler of Adam; the setting
of Beatrice's prophecy into the scenarium of the terrestrial para-
dise—so numerous and so chiastically intertwined are the cross-

---

[121] *Purg.* I,51.　　　[122] *Purg.* XXXII,100ff.

relations and inter-relations that it would be hopeless to analyze at length what poetic felicity was able to express by one image. And yet, the imagery of Dante is by no means exhausted.

Adam, of course, who in paradise was the only man and therefore identical with mankind, was at that particular time the full actuality of all intellectual potencies of man, or of *humanitas*. Crowned with glory and honor, he was the sovereign lord not only of the creation in general over which he was set, but also of mankind which he himself represented. He was both species and individual at the same time; he, therefore, quite logically was "angel-like" and he, therefore, was (as we might say) the only genuine corporation sole of this world. Now, however, Dante was crowned Adam's fellow-ruler. His "baptismal" crowning was, metaphorically, his investiture with the *Adam subtilis*, with that supraindividual *humanitas* of which he himself, like Adam, was the actuality; or (as we might say) he was invested with man's body corporate and politic. Hence, he was entitled to receive the insignia of his universal and sovereign status, crown and mitre, which conferred on him not so much the dignity of emperor and pope (these two directives, instituted after the fall of man as a remedy, were superfluous in the state of innocence) but conferred that almost objectified "Dignity of Man" which "never dies," of which Dante was the mortal incumbent, and which in later centuries was to fascinate Renaissance scholars—for example, Gianozzo Manetti and Pico.[123] Indeed, "Man" appeared as a sovereign Dignity and a universal Office whose holder was probably that "best man, who is the standard of all others and, so to say, their Idea, *whosoever he may be*." And that Dignity of Man included supreme jurisdiction over man *qua* mortal man, regardless of position and rank, while he "who was in the highest degree One within his kind," acted as the instrument of that Dignity—*homo instrumentum humanitatis*.

Admittedly, those legal theories most certainly did not cross Dante's mind. But the essence of the doctrine of the Two Bodies, of "Man's Two Bodies," was just as certainly present to his mind.

---

[123] Gianozzo Manetti (1396-1459) wrote a tractate *De dignitate et excellentia hominis*, dedicated to Alfonso of Aragon, which is not easily accessible; for some excerpts, see, however, *Prosatori Latini del Quattrocento*, a cura di Eugenio Garin (Milan and Naples, n.d.), 421-487. For Pico della Mirandola's *De hominis dignitate*, see the edition by Eugenio Garin (Florence, 1942).

"Free, upright, and whole in judgement," Dante had become a likeness of the *Adam subtilis* in paradise, who was supreme over mankind, and that meant, in Adam's particular case, supreme over himself. When Vergil invested Dante with the insignia of crown and mitre, that ceremony meant the coronation of the *Adam subtilis* in Dante over the *Adam mortalis* in Dante. Lapidarily, as a Roman would, Vergil expressed that idea in six all-embracing words when, at the dismissal of his pupil, he concluded his address with the words:

TE SOPRA TE *corono e mitrio.*

Dante crowned and mitred[124] over Dante himself: there is no need to emphasize that this verse is pregnant with implications and allusions, and that its fulness, radiating into so many directions, is as inexhaustible as that of any work of art charged with life. The image is a reflexive one: object and subject coincide and are turned back each upon itself as well as to each other. And in this respect there was, on the human level, some similarity with the likewise reflexive vision on the divine level, at the very end of the *Comedy*, when Dante visualizes the circle of light of the Second Person "painted, of its own color, with our effigy"—the coincidence of God and Son of Man and of Man in general and of the beholder in the state of perfection, each turned back upon himself and to each other.

The intention was here only to bring one aspect into focus: Dante's Adam-centered or man-centered concept of kingship, the reflexiveness of "man" and "Man," of *homo* and *humanitas*, of *Adam mortalis* and *Adam subtilis*, and, by transference, of body natural of man and body corporate of Man. Perhaps we will find it easier now, or perhaps more difficult, to understand the later definitions of English jurists, opining that "to the natural Body [of the king] there is conjoined his Body politic which contains his royal Estate and Dignity," or that "the Body politic, annexed to his Body natural, takes away the Imbecility of the Body natural." We now

---

[124] According to *Ecclus.* 45:14, Aaron receives from Moses a golden crown over a mitre *signo sanctitatis et gloria honoris,* a passage quoted sometimes in connection with the Dante verse; see, e.g., Koenen, "Busswesen" (above, n.98), 100,n.34. Though this place, together with other passages of the Old Testament, certainly had some bearing on the development of the papal headgear (see Schramm, *Herrschaftszeichen,* 1,57f), it has hardly any relevance with regard to Dante's coronation.

know that the seemingly strange talk of these jurists simply means that, philosophically speaking, the king as King, or as Crown, is full actuality—perpetually and at any moment—whereas the individual body natural is mere potentiality. Here, then, we find also the philosophical explanation for other features of the king as King: that he never dies; that he is free from the imbecility of infancy and the defects of old age; that he cannot sin or do wrong. For he is the perpetual actualization of all royal potencies and therefore owns the *character angelicus* which the political theorists tried to understand, sometimes in terms of the two-natured God, sometimes in the sense of Justice and Law, and sometimes on the basis of People and Polity. It remained, however, to the poet to visualize the very tension of the "Two Bodies" in man himself, to make *humanitas* (according to Roman Law the medium of God-imitation[125]) the sovereign of *homo*, and to find for all those intricate cross-relations and interrelations the most complex, terse, and simple, because most human, formula: "I crown and mitre you over yourself."

[125] Cf. *C.*5,16,27,1: ". . . cum-nihil aliud tam peculiare est imperiali maiestati quam *humanitas*, per quam solam *dei* servatur *imitatio*." Actually *humanitas nostra* (*vestra*) served, like *maiestas, aeternitas,* and similar notions, also as an imperial title; see, e.g., *Nov.*23,4, or *C.*11,56,1; also *Thesaurus linguae latinae,* s.v. "*humanitas.*" Most baffling is, in this connection, Dante's contemporary Andreas of Isernia (d. 1316). He wrote a lengthy gloss on Barbarossa's *Authentica "Habita"* (published at Roncaglia, in 1158; cf. *MGH, Const.,*I,249,No.176), the so-called *Privilegium Scholasticum* granting protection to students and studies, which was incorporated in Roman Law (*C.*4,13,5 post) and which cannot have failed to attract Dante's curiosity. In this gloss (n.4) Andreas of Isernia (*In usus feudorum,* fol. 318) writes "QUILIBET autem EST REX SUI IPSIUS, dicit Augustinus super illud Psalmum 'Terribili apud omnes Reges terrae' [Ps. 75:13]. Multum debent reges virtuose et in virtuosis actibus sequi Deum, maxime in humanitate, per quam Dei servatur imitatio [*C.*5,16,27,1]." There is no point in drawing rash conclusions; but the passage is important enough to call attention to it. See, for the history of Barbarossa's Law, Walter Ullmann, "The Medieval Interpretation of Frederick I's Authentic 'Habita,' " *L'Europa e il Diritto Romano: Studi in memoria di Paolo Koschaker* (Milan, 1954), I,99-136.

CHAPTER IX

EPILOGUE

"All precepts concerning kings are in effect comprehended in those two remembrances: *Memento quod es homo*, and *Memento quod es Deus*, or *vice Dei*." Of these two mottos, writes Francis Bacon in his essay *Of Empire*, the first bridles the power and the other the will of princes who, in other respects, appeared "like to heavenly bodies, which cause good or evil times, and which have much veneration, but no rest."[1]

Bacon's first "remembrance" should not be mistaken for the famous Camaldolite motto *Memento mori* which, especially in connection with its artistic symbol, the skull, had a singular appeal to the religious sentiment of the later Middle Ages. *Memento quod es homo* is not of monastic origin, but descended from classical Antiquity; and Francis Bacon could not have been ignorant of its proper Roman setting. When, on the day of his triumph, the victorious Roman imperator rolled on the chariot drawn by four white horses from the Campus Martius to the Capitol—a living god clothed in the embroidered purple toga of Jupiter Capitolinus, in his hand the eagle sceptre of the god, and his face painted red with cinnabar—the slave riding with him on the chariot and holding the golden wreath over his head, whispered to him: "Look behind thee. Remember thou art a man."[2]

This, apparently, was the scene to which Bacon's first motto alluded. His other remembrance may have referred to Psalm 81:6, "Ye are gods," a versicle very much to the taste of political writers in the age of absolutism and most certainly to that of James I, who quoted it and gave his own interpretation of it in great detail.[3]

---

[1] Bacon, *Essays*, ed. Spedding (Boston, 1860), xii, 146. For the king who has no rest (*rex exsomnis*), see above, Ch.iv,nos.131,146,167. The passage is quoted by Per Palme, *Triumph of Peace: A Study of the Whitehall Banqueting House* (Stockholm, 1956), 173, a book to which Professor Erwin Panofsky called my attention.

[2] Cf. W. Ehlers, "Triumphus," *RE*, viiA:1, 507; Tertullian, *Apologeticus*, xxxiii,4. That Roman emperors could be very conscious of their "manhood" is demonstrated, not to mention Marcus Aurelius, by Tiberius; see, for his letter to the community of Gytheion, near Sparta, E. Kornemann, *Neue Dokumente zum lakonischen Kaiserkult* (Breslau, 1926), 7, line 20. My thanks go here, as well as in the following pages, to Professor Andreas Alföldi and the kind interest he took in this brief Epilogue.

[3] See James' "Speech of 1609," ed. McIlwain, *The Political Works of James I* (Cambridge, Mass., 1918), 307ff; also Kantorowicz, "Mysteries of State," 68, n.9, and (for

Bacon's dialectical combination of these two mottos is skilful, but not really surprising. Others expressed similar ideas in those days,[4] and the antithesis itself implies no more than just another variety of a theme on which Bacon fell back quite frequently: the king a mortal being, and yet immortal with regard to his Dignity and his Body politic. Bacon's allusion, however, to the ancient Roman custom of whispering a *Memento* to the triumphant general in the moment when he acted as the *deus praesens*, may be a "remembrance" to us that a final question should at least be broached here, a question which has loomed more than once in the foregoing pages: Has the late-mediaeval juristic concept and constitutional figure of speech, the King's Two Bodies, in any respect classical antecedents or parallels? Is there a classical pagan parentage of the metaphor? Or, more succinctly and more crudely, is the concept of the King's Two Bodies of pagan or of Christian origin?

The answer is that there are indeed certain features suggesting that the dichotomous concept of rulership might have had roots in classical Antiquity.[5] The doctrine of capacities—that is, the plain distinction between a man and his office (or offices)—was certainly not beyond the imagination of classical thinkers. We do not have to look for such extreme cases as might be detected in the monarchies of the ancient Near East.[6] It will suffice here to

---

Bossuet) "Deus per naturam," 274,n.72. Also Ussher (below, n.15), 269, and passim, refers to the Psalm; so do De La Guesle (below, n.13), 42, and innumerable other authors.

[4] Cf. Palme, *Triumph of Peace*, 174, quoting from Ben Jonson, *A Panegyrie on the Happie Entrance of James, our Soveraigne, to his First High Session of Parliament . . . 1603*, in *Poems*, ed. B. H. Newdigate (Oxford, 1936), 275ff, esp. 277:

> She [Themis] tells him first, that Kings
> Are here on earth the most conspicuous things:
> That they, by Heaven, are placed upon his throne
> To rule like Heaven; and have no more, their owne,
> As they are men, then men.

[5] It is beyond the scope of this study and the competence of its author to review in any detail the classical parallels. But my brief notes might be a stimulant to others to pursue the problem more successfully.

[6] In Egypt, the representation of the *Ka* would lead *ipso facto* to duplication; see, e.g., for Ramses II inaugurating his own sanctuary and worshipping his own image, A. D. Nock, "Σύνναος Θεός," *Harvard Studies in Classical Philology*, XLI (1930), 14, n.1; also Kantorowicz, "Quinity," 81f, nos.48ff. Most intriguing is the Egyptian custom sporadically observed of entombing two statues of a dead officer: one, attired with wig and loincloth, in his capacity of a royal officer; and the other

recall Alexander the Great who, according to Plutarch, distinguished between a friend of Alexander (φιλαλέξανδρος) and a friend of the king (φιλοβασιλεύς).[7] It is not even impossible that this remark was inspired ultimately by Aristotle, who, in the *Politics*, made a clear distinction between the friends of the prince and the friends of the princedom.[8] Moreover, we may recall what Seneca said about the pilot of a ship.

> *Duas personas habet gubernator*—Two persons are combined in the pilot: one he shares with all his fellow-passengers, for he also is a passenger; the other is peculiar to him, for he is the pilot. A storm harms him as a passenger, but it harms him not as a pilot.[9]

Here, at any rate, the principle of "gemination" is put forth in so many words, and it is quite likely that, for a conclusion *de similibus ad similia*, this passage may have been used also by one of the mediaeval jurists who all liked to quote Seneca for their special purposes.[10]

Related ideas with regard to kingship had been advanced independently by the so-called Neo-Pythagorean writers "On Kingship" whose works have been handed down to us fragmentarily by Stobaeus. In a fragment bearing the name of Ecphantus, the author explains that the king in his earthly tabernacle (that is, in the flesh) is like the rest of mankind; as a king, however, he is the

---

one, bald and in a long garment, as the "man" that the dead was; cf. Jean Capart, "Some Remarks on the Sheikh El-Beled," *Journal of Egyptian Archaeology*, VI (1920), 225-233; also A. Wiedemann, "Ägyptische Religion," *Archiv für Religionswissenschaft*, XXI (1922), 457, who calls attention also to occasional double entombments of Egyptian kings. A Roman *funus duplex* should be admitted in several cases, certainly in those of Pertinax and Septimius Severus, although it was not so general a custom, as Bickermann, "Die römische Kaiserapotheose," *Archiv für Religionswissenschaft*, XXIX (1929), 1-34, ingeniously tried to prove; cf. Ernst Hohl, "Die angebliche 'Doppelbestattung' des Antoninus Pius," *Klio*, XXXI (1938), 169-185. For duplications in Achaemenian seals (King and Ahuramazda), see, e.g., H. P. L'Orange, *Studies on the Iconography of Cosmic Kingship in the Ancient World* (Oslo, 1953), 93, fig.65b.

[7] Plutarch, *Alexander*, c.47.

[8] Aristotle, *Politics*, III,16,13,1287b; cf. W. L. Newman, *The Politics* (Oxford, 1887), III,301f. Above, Ch.VII,n.180.

[9] Seneca, *Epistolae*, LXXXV,35. The distinction between man and his profession (in the exercise of which man is "playing a certain role") has been carefully worked out by the physician Scribonius Largus (first century A.D.); cf. Ludwig Edelstein, "The Professional Ethics of the Greek Physician," *Bulletin of the History of Medicine*, XXX (1956), 412ff.

[10] The place, actually, was quoted in 1625 by Hugo Grotius, *De iure belli ac pacis*, II, c.IV, §12 (Amsterdam, 1720), 234; cf. Vassalli, "Fisco," 205; above, Ch.V,n.230.

copy of the "supreme Artificer who, when fashioning the king, used himself as an archetype."[11] This author was, after Stobaeus had been edited and translated into Latin during the first half of the sixteenth century, not without influence on the political theorists of absolutism.[12] By the end of the century, Jacques de La Guesle, *Procureur général* of the Crown, worked into his solemn speeches before the French Parlement long passages from Ecphantus, including the passage quoted here.[13] The latter was used also, though in the guise of a quotation from Agapetus,[14] by Archbishop James Ussher in a tractate handling *Of the Power Communicated by God to the Prince*, which originally he intended to dedicate to Charles I.[15] In another Pythagorean tractate, likewise transmitted by Stobaeus and quoted by absolutists, the author, Diotogenes, declared that the king, "who has an absolute rulership and is himself the animate Law, has been metamorphosed into a deity

[11] Goodenough, "The Political Philosophy of Hellenistic Kingship," *Yale Classical Studies*, I (1928), 76; Delatte, *Traités de la Royauté*, 26,2ff, and 47; also 177ff, for a similar fragment by Eurysus. Another related fragment, falsely ascribed to Philo, derives from Agapetus who himself depended on the Neo-Pythagorean treatises; cf. Ševčenko (below, n.14), 145ff, who has dispelled the myth of Philonic authorship.

[12] The *editio princeps* of Stobaeus was published in Venice, 1535, and the first Latin translation, by C. Gesner, in Zürich, 1543; cf. Delatte, *op.cit.*, 7 and 21.

[13] Jacques de La Guesle, *Les Remonstrances* (Paris, 1611), 42 (Remonstrance of 21 July 1588): "La Iustice est la fin de la loy, la loy l'oeuvre du Roy, le Roy l'ouvrage et le chef-d'oeuvre du grand Dieu (cf. Plutarch, *Ad principem ineruditum*, c.3, 780E). Et combien qu'il ne soit point dissemblable en apparence des autres hommes, comme estant faict et crée de mesme matiere, si est-ce qu'il est fait et fabriqué de ce tres-grand et tres-parfaict artisan, lequel en soy, et sur soy en a pris le modelle." A few lines later he refers to *un certain Pythagoricien*. His speech of 1595 actually opens with the words of Ecphantus; cf. the passage quoted by Church, *Constitutional Thought*, 266,n.54.

[14] Agapetus Diaconus, *Capita admonitoria*, c.21, *PGr*, LXXXVI:1,1171A. This chapter, though paraphrased, is taken from Ecphantus; Agapetus betrays also in other passages the influence of the Pythagorean political philosophers. Ever since the 12th century, Agapetus (and, through his agency, Ecphantus) exercised some influence on Russian political theory also, as has been convincingly demonstrated by Ihor Ševčenko, "A Neglected Byzantine Source of Muscovite Political Ideology," *Harvard Slavic Studies*, II (1954), 141-179. The first Latin translation of Agapetus seems to be that of 1509 (*PGr*, LXXXVI:1,1155ff); a French translation of the Greek was published by Jean Picot, in 1563; and King Louis XIII added a translation from Latin into French (1613). Two English translations were published in the 16th century, the first by Thomas Paynell (ca. 1530); the second, by James Whit (London, 1564), whose work was dedicated to Mary Stuart. (I was able to avail myself of microfilms of both treatises at the Firestone Library, in Princeton.)

[15] See James Ussher, *The Whole Works* (Dublin, 1864), XI,281. I am grateful to Mrs. Margaret Bentley Ševčenko for calling my attention to Ussher's numerous quotations from the Neo-Pythagorean tractates.

among men."[16] A metamorphosis of the king was not unknown in mediaeval political thought either, even though this doctrine was inspired not by Pythagorean theorists, but by the Old Testament. One could, however, almost believe that one is hearing Diotogenes—or Sthenidas of Locri,[17] another author of the same school —in the words of the Norman Anonymous, saying:

> We have to recognize [in the king] a twin person, one descending from nature, the other from grace . . . ; one through which, by the condition of nature, he conformed with other men: another through which by the eminence of [his] deification and by the power of the sacrament [of consecration], he excelled all others.[18]

Admittedly, the Norman Anonymous would claim that his king was metamorphosed by the power of Grace which "leaps" into him at his consecration; whereas the Pythagoreans claimed that the metamorphosis was the result of the king's *mimesis*, his imitation of the godhead. Grace and *mimesis*, however, are not mutually exclusive, since Grace (at least in this connection) is the power enabling man to be, or act as, the "image of God."[19]

The antique problem of royal duplication becomes increasingly complex and involved once we include certain cultual aspects and feel inclined to "equiparate" the king's Body politic, in one way or another, with the divinity of Hellenistic kings and Roman emperors. Would it be permissible to say that in Antiquity the immortal super-body of the ruler coincided with his supposedly divine nature? Certainly the duplication of human and divine natures in one man was an idea not at all foreign to classical thought: Herodotus praised those Greek cities which devoted two cults to Heracles, "sacrificing to one Heracles as to an immortal and calling him the Olympian, but bringing offerings to the other as to a dead hero."[20] Heracles, of course, was a mythical figure; but there

[16] Goodenough, "Hellenistic Kingship," 68; Delatte, *Traités de la Royauté*, 39,10ff; also p.53. That the king holds a rule of which no accounting is to be rendered (ἀρχὰν ἔχων ἀνυπεύθυνον; Delatte, 140 and 248) must have been grist to the mills of absolutists. Diotogenes was repeatedly quoted by name in the tractate of Ussher, pp.266, 280f, 285.

[17] For Sthenidas, arguing that "God is the first king and ruler *by nature,* and the king only *by becoming* and *by imitation* of God" (Delatte, 45f; cf.56 and 274ff), see my remarks in "Deus per naturam," 268ff.

[18] Above, Ch.III,n.8.

[19] Kantorowicz, "Deus per naturam," 274ff.

[20] Herodotus, II,44.

is no dearth of historical equivalents. What, for instance, did it imply when King Philip II of Macedonia took his seat in the theatre at Aigai, while in solemn procession the images of the Twelve Gods were carried into the theatre with the image of Philip added to their number as that of the Thirteenth?[21] Was, in that case, the king in his body natural seated in his royal box (in which, incidentally, this natural body was murdered), whereas in his body politic, or the equivalent thereof, he was displayed on the couches prepared for the deities? Strange situations could easily arise in imperial Rome. Gods who themselves offered sacrifices, were not at all unheard of in Antiquity;[22] but it is more perplexing to find Roman emperors in a somewhat similar attitude. As early as 7 B.C. altars were dedicated in Rome to the *genius* of Augustus, and for the cultual functions at the *ara numinis Augusti* a very noble college of priests was instituted.[23] Hence, in his capacity of *Pontifex Maximus*, the emperor could offer sacrifices and also receive them, could be at once offerer and recipient of offerings.[24] Caligula, according to Suetonius, went so far as to dedicate a temple with priests to his own *numen* and to put up within the shrine his golden cult statue which was clad daily with the same clothes as were worn, on that day, by the emperor himself[25]—indeed a perfect, though a rather baffling, form of duplication. What it all implied was an "objectification" of the ruler's *persona publica*. This is true also for the obligation to deliver the oath in court by the τύχη, the *genius* of the emperor (a custom observed from Domitian until well beyond the time of

---

[21] Diodorus, XVI,92,5.

[22] Cf. Erika Simon, *Opfernde Götter* (Berlin, 1953), who has discussed very efficiently the material found in vase paintings. See also S. Eitrem, "Zur Apotheose," *Symbolae Osloenses*, XV-XVI (1936), 137, for various examples of "self-worship" ("*kultische Ungereimtheiten*").

[23] See D. M. Pippidi, *Recherches sur le culte impérial* (Paris, 1939), Chapters I, II, and VII; Georg Niebling, "Laribus Augustis Magistri Primi," *Historia*, V (1956), 303-331.

[24] The Christian version of this duplication, or interaction of divine and human natures, has found its most pointed expression in the Cherubic Hymn, sung in the Eastern Churches at the Great Entrance: "Thou art he that offerest, and art offered; and that acceptest and art distributed." Cf. F. E. Brightman, *Liturgies Eastern and Western* (Oxford, 1896), I,318,34; 378,5; 431,6. See above, Ch.III,n.43, and also my remarks, "Quinity," 83f, for the resulting controversy as well as for the pictorial representations of that duplication.

[25] Suetonius, *Caligula*, 22,3: "Templum etiam numini suo proprium et sacerdotes et excogitissimas hostias instituit. In templo simulacrum stabat aureum iconicum amiciebaturque cotidie veste, quali ipse uteretur."

Justinian); consequently, it could, and did, happen that a subject had to swear an oath by the *Emperor* to be loyal to the emperor.[26]

While there is no doubt that these are features vaguely related to the later objectification of the king's immortal body politic, the differences are at least as great as the similarities. After all, the *genius* or *numen* of an emperor, though an object of public worship, was not separated from the individual but was still an immanent component of the individual human being. It would, therefore, be difficult to maintain that the emperor became the *instrumentum numinis* or *genii* in the sense in which the late-mediaeval Prince became the *instrumentum Dignitatis* and the incarnation of his immortal office. Yet, "incarnation" as well as "instrumentality" likewise were within the compass of ancient ruler cults.

Instead of worshipping the *numen* or *genius* of an individual emperor, the ruler could be identified with an existing and recognized deity which he represented as a *novus Hercules*, a *novus Sol*. Caligula, it is true, was ridiculed because he consecrated himself to his own service as Jupiter Latiaris—αὐτὸς ἑαυτῷ ἱερᾶτο, as Cassius Dio expressed it.[27] Gallienus carried his identity with the goddess Ceres to curious extremes when on coins he not only displayed his bristle-bearded portrait with the attribute of the goddess, the crown of corn-ears, but also surrounded it with the telling inscription GALLIENAE AUGUSTAE.[28] Other features have to be taken more seriously. When, in the third century, Diocletian established the Tetrarchy and therewith the "Jovian" and "Herculean" dynasties, the multiplicity of *genii* was difficult to disentangle, because "the Genius of each emperor, itself divine and an object of worship, was declared to be the very Genius of Jupiter

---

[26] See E. Seidl, *Der Eid im römisch-ägyptischen Provinzialrecht* (Münchener Beiträge zur Papyrusforschung, XVII and XXIV [Munich, 1933 and 1935]), I,11ff, and II,5ff, for the formulae, which show τύχη still invoked under Heraclius I; cf. I,23f, and II,16f. For the oath by the *Emperor* to the emperor, see Fitrem, "Zur Apotheose" (above, no.22), 137.

[27] Cassius Dio, LIX,28,5. See, for the *novus* praedication, A. D. Nock, "Notes on Ruler-Cult," *Journal of Hellenic Studies*, XLVIII (1948), 30ff; and, for the Middle Ages, my remarks in *Laudes regiae*, 57,n.148, 69,n.15, 74,n.31.

[28] A. Alföldi, "Zur Kenntnis der Zeit der römischen Soldatenkaiser," *Zeitschrift für Numismatik*, XXXVIII (1928), 174ff, esp. 188ff (see above, Ch.III,n.93); cf. 193ff, for the androgyne hybridism (*zweigeschlechtliches Zwitterwesen*) expressed by the inscription. See above, Ch.I,n.8, for the jurists on hermaphrodites.

and Hercules themselves."[29] It belonged to the same compound of ideas when a god was recognized as the *comes Augusti*, the perpetual companion of an emperor,[30] whereby the *genius Augusti* and the god became almost indistinguishable, as a number of coins may easily prove. Postumus issued a coin which by means of jugate busts combined the profiles of the emperor and of Hercules—a Hercules, to wit, whose features were so strongly assimilated to those of his human-imperial double that the image unfailingly suggested "twinship" or some kind of identity of the god and the ruler (fig. 32a).[31] The same is true for the jugate busts of Probus and SOL COMES PROBI AUGUSTI, the emperor's unconquered companion, that is, the Sun god whose head with upright rays appears like a mirage behind the helmeted head of Probus (fig. 32b).[32] It should be stressed, however, that it was not the emperor's features that were idealized to match those of his divine companion but the features of the god that were formed to appear as a likeness, or a super-face, of the individual emperor. This assertion is borne out strikingly by coinages of Constantine the Great in which the same SOL INVICTUS COMES has changed his features so completely that the god now appears as though "created in the own image of Constantine" (figs. 32d-f).[33] We recognize a gemination indicating that some kind of double-being was suggested—a human-divine duplication representing Constantine and *Sol invictus* as interchangeable magnitudes and displaying the ruler's

[29] Harold Mattingly, in *Cambridge Ancient History* (Cambridge, 1939), XII,330. Cf. C. H. V. Sutherland, "Flexibility in the 'Reformed' Coinage of Diocletian," *Essays in Roman Coinage Presented to Harold Mattingly* (Oxford, 1956), 174-189.

[30] A. D. Nock, "The Emperor's Divine *Comes*," *Journal of Roman Studies*, XXXVII (1947), 102-116.

[31] H. Mattingly and E. A. Sydenham, *The Roman Imperial Coinage* (London, 1923-33), V:2, pl.XIII, fig.11, also figs.9-10; for a slightly different type, where the similarity is less outspoken, see Alföldi, *op.cit.*, pl.VII,fig.10, who stresses (p.192) "dass ein Doppelwesen gemeint ist"; also Jocelyn M. C. Toynbee, *Roman Medallions* (New York, 1944), pl.XLVI,fig.8. For the general religious background of the "jugate heads," see Hermann Usener, "Zwillingsbildung," *Kleine Schriften* (Leipzig and Berlin, 1913), 334ff, esp. 355f, who unfortunately did not discuss the imperial coins.

[32] Toynbee, *op.cit.*, pl.II, fig.7.

[33] Cf. Toynbee, *op.cit.*, pl.XVII, fig.11; J. Maurice, *Numismatique Constantinienne* (Paris, 1908-1912), II,238ff; E. Babelon, "Un nouveau médaillon en or de Constantin le Grand," *Mélanges Boissier* (Paris, 1903), 49f; see also Maurice, *op.cit.*, p.236, pl.VII, fig.14. See further, for Constantinian coins, Alföldi, "The Helmet of Constantine with the Christian Monogram," *Journal of Roman Studies*, XXII (1932). pl.II. figs. 15-16. Cf. Kantorowicz, "Quinity," figs.27-29, and p.82.

human body which is mortal together with his concomitant super-body which, being a god, is immortal and divine.[34] *Deus imago regis*—so we are inclined to think while twisting the Christian maxim of *rex imago Dei*, a concept responsible also in Christian art for occasional facial similitude between the deity and the ruler, between Christ and his vicar on earth.[35]

Moreover, when we recall other sets of Roman inscriptions, we seem to close in also on the problem of instrumentality. Ever since late Republican times, the *Genius populi Romani* was represented on coins: Hercules-like, with sceptre and cornucopiae, his feet on the globe of the world or on the footstool of divinity; or else his head only, "accompanied by sceptre, royal wreath, and globe."[36] In the third century, we find coins in which the emperor himself was hailed as the GENIUS POPULI ROMANI, the incarnation or personification of the eternally productive power of the Roman people.[37] Here, then, the emperor may safely be conceived of as an "instrument" of something that was not identical with him and not an immanent component of his own self—indeed, the *instrumentum Genii populi Romani* and the exponent of an immortal polity "which never dies." Or, when, in the third century, inscriptions were dedicated, time and again, *numini maiestatique*, to the emperor's divine *numen* and his earthly *maiestas*, we may remember that it was ultimately the *Maiestas populi Romani* of which he was the incarnation.[38] Nor should we forget that a formulation

[34] Less suggestive are certain images on coins of Carus where god and emperor face each other; but the imperial title of *deus et dominus*, customary by that time (cf. Alföldi, "Insignien," 92ff), surrounds the two heads as an inscription and tells, in fact, a story similar to that of the *numini maiestatique* inscriptions of the same period (see below, n.38). For the coin of Carus, cf. Mattingly and Sydenham, *op.cit.*, v:2, pl.vi, fig.13.

[35] See above, Ch.III,n.50.

[36] Cf. Alföldi, "The Main Aspects of Political Propaganda on the Coinage of the Roman Republic," *Essays . . . Mattingly* (above, n.29), 87, 93f.

[37] Alföldi, "Zeremoniell," 91, and fig.3 (Gallienus); also in *Zeitschrift für Numismatik*, xxxviii, pl.vii,fig.1, and p.192.

[38] That the *maiestas* of the Roman People itself was a continuation of the ancient *maiestas* of the regal power, is a different matter. The formula of dedication is found indeed very often during the third century; see, e.g., H. Dessau, *Inscriptiones Latinae selectae* (Berlin, 1916), iii:2, p.779, Index, *s.v.* "N N M QE." For an example, see Dessau, No.499 (vol.I, p.120): "Imperatori Caesari M. Antonio Gordiano etc. Numisius Quintianus v(ir) p(erfectissimus) ab epistulis Latinis, *devotus numini maiestatique eius.*" As Professor Alföldi kindly informs me, the formula itself, probably on account of its frequency, has as yet not been made the subject of a special study.

such as Seneca's "The Prince is the soul of the *res publica*; and the *res publica*, the body of the Prince," implies, philosophically, a very similar idea—no less "antique" than Cyprian's "The Church is in the bishop; and the bishop, in the Church."[39]

To summarize, it cannot be denied that isolated features are recognizable in classical political philosophy and political theology which would suggest that the substance of the idea of the King's Two Bodies had been anticipated in pagan Antiquity. Moreover, it sounds plausible enough that one or another of those antique theorems became effective in the High Renaissance when, in addition to the literary sources, the archaeological and numismatic material also became available again. There is no doubt that the classical model occasionally served to *rationalize* certain phenomena (as, for example, the display of effigies at royal funerals) which had originated and developed from totally different conditions and strata.[40] It remains, however, more than doubtful whether a summing-up of all the individual classical features of duplications would result in a compact theory comparable to that of the late mediaeval lawyers. For despite all the parallels, similarities, and "antecedents" in classical times, there is nevertheless *one* detail which would exclude a pagan origin of the Tudor formula from the outset; that is, the concept of the king having two *Bodies*. There is apparently nothing in pagan thought that would justify this diction, and therefore it has a false ring if, by modern scholars, the Roman emperor is sometimes called a "corporation sole."[41] It is true, of course, that in Greek philosophy the cosmos, the polis, or the individual could be interpreted each as a body ($\sigma\hat{\omega}\mu\alpha$), and it is true also that St. Paul's definition of the Church as *corpus Christi* reflects that philosophy.[42] On the other hand, however, this aggressive Pauline concept eventually endowed the late antique "corporations" with a philosophico-theological impetus which apparently those bodies were lacking before Constantine the Great referred to the Church as a *corpus* and thereby

---

[39] Seneca, *De clementia*, I,5,1; above, Ch.V,n.65, and Ch.VII,n.405, also n.408.

[40] See above, Ch.VII,nos.372f.

[41] Cf. F. Schultz, *Classical Roman Law* (Oxford, 1951), 90f: "Adopting the English conception of 'corporation sole,' we may simply say that the *princeps* is a corporation sole." Cf. p.89, for the statement: "The Roman people is a corporation."

[42] For the whole problem, see Arnold Ehrhardt, "Das Corpus Christi und die Korporationen im spät-römischen Recht," *ZfRG.*, rom.Abt., LXX (1953), 299-347, and LXXI (1954), 25-40.

introduced that philosophical and theological notion into the language of law.[43] Besides, the influence of the *corpus Christi* doctrine on the interpretation of legal *universitates*, and thereby also on the mediaeval corporational theories, is a fact to be reckoned with.[44]

It might be possible to argue that the general concept of the Norman Anonymous still drifted in the wake of ancient ruler deification. The tenet, however, of the Tudor jurists definitely hangs upon the Pauline language and its later development: the change from the Pauline *corpus Christi* to the mediaeval *corpus ecclesiae mysticum*, thence to the *corpus reipublicae mysticum* which was equated with the *corpus morale et politicum* of the commonwealth, until finally (though confused by the notion of *Dignitas*) the slogan emerged saying that every abbot was a "mystical body" or a "body politic," and that accordingly the king, too, was, or had, a body politic which "never died." Notwithstanding, therefore, some similarities with disconnected pagan concepts, the KING'S TWO BODIES is an offshoot of Christian theological thought and consequently stands as a landmark of Christian political theology.

[43] Ehrhardt, *op.cit.*, LXXI, 37-40; also Roberti (see next note), 79f.
[44] Cf. M. Roberti, "Il corpus mysticum di S. Paolo nella storia della persona giuridica," *Studi in Onore di Enrico Besta* (Milan, 1939), IV, 37-82; Tierney, *Conciliar Theory*, 131ff; also Gierke, *Gen.R.*, III,108ff,111ff.

LIST OF ILLUSTRATIONS

1. Medallions of 1642 [pp. 21f]

    a. King Charles I in Parliament (no reverse image)
    New York, The American Numismatic Society (Photo:
    courtesy of the Society).

    b-c. Obv.: Portrait of Charles I
    Legend: PRO·RELIGIONE·LEGE·REGE·ET·PARLIAMENTO
    Rev.: The King in Parliament

    d-e. Obv.: Portrait of Robert Devereux, 3rd Earl of Essex,
    Commander-in-Chief of the Parliamentary Army
    Legend (outer): SHOULD HEAR BOTH HOUSES OF PARLIA-
    MENT FOR TRUE RELIGION AND SUBJECTS
    FREDOM STANDS
    (inner): PRO·RELIGIONE·LEGE·REGE·ET·PARLIA-
    MENTO
    Rev.: The King in Parliament

    f-g. Obv.: Portrait of Charles I
    Legend: SHOULD HEAR BOTH HOUSES OF PARLIA-
    MENT FOR TRUE RELIGION AND SUBJECTS
    FREDOM STANDS
    Rev.: The King in Parliament
    The medallion of Essex (d-e) combines the inscriptions
    of the two royal medallions (b-c, f-g). The reverse re-
    mained unchanged (see also fig. 2). These three medal-
    lions are in Glasgow, The Hunterian Museum; plaster
    casts were obtained by the kindness of Miss Anne S.
    Robertson, Curator of the Hunter Coin Cabinet. Cf.
    Hawkins, *Medallic Illustrations*, pl. xxv, figs. 5, 6, 11.

2. Medallion of 1642, enlarged [p. 22]

    Obv.: Battleship
    Rev.: The King in Parliament
    Legend: PRO:RELIGIONE:GREGE:ET:REGE:
    London, British Museum (Photo: courtesy of Mr. J. K.
    Jenkins of the British Museum).

3. Seal (so-called "Fifth Seal") of King Charles I [p. 22]

    From: *Trésor de numismatique et de glyptique: Sceaux des
    rois et reines d'Angleterre* (Paris, 1858), pl. xx

12. Triumph of Basil II [pp. 69, 78]

Miniature, Byzantine (11th cent.); Venice, Bibl. Marciana, MS gr. 17.
Photo: Princeton University, Dept. of Art and Archaeology.

13. Christ Triumphant [p. 72]

Mosaic (6th cent.); Ravenna, Archiepiscopal Chapel.
Photo: courtesy of K. Weitzmann.

14. Christ Disappearing: Ascension [p. 74]

Miniature, Gospel Book of St. Bernward (11th cent.); Hildesheim, Cathedral Treasury, MS 18, fol. 175ᵛ.
From: S. Beissel, *Des Hlg. Bernward Evangelienbuch* (Hildesheim, 1891), pl. XXIV.

15. Christ in Majesty with 24 Elders [p. 76]

a. Miniature, Carolingian; Rome, San Paolo f.l.m., Bible, fol. 116ᵛ.

b. Miniature, Carolingian; Trier Apocalypse, Stadtbibl., MS 31, fol. 61.
Photos: Princeton University, Dept. of Art and Archaeology.

16. Charles the Bald Enthroned [pp. 63 n.46, 66, 76]

a. Miniature, Carolingian; Vivian Bible (above, fig. 9), fol. 423.
From: W. Köhler, *Die Schule von Tours* (1930), pl. 76.

b. Miniature, Carolingian; Gospel Book from St. Emmeram (*Codex aureus*): Munich, Staatsbibl., Clm. 14000, Cim. 55, fol. 5ᵛ.
From: G. Leidinger, *Codex aureus* (1921), I, pl. 10.

17. Capuan Gate of Emperor Frederick II [p. 111]

13th century (reconstruction).
From: C. A. Willemsen, *Kaiser Friedrichs II. Triumphtor zu Capua* (Wiesbaden, 1953), fig. 106.

18. Ambrogio Lorenzetti [p. 112]

a. Iustitia, b. Buon Governo.
Fresco, Siena, Palazzo Pubblico (14th cent.).
Photo: Alinari.

Medallion by Thomas Rawlins, struck by Royalists after the execution of Charles I; Glasgow, Hunter Coin Cabinet, of which Mr. J. K. Jenkins of the British Museum kindly provided a plaster cast; the photos were made by the American Numismatic Society. Cf. Hawkins, *Medallic Illustrations*, pl. xxx, 19.

24. Jetton, Design for 1643 [p. 414]

    Paris, Bibl. Mazarine, MS 4395, fol. 1ᵛ.
    Photo: courtesy of Dr. R. E. Giesey.

25. Medallion (Design): *Lit de Justice* of Louis XIV [p. 414]

    From: Claude-François Menestrier, *Histoire de Louis le Grand* (Paris, 1691), pl. 28; photo: Dumbarton Oaks Research Library and Collection, Washington, D.C.

26. Caricature by Thackeray of Rigaud's Portrait of Louis XIV [p. 423]

    The Caricature is taken from the first edition (1840) of *The Paris Sketch Book by Titmarsh* in the Pierpont Morgan Library; cf. *Works of Thackeray* (Charterhouse Edition; London, 1901), vol. xvi, facing p. 313. Photo: courtesy of the Pierpont Morgan Library.

27. King Henry IV of France on the Lit d'Honneur [p. 425]

    a-b. Engravings by Isaac Briot (1558-1670). Paris, Bibl. Nat., MS Clarembault 1127, fol. 25ᵛ. Cf. P. Mathieu, *Historia della morte d'Enrico quarto Rè di Francia* (Modena, 1625), 757; E. Benkard, *Undying Faces*, fig. 1, facing p. 18. Photo: courtesy of Dr. R. E. Giesey.

28. Tomb of John Fitzalan, 17th Earl of Arundel [p. 435]

    Arundel, Essex (ca. 1435).
    Photo: courtesy of Mr. Francis Wormald and The Warburg Institute, London.

29. The Effigy under the Canopy [p. 430]

    Frontispiece of *L'obsèque et enterrement du roy (Louis XII)*, [Paris, 1515].
    Photo: courtesy of Dr. R. E. Giesey.

Fig. 1. a, c, e, g: Charles I in Parliament; b, f: Charles; d: Essex.

Fig. 2. Charles I in Parliament (Medallion of 1642)

a. Banner

b. Standard

Fig. 4. Personal Badges of Richard II

Fig. 3. "Fifth Seal" of Charles I

Fig. 5. Otto II in Majesty (Aachen Gospels, ca. 975)

Fig. 6. Christ in Majesty (Ivory Book Cover, Darmstadt, ca. 900)

Fig. 7. Christ in Majesty (Ivory Book Cover, St. Gall, ca. 900)

Fig. 8. Terra Carrying the Crucified (Ivory, 11th century)

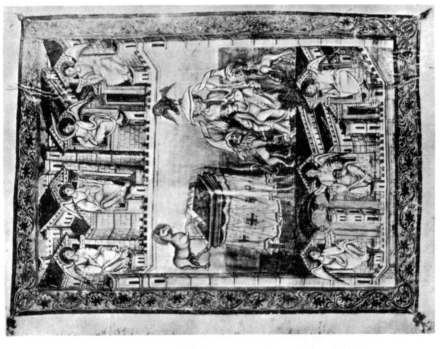

Fig. 10. Eschatological Scene
(San Paolo f.l.m. Bible, 9th century)

Fig. 9. Eschatological Scene (Vivian Bible, 9th century)

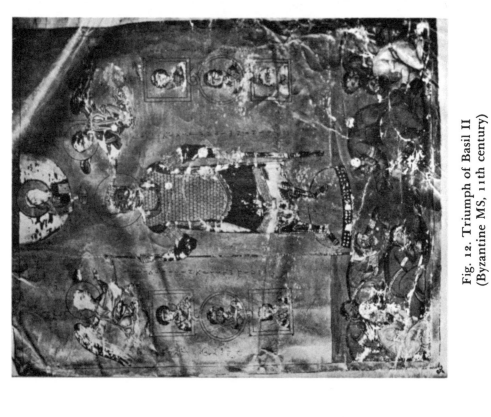

Fig. 12. Triumph of Basil II
(Byzantine MS, 11th century)

Fig. 11. Maiestas Domini supra Caelum
(Junius Bassus Sarcophagus, A.D. 359)

Fig. 14. Christ Disappearing
(Bernward Gospels, Hildesheim, 11th century)

Fig. 13. Christ Triumphant
(Ravenna, Archiepiscopal Chapel, 6th century)

b. Trier Apocalypse, 9th century

a. San Paolo Bible, 9th century

Fig. 15. Christ in Majesty with 24 Elders

b. St. Emmeram Gospels (*Codex Aureus*)

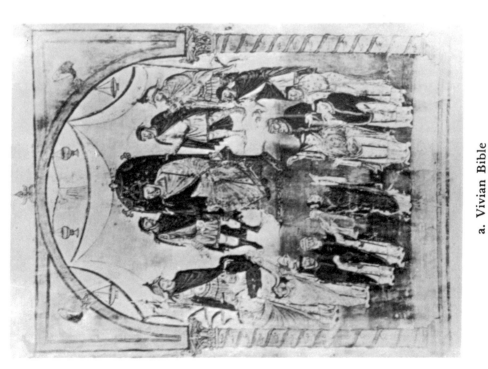

a. Vivian Bible

Fig. 16. Charles the Bald Enthroned

Fig. 17. Capuan Gate of Frederick II (reconstruction)

a. Iustitia

Fig. 18. Fresco by Ambrogio Lorenzetti (Palazzo Pubblico, Siena)

b. Buon Governo

Fig. 19. Last Judgment with Iustitia
(Enamel Triptych from Stablo, 12th century)

Fig. 20. Emperor Henry II as Judge
(Monte Cassino Gospels, A.D. 1022-1023)

Fig. 22. Queen Elizabeth: *Unica Phoenix* (Medallion, 1603)

Fig. 23. Charles I and Charles II as Phoenix (Medallion, 1649)

PRINCEPS

Quod non capit Chriſtus,
rapit fiſcus.

Exprimit humentes, quaſi cum madeſceret amiſſ
Spongias, cupidi Principis acta manus.
Proculit ad ſummam fures: quas deinde coercet,
Vertit uim fiſcum quæ malè parta ſuum.

Fig. 24. Andrea Alciati: Emblem (1621)

Fig. 24. Design for Jetton (1643)

Fig. 25. Lit de Justice of Louis XIV
(Design for Medallion)

Fig. 26. Caricature by Thackeray of Rigaud's Portrait of Louis XIV

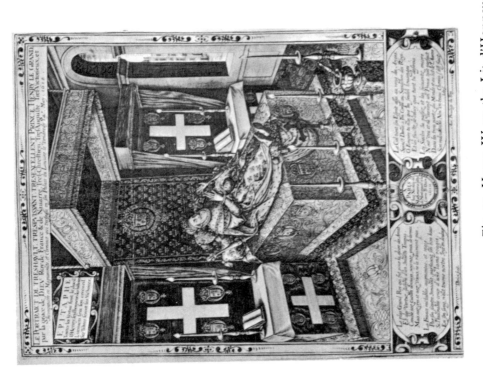

Fig. 27. Henry IV on the Lit d'Honneur (Engravings, MS Clarembault, 1127)

Fig. 28. Tomb of John Fitzalan, 17th Earl of Arundel (ca. 1435)

De l'imprimerie de Rob. Eltienne Imprimeur du Roy
Auecq' Priuilege dudict seigneur. 1547.

Fig. 29. The Effigy under the Canopy

Fig. 30. Tomb of Archbishop Henry Chichele, Canterbury Cathedral (1424)

Fig. 31. Tomb of Bishop Thomas Bekington, Wells Cathedral (ca. 1451)

a. Postumus and Hercules   b. Probus and Sol Invictus

JUGATE BUSTS

c. *Oriens Augusti*
Aureus of Aurelian

d-f. Jugate Busts: Constantine and Sol Invictus

Fig. 32. Coins

Bibliography

Index

A. ABBREVIATIONS

AHR	*American Historical Review*
AKKR	*Archiv für katholisches Kirchenrecht*
ArchUF	*Archiv für Urkundenforschung*
BZ	*Byzantinische Zeitschrift*
C.	*Codex Justiniani* (see *Corpus Iuris Civilis* [1584], vols. V and IV)
CSEL	*Corpus scriptorum ecclesiasticorum latinorum*
D.	*Digesta* (see *Corpus Iuris Civilis* [1584], vols. I-III)
DA	*Deutsches Archiv für Erforschung des Mittelalters*
DACL	*Dictionnaire d'archéologie chrétienne et de liturgie*
EHR	*English Historical Review*
Erg. Bd.	see Kantorowicz, *Kaiser Friedrich der Zweite, Ergänzungsband*
Feud.	*Libri feudorum* (see *Corpus Iuris Civilis* [1584], vol. IV)
Glos. ord.	see *Glossa ordinaria*
HZ	*Historische Zeitschrift*
Inst.	*Institutiones Justiniani* (see *Corpus Iuris Civilis* [1584], vol. IV)
JRS	*Journal of Roman Studies*
Lib. aug.	See *Liber augustalis*
MGH	*Monumenta Germaniae Historica*

The series cited in abbreviation are:

Epp. sel.	*Epistolae selectae* (octavo)	
LdL.	*Libelli de Lite*	
SS.r.Germ.	*Scriptores rerum Germanicarum* (octavo)	
Const.	*Constitutiones et acta publica*	

MÖIG [MIÖG]	*Mitteilungen des Österreichischen Instituts für Geschichtsforschung*
Nov.	*Novellae* (see *Corpus Iuris Civilis* [1584], vol. IV)
PGr	Migne, *Patrologia graeca*
PL	Migne, *Patrologia latina*
QF, QFiAB	*Quellen und Forschungen aus italienischen Archiven und Bibliotheken*
RE	*Realencyclopädie der classischen Altertumswissenschaft*, edd. Pauly, Wissowa, Kroll, and others
Rev. bénéd.	*Revue bénédictine*
RM	*Mitteilungen des deutschen archäologischen Instituts: Römische Abteilung*
Sitz. Ber.	*Sitzungsberichte*
VI	*Liber Sextus* (see *Corpus Iuris Canonici* [1588], vol. III)

Warburg Journal	*Journal of the Warburg and Courtauld Institutes*
X	*Liber Extra* (see *Corpus Iuris Canonici* [1588], vol. II)
ZfKT	*Zeitschrift für Katholische Theologie*
ZfRG	*Zeitschrift der Savigny-Stiftung für Rechtsgeschichte*

B. SELECTED BIBLIOGRAPHY

Accursius, *Glossa ordinaria* to Roman Law (*Corpus iuris civilis* [Venice, 1584]).

Aegidius Romanus, *De ecclesiastica potestate*, ed. R. Scholz (Weimar, 1929).

Albericus de Rosate, *In Digestum vetus* (*Infortiatum, Digestum novum*) *Commentaria* (Venice, 1585).

————, *In Codicem Commentaria* (Venice, 1585).

————, *Dictionarium Iuris tam Civilis quam Canonici* (Venice, 1601).

Andreas de Barulo, *Commentaria super tribus libris Codicis* (Venice, 1601).

Andreas de Isernia, *Commentaria in Usus Feudorum* (Naples, 1571).

————, *Peregrina Lectura super Constitutionibus et Glossis Regni Siciliae*, in: *Liber augustalis*, ed. Cervone.

Andrieu, M., *Le Pontifical Romain au moyen-âge* (Studi e Testi, 86-88, 99 [Vatican City, 1938-1941]).

Angelus de Ubaldis, *In Digestum vetus* (*Infortiatum, Digestum novum*) *Commentaria* (Venice, 1580).

————, *In Codicem Commentaria* (Venice, 1579).

————, *In Authenticorum volumen Commentaria* (Venice, 1580)

Aquinas, see Thomas Aquinas.

Arbusow, Leonid, *Liturgie und Geschichtsschreibung im Mittelalter* (Bonn, 1951).

Aristotle, Latin Version, see Thomas Aquinas.

Aubert, Jean-Marie, *Le droit romain dans l'oeuvre de Saint Thomas* (Bibliothèque Thomiste, xxx [Paris, 1955]).

Augustinus Triumphus de Ancona, *De summa potestate ecclesiastica* (Augsburg, Johannes Schüssler, 1483).

Azo, *Summa* [*Codicis, Institutionum, Novellarum*] (Lyon, 1530).

————, see Maitland.

Bacon, Francis, *The Works of Sir Francis Bacon*, edd. J. Spedding and D. D. Heath, 7 vols. (London, 1859-1870); also edd. Spedding, R. L. Ellis, and Heath, 15 vols. (Boston, 1861).

Baethgen, Friedrich, "Der Anspruch des Papsttums auf das Reichsvikariat," *ZfRG*, kan. Abt., x (1920).

Baldus de Ubaldis, *Consilia* (Venice, 1575).

————, *In Decretalium volumen Commentaria* (Venice, 1580).

————, *In Digestum vetus, Infortiatum, Digestum novum, Libros Codicis Commentaria* (Venice, 1586).

————, *Liber de Pace Constantiae*, in: *Corpus Iuris Civilis*, vol. IV, 159-190 (following after the *Libri Feudorum*).

Barbi, Michele, "Nuovi problemi della critica dantesca: VI. L'ideale politico-religioso di Dante," and "VIII. Impero e Chiesa," *Studi danteschi*, xxiii (1938), xxvii (1942).

Bartolus de Saxoferrato, *Commentaria in Digestum vetus, Infortiatum, Digestum novum, Codicem* (Venice, 1567).

——, *Super Authenticis et Institutionibus* (Venice, 1567).

——, *Consilia, Quaestiones et Tractatus* (Lyon, 1547).

Beda Venerabilis, *Expositio Actuum Apostolorum et Retractatio*, ed. M. L. W. Laistner (Cambridge, Mass., 1939).

Beemelmans, F., *Zeit und Ewigkeit nach Thomas von Aquino* (Beiträge zur Geschichte der Philosophie im Mittelalter, xvii, 1 [Münster, 1914]).

Beissel, Stephan, *Die Bilder der Handschrift des Kaisers Otto im Münster zu Aachen* (Aachen, 1886)

——, *Geschichte der Evangelienbücher in der ersten Hälfte des Mittelalters* (Stimmen aus Maria-Laach, 92-93 [Freiburg, 1906]).

Benkard, Ernst, *Das ewige Antlitz* (Berlin, 1927); English transl. by Margaret M. Green, *Undying Faces* (New York, 1929).

Berges, Wilhelm, *Die Fürstenspiegel des hohen und späten Mittelalters* (*MGH, Schriften*, ii [Leipzig, 1938]).

Bernard (de Botone) of Parma, *Glossa ordinaria* to *Decretales Gregorii Papae IX* (see *Corpus iuris canonici* [Turin, 1588], vol. ii).

Bibliotheca juridica medii aevi, ed. A. Gaudenzi, 3 vols. (Bologna, 1888-1901).

Blackstone, Sir William, *Commentaries on the Laws of England* (London, 1765).

Bloch, Marc, *Les rois thaumaturges* (Strasbourg, 1924).

Bodin, Jean, *Les six livres de la république* (Paris, 1583).

Böhmer, Heinrich, *Kirche und Staat in England und in der Normandie im 11. und 12. Jahrhundert* (Leipzig, 1899).

Böhmer, Johann Friedrich, *Acta imperii selecta*, 2 vols. (Innsbruck, 1870).

Boncompagno, Magister, *Rhetorica novissima*, ed. A. Gaudenzi, in: *Bibl. jurid. med. aevi*, ii (Bologna, 1892).

Bossuet, J.-B., *Oeuvres oratoires*, ed. J. Lebarq (Lille and Paris, 1892).

Bracton, Henry of, *De legibus et consuetudinibus Angliae*, ed. G. E. Woodbine, 4 vols. (New Haven, 1915-1942).

Budé, Guillaume, *Annotationes in XXIIII Pandectarum libros* (Lyon, 1551).

Burdach, Konrad, *Rienzo und die geistige Wandlung seiner Zeit, Vom Mittelalter zur Reformation*, ii, 1 (Berlin, 1913-1928).

Calasso, F., *I glossatori e la teoria della sovranità* (Milan, 1951).

Capasso, B., "Sulla storia esterna delle costituzioni di Federico II," *Atti della Accademia Pontaniana*, ix (1871).

Carlyle, R. W. and A. J., *A History of Mediaeval Political Theory*, 6 vols. (Edinburgh and London, 1903-1936).

Cases before the King's Council, 1243-1482, ed. I. S. Leadam and J. F. Baldwin (Selden Society, xxxv [Cambridge, 1918]).

Cervone, A., see *Liber augustalis*.

Chiappelli, Luigi, "Dante in rapporto alle fonti del diritto," *Archivio storico Italiano*, Ser. v, vol. XLI (1908).

Choppin, René, *De Domanio Franciae* (Paris, 1605).

Chrimes, S. B., *English Constitutional Ideas in the Fifteenth Century* (Cambridge, 1936).

Church, William Farr, *Constitutional Thought in Sixteenth-Century France* (Harvard Historical Studies, XLVII [Cambridge, 1941]).

Coester, Hildegard, *Der Königskult in Frankreich um 1300 im Spiegel der Dominikanerpredigten* (Staatsexamens-Thesis, typescript, Frankfurt, 1935-1936).

Coke, Sir Edward, *Reports*, ed. G. Wilson, 7 vols. (Dublin, 1792-1793).

——, *The Institutes of the Laws of England* (editions London 1681 and 1809).

Coquille, Guy, *Les oeuvres*, 2 vols. (Paris, 1666).

Coroner's Roll, Select Cases from the, ed. Charles Gross (Selden Society, IX [London, 1896]).

Corpus iuris canonici, 3 vols. (Turin, 1588), containing the *Glossae ordinariae* to *Decretum Gratiani* (vol. I), *Decretales Gregorii IX*, *Liber Extra* (vol. II), *Liber Sextus* and the later Decretals (vol. III).

——, ed. Emil Friedberg, 2 vols. (Leipzig, 1879-1881).

Corpus iuris civilis, 5 vols. (Venice, 1584), containing Accursius' *Glossa ordinaria* to *Digest* (vols. I-III), *Codex* (vols. V and IV), *Institutes* and *Novels*, also the *Libri Feudorum* and other material (vol. IV).

Crompton, Richard, *L'Authoritie et Jurisdiction* (London, 1594).

Cuias, J., *Opera*, 12 vols. (Prato, 1836-1843).

Cynus de Pistoia, *Commentarium in Codicem et Digestum vetus* (Frankfurt, 1578).

Dante Alighieri, *De Monarchia*, ed. Gustavo Vinay (Florence, 1950).

——, *Le opere*, ed. E. Moore and P. Toynbee (4th ed., Oxford, 1924).

Davies, J. C., *The Baronial Opposition to Edward II* (Cambridge, 1918).

Davis, Gifford, "The Incipient Sentiment of Nationality in Mediaeval Castile: The *Patrimonio real*," *Speculum*, XII (1937).

De la Guesle, see Guesle.

De la Roche Flavin, Bernard, *Treize livres des Parlemens de France* (Geneva, 1621).

Delatte, Louis, *Les traités de la royauté d'Ecphante, Diotogène et Sthénidas* (Bibl. de la Faculté de Philosophie et Lettres de l'Université de Liège, XCVII [Liège, 1942]).

Deusdedit, *Collectio canonum*, ed. Victor Wolf von Glanvell, *Die Kanonessammlung des Kardinals Deusdedit* (Paderborn, 1905).

Diehl, C., *Manuel d'art byzantin*, 2 vols., 2nd ed. (Paris, 1925).

Dölger, F. J., *Sol Salutis*, 2nd ed. (Münster, 1925).

——, *Die Sonne der Gerechtigkeit und der Schwarze* (Münster, 1918).

Dubois, Pierre, *De recuperatione Terrae Sanctae*, ed. Ch.-V. Langlois (Collection des textes, IX [Paris, 1891]).

——, *Summaria brevis et compendiosa doctrina felicis expedicionis et abbreviacionis guerrarum ac litium regni Francorum*, ed. H. Kämpf (Leipzig and Berlin, 1936).

Dupré-Theseider, Eugenio, *L'idea imperiale di Roma nella tradizione del medioevo* (Milan, 1942).

Dupuy, Pierre, *Histoire du différend d'entre Pape Boniface VIII et Philippe le Bel, Roy de France* (Paris, 1655).

Durandus, Gulielmus, *Rationale divinorum officiorum* (Lyon, 1565).

——, *Speculum iuris*, 4 vols. (Venice, 1602).

Du Tillet, Jean, *Recueil des Roys de France* (Paris, 1618).

Egenter, Richard, "Gemeinnutz vor Eigennutz: Die soziale Leitidee im *Tractatus de bono communi* des Fr. Remigius von Florenz (+ 1319)," *Scholastik*, IX (1934).

Ehrhardt, Arnold, "Das *Corpus Christi* und die Korporationem im spätrömischen Recht," *ZfRG*, rom. Abt., LXX (1953), LXXI (1954).

Ehrlich, L., *Proceedings against the Crown, 1216-1377* (Oxford, 1921).

Eichmann, Eduard, *Die Kaiserkrönung im Abendland*, 2 vols. (Würzburg, 1942).

——, "Königs- und Bischofsweihe," *Sitz. Ber. bayer. Akad.*, phil.-hist. Klasse (Munich, 1928), No. 6.

Eitrem, S., "Zur Apotheose," *Symbolae Osloenses*, XV-XVI (1936).

d'Entrèves, A. Passerin, *Dante as a Political Thinker* (Oxford, 1952).

——, "La teoria del diritto e della politica in Inghilterra all' inizio dell' età moderna," *R. Università di Torino: Memorie dell'Istituto Giuridico*, Ser. II, No. IV (1929).

Ercole, Francesco, *Il pensiero politico di Dante* (Milan, 1927-1928).

Erdmann, Carl, *Die Entstehung des Kreuzzugsgedankens* (Stuttgart, 1935).

——, *Forschungen zur politischen Ideenwelt des Frühmittelalters* (Berlin, 1951).

Esmein, A., "La maxime *Princeps legibus solutus est* dans l'ancien droit public français," *Essays in Legal History*, ed. P. Vinogradoff (Oxford, 1913).

Ettlinger, L., "The Duke of Wellington's Funeral Car," *Warburg Journal*, III (1939-1940).

Figgis, J. N., *The Divine Right of Kings*, 2nd ed. (Cambridge, 1934).

Finke, H., *Acta Aragonensia*, 3 vols. (Berlin and Leipzig, 1908-1922).

Fitting, H., *Juristische Schriften des früheren Mittelalters* (Halle, 1876).

——, *Quaestiones de iuris subtilitatibus des Irnerius* (Berlin, 1894).

Fitzpatrick, Mary Cletus, *Lactantii De Ave Phoenice* (University of Pennsylvania thesis [Philadelphia, 1933]).

Fleta, ed. John Selden, 2nd ed. (London, 1685).

Folz, Robert, *Le souvenir et la légende de Charlemagne dans l'empire germanique mediéval* (Paris, 1950).

Fortescue, Sir John, *De laudibus legum Angliae*, ed. S. B. Chrimes (Cambridge, 1942).

——, *The Governance of England*, ed. Charles Plummer (Oxford, 1885).

Frederick II, see *Liber augustalis*.

Friedberg, Emil, see *Corpus iuris canonici*.

Geoffrey of Monmouth, *Historia Regum Britanniae*, ed. Jacob Hammer (Mediaeval Academy of America Publications, N.57 [Cambridge, 1951]).

Gerson, Jean, *Opera omnia*, ed. Ellies du Pin, 5 vols. (Antwerp, 1706).

Gierke, Otto von, *Das Deutsche Genossenschaftsrecht*, 4 vols. (Berlin, 1868-1913).

——, *Political Theories of the Middle Age*, transl. by F. W. Maitland (Cambridge, 1927).

——, *Johannes Althusius*, 3rd ed. (Breslau, 1913).

Gilbert of Tournai, *Eruditio regum et principum*, ed. A. de Poorter (Philosophes Belges, IX [Louvain, 1914]).

Gilbert, Felix, "Sir John Fortescue's *Dominium regale et politicum*," *Mediaevalia et Humanistica*, II (1943).

Gilson, Étienne, *Dante et la philosophie* (Paris, 1939), Engl. transl. by David Moore, *Dante the Philosopher* (New York, 1949).

——, *Jean Duns Scotus* (Études de philosophie médiévale, XLII [Paris, 1952]).

Glanvill, *De legibus et consuetudinibus regni Angliae*, ed. G. E. Woodbine (New Haven, 1932).

Glossa ordinaria, see *Corpus iuris canonici* (Turin, 1588), *Corpus iuris civilis* (Venice, 1584), and Accursius, Bernard of Parma, Johannes Andreae, Johannes Teutonicus.

Godefroy, Th., *Le céremonial de France* (Paris, 1619).

Goldast, M., *Monarchia S. Romani Imperii*, 3 vols. (Hanau and Frankfurt, 1611-1613).

Goldschmidt, A., *Die Elfenbeinskulpturen aus der Zeit der karolingischen und sächsischen Kaiser*, 4 vols. (Berlin, 1914-1926).

——, *German Illumination, II: Ottonian Period* (New York, n.d.).

Goodenough, Erwin R., "The Political Philosophy of Hellenistic Kingship," *Yale Classical Studies*, I (1928).

Gottlob, Th., *Der kirchliche Amtseid der Bischöfe* (Kanonistische Studien und Texte, IX [Bonn, 1936]).

Grabar, André, *L'Empereur dans l'art byzantin* (Paris, 1936).

Grabmann, Martin, *Der lateinische Averroismus des 13. Jahrhunderts und seine Stellung zur christlichen Weltanschauung* (Sitz. Ber., Munich, 1934, No. 2).

——, *Mittelalterliches Geistesleben*, 3 vols. (Munich, 1926-1956).

——, *Studien über den Einfluss der aristotelischen Philosophie auf die mittelalterlichen Theorien über das Verhältnis von Kirche und Staat* (Sitz. Ber., Munich, 1934, No. 2).

Grassaille, Charles de, *Regalium Franciae libri duo* (Paris, 1545).

Grégoire, Pierre, *De Republica* (Lyon, 1609; first published 1578).

Gregory VII, *Das Register Gregors VII.*, ed. Erich Caspar (*MGH, Epp. sel.*, II [Berlin, 1920-1923]).

Gregory of Bergamo, *De veritate corporis Christi*, ed. H. Hurter, *Sanctorum patrum opuscula selecta* (Innsbruck, 1879).

Grotius, Hugo, *De iure belli et pacis* (Amsterdam, 1720).

Guesle, Jacques de la, *Les Remonstrances* (Paris, 1611).

Guido Vernani, see Vernani.

Güterbock, Carl, *Bracton and his Relations to the Roman Law*, transl. by Brinton Coxe (Philadelphia, 1866).

Hackelsperger, Max, *Bibel und mittelalterlicher Reichsgedanke* (Diss. Munich, 1934).

Hahn, August, *Bibliothek der Symbole und Glaubensregeln der alten Kirche*, 3rd ed. (Breslau, 1897).

Hawkins, E., *Medallic Illustrations of the History of Great Britain and Ireland* (London, 1911).

Hamburger, Max, *Morals and Law: The Growth of Aristotle's Legal Theory* (New Haven, 1951).

Henry of Ghent, *Quodlibeta magistri Henrici Goethals a Gandavo* (Paris, 1518).

Heydte, F. A. Freiherr von der, *Die Geburtsstunde des souveränen Staates* (Regensburg, 1952).

Hinschius, P., *Decretales pseudo-Isidorianae et Capitula Angilramni* (Leipzig, 1863).

Hofmeister, Philipp, *Die heiligen Öle in der morgen- und abendländischen Kirche* (Das östliche Christentum, N.F., VI-VII [Würzburg, 1948]).

Holdsworth, W. S., *A History of English Law* (London, 1922-1952).

Holtzmann, Robert, *Französische Verfassungsgeschichte* (Munich and Berlin, 1910).

——, *Wilhelm von Nogaret* (Freiburg, 1898).

Hope, W. H., "On the Funeral Effigies of the Kings and Queens of England," *Archaeologia*, LX:2 (1907), 518-565.

Hostiensis (Henry of Segusia), *Summa Aurea super titulis Decretalium* (Venice, 1586).

Hotman, François, *Francogallia* (Frankfurt, 1586).

Hoyt, Robert S., *The Royal Demesne in English Constitutional History: 1066-1272* (Ithaca, N. Y., 1950).

Hubaux, Jean, and Leroy, Maxime, *Le mythe du Phénix* (Bibl. de la Faculté de Philosophie etc. de Liège, LXXXII [Liège and Paris, 1939]).

Hugelmann, K. G., "Die Wirkungen der Kaiserweihe nach dem Sachsenspiegel," *ZfRG*, kan. Abt., IX (1919).

Huillard-Bréholles, J. L. A., *Historia diplomatica Friderici Secundi*, 7 vols. (Paris, 1852-1861).

Innocent IV, *In quinque libros Decretalium apparatus* (Lyon, 1578).

James of Viterbo, *De regimine Christiano*, ed. H. X. Arquillière, *Le plus ancien traité de l'Église* (Paris, 1926).

Jenkins, Marianna, *The State Portrait* (Monographs on Archaeology and Fine Arts, III [New York, 1947]).

Johannes Andreae, *Glossa ordinaria* to *Liber Sextus Decretalium* (see *Corpus iuris canonici* [Turin, 1588], vol. III).

——, *Novella super Decretalibus* (Venice, 1612).

Johannes de Terra Rubea, see Terre Rouge.

Johannes Teutonicus, *Glossa ordinaria* to *Decretum Gratiani* (see *Corpus iuris canonici* [Turin, 1588], vol. I).

John of Paris, *De potestate regia et papali*, ed. Dom Jean Leclerq, *Jean de Paris et l'ecclésiologie du XIIIᵉ siècle* (Paris, 1942).

John of Salisbury, *Policraticus*, ed. C. C. J. Webb, 2 vols. (Oxford, 1909).

John of Viterbo, *De regimine civitatum*, ed. Gaetano Salvemini, in *Bibliotheca iuridica medii aevi*, III (Bologna, 1901).

Jungmann, Josef Andreas, "Die Abwehr des germanischen Arianismus und der Umbruch der religiösen Kultur im frühen Mittelalter," *Zeitschrift für katholische Theologie*, LXIX (1947).

——, *Die Stellung Christi im liturgischen Gebet* (Liturgiegeschichtliche Forschungen, VII-VIII [Münster, 1925]).

Kämpf, Hellmut, *Pierre Dubois und die geistigen Grundlagen des französischen Nationalbewusstseins um 1300* (Leipzig und Berlin, 1935).

Kail, J., *Political and Other Poems* (Early English Text Society, Orig. Series, CXXIV [London, 1904]).

Kallen, Gerhard, *Aeneas Silvius Piccolomini als Publizist* (Stuttgart, 1939).

Kantorowicz, E. H., "An 'Autobiography' of Guido Faba," *Mediaeval and Renaissance Studies*, I (1943).

——, "Deus per naturam, deus per gratiam," *Harvard Theological Review*, XLV (1952).

——, "Inalienability: A Note on Canonical Practice and the English Coronation Oath in the Thirteenth Century," *Speculum*, XXIX (1954).

——, *Kaiser Friedrich der Zweite* (Berlin, 1927) and *Ergänzungsband* (Berlin, 1931).

——, *Laudes Regiae: A Study in Liturgical Acclamations and Mediaeval Ruler Worship* (Berkeley and Los Angeles, 1946).

——, "Mysteries of State: An Absolutist Concept and its Late Mediaeval Origins," *Harvard Theological Review*, XLVII (1955).

——, "Petrus de Vinea in England," *MÖIG*, LI (1937).

Kantorowicz, E. H., "*Pro patria mori* in Mediaeval Political Thought," *AHR*, LVI (1951).

———, "The Quinity of Winchester," *Art Bulletin*, XXIX (1947).

———, "Σύνθρονος Δίκη," *American Journal of Archaeology*, LVII (1953).

Kantorowicz, Hermann, *Bractonian Problems* (Glasgow, 1941).

———, "The Poetical Sermon of a Mediaeval Jurist," *Warburg Journal*, II (1938-1939).

———, *Studies in the Glossators of the Roman Law* (Cambridge, 1938).

Keeton, George W., *Shakespeare and His Legal Problems* (London, 1930).

Kempf, Friedrich, *Papsttum und Kaisertum bei Innocenz III.* (Miscellanea Historiae Pontificiae, XIX [Rome, 1954]).

Kern, Fritz, *Die Anfänge der französischen Ausdehnungspolitik* (Tübingen, 1910).

———, *Gottesgnadentum und Widerstandsrecht im früheren Mittelalter* (Leipzig, 1914).

———, *Humana Civilitas* (Leipzig, 1913).

———, "Die Reichsgewalt des deutschen Königs nach dem Interregnum," *HZ*, CVI (1911).

Kloos, Rudolf M., "Ein Brief des Petrus de Prece zum Tode Friedrichs II.," *DA*, XIII (1957).

———, "Nikolaus von Bari, eine neue Quelle zur Entwicklung der Kaiseridee unter Friedrich II.," *DA*, XI (1954).

Koenen, Ferdinand, "Anklänge an das Busswesen der alten Kirche in Dantes Purgatorio," *Deutsches Dante-Jahrbuch*, VII (1923).

Koht, Halvdan, "The Dawn of Nationalism in Europe," *AHR*, LII (1947).

Kristeller, P. O.,"A Philosophical Treatise from Bologna Dedicated to Guido Cavalcanti: Magister Jacobus de Pistoria and his *Questio de Felicitate*," *Medioevo e Rinascimento: Studi in onore di Bruno Nardi* (Florence, 1955).

Kuttner, Stephan, *Kanonistische Schuldlehre von Gratian bis auf die Dekretalen Gregors IX.* (Studi e Testi, LXIV [Vatican City, 1935]).

———, *Repertorium der Kanonistik* (Studi e Testi, LXXI [Vatican City, 1937]).

——— and Rathbone, Eleanor, "Anglo-Norman Canonists in the Twelfth Century," *Traditio*, VII (1949-1951).

Ladner, Gerhart B., "Aspects of Mediaeval Thought," *Review of Politics*, IX (1947).

———, "The Concepts: Ecclesia, Christianitas, Plenitudo Potestatis," *Sacerdozio e regno da Gregorio VII a Bonifacio VIII* (Miscellanea Historiae Pontificiae, XVIII [Rome, 1954]).

———, "Die mittelalterliche Reform-Idee und ihr Verhältnis zur Idee der Renaissance," *MIÖG*, LX (1952).

———, "St. Augustine's Conception of the Reformation of Man in the Image of God," *Augustinus Magister* (Congrès International Augustinien: Communications [Paris, 1954]).

Laehr, Gerhard, *Die Konstantinische Schenkung in der abendländischen Literatur des Mittelalters bis zur Mitte des 14. Jahrhunderts* (Berlin, 1926).

Lagarde, G. de, "Individualism et corporatism au moyen âge," *L'Organisation corporative du moyen âge à la fin de l'ancien régime* (Recueil de travaux d'histoire et de philologie, 2me sér., XLIV [Louvain, 1937]).

————, "La philosophie sociale d'Henri de Gand et de Godefroid de Fontaines," *L'Organisation corporative* etc. (Recueil de travaux etc., 3me sér., XVIII [Louvain, 1943]).

————, *La naissance de l'esprit laïque au declin du moyen âge*, vol. I (Vienna, 1934).

Langlois, Ch.-V., *La connaissance de la nature et du monde au moyen âge* (Paris, 1911).

Lapsley, Gaillard, "Bracton and the authorship of the 'Addicio de Cartis,'" *EHR*, LXII (1947).

Le Bras, G., "Le droit romain au service de la domination pontificale," *Revue historique de droit français et étranger*, XXVII (1949).

Leclercq, Dom Jean, "Un sermon prononcé pendant la guerre de Flandre sous Philippe le Bel," *Revue du moyen âge latin*, I (1945).

Lemaire, A., *Les lois fondamentales de la monarchie française d'après des théoriciens de l'ancien régime* (Paris, 1907).

Lesky, Erna, *Die Zeugungs- und Vererbungslehren der Antike und ihr Nachwirken* (Abh. d. Mainzer Akad. d. Wissensch. und der Literatur: Geistes- und Socialwiss. Kl., 1950, No. 19 [Mainz, 1951]).

Liber augustalis, ed. Cervone = *Constitutionum Regni Siciliarum libri III* (Sumptibus Antonii Cervonii, Naples, 1773), containing the *Glossa ordinaria* of Marinus de Caramanico and the commentary of Andreas de Isernia.

Liber censuum, ed. Fabre, M. P., and Duchesne, L. M. O. (Paris, 1895ff).

Liebermann, F., *Die Gesetze der Angelsachsen*, 3 vols. (Halle, 1903-1916).

Lizerand, Georges, *Le dossier de l'affaire des Templiers* (Paris, 1932).

Lodge, E. C., and Thornton, G. A., *English Constitutional documents 1307-1485* (Cambridge, 1935).

Loyseau, Charles, *Cinq livres du droit des offices* (Cologne, 1613).

Lubac, Henri de, *Corpus mysticum* 2nd ed. (Paris, 1949); also in: *Recherches de science religieuse*, XXIX (1939), and XXX (1940).

Lucas de Penna, *Commentaria in Tres Libros Codicis* (Lyon, 1597; also Lyon, 1544, and other editions).

Maccarone, Michele, "Teologia e diritto canonico nella *Monarchia*, III, 3," *Rivista di Storia della Chiesa in Italia*, V (1951).

Maccarrone, Michele, *Vicarius Christi: Storia del titolo papale* (Lateranum, N. S., XVIII [Rome, 1952]).

McIlwain, C. H., *Constitutionalism Ancient and Modern*, 2nd ed. (Ithaca, N. Y., 1947).

——, *The High Court of Parliament and its Supremacy* (New Haven, 1910).

Maisonobe, A., "Mémoire relatif au Paréage de 1307," *Bulletin de la société d'agriculture, industrie, sciences, et arts du Departement de la Lozère* (Mende, 1896).

Maitland, F. W., *Selected Essays* (Cambridge, 1936).

——, *Select Passages from the Works of Bracton and Azo* (Selden Society, VIII [London, 1895]).

——, see Pollock, Sir Frederick.

Marinus de Caramanico, *In Constitutiones Regni Siciliae* (= *Glossa ordinaria*), see *Liber augustalis*, ed. Cervone.

Marongiu, A., "Concezione della sovranità ed assolutismo di Giustiniano e di Federico II," *Atti del Convegno Internazionale di Studi Federiciani* (Palermo, 1952).

——, *L'Istituto parlamentare in Italia dalle origini al 1500* (Rome, 1949).

——, "Note Federiciane," *Studi Medievali*, XVIII (1952).

Martène, E., *De antiquis Ecclesiae ritibus* (Rouen, 1700; Bassano, 1788).

Matthaeus de Afflictis, *In utriusque Siciliae Neapolisque sanctiones et constitutiones novissima praelectio* (Venice, 1562).

Meer, F. van der, *Maiestas Domini* (Vatican City, 1938).

Meyers, E. M., *Juris interpretes saec. XIII* (Naples, 1924).

Michels, Dom Thomas, "Die Akklamation in der Taufliturgie," *Jahrbuch für Liturgiewissenschaft*, VIII (1928).

Mirbt, Carl, *Quellen zur Geschichte des Papsttums und des römischen Katholizismus*, 4th ed. (Tübingen, 1924).

Mitteis, Heinrich, *Die deutsche Königswahl: Ihre Rechtsgrundlagen bis zur Goldenen Bulle*, 2nd ed. (Brünn, Munich, and Vienna, 1944).

Most, Rudolf, "Der Reichsgedanke des Lupold von Bebenburg," *DA*, IV (1941).

Nardi, Bruno, *Dante e la cultura medievale*, 2nd ed. (Bari, 1949).

——, "Note alla *Monarchia*, I: La *Monarchia* e Alberico da Rosciate," *Studi danteschi*, XXVI (1942).

——, *Saggi di filosofia dantesca* (Milan, 1930).

Nicholas of Bari, see R. M. Kloos, ed.

Nock, A. D., "Notes on Ruler-Cult," *Journal of Hellenic Studies*, XLVII (1948).

——, "The Emperor's Divine *Comes*," *JRS*, XXXVII (1947).

Oldradus de Ponte, *Consilia* (Venice, 1571; also Lyon, 1550).

Onory, Sergio Mochi, *Fonti canonistiche dell'idea moderna dello stato* (Milan, 1951).

Oppenheim, Philipp, "Die sakralen Momente in der deutschen Herrscherweihe bis zum Investiturstreit," *Ephemerides Liturgicae*,
LVIII (1944).

Ott, Irene, "Der Regalienbegriff im 12. Jahrhundert," *ZfRG*, kan. Abt.,
XXXV (1948).

Parliamentary Writs, ed. F. Palgrave, 2 vols. in 4 (London, 1827-1834).

Palmer, John Leslie, *Political Characters of Shakespeare* (London,
1945).

Paris de Puteo, *De Syndicatu* (Lyon, 1548).

Peregrinus, Marcus Antonius, *De privilegiis et iuribus fisci libri octo*
(Venice, 1611).

Perrot, Ernest, *Les institutions publiques et privées de l'ancienne
France jusqu'en 1789.* (Paris, 1935).

Peterson, Erik, "Der Monotheismus als politisches Problem," in his
Theologische Traktate (Munich, 1951).

Petrus de Ancharano, *Consilia* (Venice, 1574).

———, *In quinque Decretalium libros . . . Commentaria* (Bologna,
1581).

Petrus de Vinea, *Epistolarium*, ed. Simon Schard (Basel, 1566).

Philip of Leyden, *De cura reipublicae*, edd. R. Fruin and P. C. Molhuysen (The Hague, 1915).

Piccolomini, Aeneas Silvius, *De ortu et auctoritate imperii Romani*,
ed. R. Wolkan, *Der Briefwechsel des Eneas Silvius Piccolomini*
(Fontes rerum Austriacarum, LXVII [Vienna, 1912]); see also Kallen, G., for another edition.

Pickthorn, Kenneth, *Early Tudor Government: Henry VII* (Cambridge, 1934).

[Placentinus], *Quaestiones de iuris subtilitatibus*; cf. Fitting, *Quaestiones.*

Placentinus, *Summa Institutionum*, ed. H. Fitting, in *Juristische Schriften* (Halle, 1876).

Plowden, Edmund, *Commentaries or Reports* (London, 1816).

Plucknett, T.F.T., "The Lancastrian Constitution," *Tudor Studies*,
ed. by R. W. Seton-Watson (London, 1924).

Pollard, A. F., *The Evolution of Parliament* (London, 1926).

Pollock, Sir Frederick, and Maitland, F. W., *The History of English
Law Before the Time of Edward I*, 2 vols., 2nd ed. (Cambridge,
1898).

Post, Gaines, " 'Blessed Lady Spain'—Vincentius Hispanus and Spanish National Imperialism in the Thirteenth Century," *Speculum*,
XXIX (1954).

———, "A Romano-Canonical Maxim, *Quod omnes tangit*, in Bracton," *Traditio*, IV (1946).

———, "Some Unpublished Glosses (ca. 1210-1214) on the *Translatio Imperii* and the Two Swords," *AKKR*, CXVII (1937).

———, "The Two Laws and the Statute of York," *Speculum*, XXIX
(1954).

Post, Gaines, "Two Notes on Nationalism in the Middle Ages: I. *Pugna pro patria*, II. *Rex imperator*," *Traditio*, IX (1953).

Powicke, F. M., *King Henry III and the Lord Edward*, 2 vols. (Oxford, 1947).

Pseudo-Isidorus, see Hinschius.

Rapisarda, E., *L'Ave Fenice di L. Cecilio Firmiano Lattanzio* (Raccolta di studi di letteratura cristiana antica, IV [1946]).

Remigio de' Girolami, see Egenter, ed.

Richardson, H. G., "The English Coronation Oath," *Transactions of the Royal Historical Society*, 4th Ser., XXIII (1941).

——, "The English Coronation Oath," *Speculum*, XXIV (1949).

Richier, *La vie de Saint Remi: Poème du XIIIᵉ siècle*, ed. W. N. Bolderston (London, 1912).

Roberti, M., "Il *corpus mysticum* di S. Paolo nella storia della persona giuridica," *Studi in Onore di E. Besta*, vol. IV (Milan, 1939).

Rossiter, A. P., *Woodstock* (London, 1946).

Saint-Gelais, Jean de, *Chronique*, in Th. Godefroy, *Histoire de Louys XII* (Paris, 1622).

Sauer, J., *Die Symbolik des Kirchengebäudes* (Freiburg, 1902).

Sayles, G. O., *Select Cases in the Court of King's Bench under Edward I*, vol. III (Selden Society, LVIII [London, 1939]).

Schäfer, Carl, *Die Staatslehre des Johannes Gerson* (Cologne diss., 1935).

Schaller, Hans-Martin, *Die Kanzlei Kaiser Friedrichs II.: Ihr Personal und ihr Sprachstil* (Göttingen diss. [type-script], 1951).

Schapiro, Meyer, "The Image of the Disappearing Christ," *Gazette des Beaux Arts*, LXXXV (1943).

Scholz, Richard, *Die Publizistik zur Zeit Philipps des Schönen und Bonifaz' VIII.* (Kirchenrechtliche Abhandlungen, H.6-8 [Stuttgart, 1903]).

——, *Unbekannte kirchenpolitische Streitschriften aus der Zeit Ludwigs des Bayern (1327-1354)*, (Bibliothek d. Preussischen Historischen Instituts in Rom, IX-X [Rome, 1911-1914]).

Schrade, Hubert, "Zur Ikonographie der Himmelfahrt Christi," *Vorträge der Bibliothek Warburg 1928-9* (Leipzig, 1930).

Schramm, Percy E., *Die deutschen Kaiser und Könige in Bildern ihrer Zeit*, 2 vols. (Leipzig, 1928).

——, *Herrschaftszeichen und Staatssymbolik* (Schriften der *MGH*, XIII:1-3 [1954-1956]).

——, "Das Herrscherbild in der Kunst des Mittelalters," *Vorträge der Bibliothek Warburg 1922-3*, I (1924).

——, *A History of the English Coronation* (Oxford, 1937).

——, *Der König von Frankreich*, 2 vols. (Weimar, 1939).

——, "Die Krönung in Deutschland bis zum Beginn des Salischen Hauses," *ZfRG*, kan. Abt., XXIV (1935).

————, "Die Ordines der mittelalterlichen Kaiserkrönung," *ArchUF*, XI (1929).

————, "Sacerdotium und Regnum im Austausch ihrer Vorrechte," *Studi Gregoriani*, II (1947).

Schulz, Fritz, "Bracton on Kingship," *EHR*, LX (1945).

Ševčenko, Ihor, "A Neglected Byzantine Source of Muscovite Political Ideology," *Harvard Slavic Studies*, II (1954).

Silverstein, Theodore, "On the Genesis of *De Monarchia*, II,v," *Speculum*, XIII (1938).

Steinwenter, Artur, "Νόμος ἔμψυχος: Zur Geschichte einer politischen Theorie," *Anzeiger d. Akad. d. Wissensch. in Wien*, phil.-hist.Kl., LXXXIII (1946).

Stengel, Edmund E., "Kaisertitel und Suveränitätsidee," *DA*, III (1939).

————, *Nova Alemanniae*, 2 vols. (Berlin, 1921-1930).

Stickler, A. M., "Imperator vicarius Papae," *MIÖG*, LXII (1954).

————, "Der Schwerterbegriff bei Huguccio," *Ephemerides Iuris Canonici*, III (1947).

————, "*Sacerdotium et Regnum* nei decretisti e primi decretalisti," *Salesianum*, XV (1953).

Strayer, Joseph R., "Defense of the Realm and Royal Power in France," *Studi in onore di Gino Luzzatto* (Milan, 1949).

Stubbs, William, *Select Charters and other Illustrations of English Constitutional History*, 9th ed. (Oxford, 1921).

Terre Rouge, Jean de, *Tractatus de iure futuri successoris legitimi in regiis hereditatibus*, in: François Hotman, *Consilia* (Arras, 1586), Appendix.

Thomas Aquinas, *In decem libros Ethicorum Aristotelis ad Nicomachum expositio*, ed. R. M. Spiazzi (Turin and Rome, 1949), with the Latin version of Aristotle.

————, *In duodecim libros Metaphysicorum Aristotelis expositio*, ed. M.-R. Cathala and R. M. Spiazzi (Turin and Rome, 1950), with the Latin version of Aristotle.

————, *In libros Politicorum Aristotelis expositio*, ed. R. M. Spiazzi (Turin and Rome, 1951), with the Latin version of Aristotle.

————, *De regimine principum*, ed. Joseph Mathis, 2nd ed. (Turin and Rome, 1948).

Thomson, S. Harrison, "Walter Burley's Commentary on the *Politics* of Aristotle," *Mélanges Pelzer* (Louvain, 1947).

Tierney, Brian, "A Conciliar Theory of the Thirteenth Century," *Catholic Historical Review*, XXXVI (1950-1951).

————, *Foundations of the Conciliar Theory: The Contribution of the Medieval Canonists from Gratian to the Great Schism* (Cambridge, 1955).

Tolomeus de Lucca, *Determinatio compendiosa de iurisdictione Imperii*, ed. Mario Krammer, in: *MGH, Fontes iuris germanici antiqui* (Hannover and Leipzig, 1909).

Toynbee, Jocelyn M. C., *Roman Medallions* (New York, 1944).

Treitinger, O., *Die oströmische Kaiser- und Reichsidee nach ihrer Gestaltung im höfischen Zeremoniell* (Jena, 1938).

Überweg, F. and Baumgartner, M., *Grundriss der Geschichte der Philosophie der patristischen und scholastischen Zeit*, 10th ed. (Berlin, 1915).

Ullmann, Walter, "The Influence of John of Salisbury on Mediaeval Italian Jurists," *EHR*, LIX (1944).

———, "Baldus' Conception of Law," *Law Quarterly Review*, LVIII (1942).

———, *The Medieval Idea of Law as Represented by Lucas de Penna* (London, 1946).

———, *Medieval Papalism* (London, 1949).

Ussher, James, *The Whole Works* (Dublin, 1864).

Vassalli, Filippo E., "Concetto e natura del fisco," *Studi Senesi*, XXV (1908).

Vernani, Guido, *De reprobatione Monarchie composite a Dante*, ed. Thomas Käppeli O.P., "Der Dantegegner Guido Vernani O.P. von Rimini," *QFiAB*, XXVIII (1937-1938).

Vieilleville, Marquis de, *Mémoires*, ed. J. Michaud and P. Poujoulat, *Nouvelle collection des mémoires sur l'histoire de France*, vol. IX (Paris, 1850).

Watkins, Robert D., *The State as a Party Litigant* (Johns Hopkins diss., Baltimore, 1927).

Wieruszowski, Helene, *Vom Imperium zum nationalen Königtum* (*HZ*, Beiheft, 30 [Munich and Berlin, 1933]).

Wilkinson, B., "The Coronation Oath of Edward II and the Statute of York," *Speculum*, XIX (1944).

———, "The 'Political Revolution' of the Thirteenth and Fourteenth Centuries in England," *Speculum*, XXIV (1949).

Willemsen, Carl A., *Kaiser Friedrichs II. Triumphtor zu Capua* (Wiesbaden, 1953).

Williams, George H., *The Norman Anonymous of ca. 1000 A.D.: Toward the Identification and the Evaluation of the So-called Anonymous of York* (Harvard Theological Studies, XVIII [Cambridge, Mass., 1951]).

Wilson, John Dover, ed., *King Richard II*, in: *The Works of Shakespeare* (Cambridge, 1939).

Wipo, *Gesta Chuonradi*, ed. H. Bresslau (*MGH*, SS.rer.germ., 1915).

Woodbine, G. E., see Bracton, Glanvill.

Woolf, C.N.S., *Bartolus of Sassoferrato* (Cambridge, 1913).

Wunderlich, Agathon, *Anecdota quae processum civilem spectant* (Göttingen, 1841).

Yates, Frances A., "Queen Elizabeth as Astraea," *Warburg Journal*, X (1947).

INDEX

Whereas the index of proper names at least aspires to reasonable completeness, a warning should be sounded with regard to that of subjects: it is not complete nor could it have been expanded without approximating a concordance. For all its omissions and shortcomings, however, it still may have its usefulness as a convenient guide for the scholar. Index references to a footnote refer, as often as not, also to the text to which the note belongs. The abbreviations (abp. = archbishop, bp. = bishop, emp. = emperor, k. = king, q. = queen) follow the customary pattern, and those of proper names will be (it is hoped) intelligible without further explanation.

Aachen: 83 n.100 (*Roma futura*), 89 n.6, 204 n.34 (another Rome)

Abingdon, Edmund, abp. of Canterbury: 350

Absolutism: 98 n.31, 151, 194, 220, 230 n.112, and passim

Acclamations: 68 n.57 (to king), 81 (Louis the Pious), 80 n.93 (queens), 83 n.102, 85 n.105, 410ff (*le Roy est mort . . .*), 490 (baptismal)

Accursius (see Law: Roman, *Glos. ord.* [c.1227-1240]); 103, 121 n.102, 122f, 126, 140, 171 n.246, 295 n.48, 297, 306, 324 n.29, 452 n.4, passim

Accursius, Francis: 44 n.4, 361

Acre: 243, 251 n.182

Adam: 66 n.52, 70 (giant), 308 (belongs to *corpus mysticum*), 450 (prototype of corporation sole), 468ff passim (see Dante)

Adoption, Adoptionism: 49, 52 n.21

Adventus: 70 n.64, 255 n.191 (Christ), 430 n.377 (effigy)

Aegidius Romanus (d.1316): 130 n.128, 131 n.131, 134 (*De reg. princ.*), 135, 139 n.161, 148, 466 n.43

Aelia Capitolina (Jerusalem): 83

Aelfric: 85 n.105, 150 n.182

Aeneas: 253

Aeschylos: 230 n.113

Aethelwold Benedictional: 52 n.22

Africa: 328

Agapetus Diaconus: 499 nos.11 and 14

Aigai: 501 (theatre at A.)

Ailly, Cardinal Pierre d': 124

Albericus de Rosate (d.1354): 122 n.104 (jurists priests of Justice), 130 n.129 (Prince *in lege*, not *sub lege*), 136 n.154 (*lex animata*), 175 n.260 (Christ and fisc), 213 n.57 (Prince's marriage to realm), 310 n.90 (*universitas*), 324 n.29 (regnal years), 392 n.263 (identity

of testator and heir), 397 n.280 (perpetuity), 399 n.290 (*dignitas perpetua*), 455 n.13 (Prince *philosophissimus*), 457 n.17, 460 n.28, and 463 n.35 (references to Dante)

Albertus Magnus: 133, 389 n.247

Alchemy: 307 n.81

Alciati, Andrea: 174 n.254, 175

Alcuin: 280 n.14 (*aevum*), 320 n.15

Alexander of Roes: 202 n.28, 254 n.187

Alexander the Great: 498

Al-Fārābī: 387 n.240

Alvarus Pelagius: 204, 205 n.35

Amalar of Metz: 81

[Ps.-]Amalar of Trier: 490 n.113

Amanieu of Armagnac, abp. of Auch: 351 n.136

Amarcius: 54 n.26

Amboise: 429

St. Ambrose, bp. of Milan: 50 n.19, 53 n.24, 70f (*gigas geminae substantiae*), 91 n.12, 188, 205 n.36 (*ubi Christus ibi Jordanis*), 280 n.14, 389 n.247, 390 n.253, 391, 490

Ambrosiaster: 89 n.7, 91 n.12, 161

amicus regis (title; cf. Bible: Apostles): 406 n.341 (privy councillor)

Anagni: 250 n.177, 454

Andreas de Barulo (fl. 1260-1290): 99 n.36 (*vigor iustitiae*), 106 n.54 (*lex digna*)

Andreas of Caesarea: 71 n.65

Andreas of Isernia (d. 1316): 92 n.16 (Prince: *numen divinum*), 97 n.29 (*rex imperator*), 109 n.63 (*templum iustitiae*), 111 n.72 (images, royal and holy), 117 n.86 (juristic authority of Bible), 124 n.111 (Prince *iudex iudicum*), 130 n.131 (*lex animata*), 136 n.154 (*vis directiva* of law above the Prince), 138 n.159 (*iurisiurandi religio*), 153 n.191 (*raro princeps iuris-*

Plato: 134 (*Politicus*), 135 n.149, 200 n.20
(Timaeus), 244 (Cicero, *De off.*), 280
n.14 (Ambrose), 281 (ideas), 332 n.63
(Loyseau), 391 n.258 (*hereditas*)
Pliny: 237, 238 n.136 (*nat. hist.*), 389
n.249 (Phoenix)
Plowden, Edmund: 7-23 passim, 24f, 230
n.114, 370f, 404 n.307, 405, 407 nos.313-
315, 438 nos.398 and 400
Plurality of worlds: 276 n.6
Plutarch: 199 (see Ps.-Plutarch), 235
n.126 (κοινὴ πατρίς), 247 n.165, 481
n.83 (trichotomy), 498 n.7 (Alexander), 499 n.13 (*ad princ. inerud.*, quoted by De la Guesle)
    Ps.-Plutarch's *Institutio Traiani*: 94
n.20, 199 n.19, 216 n.66
Pole, Cardinal: 229
Policraticus (see John of Salisbury): 94ff
Poliziano, Angelo: 427
Pomponius, Roman jurist: 295 n.48
Pope, Papacy: Individual Popes: Alexander III: 349, 385, 393, 409; Alexander
IV: 36 n.22; Benedict XI: 250 nos.177-
178, 259 n.202; Benedict XII: 336;
Boniface VIII: 28 n.15, 195f, 202, 206
n.39, 215 n.61, 229, 249, 250 n.177, 251
n.179, 258 n.262, 346 n.115, 361 n.165,
386, 396f, 454f; Celestine III: 246 n.163,
350ff; Celestine V: 35f, 215 n.61; Clement II: 215 n.61; Clement V: 238 n.135,
250 n.177; Gelasius I: 81 n.94, 153
n.192, 456, 463 n.33, 481 n.83 (Sacramentary); Gregory I: 50 n.18, 63 n.47,
68 n.55, 81 n.94, 118 n.88, 153 n.192;
Gregory VII: 28f n.15 (*dictatus papae*),
42 (anti-Gregorian), 58, 81, 335, 349
nos.126-127, 353 n.140; Gregory IX:
290, 347, 350, 353 n.140, 355 nos.144-
145, 385 (see also Decretals, *Liber Extra*); Gregory X: 361; Hadrian I: 334,
335 n.70; Honorius III: 354, 355 nos.-
143-145, 356f, 358 n.158, 377 n.215;
Honorius IV: 285 n.23; Innocent III:
10 n.7, 36 n.22, 91, 163 n.223, 181 n.279,
199, 213 n.55, 215 n.61, 238 n.137, 319,
320 n.17, 321, 350, 351 n.135, 353 n.140,
354 n.142, 356 n.148, 358ff, 372 n.197,
440 n.405, 452 n.4; Innocent IV: 186
n.297, 205 n.35, 282 n.18, 298 n.35, 305,
306 nos.77-78, 307 n.82, 308 n.83, 314,
384 n.231, 385 n.237, 386, 394 n.270,
396 n.277; John VIII: 87, 127, 335 n.70;
John XXII: 177, 321; Leo I: 14 n.5,
50 n.18, 74 n.76; Martin IV: 285 n.23;

Nicholas II: 349; Nicholas IV: 373
n.199; Pelagius: 292; Pius II (see Piccolomini, Enea Silvio): 260; Pius XII:
88 n.5; Urban II: 241
    Papal titles of honor: general: 193;
Christus in terris: 92; *canon vivus*: 129
n.127; *haeres apostolorum*: 44 n.4; *lex
animata*: 129 nos.127-128; *pontificalis
maiestas*: 193; *potest dici ecclesia*: 4,
204 n.32; *primus princeps*: 203; *princeps*: 193; *princeps episcoporum*: 44
n.4; *qualis Petrus officio*: 58; *quasi
rex in regno*: 203 n.29; *servus servorum Dei*: 255 n.191; *unctione Christus*:
44 n.4; *verus imperator*: 193; *vicarius
(Christi, Petri)*: see s.v. Vicarius
    Papal functions and relations: above
and under the law of the Church: 129
n.128; appeal from pope to God: 264
n.220; *caput corporis ecclesiae mystici*:
203f; *caput ecclesiae* above *corpus ecclesiae*: 264f; cardinals *pars corporis
papae*: 208 n.42; Church a *principatus
papalis*: 202; guardian of the Church
iure minoris: 376 n.210; immortality
of *Dignitas*: 386ff passim (see Immortality); *indignatio papae*: 257 n.199;
interrex and *vicarius imperii*: 335;
married to States of the Church: 223
n.87; *patrimonium Petri*, the dowry
of the Church: 217 n.71; maxim *Omnia
iura*: 153; sacramental power above
emperor: 456f; under king's law
(Matth. 22:21): 157 n.206; wears no
mourning: 429 n.376
    Papacy: imperialization of: 90, 257
n.199; *limina Apostolorum*: 349, 351
n.136; *papatus*: 349 (defense of), 354;
promotes secularism: 320f; Reform
Papacy: 60, 185 n.293, 322 (see Investiture Struggle); *regalia S. Petri*:
349 (defense of)
    Cardinals: 36, 208 n.42, 264, 297 n.53
Porphyrius: 139 n.161
Porrée, Gilbert de la: 279
Portugal: 326 n.38
Potestas, power: See Ch. III, passim; 48
(divine and royal), 54ff (Tiberius), 56
n.30 (*pot. ordinis et iurisdictionis*), 80
(sempiternal and sexless, personified
by emperor)
Poverty struggle: 176
Prescription (see Fisc): 165 n.226, 166,
168ff, 179, 180f (hundred years), 182ff,
345, 374 (runs not against a minor)

ADDENDA

223 n.85: The *mariage saint et politique* of the French king is probably reflected in a curious remark of Louis XIV to which Ruth M. Cherniss kindly called my attention. Saint-Simon, *Mémoires*, ed. Gonzague Truc (Pléiade edition, Paris, 1953), IV, 1069, Ch. 58, reports about the distinction made by Louis XIV between princes of the royal blood and royal bastards: "Il considéra les premiers [les princes du sang] comme les *enfants de l'État et de la couronne* . . . , tandis qu'il chérit les autres comme les enfants sortis de ses amours."

424 n.366: Cf. Lucas de Penna, on *C*.10,74[76], fol.115ʳ (Lyon, 1544): ". . . videtur quod rex sine corona sepeliri non debeat."

480 n.79: It is not impossible that Remigio de' Girolami (as Mrs. Enrico de Negri kindly pointed out to me) had Romans 9:3 in mind: "Optabam enim ego ipse anathema esse a Christo pro fratribus meis."